CONTINUITY
AND DISCONTINUITY IN
CHURCH HISTORY

STUDIES IN THE HISTORY OF CHRISTIAN THOUGHT

EDITED BY

HEIKO A. OBERMAN, Tübingen

IN COOPERATION WITH

HENRY CHADWICK, Oxford
EDWARD A. DOWEY, Princeton, N.J.
JAROSLAV PELIKAN, New Haven, Conn.
BRIAN TIERNEY, Ithaca, N.Y.
E. DAVID WILLIS, Princeton, N.J.

VOLUME XIX

F. F. CHURCH AND T. GEORGE (Eds)

CONTINUITY
AND DISCONTINUITY IN
CHURCH HISTORY

LEIDEN
E. J. BRILL
1979

CONTINUITY AND DISCONTINUITY IN CHURCH HISTORY

Essays Presented to

GEORGE HUNTSTON WILLIAMS

on the Occasion of his 65th Birthday

EDITED BY

F. FORRESTER CHURCH AND TIMOTHY GEORGE

LEIDEN
E. J. BRILL
1979

ISBN 90 04 05879 6

TABLE OF CONTENTS

Tabula Gratulatoria IX
    F. Forrester Church and Timothy George
Editors' Preface XX

*

George Huntston Williams: A Portrait I
    James Luther Adams
The Periodization of History 18
    Franklin H. Littell

COMMUNION AND ATONEMENT
Essays in Ancient and Medieval Church History

I Thessalonians—Experiment in Christian Writing 33
    Helmut Koester
The Pre-Cyprianic Doctrine of the Priesthood of All Christians 45
    James Leo Garrett, Jr.
Civilization as a Preparation for Christianity in the Thought of
    Eusebius 62
    Robert M. Grant
A First-Generation Anselmian, Guibert of Nogent 71
    Jaroslav Pelikan
Nudus nudum Christum sequi and Parallel Formulas in the
    Twelfth Century: A Supplementary Dossier 83
    Giles Constable
The Church as Eucharistic Communion in Medieval Theology . 92
    George H. Tavard
The Byzantine Recovery of Constantinople from the Latins in
    1261: A Chrysobull of Michael VIII Palaeologus in Favor
    of Hagia Sophia 104
    Deno J. Geanakoplos
The Christian Gospel and Social Responsibility: the Eastern
    Orthodox Tradition in History 118
    John Meyendorff

THE RADICAL REFORMATION

Essays in Radical, Magisterial, and Catholic Reformation Church History

Humanism, Scholasticism, and the Intellectual Origins of the
    Reformation   133
    Steven Ozment

Luther's Hexameral Anthropology   150
    Charles Trinkaus

The Baptism of John and the Baptism of Jesus in Huldrych
    Zwingli, Balthasar Hubmair and Late Medieval Theology . 169
    David C. Steinmetz

The Role of Nuremberg in the Spread of the Reformation .   . 182
    Harold J. Grimm

Peter Martyr Vermigli and the Marks of the True Church .   . 198
    Robert M. Kingdon

The Bishop Confronts the Queen: John Jewel and the Failure
    of the English Reformation   215
    John E. Booty

Preliminary Observations on Writing a History of the Roman
    Inquisition   232
    John Tedeschi

Fausto Sozzini and Justification   250
    John C. Godbey

WILDERNESS AND PARADISE

Essays in Modern Church History

Religion and Bacon's New Learning: From Legitimation to
    Object   267
    J. Samuel Preus

Socinian Historiography in the Late 17th Century (Benedykt
    Wiszowaty and his "Medulla historiae ecclesiasticae") .   . 285
    Lech Szczucki

Wilderness Experiences of Religion in America .   .   .   301
    Robert T. Handy

Annuit Coeptis: America as the Elect Nation, the Rise and
    Decline of a Patriotic Tradition   315
    Sydney E. Ahlstrom

John Cotton Washed and Made White 338
    Conrad Wright

American Missionary Ideologies: "Activism" as Theory, Practice,
    and Stereotype 351
    William R. Hutchison

The Ecumenical Commitment to a Transforming Social Justice . 363
    John C. Bennett

Model Man, Modern Man, Reformation Man 379
    Lewis W. Spitz

*

A Letter from Roland Bainton on Immortality 391

*

Bibiography of the Writings of George Huntston Williams . 397

*

Index of Subjects 413

Index of Selected Names 417

Rafal and Bozena Cholodzinscy
Ibadan, Nigeria

Amy Furth Church
New York, NY

Senator and Mrs. Frank Church
United States Senate

Prof. David L. Clark
Hope College
Holland, MI

John Ruskin Clark, Minister Emeritus
First Unitarian Church of San Diego

Martin Clark
Huntingdon, PA

John Coakley
Harvard Divinity School

The Right Reverend John B. Coburn
Episcopal Diocese of Massachusetts

Rev. John M. Coffee, Jr.
Emerson College

Ralph John Coffman, Jr.
Marblehead, MA

Rev. Joseph I. Collins
Pastor, St. Pius V Parish
Lynn, MA

Prof. Demetrios J. Constantelos
Stockton State College

J. Harry and Luella G. Cotton
Retired, Swarthmore, PA

William J. Coutenay
University of Wisconsin

Harvey G. Cox
Harvard Divinity School

Rev. James W. Crawford
Old South Church in Boston

Robert Darwin Crouse
Dalhousie University

William R. Crout
Cambridge, MA

Winston F. Crum
Seabury-Western Theological Seminary

Barbara Ritter Dailey
Boston University

Forest K. Davis
Empire State College (SUNY)

Millie DeCarlo
Harvard Divinity School

George J. Delp
Wollaston, MA

Pawel and Ingrid Depta
Cambridge Public Library

Larry and Gladys Derr
Center Ossipee, NH

Michel Despland
Concordia University

Joseph A. Devenny, S.J.
Weston School of Theology

Rev. James A. Diamond
University of Minnesota
Episcopal Chaplaincy

Ronald E. Diener
Harvard University Library

John Dillenberger
Hartford Seminary Foundation

John P. Dolan
University of South Carolina

Harriet S. Dorman
Arlington, MA

Jane Dempsey Douglass
School of Theology at Claremont

David C. Dow, M.D.
Cambridge, MA

Sterling Dow
Harvard University

Burton Dreben
Harvard University

Congressman Robert F. Drinan
U.S. House of Representatives

Marjorie Hope Dunham
Northampton, MA

Prof. Donald F. Durnbaugh
Bethany Theological Seminary

Sylvia and Arthur Dyck
Lexington, MA

Mark U. Edwards, Jr.
Wellesley College

Frederick Elder
Lexington, MA

John Dixon Elder
Oberlin, OH

Dr. Sharon Elkins
Wellesley College

Prof. Michael A. Fahey, S.J.
Concordia University, Montreal

Prof. and Mrs. Rollin J. Fairbanks
Episcopal Divinity School

De Coursey Fales, Jr.
Emerson College

Bishop Dr. Joseph Ferencz
Unitarian Church in Hungary

Everett Ferguson
Abilene Christian University

Joseph H. Fichter, S.J.
Professor of Sociology
Loyola University of the South

Paul Corby Finney
University of Missouri

The Congregation of the First
Unitarian Church
Rochester, NY

Roderick Firth
Harvard University

Charles C. Foreman
Wheaton College
Norton, MA

Stephen Foster
Northern Illinois University

William Lloyd Fox, Jr.
Washington, D.C.

Cecil L. Franklin
University of Denver

Prof. S. J. Freedberg
Harvard University

Duane K. Friesen
Bethel College

John Friesen
Canadian Mennonite Bible College

Max D. Gaebler
First Unitarian Society of Madison

Prof. Lancelot A. Garrard
Goring, Reading, England

Charles Garside, Jr.
Rice University

Dres. Ursula and Erich Geldbach
Ökumenisches Seminar
University of Marburg

Denise Wyse George
Old South Church in Boston

Stephen Gero
Brown University

Prof. Alexander Gieysztor
Warsaw University

Prof. Marshall Gilliland
University of Saskatchewan

Stephen Gilman
Harvard University

Myron P. Gilmore †
Harvard University

Elisabeth Gregorisch Gleason
University of San Francisco

Mr. Dieter Goetze
Santa Barbara, CA

Rabbi Ben-Zion Gold
Harvard-Radcliffe Hillel

Rev. Richard H. Graham
Trinity Lutheran Church
Hagerstown, MD

Rev. and Mrs. Dana McLean
  Greeley
First Parish in Concord, MA

Prof. Louis S. Greenbaum
University of Massachusetts

Prof. Egil Grislis
University of Manitoba

Eric W. Gritsch
Professor of Church History
Lutheran Theological Seminary at
  Gettysburg

Wells and Helen Grogan
First Congregational Church,
  U.C.C.

Maria Grossmann
Harvard University

Walter Grossman
University of Massachusetts

Prof. Ewart Guinier
Harvard University

Rev. Alan Hackett
East Falmouth, MA

Canon Michael P. Hamilton
Washington National Cathedral

Mrs. Alicia Hammer
Mexico City

Mason Hammond
Harvard University, Emeritus

Dean and Mrs. Harold J. Hanham
Massachusetts Institute of Technology

Paul D. Hanson
Harvard Divinity School

Allen Happe
First Church in Cambridge
Congregational, U.C.C.

Rev. Stanley S. Harakas
Holy Cross Greek Orthodox
  School of Theology

Rev. Edward R. Hardy, Ph.D.
Jesus College
Cambridge, England

Rev. Dr. Donald Szantho Har-
  rington
Community Church of New York

J. Michael Hartenstine
Sarasota, FL

Rev. Richard S. Hasty
First Parish Society
Portland, ME

John F. Hayward
Southern Illinois University

Rev. Robert W. Henderson, Ph.D.
University of Tulsa

Holly Hendrix
Harvard Divinity School

Prof. David Herlihy
Harvard University

Guy F. Hershberger
Goshen College

Rev. Theodore M. Hesburgh,
  C.S.C.
University of Notre Dame

Susannah Heschel
Dept. of Religious Studies
University of Pennsylvania

Rev. Phillip Hewett
Unitarian Church of Vancouver

Brother Blue (Hugh Morgan Hill)
  Ruth Edmonds Hill
Cambridge, MA

Harley Peirce Holden
Harvard University Archives

Rev. and Mrs. Frank O. Holmes
Jamaica Plain, MA

Stephen H. Hornbegger
Cusco, Peru

Richard A. Horsley
University of Massachusetts

Prof. Irvin B. Horst
Universiteit van Amsterdam

Rev. John W. Howard, S.J.
Boston College

Carolyn and Duncan Howlett
Lovell, ME

Po-chia Hsia
Yale University

Dr. John W. Hughston
Metropolitan Baptist Church
Cambridge, MA

Archbishop Iakovos
Greek Orthodox Archbishop of
    North and South America

Ephraim Isaac
Hebrew University

Esther W. Jack
Brookline, MA

Dr. and Mrs. James H. Jackson
First and Second Church, Boston

Prof. W. K. Jordan
Cambridge, MA

Gordon D. Kaufman
Harvard Divinity School

James Kay
United Ministries in Higher Edu-
    cation
Bemidji State University

Prof. Edwin C. Kemble
Harvard University

Dr. Robert C. Kimball
Thomas Starr King School for the
    Ministry

Ernst Kitzinger
Harvard University

Walter Klaassen
Conrad Grebel College
University of Waterloo

Prof. William Klassen
University of Manitoba

Prof. John W. Kleiner
Lutheran Theological Seminary

Rev. and Mrs. Manfred Waldemar
    Kohl

Waldemar Roy Kohl
World Vision International
Ivory Coast, West Africa

Dean Alan Kolp
Earlham College
Richmond, IN

Dr. Lajos Kovács, Bishop
Unitarian Church, Romania

Cornelius Krahn
Bethel College, Kansas

Dr. Walter Donald Kring
Unitarian Church of All Souls

Paul Oskar Kristeller
Columbia University, Emeritus

Maria H. Krisztinkovich
Vancouver, B.C.

Bishop Daniel Krstitch
Patriarchate of Serbia

Jerzy Ktoczowski
Catholic University of Lublin

G. Richard Kuch
Chicago, Illinois

Gerhart B. Ladner
University of California

Prof. Samuel Laeuchli
Temple University

Rev. N. Frederick Lang, Th.D.
Chaplain, Lt. Colonell, U.S.A.F.,
  Retired

Dr. Spencer Lavan
Tufts University

Prof. Bently Layton
Yale University

Rev. John H. Leamon
First Church in Cambridge
Congregational, U.C.C.

Paul Lehmann
Charles A. Briggs Professor of
  Systematic
Theology Emeritus
Union Theological Seminary

Dr. Marjorie LeMay
Harvard University Health Services

Prof. LeMoine G. Lewis
Abilene Christian University

Prof. Raimundo Lida
Harvard University

Ruth P. Liebowitz
Peppercll, MA

Prof. Christiaan T. Lievestro
University of Santa Clara

Carter Lindberg
School of Theology, Boston University

Klaus M. Lindner
Harvard University

Rev. Donald G. Lothrop
The Community Church of Boston

Dr.theol. Denton Lotz
Baptist Theological Seminary
Rüschlikon, Switzerland

John Mather Lurvey, Jr.
San Bernardino, CA

F. Lyra
Instytut Filologii Angielskiej
Uniwersytet M.Curie-Sklodows-
  kiej,
Lublin, Poland

Wallace T. MacCaffrey
Harvard University

Donald J. and Alyce S. Maccallum
Rockville, MD

Dr. Richard V. McCann
U.S. Office of Education

James F. McElwain
Foxboro, MA

Cushman McGiffert
Claremont, CA

Pres. Thomas D. McGonigle, O.P.
Aquinas Institute of Theology
Dubuque, Iowa

George W. MacRae, S.J.
Harvard Divinity School

Kathleen Elizabeth McVey
Ecole Biblique, Jerusalem

Humberto Cardinal Madeiros
Boston, MA

M. Albert Mahaka
Mount Silinda Mission (A.B.M.)
Chipinga, Rhodesia

Prof. Muhsin Mahdi
Harvard University

Calvin S. deWaal Malefyt
University Reformed Church

Abraham J. Malherbe
Yale Divinity School

Archbishop Torkom Mannogian
Archbishop Primate of the Diocese
  of the Armenian
Church of U.S.A.

Dr. Clyde L. Manschreck
Chicago Theological Seminary

John H. Mansfield
Harvard Law School

Juan Marichal
Harvard University

Dr. Stephen A. Marini
Wellesley College

Edward L. Mark
Harvard-Epworth United Methodist Church

Louis E. Martin
Harvard College Library

Martin E. Marty
University of Chicago

Dr. George N. Marshall
Church of the Larger Fellowship

Rex D. Matthews
Harvard Divinity School

His Grace Bishop Maximos
Titular Bishop of Diokleia

Prof. Roger Mehl
Doyen de la Faculté de Théologie
protestante
University of Strasbourg

Mrs. Frederick Merk
Harvard University

Prof. Margaret Miles
Harvard Divinity School

Diane Miller
First Unitarian Church
San Francisco, CA

Paul S. Minear
Yale Divinity School

Nelson H. Minnich
The Catholic University of America

Dr. Paul Misner
Everett, MA

Rev. Enrico S. Molnar, Th.D.,
OAR
Canon Prior, Order of Agape &
Reconciliation
St. Michael's Forest Valley Priory
Tajique, NM

Walter L. Moore, Jr.
Florida State University

Dr. Carol Morris
North Shore Community College

Karl F. Morrison
Department of History
University of Chicago

Msgr. Edward J. Murray
Cambridge, MA

Richard E. Myers
Editor, *The Unitarian Universalist Christian*

Prof. Roderich Nash
University of California

Seyyed Hussein Nasr
President, Imperial Iranian Academy of Philosophy

Rev. Dr. John R. Neal
University of Western Australia

Prof. J. Robert Nelson
Boston University

Christopher Niebuhr
Albany, NY

Prof. José C. Nieto
Juniata College

Prof. James H. Nichols
Princeton Theological Seminary

Paul L. Nyhus
Bowdoin College

Prof. Zbigniew Ogonowski
Polish Academy of Sciences
Warsaw, Poland

Prof. Albert C. Outler
Perkins School of Theology,
  S.M.U.

Prof. Frederick C. Packard, Jr.
Harvard University, Emeritus

Prof. Elaine H. Pagels
Barnard College, Columbia University

Joan Paine
University of Alaska

Robert C. Palmer
U.U. Minister, Retired
Boston, MA

Dr. and Mrs. Egidio Papa
Rochester Institute of Technology

Dr. Calvin Pater
Knox College
Toronto, Canada

Prof. Lewis J. Patsavos
Holy Cross Greek Orthodox Seminary

Rev. Prof. Lloyd G. Patterson
Episcopal Divinity School

W. Brown Patterson
Prof. of History
Davidson College

Dean W. Morgan Patterson
Golden Gate Baptist Seminary

Wilhelm Pauck
Charles A. Briggs Graduate Professor of Church History
Emeritus, Union Theological Seminary
Visiting Prof. Emeritus, Stanford University

Dean George Peck
Andover Newton Theological School

Prof. Prentiss L. Pemberton
Atlanta, GA

Prof. Klaus Penzel
Perkins School of Theology
Southern Methodist University

Mr. and Mrs. Dwight H. Perkins
Harvard University

Rodney Lawrence Petersen
Princeton Theological Seminary

Dr. Ray C. Petry
James B. Duke Professor Emeritus of Church History
Duke University

Norman Pettit
Cambridge, MA

Mr. Robert H. Pfeiffer
Cambridge, MA

Craig A. Phillips
Harvard Divinity School

Prof. Marc Philonenko
University of Strassbourg

Rabbi Herman Pollack
Emeritus, Massachusetts Institute of Technology
Hillel Rabbi

Dr. Mina W. Power
New York, NY

Rev. David M. Powers, S.T.B.
Dennis Union Church

Dr. Eugene G. Prater
University of Southern California

Charles P. Price
Virginia Theological Seminary

Omeltan Pritsak
Director, Harvard Ukrainian Research Institute

Oksana Procyk
Harvard College Library

Wayne Proudfoot
Columbia University

Cyriac K. Pullapilly
St. Mary's College, Notre Dame

Richard Quebedeaux
Nevada City, CA

Willard V. Quine
Harvard University

Jill Raitt
Duke University, Divinity School

Mary Rakow
Boston College

Gene Reeves
Wilberforce University

Lucien S. Richard
Weston School of Theology

Herbert Richardson
Université du Québec à Montréal

Prof. Nancy L. Roelker
Boston University

Prof. and Mrs. William R. Rogers
Harvard University

Prof. and Mrs. Jakob Rosenberg
Arlington, MA

Mark Roskill
University of Massachusetts

Prof. Lionel N. Rothkrug
Concordia University
Montreal, Canada

Prof. Joseph and Dr. Jean Runzo
Chapman College

George Rupp
University of Wisconsin-Green
  Bay

Rousas John Rushdoony
Chalcedon Foundation

J. Joseph Ryan
St. John Seminary

Margaret Amy Schatkin
Princeton Theological Seminary

Dr. Hedwig Schleiffer
University of Vienna

Prof. Dr. M. A. Schmidt
University of Basel, Switzerland

Robert A. Schneider
Harvard University

David M. Scholer
Gordon-Conwell Theological Seminary

Peggy R. Schreiner
Harvard University

Alan Seaburg
Andover-Harvard Theological Library

Prof. Eduard F. Sekler
Harvard University

Philip H. Sellew
Harvard Divinity School

Ihor Ševčenko
Harvard University

Prof. Massey H. Shepherd, Jr.
The Church Divinity School of the
  Pacific

Frank Shuffelton
University of Rochester

Dr. Muzammil H. Siddiqi
Muslim World League

Prof. Ian D. K. Siggins
Harvard Divinity School

Mrs. Grazyna Slanda
Natick, MA

Rev. Robt. S. Slater
Swampscott, MA

Abigail Abbot Smith
Hamden, CT

George Putnam Smith
Hamden, CT

H. Shelton Smith
James B. Dubke Professor, Eme-
ritus
Duke University

Rev. and Mrs. James D. Smith, III
Harvard Divinity School

Timothy L. Smith
Johns Hopkins University

Wilfred Cantwell Smith
Harvard University

Keith L. Sprunger
Bethel College

Max L. Stackhouse
Andover Newton Theological
School

Pastor Denver L. Stanford, Sr.
Boston's United Pentecostal
Church

James M. Stayer
Queen's University

Dr. Arvel M. Steece
The First Church of Christ in
Lynn Congregational

Jeffrey N. Steenson
Cummings, ND

Douglas V. Steere
Haverford College

Dean and Mrs. Krister Stendahl
Harvard Divinity School

Prof. Zeph Stewart
Harvard University

Mr. Harry M. Stokes
Boston, MA

David M. Stowe
New York, NY

Prof. John Strugnell
Harvard Divinity School

Florence and Dick Sund
Palo Alto, CA

Shauna I. Sutliff
Harvard Divinity School

Frank Sysyn
Ukrainian Research Institute
Harvard University

Dr. Charles L. Taylor
Wellesley Hills, MA

Bunn Thompson
Wellesley, MA

Gordon and Maude Thompson
Clearwater, FL

Paula and Robert Tonis
Harvard University

Prof. John T. Townsend
Episcopal Divinity School

Rev. Prof. Robert Trisco
The Catholic University of America

Pres. Étienne Trocmé
University of Strasbourg

Prof. Isadore Twersky
Harvard University

James A. Vendettuoli, Jr.
Oakland Community College

Masha Vorobiov
New York, NY

Prof. Dennis N. Voskuil
Hope College

Walter and Mariana Wagoner
Hartford, CT

Grant Wacker
University of North Carolina

Robert Cutler Walton
Fachbereich Ev. Theologie der
Universität Münster

William B. Watson
Massachusetts Institute of Technology

(Alexander) Frederick Cameron
Webster
Catholic High of Pointe Coupee

Mr. and Mrs. Lewis H. Weinstein
Waban, MA

Wiktor Weintraub
Harvard University

Rev. and Mrs. Frank M. Weiskel
Prospect Congregation Church

Victor F. Weisskopf
Massachusetts Institute of Technology

David F. Wells
Trinity Evangelical Divinity School

R. J. Zwi Werblowsky
The Hebrew University of Jerusalem

Prof. Dorothy Corbett Wertz
Suffolk University

Dr. Richard W. Wertz
Westport Pt., MA

Prof. and Mrs. Amos Wilder
Harvard Divinity School

Helen D. Willard
Cambridge, MA

Prof. David Willis
Princeton Theological Seminary

Mrs. Albert Rhys (Lucita) Williams
Boston, MA

Drs. David and Polesta Williams
Bay Village, OH

Edwin E. Williams
Harvard University Library

Rev. and Mrs. Rhys Williams
Boston, MA

Nancy Elizabeth Wilson
Harvard University

Donald F. Winslow
Episcopal Divinity School

Rev. Dr. Prescott B. Wintersteen
Milton, MA

Eugeniusz Wisniowski
Lublin-KUL

Anatoly Stephan Wojcechowskyj
Harvard Divinity School

Zbigniew Wojcik
Institute of History of Polish Academy of Sciences
Warsaw, Poland

Karol Cardinal Wojtyła
olim, Archbishop of Kraków
nunc, Pope John Paul II

Prof. William Wolf
Episcopal Divinity School

John Dunning Woodbridge
Trinity Evangelical Divinity School

Rev. Dr. Herman E. Wornom
General Secretary, Emeritus
The Religious Education Association of the United States and Canada

Rev. Dr. Harold F. Worthley
The Congregational Library, Boston

John Cardinal Wright
Rome

Mrs. G. Ernest Wright
Lexington, MA

Prof. Basil Yankakakis
Suffolk University Law School

Dr. M. O. Young
Surry, VA

Dr. John K. Yost
University of Nebraska

Dr. George Zhmysson, Jr.
Providence Baptist Church
Philadelphia, PA

Lowell H. Zuck
Eden Theological Seminary

EDITORS' PREFACE

It is with pleasure that we present this volume of essays in honor of George Huntston Williams, Hollis Professor of Divinity, Harvard University, on the occasion of his sixty-fifth birthday. Our title, *Continuity and Discontinuity in Church History,* is adapted from that of one of Professor Williams' courses. It is intended not only to reflect the nature of this volume itself, but also to recall an important motif that recurs throughout his scholarship. George Williams is deeply committed both to the integrity of Church History as a theological discipline and to the specific histories of, in his words, "the New Testament People." Picking up threads while matching fabrics, respecting the new while revering the old, he combines an ability for specialized research, intimidating in its detail, with a rare sensitivity to the interlocking patterns that identify each piece as but a part of a greater whole. The essays in this volume embody, in their diversity and their range, both of these dimensions of his work: his desire to take the larger view, to synthesize, to be a generalist, while yet never taking his finger off the pulse-beat of living persons and living ideas.

We have divided the following essays into three sections, each under the gathering rubric of one of Williams' major works. Of course, in keeping with his own approach to Church History, the themes of Communion and Atonement, Radical Reformation, and Wilderness and Paradise are in no sense confined to those periods (Ancient and Medieval; Reformation; Modern) to which they are assigned. However, they serve to underscore the major chords of Williams' thought, while permitting the convenience of a roughly chronological presentation.

If these essays attest to Williams' profound contribution to the substance and spirit of Church historical scholarship, we would here add a word on behalf of those who have studied under him. For nearly four decades he has exerted a remarkable influence on several generations of students, graduates and undergraduates alike. Those of us who have attended his 9 a. m. lectures in Sever Hall have witnessed a master who could move with equal ease and expertise from Constantine through Calvin to Channing, from Celtic spirituality and Orthodox mysticism to the Charismatic Movement and Third World Christianity. When participating in his graduate seminars we have felt the keen edge of his critical acumen. In serving him as teaching fellows, we have sensed his personal concern for individual students and his passion for fairness, and have shared—at least by osmosis—the burden of his calling as *verax historicus*.

Finally, we have many to thank for helping to make this book possible. First, our editorial advisory committee, Dean Krister Stendahl and Professors James Luther Adams and Amos Wilder, all of Harvard Divinity School, for their encouragement and guidance. Then, Professor Heiko A. Oberman, for including this volume in his series, "Studies in the History of Christian Thought." And, also, our colleagues Gary Bisbee, Rex Matthews, Manfred Schulze, and James Smith for assisting us in preparing the manuscript for press. As always, Amy Furth Church and Denise Wyse George have given of themselves beyond the measure of our words to thank them for it. To so many others, our contributors and all of those whose financial support has helped to defray the expense of publication, we are grateful indeed.

F. Forrester Church
Unitarian Church of All Souls
New York City

Timothy George
Southern Baptist Theological Seminary
Louisville, Kentucky

GEORGE HUNTSTON WILLIAMS

A Portrait

JAMES LUTHER ADAMS *

Emeritus, Harvard Divinity School

George Williams entered his theological studies in 1936 with the "Horst Wessel" of a goose-stepping Germany ringing in his ears. At that time he became one of my students in the first classes I taught at The Meadville Theological School (Unitarian), affiliated with the Divinity School, the University of Chicago.

Williams and I began our association there out of strikingly similar experiences—he as a student from St. Lawrence University (Universalist), having spent his junior year, 1934-35, at the University of Munich, and I in the next year having joined Dr. Peter Brunner in the underground movement of the Confessing Church's opposition to Nazism. Brunner, now Professor Emeritus at Heidelberg, had previously been incarcerated for some months in Dachau Concentration Camp.

During the days of turmoil in Munich, Williams became vividly aware of a plumbline in the witness of Cardinal Faulhaber. On one occasion Williams, in a casual conversation in a Munich museum, apparently quite accidentally used a code word. To his surprise he found himself led immediately to an underground meeting of opposition conspirators taking place near the infamous Braun House, only to have the frightened group abruptly disappear when they discovered that he was not the anti-Nazi courier whom they had expected. On another occasion a Nazi student who was absent when Williams brought a Jewish student as a guest into the home for a meal, told him that if he had been home he would have kicked Williams and the Jewish guest down the stairs—whereupon Williams demanded an apology.

Only a few months later I, along with some Confessing Church students in a clandestine seminary in Barmen-Wuppertal, had an encounter with the police who were searching in our pension for a

* The author is indebted to research assistant Elizabeth Findley for aid in the preparation of this essay.

pamphlet published secretly by one of these students, a pamphlet that
had been distributed through the post office by sympathetic postal
clerks. Later on in Marburg I was apprehended by Gestapo officers
equipped with full regalia (including bloodhounds) who had searched
in my room for Confessing Church documents or other evidence
against me, and who required me to face an exhaustive hearing at the
Gestapo headquarters.

In the light of our somewhat similar experience in Hitler's Germany
Williams and I recognized that we had separately been involved in
what the Heidelberg theologian Edmund Schlink was to describe as a
unique and important chapter in church history.

Because of our experience in Nazi Germany Williams early took
an interest, as did I, in the writings of Paul Tillich whom we recognized as the crucial theological and religious-socialist critic of Nazism.
In his senior year, 1939, at Meadville Williams completed his B.D.
dissertation on Tillich's Doctrine of Sin, probably the first dissertation
on Tillich to appear in English. By virtue of this study Williams
became familiar with an elaborate exposition of characteristic demonries
of the modern period—for example, imperialist capitalism, nationalism,
racism, elitism, sexism and unengaged intellectualism. He became
aware also of the fundamental importance of dissent. I recall reporting
to Williams a conversation with Tillich in which he agreed that modern
democracy had been of retarded growth in Germany because of the
early systematic liquidation of the dissent of the Radical Reformers
of the sixteenth century—Nonconformity had become thereafter largely
alien to the German ethos. Williams in time came to the view that
rational dissent is a channel of grace and renewal in human affairs,
indeed that when it does not issue from explicitly religious motivation
the divine Spirit finds an opening among so-called unbelievers. In
any event, the quality of the dissent depends in large part upon the
dissenters' grasp of tradition. To be sure, dissent can move in the
direction of atavism—or of barbarism, as in Nazism. Moreover,
Williams early recognized that ordinarily dissent, creative as well as
destructive, requires institutional power in order to be effective in
history. He saw also that dissent and renewal very often take the
form of re-interpretation of a motif, a doctrine, or an institution that
has found earlier articulation. To understand these motifs and their
reincarnations the church historian must attempt to grasp the relations
between them and the milieu out of which they emerged—priest,
prophet, institution, layman and theologian are to be seen in interplay.

In carrying out this task the historian must find a unity of pattern in a variety of particular incidents. When this pattern repeats itself, it becomes a tradition. The church historian dealing with it recognizes with Goethe that a tradition cannot be inherited, it must be earned. That is, once the main ingredients of a tradition have been discovered, only the words of the historian as artist can give it tangible form by bringing it into focus. Once this happens, it then has the impact of an emblem on the society or the community of faith.

Here we have a preliminary indication of Williams' conception of the vocation of the church historian. One must add, however, that for Williams, the earning of a tradition must be attempted in the context of a growing community of faith in face of historical change. The historian who lives within a community of faith does not sit on a pedestal outside history. He shares the agonies, the frustrations, and the sense of promise in history. Like the jurist, he is aware of precedents of the past which are pregnant with new relevance, new life. Therefore, also in order to take time by the forelock, the historian must participate with a sense of social responsibility in the processes that define current conflicts and policies. The church historian accordingly writes of the past not merely for the past itself, but also for its impact on the present.

When I consider Williams' range of interests in nature as well as in history, in the natural sciences as well as in the humanities, in the variety of languages and literatures, and when I consider his view of the church historian as artist, I think of the paintings of an eminent contemporary artist, Al Held of Yale University. His paintings, black-and-white, are made up entirely of geometric forms (rectangles, squares, circles and the like), some of the paintings being as large as nine feet by nine, canvases of luminous, sprawling complexity. The ingredients of these paintings, the geometric forms, are in consonance and also in tension with each other. Moreover, they lend themselves to a variety of shifting perspectives. At least in its parts this congeries of forms is amenable to rational scrutiny and ordering. In some instances a form seems to extend beyond the edge of the canvas into an indeterminate future or into patterns that are to be lost. The forms do not present simply a pathless forest. Major paths are signalled by heavier, thicker lines. The forms, moreover, are depicted on different levels or layers within the depth of the painting, the lower levels being seemingly earlier partial manifestations of later forms, all of the forms in juxtaposition lending themselves to a variety of perspectives. Moving from one point of vantage to another and then to another the perceptive eye comes to recognize that although no embracing order is discernible there are in the house of reason (and unreason) many mansions seeking permanence, each mysteriously and independently related to others in unresolved tensions and in evanescent and partial integration. These are the dimensions of George Williams' depiction as church historian of the human scene, though (unlike Held) he discerns within and beyond the polarities "a deep purpose in the universe," an ecology of grace, an ecology that warns against premature closure or utopian expectations. Yet, the whole is more complex than human reason can embrace; it out-tops our knowledge.

Because of the vastness of the canvas and the complexity of detail many a historian tends to carry on research as a specialist, largely confining attention to carefully limited areas or problems. From early in his career Williams resolved to work as a generalist, here following the venerable model of the German Professor Ordinarius of Church History. Williams thought of the work of the generalist as providing an introduction to Western civilization. He also considered it an opportunity to study all types of Christianity.

When in 1952 he was appointed at Harvard Divinity School, Dean Willard L. Sperry informed him that as successor to Professor George La Piana he was to have responsibility for church history up to the Reformation. Williams was unwilling to confine himself to this, wishing rather to assume responsibility for ancient, medieval and modern church history, with the exception of American church history. His major course, attended by large numbers of students from the College and the Graduate School (including future members of the Harvard faculty) required two years of four semesters. As in his earlier work at the (Unitarian) Starr King School for the Ministry and the Pacific School of Religion in Berkeley, the breadth of scholarly concern always included his maintenance of familiarity with source materials, manuscripts, and monographs in a variety of languages. But the question was to nag him, how was he to do all of this without becoming a dilettante?

He found some of the answers to these problems under the tutelage of the eminent medievalist Ernst Kantorowicz at Berkeley and also under his previous Chicago teacher, Wilhelm Pauck, who in his work traversed the full arc of historical theology. Kantorowicz was a scholar who in political preference remained a monarchist and who was so deeply immersed in the life and literature of the Middle Ages as to make the diligent student feel that he was living in that period, in "its native surroundings, its time and space." Kantorowicz gave structure to the period by rendering luminous certain dominant themes such as the traditional liturgical tricolon of the "Medieval Ruler Cult": "Christus vincit, Christus regnat, Christus imperat," displaying "as it were the cosmic harmony of Heaven, Church and State, an interweaving and twining of the one world with the other and an alliance between the powers on earth and the powers of heaven." To be sure, this harmony is all too often broken. These shifting transcendent concepts were used to sanction the exercise of power, to legitimate established or changing distribution of power. The "Ruler Cult" with the old acclamations was traced by Kantorowicz into modern nationalism down to National Socialism and Fascism, not to speak of its revival in papal triumphalism. The "human and Christian virtues were perverted to intoxicate people into fighting for unjust causes." Williams was able to supplement his background in the Social Gospel and in the socio-historical method he acquired from Chicago with the knowledge of specific ways in which forces for change are perverted in the course of history.

Stimulated by these studies, Williams began to map out major routes through church history. For him these routes or trenches are irrigation ditches (Thomas Mann called them "coulisses") which vitalized the landscapes through which they passed. Sometimes the characterizations by the historian provisionally assume the form of a cartoon, offering the intense visual dynamics of simplified line and color and providing an effective pedagogical device. Williams has said that the characterization of a route in history may acquire the forefulness of a Japanese print with its few brush strokes. The heavier lines of Williams' canvas became such motifs as church and state, the ministry and the sacraments, the role of the laity, justification by faith, atonement and sacrament, the Radical Reformation, the reluctance to inform, the idea of the university in Puritanism, wilderness and paradise, and attitudes toward nature. They are never presented as merely the organization of data in terms of an integrating idea. In Troeltschean fashion Williams colors in his ideas, fills out their basic outlines in relation to institutions, places and historical figures. Thus he gives to statistics body, locale and voice. Moreover, these recurring motifs of the iconography are seen also as analogues of the birth and rebirth of individual figures. In short, these outlines aim to trace the transmutation (and perversion) of values, the Phoenix-like death and rebirth of motifs which sometimes go underground and then reappear under new names and guises.

Williams' pathos for particularity is especially evident in his sense of the genius of place. The thick lines of his canvas are always delineated topographically. Maps, maps, maps are always in evidence. Nicaea or Kiev or Warsaw or Trent is a place on a map of a particular period. Such mappings of church history are not unilinear, precisely because they do not represent undisturbed balance or symmetry. In fact, they acquire multidimensional form through the discernment of polarities which strive for resolution.

*

We turn now to trace largely in anecdotal fashion some aspects of his personal *curriculum vitae*. John T. McNeill, one of his mentors in church history, once told Williams that as church historian he should speak from his own community of faith, ever aware of its needs. This admonition only confirmed his own instinct and habit. The past has never been for him a sanctuary in which to hide from the present. For one thing, it is capable of ringing an alarm, recalling the present church to its authentic mission. More than that, the present is rooted for Williams personally in the community of faith and in his family of orientation as it has related itself for several generations to that community—he is a minister of the fourth generation. Many of the motifs in polarity which give continuity and structure to his understanding of church history appear in a preliminary way, as we shall see, in the polarities of his own personal experience in the days of his youth and maturation. In this sense the child is father of the man.

As in his conception of church history, moreover, these polarities in his life are associated in emphatic ways with geography, with special places extending from his earlier years in rural Huntsburg, Ohio (thirty miles from Cleveland) where he was born in 1914, to urban Cleveland, Chicago and Rochester, though for him the flora and fauna of the countryside are characteristically never forgotten. Williams later on adopted the middle name *Huntston*, invented intentionally to resemble the word *Huntsburg*, since he had often been teased by his peers for his baptismal name, Pease. His grandparents Pease were never willing to accept the substitution and continued to call him George Pease Williams.

Williams dedicated his monograph on *Norman Anonymous of 1100 A.D.* (published in 1951), originally his doctoral dissertation

CONTINUITY AND DISCONTINUITY IN CHURCH HISTORY

Essays presented to George Huntston Williams

SOCINIAN HISTORIOGRAPHY IN THE LATE 17TH CENTURY

by Lech Szczucki

ERRATA

p. 285: *instead of* University of Warsaw *read* Polish Academy of Sciences, Warsaw, Institute of Philosophy and Sociology

p. 285, n. 2, 1.3: *instead of* but see *read* see also

p. 286, n. 4: *read*

4 But cf. K. Pomian, "Piotr Bayle wobec socynianizmu" [Pierre Bayle and Socinianism], Archiwum Historii Filozofii i Myśli Społecznej, 6 (1961), 101-82; Z. Ogonowski, *Socynianizm i Oświecenie. Studia nad myślą filozoficzno-religijną arian w Polsce XVII wieku* [*Socinianism and Enlightenment. Studies in the Philosophical and Religious Thought of the Unitarians in Seventeenth-century Poland*] (Warszawa, 1966); M. Firpo, "Pierre Bayle, gli eretici italiani del Cinquecento e la tradizione sociniana," *Rivista storica italiana*, 65 (1973), 612-66.

p. 287, l. 17: *instead of* second edition *read* second, enlarged, edition

p. 287, n. 6, l. 2: *instead of* (1975). *read* (1976), 197-212.

p. 288, l. 5: *instead of* athough *read* although

p. 288, l. 7: *instead of* Lubienicki *read* Lubieniecki

p. 288, l. 16: *instead of* Benedikt *read* Benedykt

p. 289, n. 9, l. 4: *instead of* Prypcovii-L.S. *read* Przypcovii-*L.S.*

    n. 9, l. 6: *instead of* ms. III e. 3, *read* m.s. III E. 3,

    n. 11, l. 1: *instead of* Regiomenti *read* Regiomonti

    n. 11, l. 7: *instead of* beryllo *read* Beryllo

p. 291, l. 11: *instead of* promere *read* premere

p. 293, l. 1: *instead of* (nucleus!) *read* (*nucleus!*)

p. 293, n. 18: Archiwum Filozofii i Myśli Społecznej *should be italicized*

p. 300, l. 22: *instead of* libertate *read* *libertate*

p. 300: at the end of the article add:

    Florence, Villa I Tatti, February-March, 1978.

at Union Theological Seminary, jointly to his paternal grandfather, David Thomas Williams, D.D. (1851-1946), *"Churchman,"* and to his maternal grandfather George W. Pease (1853-1949), *"Citizen."* The dissertation deals with "the bearing of Christology on the relationship between church and state." As we shall observe, Williams through his grandparents had already seen in action the conflicts and the intertwining of church and society.

His *magnum opus* of 924 pages, *The Radical Reformation* (1962), besides being dedicated to his first teacher of theology, is dedicated to his mother, Lucy Adams Williams whose "loving understanding of all individuals in their diversity encouraged me in the study of their varied tongues." From her he also gained an interest in the personal history of his students. "George Williams felt that every person has his own story to tell," says his teaching fellow, Royal Rhodes. He dedicated the book also to his father whose "prophetic sermons opened for me the vision of that world where thrones are crumbled and where kings are dust." Through his parents, he had an intimate view of the ways in which differing personalities could generate great tension, yet at the same time bolster each other up. For Williams it is clear that the members of his family, including his wife Marjorie Derr, were the decisive sinews in his personal development.

Williams was fortunate in that there was such a diversity of personality in his own family. Huntsburg, where he spent much of his childhood, was a rural community, where it was common for extended families to live together or near to each other. The flow of ideas coming from this well-loved, closely knit cluster of relatives had a much more powerful effect on Williams than would the diverse, but anonymous, stimuli of an urban setting.

From stories about his grandparents, Williams at an early age learned about social action as a means of effecting social change. The parental grandfather, David Thomas Williams, born in Wales, was the son of a Congregationalist minister, both father and son having worked in the coal mines surrounded by great mounds of slag. On migrating to the States he secured his theological education at Bangor, Oberlin and Western Reserve University, and he served virtually as itinerant minister in several states. His act of courage in the midst of a bitter labor-management struggle became a legend in the family and the neighborhood. In the middle of winter the owners "locked out" the miners—from their homes as well as from the credit of the stores. The workers were spurned by the respectable people in the town, and indeed also in the surrounding territory. In face of this tense struggle David Williams opened the local church building to the miners, and also solicited funds for their relief.

Everyone in the family knew also that his wife in her earlier days in Wales had led a protest against the British Establishment by organizing a picnic for ministers' wives to be held outside the town precisely when the Prince of Wales was to visit the town. They knew also that later on from the parsonage in South Boston she had pushed aside the police in a protest against the broken promise of the authorities regarding the workers' use without charge of a new bridge.

After her death David Thomas Williams lived with George's parents, and later on he was honored with a D.D. Degree from Western Reserve University as a representative rural minister; and still later on as an aged man he in prayer laid his hands on the head of his grandson George when in 1930 he was ordained in Rockford, Illinois, to the Unitarian ministry, the present writer also participating in this Ordination Service.

His mother's side of the family was named Pease—one of the first families in Huntsburg, Ohio, a town served by Grandfather Williams. In the town that aspired to a Shakespeare Society and other literary groups, George W. Pease, having assisted in the raising of funds, laid the cornerstone of the local Academy. A member of the Congregational Church, the grandmother was of a mystical temper prone to absorption in an ecstasy of peace, particularly during the celebration of the Lord's Supper. The grandfather Pease, on the other hand, felt himself unworthy to receive the communion, a cause of some puzzlement for the grandmother who held him in highest esteem for his sterling character. The young child George who lived with the family for a time and sat between the grandparents in church did not know, he says, which was the greater God, the God of his grandmother in her ecstacy or the God of the grandfather in his sense of moral inadequacy.

Williams' father, David Rhys Williams, graduated from Harvard Divinity School in 1914, when it was associated with Andover Theological School. A variety of stories has gathered about an episode in his graduation exercises of 1914. David Williams felt that much that went on in the School was irrelevant to the tasks of the minister and to the needs of the churches. No doubt mindful of his father's experience in the milltown controversy in Huntsburg and of his mother's even greater concern for social justice, he as a socialist had gone to Lowell,

Mass., to observe the strike of the textile workers. There he had seen a mounted policeman who with murderous intent had caused his horse to trample on one of the striking women, and he had seen her lie in the street in blood. Being shocked by what he had witnessed he was determined to exercise the liberty of prophesying during the graduation ceremony. Former President of Harvard, Charles William Eliot, was on the platform. Never timid, Williams after the speeches were concluded arose and approached the podium. The faculty member in charge gestured for him to return to his seat, but instead of acquiescing he beckoned for the faculty member to take his seat. It is said that President Eliot gave a welcoming gesture. With the eloquence for which he was later to become noted, Williams asserted that theological education at Harvard fell short if it did not show concern for social justice. If the study of the Old and the New Testament did not induce the faculty and students to do something in face of the cruelty to the workers in Lowell, then they had not understood Amos and the prophets and Jesus. (From the outset of his ministry David Williams was an advocate also of women's rights and of pacifism.) The incident at the graduation exercises received wide publicity in the press.

With the entry of the United States into the World War David Williams, minister of the Congregational Church in Edgartown, Martha's Vineyard, protested against the war and later also against the "peace" imposed on Germany. Being a pacifist, he did not enter into the fighting. Instead, he served in France as a volunteer in a canteen near the front lines. After the war, David Williams became minister of a Congregational church in an industrial, blue-collar section of Cleveland where in the post-war years he inaugurated the first forum in the city. Speakers were always chosen to take opposing sides and there were always refreshments and conversation in the parsonage following the forum. The young George was supposed to be asleep by this time, but his mother allowed him to lie on a couch in the adjoining room. He peeked through the opening to see and hear such figures as Eugene V. Debs, W. E. B. DuBois, and Newton D. Baker. This was only the beginning of this eavesdropping on the great, for in the succeeding pastorates in Chicago and Rochester his father also introduced a forum. Moreover, against great opposition his father established the first birth-control clinic in Rochester.

When George was in his early teens his father, transferring from the Congregationalist denomination, became minister of the Third

Unitarian Church in Chicago. There George intensively cultivated his interests not only in history and natural history, but also in the fine arts. Saturday after Saturday he visited the Field Museum, gaining virtual command of the exhibits, also making regular trips to the Forest Reserves, the while assembling his own elaborate collections of flowers and animals both alive and stuffed. He became familiar with the exhibits at the Institute of Fine Arts, and even took a course in drawing there in order to improve his sketches of flowers, animals, and landscapes. At the family summer place in Westfield, N.Y., he planted a thousand trees. For him, the earth had become not a place to quarry, but an extension of body, family and soul. Things outward draw the inward quality after them.

During these years, his mother's "loving understanding of all individuals" entered fully into the boy's consciousness, encouraging him to acquire precision of observation and reverence for the diversity of life.

In his father's pastoral calls in the parish his mother generally accompanied him. On their return home Mrs. Williams would tell him of the problems and anxieties he had not noticed. Actually, the father at home and often abroad would display a strongly authoritarian temper. Indeed, the conflicts between the father and other members of the family sometimes reached the level of vehemence. The tension remains deeply embedded in the son's memory. This element of tension he was later to recognize also in the polarities of church history. One may say that as in abstract expressionist paintings, the curvilinear shapes are in Williams' writing presented with a counterpoint of jagged, brittle lines that heighten the energy of the canvas, an energy to be observed also in Williams' indefatigable probing into the minutest details of research.

*

Williams' fundamental personal commitment as an individual and as a church historian is to the church universal and to the prophetic obligation of rational dissent. How this came about we have seen as stemming from his family heritage and his experience in the local congregation. His sense of the Body of Christ is informed by the richness of communal experience which comes to a focus in liturgy and sacrament and in the prophetic moments when the church as a corporate entity shows its sacrificial concern for the world and its transcendent independence of the world. I have heard him say that when he is in a worship service he feels almost a physical pressure on his temples by

reason of his awareness of the community of faith. In large degree
he has chosen the iconography he has delineated because of his interpretation of the perennial and current needs of the community of
faith. He says that when he made the decision to resign his pastorate
in Rockford in order to accept a teaching position in Berkeley he wept
and then wrote an individual letter to each member of the congregation. His wife Marjorie Derr who cherished the teamwork with him in
the parish, shared this lament, and has continued to perform pastoral
duties as a vigorous church member, serving also in numerous community enterprises.

On his traveling fellowship from Meadville he first went, as I had
done previously, to study at L'Institut Catholique in Paris under the
historical theologian Le Breton who was giving his lectures on the
Doctrine of the Trinity, all in Latin. (Wilhelm Pauck at Chicago
had sometimes teased Williams by saying that as a "birthright Unitarian" he would not be able to understand this Doctrine.) From Paris
he transferred to Strasbourg because he would find there both a
Protestant and a Catholic faculty. Later, as Acting Dean of Harvard
Divinity School he aimed to introduce an ecumenical pattern which
previously had been neglected.

When he served from 1962 to 1965 as an official Observer at
Vatican Council II, he noted that the liberals and the free churchmen
were often among the most positive in evaluating the progress of the
Council. He was dismayed by the comment of a Heidelberg theologian
who said, "It is more pleasant to feel the warmth of fraternal embrace
here than the acrid heat of inquisitional flames—but the purpose is
the same!" The open-mindedness on the part of liberal Protestants
toward Catholics was not entirely new. In his Sermon on the Council
entitled "A Time to Rend and a Time to Sew" (December, 1962)
Williams recalled that William Ellery Channing was a personal friend
of Bishop John Cheverus of Boston who, on later becoming a Cardinal
Archbishop of Bordeaux, was a factor in making Channing's writings
on social justice and toleration known in France. Especially noteworthy for Williams, in addition to the stress on collegiality and on
the lay apostolate, was the recognition in the Council that the church
can be truer to her mission if she is independent of the state, not only
of the Communist state but also of the democratic state. Equally
important for all was the renewed emphasis on the de-Europeanization
of the church and on a pluralistic ecumenism.

This ecumenical thrust was seen by Williams as working not only against the demonry of nationalism but also against the racism which he had opposed in determining to attend the inner-city East High School in Rochester and, later, in marching in Montgomery. He believes that in America and in the Third World a new more inclusive conception of covenant is being engendered which will bring political as well as religious renewal. Asa Davis, one of his doctoral students, unbeknownst to Williams, brought the young Martin Luther King to one of his lectures at Harvard. In this lecture he predicted that the next great theologian would be a black.

When Williams in 1968 visited Russia at the invitation of Metropolitan Nikodin of Leningrad and under the auspices of La Société Européenne de Culture he found special satisfaction in becoming personally acquainted with churchmen who were suffering under the heel of Soviet oppression, though he felt constrained to lament to the Baptists that they had lost their savor as Dissenters.

Williams' ecumenical outlook found singular expression many years earlier in the days of the Scopes Trial of 1925 in Tennessee. At the age of eleven he was in full sympathy with Scopes' position—his claim to freedom to teach the theory of evolution—but he deplored the contemptuous attitude of those who made fun of Williams Jennings Bryan and the Fundamentalists whom he represented in the court. He felt that sincere conviction deserved respect. Years later when in 1978 he testified before the Supreme Court of Kentucky he came to the defense of the Fundamentalists in their maintenance of private schools. He took this position in the name of cultural pluralism and in opposition to the encroachments of the state in its oppression of civil liberty and of freedom of association. To be sure, he made it clear that he was opposed to racial discrimination in private as well as in public schools.

Although a liberal in religion and politics, Williams has the independence of mind not to adopt every allegedly liberal tenet. Despite his years of support of the American Civil Liberties Union, he has expressed in numerous articles his impassioned opposition to abortion on demand. In his formal statement on February 26, 1971, before the Massachusetts House Judiciary Committee he rejected the view that opposition to abortion on demand represents the attempt of a sectarian faction to impose its restrictions upon the public domain. The ground of the rejection of abortion on demand, he said, is not sectarian, nor is it peculiarly Christian, it is humane. It asserts the inherent right of embryonic being, once conceived, to be brought into the world. The claim that freedom of decision for the mother is a matter of private morality is invalid. The issue is one of public morality, and it belongs to the public authorities to safeguard whatever new life may issue from privatized sexual activity, and thus to protect the civil liberty of the unborn. In ancient Rome, he said, the sire could abort the fetus in his wife or servant without their consent. This claim to sire-sovereignty has long ago been rejected. Yet, there is no ethical difference between the ancient sire-sovereignty and the present claim for the sovereignty of the mother over the life in her womb.

In the period of McCarthy-inspired anti-Communist hysteria Williams' alertness to the dangers of statism became cogently evident in his article on "Reluctance to Inform" (1957), an article drawing warnings from church history and showing the similarity between former ecclesiastical oppression and the present punishment of journalists and others who refuse to inform regarding sources of information. From Supreme Court Justices Earl Warren and Felix Frankfurter he received letters of thanks for this article, indicating that the Court had been influenced by it in its deliberations.

Numerous other activities of Williams attest to his sense of social responsibility as citizen and churchperson, such as his participation in 1967 with William Sloane Coffin and others in the ceremonial supporting those who burned their draft cards at Arlington Street Church in Boston as well as his joining in the anti-discrimination protests in Alabama and elsewhere, and in an anti-pollution campaign in his suburban town.

These examples of Williams' combination of pluralistic ecumenicity and the prophetic freedom of dissent and social criticism gives occasion to recall his keen interest in the writings of Frederic Henry Hedge (1805-1890) who was probably the first American theologian to use the term *ecumenical* in its present sense. A Christian Transcendentalist and for a time the president of the American Unitarian Association, Hedge served as the first professor of ecclesiastical history (1857-1876) at Harvard Divinity School. In this position he was, then, one of Williams' predecessors.

It would be difficult to find in the nineteenth century any American theologian, except perhaps Philip Schaff, who stressed the ecumenical ideal more than did Hedge. "The church," Hedge said, "must be catholic, it must embrace the whole, it must gather into one all the elements which are scattered abroad." It is not surprising, therefore,

that Williams' brochure of 1949 on Hedge is one of his most sug-
gestive essays on the doctrine of the church, and specifically of the
liberal church in its concern for social justice and in its relations to
the various types of Christianity in past and present.

Since the doctrine of the atonement is one of the principal items
in his iconography, Williams finds much to his liking Hedge's adoption of a form of the doctrine. Hedge's doctrine of at-one-ment serves
as the basis for his conception of the reconciliation of differentiating
elements in Christian history. In his view this reconciliation comes as
the interpenetration of the transcendent and the immanent. Interpreting
the atonement in corporate terms rather than as merely the "particular
redemption" or election of the individual, Hedge urged the churches
to yearn for "a public grace of which the individual becomes a partaker
through his social relations and not by private negotiations, and the
realization of which is society itself in the measure of its moral and
Christian progress." This is the nerve of Hedge's "social gospel." One
is reminded here of the view of Hedge's famous German contemporary,
Friedrich Julius Stahl, who held that conversion and salvation belong
to institutions as well as to individuals. Hedge for his part aimed to
recover the Pauline social conception of atonement (and at the same
time perhaps to pay his respects to Hegelianism). Accordingly, any
radically sectarian movement was to Hedge inimical to the working of
the Holy Spirit in its engendering of a variety of authentic witness
and in its reconciling of these differentiations in the unity of the
Spirit.

From Williams' perspective it is this sectarian spirit that causes
him to qualify radically his assessment of the Radical Reformers
whom he has dealt with in unprecedented amplitude. They cultivated
the inner disciplines that nourish conscience and independence of the
world. Moreover, through their separation of church and state they
prepared the West for the modern world. But insofar as they promoted
the temper of withdrawal they failed to maintain the Constantinian
legacy entailing the churches' sharing of responsibility for the character
of the society as a whole. The Radical Reformers who did not surrender this legacy were those of the aggressive sects which, like the
Levellers and others in England and America, initiated the movement
towards the dispersion of power and responsibility in society as well
as in the churches, thus giving impetus to the democratization of the
organization of the church, the state and education, and finally also
to the laborers in the work force. Williams saw in Channing not

only the insistence upon rationality in approaching religion and the Scriptures ("the liberal intellect") but also the maintenance of the Constantinian legacy, as in his classical statement on "Religion as a Social Principle." These themes are all freshly examined in Williams' forthcoming work on the Polish Brethren of the sixteenth century.

Having emphasized the variety of the forms of Christianity, Hedge was concerned also to find a classification of these differentiations. Here again Hedge's approach is of special interest to Williams who, as we have noted, possesses a strong sense of the genius of place. Hedge's classification of the types of Christianity is accomplished in terms of place or space. We should recall here that having in his youth studied in Germany for four years under the tutelage of the future American historian, George Bancroft, also a Unitarian, Hedge was familiar with (and later published translations of) the writings of the philosophical idealists on philosophy of history and of church history. Schelling, for example, had developed a chronological scheme, dividing church history into three stages, the Petrine (Catholic), the Pauline (The Reformation), and the Johannine (the coming Age of the Spirit).

Hedge envisaged the major segments of historical Christianity in terms of space and not of time. He identified the different types of Christianity according to their principal geographical areas— eastern, western, northern and southern sectors. In almost misleading simplicity we can note that for Hedge the cast represents stability, conservatism; the west, mobility, innovation, progress; the north, internal activity (the inner life), idealism, mysticism; and the south, external productiveness, ritual, symbolism, and ecclesiastical organization. Particularly significant for the New Englander is Hedge's view that Unitarianism and Congregationalism combined the Dissenting heritage of sectarian localism and the view of the church as a territorial establishment promoting a "public theology" entailing the church's sense of corporate responsibility for the character of the society as a whole—the best of the polar opposites, sect and church, as Troeltsch called them.

The elements in Hedge's composite, geographically mapped-out sectors of Christian history past and present appear in Williams' landscape with its many "trenches," but one sector is missing in Hedge, "our neighbor the universe." Williams, a lover of nature since boyhood, includes a theological interpretation of the embedment of the human and religious enterprise in the context of nature as well as of history. Christianity is part of something larger than itself. The God who acted in Israel and in the raising up of Jesus in the prophetic line works in all peoples and their religions. Especially significant for Williams is the relationship between Christianity and Islam and modern Judaism. His positive interest in the State of Israel and his active participation in her support has been noteworthy in a multitude of ways, some of them being highly dramatic.

But the attitude toward nature must also be taken into account. In his elaborate history of attitudes toward nature in Western history (1971) he traces the antinomies suggested by seven sets of Scriptural passages. The great achievement of the covenantal religion of Israel was to disengage itself from the cults of fertility of the Canaanites and to think of man as in this sense overcoming nature. In our time American Protestant Neo-orthodoxy has tended to overstress the view that God is to be understood not so much as the Creator of nature as the redemptive Lord of history.

Williams has not been willing to put to one side the theological concern for the cosmos and for the earth and its diversified world in which all creatures have a precious place in God's eyes. There is grace from below as well as grace from above. We are both a part of nature and are separated from it. "There is surely a piece of divinity within us," says Sir Thomas Browne, "something that was before the elements and owes no homage unto the sun." We come from below in one sense: the very salt solution of our blood corresponds to that of the salt density of the sea. We are nevertheless brought out of the water and the seas and lifted up to be reborn as rational, responsible creatures sustained by grace. But the water and the seas are still a part of us. Indeed, water becomes in baptism a symbol for creation and re-creation, of spiritual birth and regeneration through grace from above. In this sacrament, and also through the elements of the Lord's Supper, nature is brought into the history of salvation in a community of faith. Sight, sound, touch, and the olfactory all belong in the liturgy and the sacraments, that is, in the liturgy and the sacraments that do not submerge us in the sub-human, the biological sphere.

Yet, we again and again in our corporate life face the temptation of reverting to a naturistic religion, as in Social Darwinism and in Hitlerism. In the first, "survival of the fittest" becomes the criterion; and in the second, race is raised to demonic prominence.

The authentic religious community is the only community in which we are protected from the demonries to which flesh is heir. Only in this community are we completely human because we have transcended the limitations of our biological provenance. Nor can we be saved by reason alone, for reason must itself be saved. With the help of a superior power whom we address in prayer and in anguish, we prepare for the grace of "regeneration which makes us purposeful, illumined and whole in the community of faith."

*

Despite the originality of his concern for a philosophy of church history, the writings of Hedge on church history are not numerous. If we look for an American church historian of greater stature who was a generalist possessing a temper similar to that of Williams, we can readily see a kindred spirit in Philip Schaff (1819-1893). Although their philosophies of church history are not the same, they both stem in large measure from a Calvinist heritage, and they are similar in their search for a better understanding of the various types of Christianity. Both of them have worked for reconciliation between these types, though they have recognized that adjustments can be only partial and temporary. Both of them have exhibited a profound interest in liturgy and sacrament, both have cultivated a consistent respect for minorities, both have allowed for diversity of education as well as urging cooperation in all that pertains to the commonweal of humanity. Both of them have promoted appreciation for the worth of every confession. Yet, as was once said of Schaff, of Williams too it may be said that his is "a devotion to Christianity which rises superior to all denominations." They belong to John Bunyan's House of the Interpreter, offering light and guidance and warning to the pilgrim "in the difficult places he meets with in the way."

Both men, I doubt not, would accept with alacrity Nicholas of Cusa's "icon of God" (1454), an omnivoyant portrait which, regardless of the quarter from which the pilgrim regards it, "Looks upon him as if it looked on none other," each experiencing the directness of its gaze, each being precious in its sight but none claiming to possess the icon as his own prerogative, and each knowing that "it taketh the same most diligent care of the least of creatures as of the greatest, and of the whole universe."

THE PERIODIZATION OF HISTORY

FRANKLIN H. LITTELL

Temple University

The ocean of facts is infinite. Every writer reveals his presuppositions in several ways, and never more clearly than by selecting certain persons to feature, certain reports to highlight, certain events to emphasize in telling the story. The useful "facts" are organized in ways that seem to him significant; the "facts" that never surface in the account, always far more numerous than those for which space is provided, by their absence also indicate the writer's stance. "Facts" may be included because they come to attention from credible reporters, even though they are inconvenient to the effort to make out a certain sense in the tale. Other "facts" may be dropped, or at most noted briefly in a footnote, simply because they lack the note of probability provided by a credible witness. As in a court of law, the establishment of a witness' credibility—or, conversely, the discrediting of an account —is a fudamental exercise of the careful scholar.

Aware of his own fallibility and mortality, the writer may deliberately brief the reader, as did Kenneth Scott Latourette in the Introduction to the first volume of his great seven-volume *History of the Expansion of Christianity,* [1] pledging his effort toward fairness and accuracy but conscious of his own inevitable biases—and being convinced that the reader is entitled to know the probabilities. Or he may be silent, letting the careful reader check his academic pedigree and past performance, and providing only the footnotes which make possible a check on his use of sources. But every writer, including the historian, has presuppositions. Presuppositionless history does not exist. The facts do not speak for themselves. Every translation, however careful, is an interpretation. There are only two kinds of historians: 1) those who know their own fallibility, work with utmost fairness and care, and sign their names to their work; 2) those who claim a sterile "objectivity" and deceive themselves and, perhaps, their readers.

When certain persons are considered important and given center

---

[1] Kenneth Scott Latourette, *A History of the Expansion of Christianity,* vol. I (New York, 1937), xvi-xvii.

stage, or when certain events are singled out for emphasis, a complex set of choices has been made—consciously or unconsciously—by the interpreter. The organization of a narrative into chapters, with titles and sub-titles, also clearly shows what the writer considers to be meaningful in the dialogue with the past. By such means the writer deals in "the thoughts that wound from behind" (SK) and may in fact communicate ideas and interpretations which stay with the reader long after the subject matter has been forgotten.

Awareness of this truth led James Harvey Robinson to write his great book, *The New History*. [2] Robinson was convinced that most earlier writings, concentrating upon the dynastic and military chronicles, implanted a false view of history in the student's mind—a false view that remained long after the "facts" were forgotten. He went on to challenge certain events traditionally used to periodize history to the glory of dynasts and generals and urged that major attention be given to the common life of the common people. Translated into Christian history, this would mean major attention to the life of the laity (the whole people of God) rather than concentration upon the affairs of Christian princes and hierarchs. In any case, the featuring of certain periodizing events conveyed a message he believed to be false. Choosing them and rejecting others revealed a basic philosophy of history. Robinson, devoted to the idea of the continuity of the common life, with no abrupt turns or sudden changes, was perhaps too sanguine that events and periodizations he abhorred could be erased rather than overpowered by other myths conveying another message. But he read the "unwritten agenda" of the traditional chronicles—and rejected it.

As a church historian in America, one of the few in his generation well enough trained and secure enough in his vocation to avoid the flight into specialization and mere facticity, George H. Williams has been a master of the scientific tools of his craft. At the same time he has not hesitated to be a protagonist as well as observer and interpreter. He is a credible witness, as both scholar and churchman. He has taken his stand with a "new Church History," well beyond most earlier writers—to whom Christian history was either an exercise in filial devotion or an attempt to present the history of Christianity as a sterile sector of the history of mankind. One of his most massive

---

[2] James Harvey Robinson, *The New History* (New York, 1920); of the traditional history he (p. 6) wrote, "It recommends itself, it is true, as the easiest kind of history to teach, since it requires no thought,—only memory."

contributions has been in exposing and interpreting the contribution
of the Radical Reformation.

Attention to the Radical Reformation has grown, in good part as a
consequence of his work, as the old monolith of Christendom—to which
Christian Europe, both Roman Catholicism and "the magisterial Reformation," were devoted—has lost credibility in the modern world.

Nothing has contributed more to that loss of credibility than study of
the lessons of the German Church Struggle and the Holocaust. Among
the minority of Christians who resisted Nazism, the question of
breaking from the traditional state-church system (*landesherrliches
Kirchenregiment*) was seriously debated. The Augsburg Synod (1935)
of the Confessing Church (*Bekennende Kirche*) rejected the option,
and after the war a modified system of establishment was restored in
the British, American and French zones of military government.
Although the Evangelical Church of Württemberg experimented
briefly (1952) with separation, such remains the pattern in West
Germany to the present day. The continuity of the self-image of
"Christian civilization," in which all subordinate structures of being are
coordinated to implement a single sacral ideal, is thus preserved.

Nevertheless, there is an underground stream of Christian discontent
with the long-lived tradition of the *corpus christianum*. Marxism and
Nazism, of course, represent substantial "post-Christian" worlds
which have adopted a quite different set of events and historical
periodizations to comprehend their dogmatic systems. But some
Christian thinkers also raise fundamental questions. The case for a
radical break from the traditional theology of history was sharply
stated in the midst of what some called "the second Church Struggle"
(in Communist East Germany). At the 1956 Special Synod of the
Evangelical Church in Germany, Superintendent Günter Jacob of
Cottbus stated:

> Alert minds characterize the Christian situation in Europe today in this
> way: that the end of the Constantinian age has arrived.... The Constan-
> tinian alliance marked the betrayal of the genuine style of the Church of
> Jesus Christ, which according to the view of the New Testament is to be
> in this world a course of suffering from the contradiction and resistance
> of the world....
>   After the end of illusions about the Constantinian era, and in return to
> the early Christian witness, we have no right to appeal to the state for
> privileges and monopoly in support of the Gospel. [3]

---

[3] Günter Jacob, "Der Raum für das Evangelium in Ost und West," in
*Bericht über die ausserordentliche Synode der evangelischen Kirche in Deutsch-
land, 1956* (Hanover, 1956), 17-29.

True to a long line of radical Christian apologetic, Dr. Jacob expressed his discontent with the blind alley into which the intimate association of church and state had led Christians during the Nazi period and again under Communist control of East Germany by welding it to a radical periodization of history. Abandoning the theme of continuity, he in effect put brackets around the more than sixteen centuries between the triumph of Christianity as the religion of the Roman Empire and the battle of Christianity with its militant alternatives in the present age.

Periodization in Protestantism

The Roman Catholicism which was formulated at the Council of Trent (1545-63), holding together those sectors of Christendom which remained loyal to the papacy, claimed to continue unbroken the authentic practices and teachings of the origins. Rejecting an un-reformed papacy as guarantor of continuity, Reformers generally followed Luther in identifying a continuity of the preaching of the Word of God. Both Luther and Calvin perceived falls and recoveries in Christian history, but none so radical that the line was broken or all but hidden remnants expunged. To the affirmation of continuity the Church of England, in time, added the guarantee of "apostolic succession" (episcopal).

Only the Radical Reformers of the sixteenth century, [4] followed by radical Puritans and radical Pietists in the seventeenth and eighteenth centuries, declared that a rupture of continuity had occurred—a rupture so basic that the True Church (*rechte Kirche*) was condemned to wander in the wilderness (Christendom) for centuries, to be restituted in their own ranks. Among many Free Churches of the modern period, especially in America (e.g., Alexander Campbell's "Restoration Movement"), the "Fall of the Church" with Constantine and the restitution or restoration of "the New Testament order" became basic motifs. The normative use of "the Early Church" or even "the Church at Jerusalem" and the condemnation of "the Constantinian compromise" became vehicles for articulating a set of affirmations and negations about the Christian life.

All wings of the Radical Reformation agreed that the Constantinian establishment brought about a basic corruption of Christian life and

---

[4] Franklin H. Littell, *The Origins of Sectarian Protestantism* (New York, 1964), PB of revised edition: ch. II—"The Fall of the Church," ch. III—"The Restitution of the True Church."

teaching. Spiritualizers like Sebastian Franck and Caspar Schwenckfeld saw it signalized by the enforcement of dogmatic orthodoxy and the suppression of spiritual liberty. Religious revolutionaries like Thomas Müntzer and John of Leyden saw the fall of the church in the acceptance of private property and the emergence of economic exploitation of Christians by Christians. (The Hutterite wing of Anabaptism, still extant, shared this view but eschewed revolution and violence.) Anti-Trinitarians saw it in the enforcement of the theologians' Trinitarian dogma at Nicaea (325 C.E.). The Anabaptists (Swiss Brethren, South German Brethren, Dutch Mennonites and Hutterites) singled out the union of church and state as the chief mark of "the Fall of the Church."

In their affirmations about "the True Church" the Anabaptists differed little from the mainline Reformers on matters of doctrine. In the sacramental life, however, a radical discontinuity was evident. Most basic, they rejected Infant Baptism as the door through which whole populations—unwitting and unschooled—had been led into a formless, undisciplined "baptized heathenism." In observance of the Lord's Supper, they observed "the Lesser Ban" and "the Greater Ban": none but those in good standing were admitted to the table. In measuring practical differences, probably most important was their emphasis upon the apostolic order and primitive style of life of the Christian community. The Anabaptists believed the proclamation of the Word and the right observance of the sacraments to be insufficient by themselves: the new life in Christ should be evident in a Christian style of life, supported and enforced by church discipline.

The Anabaptist emphasis upon a community of witness as fundamental to the True Church was so strenuous that the scholar Robert Friedmann was moved to refer to the Anabaptist-Mennonite testimony as a "Third Type"—basically different from both Roman Catholicism and Protestantism. [5] Certainly, to use contemporary language, they conceived of themselves as a "counter-culture" to Christendom. And it is clear that, by their rejection of both Roman Catholic and Protestant establishments, they closed the historical parentheses around the "Constantinian era."

Since the eighteenth century, Protestantism of restitutionist origins has oscillated between considering itself a "root and branch Reforma-

---

[5] Robert Friedmann, *Mennonite Piety Through the Centuries* (Goshen, Ind., 1949).

tion" and a new (or restored) manifestation of primitive Christianity. Both themes, mutually contradictory so far as periodization is concerned, can be found at times in the same denomination. Among the Free Churches, the line of distinction today runs between those that have accepted social establishment and promiscuous membership practices (a social, but not legal, *Kulturprotestantismus*) and those that still maintain church discipline and some measure of "separation."

"Separation" begins, of course, not with the simple question of relationship to government, but with the whole issue whether the Christian community is a "counter-culture" to this age or a part of the social fabric sustaining a given society. The "fall of the church" remains a common theme to be verbalized, even where evidences of "separation" can no longer be found. The question whether the parentheses around "the Dark Ages" were closed in the sixteenth century or later remains—even among the American Free Churches—an unsettled issue. And among those that have attained success and a popular following, the notion of a present Christian civilization, a Christian civilization, a Christian society, a Christian nation here and now, also has a seductive appeal.

"Secular Religions" and Periodization Schemes

Among modern "secular religions," i.e. those ideologies which function as substitute religions (*Ersatzreligionen*) for numbers of people, a suitable scheme of periodization has an important place in the arsenal of ideas as weapons. The most dramatic illustration of this has been the dogma elaborated by National Socialism during the Third Reich.

German National Socialism has been treated as a "secular religion," a "post-Christian *Ersatzreligion*," and as a "New Islam" with an interpretation of history competitive to Christianity. More accurately, Nazism represented not a secularization process but a re-sacralization within tribal boundaries. Certainly in the minds of the "true believers," as well as in the historical perspectives of those who adjusted Christian teachings to accommodate the Nazi dispensation, a special periodization of history was involved. [6]

The Nazi use of the concept of "Third Reich," which had many antecedents in German political philosophy, is a classic case of an idea

---

[6] The writer is grateful to Prof. Michael Ryan of Drew University and Prof. Thomas Flanagan of the University of Calgary for their recent writings on the religious aspects of the Third Reich in idea and history.

used as a political-religious weapon. The concept was popularized by
Arthur Moeller van den Bruck's book *Das dritte Reich* (1923), and it
was introduced into Nazism by Otto Strasser. It was Moeller's aim
and achievement to give political content to a philosophical idea which
can be found in many earlier German writers, including Lessing, Hegel
and Schelling. Moeller's immediate forerunners—including Henrik
Ibsen, Johannes Schlaf, Eugen Diedrichs, Ernst Krieck—had already
given the concept its emphasis upon the New Man of the New Age.
The First Reich was the Holy Roman Empire of the German Nation
(ended by Napoleon in 1806); the Second Reich was the Bismarckian
empire (ended by Wilhelm II's abdication in 1918); the Third Reich,
"post-Christian" in content and intention, carried by the man of
will and action (vs. reason and theory), was to be a new era in human
history.

It was Ernst Krieck, author of *Die deutsche Staatsidee,* a conservative during the Weimar Republic who became a Minister of Education
during the Third Reich, who gave the concept its peculiarly German
antecedents and direction. It was Moeller van den Bruck who transformed it from speculative symbolism to political propaganda. Although
Moeller died a despairing suicide in 1925, in less than a decade the
Nazi one-party government had made it a fundamental section of the
unity of dogma which was the world of the Nazi true believer. It
was also a powerful ideological weapon to batter the defenses of the
uncommitted, for it led politics out of the realm of pedestrian problem-
solving into the excitement of political realized eschatology.

Among writers who have traced the triadic typology back behind
German writers to such medieval shapers of Western historical thought
as Otto von Freising (c. 1114-1158) and Joachim of Fiore (c. 1145-
1202) have been Norman Cohn (*The Pursuit of the Millenium*) and
Klemens von Klemperer (*Germany's New Conservatism*).

Joachimite Origins of Radical Periodization

With the popularization—during the battle of the radical Franciscans
with the papacy—of the idea that history was entering its third and final
age, a motif of historical discontinuity was injected into Western
thought. Since the thirteenth century it has been a powerful source of
both religious and political radicalism, an underground river which
has surfaced from time to time to arm protest movements and launch
revolutions. The teachings which proved so potent a challenge to

traditional Christian ideas of continuity were attributed to the Abbot Joachim of Fiore. [7]

Until Joachim's time, Christian history traversed as it were a level plain between two mountainous events: the Ascension of Christ and His Second Coming. History was conceived in such a way that nothing very important could happen in the intermediate period—except in the histories of individuals and their souls. Joachim, however, introduced a radically different periodization of history. His scheme elaborated a superseding myth, defining historical periods which he related to the Trinitarian formula. In the Age of the Father, the Law was given on tablets of stone. In the Age of the Son, the message was taught by voice and sealed by the sacramental system. In the Age of the Spirit, divine truth would be communicated directly to the hearts of men.

In Joachimitism, each succeeding age replaced the former in a passage of struggle, tribulation and resistance of the old order to the new. Each age was introduced by a prophet—Moses, Jesus, and a third. (According to those who later applied Joachim's scheme to battle with the papacy, the third figure was Francis of Assisi.)

In the final age the church would wither away, the hierarchy and sacramental rites disappear, and the humble, the oppressed and anonymous would stand forth as the carriers of history. The Great Church of Christendom would be replaced by a band of brothers recapitulating the holy relationships of an earlier period, when the people were of one faith and soul—as in the Early Church. The prophet of the last age, according to the Joachimites, would be spiritual Constantine—freeing the church from the slavery into which the imperial Constantine had bound her.

For the student of religions, it is interesting to note that the center of Joachim's work was Calabria, in the boot of Italy, but a few years removed from two centuries of Muslim rule. Roger, the first Norman king of Calabria and Sicily, retained many Islamic institutions, kept Arabic advisors, struck coins with Koranic motifs. Roger II, king of the Two Sicilies, spoke Arabic, used a Muslim royal seal, and ran a court and palace school with Muslim staffing.

---

[7] The classic treatment of Joachim's thought remains Ernst Benz' *Ecclesia Spiritualis* (Stuttgart, 1934). Cf. also, on Joachim and his popularizers, Herbert Grundmann, *Studien über Joachim von Floris* (Leipzig & Berlin, 1927); Decima L. Douie, *The Nature and Effect of the Heresy of the Fraticelli* (Manchester, Eng., 1932); and Marjorie Reeves, *The Influence of Prophecy in the Later Middle Ages* (Oxford, 1969).

A three-fold periodization, with human history culminating in a final spiritual age superseding the age of Judaism and the age of Christianity, is a standard line of interpretation among Muslim teachers. Thus some scholars of the twelfth and thirteenth centuries have concluded that, as G. G. Coulton put it, Joachimitism is heavily indebted to Muslim views of history, "which essentially rests upon this idea of successive revelations, each complementing and to a great extent superseding its predecessor, and all culminating finally in the Prophet." [8]

We know that some of the radicals of the sixteenth century, Thomas Müntzer among them, studied both Joachim's *Evangelium Aeternum* and the Koran. And we know that Joachim and his followers were the first to break through the traditional periodization of history. In the modern age, prophets—both political and religious—who are said to be the culmination of the historical process are like the sands of the seashore in number. Sectarian Protestantism provides a gallery of culminating prophets and ages, of which David Joris—with three ages of history, each introduced by a "David"—is but one of the more exotic birds. Mother Ann Lee of the Shakers and Mary Baker Eddy of the Christian Scientists add another note to some movements' vision of the final age: the reaffirmation of the female principle in an originally (and finally) androgynous redeemed Humanity.

A significant illustration of the pervasiveness of the Joachimite motifs in "left wing Protestantism" is provided in the correspondence of the Pietist, August Hermann Francke (1663-1727), with the Puritan, Cotton Mather (1663-1728). In their discussions of the impending triumph of a world-spanning Christianity, of which the tangible evidences were the rapid conversion of many tribes and peoples and the cooperation and coming reunion of purified spiritual churches, they used without question such terms as "Age of the Spirit" and "Eternal Gospel." [9]

Whether the Unification Church is "Protestant" or even "Christian" is currently disputed. But we may note that the historical periodization scheme proclaimed by Rev. Sun Myung Moon and his followers illustrates a familiar triadic typology. And he has attracted reputable theologians to his entourage, just as leading theologians of Erlangen a few years ago were able to work out a (temporary) accommodation

---

[8] G. G. Coulton, *Five Centuries of Religion* (Cambridge, 1927), 2:120.

[9] Ernst Benz, "The Pietist and Puritan Sources of Early Protestant World Missions (Cotton Mather and A. H. Francke)," *Church History* 20 (1951), 28-55.

between Christianity and a promised *Wundermensch* (A. Hitler) and a promised New Age (Third Reich).

Early Christian Thought and Periodization

Radical Protestantism has for more than four centuries made normative use of the pre-Constantinian church, as though a fixed entity could be there located. Until the emergence of Joachimite periodization, and in substantial church circles to the present day, history was portrayed as a basically uneventful stretch of time between the Ascension and the Last Judgment. Here too a fixed view, a glassy sea where nothing happened, was fixed.

Yet study of the church before Constantine's accession to power will reveal that Christians of the first generations had their own problems of interpretation to work out, e.g., in regard to the destruction of the Second Temple (70 C.E.), the profanation of the Holy City by Titus (135 C.E.), and the great change which came with imperial acceptance and favor of the previously illicit and persecuted religion (313, 324 C.E.).

The normative use of "the Early Church," "the apostolic Church," "the New Testament Church," "primitive Christianity," or even "the Church at Jerusalem" has been a standard weapon of radical Christianity's attack upon Christendom. It has been a memorization device, expressive of a teaching method. Technically, the perspective is an expression of "primitivism." [10] The transfer into Christian historical views of the themes of Golden Age, Fall and Restitution, familiar enough in classical poetry and philosophy, [11] introduced a radical discontinuity where previously a principle of continuity had governed post-Constantinian theology of history. Equally important to this discussion, the glorification of "the Golden Age of the Church" (i.e., the pre-Constantinian, pre-establishment churches) brought with it an assumption of coherence, uniformity and consistency in the first generations of Christianity which the records scarcely support.

Modern man is preoccupied with "history," and has of course a far

---

[10] Cf. "Primitivismus," in Franklin H. Littell, and Hans Hermann Walz, eds., *Weltkirchenlexikon* (Stuttgart, 1960), cols. 1182-87.

[11] Primitivism was explored extensively by Professor A. O. Lovejoy of Johns Hopkins University and his students. In addition to numerous articles in the early years of *The Journal of the History of Ideas,* useful materials are found in Lovejoy's *A Documentary History of Primitivism and Related Ideas ... in Antiquity* (Baltimore, 1935) and George Boas, *Essays on Primitivism and Related Ideas in the Middle Ages* (Baltimore, 1948).

more awesome sense of the duration of human affairs than the early
Christians or their contemporaries could conceive. He is not only
subject to the sense of alienation which is the mature human predicament: he has been trained to scepticism, to comparison, to analysis.
Early Christian faith rested not upon a view of the future nor upon
the truth of certain propositions or abstractions, but upon the meaning
of certain present events foretold in the Scriptures. Those who spoke
of Him centered the message in His resurrection. In doing so, they
broke with the perspective then dominant among Jews: He was not
the One who is to come, but the One who has arrived. The distinction
between *Historie* and *Geschichte,* commonly associated with the work
of Rudolf Bultmann, is a contemporary Christian intellectual exercise
which would not have made sense to early Christians. They did not
know a "history" so divided. They were taught the worth of spontaneous, uncalculating goodness. They expected the Lord's return in a
consummating event in their own lifetime.

Yet Paul had to deal already with a problem of time between His
resurrection and His coming again (Rom. 9:1-11:36). Justin Martyr
(100-165 C.E.) made an attempt to gain elbow room within the
historical view of the Scriptures (those still shared by Jews and
Christians) by writing of two comings of Christ, one that had happened and the second yet to come. His solution did not commend
itself to others of the time, for most of them were working out a
relationship of Christianity to the philosophical tradition. "The fact is
that a really serious grasp of the contemporary philosophical understanding of the human problem would appear, on the basis of Clement's
evidence, to involve crossing over into the world of ideas in which it is
difficult to invest any specific course of events with unique significance." [12] With Clement of Alexandria (c. 150 - c. 215 C.E.) the
Hellenization of Christian perspectives was well under way. Tertullian
(c. 160 - c. 230 C.E.), with his vivid sense of God's present action,
of God's rule of "times" in which one ruler after another was allowed
to control, was a mutation among the Church Fathers. As the *parousia*
was delayed, as the Christian intellectuals laid conquest the philosophical concern for timeless truths, as Christian leaders built up structures of responsible administration and planned for the future, the
Christians acquired a sense of "history."

---

[12] L. G. Patterson, *God and History in Early Christian Thought* (London,
1967), 47.

Eusebius of Caesarea (c. 260 - c. 340 C.E.) made the final crossing over from the Jewish and early Christian language of events, told or foretold in the Scriptures, to the classical style of handling materials. He also completed the reversal of the attitude of the early Christians and earlier Church Fathers to Rome: for them, Rome was the last of the world empires, its doom already pronounced. For Eusebius, the Eternal Rome of the Augustan Empire was to be perfected by the Christian Emperor, and its time stretched far forward. Whether an Arian or not, Eusebius in his Panegyric to Constantine purposed the *apotheosis* of a human ruler.

For those who followed the line of imperial Christianity, with its triumphalist view of accomplished history, an unbroken course of human history would run until Christ's coming again. The early Christian view of the earthly Jerusalem as a foreshadowing of the Heavenly City to come at the end of the age was superseded by a baptized version of the old Roman religious meaning ascribed to *Roma aeterna*. Even the sack of Rome (410 C.E.), a major trauma at the time, would be forgotten by posterity, and the great book— *On the City of God*—written by Augustine (354-430 C.E.) to give the event a Christian meaning would be misinterpreted by Christian rulers of later centuries to justify their uses of religious and political power.

In later centuries other events have been singled out by major thinkers and/or sections of Christianity to bracket periods of history: e.g., the coronation of Otto the Great as "Holy Roman Emperor" (962 C.E.), the fall of Constantinople (1453), Luther's posting of the Ninety-Five Theses (31 October 1517), Holy Russia's defeat of Napoleon at Moscow (October, 1812). In recent years, the murder of 6,000,000 Jews by baptized Christians in the heart of Christendom has been identified by some writers as an "epic event," a *"novum,"* a "unique event" (even, "uniquely unique"), a "watershed event," and the claim has been entered that the history of Christendom, even Western civilization, must be periodized before and after the Holocaust (1941-45).

Every such designation of an "Alpine event" (Bialik's term), like the periodization built around it, involves a whole set of affirmations and negations about the Christian's predicament until the Lord come. Neither Christians today, nor those who first realized that the Messianic Age was delayed in its coming, can escape the toils of recapitulating old myths or struggling through to newer ones that seem to convey a larger truth.

There are true myths and false myths, and there are myths once true that have joined the customs that corrupt the world. Of the latter order, the myth of a monolithic Christendom—unable to comprehend the great worth of soul liberty, unwilling to share the radical Christian confidence that "the Lord hath yet more light and truth to break forth from his Word"—has brought the most misery to persons of sensitive conscience and openness to new leadings of the Spirit. And now, perhaps most serious of all, through centuries of flight from confrontation with events of unique significance, with centuries of teaching of contempt for the Jewish people culminating in the Holocaust, Christendom has precipitated Christianity's major credibility crisis.

If this argument be true, a radical reconstruction of the Christian periodization of history is called for. Those who defend continuity, as well as those who demand a re-assessment, should know that in their structuring of the teaching of history they are confessing the substance of the faith that is in them.

COMMUNION AND ATONEMENT

Essays in Ancient and Medieval Church History

I THESSALONIANS—EXPERIMENT IN CHRISTIAN WRITING

HELMUT KOESTER

Harvard Divinity School

The first Letter of Paul to the Thessalonians appears as one of the minor letters of Paul, albeit his first. It is short and relatively insignificant, dwarfed by such giants as the letters to the Romans, Corinthians, and Galatians. This is the general opinion.

However, this carefully composed writing is actually an experiment in the composition of literature which signals the momentous entry of Christianity into the literary world of antiquity. The consequences of this experiment cannot be underestimated. With the creation of the letter, Paul had forged for himself a powerful political weapon in his struggle to organize and sustain the churches he had founded; the first collection of his letters spawned the composition of more letters written in his name; numerous endeavours followed in the use of this literary genre as a political and theological agency—from I Peter, *I Clement* and Ignatius to Dionysios of Corinth, Irenaeus, Cyprian and many others. I Thessalonians testifies to the creative moment, it is "the Christian letter in the making." [1]

The analysis of established genres in art, literature, and architecture has provided most of our critical canons. Scientific research and its methods have taught us to consider each individual phenomenon as an instance of a group or species. But when I Thessalonians was composed, no species or genre of the Christian letter existed, nor was there a pattern for the incorporation of particular sub-genres and forms, nor had the literary vocabulary and terminology for this type of writing been established.

To be sure, a treatment of I Thessalonians can draw on the wealth

---

[1] This formulation is an adaptation of the title of the recent book of Ernst Kitzinger, *Byzantine Art in the Making* (Cambridge, MA, 1977). I gratefully acknowledge my great indebtedness to this rich and instructive work. It has provided important intellectual stimulus for my work on I Thessalonians. It seems to me a fitting tribute to my colleague and friend, George H. Williams, if this essay can demonstrate that the historian of literature can learn much from the historian of art.

of information which is available to us from the rest of the Pauline
Corpus and from other Christian literature, and thus treat this letter
as an instance of the genre "Pauline letter." The most detailed and
comprehensive recent commentary, that of Beda Rigaux,[2] utilizes
these resources extensively and with great erudition. But precisely this
approach obscures the real task, because all the other Pauline letters
are continuations and results of the experiment which began with 1
Thessalonians. They reveal its direction, further development and success, but cannot explain the creative process itself.

On the other hand, non-Christian analogies for the genre of the
letter can only explain some aspects of the formal composition and
the material resources for the creation of the Pauline letter.[3] Such
studies, however successful, do not provide a model for the first experiment, nor are they capable of explaining its success.[4] A new message
and a new community which is utilizing old forms and traditions
remains indebted to the language of its culture, but is also faced with
the need to make explicit its departure for new shores. I will try to
demonstrate the resulting *concordia discors* in the consideration of two
aspects of the creation of the first Christian letter: (1) the genre
of the letter, (2) the use of traditional materials.

(1) *The genre of the letter.*

Numerous letters and epistles from antiquity, particularly from the
late Hellenistic and Roman Imperial period, are extant. They have
been analyzed and classified repeatedly: private communications, official letters, treatises in letter form, etc., not to speak of the pseud-
epigraphical letters and letter collections.

---

[2] B. Rigaux, O. F. M., *Saint Paul: Les Épitres aux Thessaloniciens* (Etudes
Bibliques; Paris, 1956).

[3] Great progress has indeed been made in recent years in analyzing formal
structures and literary genres which must be presupposed for the Pauline letters.
For a survey of such studies see William G. Doty, *Letters in Primitive Christianity*
(Philadelphia, 1973). Most influential was the work of Robert W. Funk, *Language,
Hermeneutic, and the Word of God* (New York, 1966); and "The Apostolic
Parousia: Form and Significance," in *Christian History and Interpretation:
Studies Presented to John Knox,* eds. W. R. Farmer, C. F. D. Moule and R. R.
Niebuhr (Cambridge, 1967) 249-68.

[4] This is most clearly evident in the otherwise most instructive essay of
Hendrikus Boers, "The Form Critical Study of Paul's Letters. 1 Thessalonians
as a Case Study," *NTS* 22 (1975-76), 140-58. Characteristically, Boers concludes his investigation with the statement: "The letter (i.e., 1 Thessalonians) has
a completely normal form" (p. 158)—a statement which is quite correct, but
misses the excitement of the analysis of the "Christian letter in the making."

It is difficult to classify I Thessalonians according to any of the known genres of ancient letters. [5] Paul seems to use the form of the private letter: prescript with sender introduced by name (no title), proem with personal remembrance and thanksgiving, personal greeting in the conclusion. But one looks in vain for analogies among private letters which have such extensive and elaborate thanksgiving sections, let alone the lengthy moral and eschatological instructions.

That I Thessalonians as a letter substitutes for the personal presence of the apostle, [6] is also paralleled in private letters. But Paul's presence has an official function and is not simply serving a personal relationship, although signs of the genre of the official letter are otherwise absent. Only in later letters does Paul introduce himself with his title (apostle) or an equivalent designation. [7] Instructions appear also in the official letter; yet such instructions as given in I Thessalonians, coupled with eschatological exhortations, rather resemble the protreptic letter which invites the reader to the true way of philosophy and moral life. This observation, however, should not mislead us to assume that Paul composed a philosophical or religious treatise, or used the letter form simply in order to expound his theology and his invitation to a moral life.

Faced with such difficulties, one is tempted to describe the literary form and dynamics of composition of this letter as *sui generis*. That explanation, however, disregards the indispensible presuppositions for the identification of a "genre." Any production of literature implies cultural establishment, convention, and continuity—or at least development along set lines. Development, however, can be continuous or discontinuous; it may be defined in terms of utilization or alteration, old forms in a new frame or old frames for new images. If a letter does not fit the established conventions, although it is still dependent upon them, how are traditional elements used, altered, bent, reshaped? What is the new message or experience which reveals the motivation for the transforming of traditional patterns?

---

[5] Boers' definition, "a paraenetic letter with two characteristic main parts, philophronesis and paraenesis" ("Form Critical Study of Paul's Letters," 158, referring to an unpublished SBL Seminar paper of 1972 by Abraham Malherbe) points to the constituent parts of I Thessalonians; but there is no extant example of such a parenetic letter with the same formal characteristics, i.e., those of a personal and private letter.

[6] On this aspect of the Pauline letter see Funk, "The Apostolic *Parousia.*"

[7] *doulos* as a title appears even in the otherwise deceptively "private" letter to Philemon.

The *thanksgiving section* (proem; 1 Thess 1:2-3:13) may serve as an example. The disproportionate length of this section is striking [8] if one compares 1 Thessalonians with other Pauline letters. But the proem of 1 Thess 1:2-3:13 corresponds more closely to the conventions of the private letter than the proem of any other letter of Paul. Its three major sections—remembrance of the relationship in the past (1 Thess 1:2-10), explanation of and apology for one's past behavior (2:1-12), and discussion of the present situation (2:17-3:13)—are standard features of proems in private correspondence. Thus, the general form of a traditional genre is very clearly visible. However, in each instance Paul forces the traditional topos to convey a message which cannot be contained in the conventional frame. The unusual length of Paul's proem is only the external documentation of a clear break with a traditional form.

The first topos of the thanksgiving section—remembrance of past relationships between sender and addressee—breaks out of the description of a personal relationship for which the deity (if mentioned at all) functions simply as benign protector. In contradistinction, 1 Thess 1:2-10 describes this relationship with the church not as a private matter, but as an event before God in which the Holy Spirit is the primary agent. Repeatedly Paul introduces "God" as the reference point of this relationship in an almost importunate fashion: "... faith ... love ... and hope before God" (1:3); "brothers and sisters beloved by God" (1:4); "your faith which is faith towards God" (1:8); "how you turned to God"; "to serve the living God" (1:9). Furthermore, the characterization of the church moves this church out of the realm of personal relationship with the apostle into a universal horizon of participation in an eschatological event ("From you the word of the Lord has sounded forth not only in Macedonia and Greece, but your faith in God has gone out everywhere" 1:8). This also implies that the addressees are released from their dependence upon the writer: "there is no need for us to say anything (about you)" (1:8). In this way, the thanksgiving section of the letter radically departs from its conventional purpose. Rather than binding writer and addressee more closely together in their personal relationship, it establishes a situation for the addressee that is independent of the writer and seen within the context of a universal eschatological event.

---

[8] This long thanksgiving section has been in the center of attention ever since the classic monograph of Paul Schubert, *Form and Function of the Pauline Thanksgiving* (BZNW 20; Berlin, 1939).

The second topos of the proem (2:1-12), explanation of the writer's behavior and actions, similarly transcends the conventional concentration upon the writer's motivations, his fortune or misfortune, and his justified actions or deplorable failures. To be sure, the elements of this topos are clearly present. But what the author has done in the past is justified as a behavior which does not want "to please people, but God" (2:4), and his actions are not just explained as contributions to a personal relationship; rather, they seek to strengthen the addressees' relationship to God's coming kingdom (2:12). I will return to this section below.

Elements of the private letter are clearly visible in the third topos of the proem, the discussion of the present situation (2:17-3:13). The emphasis upon the physical separation and the desire to communicate (2:17, 18; 3:1-2, 5-6, 10-11) are almost pathetic and quite in style. But Robert Funk has already demonstrated that these familiar items of the common letter have been gathered into a discrete section in which Paul discusses the media through which "his apostolic authority and power are made effective." [9] The traditional topic "friendship" (*philophronesis*) has been transformed into a new topic of the genre of the Christian letter, namely "apostolic *parousia*." However, Paul goes even further in his transformation of the *philophronesis*: even the Apostle's presence is transcended by the coming (*parousia*) of Christ. In 1 Thessalonians, Paul never uses the term *parousia* of his own anticipated or prevented personal presence, but always for the "coming of the Lord"—1 Thess 4:15 and 5:23 and twice in this third section of the proem, i.e., in its first and last paragraph (2:19; 3:13). Outside of 1 Thessalonians, 1 Cor 15:23 is the only passage in which Paul speaks of Christ's *parousia*. [10] The sorrow and concern caused by the absence of the Apostle is therefore not overcome by the joy that will be brought with Paul's presence (be it in his personal arrival, or through an emissary or through his letter), but by the outlook to the expected coming of the Lord (see especially 2:19). Paul thus relativizes the theme of friendship. No longer is the letter a substitute for physical presence for friendship's sake, but a medium through which both writer and addressees are bound together in the eschatological perspective of a new message. Closely related to this

---

[9] Cf. Funk, "The Apostolic *Parousia*," 266.

[10] Elsewhere in Paul's letters the term *parousia* always refers to the arrival of a human being; cf. 1 Cor 16:17; 2 Cor 7:6; 10:10; Phil 1:26; 2:12; in the last three passages to Paul himself.

new Christian view of the traditional theme is the reinterpretation of the sorrows and tribulations (θλίψεις). They are no longer caused by temporary physical separation, but are seen as the fundamental condition of Christian existence (3:3-4; cf. 1:6) which can neither be remedied by the letter nor by the personal presence, although personal communications bring consolation (παράκλησις 3:2, 7).

A brief discussion of 1 Thess 2:13-16 is in order here. If the whole proem of 1 Thessalonians (1:2-3:13) is a conscious and careful creation of a part of a Christian letter, this section is obviously a foreign element. The arguments against the Pauline authorship of this anti-Jewish polemic seem to me fully convincing: [11] unnecessary resumption of the "Thanksgiving"; interruption of the close connection between 2:12 and 2:17; non-Pauline use of Pauline terms (especially μιμηταί 2:14); characterization of the Jews which conflicts with Rom 9-11; lack of a historical point of reference for the last phrase ("the wrath to the end has come upon them" 2:16) before A.D. 70; absence of any allusion to 1 Thess 2:13-16 in 2 Thessalonians. But also as part of Paul's effort to create a Christian form of the conventional proem, this section makes no sense whatsoever. A polemic against the Jews, consisting of statements from a traditional topos, is completely unwarranted in a proem that makes every effort to reshape the theme of the writer-recipient relation in the conventional proem of the private letter. A polemic against a third party would destroy the very result which Paul wants to accomplish. [12]

The instructions which follow upon the proem, 1 Thess 4:1-12, appear in the appropriate position according to the usual conventions of letter writing. However, they differ insofar as they are not specific but general. They are not occasioned by the situation, rather they

---

[11] Arguments against Pauline authorship were brought forth first by Ferdinand Christian Baur in his *Paulus, der Apostel Jesu Christi* in 1845; several scholars of the last century accepted Baur's judgment. But a conclusive case was made only recently by Birger A. Pearson, "1 Thessalonians 2:13-16: A Deutero-Pauline Interpolation," *HTR* 64 (1971), 79-94. See also Boers, "Form Critical Study of Paul's Letters," 151-52.

[12] With the elimination of 1 Thess 2:13-16 one significant argument for the division hypothesis of 1 Thessalonians as proposed by Walter Schmithals disappears ("Die Thessalonicherbriefe als Briefkomposition," in *Zeit und Geschichte: Dankesgabe an Rudolf Bultmann zum 80. Geburtstag* [Tübingen, 1964] 295-315). Other arguments for this hypothesis are less weighty. Any attempt to assign parts of 1 Thess 1:2-3:13 to two different letters (see also Karl-Gottfried Eckart, "Der zweite echte Brief des Apostels Paulus an die Thessalonicher," *ZThK* 58 [1961], 30-44) disregards the careful composition which elaborates and transforms an established literary genre.

elaborate a tradition. The basis for part of the instruction seems to be a catalogue; the vices of this catalogue are common enough, but Col 3:5 has independently preserved the same brief catalogue which is used in 1 Thess 4:3-7: πορνεία, πάθος, ἐπιθυμία, πλεονεξία, ἀκαθαρσία (only εἰδωλολατρία is missing in 1 Thess 4). The generalizing tendency of these instructions is even more patent in the positive admonitions (4:9-12); no specific advice is given. [13] On the contrary, in 4:9 Paul coins a new term, θεοδίδακτοι, [14] in order to characterize a relationship between writer and recipients which differs fundamentally from the common letter. "Taught by God" emphasizes that the recipients are not dependent upon the writer's instructions. An analogy may be found in the philosophical parenesis, which stresses the independence of moral action, and in Philo's use of αὐτοδίδακτος: the truly wise man is a "self learner"(αὐτομαθής)and "self-taught" (αὐτοδίδακτος) and "finds wisdom readily prepared, rained down from heaven above" (*De fuga et inventione*, 166). [15]

Paul has thus accomplished two things: He has made room for the use of traditional parenetic materials in the frame of the Christian letter—this became very important in the composition of letters dependent upon Paul [16]—and he has liberated the addressees from the dependence upon the writer's demands; their responsible action is bound to their relationship to God.

In the case of the "instructions" it is still possible to cite the philosophical moral epistle as an analogy or parallel; but no analogies exist in letters of any kind for the eschatological admonitions which are found in 1 Thess 4:13-5:11. The reason for writing 1 Thess 4:13-18 has been sought in a specific problem of the church, i.e., that

---

[13] Even the admonitions to lead a quiet life and work with one's own hands are general, albeit concrete, requests to insure the moral and economic independence of the church, not attacks upon some lazy church members; cf. Martin Dibelius, *An die Thessalonicher I, II, An die Philipper* (HNT 11; 3rd ed.; Tübingen, 1937) 23.

[14] There is no evidence for the use of this term in pre-Christian literature. The only non-Christian use I am aware of is θεοδίδακτος ἡ ῥητορική in *Prolegomenon Sylloge*, ed. Hugo Rabe (Rhet. graeci 15; Leipzig, 1931), 91, line 14. This is apparently a phrase from a late introduction to one of the rhetorical theorists. But since I was unable to get access to this book, I cannot say more about the exact date. That the word was coined on the basis of such passages as Isa 54:13 and Jer 31 (38): 33-34, as is usually assumed (cf. Rigaux, *Aux Thessaloniciens*, 517), is not impossible. See, however, the following.

[15] This term occurs more frequently in Philo, especially of Isaac (*De somnis*, 159).

[16] Cf., e.g., Eph 4-5; 1 Pet 2:11-4:6; *1 Clement passim*; etc.

members had died and that Paul felt compelled to address this
problem. But for 1 Thess 5:1-11 no such immediate and urgent problem
which called for an answer can be identified. For this entire eschatological section, the search for a specific problem in the church of
Thessalonike as cause for Paul's writing is awkward in any case: Had
Paul during his stay in Thessalonike forgotten to speak about the
possibility that some Christians might die before the parousia? Or
had he failed to tell them that the parousia would happen suddenly?

The cause for this eschatological section can be more easily found
if one considers Paul's effort to transform the conventional genre
of the letter into a Christian medium of communication. It was the
message of the Christian gospel which demanded this drastic expansion
of the traditional genre. The gospel did not endeavour to add another,
albeit better, religious movement to the religions of the world. In that
case the letter could have been satisfied with responses to problems
in the ongoing life of the churches. Rather, the gospel announced the
end of the world, the coming of a new age, an expectation that the
future of God which was at hand would make everything new. The
"letter" could become a *Christian* medium only by expressing this
perspective. How traditional apocalyptic materials, drawn from a
genre that has no relationship to the common form of the letter, are
utilized and interpreted for his purpose will be discussed below. In
1 Thessalonians, as well as in later Christian letters, the eschatological
section became the most distinctive mark of the new genre, be it as
the typical final paragraph as in 1 Cor 15 or 2 Peter 3, or as the
primary corpus of a letter as in Romans 3:21-11:36.

(2) *The use of traditional materials.*

No work of art or literary creation can be fashioned without the
use of traditional forms and materials. Its message is conveyed not
through forms and materials themselves, but through the reshaping
of the form and the interpretation of the material.

The writing of the first Christian letter could not rely on established
Christian conventions for the use and interpretation of traditional
materials in the form of literary communications. There were no
precedents. Moreover, whatever traditions there were, very few could
be termed specifically "Christian." An alternative might have existed in
the cultivation of traditions which could claim to derive directly from
the originator of the Christian movement, i.e., Jesus of Nazareth. But
the tradition of the words and works of Jesus, at the time of the writing

of 1 Thessalonians, was still in the process of being formed and had certainly not yet reached the stage of literary production. In any case, Paul exhibits very little knowledge of this tradition. It is characteristic that the only "word of the Lord" which he quotes in 1 Thessalonians (4:15-17) is the word of a Christian prophet which uses traditional Jewish apocalyptic imagery. [17] One may also point to a few kerygmatic or baptismal formulae as parts of a specifically Christian tradition. 1 Thess 1:10 and 4:14 seem to utilize such formulae. But these are very small portions of the total writing, and even if such formulae may have been stable in their ecclesiastical usage (which I doubt), Paul's letters demonstrate that, in their literary usage, their wording is not yet fixed (not a single formula is ever repeated by Paul!).

When Paul wrote 1 Thessalonians he could not rely to any major extent upon traditional materials which were clearly shaped by the new departure and the message of the Christian movement. Almost all traditions used here were not yet very far removed from their non-Christian origin. Three examples must suffice here.

The second section of the proem explains the writer's behavior and actions, and thus in 2:1-12 Paul uses the traditional topos and vocabulary of the description of the "philosopher." Applied to himself, he seeks to respond to the standard criticism of the wandering philosopher, preacher, or magician [18]—not, however, to specific attacks directed at his own behavior. Was anything accomplished? Did the philosopher stand the test of a public appearance? Did he use dirty tricks and deceit? Did he simply try to please the audience? Did he just play games in order to make money and gain honor? These and similar questions are all part of the conventional polemic and apology. So are the answers: no deceit, public appearance, following a divine call, no desire for money, gentle and kind. Except for the quotation of Jer 11:12 in 1 Thess 2:4, all the answers Paul gives belong to the general requirements of behavior for the philosopher, in particular the Cynic preacher. Had Paul said no more than this, his image of himself would have fitted perfectly into the accepted image of the morally respectable, honest, and skilled preacher. But in 1 Thess

---

[17] To be sure, such sayings of revelation, circulating as "words of the Lord," were later incorporated into the gospel tradition (cf. Mark 13 and similar materials), but they have no claim to derive from Jesus of Nazareth.

[18] On the general philosophical background of this "apology" of Paul see the illuminating discussion by Abraham J. Malherbe, "'Gentle as a Nurse': The Cynic Background to 1 Thess ii," *NovT* 12 (1970), 203-17.

2:7-11, Paul expands a specific argument for the good philosopher in a non-conventional way. Gentleness, for the Cynic philosopher, was a rhetorical device, used in order to be more effective, because human nature does not always respond well to harshness; thus one should be careful to choose either harshness or gentleness, depending upon the situation. [19] For Paul, however, gentleness is not a device, but the first step in the direction of establishing a new relationship between Apostle and church. Therefore, the traditional image of the nurse is further expanded. Unfortunately, one word used in this context, ὁμειρόμενοι (2:8), has so far withstood all attempts at translation. [20] It seems to be a vernacular term from the nursery. [21] The use of such terms as well as the following statements ("I gave myself to you," "I worked day and night") demonstrate that Paul does not understand gentleness as a device, but as a commitment. That would not be required from the professional philosopher, indeed it would violate his freedom. The people in Thessalonike have become Paul's "beloved" (1 Thess 2:8) to whom he has committed his own being and status as an apostle. This undercuts the authority structure implied in the tradition of the true philosopher used here. No longer is the apology of the philosopher used to establish his dignity and integrity. Instead, it establishes a relationship between partners who are tied together by an almost embarrassingly intimate bond of affection.

In 1 Thess 4:1-12 Paul uses and interprets, as has been stated before, a catalogue of vices. The catalogue derives from Hellenistic Judaism, and it may have been used in Christian baptismal instruction. There is nothing new about the use of such catalogues in order to construct moral teachings which make explicit what one should avoid and what one should do. Paul brackets his interpretation by the

---

[19] Malherbe, *ibid.*, 212-13.

[20] This word is attested elsewhere only in a 4th century A.D. tomb inscription from Lycaonia: ὁ[μει]ρόμενοι περὶ παιδός (*CIG* 3.4000.7). Job 3:21 οἱ ὁμείρονται τοῦ θανάτου ("those who long for death") is probably a scribal error for ἱμείρονται ("to be desirous of"). It is on the basis of this passage that the translation "desirous" arose which is, however, complete nonsense because Paul speaks of the time when he was right there and had no reason to "long for" the Thessalonians. Etymologically there is no relation of ὁμείρεσθαι to either ἱμείρεσθαι or μείρεσθαι ("to receive one's portion").

[21] This would fit the other words used here: τροφός "nurse" or "mother breast-feeding the children"; θάλπειν "to cuddle," "to pet," cf. *Pap. Rainer* 30.20 of the husband's behavior towards his wife: ἀγαπᾶν καὶ θάλπειν καὶ θεραπεύειν. As these words also ὁμείρεσθαι must belong to the nursery or bedroom slang.

traditional term ἁγιασμός, "sanctification" (1 Thess 4:3 and 4:7). [22] But his use of this term neither point to ritual purification, nor does it indicate personal moral perfection. The two exhortations which are given speak about mutual behavior in matters of sex (4:3b-5) and of business (4:6): "treat your marriage partner with respect, not in blind passion" —that seems the best way to understand the difficult term σκεῦος—[23] and "don't rip off your brother in a business deal." The exhortations are obviously concerned with relationships. That is underlined in the sentence of "sacred law" in 4:8: [24] disregard for one's brother or sister is disregard for God, because all members of the church have received the Holy Spirit. "Sanctification," therefore, cannot be understood as a task of moral perfection for the individual, as the traditional use of such catalogue instruction in Hellenistic Judaism suggests. Rather, "sanctification" involves a reassessment of the values for dealing with each other in everyday life.

A final comment regarding the use of traditional material concerns the "eschatological" section, specifically 1 Thess 5:1-11. These verses are full of traditional eschatological metaphors and cliches. But Paul has used a method of interpretation which is particularly applicable in a literary composition: the play with words and their different connotations. The traditional saying about the day of the Lord coming like a thief in the night (1 Thess 5:2) conventionally connotes unexpectedness; [25] but "night" also connotes "darkness" (5:4). This allows Paul to conclude that the "day" cannot surprise us, since we are already living as "children of the day" (5:5). Thus the significance of the future day of the Lord is relativized for the believer. A second connotation of the contrast of "night" and "day," i.e., "to sleep" and "to be awake," leads to a new set of metaphors for Christian life in the present: "to be awake" and "to be sober" (5:6-8). The latter term

---

[22] This term, not used outside of Biblical and Christian literature, specifically designates cultic sanctification (cf. Judg 17:3; Ezek 45:4); in *1 Clement* 30.1 it is used together with ἐγκράτεια "self-control."

[23] This term has been discussed extensively; cf. Christian Maurer, "σκεῦος," TDNT 7, 359-68 for literature. In the space of this article it is impossible to debate the suggestions for translation which range from *membrum virile* to "woman." The phrase σκεῦος κτᾶσθαι seems to resist any rational attempt of translation. I would suggest that Paul uses this formulation because he does not want to say γυνή ("wife"). The choice of the neuter term σκεῦος emphasizes mutuality of sexual control.

[24] Cf. Ernst Käsemann, "Sentences of Holy Law in the New Testament," in his *New Testament Questions of Today* (Philadelphia, 1969) 66-81.

[25] Rev 3:3 makes this quite clear; cf. also Luke 12:39 (Matt 24:43).

3

is associated with another set of traditional imagery: the armor of God which, in turn, is interpreted as faith, love and hope (5:8-9). What started as apocalyptic instruction has thus become demythologized eschatology, describing faith, love, and hope as the presence of eternity. A final daring play on the terms "death" (of Jesus), "being awake" and "being asleep" (of Christians) and "life" (with Jesus) seems to relativize also the problem of being alive or dead at the parousia. The timetable of the eschatological expectation has been rendered meaningless.

Here and elsewhere in this first Christian piece of literature, Paul has set the stage for the incorporation of traditional materials and their critical reinterpretation: never are such materials simply repeated or only expanded and further elaborated. That this genre of literature demands critical assessment of tradition, imitators of Paul—including the author of 2 Thessalonians—have sometimes overlooked: to their own detriment.

What I can present here is only a suggestion, not a set of solutions. All that is to be learned is that this earliest Christian letter is neither a reflection of a fixed form nor a quarry of information for pieces of a genre or established traditions. Rather, it is a composition using inherited themes in the context of a new counterpoint. In the formation of the Christian letter, some laws of this counterpoint that Paul introduced were forgotten, or the inherited themes simply prevailed; but more often than not attempts were made by Paul himself and by his successors to write new fugues using Paul's rules of counterpoint— or, to use another image, Christian artisans tried to present individual figures in their reliefs in such a way they faced the experience of a new message.

THE PRE-CYPRIANIC DOCTRINE OF THE PRIESTHOOD
OF ALL CHRISTIANS

JAMES LEO GARRETT, Jr.

Baylor University

The doctrine [1] of the priesthood of all Christians as taught during the patristic era has been the subject of detailed research by neither patristic scholars [2] nor historians of this particular doctrine. [3] The more surprising is this fact when one discovers that, whereas the universal Christian priesthood did not constitute a major theme for controversy during the age of the Church Fathers, there are numerous passages in extant patristic literature pertaining to this doctrine.

To understand the development of the doctrine of the priesthood of all Christians during the age of the Fathers, one should perceive as clearly as possible the Old Testament background to and the New Testament meaning of the doctrine. Rooted in the concept of the entire People of Israel as "a kingdom of priests" (Exod. 19:6) and related to, but in no sense identical with, the doctrine of the high priesthood of Jesus as set forth in the Epistle to the Hebrews, the royal priesthood was ascribed to all Christians by New Testament writers (1 Pet. 2:9; Rev. 1:5b, 6; 5:9, 10). Its chief function was identified as the offering of "spiritual sacrifices" (1 Pet. 2:5), such as in worship, witness, gifts to an apostle, and diakonic ministry. [4]

---

[1] The term "doctrine" is utilized in preference to "dogma," which would wrongly imply ecclesiastical or conciliar definition, and to "idea" or "concept," which would tend to suggest only the personal beliefs of certain individual Christians during the patristic age.

[2] No extensive monograph concerning the patristic doctrine of the priesthood of all Christians has been produced in the modern age, to the knowledge of the author.

[3] Cyril Eastwood, *The Royal Priesthood of the Faithful*: *An Investigation of the Doctrine from Biblical Times to the Reformation* (London, 1963) 56-101, has interpreted the doctrine according to Clement of Rome, the *Didache*, Polycarp, Justin Martyr, Irenaeus, the *Epistle to Diognetus*, Clement of Alexandria, Tertullian, Origen, Cyprian, John Chrysostom, Augustine, and Narsai. Eastwood's responsible interpretation of the doctrine during the patristic age is not, however, based upon an extensive location and examination of all pertinent passages in extant patristic literature.

[4] See the author's "The Biblical Doctrine of the Priesthood of the People of

The first epoch or era in the post-biblical development of the priest-hood of all Christians extended from the Apostolic Fathers and the so-called Apocryphal New Testament to the writings of the third-century bishop of Carthage, Cyprian, whose emphasis on the clerical priesthood marked the advent of a new era in the development of the doctrine under investigation.

The priesthood of all Christians does not figure prominently in the theology of the Apostolic Fathers; yet there are a few passages per-tinent to this priesthood. The *Didache* refers to true Christian prophets and teachers as "high priests" [5] and admonishes:

> On the Lord's own day, assemble in common to break bread and offer thanks;
> but first confess your sins, so that your sacrifice may be pure. [6]

The "sacrifice" seems to be worship, of which breaking of bread and offering of thanks are integral parts, and is to be preceded by confession of sin. The most detailed passage [7] in the *Didache* concerning thanks-giving and the breaking of bread contains no reference to priesthood or sacrifice but is characterized by a servant Christology. Clement of Rome refers to Jesus Christ as "the High Priest and Ruler of our souls" [8] and as "the High Priest who offers out gifts, the patron and helper in our weakness." [9] Clement likens the proper conduct of Christian worship to the divine prescriptions for the sacrifices in ancient Israel's worship.

> For the high priest has been given his own special services, and the priests
> have been assigned their own places and Levites have their particular duties.
> The layman [λαϊκός] is bound by the rules for laymen. [10]

God" in Huber L. Drumwright and Curtis Vaughan, eds., *New Testament Studies: Essays in Honor of Ray Summers in His Sixty-Fifth Year* (Waco, Tex., 1975), 137-49.

[5] 13.1-3.

[6] 14.1, tr. James A. Kleist, ed., *The Didache, The Epistle of Barnabas, The Epistles and Martyrdom of St. Polycarp, The Fragments of Papias [and] The Epistle to Diognetus,* ACW, 6 (Westminster, Md., 1948). This "sacrifice" is connected with Mal. 1:11, 14.

[7] 9.1-10.6.

[8] *Epistle to the Corinthians* 61.3; 64, tr. James A. Kleist, ed., *The Epistles of St. Clement of Rome and St. Ignatius of Antioch,* ACW, 1 (Westminster, Md., 1949).

[9] *Ibid.,* 36.1. The word "gifts" may also be translated "offerings." W. K. Lowther Clarke (*The First Epistle of Clement to the Corinthians* [London, 1937], 40) concludes that "The 'offerings' (προσφορῶν) are the prayers of the worshipping congregation.... To the early Church, which used the same technical term for prayers and for the Eucharist gifts, the two things must have seemed closely connected."

[10] 40.5, tr. Edgar J. Goodspeed, *The Apostolic Fathers* (New York, 1950).

Clement extends this analogy to apply to a single place of worship, i.e., "Jerusalem only." [11] He also quotes the Psalms relative to the sacrifice of confession of sin and the "sacrifice of praise." [12] All these texts should be understood in the context of the epistle's major concern, namely, schism in the Corinthian congregation. Ignatius of Antioch applies the language of sacrifice to the martyrdom of Christians [13] and asserts the superiority of Jesus as high priest to the Jewish priests, "for he is himself the door to the Father, through which Abraham and Isaac and Jacob and the prophets and the apostles and the church enter." [14] Polycarp refers to Jesus as "the eternal high priest himself" and "the eternal heavenly high priest" [15] and to Christian widows as "God's altar" [16] and is reported to have prayed that his own forthcoming martyrdom might be accepted before God "as a rich and acceptable sacrifice." [17] *The Epistle of Barnabas* contains no reference to Christians as "priests." This omission was perhaps due to the author's regarding such a term as belonging to the Jewish dispensation and, unlike the epistle's major motifs—new people, new covenant, second creation, new and circumcised heart, new temple, etc., not reflective of the uniquely Christian in an anti-Judaic interpretation of Christianity. Similarly, the *Shepherd* of Hermas, with the possible exception of one passage, [18] is silent on the royal priesthood, and the so-called *Second Letter of Clement of Rome* and the fragments from Papias are likewise silent. Among the Apostolic Fathers only the *Didache*, Clement, Ignatius, and Polycarp specifically refer to the offering of spiritual sacrifices by Christians; for the *Didache* and Clement there are the sacrifices of worship or praise, whereas Ignatius and Polycarp allude to the sacrifice of martyrdom.

The writings which comprise the Apocryphal New Testament do

---

[11] 41.2.

[12] 52.1-4.

[13] *Romans*, 2.2; 4.2.

[14] *Philadelphians*, 9.1.

[15] *Philippians*, 12.2 and *The Martyrdom of Polycarp*, 14.3. The latter passage is part of a prayer ascribed to Polycarp and said to have been offered just prior to his martyrdom.

[16] *Philippians*, 4.3. The context suggests that the conduct of the widows is always seen by God.

[17] *The Martyrdom of Polycarp*, 14.2.

[18] Bk. 3, similitude 2, contrasts the poor man who is rich in intercession and confession and who prays for the rich man with the rich man who out of his wealth supplies the necessities of the poor man but then concludes that both are partners and accomplish their work in a manner acceptable to God.

not set forth the theme of a common priesthood of Christians except possibly in the statement in the Gnostic *Gospel of Philip* that "some" who "are in the tribe of the priesthood ... will be able to go within the veil with the high priest." [19] The absence of mention of Christians —or of Gnostics—as priests prevails throughout the extant Gnostic literature. One notable exception is to be found in Ptolemy's three-fold classification of the laws, i.e., those pure laws which the Saviour fulfilled, those laws "bound up with lower things and wrongdoing" which He abrogated, and those "typical and symbolical" laws which He "transformed from the sensible and phenomenal into the spiritual and invisible." Under the last Ptolemy declares:

> For the Saviour commanded us to offer sacrifices, but not of irrational animals or incense but of spiritual praises and gloryings and thanksgiving, and through fellowship and beneficence toward neighbours. [20]

In the *Odes of Solomon*, sometimes regarded as Gnostic, sometimes as Essene, appears the text:

> I am a priest of the Lord, and to Him I do priestly service: and to Him I offer the sacrifice of His thought. For his thought is not like the thought of the world nor the thought of the flesh, nor like them that serve carnally. The sacrifice of the Lord is righteousness, and purity of heart and lips. [21]

The second-century apologists had little place for the priesthood of all Christians in their writings, chiefly, it seems, because sacrifices tended to be identified exclusively by the apologists with the system of pagan sacrifices which they were seeking to refute. The earliest of the extant writings, the *Apology* of Aristides, declares that the true God "requires not sacrifice and libation nor any one of the things that appear to sense" [22] but does acknowledge that Christians "are ready to sacrifice their lives for the sake of Christ." [23] Justin Martyr mentions in his *First Apology* in the context of pagan worship that sacrifices are offered to idols or images, to demons, and to pagan deities of all kinds. [24] He insists that "God does not need the material

---

[19] 133.1-5, tr. R. McL. Wilson, *The Gospel of Philip: Translated from the Coptic Text, with an Introduction and Commentary* (London, 1962).

[20] *Letter of Ptolemaeus to Flora*, 3, tr. Robert M. Grant, ed., *Second Century Christianity: A Collection of Fragments* (London, 1946).

[21] 20.1-3, as trans. by J. Rendel Harris and ed. J. H. Bernard, *The Odes of Solomon*, Texts and Studies, 8, 3 (Cambridge, 1912), 89.

[22] From the Gk., ch. 1, tr. D. M. Kay in *The Ante-Nicene Fathers*, eds. Alexander Roberts and James Donaldson, 10 vols. (New York, 1896), 10:264.

[23] Ch. 15.

[24] Chs. 9, 12, 62, and 24.

offerings which men can give, seeing, indeed, that He Himself is the provider of all things." [25] Moreover, God

> has no need of bloody sacrifices, libations, and incense. But we praise Him to the best of our power by prayer and thanksgiving for all our nourishment.... [Indeed,] the only worship worthy of Him is not to consume by fire those things that He created for our sustenance, but to employ them for the good of ourselves and the needy, and, with thankful voices, to offer Him solemn prayers and hymns... [26]

Justin does not specifically connect the royal priesthood and the Eucharist, although in reference to the latter he speaks of "prayers and thanksgiving." [27] In his *Dialogue with Trypho* he is more explicit concerning the royal priesthood. Christians refuse to offer sacrifices to pagan deities which they formerly worshipped, even when it means their own death. [28] God did not need, according to Justin, sacrifices from the Israelites but ordained and received them on account of the sins of the Israelites, principally idolatry. [29] Jesus Christ is the Melchizedekan high priest, [30] indeed an eternal priest [31] whose priesthod is conjoined with kingship. [32] A Gentile, e.g., "a Scythian or a Persian," and his offerings can now through the Son of God be acceptable to God. [33] In another context Justin affirms:

> Having been set on fire by the word of His calling, we are now of the true priestly family [34] of God, as He Himself testifies when He says that in every place among the Gentiles pure and pleasing sacrifices are offered up to Him. But God receives sacrifices from no one, except through His priests. [35]

Justin refuses to accept the Jewish interpretation of Malachi 1:10-12, which applies the passage to "the prayers of the Jews who were then in the Dispersion" but instead gives it a Christian eucharistic interpretation. [36] Pressing his polemic against Trypho, Justin insists that

---

[25] Ch. 10.

[26] Ch. 13, tr. Thomas B. Falls in *Saint Justin Martyr*, The Fathers of the Church, 6 (New York, 1948).

[27] Chs. 65-67.

[28] Ch. 46.

[29] Chs. 22, 67.

[30] Chs. 32, 33, 63, 83, and 118.

[31] Chs. 33, 36, 42, 96, and 118.

[32] Chs. 36, 86, 96, and 118.

[33] Ch. 28.

[34] The Greek word is γένος. *ANF* translates γένος as "race." It is possible that Eastwood (*The Royal Priesthood of the Faithful*, 61-66) has overdrawn the relation in Justin between the priesthood of all Christians and Christians as a third race.

[35] Ch. 116.

[36] Chs. 117, 41.

there is not one single race of men—whether barbarians, or Greeks, or persons called by any other name, nomads, or vagabonds, or herdsmen dwelling in tents—among whom prayers and thanksgivings are not offered to the Father and Creator of the universe in the name of the Crucified Jesus. [37]

Even at the parousia of Jesus, according to Justin, the sacrifices to be offered will not be "of blood" but "only of true and spiritual praises and thanksgiving." [38] Athenagoras makes no direct reference to Christians as priests but reiterates Justin's point that God has no need of sacrifices. [39] Sextus declares: "The only sacrifice acceptable to God is through God to do good to one's fellow men." [40] Coupled with the apologists' polemic against pagan sacrifices, therefore, one finds in Justin that Christians are regarded as a priestly people among whom Gentiles can offer to God acceptable sacrifices and among whom prayers and thanksgivings are universally offered.

Melito of Sardis interprets the priesthood of Christians in language obviously drawn partly from 1 Peter 2:9:

This is he who rescued us from slavery to freedom, from darkness to light, from death to life, from oppression to an eternal kingdom, and made us a new priesthood and a chosen people for ever. [41]

In the writings of Irenaeus of Lyons priestly sacrifices continue to be identified with the Eucharist. He reiterates the emphasis made by the apologists that God did not need the sacrifices made by the Israelites but ordained them as an antidote to idolatry, [42] although now God rejects these in view of the true sacrifice of Christ. [43] Irenaeus concludes that "God did not seek sacrifices and holocausts from them, but faith, and obedience, and righteousness, because of their salvation." [44] Jesus fulfills the high priestly role [45] and is akin to

---

[37] Ch. 117.

[38] Ch. 118.

[39] *A Plea for the Christians,* 13.

[40] Line 47. The Greek text and the Latin translation by Rufinus of Aquileia are given by Henry Chadwick, *The Sentences of Sextus: A Contribution to the History of Early Christian Ethics,* Texts and Studies, n.s., 5 (Cambridge, 1959). Chadwick (pp. 16, 17, 106) interprets διὰ θεόν and *pro deo* as meaning "with God's help."

[41] Sect. 68, tr. Campbell Bonner, ed., *The Homily on the Passion by Melito, Bishop of Sardis, with Some Fragments of the Apocryphal Ezekiel,* Studies and Documents, 12 (Philadelphia, 1940).

[42] *Against Heresies,* 4.14.3.

[43] *Ibid.,* 4.17.2. Irenaeus quotes, as if from Scripture, the following: "The sacrifice to God is an afflicted heart: a sweet savour to God is a heart glorifying Him who formed it."

[44] *Against Heresies,* 4.17.4.

[45] *Ibid.,* 4.8.2.

Melchizedek [46] and to the about-to-be-offered Isaac. [47] Even his second advent may be described as "sacerdotal." [48]

The reader of *Against Heresies* can find passages in which Irenaeus could easily have become more explicit about the royal priesthood of Christians. [49] For example, mention of the Old Testament "sacerdotal and liturgical service" could have led to a comparable mention of the sacerdotal functions under the New Covenant, but instead Irenaeus refers to the giving of the Holy Spirit. [50] Likewise, the prayers of the church "to the Lord, who made all things, in a pure, sincere, and straightforward spirit, and calling upon the name of our Lord Jesus Christ" are not described as a priestly sacrifice but as the opposite of "angelic invocations" and "incantations." [51] Cyril Eastwood has attempted to connect the royal priesthood with the doctrine of recapitulation in Irenaeus, [52] but the two are never mentioned by Irenaeus in the same context. Irenaeus, when referring to the Old Testament incident in which David ate the shewbread reserved for priests, calls "all the apostles of the Lord" and "the disciples of the Lord" "priests." [53]

According to Irenaeus, the church's "oblation" is "reckoned a pure sacrifice with God." [54] The New Covenant has not dispensed with sacrifice; rather "the species alone has been changed, inasmuch as the

---

[46] *Proof of the Apostolic Preaching*, 48, tr. Joseph P. Smith, ACW, 16 (Westminster, Md., 1952), 79.

[47] *Against Heresies*, 4.5.4.

[48] *Ibid.*, 4.20.11.

[49] John Lawson, *The Biblical Theology of Saint Irenaeus* (London, 1948), 254-55, says concerning *Against Heresies*, 4.17.5, that "Irenaeus gives a hint that he held a doctrine of the universal priesthood of all believers" and that logically this "does not ... preclude the conception of a special priesthood in addition, representatively exercising the function which in principle belongs to the whole priestly community." Paul Beuzart (*Essai sur la théologie d'Irénée* [Le Puy-en-Velay, 1908], 158-60), while stating that Irenaeus holds to the universal priesthood, observes that he "assimilates the disciples to the Levites of the old law" and admits and develops the distinction between clergy and laity.

[50] *Against Heresies*, 3.11.8.

[51] *Ibid.*, 2.32.5. Eastwood (*The Priesthood of the Faithful*, 69) quotes this passage presumably as evidence that Irenaeus teaches the royal priesthood.

[52] *The Royal Priesthood of the Faithful*, 68.

[53] *Against Heresies*, 4.8.3. This passage contains the difficult text which *ANF* translates: "For the righteous possess the sacerdotal rank." However, from Antonius Melissa and John of Damascus has been derived an alternate reading which *ANF*, 1:471.6, translates: "Every righteous king possesses a priestly order."

[54] *Ibid.*, 4.18.4; cf. 4.18.1.

offering is now made, not by slaves, but by freemen." [55] Such sacrifices are not to be offered "merely to outward appearance," as the history of sacrifice from the age of Cain and Abel shows. They "do not sanctify a man, ... but it is the conscience of the offerer that sanctifies the sacrifice when it is pure, and thus moves God to accept (the offering) as from a friend." [56] That Irenaeus regards the Eucharist as *an* offering or oblation of the church is clear; whether he reckons it *the* oblation may be debated. The Eucharist as thanksgiving constitutes "first-fruits of His own things," is offered with altar and temple in heaven, and glorifies God's name among the Gentiles. [57]

Irenaeus, who could have been more explicit about the priesthood of all Christians, nevertheless does acknowledge the same, together with the true sacrifices which Christians are to offer. For Irenaeus the chief oblation is the Eucharist.

Clement of Alexandria tends to interpret the royal priesthood in the light of his Christian gnosis. Frequently he refers to the high priestly office of Jesus Christ. Melchizedek is "a synonym for righteousness and peace," [58] and Jesus is the antitype of Isaac, who "was the son of Abraham, as Christ the Son of God, and a sacrifice as the Lord, but he was not immolated as the Lord." [59] As high priest Jesus is identified with "the first Administrator of the universe," [60] "prays for and exhorts men," [61] alone knows "the worship of God," [62] and reveals the good and the right. [63] Through adoption he "has deigned to call us brethren and fellow-heirs." [64]

---

[55] *Ibid.*, 4.18.2.

[56] *Ibid.*, 4.18.3.

[57] *Ibid.*, 4.18.4; 4.18.6; 4.17.5. Recent interpreters of Irenaeus have tended to agree that according to Irenaeus it is not Christ but gifts from the created order that are offered in the Eucharist. Cf. Gustaf Wingren, *Man and the Incarnation: A Study in the Biblical Theology of Irenaeus* (Philadelphia, 1959), 165-66; Juan Ochagavía, *Visibile Patris Filius: A Study of Irenaeus' Teaching on Revelation and Tradition,* Orientalia Christiana Analecta, 171 (Rome, 1964), 137-38.

[58] *The Stromata,* 4.25 (*ANF,* 2).

[59] *The Instructor,* 1.5 (*ANF,* 2).

[60] *The Stromata,* 7.2.

[61] *Exhortation to the Heathen,* 12 (*ANF,* 2).

[62] *The Stromata,* 2.5.

[63] *Ibid.*, 2.9.

[64] *Ibid.*, 2.22. Charles Bigg's (*The Christian Platonists of Alexandria,* 2nd rev. ed. [Oxford, 1913], 106) statement, "Clement speaks of Jesus as our High Priest, but only in the Philonic sense, as our Representative and Intercessor," seems dubious if it means that the High Priest, according to Clement, is not fully and essentially the Son of God. R. B. Tollinton, *Clement of Alexandria:*

Only in *The Stromata* does Clement specifically set forth the royal priesthood in its application to Christians. Here he exhibits the most distinctive aspect of his teaching on the priesthood, namely, that the high priesthood is to be identified with the gnostic or spiritual Christians. Of the gnostic Clement declares: "He is .. the truly kingly man; he is the sacred high priest of God." [65] He elaborates on this gnostic priesthood:

> This is the function of the Gnostic, who has been perfected, to have converse with God through the great High Priest, being made like the Lord, up to the measure of his capacity, in the whole service of God, which tends to the salvation of men, through care of the beneficence which has us for its object; and on the other side through worship, through teaching and through beneficence in deeds. [66]

The gnostic's virtues of moderation such as "mildness, . . . philanthropy, and eminent piety" " 'are a sacrifice acceptable in the sight of God,' " [67] and " 'the humble heart with right knowledge is the holocaust of God.' " [68] The gnostics' progress will continue until "they come to the Good itself, to the Father's vestibule, so to speak, close to the great High Priest." [69] Clement gives to certain Old Testament passages pertaining to the Jewish priesthood and the tabernacle an allegorical interpretation leading to Christian gnosticism. The ark of the covenant is either "the eighth region and the world of thought, or God," the high priest's robe is "the symbol of the world of sense" and points to the Saviour's "ministry in the flesh," and "the broad gold mitre indicates the regal power of the Lord." [70] The gnostic high priest, having put off the created world, having been washed, "not in water" but "by the gnostic Word in his whole heart," and having risen "above other priests," enters into "face to face" "contemplation" and "hearing" of "the Word Himself." [71]

By emphasizing that God does not need that sacrifices be offered to Him, Clement stands with the apologists, of whom he is one. Indeed, "neither by sacrifices nor offerings, nor on the other hand by glory and honour, is the Deity won over." Instead "we glorify Him who

---

A Study of Christian Liberalism (London, 1914), 2:227, sees Clement's doctrine as a blending of the Epistle to the Hebrews with Egyptian ritual.

[65] *The Stromata*, 7.7.
[66] *Ibid.*, 7.3.
[67] Cf. Phil. 4:18.
[68] *The Stromata*, 7.3; cf. Ps. 51:17, 19.
[69] *The Stromata*, 7.7.
[70] *Ibid.*, 5.6.
[71] *Ibid.*

gave himself in sacrifice for us, we also sacrificing ourselves," [72] and "the sacrifice which is acceptable to God is unswerving abstraction from the body and its passions." [73] Clement also identifies prayer as "the best and holiest" expression of Christian sacrifice and the "common voice" of the church at prayer as the "breathing together" (σύμπνοια) of the church. God does not desire "costly" material sacrifices but is pleased with "that compounded incense ... which consists of many tongues and voices in prayer ... and [is] brought together in praises." [74] Indeed the gnostic's

> whole life is a holy festival. His sacrifices are prayers, and praises, and readings in the Scriptures before meals, and psalms and hymns during meals and before bed, and prayers also again during night. By these he unites himself to the divine choir, from continual recollection, engaged in contemplation which has everlasting remembrance. [75]

Clement does not explicitly connect the priesthood of Christians with his concepts of Christians as a "third form" beyond Greeks and Jews [76] and of martyrdom as sacrifice. [77] He is quite specific in applying the priestly office and role to the gnostic Christian. Eastwood is correct in noting the importance of Clement's statement:

> Those ... who have exercised themselves in the Lord's commandments, and lived perfectly and gnostically according to the Gospel, may be enrolled in the chosen body of the apostles. Such an one is in reality a presbyter of the Church, and a true minister (deacon) of the will of God, if he do and teach what is the Lord's; not as being ordained by men, nor regarded righteous because a presbyter, but enrolled in the presbyterate because righteous. [78]

Ascribing to Clement a concept of "hierarchical clericalism," Eastwood finds that Clement "does not hesitate to place the true spiritual gnostic on the same level as the cleric" and that the Christian gnostic's "spiritual qualifications" give to him "clerical honour, if not all the clerical functions." [79] Taking Clement's thought in its entirety, how-

---

[72] *Ibid.*, 7.3.
[73] *Ibid.*, 5.11.
[74] *Ibid.*, 7.6. Walther Völker (*Der wahre Gnostiker nach Clemens Alexandrinus*, Texte und Untersuchungen, 57 [Berlin, 1952], 549), says concerning Clement: "Er halt sich hier völlig in der neutestamentlichen Linie: die Gebete sind das eigentliche Opfer der Christen, sie sind der Weihrauch, der vom Altar des Herzens aufsteigt."
[75] *The Stromata*, 7.7.
[76] *Ibid.*, 6.5; 6.17.
[77] *Ibid.*, 4. esp. 13, 16, and 18.
[78] *Ibid.*, 6.13.
[79] *The Royal Priesthood of the Faithful*, 72.

ever, one may more aptly ask to what extent Clement has narrowed or constricted gnostically rather than clerically the apostolic doctrine of the priesthood of all Christians.

In view of his relation to Clement of Alexandria and of his work as a biblical exegete, Origen would be expected to have formulated a more precise concept of the royal priesthood than Clement or to have made it an integral part of his thought. Such, however, is not the case, for seemingly only in his biblical homilies and scholia does he unambiguously teach the general priesthood. In *On First Principles* he mentions only the Jewish priesthood. [80]

Most of Origen's other extant writings contain passages in which the high priesthood of Jesus is mentioned. He is the high priest "through" whom but not "to" whom men are to pray, [81] for he is

praying for those who pray and pleading with those who plead. He will not pray for us as His friends if we do not pray constantly through His intercession. Nor will He be an advocate with God for His followers if we do not obey His teaching that we ought always to pray and not to faint. [82]

As high priest Jesus "offered Himself in sacrifice;" [83] he is "the highpriest of all angels;" [84] he who is asked to "bear our prayers and sacrifices and intercessions to the supreme God" is to be worshipped. [85] Both "the more intelligent people" and "the common folk" pray to the Creator "by the mediation of a high priest who has shown to men the pure way to worship God." [86] Hence men ought not to pray to demons. [87] Jesus is "the absolute Word holding converse with the Father" [88] and "restores all things to His Father's kingdom, and arranges that whatever defects exist in each part of creation shall be filled up so as to be full of the glory of the Father." [89]

In ascribing priesthood to men within Christianity, Origen makes a place for a limited or special priesthood, although not that of the

---

[80] 4.1.3.
[81] *Prayer*, 15.4; tr. John J. O'Meara, ed., *Origen : Prayer [and] Exhortation to Martyrdom*, ACW, 19 (Westminster, Md., 1954), 42.
[82] *Ibid.*, 10.2.
[83] *Exhortation to Martyrdom*, 30.
[84] *Against Celsus*, 5.4, tr. Henry Chadwick, *Origen : Contra Celsum* (Cambridge, 1953).
[85] *Ibid.*, 8.13.
[86] *Ibid.*, 7.46.
[87] *Ibid.*, 8.26.
[88] *Commentary on the Gospel of Matthew*, 12.39 (*ANF*, 10).
[89] *Commentary on the Gospel, of John*, 1.40 (*ANF*, 10).

Christian gnostic. This special priesthood is variously identified by
Origen. In a context pertaining to the limitations on the apostolic
granting of remission of certain sins, [90] he seems to ascribe priesthood
to the apostles, who "know from their instruction by the Spirit for
what sins, when, and how they must offer sacrifice" and "also the
sins for which they must not do so." [91] Origen then decries those who
"have taken to themselves powers beyond the priestly dignity, perhaps
because they are unversed in the craft of the priesthood, and boast
that they can forgive idolatries, and remit fornications and adul-
teries." [92] Furthermore, in introducing his *Commentary on the Gospel
of John* he draws an analogy between the people of God under the Old
Covenant who offered "tithes and first fruits" to God "through
levites and priests" who had "no possessions but tithes and first
fruits" and "the whole people of Christ" who ought to provide support
for Christian scholars "who devote themselves to the divine word and
have no other employment but the service of God." According to
Origen, "those who fulfill a more distinguished office than their kins-
men will perhaps be high-priests, according to the order of Aaron." [93]
In yet a third context Origen identifies martyrs as "priests" who
"offer themselves in sacrifice" both as priests "without blemish" and
as victims "without blemish." Such martyrs "do not assist in vain at the

---

[90] I.e., idolatry, murder, and adultery. *Prayer*, 28.9-10.

[91] *Ibid.*, 28.9.

[92] *Ibid.*, 28.10, tr. Eric George Jay, ed., *Origen's Treatise on Prayer* (London,
1954). William Fairweather (*Origin and Greek Patristic Theology* [Edinburgh,
1901], 198), comments: "According to Origen every Christian is a priest in
virtue of the spiritual sacrifice which he offers. Through almsgiving, charity,
self-mortification, martyrdom, we share in the sacrifice of Christ, and so in
His priesthood. But it is only in this moral and figurative sense that any layman
can be called a priest. Origen did not allow the treatment meted out to himself
to lead him to belittle the office of the ministry. He magnifies it more than
Clement does, and shows a distinct leaning towards a restricted use of the
priestly name. Those who bear it, however, must have a character in keeping
with it." René Cadiou, *Origen: His Life at Alexandria* (St. Louis, 1944) 311ff.,
defends Origen's high regard for ministerial ordination even by citing his
criticisms of the conduct of the ordained, in an anti-Protestant context. Jean
Daniélou, *Origen* (New York, 1955), 44-51, sees in the era of Origen (1) the
existence of "two distinct types of authority," that of the Scripture-oriented
didaskaloi, of whom *Origen* was a leading example, and that of the worship-
oriented priests and (2) the incorporation of the former into the latter. Although
acknowledging (pp. 44-45) in Origen "a certain depreciation of the whole
clerical hierarchy," Daniélou (p. 50) insists that "he does not at all deny that
ordination to the priesthood confers special powers on the visible hierarchy."

[93] 1.3.

altar of heaven, but procure for them that pray the remission of sins." [94] Origen even speaks of "heavenly elders" and "diviner high-priests who are ordained under the one High-Priest." [95] In summary, Origen's concept of the special priesthood is variously identified with the apostles, the scholars, and the martyrs.

Only in a few pasages does Origen specifically mention the priest-hood of all Christians. These involve the quoting or paraphrasing of 1 Peter 2:5, 9 in contexts in which Origen is expounding other biblical texts. [96] While commenting on John 2:21, he clearly says: "The body is the Church, and we learn from Peter [1 Pet. 2:5] that it is a house of God, built of living stones, a spiritual house for a holy priesthood." [97] Similarly, when expounding Leviticus, he writes:

> He has given instructions so that we may know how we may approach God's altar. For it is an altar upon which we offer our prayers to God. That we may know, then, how we ought to offer them, He bids us put aside our soiled garments—the uncleanness of the flesh, the faults of character, the defilements of lust. Or do you not recognize that the priesthood has been given to you also, that is to the whole Church of God and the nation of believers? Hear, how Peter says concerning believers: "chosen race," says he, "royal priesthood, holy nation, a people in possession" [1 Pet. 2:9]. You have therefore a priesthood being a priestly nation. Therefore you ought to offer God a sacrifice of praise, of prayers, of pity, or purity, of righteousness, of holiness. [98] .... You have heard of the two sanc-tuaries; one as it were visible and open to the priests; the other invisible, to which the High Priest alone had access, while the rest remained out-side.... And pray do not marvel that the sanctuary is open to priests only. For all who have been anointed with the unction of the sacred chrism have been made priests, just as Peter says to the whole church, "But you are a chosen race, a royal priesthood, a holy nation" [1 Pet. 2:9]. You are, there-fore, "a priestly race," and thus you draw near to the holy places. [99]

Origen, in distinction from his identification of apostles, of scholars, and of martyrs as special priests, mentions the priesthood of all

---

[94]. *Exhortation to Martyrdom*, 30.

[95] *Commentary on the Gospel of Matthew*, 12.20.

[96] When 1 Peter 2:5 or 2:9 is quoted by Origen, the emphasis does not always rest upon priesthood. In *Exhortation to Martyrdom*, 5, 1 Peter 2:9 is quoted, but the comments pertain to "the chosen generation." In *Against Celsus*, 5.10, Origen applies this text to the Hebrew people only. He quotes 1 Peter 2:5 in his argument that Christians do not build "lifeless and dead temples to the author of all life" but stress the temple of the body and its future resurrection (*Against Celsus*, 8.19).

[97] *Commentary on the Gospel of John*, 10.23.

[98] *Homilia in Leviticum*, 9.1, quoted by Eastwood, *The Royal Priesthood of the Faithful*, 79, and revised by the present author.

[99] *Ibid.*, 9.9.

Christians only when commenting on or expounding Holy Scripture. Tertullian, on the other hand, alludes to it in his ethical and apologetic writings.

Priesthood for Tertullian, however, does not always mean the priesthood of all Christians. Frequently the North African alludes to pagan and to Jewish priests. Christians refuse "to offer sacrifice for the well-being of the emperor," although they customarily pray for him and other rulers. [100] In a Montanist treatise he identifies the wearing of the soldier's crown with idolatry, for "crowns adorn the very doors, victims, and altars of idols; their ministers and priests wear them, also." [101] Tertullian chides non-fasting Christians in a pungent contrast with the pagans:

> Hence *you are* more irreligious, in proportion as a heathen is more conformable. He, in short, sacrifices his appetite to an idol-god; *you* to (the true) God will not. For to you your belly is god, and your lungs a temple, and your paunch a sacrificial altar, and your cook the priest, and your fragrant smell the Holy Spirit, and your condiments spiritual gifts, and your belching prophecy. [102]

In *On Idolatry* Tertullian frequently refers to pagan priests and sacrifices. [103] Yet he allows Christian attendance of "private" pagan marriage ceremonies provided that the ceremony be not entitled " 'assisting in the sacrifice' " and that one is not "invited to act as priest and perform a sacrifice." [104] In reply to Jews, Tertullian interprets the history of sacrifices under the Old Covenant as being characterized by both "earthly sacrifices" which foreshadowed Israel and "spiritual sacrifices" which foreshadowed Christianity. "Thus, accordingly, the spiritual 'sacrifices of praise' are pointed to, and 'an heart contribulate' is demonstrated an acceptable sacrifice to God." [105]

Tertullian frequently refers to Jesus Christ in priestly terms. He is "the Priest of God the Father unto eternity," [106] "the universal high

---

[100] *Apology,* 27-33, esp. 28.2, tr. Sister Emily Joseph Daly, *Tertullian: Apologetical Works and Minucius Felix: Octavius,* FC, 10 (New York, 1950).

[101] *The Chaplet,* 10.9, tr. Edwin A. Quain, *Tertullian: Disciplinary, Moral and Ascetical Works,* FC, 40 (New York, 1959), 255.

[102] *On Fasting,* 16 (*ANF,* 4).

[103] Chs. 2, 5, 12, 13.

[104] *Ibid.,* 16, tr. S. L. Greenslade, ed., *Early Latin Theology,* LCC, 5 (Philadelphia, 1956), 102.

[105] *An Answer to the Jews,* 5, (*ANF,* 3). Tertullian quotes Gen. 4:2-14; Mal. 1:10-11; Ps. 51:17; 50:14; and Isa. 1:11-14.

[106] *Ibid.,* 14.

priest of the Father," [107] "the high priest of salvation," [108] and "the successful Suppliant of the Father" for remissible sins. [109]

Priesthood is also a term which Tertullian applies to the clergy, especially in contexts in which he is arguing against digamy, or second marriages for Christians who are widows or widowers. He argues:

> The pagans have a priesthood of widows and celibates—though, of course, this is part of Satan's malevolence; and the ruler of this world, their *Pontifex Maximus,* is not permitted to marry a second time. How great purity must please God, since even the Enemy affects it! [110]

Tertullian even claims to have found in Leviticus a text which reads "My priests shall not pluralize marriages," but modern scholars have been unable to locate such a text. Arguing as to a higher standard in Christianity, he asserts that

> with us the law which requires that none but monogamists are to be chosen for the order of the priesthood, is more comprehensive in its scope and exacting in details. So true is this that . . . there have been men deposed from office for digamy. [111]

Rejecting the view of his opponents that only ordained clerics are forbidden to remarry, the Montanists ask:

> Whence do we take our bishops and clergy? Is it not from among all of us? And if not all are obliged to monogamy, whence will we have mono- gamists for the clergy? Are we to institute some special order of mono- gamists so that we may choose the clergy from its ranks? [112]

The question expects a negative answer, for Tertullian continues:

> Indeed, whenever we are minded to exalt ourselves with swelling pride at the expense of the clergy, then "we are all one" [cf. John 17:21; Gal. 3:28], then we are all priests, for "He hath made us priests to God and His Father" [cf. Rev. 1:6; 5:10]! But when we are called upon to be the peers of priests in discipline, we lay aside our fillets—and pair off! [113]

Both in the latter passage in *Monogamy* and in a similar one in *An Exhortation to Chastity* one may see how Tertullian, accepting both the general priesthood of Christians and the special clerical priesthood,

---

[107] *Against Marcion,* 4.9, tr. Ernest Evans, ed., *Tertullian: Adversus Marcionem* (Oxford, 1972). Cf. *Monogamy,* 7.

[108] *On the Flesh of Christ,* 5, tr. Ernest Evans, ed., *Tertullian's Treatise on the Incarnation* (London, 1956), 21.

[109] *On Modesty,* 19 (*ANF,* 4).

[110] *To His Wife,* 1.7, tr. William P. LeSaint, ed., *Tertullian: Treatises on Marriage and Remarriage,* ACW, 13 (Westminster, Md., 1951), 20.

[111] *An Exhortation to Chastity,* 7.

[112] *Monogamy,* 12.

[113] *Ibid.*

argues from one to the other. In the former he, assuming that clerical priests can marry only once, argues from the priesthood of all Christians in behalf of singular marriages for all Christians. In the latter he, assuming that clerics are in a special sense priests, argues from the general priesthood and the occasional clerical functions of laymen to singular marriages for all Christians. There must be no double standard! He says:

> It would be folly to imagine that lay people may do what priests may not. For are not we lay people also priests? It is written: "He hath made us also a kingdom, and priests to God and His father" [Rev. 1:6]. [114]

Moreover, since lay people in cases of necessity do baptize and offer the Eucharist, "How much more serious a crime is it for a lay digamist to perform sacerdotal functions, when a priest who becomes a digamist is removed from his priestly office!" [115]

In a context utterly distinct from the issue of digamy, Tertullian expounds the priesthood of all Christians in terms of prayer:

> For this is the spiritual oblation which has wiped out the ancient sacrifices.... We are the true worshippers and the true priests, who, praying in the Spirit, in the Spirit offer a sacrifice of prayer as an oblation which is God's own and is well pleasing (to him), that in fact which he has sought after, which he has provided for himself. [116]

Tertullian is, therefore, both a witness to the general priesthood of all Christians as taught in the New Testament and by Christian writers of the second and early third centuries and a pioneer in applying to the ordained clergy in a very special sense the category and language of priesthood. James Morgan has interpreted this dual usage as follows:

> Tertullian is the first, who expressly advances sacerdotal claims on behalf of the Christian ministry and calls it "sacerdotium," although he also emphatically affirms the universal priesthood of all believers. [117]

---

[114] *An Exhortation to Chastity,* 7.
[115] *Ibid.*
[116] *On the Prayer,* 28, tr. Ernest Evans, ed., *Tertullian's Tract on the Prayer* (London, 1953), 37. Robert E. Roberts, *The Theology of Tertullian* (London, 1924), 188-89, is hardly justified in stating that this "passage may be understood in a figurative sense, so as not to oppose the view ... of the office of the bishop as a priest" and concluding that Tertullian's question, "Are not we lay people also priests?" involves "the notion of the layman as a literal priest."
[117] *The Importance of Tertullian in the Development of Christian Dogma* (London, 1928), 122. Quoting Edwin Hatch, *The Organization of the Early Christian Churches,* 142, Morgan concludes that the general acceptance of the clerical priesthood and the expression of its corollaries came about a century and a half after Tertullian's time. Adolf Harnack (*A History of Dogma* [1894; repr. New York, 1961], 2:129) associates Tertullian's concept of priesthood more closely with that of Irenaeus than with that of Cyprian.

The extant writings of Hippolytus afford no evidence of his teaching the priesthood of all Christians. In the fragments from his *Commentary on Daniel* Jesus is called "the perfect King and Priest," "the Priest of priests," and "the heavenly Priest." [118] In *The Apostolic Tradition* bishops are referred to three times as God's "high priests," presbyters offering to God "the bread and the cup" are identified as "priests," the deacon is said to be "not ordained for a priesthood," and the Holy Spirit is called "the high priestly Spirit." [119]

Four of the Apostolic Fathers recognize that Christians offer to God "spiritual sacrifices." Although the apologists characteristically refute any necessity for offering sacrifices, Justin Martyr identifies Christians as "the true priestly family of God" and Gentile prayers as acceptable to God. Melito of Sardis points to the *locus classicus*, 1 Peter 2:9. Obliquely acknowledging the general priesthood, Irenaeus regards the Eucharist as the chief sacrifice offered by Christians. Clement of Alexandria limits the general priesthood to the gnostics or pneumatics. Origen at various times identifies apostles, scholars, and martyrs as "priests" but in his exegetical works clearly teaches the priesthood of all Christians when quoting 1 Peter 2:5, 9. Tertullian applies the sacerdotal category and language both to all Christians and to clerics, and by the latter usage, in which he is joined by Hippolytus, he prepares the way for Cyprian's exclusive application of the term "priests" to the clergy, especially the bishops.

---

[118] *Fragments from the Commentary on Daniel*, 2.14, 15, 17 (*ANF*, 5).

[119] 3.4; 9.11; 30; 4.11; 9.2; 3.5, tr. Gregory Dix, ed., *The Treatise on the Apostolic Tradition of St Hippolytus of Rome*, rev. Henry Chadwick (London, 1968).

CIVILIZATION AS A PREPARATION FOR CHRISTIANITY IN THE THOUGHT OF EUSEBIUS

ROBERT M. GRANT

University of Chicago

In the preface to his *Church History* Eusebius of Caesarea explains why the divine Word came among men and was proclaimed to all, just at the time when this occurred and not earlier (I 2, 17-27). His answer is that the wickedness of primitive man was such that only a succession of divine revelations could gradually instruct him. First came punishments by flood and fire, then revelations to a few (such as the patriarchs), then the "images and symbols" delivered to Moses. After Moses came legislators and philosophers among the gentiles, changing "wild and fierce brutality" into "a gentler mood." Then the Word himself appeared "in the early days of the Roman empire."

Eusebius does mention the fall, when the first man "fell to this mortal and perishable condition and received this earth, laid under a curse, in exchange for his former God-given delights." But for him the fall is an item in the general history of mankind and its struggle toward civilization. Adam's descendants were much worse than he was. They entered upon

> a bestial, intolerable mode of existence. And what is more, they took no thought for city or state, arts or sciences; they did not possess even the name of laws and ordinances nor, still further, of virtue and philosophy, but passed a nomadic life in the desert like wild and fierce creatures. The powers of reasoning that nature gives for man's possession, and the seeds of thought and culture implanted in the human soul, they destroyed by an excess of self-chosen wickedness (Oulton, revised).

Eusebius is not interested in any original golden age. He is concerned with the gradual progress and development of mankind.

We should never overestimate Eusebius' originality even, or especially, at points where he insists upon it. The present passage is a mosaic of Graeco-Roman commonplaces. Thus the bestial θηριώδης life of primitive man was well-known to all those who spoke of human progress. [1] We need mention only the pre-Socratics Democritus (68

---

[1] Examples in L. Edelstein, *The Idea of Progress in Classical Antiquity* (Baltimore, 1967), 25 n. 7, 55 n. 73; K. Thraede, "Fortschritt," *Reallexikon für Antike und Christentum* VIII (1972), 143.

B 5 Diels-Kranz) and Critias (88 B 25) and the influential rhetorician Isocrates (*Nicocles* 6 = *Antidosis* 254). The fragment of Democritus actually comes from Diodorus Siculus I 8, and Eusebius cited this passage in his *Praeparatio Evangelica* (I 7, 10). The significant verses from Critias are ascribed to Euripides and cited in Aetius' doxography (I 7, 2, p. 298, 15-17 Diels), and Eusebius notes the ascription but omits the verses because they are not relevant to his discussion in the *Praeparatio* (XIV 16, 1). Unfortunately we cannot prove that Eusebius knew Isocrates. Two different dates for the orator's *floruit* appear in the Latin *Chronicle,* while in the *Praeparatio* he is known only through Clement and Porphyry—as a victim of plagiarism (X 2, 6; 3, 4; 3, 17). On the other hand, Eusebius may well have noticed that the Christian rhetorician Tatian referred to "the end of bestial and nomadic life" in a passage quoted in *Praeparatio* X 11, 18. In his reading of Clement of Alexandria he probably encountered the expression several times. 2

In our search for Eusebius' background at this point, references to a bestial life are obviously inconclusive. We need to find a context in which this kind of life is followed by the rise of civilization. As a matter of fact, such a picture is given us precisely by Isocrates. Even if Eusebius never read a line of Isocrates he could have heard declamations related to the *Nicocles.* 3

In the *Nicocles,* Isocrates speaks in the person of the king of Salamis on Cyprus and vigorously defends monarchy as the ideal form of government. Since Eusebius certainly shared this point of view we may suspect that he would have read Isocrates at least on this subject. As he begins to get to the point, Isocrates speaks of eloquence (λόγοι) as the power which brought men out of barbarism into civilization.

> Not only have we escaped the life of wild beasts (θηριώδης) but we have come together and founded cities and made laws and invented arts; and generally there is no institution devised by man which the power of speech (λόγος) has not helped us to establish (tr. Norlin).

This is exactly what Eusebius had in mind, as we see throughout his preface to the *Church History.* There he tells us repeatedly that the Logos divine not human, guided mankind and planted "the seeds of godliness in a multitude of men" (I 2, 22). The Logos led mankind to civilization (I 2, 23).

---

2 *Paed.* I 54, 3; *Str.* VI 50, 3; VII 22, 1; VIII 5, 3.
3 He could allude to Thucydides without close contact (*H.E.* V pr. 3-4); cf. Dionysius of Alexandria in *H.E.* VII 22, 6 (Thuc. II 64, 1).

It appears that Isocrates provided Eusebius with his basic ideas about primitive man, whether directly or, indeed, through some manual of rhetoric. In addition, we may suppose that Eusebius envisioned the cooperation of human minds with the divine, since in a work he certainly knew, the *Contra Celsum* of Origen, there is a strong emphasis upon this work of cooperation (*C. Cels.* IV 74 ff., especially IV 80-81).

For completeness' sake we should mention what Graf Uxkull-Gyllenbrand pointed out: that Isocrates' picture in turn in based on a theory held by Archelaus, the pupil of Anaxagoras. [4] What we know of Archelaus' teaching on this subject comes from doxographical information preserved by the Christian author Hippolytus. [5]

> Mankind came to be differentiated from the other animals and instituted rulers and laws and arts and cities and the rest. Mind is implanted in all animals in similar fashion. Each of the animals uses its mind either more slowly or more rapidly.

Obviously this is not Eusebius' direct source. The ideas of an ancient "naturalist" did not appeal to him. Archelaus' principle of mind could not be connected with Eusebius' Logos as Isocrates' λόγος could. But our citation of a passage preserved in the third-century writing of Hippolytus shows that ideas like those of Isocrates were not necessarily surprising. Eusebius' readers could find them attractive.

Certainly Eusebius himself found the ideas attractive. Since he wrote all his major works after the end of the Diocletianic persecution, he welcomed ideas about progress and civilization as pointing onward toward the triumph of the Christian church in the Roman empire. The early history of civilization had prefigured the history of his own time, just as the passage from darkness to light at creation had anticipated the transmission of the gospel message. [6] In his sermon for the rededication of the basilica at Tyre he touched on the theme of the Word as civilizing agent (X 4, 18).

> Who abolished the barbarous and uncivilized customs of uncivilized nations by his civilized and most humane laws?

---

[4] *Griechische Kultur-Entstehungslehren* (Berlin, 1924), 11 n. 21.

[5] *Ref.* I 9, 6, p. 15, 24-28 Wendland = H. Diels, *Doxographi Graeci* (Berlin, 1879), 564, 6-10.

[6] The light of the gospel (*H.E.* II 3, 1) against Simon Magus (II 14, 3-4. 6; 15, 1); the truth and the church (IV 7, 12-13); toleration (IX 1, 8) and peace (8, 15); revelation (X 4, 13); Constantine (8, 19) and his victory (9, 7). Dionysius used the language in regard to Gallienus (VII 23, 2), Maximin to his own revival of paganism (IX 7, 3; cf. W. Dittenberger, *Sylloge Inscriptionum Graecarum*, ed. 3, Leipzig, 1915/24, no. 900, lines 23-26).

Eusebius is referring both to primitive times and to recent experiences. The tetrarchic persecution had been a lapse into barbarism.

The passage from the *Nicocles* of Isocrates which Eusebius used for his picture of civilization comes from an oration which has created grave difficulties for historians of culture. The oration is put in the mouth of the young king of Cyprus and sets forth the duties of subjects toward a monarch. As Isocrates had earlier idealized Athenian democracy, so now he eulogized the first king of New Salamis *(Evagoras)*, addressed his son on the duties of monarchs *(To Nicocles)*, and wrote on the duties of subjects as well *(Nicocles)*. His praise of eloquence as the prime civilizing force (repeated in *Antidosis* 253-57)—eloquence which for Eusebius becomes *the Logos*—can thus be taken either as a notable expression of Greek παιδεία or as a witness to his selling out to dictatorship. Werner Jaeger naturally took it the first way, [7] and H.-I. Marrou, though without quite so much enthusiasm, did so too. [8] On the other hand, N. H. Baynes, who had given a Romanes lecture on "Intellectual Liberty and Totalitarian Claims" and for the Foreign Office was translating the speeches of Adolf Hitler, vigorously attacked both Isocrates and Jaeger, claiming that the *Nicocles* was none other than a "eulogy of Führertum." His criticism was not published until 1955, when it appeared in his *Byzantine Studies and Other Essays*. By coincidence, this volume also contained his earlier study of "Eusebius and the Christian Empire," in which he traced Eusebius' attitude and expressions back to Neopythagorean sources. [9] Use of the *Nicocles* by Eusebius, which Baynes did not note, obviously reinforces his view and reminds us that uncritical acceptance of contemporary culture is almost as questionably Christian as is uncritical denunciation.

Is it really likely that Eusebius was relying on Isocrates for this thought? One cannot be sure how close he was to Isocrates' own orations, especially when we recall how they had been cannibalized by anthologists like Stobaeus—precisely when he collected texts on monarchy. For that matter, we cannot be confident that two second-century bishops of Antioch had recourse to Isocrates for some of the

---

[7] W. Jaeger, *Paideia* III (New York, 1944), 147-57; on *logos* and civilization, 150-51.

[8] H. I. Marrou, *History of Education in Antiquity* (E.T., London, 1956), 79-91.

[9] *Byzantine Studies and Other Essays* (London, 1955), 144-67 (Isocrates); esp. 149-51 *(Nicocles)*; 168-72 (Eusebius).

proverbial expressions they used. [10] The indubitable use of the *Pana-thenaicus* in Clement's *Stromata* may be second-hand, since the passage is to be found in Stobaeus as well. [11] But whether at first-hand or second, the idea is Isocratean and it recurs in the firmly monarchist author Eusebius. [12]

The ideas about civilization are present in all Eusebius' major writings, even though various aspects of it are emphasized at various points. We have seen that in the *Church History* what Eusebius chiefly deals with is the civilizing effect of urban society with its institutions. This was the point made by Isocrates. The same point occurs in two passages in the *Praeparatio*. In summarizing the effect of the gospel, Eusebius says that even "the most savage barbarians ... refrain from their irrational brutality and adopt the opinions of a wise philosophy" (I 4, 13). The situation of primitive, savage men is described thus: "there were no laws yet established for the guidance of life, no civilized government set in order among men, but they led a loose and wandering life like that of the beasts" (II 5, 4 tr. Gifford).

A similar but more highly developed passage in the *Demonstratio* (VIII praef. 6-11) is almost certainly based on the account in the *Church History*. Indeed Eusebius says that he has already explained why the Christ appeared recently, "in the last times," and not before (*Dem*. VIII pr. 5); in the *Church History* (I 2, 17-23) much the same account served just the same purpose. The account in the *History* tells of nomads living in the desert. According to the *Demonstratio* primitive men lived in lonely deserts, in mountains, caves and villages. [13] "They preyed on their neighbors like robbers, and gained their livelihood mostly by tyrannizing over those weaker than themselves" (tr. Ferrar). Similarly in Lucretius' poem *De rerum natura* we learn how magistrates and law were introduced in order to put an end to anarchy (V 1136-47). Protagoras had also pointed out that men treated one another unjustly because they had no political ability. [14] And Cicero, like Lucretius relying on Greek sources, claimed that primitive

---

[10] Ignatius, *Polyc*. 1, 3; 4, 2; cf. *Ad Demonicum* 20; Theophilus, *Ad Autol.* II 38; III 15; cf. *Ad Demonicum* 18.

[11] *Panathenaicus* 30-32; Clement, *Str.* IV 69, 1-5; Stobaeus I 44.

[12] On other patristic authors cf. F. A. Spencer, *The Influence of Isocrates in Antiquity* (Diss. Chicago, 1923), 91-104 and summary, p. 3.

[13] Perhaps an echo of mountains and caves in Hebrews 11:38 (after deserts); but *nemora atque cavos montis silvasque* (Lucret. V 955).

[14] Plato, *Protagoras* 322B.

men abused their strength in order to dominate those who were weaker. [15]

Obviously such a view of primitive man is the opposite of what Posidonius taught. (It is important to note this because of the supposed influence of Posidonius on many fourth-century Christian exegetes of Genesis. [16]) Posidonius maintained that in the golden age the wise governed and protected the weaker from the stronger. "After vice slipped in and kingdoms were transformed into tyrannies, there began to be need for laws." [17] He depicted the development of tyranny when he spoke of Moses and his successors. Moses proclaimed a pure religion; then came superstitious successors; then tyrants, who practised robbery. [18] According to Eusebius, on the contrary, mankind developed away from such vices, not toward them.

In Eusebius' view, the movement away from beast-like life involved movement toward monarchy (to be precise, the monarchy of the Roman empire) and away from various forms of polyarchy. He develops this theme in relation to civilization especially in the *Praeparatio* (I 4, 2-5) and the late *Commentary on Isaiah* (p. 80, 10-11. 26; 81, 3 Ziegler), more generally in various passages in the *Demonstratio* (VII 1, 50; VIII pr. 3; 3, 14; 4, 13; IX 17, 18). These passages have been discussed by Erik Peterson and Raffaele Farina, among others, and we shall not go into them here. [19]

It is equally significant that beast-like life is characterized by immorality. According to the *Church History* (I 2, 19) primitive men "corrupted one another" (ἀλληλοφθορεῖν), "killed one another" (ἀλληλοκτονεῖν), and (though one would expect ἀλληλοβορεῖν) "practised cannibalism" (ἀνθρωποβορεῖν). Changes are rung on this in *Praeparatio* and *Demonstratio*, as we should expect; more surprisingly, in the *Laus Constantini* and the *Theophany*. [20] In the first passage cited, Eusebius gives examples of "beast-like and barbarous customs." To the Persians he ascribes marriage with mothers, cannibalism to the

---

[15] Cicero, *De invent*. I 2.

[16] K. Gronau, *Poseidonios und die jüdisch-christliche Genesisexegese* (Leipzig-Berlin, 1914); carried *ad absurdum,* says (rightly) Uxkull-Gyllenband, *op. cit.,* 45 n. 9.

[17] Seneca, *Epist*. 90, 5-6.

[18] Strabo XVI 2, 37.

[19] Peterson, *Theologische Traktate* (Munich, 1951), 45-147 ("Der Monotheismus als politisches Problem"); on Eusebius, 86-93; R. Farina, *L'Impero e l'imperatore cristiano in Eusebio di Cesarea* (Zurich, 1966).

[20] *Praep. ev.* I 4, 6; VII 2, 6; *Dem. ev.* I 2, 14; 6, 56; IV 10, 2; *Laus* 13, 14; *Theoph.* II 15.

Scythians, sexual intercourse with daughters and sisters to others not identified, and to still others male homosexual practises, casting corpses to dogs and birds, strangling the aged, eating the dead, or offering human sacrifice. Most of these items actually come from the treatise of Porphyry *On abstinence from meat,* a work which Eusebius used extensively in the *Praeparatio* (naming its author) and even in the *Laus Constantini* (not naming the author, presumably because like the Arians his memory incurred imperial displeasure in 333 [21]). He seems to have added Persian (and Egyptian) incest from the treatise of Bardesanes employed later in the *Praeparatio* (VI 10, 15-16), male homosexual practises from Romans 1:27. More interesting is the use made of these examples. They are obviously characteristic of barbarians, as anyone knew who had looked at the studies made by Graeco-Roman ethnographers or the works of philosophers, especially Skeptics, who relied on the studies when showing how relative moral standards were. It is not surprising to find almost everything Eusebius mentions already noted in the writings of Sextus Empiricus. [22] What is surprising is to find Eusebius suggesting that all this uncivilized behavior belongs to a primitive stage of society. Modern man has outgrown such activities, by the guidance of the Logos.

The reason Eusebius thinks this is the case, or can be the case, is that he has carefully studied the arguments of Porphyry against eating meat and those of Bardesanes against astrological determinism, and he has made the progressivist approach his own. Porphyry saw a decline when the earlier offerings of first-fruits were replaced by animal sacrifices, [23] but he also insisted on the improvement that was made when, with the passage of time, human sacrifice was stopped. [24] (Unfortunately Porphyry, followed by Eusebius, went on to speak of contemporary human sacrifices at Rome.) The improvement was not merely theoretical. Eusebius was aware that sacred prostitution continued to his own day at Baalbek, and he referred to it in both the *Praeparatio* and the *Theophany.* [25] When he rewrote (it appears) the *Theophany* passage in the *Laus Constantini* parallel, he left out mention of happenings at Baalbek. The obvious reason for the omission was that moral improvement had occurred when Constantine closed down

---

[21] Cf. H. G. Opitz, *Athanasius Werke* III (Berlin, 1933), 66-68 = Urkunde 33.
[22] *Pyrrh. hypot.* I 152; III 199. 205. 207.
[23] Porphyry, *De abst.* II 7, p. 138, 2 Nauck[2]; Eusebius, *Praep. ev.* IV 14, 1.
[24] Porphyry, *op. cit.,* II 54-55, p. 179, 7-181, 14; Eusebius, *op. cit.,* IV 16.
[25] *Praep. ev.* IV 16, 22; *Theoph.* II 14.

the operations there. [26] Divine guidance in history and a favorable imperial policy obviously went hand in hand.

Finally it should be noted that the course of debestialization and debarbarization could be regarded as the fulfilment of biblical prophecy. [27] The key passage for the domestication of wild animals was, of course, Isaiah 11:6-9, where we learn about the wolf and the lamb together, not to mention the leopard with the kid, and the cow and the bear. As early as the *Eclogae propheticae* (IV 8) Eusebius referred this passage to human behavior, "changed from the depths of wickedness into gentleness through the epiphany of our Savior." In the *Demonstratio* (II 3, 111) he refers the words to "the change of savage and uncivilized nations, in no way differing from wild beasts, to a holy, mild, and social way of life." All races of men, by conversion to Christianity, are transformed "from savagery and barbarism to gentleness and mildness" (II 2, 40. 42; cf. VII 3, 34). The same points, with an emphasis more strictly political, recur in the late *Commentary on Isaiah* (I 62, p. 80 Ziegler). There is nothing especially surprising or even predictive in Isaiah's prophecy, for it points to the victory of Christ and that has already taken place.

Here as usual we find spiritualizing exegesis correcting more primitive literal interpretations of prophecy. Irenaeus (*Adv. haer.* V 33, 4) knew exegetes who took the line followed by Eusebius, but he himself, adhering to the apocalypticism of Papias, took the prophecy literally. At the same time he did hold that the Logos had brought civilization to savages (V 24, 2). What Eusebius does is to take one side of Irenaeus' twofold interpretation.

A final question remains. Should what we have been discussing be described as "progress," or is there any such thing in the thought of Eusebius or, indeed, of other Christian writers? Probably the first occurrence of a term like "progress" among Christian writers is to be found in the gospel of Luke, where the child Jesus is described as "advancing" (προέκοπτεν, cf. προκοπή, Luke 2:52) in wisdom and age and favor with God and men. There are other New Testament examples of the use of the word, but in the Apostolic Fathers it occurs only in 2 Clement 17:3: "Let us try . . . to advance in the commandments of the Lord." In the writings of the apologists we find it only in Justin's *Dialogue with Trypho* (2, 6): Justin advanced in Platonic studies (the

---

[26] *Laus* 13, 11; *Vit. Const.* III 58, 1-2.

[27] Eusebius does not relate bestial behavior to old charges against Christians; these are now outmoded (*H.E.* IV 7).

other instances have to do with the passage of time). "Progress" comes up again in Theophilus of Antioch (*Ad Autol.* II 24), from whom we learn that God gave Adam an "opportunity (ἀφορμή) for progress (προκοπῆς), so that as he grew (αὐξάνων, Gen. 1:28) and became perfect he might be ... shown forth as a god and ascend into heaven." Here we find real progress, but it is not the innate or natural progress of the modern world-view. It is a progress clearly controlled and desiderated by God, not something spontaneous or, should we say, Darwinian. And when we come to the προκοπή, advancement or even progress, of which the Alexandrians, deeply influencing Eusebius, made so much, [28] there is no reason whatever to suppose that any of them, or Eusebius himself, ever thought of progress as if it were some spontaneous force apart from divine providence. In the view of all these writers, providence was in complete control of the course of history and in so far as there was progress it was due to the action of God. [29]

Thus Edelstein and others may be right when they speak of "progress" as a theme developed by ancient writers. But if Eusebius' sources had in mind a progress independent of divine action, he himself and other Christians never supposed that the progress occurred outside God's plan.

---

[28] Cf. Hal Koch, *Pronoia und Paideusis* (Leipzig, 1932).

[29] I owe this point to the article of C. J. Berry, "On the Meaning of Progress and Providence in the Fourth Century," *Heythrop Journal* 18 (1977), 257-70, kindly given me by the editor, Robert Murray, S.J.

A FIRST-GENERATION ANSELMIAN,
GUIBERT OF NOGENT

JAROSLAV PELIKAN

Yale University

In his monograph of 1960 on Anselm of Canterbury, from which this section of the present volume has derived its title, George H. Williams has set the *Cur Deus Homo* into the liturgical and apologetic contexts of the time, as reflected in the work of Anselm himself and in that of his pupils and colleagues. [1] And in his doctoral dissertation of 1946, published in 1951 as *The Norman Anonymous of 1100 A.D.*, he has identified that text as "strictly Christocentric," [2] thereby contributing, as Ernst Kantorowicz acknowledged, to the latter's characterization of the age of Anselm as "the uncompromisingly christocentric period of Western civilization." [3] As an expression of my own gratitude to Professor Williams, I propose here to examine the Anselmian elements in the thought of one of Anselm's foremost disciples, Guibert of Nogent (1053-1124). The *Dictionnaire de théologie catholique* contains no entry on Guibert, and the second edition of the *Lexikon für Theologie und Kirche* gives him ten lines plus a bibliography. [4] Nevertheless, he would seem to merit greater attention both in his own right and for his affinities with the theology of his master. Within the confines of the length prescribed for this article, I want to look briefly at several of these affinities.

The specific feature of Anselm's theology with which George Williams has dealt in his study is the replacement of baptism by the

---

[1] George Huntston Williams, *Anselm: Communion and Atonement* (Saint Louis, 1960), 18-28.

[2] George Huntston Williams, *The Norman Anonymous of 1100 A.D.: Toward the Identification and Evaluation of the So-Called Anonymous of York,* Harvard Theological Studies, 18 (Cambridge, Mass., 1951), 175.

[3] Ernst H. Kantorowicz, *The King's Two Bodies: A Study in Mediaeval Political Theology* (Princeton, 1957), 61; see also p. 42.

[4] Ludwig Ott, "Guibert v. Nogent," *Lexikon für Theologie und Kirche,* 2d ed., 4:1266. The only full-length study of Guibert is that of Bernard Monod, *Le moine Guibert et son temps (1053-1124)* (Paris, 1905), but the section on "Guibert théologien" (pp. 302-25), while hailing him as "le premier, a osé l'introduire [l'esprit critique et scientifique] dans le domaine religieux," is not very instructive.

Eucharist as the root metaphor for the doctrine of the atonement.
As he has noted, there is "an embryonic formulation of the *Cur Deus
Homo* ... in the *Disputatio Judaei cum Christiano* of Gilbert Crispin,
Abbot of Westminster"; Gilbert Crispin was a protégé of Anselm in
his doctrine of the atonement and in his apologetic method. [5] Similarly, Réginald Grégoire has called the treatise *De incarnatione Domini
et ejus sepultura* ascribed to Bruno of Segni "un '*Cur Deus Homo*'
rudimentaire." [6] Others of Anselm's contemporaries, including Honorius of Autun (ca. 1080 - ca. 1156), also reflected his theories on the
work of Christ and the plan of salvation. Among these, Guibert stands
out as the author of treatises not only on the person and work of
Christ but also on the Eucharist, and therefore as the one disciple of
Anselm who had the opportunity to develop *in extenso* the eucharistic
presuppositions of the atonement; for, as Williams points out in a
bibliographical footnote, these were not the subject of a discrete
treatise by Anselm, but appeared in a work that has been frequently,
though mistakenly, attributed to him, the letter *De corpore et sanguine
Domini*. [7]

The eucharistic theology of Guibert of Nogent was examined in
a study published fifty years ago by Geiselmann, although his interest
was in Guibert's role in the controversy with Berengar of Tours. [8]
In connection with our earlier references to Kantorowicz and Williams
on the matter of "christocentrism," it is interesting to note that a
passage from Guibert quoted by Kantorowicz on the leitmotiv of
Kantorowicz's book, the idea of the "bipartite body [*corpus biper-
titum*]," is followed immediately by a statement of the theme of
Williams's book, a comparison between "the temporary, in fact only
hour-long power [*temporalem, imo horariam potestatem*]" of the
baptismal water and the "continuing [*semper*]" power of the eucharistic
host to avail before the throne of glory. [9] Elsewhere, too, Guibert
contrasted baptism and the Eucharist, to the advantage of the

---

[5] Williams, *Communion and Atonement*, 27.

[6] Réginald Grégoire, *Bruno de Segni exégète médiéval et théologien monastique* (Spoleto, 1965), 261.

[7] Williams, *Communion and Atonement*, 60, n. 135. The treatise appears in
Book IV, Epistle 107 of Migne's edition of Anselm's letters (*PL* 159:255-58).

[8] Josef Rupert Geiselmann, "Die Stellung des Guibert von Nogent (+ 1124)
in der Eucharistielehre der Frühscholastik," *Theologische Quartalschrift* 110
(1929) : 66-84, 279-305.

[9] Guibert *De pignoribus sanctorum* 2.3.1 (*PL* 156: 634-35) ; Kantorowicz, *Two
Bodies*, 198.

Eucharist. [10] He did point out that "without the faith in baptism the other sacraments are null and void," and that without baptism and the Eucharist, "inasmuch as they are common to Christianity, our faith is not able to subsist." [11] In his statements about the sacraments as "that which takes place mystically in the church," it was only to baptism and the Eucharist, together with "the gift of the Spirit," that he referred, [12] although he proposed various definitions of "sacrament" that could include other actions of the church sometimes given that designation. [13]

As is evident from the full title of his eucharistic treatise, *Epistola de buccella Judae data et de veritate dominici corporis,* [14] Guibert's principal polemical concern was with the objective reality of the presence of the body of Christ in the Lord's Supper. The doctrine of the real presence was necessary because the notion of the Eucharist as a "figure" among other figures or as a "memorial" akin to the memorials of the saints would depress it to a "perfunctory" and trivial status. To be sure, Christ was called a "rock" in Scripture (1 Cor. 10:4), as well as other things; but about none of these did the eucharistic prayer of the church declare that it was to be "borne by the hands of the angel to the sublime altar of God," as it did about the elements in the Sacrament. [15] As for the "morsel given to Judas" referred to in the title, Guibert averred that "the more eminent teachers of the church, such as Augustine and Leo, agree that Judas received the Eucharist from the hands of the Lord, together with the other apostles," but that other church fathers disagreed. [16] Although this patristic question did continue to agitate the minds of the participants in the controversy against Berengar, a more recent issue was whether or not a mouse that nibbled a consecrated host was, by virtue of the objectivity of the real presence, eating the true body of Jesus Christ. [17]

---

[10] Guibert *Epistola de buccella Judae data et de veritate dominici corporis* 3 (*PL* 156:532).

[11] *De pignoribus* 1.1 (*PL* 156:613).

[12] Guibert *Quo ordine sermo fieri debeat* (*PL* 156:23).

[13] *De pignoribus* 2.3.6 (*PL* 156:638).

[14] *PL* 156:527-38.

[15] *De veritate corporis* 3 (*PL* 156:531). The use of this argument from the eucharistic prayer went back at least to Ambrose *De sacramentis* 4.27 (*SC* 25-II:116) and had been introduced into the medieval eucharistic controversies by Paschasius Radbertus *De corpore et sanguine Domini* 8 (*CCCM* 16:41-43).

[16] *De veritate corporis* 1 (*PL* 156:529).

[17] Artur Michael Landgraf, *Die Lehre von den Sakramenten* part 3 of *Dogmengeschichte der Frühscholastik* (Regensburg, 1952), 2:207-22: "Die in der Frühscholastik klassische Frage 'Quid sumit mus.'"

Guibert saw this issue as an effort to disparage the doctrine of the
real presence through a *reductio ad absurdum,* as though this doctrine
required that the body of Christ be "something that is common to
beasts and to human beings," and he concluded that "we by no means
[*nulla ratione*] believe" that a dumb animal could devour the true body
of Christ. [18]

As Professor Williams has observed, "the sacrament of the Eucharist [was] systematically defined for the first time in theological
debate and conciliar decision in the anti-Berengarian controversy," by
Guibert among others, and this "could not but have its effect in any
fresh formulation of the manner of man's objective salvation." [19] Like
penance and unlike baptism, the Eucharist was, as Williams puts it,
"reiterative." According to Guibert, someone had claimed, apparently
for that reason, "that in the confecting of the host that brings salvation
the Lord Jesus is crucified every day on the altar." [20] But New
Testament passages such as I Peter 3:18 and Hebrews 9:24-28
emphasized that Christ had died "once and for all [*semel*]" and that the
sacrifice of Calvary was not offered up "repeatedly [*saepe*]" but
"once [*semel*]." [21] Reiterative though the sacrifice of the Mass was,
this did not mean that Christ performed his priestly function over and
over again, but that he was, as Psalm 110:4 said, "a priest for ever." [22]
Therefore the notion of a daily crucifixion of Christ was to be rejected
as execrable; for "the fact that the same sacrifice is carried out over
and over [*frequentatur*] through daily iteration is to be explained not
as a repetition each day of the punishment of the crucifixion, but
rather as a means of washing away, through the daily re-presentation
of this great mystery, the daily evil incurred by the variety of our
transgressions." [23] There was in this sense only one sacrifice, once
and for all, as there was only one high priest, and, as Guibert stressed
against Berengar, only one body of Christ, to which notions of quantity
or measure were not applicable, since he who received the tiniest bit
of the consecrated host received the total Christ. [24]

Such was the eucharistic doctrine that provided the framework for

---

[18] *De pignoribus* 2.3.8; 2.4.3 (*PL* 156:640-41; 643).
[19] Williams, *Communion and Atonement,* pp. 22-23.
[20] *De pignoribus* 2.6.1 (*PL* 156:646).
[21] *De pignoribus* 2.6.1 (*PL* 156:647-48).
[22] Guibert *De incarnatione contra Judaeos* 3.7 (*PL* 156:322).
[23] *De pignoribus* 2.6.1 (*PL* 156:648). There is a close parallel in William of
Saint-Thierry *De sacramento altaris* 10 (*PL* 180:358).
[24] *De pignoribus* 2.2.2 (*PL* 156:632-33).

Guibert's Anselmian view of the redemptive work of Christ. Like Anselm, he was conscious of the figures and metaphors that Scripture employed in speaking of God, and he joined himself to the consensus of the church fathers in identifying what John Courtney Murray once called "the towering text that tells the story of the theophany to Moses at the burning bush," Exodus 3:14, as the only passage in the Old Testament that spoke of God in his essential being, which was absolute and unchangeable. [25] Yet this unchangeable God had accommodated himself to human ways and had spoken and acted as though he were changeable. [26] This he had done by manifesting wrath against sin and yet, in the midst of wrath, continuing to manifest mercy. [27] The omnipotence of God was evident above all in his being able to undertake the redemption of the human race from sin. [28] The devil was God's servant and executioner, who carried out the punishment of human sin. [29] But "it would not have been fitting [congruum] for that which humanity had committed to be expiated by someone from the angelic order," and therefore it had to be a human being, yet one who was not captive to the devil, who achieved the salvation of man. [30] Although it was correct to call Christ a "prophet," a new prophetic message from God would not have been sufficient to bring about salvation. [31] The Messiah who was to come for salvation had to be both God and man. [32] "Therefore it was just [justum] that the one who was to act on behalf of men should, being a man, be able to die for man; should, being nevertheless free of sin, bear the sins of men; and should, being God, reconcile man to God and to Himself, since these are one and the same." [33]

What was "fitting" and "just," in short, was the incarnation and crucifixion of Christ. There had been theophanies before, as on the plain at Mamre, but this was more. [34] For "if all [the saints] have been entangled in their own offenses, who is there who is capable of

---

25 De pignoribus 4.1.2 (PL 156:666); John Courtney Murray, The Problem of God: Yesterday and Today (New Haven, 1964), 5.

26 De incarnatione 3.6 (PL 156:519).

27 Guibert De vita sua sive monodiarum libri tres 1.1, ed. Georges Bourgin (Paris, 1907), 2.

28 De incarnatione 1.3 (PL 156:493).

29 De pignoribus 4.3 (PL 156:672).

30 De incarnatione 3.3 (PL 156:509).

31 De incarnatione 2.4 (PL 156:504).

32 De incarnatione 2.2 (PL 156:500).

33 De incarnatione 3.2 (PL 156:509).

34 De incarnatione 1.4 (PL 156:495).

bearing the burden of the sin of all?... Who can wash sin away
and by what kind of satisfaction [*qua satisfactione*] unless he has as his
faithful advocate the very one whom he has offended?" [35] The God
who had manifested himself as absolute and unchangeable became,
through the incarnation, changeable and human, "passible and mortal
solely because he wanted to suffer and die for human redemption." [36]
Thus God himself resolved the dilemma of the atonement, which was
that "he who was God could not accomplish this unless he died." [37]
Hence the incarnation had to be total, involving "all that there is
to man ... except sin," in other words, human nature as God had
created it before the fall. [38] As the instrument of this atonement
through satisfaction, the cross was deserving of the veneration that
Christians paid to it. [39] It was an echo of what Williams calls Anselm's "basic and characteristic emphasis that man redeemed is superior
to paradisic man as first created" when Guibert, in a prayer addressed
to Jesus, declared: "Oh, what purity, what tranquillity we lost in
our first parent, although we have gained even greater benefits
through thee!" [40] Clearly Guibert would qualify, along with Honorius
of Autun, as "one of the few immediate followers of Anselm in the
satisfaction theory of the atonement." [41]

But Anselm also "occupies a place of some importance in the
evolution of Marian doctrine," [42] and Guibert was his "immediate
follower" in this area as well. Such statements of Anselm as that
"nothing is equal to Mary, and nothing except God is greater than
Mary" or that her purity "is such than which none greater can be
thought, except in God" have their counterpart in Guibert's praise of
her as "the woman who is, after the Son, above all creatures" and as
"the one to whom, through the Son, everything in heaven is subject." [43]
Whatever may be the validity of the tradition ascribing to Anselm

---

[35] *De incarnatione* 3.2 (*PL* 156:508-9).
[36] *De pignoribus* 2.5 (*PL* 156:645).
[37] *De incarnatione* 3.3 (*PL* 156:509).
[38] *De incarnatione* 2.1; 1.3 (*PL* 156:499; 494).
[39] *De incarnatione* 3.9 (*PL* 156:524).
[40] *De incarnatione* 1.6 (*PL* 156:497); Williams, *Communion and Atonement,* 49.
[41] Williams, *Communion and Atonement,* 58.
[42] Williams, *Communion and Atonement,* 37.
[43] Anselm *Orationes* 7, ed. Franciscus Salesius Schmitt, *Sancti Anselmi opera omnia,* 5 vols. (Edinburgh, 1950-55) 3:21; Anselm *De conceptu virginali* 18 (Schmitt 2:159); Guibert *De laude Sanctae Mariae* 1 (*PL* 156:537); Guibert *De virginitate* 5 (*PL* 156:586).

the first technical use of the title *mediatrix* for Mary, [44] it seems clear that Guibert did use it as a technical term. "Is it not the consummation of our glory," he said in an apostrophe to Mary, "if only we can have thee as our mediatrix between ourselves and thy Son?" [45] In another apostrophe he prayed: "Since clearly the power is thine at will and the authority of the Son is known to overflow from the mother, from whom may I rather demand salvation than from thee?" [46] Mary was the one who had extirpated heresies all over the world. [47] Using an argument from silence that was to be a *topos* in devotion to Mary, Guibert concluded that since Christ had not appeared to Mary after he rose from the dead, she must have known about the resurrection even before his suffering and death. [48] Because the pericope for the Feast of the Assumption was Luke 10:38-42, containing the words, "Mary has chosen the best part, which shall not be taken away from her," it was the mother of Jesus rather than the sister of Lazarus who came to represent the contemplative life as contrasted with the active life represented by Martha. [49] As could be expected, Guibert was also familiar with the play on the words *"virgo"* and *"virga,"* which made possible the typological explanation of various "branches" spoken of in the Old Testament, and with the etymology *"Maria = maris stella,"* which helped to shape an entire genre of poetry. [50]

In all of these ways Mary was "the standard-bearer of piety." [51] It was unthinkable that the church could be without Mary. [52] She was a model to all the saints, but she was also preeminent over all of them, since only of her could it be said that she had "never faltered from the vision of God." [53] Only to her had the full measure of all spiritual charisms been granted in this present life. [54] She was the

---

[44] Eadmer *De excellentia Virginis Mariae* 9 (*PL* 159:574), cited in Williams, *Comunion and Atonement,* 37. It is noteworthy that at least two of Anselm's pupils should have made use of the term.

[45] *De laude Mariae* 14 (*PL* 156:577).

[46] *De vita sua* 1.3 (Bourgin 11), quoting the translation of C. C. Swinton Bland, *Self and Society in Medieval France: The Memoirs of Abbot Guibert of Nogent (1064?-c. 1125)* (New York, 1970), 16.

[47] *De incarnatione* 1.1 (*PL* 156:491).

[48] *De pignoribus* 3.5.5 (*PL* 156:664).

[49] *De laude Mariae* 7 (*PL* 156:558-60).

[50] *De incarnatione* 2.4; 3.3 (*PL* 156:503; 514).

[51] *De vita sua* 1.16 (Bourgin 62).

[52] *De laude Mariae* 4 (*PL* 126:543).

[53] *De laude Mariae* 7 (*PL* 156:561).

[54] *De laude Mariae* 1 (*PL* 156:539).

model for special reasons to all those who had followed her in electing
a life of virginity in the service of God. Such a life meant following
in her footsteps. [55] As a way of life, virginity, and *a fortiori* her
virginity, was even purer and more glorious than the primitive state
of Adam and Eve had been. [56] By choosing to be born of Mary the
Virgin, Christ was saying to the human race: "Even though, for the
sake of your weakness, I am afraid to make it a command that you
cultivate virginity, lest you regard marriage as an evil, nevertheless I
am indicating, by the clear evidence of my conception and of my way of
life, what it is you should strive for, since I have come down to you by
being born of one whose virginity is intact." [57] Christ was different
from other men because his birth was different from theirs, [58] but in
this respect they could be like him. Mary was different from other
men because she alone had been united with God "in substance," [59]
but in this respect they could be like her. And because of her virginity,
the hosts of angels venerated all virginity. [60]

There were several other questions about Mary, at least two of them
matters of great importance for the future development of doctrine,
on which Guibert also commented. One was the relation between the
maternity of Mary and her virginity. It was suggested to him by the
idea just mentioned, that the angels were subject to the Virgin. Strictly
speaking, he explained, it was not to her as Virgin, but to her as
Mother of God, that they owed obeisance. [61] In this connection he
spoke of a *privilegium* of Mary, though probably not in the technical
sense of later tracts on mariology, where the term referred especially
to such "privileges" as the immaculate conception and the assumption.
On the first of these issues, the immunity of the Virgin from both
original and actual sin, the Augustinian tradition had always faced a
quandary. In the course of formulating his doctrine of original sin,
Augustine had been unable to work out a schema for harmonizing it
with the historical fact, which was to him incontrovertible, that Mary
was free of sin. [62] Two centuries before the time of Guibert and
Anselm, Paschasius Radbertus (ca. 790-865) had begun to move toward

---

55 *De virginitate* 4 (*PL* 156:584).
56 *De incarnatione* 2.5 (*PL* 156:505).
57 *De virginitate* 4 (*PL* 156:585).
58 *De incarnatione* 3.7 (*PL* 156:523).
59 *De laude Mariae* 2 (*PL* 156:539).
60 *De virginitate* 5 (*PL* 156:586).
61 *De virginitate* 5 (*PL* 156:586).
62 Augustine *De natura et gratia* 36.42 (*CSEL* 60:263-64).

such a schema, but many issues were still a long way from being settled. Guibert took up the question as part of an attempt to explain the meaning of the phrase in the Ave Maria (Luke 1:28), "full of grace [*gratia plena*]." If "grace" was synonymous with the forgiveness of sins, the angelic salutation must mean that "whether it be original sin or actual sin, this is purged away by the Holy Spirit." [63] A little later on in the same treatise he elaborated on this purification, specifying that the Holy Spirit had "abolished actual sin together with original sin" in the Virgin. [64] This was ambiguous enough to call for a lengthy explanation by Guibert's editors, endeavoring to bring him into conformity with (later) dogmatic formulations. [65] In his teaching on the assumption, on the other hand, Guibert did anticipate later doctrine; for he personally held that Mary had been raised from the dead, even though the evidence for this from Scripture and dogma was insufficient. [66] This attitude was in keeping with his recognition that there were certain theologoumena, which could be "held but not taught" and on which there could be a difference of opinion. [67]

There were also differences of opinion, some of them having to do with Mary, in another area of church practice, and the one for which Guibert is probably best known, the cult of relics. [68] Here, too, the Anselmian character of his thought is very much in evidence, for the underlying assumption of his treatise *De pignoribus sanctorum* may well be summarized in Gerald B. Phelan's statement of the governing principle of Anselm's theology: "Where anything is proposed as unfitting to God as by faith we know Him to be, we must conclude that it is impossible; on the other hand, whenever we see even the slightest reason, provided there is nothing else contrary to it, we may conclude to its necessity." [69] It was patently "unfitting to God as by faith we know Him to be" when a cleric touting relics said to his congregation: "You should know that within this capsule there is contained a morsel of the bread that the Lord chewed with his very

---

[63] *De laude Mariae* 5 (*PL* 156:550-51).

[64] *De laude Mariae* 8 (*PL* 156:562).

[65] *PL* 156:1017-20, with references to Radbertus.

[66] *De pignoribus* 1.3 (*PL* 156:623-24).

[67] *De pignoribus* 1.1; 2.3.9 (*PL* 156:612; 641).

[68] Cf. Max Manitius, *Geschichte der lateinischen Literatur des Mittelalters,* 3 vols. (1911; reprint ed., Munich, 1965), 3:420.

[69] Gerald B. Phelan, *The Wisdom of Saint Anselm* (Latrobe, Pa., 1960), 30-31. On the Anselmian elements in Guibert's *De pignoribus sanctorum,* see Klaus Guth, *Guibert von Nogent und die hochmittelalterliche Kritik an der Reliquienverehrung* (Ottobeuren, 1970), 47, n. 68, and p. 75.

own teeth." [70] Guibert was even more exercised at the monks of Saint-Médard (a saint revered for his cure of toothache) when they claimed to possess "a tooth of the Savior, which he shed in the natural course when he was nine years old," as well as the umbilical cord and the foreskin of Christ. [71] Such preoccupation with "superfluous portions" of the body of Christ was inconsistent with the institution of the Eucharist. [72] The Eucharist, not any purported relic of Christ, "is and can be called the fundamental reality [*veritas principalis*]." [73]

The same strictures did not apply, at least not in the same way, to the supposed relics of the saints, including those of Mary. Thus, as Otto von Simson has observed, "the abbot of Nogent did not regard without skepticism the cult of relics as he encountered it among many contemporaries. Yet he looked with the most reverent affection upon the Sacred Tunic of Chartres." [74] Guibert spoke of the tunic as enjoying "the veneration of almost the entire Latin world." [75] At the same time he was more acutely aware than any of his contemporaries of the abuses to which the cult of saints' relics was subject. [76] His history of the First Crusade included the report of two heads of John the Baptist, one at Saint-Jean-d'Angély and the other at Constantinople. [77] The basic rule governing the cult of relics, then, was that the relic must be authentic and that the saint must be genuine. [78] For "when something is worshipped or said about God that clearly contradicts the evidence of the truth itself," it was to be rejected, since "there is nothing worse than to do evil and to regard what is done without sound advice as the exercise of a good work." [79] On the same grounds it was a sin to pray to an unknown saint. [80] Guibert reminded his readers, moreover, alluding to the axiom of Augustine, "It is not the punishment they suffer, but the cause for which they suffer it, that

---

[70] *De pignoribus* 1.2 (*PL* 156:621).

[71] *De pignoribus* 3.12; 2.1 (*PL* 156:651; 629).

[72] *De pignoribus* 3.2.2 (*PL* 156:656-57).

[73] *De pignoribus* 2.1.1 (*PL* 156:630).

[74] Otto von Simson, *The Gothic Cathedral: Origins of Gothic Architecture and the Medieval Concept of Order*, Bollingen Series, 48 (New York, 1956), 160.

[75] *De vita sua* 1.16 (Bourgin 61); see also *De vita sua* 3.12 (Bourgin 187).

[76] Thus Guth, *Guibert von Nogent*, 72, calls *De pignoribus sanctorum* "ein einzigartiges Zeugnis für die Entwicklung des wissenschaftlichen Geistes im Mittelalter."

[77] Guibert *Gesta Dei per Francos* 1.5 (*PL* 156:695).

[78] *De pignoribus* 1.1 (*PL* 156:613).

[79] *De pignoribus* 3.1.1 (*PL* 156:649-50).

[80] *De pignoribus* 1.3 (*PL* 156:623).

makes men martyrs," that heretics and schismatics could have their martyrs, too, so that even authenticated martyrdom did not of itself justify the cult of a supposed saint or of his relics. [81] On all of these objective grounds, then, it was necessary to look critically at the way the putative relics of the saints, and above all the putative relics of Christ, were being treated.

Yet in *Communion and Atonement* Professor Williams has reminded us that in reading Anselm, and therefore also in reading such Anselmians as Guibert, we should look not only at "the manner of man's objective salvation," but also at "the means of the believer's subjective appropriation" of it. [82] After examining the objective arguments against the claim that the monks of Saint-Ménard had in their possession a tooth of Christ, Guibert went on, in an analysis that cannot help reminding a modern reader of the apophthegm in Goethe's *Faust* (766), "*Das Wunder ist des Glaubens liebstes Kind*," to assert: "And even if [the tooth] did not come from any saint, the faith of simple believers would bring it about that it would obtain what it hoped for. For many things can be accomplished not by the merit of the one through whom they are requested, but by that of the one who is concerned about them." [83] The existential element was even more explicitly present in Guibert's doctrine of Mary. Before his birth he had been "dedicated to her who is Queen of all next to God," and in later life she remained his "only refuge in every need." [84] In his eucharistic doctrine, too, there was an acute awareness of subjective considerations, particularly in his treatment of what came later to be called *manducatio indignorum*, the question of whether or not an unworthy communicant received the true body and blood of Christ. Characteristically, he resolved the question with the observation: "Even if the bread had nothing sacred about it beyond what common bread has, but he who ate it regarded it as the Lord's body and took it upon himself to receive it shamelessly, he would undoubtedly be as liable to damnation as if it were the utterly real body of Jesus." [85]

In each of these doctrines, therefore, Guibert concerned himself with the relation between knowledge of self and knowledge of God.

---

[81] Augustine *Epistolae* 89.2 (*CSEL* 34:419); Guibert *De pignoribus* 1.3 (*PL* 156:622).

[82] Williams, *Communion and Atonement*, 23-24.

[83] *De pignoribus* 3.5.2 (*PL* 156:663).

[84] *De vita sua* 1.3; 1.19 (Bourgin 9-10; 77).

[85] *De pignoribus* 2.3.3 (*PL* 156:636).

He urged a cultivation of this relation as the key to sound preaching, [86] and in his *De vita sua* he made it the theme of his autobiographical reflection "to seek knowledge of thee through knowledge of myself [*ut per mei notitiam tuam petam*]." [87] This Augustinian method of probing the self and sounding its depths as a way of coming to know God had achieved its most brilliant expression in the ontological argument of Anselm, but Guibert's theology is an illustration of its further implications—implications that were to be drawn even more profoundly by Bernard of Clairvaux and by Bonaventure. Guibert regarded himself as a disciple of Anselm, one whom Anselm had "inducted into his knowledge [*suae me cognitioni ascivit*]," and throughout his life he retained his loyalty to his master as "the light of all France, indeed, of the whole Latin world in the liberal disciplines and in serenity of character." [88] He showed this not only in what he taught, but in how he taught it, and he deserves consideration, in the company of Gilbert Crispin and Honorius of Autun, as a first-generation Anselmian.

---

[86] *Quo ordine sermo fieri debeat* (PL 156:27).

[87] *De vita sua* 1.1 (Bourgin 3). Karl Joachim Weintraub, *The Value of the Indnvidual: Self and Circumstance in Autobiography* (Chicago, 1978), 64-65, finds Guibert's account "perplexing."

[88] *De vita sua* 1.17; 3.4 (Bourgin 66; 139).

NUDUS NUDUM CHRISTUM SEQUI AND PARALLEL FORMULAS IN THE TWELFTH CENTURY

A Supplementary Dossier

GILES CONSTABLE

Dumbarton Oaks, Harvard University

The formulas *nudus nudum Christum sequi, nudus nudam crucem sequi, pauper pauperem Christum sequi,* and parallel phrases with *humilis, egenus,* and other terms are among the most characteristic and popular expressions of the desire to imitate Christ in the Middle Ages. They first appear in the letters and homilies of St Jerome, who used both *nudum Christum* and *nudam crucem,* [1] but their more distant origins can be found in the ancient tradition, which drew on both Scriptural and Platonic elements, emphasizing the assimilation of the individual Christian to the human and divine aspects of Christ. [2] Gregory of Nyssa in his first sermon on the Beatitudes told his listeners that, "The Lord became poor, so be not afraid of poverty. But He who became poor for us reigns over all creation. Therefore, if you become poor because He became poor, you will also reign because He is reigning." [3] The linking of the poverty of Christ with that of man and of the divinity of Christ with that of man is clear in this passage, although the formula *nudus nudum* is not used. John Climacus came closer in his *Scala paradisi,* where he said that, "He who truly loves the Lord . . . naked with respect to these [earthly] things and without care and unhesitatingly follows Christ." [4] The persistence of this theme in the spirituality of the Eastern church deserves further study.

Its formulation in Latin by St Jerome and frequent use in the West throughout the Middle Ages has been studied by several scholars.

---

[1] See Paul Antin, "Saint Jérôme," *Théologie de la vie monastique* (Théologie, 49; Paris, 1961), 195, esp. n. 24.

[2] I owe this point to Professor John Callahan of Georgetown University, who drew my attention to the two Greek texts cited below and also pointed out the element of paronomasia in the use of the term *nudus,* which refers in somewhat different senses to Christ's humanity and to His divinity.

[3] Gregory of Nyssa, *The Lord's Prayer. The Beatitudes,* tr. Hilda C. Graef (Ancient Christian Writers, 18; Westminster, Md. — London, 1954), 96.

[4] John Climacus, *Scala paradisi,* II, in *Pat. greca,* LXXXVIII, 653C.

Matthäus Bernards in 1951 wrote a short but dense article entitled *Nudus nudum Christum sequi,* in which he cited over fifty examples of its use in the works of some three dozen writers from the fourth to the fourteenth century. [5] In an article on the ideal of the imitation of Christ in monastic hagiography, published in 1966, Gregorio Penco listed almost twenty-five examples in the *Vitae* of monastic saints down to the eleventh century. [6] And Réginald Grégoire in an article published in 1972 collected forty-nine "principal" and fifteen "parallel" examples beginning with St Jerome and ending with the *Imitatio Christi.* [7]

The purpose of this article is not to repeat the references given by these scholars but rather to cite some additional examples, together with a few secondary references, showing the importance of the formula in the twelfth century and the way in which it was used at that time. Bernards found *nudus nudum Christum sequi* and its parallels in the works of Abelard, Anselm of Havelberg, Ellenhard of Freising, Hildegard of Bingen, Peter the Venerable, Robert of Arbrissel, and Walter Map, in the *Vitae* of Godfrey of Cappenburg and Bernard of Tiron, and in the *Exordium parvum Cistercii, Speculum virginum,* chronicle of Engelberg, and a charter for Siegburg. [8] Grégoire added to these examples those in the works of Aelred of Rievaulx, Achard of St Victor, Hugh of Fouilloy, and Prevostin of Cremona, and in the *Vita* of St Norbert, the *Libellus de diversis ordinibus et professionibus qui sunt in aecclesia,* the so-called Premonstratensian continuation of the chronicle of Sigebert of Gembloux, and a late twelfth-century sermon from Piedmont. [9] Bernards and Grégoire also gave secondary referen-

---

[5] Matthäus Bernards, "Nudus nudum Christum sequi," *Wissenschaft und Weisheit,* 14 (1951), 148-51; cf. *idem, Speculum Virginum* (Forschungen zur Volkskunde, 36-38; Cologne-Graz, 1955), 153, where he stressed that the formula was not restricted to reforming circles and was almost a commonplace of eleventh- and twelfth-century piety and added (n. 169) several late medieval examples.

[6] Gregorio Penco, "L'imitazione di Cristo nell'agiografia monastica," *Collectanea Cisterciensia,* 28 (1966), 29-32.

[7] Réginald Grégoire, "L'adage ascétique 'Nudus nudum Christum sequi'," *Studi storici in onore de Ottorino Bertolini* (Pisa, 1972) I, 395-409.

[8] To the editions cited by Bernards may be added, for Walter Map, the edition of the *De nugis curialium* by Montague Rhodes James (Anecdota Oxoniensia: Mediaeval and Modern Series, 14; Oxford, 1914), 61; for the *Vita* of Bernard of Tiron by Geoffrey the Fat, *Pat. lat.,* CLXXII, 1432B; and for the *Exordium parvum Cistercii,* the edition by Jean de la Croix Bouton and Jean Baptiste Van Damme, *Les plus anciens textes de Cîteaux* (Achel, 1974), 77.

[9] To the editions cited by Grégoire may be added that of the *Libellus de diversis ordinibus et professionibus qui sunt in aecclesia,* eds. Giles Constable and

ces on the formula, showing its use in the twelfth century, to the works of Johannes von Walter on the earliest wandering preachers in France (1903-6) and on the history of Christianity (1939), Michael von Dmitrewski on the history of voluntary Christian poverty (1913), Ernst Werner on *Pauperes Christi* (1956), Jean Leclercq on the theme of separation from the world (1961), Jean Becquet on hermits (1962) and Ilarino da Milano on evangelical piety before St Francis of Assisi (1963). [10]

To these secondary references can be added one (the earliest I have found) on the popularity of the formula *nudus nudum Christum sequi* in twelfth-century sermons in L. Bourgain, *La chaire française au XIIe siècle d'après les manuscrits* (Paris-Brussels, 1879) p. 337. Hans von Campenhausen noticed its presence in the *Vita* of Marianus Scotus, who died after 1080, in his pioneering work on *Die asketische Heimatslosigkeit* (Tübingen, 1930) p. 16. Jean Leclercq in 1955, remarking on its use in a letter by Matthew of Rievaulx (see below), called it "a frequent theme in traditional ascetic literature" and cited its presence in a sermon by Abbot Thiofrid of Echternach, who died in 1110, and its popularity among the Cistercians. [11] Josef Siegwart mentioned it in his *Die Chorherren- und Chorfrauengemeinschaften der deutschsprachigen Schweiz vom 6. Jahrhundert bis 1160* (Freiburg S., 1962) p. 160. Both Léopold Genicot and Étienne Delaruelle, writing in the proceedings of the second La Mendola conference on *L'eremitismo in occidente nei secoli XI e XII* (Milan, 1965) pp. 45 and 226, commented on the popularity of the formula *nudus nudum* in the twelfth century. [12]

It is found in the twelfth century in four basic patterns, each with a few variants. The first and most frequent is the basic *nudus nudum Christum sequi,* which was used by St Jerome in his Letter 125 and

---

Bernard Smith (Oxford, 1972), 46. On the use of the formula by Aelred of Rievaulx, with two other examples (cited below), see Charles Dumont, in *Théologie* (cited n. 1 above), 529, n. 17.

[10] To the references to Werner, *Pauperes Christi,* given by Grégoire may be added p. 43 (Robert of Arbrissel), p. 48 (*Vita* of St Norbert), and p. 81 (continuation of Sigebert).

[11] Jean Leclercq, "Lettres de vocation à la vie monastique," *Analecta monastica,* III (Studia Anselmiana, 37; Rome, 1955), 174.

[12] Delaruelle noted its use, not mentioned in previous literature, in the chronicle of Regino of Prüm, ed. F. Kurze (Monumenta Germaniae historica, Scriptores in usum scholarum; Hanover, 1890), 41, s.a. 746, where Carloman was described as entering monastic life "nihil secum portans ex omnibus bonis, quae corpori erant necessaria, nudus nudum Christum secutus est."

homily on Luke and which emphasized the nakedness of Christ as well
as that of the follower. [13] The second, which was used by Jerome in his
Letters 52 and 58, had *crux* rather than *Christus* and thus emphasized
the austerity of the cross rather than the personal nakedness of Christ. [14]
The third form substituted *pauper* for *nudus,* becoming *pauper pauperem Christum sequi.* [15] The fourth form omitted any description of
Christ, referring only to the nakedness of the follower—*nudus Christum
sequi*—, though it is probable that the reader or listener would have
assumed the corresponding nakedness of Christ. [16] A fifth form, of
which the earliest example I have found is in the early thirteenth
century and to which I shall return at the end of this article, omitted
the reference to Christ and read simply *nudus nudum sequi.*

The examples listed here are classified according to these types,
with the variants cited after the principal examples. In view of the
difficulty of establishing the dates of individual passages, no effort
has been made to put them into chronological order.

> I. . . . et *nudum Christum nudi sequuntur*: Aelred of Rievaulx, *Sermo
> de oneribus* XXVII, in *Pat. lat.,* CXCV, 472C (cf. the example
> cited by Grégoire, p. 402).
>
> *Nudus, proprie, non habens proprium, unde dicit auctoritas quod
> nudi nudum Christum sequi* debemus: Alan of Lille, *Liber in
> distinctionibus dictionum theologicalium,* in *Pat. lat.,* CCX, 677C.

---

[13] Among the examples cited above, this pattern is found in the works of
Abelard, Achard of St Victor, Aelred, Anselm of Havelberg, Prevostin of
Cremona, and Walter Map and in the *Speculum Virginum* and the sermon from
Piedmont.

[14] Among the examples cited above, this pattern is found in the *Vitae* of
Godfrey of Cappenburg and Norbert and in the continuation of Sigebert of
Gembloux. An earlier example of this form is found in Odo of Cluny, *Collec-
tionum libri tres,* II, 34, in *Pat. lat.,* CXXXIII, 581A: "Et certe nulla hoc
regula jubet, sed magis nudam crucem esse clamat a nudo sequendam."

[15] This form and its variants were used by Hildegard of Bingen, Hugh of
Fouilloy (together with *humilis*), Peter the Venerable (both with *pauper spiritu*
and with *humilis*), in the *Vita* of Bernard of Tiron (*pauper spiritu*), the *Exordium
parvum* (*cum paupere Christo pauperes*) and the *Libellus de diversis ordinibus.*
An earlier example of this form is found in Ademar of Chabannes, *Chronicon,* III,
26, ed. Jules Chavanon (Collection de textes pour servir à l'étude et à l'enseignement
de l'histoire, 20; Paris, 1897), 148: two canons of Tours "pauperes pauperem
Christum secuti sunt" and became monks at Cluny.

[16] See also the *Epistola apologetica* attributed to Anselm of Havelberg and
the continuation of Sigebert. An earlier example of this form is the description
of Otto III's promise to leave his realm, "tota anima nudus sequar Christum," in
Bruno of Querfurt, *Vita quinque fratrum,* in Monumenta Germaniae historica,
Scriptores in-fol., XV.2, 719.

Qui cum dives esset in coelis, pauper factus pro nobis est in terris, ut sua paupertate nos divites faceret. In exemplum etiam veniant antiqui patres, qui *nudi Christum nudum secuti sunt*: Alan of Lille, *Summa de arte praedicatoria*, in *Pat. lat.*, CCX, 185A.

Ergo parentes, agros et possessiones nostros sine differentia relinquamus, et *nudi nudum Christum sequamur*: *De ordine Vallisscholarium*, in Philippe Labbe, *Nova bibliotheca manuscriptorum librorum* (Paris, 1651) I, 392.

Contempsit enim nomen et genus, seculi divitias et honores, ut *nudus nudum Christum sequeretur*: *Gesta comitis Lodewici*, ed. S. Widmann, "Die Lebensbeschreibung des Grafen Ludwig III. von Arnstein," *Annalen des Vereins für Nassauische Altertumskunde und Geschichtsforschung*, XVII (1882) 263.

... ordinatus rebus suis, *nudum Christum nudus sequens*, arctiorem, et ideo feliciorem vitam sub sancti Benedicti regula aggressus est in Cluniacensi coenobio: Nicholas of Liège, *Elogium Algeri scholastici*, in Jean Mabillon, *Vetera analecta* (Paris, 1723) p. 130.

... si vero perfecta desideras, exi cum Abraham de terra tua, *nudus nudum Christum sequens*: letter of Rainald the Hermit, ed. G. Morin, "Rainaud l'ermite et Ives de Chartres: Un épisode de la crise du cénobitisme au XIe-XIIe siècle," *Revue bénédictine*, XL (1928) 102.

(description of the apostles as followers of God, in a sentence on poverty) *nudo Christo, nudi adhaerentes*: Henri Rochais, "Textes Bernardins dans un manuscrit de Berlin," *Analecta Cisterciensia*, XXIII (1967) 173.

Primum quippe necesse est ut per mundi abrenuntiationem *imitetur nuditatem Christi*: Aelred of Rievaulx, *Sermo in Ascensione Domini*, ed. C. H. Talbot, *Sermones inediti B. Aelredi abbatis Rievallensis* (Series scriptorum S. ordinis Cisterciensis, 1; Rome, 1952) p. 103.

II. Eligat propensius utilis frater, qui *nudus* tenet *sequi nudam crucem* Crucifixi: Matthew of Rievaulx, ed. Jean Leclercq, *Otia monastica* (Studia Anselmiana, 51; Rome, 1963) p. 174.

Ecce quomodo *nudi nudam crucem sequebantur* apostoli: Godwin of Salisbury, *Meditationes*, in MS Oxford, Bodleian Library, Digby 96, f. 17v.

(quoting Jerome) Habens victum et vestitum his contentus ero, et *nudam crucem nudus sequar*: Peter de Honestis, *Regula clericorum*, I. 1, in *Pat. lat.*, CLXIII, 706B.

(description of married people) non valentes illos imitari qui per arctam et arduam continentiae viam gradiuntur et voluntatibus et

rebus propriis abrenuntiantes *nudi nudam crucem sequuntur*:
Richard of St Victor, *Sermo LXXII,* in *Pat. lat.,* CLXX, 1127A.

(the Cistercians at Stella) in hanc semotam, et inclusam oceano
insulam nudi ac naufragi *nudam nudi* Christi *crucem amplexi*
pauci evasimus: Isaac of Stella, *Sermo XVIII,* in *Pat. lat.,*
CXCIV, 1750A. (It is uncertain whether the *Christi* applies to
the *nudi* or the *crucem.*)

(Herman joined Cappenburg) *nudus cum nudo hoste luctaturus*:
Hermannus quondam Judaeus, *Opusculum de conversione sua,*
c. 20, ed. Gerlinde Niemeyer (Monumenta Germaniae historica,
Quellen zur Geistesgeschichte des Mittelalters, 4; Weimar, 1963)
p. 121.

III. ... cum eisdem fratribus et inter eos *pauperem Christum* delibe-
rarem *pauper sequi*: letter from former prior of St Barbe, who
became a Premonstratensian, in Edmond Martène and Ursin
Durand, *Amplissima collectio* (Paris, 1724-33) I, 782C.

pauperes pauperem sequimur Christum: C. H. Talbot, "A Letter
of Roger, Abbot of Byland," *Analecta Sacri Ordinis Cisterciensis,* VII (1951) 227.

(mortuary encyclical for Marbod of Rennes) *pauperem Christum
pauper* et ipse *secutus est*: Léopold Delisle, *Rouleaux des morts
du IXe au XVe siècle* (Société de l'histoire de France, 11; Paris,
1866) p. 345.

... ut, terrenis curis abjectis, *pauperem Christum pauper* ipse ac
nudus, expedito gressu, continuo *sequeretur*: *Vita* of Stephen of
Obazine, I. 2, ed. and tr. Michel Aubrun (Faculté des lettres et
sciences humaines de l'Université de Clermont-Ferrand: Publications de l'Institut d'Études du Massif Central, 6; Clermont-
Ferrand, 1970) p. 46.

... qui omnia sua pro Christo contempnentes, et *pauperes pauperem
Christum sequentes*: treatise by provost Meingot of Utrecht, ed.
S. Muller and A. C. Bouman, *Oorkondenboek van het Sticht
Utrecht tot 1301,* I (Utrecht, 1920-25) p. 237.

Relinque pallium cum Ioseph, teloneum cum Matthaeo, ... et
pauper pauperem Christum imitare, qui reliquit nobis exemplum
ut *sequamur* uestigia eius: Matthew of Rievaulx, Letter, ed. Jean
Leclercq, *Analecta monastica,* III (Studia Anselmiana, 37; Rome,
1955) p. 176.

Inter opes esto *pauper cum paupere Christo*: Baudri of Bourgueil,
Poem XXVI, ed. Phyllis Abrahams, *Les oeuvres poétiques de
Baudri de Bourgueil (1046-1130)* (Paris, 1926) p. 7.

Sis mecum *pauper,* immo *cum paupere Christo*; / Cum Christo
vives, cum Christo divite dives: Baudri of Bourgueil, Poem
CXXXIX, *ibid.,* p. 114.

Haec videns, levavi me super me, et in mentis excessu raptatus, juravi et statui *pauperem Christum cum pauperibus sequi*: Nicholas of Montiéramey, Letter 7 to the monks of Clairvaux, in *Pat. lat.*, CXCVI, 1602B.

... quia Philippus *ad paupertatem pauperum Christi descendit*: Nicholas of Montiéramey, Letter 33 to Philip of Clairvaux, in *Pat. lat.*, CXCVI, 1624C.

... tollens se super se, *pauper spiritu pauperiem Christo recompensans*: Gilo, *Vita sancti Hugonis abbatis*, I.3, ed. H. E. J. Cowdrey, *Two Studies in Cluniac History* (Offprint from *Studi Gregoriani*, XI; Rome [1978]) p. 50.

IV. Si enim Christum vis habere: *Christum nuda sequere*: *The Life of Christina of Markyate*, ed. C. H. Talbot (Oxford, 1959) p. 72.

... venit Christus, ut reiteraret vestem cilicinam, saccum scilicet, et nudus nudis obtutibus paternis in carne nostra, imo sua appareret. Filii itaque nudi Christi, nuda adinvicem corda pandamus. Peter of Celle, Letter I, 56 (III, 10), in *Pat. lat.*, CCII, 481D-482A.

These examples, taken together with those cited by Bernards and Grégoire, doubtless represent no more than a fraction of the total number of uses of *nudus nudum Christum sequi* and parallel formulas in the twelfth century. Without extensive research it would be impossible to determine whether it was more used by writers at that time than in other centuries, but the evidence points in that direction and counteracts the impression given by Penco (most of whose examples derive from Mabillon's *Acta sanctorum OSB,* which goes only to 1157) that it was less popular in the twelfth century than in the early Middle Ages. It may be true that it was less exclusively used in monastic hagiography, however, since these examples show that it is also found in chronicles, treatises, sermons, mortuary rolls, letters, poems, and charters.

Its extensive use and adaptation in the twelfth century show that it expressed a widely felt need to associate the virtues of the individual Christian with those of Christ and to model human behavior on that of Christ. The essence of the formula was to link the follower to Christ in a common nakedness or poverty in the sense of a stripping not only of worldly goods but also of worldly cares and associations. *Pauper* was used in the early Middle Ages as the opposite of *potens* and indicated a state of weakness and unprotectedness as much as of economic poverty. In this sense the terms *nudus, pauper, egenus,* and *humilis* were more or less interchangeable. Several of the writers cited above used more than one type of the formula probably without intending any significant difference in meaning. The desire to identify with the poverty and weakness of Christ was expressed in many ways in the eleventh and twelfth centuries, as in the arenga to a charter of 1098 from the diocese of Liège in which a layman who was joining the congregation of regular canons at Flône said that he had listened to the voice of God telling him to renounce his possessions and wished "to follow the Lord who became poor for us (sequi Dominum illum qui pro nobis factus est egens)." [17]

The formula seems to have almost part of the common culture of the twelfth century. In the *Vita* of Christina of Markyate, cited above, it was used sarcastically by her father, who in turning her out of his house told her to follow Christ naked if she wanted to have Him. The heretic Henry of Lausanne was described in the *Actus pontificum Cenomannis* as having led women to reject their possessions, "nudus nudam, debilis egrotam, pauper duceret egenam." [18] Since the author of the *Actus* was hostile to Henry, the blasphemous implication of his words, which associated Henry with Christ, the naked leader of the naked, may have escaped him. This was probably not true, however, of Gilbert Foliot, who in his famous letter *Multiplicem nobis* written to Thomas Becket in 1166 described King Henry II as a crusader "quin spretis omnibus post crucem suam portantem Dominum Iesum nudus exeat, et paupertatem contemplando quam subiit, id facto studeat implere quod docuit ipse dicens . . ." and went on to cite the Dominical injunctions in Luke 14.27 and Matthew 10.38. [19] Foliot was obviously doing the best he could, but it would be hard to think of a less apt description of Henry II in the 1160s, and the suggestion that he was following the nakedness and poverty of Christ shows that the formula had to a great extent broken loose from its ascetic and monastic moorings.

The words were probably so familiar by that time that the missing elements in the formulation were supplied unconsciously. When therefore an explicit reference to the nakedness or poverty of Christ was

---

[17] Charles Dereine, *Les chanoines réguliers au diocèse de Liège avant saint Norbert* (Académie Royale de Belgique: Classe des Lettres et des Sciences morales et politiques, Mémoires in-8°, 47.1; Brussels, 1952), 113, n. 7.

[18] *Actus pontificum Cenomannis in urbe degentium,* eds. G. Busson and A. Ledru (Le Mans, 1902), 411; cf. Johannes von Walter, *Die ersten Wanderprediger Frankreichs* (Leipzig, 1903-6) II, 135.

[19] *The Letters and Charters of Gilbert Foliot,* eds. Adrian Morey and C. N. L. Brooke (Cambridge, 1967), 241 (No. 170).

omitted, as in the fourth type of usage described above, it was doubtless assumed to be the exemplar for the naked or poor follower. In the early thirteenth century there emerged a fifth type of usage that omitted any reference to Christ. [20] James of Vitry described both the Franciscans in his *Historia occidentalis* and the Dominicans in his *Sermones vulgares* as *nudi nudum sequentes,* where the *nudum* certainly referred to Christ. [21] The formula was often used by the Franciscans, who may sometimes have identified the *nudum* with St Francis. It was less popular among the Dominicans, according to Ralph Bennett, who found only one example of its use in Dominican literature in the thirteenth century, in the commentary on 1 John by Hugh of St Cher, who, after citing the injunction to "go sell what thou hast and give to the poor and come follow Me" from Matthew 19.21, added, as if it were part of the Gospel text, "nudus scilicet nudum." [22] This conflation exemplifies the association of the formula *nudus nudum* with the Biblical commands to follow Christ and helps to explain its popularity and prominence in the new evangelical piety of the twelfth and thirteenth centuries. [23]

---

[20] I have found no example of *nudum* or *pauperem* used as a substantive for Christ before the thirteenth century.

[21] James of Vitry, *Historia occidentalis,* ed. F. Moschus (Douai, 1597), 350; *Sermones vulgares,* in *Analecta novissima spicilegii Solesmensis altera continuatio,* II, ed. J. B. Pitra (Paris, 1888), 389. In his *Vita* of Mary of Oignies, James said "casto castam [Dominus] commendavit ancillam" and "nudum Christum nuda sequeretur" (*Acta sanctorum,* June IV, 640 and 648), showing that the formula was known to him in its entirety.

[22] Hugh of St Cher, *Opera omnia* (Venice, 1754) VII, 354, col. 4; cf. R. F. Bennett, *The Early Dominicans* (Cambridge, 1937), 178. The formula also appears in the margin to Hugh's commentary on Psalm 87.16 (*ed. cit.,* II, 229, col. 3), but it may be an editorial addition.

[23] On the use of the formula by Thomas Aquinas, see Jean Leclercq, "La vie contemplative dans S. Thomas et dans la tradition," *Recherches de théologie ancienne et médiévale,* 28 (1961), 257-58.

THE CHURCH AS EUCHARISTIC COMMUNION IN MEDIEVAL THEOLOGY

GEORGE H. TAVARD

Methodist Theological School in Ohio

The classical Christian Churches have always assigned a high priority to the eucharist among the constitutive elements of the Church. The Reformers' standard definition of the recognizability of the Church took for granted such a priority. In the words of the Thirty-nine Articles of the Church of England, "the visible Church of Christ is a congregation of faithful men in which the pure Word of God is preached and the Sacraments be duly ministered according to Christ's ordinance in all those things that of necessity are requisite to the same" (Article XIX). The implications of this remain open to question. For priority is shared with the preaching of the Word, which gained first place in later Protestantism, and with baptism as the other sacrament of the gospel. At least for Calvin, baptism has priority over the eucharist, since it introduces into the Christian life, which the eucharist only nurtures. For Calvin, too, sacramental priority entails no real analogy but only a comparison between the body of Christ and the body of the Church. "As to us, let us listen to the Apostle, who says that the Church is the body of Christ: by this expression he means that those who refuse to submit to him are unworthy of the Church's communion, for the unity of the Church depends on him alone." [1] Rom. 4:5 means: "We are called to becoming united as though in one body, since Christ has ordered such a society and conjunction of all his faithful as obtains between the limbs of the human body." [2]

These quotes from Calvin help to focus attention on a central question relating to the theme of the Church as eucharistic fellowship. That the Church is an eucharistic fellowship suggests a positive relationship of the sacramental body (or the body of Christ in its sacramental presence) to the Church as the mystical body of Christ (or the body of Christ in its corporate presence among the members of the

---

[1] *Comm. on Eph.,* 1: 23.
[2] *Comm. on Rom.,* 12: 5.

Church). But what is the nature of this relation? Should it be conceived realistically as a sort of identification of the body-of-Christ-which-is-the-Church with the resurrected body of Christ offered for us and to us in the eucharist? Or is the traditional use of the expression, body of Christ, in both cases purely metaphorical? Are we dealing with a phenomenon of sacramental identity or with a linguistic form of poetic assimilation?

In the next pages I will present a series of selected *testimonia*, in reversed chronological order, to the effect that the central medieval tradition espoused the realistic view. To call the Church a eucharistic fellowship implies at least that it may be compared to the eucharistic body of Christ, and that it subsists by virtue of this eucharistic body. The medieval tradition also held that there is an identity *in mysterio* between the Church and the eucharist.

I

The theology of Thomas Aquinas on the Church as eucharistic fellowship is succinctly outlined in *Summa theologica*, II, q. 73, a.6:

> In this sacrament one can consider three points: the sacrament alone, that is, bread and wine; the reality as sacramental, that is, the true body of Christ; the reality alone, that is, the effect of this sacrament.

The eucharist has three levels: the visible signs of bread and wine, the body of Christ (in medieval discussions on real presence, the word *verum* denotes the historical, and now resurrected, body of Christ) and finally the effect of the sacrament for redemption. The level of *res tantum* is explained in a. 4, where the names of the sacrament are interpreted as pointing to different aspects of its meaning. *Sacrificium* refers to the memorial of the passion, which was *verum sacrificium*. *Communio* and *synaxis* refer to ecclesial unity, "to which men are joined by this sacrament." *Viaticum* and *eucharistia* evoke the eschatological fulfilment, "insofar as this sacrament prefigures the fruition of God which takes place in the fatherland." Aquinas adds a fourth denomination, *metalepsis*, which he translates as "assumption": through the sacrament "we assume the divinity of the Son," we are being deified.

Thus the eucharist relates the communicants to the passion of Christ, to the oneness of the Church, to their eternal fulfillment in heaven, to the divine Filiation. The faithful receive the fruits of redemption; they are incorporated into the Church; they anticipate the resurrection; they partake of the filiation of the eternal Son. Thus the level of *res tantum* is itself plurivalent, in relation to the *ephapax* of the past, to the community of the present, to the eschatological future, and to the vertical perspective of deification as effected in this threefold dimension of time. The oneness of the Church serves the eschatological future and deification, just as the redeeming act of Christ serves the oneness of the *ecclesia*. There is thus a two-way exchange between the highest effect, deification, and the steps leading to it. In the Thomist conception of causality, the final end is already present as the guiding principle of what it draws to itself. Likewise, the eucharist, where we celebrate the memorial of the passion of the Lord, is oriented toward the unity of the Church, which fosters the eschatological transfiguration of creation, which in turn brings about the assumption of humankind into the realm of the divine. On the one hand, the eucharist, in which the passion of Christ is present, effects the oneness of the Church which, being pregnant with the transfiguration of all things, will burst forth into the deification of human persons. On the other, the *metalepsis,* as God's ultimate graciousness, draws all human creatures into being transfigured to the image of the eternal Son, by way of the ecclesial unity of the disciples in the eucharistic body of the Lord.

The theology of Aquinas should of course be seen on the background of medieval eucharistic symbolism. Since Florus of Lyon the medieval liturgists explained the *fractio* or breaking of the bread at mass as the opening of the mystery, leading precisely to its significance as the *ecclesia*. [3] They exploited the theme of the bread made of many grains and the wine made of innumerable grapes: this again pointed to the *ecclesia*. And they discussed the theme of the three bodies of Christ. As William of St Thierry explained it in his *De sacramento altaris,* [4] the historical body, the sacramental body (often called, mystical body), and the ecclesial body are not three bodies, but three modes of contemplation of the one body of Christ. For Amalarius of Metz (c. 780-850) the *corpus triforme* derives from three moments of the historical body: "the first is the holy, immaculate body assumed from the Virgin Mary; the second is the body walking on this earth; the third is the body lying in the tomb." [5] Liturgically, this corresponds to the fraction in three sections, for mixtion with wine, for communion, for reservation, pointing respectively to the body of Christ rising,

---

[3] Florus, *De Expositione Missae,* 89 (Migne, Patrologia Latina, 119. 71).
[4] *De Sacramento Altaris,* 12 (PL, 180. 361-62).
[5] Amalarius, *De Ecclesiasticis Officiis,* 3, 35 (PL, 105. 1154).

ministering on earth, lying in the tomb. As Florus of Lyon pointed out, excessive subtlety marked this type of liturgical exegesis.

II

Baldwin of Canterbury (d. 1190), Cistercian, archbishop of Canterbury, provides an important testimony on the relationship between the Church and the eucharist. His *De sacramento altaris* is a commentary on the eucharistic texts of the New Testament. Commenting on the account of the institution in Matthew, Baldwin analyzes the liturgical event under two headings: "The change of the bread into the body of Christ is true and is mystical." [6]

The aspect of *veritas* is described in the language of transubstantiation: For the archbishop of Canterbury, the change of the bread into the body of Christ is more than metaphorical: "It is a true change, not one in metaphor but one in substance. For the bread is not transfigured but transubstantiated. In a new and unusual way the appearance remains and the substance is changed." Transubstantiation is contrasted with the transfiguration of Christ. There, the change was not in the reality of Jesus but in his appearance. At the eucharist, the change affects the reality of bread and wine, not their appearance. Baldwin's use of this kind of language clearly shows that the early doctrine of transubstantiation owed nothing to the metaphysics of Aristotle. It expressed the fullness of the transformation envisioned in the eucharist, but it was not a theory as to the "how" of such a *mutatio*.

The aspect of mystery relates to another transformation: those who participate in the eucharist are changed. The eucharist is the food of immortality: "See the power of this sacrament. God decided to clothe this mortal body with immortality and to transfer this mortal life to eternal life." [7] There are therefore two conjoined events: the bread is made into the body of Christ, and our mortal life becomes immortal.

The two events are similar: "The whole Church is one bread in the universal multitude of the elect, and it is the body of Christ. And whoever we are who are in and from the body of the Church, we are one bread and members of Christ, and by a kind of mutation we shall be as it were other than we are, since what we shall be has not yet been manifested." [8] The point of similarity is that the Church is one

---

[6] Bauduin de Ford, *Le Sacrement de l'Autel*, I (Sources Chrétiennes, 93; Paris, 1961) 204.

[7] *Ibid.*, 212.

[8] *Ibid.*, 214.

bread made of all members of Christ. Such a unity heralds a greater unity to come. The company of the elect, as the one bread and the body of Christ, is destined to a still greater transformation: what we shall be has not yet been manifested.

Similarity entails dissimilarity. In the eschatological transformation announced by our bread-like ecclesial unity we shall be changed into another glory and not, as in the case of transubstantiation, into another nature (*in alteram gloriam sed non in alteram naturam*). Such a dissimilarity does not belittle our eschatological transformation: "We shall be so different from ourselves that we can hardly be considered less than what we are now." In comparison with what we shall be, what we are now counts hardly for anything.

This conception is radically eschatological. That it is truly the heart of Baldwin's sacramental theology appears from his treatment of the rest of the New Testament. Mark and Luke are examined briefly, as their testimony adds nothing to, but supports, that of Matthew. One remark may sum up the doctrine. The "cup of the New Covenant" illustrates the overcoming of death by the obedience of the Son which leads to the disciples' eternal life: "The new testament is a new law, containing a new covenant and a new promise. It imposes a new obedience and it promises a new legacy. The former is obedience unto death, the latter is eternal life after death." [9]

Chapter 6 of the gospel of John, which is taken to be strictly eucharistic, is examined in the same vein. Yet the eucharistic interpretation does not rule out the ambivalence of the manducation of Christ by the faithful: there are two eatings of Christ, which reinforce and illustrate each other. "Christ is eaten in two ways, for he is participated in in two ways. One is through faith . . . Knowing through faith the flesh accepted for us and given to us as food, we eat the flesh of Christ. It is therefore the faith of unity, of union, of communion." [10] Three levels of oneness (unity, union, communion) refer to the faith that the Son is one with the Father in the Trinity, to the union of the human nature to the divine Person in the incarnation, to communion with the life-giving flesh of Christ in the eucharist. Thus Baldwin sums up the Johannine teaching: "The sum total of our faith is this: to know Christ in the Father, Christ in the flesh, Christ in participating at the altar." But faith does not exhaust our manducation

---

[9] *Ibid.*, 230.
[10] *Ibid.*, 268-72.

of Christ, for we also eat his flesh: "He is received in us in our eating, using and discerning this body."

The main eucharistic passages of Paul are also read by Baldwin in an eschatological light. They also stress the ecclesial aspect of the eucharist. Paul's use of the relationship "one bread, one body", in 1 Cor. 10, introduces a long text on the Church as *corpus Christi* in which one people is made of persons who differ both in their charisms ("important ones, humble ones, beginners, proficients, simple ones, cautious ones, some are like children, some like adults, some like old men matured in perfection" [11]) and in their situations ("innumerable persons, of diverse sexes, diverse conditions, diverse orders, diverse professions.") The cup of blessing is, "both at the supper of the Lord and at the table of the Lord, that is, at the altar," the very blood that has been shed "for the common salvation." Remarking that this may be called either *communicatio* or *communio*, Baldwin notes that both terms refer to the commonalty of the disciples:

> It can be understood as communication, since it is given and received in common. For another reason also it is called communion. It operates in us the charity of the blood through which all becomes common and what is special to each is common to all. [12]

In the last section of his book Baldwin examines some Old Testament prefigurations of the eucharist, especially the Paschal Lamb and Manna. Here again he emphasizes eschatology: "Christ, the victim of our passover, passing himself from this world to the Father, opened the way of our passage and showed the mode of it ... [13] Thus the true manna, the bread of eternal life, is now gathered and served." [14] The ecclesial dimension is not forgotten: "There is one faith and one law of justice, which is charity, and one form of faith and love, which is common to all the just and to them alone, and because of the justice of faith there is one hope of eternal life, common to all." [15]

Admittedly, Baldwin's theology of *mutatio* was not universal in his time. In his study of the period, Josef Geiselmann distinguished three conceptions, which he called "metabolism," "dynamism," and "realism." He related them, rightly or wrongly, to Ambrose, to Augustine and to "Rome," and he found them illustrated chiefly by Paschasius, by

---

[11] *Le Sacrement de l'Autel*, II (Sources Chrétiennes, 94; Paris, 1963) 362.
[12] *Ibid.*, 358.
[13] *Ibid.*, 454.
[14] *Ibid.*, 510.
[15] *Ibid.*, 498.

Ratramnus and by Florus of Lyon. [16] Yet, whatever the medieval explanation of "presence" and of "change," the ultimate purpose and the end result of the eucharist were always identified with the body of Christ which is the Church. This is patent in the doctrine of Paschasius Radbertus.

III

The theological developments of the 9th century saw a major work on the eucharist, the *Liber de Corpore et Sanguine Domini* of Paschasius Radbertus, Abbot of Corbey. This volume is famous chiefly for its identification of the historical body and the sacramental body of Christ. But Radbertus's investigation is not limited to this question. Among other concerns, the Abbot of Corbey studies the relations between the sacramental body and the mystical body which is the Church. The one expression, body of Christ, has three dimensions. It denotes the Church, or the *corpus mysticum* of the eucharist, or the *corpus verum* born of the Virgin, thus passing from the ecclesial to the historical by way of the mystical:

> The body of Christ is named in three ways in the holy Scriptures; no doubt because his body is the universal Church of Christ, where Christ is the head and all the elect are called members of it, and from these a body is gathered everyday into a perfect man in the measure of the fulness of Christ. [17]

All is common among the elect, who are "one another's members." Those who have become "members of the devil" through sin cannot share the eucharist lawfully. But those who are truly faithful live entirely by Christ:

> Those feed on him properly who are in his body, so that only the body of Christ, while it is on the way, is nourished by its own flesh and it learns to desire nothing but Christ, to live from nowhere else, to be nothing but the body of Christ.

The sacramental body of Christ which feeds his ecclesial body can only be his historical body. By this logic, Paschasius, having defined the Church as the body of Christ living by his sacramental body, affirms that this sacramental body must be also the historical one, *corpus verum* and not only *corpus figuratum*. The realism of Paschasius's eucharistic theology rests upon a realistic ecclesiology: since the

---

[16] *Die Eucharistielehre der Vorscholastik* (1926).
[17] *Liber de Corpore et Sanguine Domini*, 7, 1 (PL, 120. 1284-85).

Church is the body of Christ, it is fed, in the eucharist, by the body of Christ.

The oneness of Christ and the elect is comparable to the unity of the Father and the Son. These are one, *unitate naturae*. Likewise, Christ, "is rightly said to dwell in us and we in him, not only by the concordance of the wills but by nature." [18] Such a union by nature between Christ and us is made possible by our communicating with his body:

> For if the Word was made flesh and if we truly eat the Word made flesh in the food of the Lord, how can Christ not be properly deemed to dwell in us naturally, he who being God born as man assumed the inseparable nature of our flesh, and united the nature of his flesh with the nature of eternity in this sacrament of the flesh to be given to us?

A dialectical relationship joins the body of Christ which is the Church and his *corpus verum*: they are one in the *corpus* which chapter IV calls both *veritas* and *figura,* that is, in the sacramental body. [19] That this is paradoxical does not escape Paschasius. We ourselves are the body which we eat: ". . . as members of Christ, we eat his flesh, so that we may be found to be nothing but his body and blood from which we live." [20] But this is the paradox of faith: "In all this we walk by faith and not by sight." [21] Paschasius understands the royal priesthood of believers in relation to the body of Christ which nurtures the faithful:

> For that reason let us hold on to this pontiff and priest Christ, and let us dwell in him, for, since he is in us and we are in him, we also are all called and we are priests. He made us a kingdom and priests for God, and thus the apostle calls us a holy nation, a royal priesthood, an acquired people. It is therefore known that we are in him and he is incorporated in us by this grace, transfigurating us in the body of his light, that with him and in him the reign of peace be with us. [22]

In other words, the eucharistic action does not derive from the royal priesthood; but the royal priesthood derives from the mutuality of Christ and the faithful in his eucharistic body.

This mutual inherence of Christ and the faithful is again stressed by the symbolism of the drop of water mixed with wine during the liturgy. Chapter XI examines this practice. This gesture signifies,

---

[18] *Ibid.,* 9, 4 (1296).
[19] *Ibid.,* 4, 1 (1278).
[20] *Ibid.,* 9, 5 (1296).
[21] *Ibid.,* 4, 3 (1279).
[22] *Ibid.,* 9, 6 (1298).

among other things, that we who are in Christ are offered to God
together with him. With forcefulness Paschasius connects this with the
unity of Christ and the Church: "... if wine is offered without water,
the blood of Christ begins to be without us; if only water is offered,
the people is seen to be without Christ. When both are mixed and
united, then rightly is the mystery of the Church spiritually effected." [23]
This is repeated in the *Epistola ad Frudegardum*: the water mixed with
wine signifies the unity of baptism and redemption. By it Christ and
the Church are one body. "Thus neither Christ is high-priest for
eternity without the Church, nor is the Church offered to the Father
without Christ." [24]

In conclusion we may say that Paschasius's eucharistic theology
implies an ecclesiology and a christology. The body which is the Church
is the historical body of Christ as spiritual food of the faithful in the
eucharistic mystery: "With such food and drink we dwell as one body
with him and in him, where Christ is the head and we are considered
the members." [25] Ratramnus himself, the monk of Corbey who attacked
his abbot's identification of *veritas*, understood as "the manifest
showing of reality," [26] and *figura*, described as "some adumbration
showing what is intended under some veils," [27] never questioned the
interrelationship between the Church and the eucharist. For him also
the eucharistic mystery signifies both the historical body and the
Church: "But in what is shown through the mystery there is the
image not only of the true body of Christ but also of the people who
believe in Christ: it carries the image of the two bodies, that of
Christ, which died and rose again, and that of the people reborn in
Christ and made alive from among the dead." [28] The eucharistic symbols are sacraments of the Church as well as of the body and blood
of Christ.

IV

Although St Augustine does not belong to the Middle Ages, the
special place that he occupies in eucharistic theology makes it imperious
to consider his thought at this point. Later historians have interpreted

---

[23] *Ibid.*, 11, 2 (1308).
[24] *Epistola ad Frudegardum* (PL, 120. 1353).
[25] *Liber de Corpore*, 15, 3 (1324).
[26] Ratramnus, *De Corpore et Sanguine Domini*, 8 (PL, 121. 130).
[27] *Ibid.*, 7 (130).
[28] *Ibid.*, 98 (169).

his theology in opposite directions, along the "dynamic," spiritualizing line of Ratramnus-Berengar-Calvin, or according to the realism of the central medieval tradition. Indeed one cannot deny that his vocabulary often seems ambiguous. Taken at face-value, some of his formulae appear to favor a real presence in the standard Catholic sense of the phrase, while others come close to a "virtual dynamism" stressing a symbolic presence. However, this is due, in my judgement, to Augustine's polemical situation rather than to any imprecision in his thought. Harnack's remark, that "the emphasis rests so strongly on the Word and faith that the sign is simply described, in many places and indeed, as a rule, as a figure," [29] understates Augustine's concern for the integrity of the sacramental action. Augustine's situation was difficult. He was combatting the Donatists, who held such a strong view of the Church as the agent of the sacraments that a synod of bishops claimed to invalidate sacraments by withdrawing the Church's salvific intent from the actions of other bishops. Thus the Donatist Council of Bagaï (April 24, 394) threatened excommunication on the supporters of Maximianus, giving them eight months (until Christmas) to submit, after which their acts would be null and void. [30] Augustine wanted to restore the unity of the Church in North Africa while preserving the once for all character of baptism, given by Christ, and therefore essentially unaffected by the faults of the ministers. He had to avoid overstressing the involvement of the Church in the sacramental acts. For this reason he insisted on the internal, spiritual aspects of sacraments. Yet his understanding of sacrifice and his explanation of eucharistic sacramentality rested on a fundamental assimilation of the sacramental body with the ecclesial body of Christ. This is all the more important as it could have given fuel to the Donatist argumentation.

The sacrifice is discussed in book X of the *De Civitate Dei*, where Augustine posits the following definition, which is both personalistic (sacrifice tends to man's beatitude) and corporate (it tends to oneness with God in the holy society). "Thus, all that is done so that we may adhere to God in holy community relatively to the good and by which we can really be blessed, is a true sacrifice." [31] Such a definition applies equally well to interior sacrifices of the heart offered by a Christian "insofar as he dies to the world and lives in God," and to the offering of the whole Church to God by our high-priest: "It is certainly done

---

[29] *History of Dogma*, 5 (New York, 1961), 156.
[30] *Traités Anti-Donatistes*, 1 (Oeuvres de saint Augustin, 28; Paris, 1963) 736.
[31] *De Civitate Dei*, 10, 6.

so that the whole redeemed city, that is, the fathering and society of the saints, be offered to God as a universal sacrifice by the high-priest, who also offered himself for us in the passion in the form of the Servant, that we may be the body of such a head." [32] This universal sacrifice is that of Christ himself who, in the form of the Servant, is the offering, the mediator, the priest and the sacrifice: "He offered it, he was offered in it, for in it he is mediator, priest, sacrifice." Again, "By this he is the priest, being the offerer and the offering." [33] By the same token, this offering is also that of the Church, of "the whole redeemed city": "He willed the daily sacrifice of the Church which, as it is the body of himself who is the head, learns to offer it through him, to be the daily sacrament of that event."

That the sacrifice is that of the Church with Christ, as of the body with the head, tallies with Augustine's repeated assertion that the sacrament of a reality is this reality: "As the sacrament of the body of Christ is somehow the body of Christ, and the sacrament of the blood of Christ is the blood of Christ, so the sacrament of faith is faith." [34] In this context infant baptism is justified by analogy with the eucharist. The sacrament of faith (baptism) amounts to the faith of the infant, just as the sacrament of the body of Christ (the eucharist) amounts to the body of Christ. So the offering made everyday *in sacramento* is also that which Christ made once for all *in seipso*. [35] In answer to Januarius, Augustine explains the paschal mystery in his *Epistola LV*: the Pasch is the *transitus,* the passage of the Lord through his dying and his rising. "The passage from death to life has been sanctified in the passion and resurrection of the Lord." [36] As taking place now in the sacrament, it necessarily involves those who celebrate it. For there is no sacrament without real participation. "There is a sacrament in a celebration when the remembering of the past even is so done that what is understood to be signified is also to be received *in holiness.*" On this basis the Christian passover is a true sacrament; but Christmas is not one. We are not born at Christmas as we die and rise with Christ at Easter and in every eucharistic celebration. Thus the reality of the eucharistic sacrament includes the eschatological *transitus* of the whole Church:

---

[32] *Ibid.,* 10, 6.
[33] *Ibid.,* 10, 20.
[34] *Epistola* 98, 9 (PL, 33. 364).
[35] *Ibid.,* (363).
[36] *Epistola* 40, 2 (PL, 33. 205).

> This universal Church, which may be seen in the pilgrimage of mortality,
> expects at the end of the world what has been pre-announced in the body
> of our Lord Jesus Christ, who is the first-born from among the dead, for
> the body of which he is the head is no other than the Church. [37]

One could hardly wish for a clearer formulation of the ecclesial
principle that the *ecclesia* is, especially at the eucharist, the body
of Christ. There is an identity "in some way;" the Church is a sacrament, which takes place "in some celebration," in "the commemoration
of an event." Such expressions abound in Augustine's writings. For
the realities that are being joined remain at different levels. But this
does not tone down the identity between the body and the head. Rather,
it suggests the yet-to-come fullness of eschatological transformation.
In keeping with the First Epistle of John, 3:2: "What we shall be has
not yet appeared," it evokes the journey from "the pilgrimage of mortality" to "the end of the world," from the "region of dissemblance" to
"ressemblance," [38] the differences between the earthly city and the city
of God. The proper locus of the Augustinian sacrament is the twilight
zone between these realms: the Church is the body of Christ in sacrament.

V

Conclusion

Nothing is especially new in the material that I have presented.
In fact, some of these texts have been scrutinized time and time again
in the course of the eucharistic controversies which followed the Reformation. It is not superfluous, however, to study them again in our day,
when ecumenical dialogues are attempting to overcome the differences
of eucharistic theology inherited from the past. If it is true that a
consensus is now emerging between the major Christian Churches on the
meaning of the eucharist, [39] this consensus should be seen in its proper
theological background. The horizon of the eucharistic presence of the
Lord is the intimate connection, which dominates theological reflection
from Augustine to Thomas Aquinas, between the body of Christ given
for the many and the body-of-Christ-is-the-Church. This connection is
not metaphorical, but real: there is an identity *in mysterio,* therefore
to be perceived through faith, between the Church and the eucharist.

---

[37] *Ibid.,* 3 (206).

[38] *Confessions,* 7, 10, 16.

[39] See the agreed statements issued by some major ecumenical dialogues, such
as *The Windsor Statement,* 1971 (Anglican-Roman Catholic), the statement on
The Eucharist as Sacrifice, 1967 (Lutheran-Roman Catholic), *The Moscow
Agreed Statement,* 1976 (Anglican-Orthodox), the document *Vers une même foi
eucharistique?* (Groupe des Dombes).

THE BYZANTINE RECOVERY OF CONSTANTINOPLE FROM THE LATINS IN 1261

A Chrysobull of Michael VIII Palaeologus in Favor of Hagia Sophia

DENO J. GEANAKOPLOS

Yale University

In 1261, after fifty-seven years of Latin occupation, the Byzantine capital of Constantinople was reconquered from the Latins by Emperor Michael VIII Palaeologus. Among the many pressing political and administrative tasks facing the emperor after return of the seat of Empire and Church from Nicaea to the Bosporus was the restoration or grant to the Church of revenues and lands for its subsistence and support. The document with which this study is concerned is a *chrysobull* issued by the same Michael VIII in favor of the Great Church of Hagia Sophia. The document's significance lies in part in its explicit, detailed enumeration of properties and privileges granted to Hagia Sophia and to the patriarch Joseph. [1] The section of the document which provides this particular information has already been analyzed by H. Ahrweiler in an essay discussing the geographical importance of areas in western Asia Minor, especially around Smyrna and Nicaea. [2] The remaining material, however, has been almost completely ignored by scholars—important material which describes how Michael restored churches, city walls, and buildings, and no less significant, which reflects the exultant mood in Constantinople at the restoration of the Queen City to the Greeks. Accordingly, this study, while making some reference to the section of the chrysobull assigning privileges to the Great Church, will focus primarily on the neglected portions of the document which reflect not only Michael VIII's

---

[1] Document printed first (in Greek) by J. Sakellion, "ˮΙσον Χρυσοβούλλου Μιχαὴλ Η' Παλαιολόγου γεγονότος τῇ μεγάλη τοῦ Θεοῦ 'Εκκλησίᾳ ἐπὶ τοῖς δωρηθεῖσιν αὐτῇ κτήμασιν (1272)," *Pandora* 15 (Athens, 1864), 27-32; reprinted in J. and P. Zepos, *Jus Graecoromanum* 1 (Athens, 1931), 659-66. Not mentioned in V. Laurent, *Les Regestes des Actes du Patriarcat de Constantinople, 1208-1309* (Paris, 1971). Dated 1272 by Sakellion and Zepos.

[2] H. Ahrweiler, "L'histoire et la géographie de la région de Smyrne entre les deux occupations Turques (1081-1317) particulièrement du XIIIᵉ siècle," in *Travaux et Mémoires* 1 (Paris, 1965) esp. 57-58. For summary of contents relating specifically to properties of Hagia Sophia see F. Dölger, *Regesten der Kaiserurkunden des oströmischen Reiches*, part 3 (Munich, 1932) 52, no. 1956.

attitude to the Latin expulsion and the Greek restoration, but the feelings evoked among the Greek population as a whole.

Let us quote first from the *proemium* which, I believe, reflects better than any other source the mood in the capital at the Greek restoration (the translation is mine):

> "Hail, hail indeed Daughter of Zion, rejoice daughter of Jerusalem. The Lord has redeemed you from your sins. He has released you from the hands of your enemies and you will suffer no more misfortunes. The Lord God will bring you joy and will renew (καινίζει) you as on a feast day." These are the words of the admirable prophet Sophonius which of old he was joyously singing for the renewal of Zion when he foresaw the return of the Hebrews from Babylon and the release of Israel from the hands of its enemies, and announced that no further trials were any longer to be expected.

Especially meaningful here is the analogy drawn by Michael (an analogy used by other Byzantine sources of the period) between the Byzantines of 1261 and the Jews of the Babylonian exile. As Michael clearly implies, the period of the Byzantine exile in Nicaea was for the Greeks their Babylon, and like the Jews they, after a period of atonement and renewal of the purity of their faith, were now being led back in triumph from Nicaea to their Zion, Constantinople. The next continues:

> Our majesty, responding to these words and relating them to our own circumstances, will now appropriately set these forth as a *proemium* to this *chrysobull*. For it is now opportune that my reign chant joyfully the "rejoice" (χαῖρε, of the liturgy) and the "exult" (εὐφραίνου) to the Great Church of God, which takes precedence over other churches and is honored as the metropolis of the metropoleis . . . This discourse will refer to her (Constantinople) as the new Zion and the New Jerusalem, and will say appropriately about her . . . The Lord of all, the God of wonders has released her (Constantinople) from her sins and from the hands of her enemies. But now the sweet fragrance of the sacrifice of lambs and of the blood of calves, does not, as of old in the Temple of Old Zion, reach the Lord's nostrils, but, rather, through the true sacrifice of the lifegiving blood from the side of the spiritual calf (Christ), the only begotten Son of God . . . This city has been delivered, not as were the Jews long ago from the hands of the Babylonians, but from the contemptible Italians, whose "nation" (ἔθνος) is worse than the Babylonian serpent (δράκων) because it (the Latin army) a long time ago crept against it (Constantinople) stealthily with the "windings" of their ships and, penetrating into the interior of its habitations (and) spreading itself through the dark places (καταδύσεις) of the city's quarters (ἐπαυλέων), it rendered desolate and destroyed everything it found which adorned the city.[3]

---

[3] For these passages see text in Sakellion, p. 27, col. 1. The sentence referring to the sacrifice in the Temple of Jerusalem and the "life-giving blood of Christ" in Hagia Sophia and also comparing the Latin army to the Babylonian serpent draws on the Book of Revelation.

Note the striking image of the Latin forces Michael projects here—
that of a serpent gradually uncoiling itself and spreading throughout
all parts of Constantinople.

> Others have tragically lamented the extent and magnitude of the de-
> struction. But today is a holiday and a festival because the city is again
> coming to life and being revived.[4] And as God in his goodness has until
> now many times bestowed his favor on my reign in many matters, He
> now has proclaimed my reign to be the instrument of this restoration
> and renewal (τοῦ καινισμοῦ τούτου καὶ τῆς ἀνανεώσεως ταύτης). Our
> Majesty has decided to spur on this renewal and restore not only the
> buildings of this New Zion, not only His church (Hagia Sophia) and
> the sacred vessels and holy objects (ἐπίπλων) but also the estates and
> properties from which the yearly revenue is drawn for the sake of the
> things of God. Thus we have decided to issue this *chrysobull* in behalf of
> this church as a kind of renovation and renewal. For these rights, which
> it had previously been granted by emperors through edicts and chryso-
> bulls, were lost to her through the things that happened during the
> Latin dynasty.

Reference here at the end is of course made to seizure of the
patriarchal properties in 1204 by the Latin church. We know that the
Latins made considerable changes in the Byzantine ecclesiastical structure, for example substituting Latin prelates for recalcitrant Greeks,
and reducing the total number of Byzantine episcopal sees by com-
bining two or more bishoprics in order to produce increased revenues
for each newly-installed Catholic prelate. [5] Moreover, owing to dif-

---

[4] See text, p. 27, col. 2. This passage, on the revivification of Constantinople, may be compared to Michael's own description in his "Typikon for
the Monastery of St. Michael" published in A. Dmitrievskii, *Opisanie
ligurgiceskih rukopisej*, vol. 1, pt. 1, *Typika* (Kiev, 1895), 771, where Michael
implies that the most immediately visible sign of the Greek restoration was
that "in Constantinople there is no longer heard the confused tongue (broken
Greek) spoken by a half-barbarian people (the Latins) but that of the Greek
population now spoken correctly by all." For other examples of the explosion of popular Greek jubilation at the capital's recovery see G. Acropolites, *Historia*, ed. Teubner (1903), 1:87-89; S. G. Mercati, "Giambi di
ringraziamento per la riconquista di Constantinopoli," *Byzantinische
Zeitschrift* 36 (1936), 289-90, written by a certain Nicetas, who calls Michael
VIII the "New David" (founder of the Hebrew dynasty in Jerusalem). Also
on the Greek elation see the encomia written by Michael's official panegyrist,
Manuel Holobolos, *Orationes*, ed. M. Treu (Potsdam, 1906-07), 58ff.; Gregory
of Cyrus, "Laudatio," in MPG, 142, cols. 346-86; and finally, the very
important "Un panegyrico inedito per Michele VIII Paleologo," *Byzantinische Zeitschrift* 42 (1942), 1-27, where some of the same epithets are used
for Michael as in the present document.
[5] On the reduction of the number of Byzantine episcopal sees as compared
to those in 1198, see R. H. Wolff, "The Organization of the Latin Patriarchate of Constantinople (1204-61): Social and Administrative Consequences of the Latin Conquest," *Traditio* 6 (1948), 56-57.

ferences in the Greek and Latin ecclesiastical rites, certain changes must inevitably have been made by the Western clergy in the internal decoration of Hagia Sophia and also in the composition of the clerical staff of the cathedral. [6] Such considerations (as well as the looting and destruction) of course would subsequently have made it difficult for Michael to restore to their original condition the church buildings and the clerical staff of Hagia Sophia and other Constantinopolitan churches.

A similar state of disorganization also obtained in the civil affairs of restored Byzantium. Thus we know that, when in 1261 many Greeks returned to their capital from exile, it was difficult in many instances to recall even the names of previous owners of properties in the city. In a document published by S. Kougeas, the case is cited of the Grand Logothete George Acropolites, who in 1261 took over the house of an Anconitan, since it could not be recalled to which Greek it had previously belonged. Since it was a difficult task to divide up equitably the houses and residences among the Byzantine nobles and people, Michael VIII declared all land and houses of the city to belong to the Emperor pending appropriate distribution. [7] Reading again from our document:

> Our Majesty therefore issues this chrysobull on behalf of the most holy Great Church of God as a beginning, as another foundation for the increase of ecclesiastical revenues which Our Majesty has inaugurated and toward which, with God's help, my reign is disposed and eager to

---

[6] See esp. R. Janin, "Les sanctuaires de byzance sous la domination latine," *Etudes byzantines* 2 (1944), 134ff. Also E. Swift, "The Latins at Hagia Sophia," *American Journal of Archaeology* 39 (1935), 458-74. Janin affirms that in Constantinople twenty churches and fourteen monasteries were occupied by the Latins (some Greek sanctuaries were deserted by Greeks who fled). Most Greek ecclesiastics and monks refused to submit to the pope. Janin, (p. 150) says we do not know of Latin changes in decoration of Hagia Sophia (to conform to Western ritual) though we do know (p. 151) that Thomas Morosini, the new Venetian patriarch, put up marble columns to ornament the altar of Hagia Sophia, and that the Latin Emperor Baldwin II, in 1261, removed from Hagia Sophia a great number of plaques of marble. The Venetian Doge Enrico Dandolo was interred in St. Sophia. Swift, *op. cit.*, pp. 464, 473, shows the Latins strengthened the building, the dome especially, by erecting a number of flying buttresses in the current Western style.

[7] See S. Kougeas, "Ho Georgios Akropolites ktetor tou parisinou kodikos tou Souida," *Byzantina Metabyzantina* 1 (1949), 61ff. On Michael's arrogation of all property to the imperial government for disposition see Pachymeres, *Historia* (Bonn) 1:391 (cf. D. J. Geanakoplos, *Emperor Michael Palaeologus and the West: A Study in Byzantine-Latin Relations, 1258-82* [Cambridge, Mass., 1959] 124). Michael assigned special lands to the θεληματαῖοι, who had helped him take the city from the Latins (p. 124).

7

build upon. Our reign is determined that it (Hagia Sophia and its revenues) will be extended and increased in beauty and greatness by our successors in authority and government.

This last statement is probably a less than veiled allusion to Michael's aim of establishing his own dynasty on the throne. In fact only a short time after Constantinople's recapture by his troops, Michael had himself *and* his son Andronicus (together with the latter's Hungarian wife) crowned for a second time in August 1261 (the previous coronation taking place on Christmas day of 1258 in Nicaea). At this time, it would seem Andronicus was granted the title of Autokrator. [8]

After a long section on the desirability of granting additional revenues and properties to Hagia Sophia, the text continues:

> And so that it may be clear how everything pertaining to the church has been arranged—since God, because of his great favor toward me (περὶ ἐμὲ ἐλέους) has entrusted to my reign the *epistemonarchian* (literally, supervision or disciplinary authority over the church—a more accurate expression, I suggest, for imperial authority over the church than the term Caesaropapism).[9] [Since God has done this and] so that it may be known how affairs were conducted before our reestablishment and recall (by God) to this Queen of Cities (τὴν βασιλεύουσαν), and to ascertain how matters were arranged and have fared since our divinely arranged return (ἐπὶ τῆδε θεοσυγκρότητον ἡμετέραν ἐπάνοδον) to this city, Our Majesty has decided to dispose of all these matters one by one through this chrysobull.

What should be noted here above all is Michael's constant repetition of what he clearly wishes to be the central theme of this document: God's divine plan for Byzantium using Michael as his divinely chosen instrument. [10] Our translation continues:

---

[8] See text, p. 27, col. 2. On the coronations see F. Dölger, "Die dynastische Familienpolitik des Kaisers Michael Palaiologos (1258-1282)," *Festschrift E. Eichmann* (Paderborn, 1940), 179ff. and A. Heisenberg, "Aus der Geschichte und Literatur der Palaiologenzeit," *Sitzungsb. d. bayerischen Akademie der Wissens. zu München* 10 (1920), 1-44. Dölger shows that Andronicus was crowned Basileus in August of 1261 when Michael was recrowned. P. Wirth, "Die Begründung der Kaisermacht Michaels VIII. Palaiologos," *Jahrbuch der Osterreichischen Byzantinischen Gesellschaft* 10 (1961), 85-91, says there were three coronations of Michael.

[9] See G. Lampe, *A Patristic Greek Lexicon* (Oxford, 1961), 535, under ἐπιστημονάρχης, defined as "a disciplinary office in a monastery"—hence supervisor or "regulator" of the church. This might be a more satisfactory term to use of the emperor's authority over the church than Caesaropapism.

[10] Text, p. 27, col. 2 and p. 28, col. 1. In Manuel Holobolos, *Orationes*, ed. Treu, p. 68, Holobolos, Michael's official encomiast, refers to Michael as θεοκυβέρνητε βασιλεῦ. (God-directed emperor). Dölger, op. cit., 45, notes that through use of this term Michael sought to give the impression of acting under divine guidance and providence.

We note the small size of the ecclesiastical estates in former times and
their division later, and [we state] this not in order that we be considered
conscientious—because what can anyone offer of worth in comparison
to that which he has received from God? For we have been taught that
no one can honor God deservedly but only rightfully.

Observe Michael's indirect disclaimer here of any responsibility for
the events of 1261, presumably in order the more to stress God's freely
bestowed gift to him and the Greeks of their capital. Then the document affirms:

> We mention all this in order to describe the former weakness of things
> and to reveal the fullness of mercy which God has shown in our behalf
> . . . The inhabitants of Constantinople fled from their fatherland
> (πατρίς) into exile, and the cup (κόνδυ) which was alloted them to drink
> was overflowing as a penalty for their sins, and the bitterness was
> emptied like water into their entrails.[11]

This latter, striking metaphor refers of course to the idea prevalent
among the Byzantines—and the Latins as well—that Constantinople
fell to the Latins in 1204 because of the many sins of the Greeks,
and would only be restored to them when their sins were fully expiated. [12] To continue with the text:

> And the ecumenical patriarch resided away from Constantinople and
> the metropoleis and archbishoprics took refuge abroad. The metro-
> politan city of Nicaea was established as the patriarchal see and
> residence for all of the patriarchal clergy. And the formerly wealthy
> estates and rich properties of this church were together at once swept
> away by the (Latin) dynasty of the time and were lost to (Byzantine)
> authority and no revenues any longer remained to the patriarch and his
> clergy except for the income from the metropolis (of Nicaea). And the
> God of mercy who punishes justly and heals benevolently (φιλανθρώπως),
> who rehabilitates ruins and releases from suffering and from our bonds,
> through much sweat and effort of the late blessed Lord Theodore (I)
> Lascaris and through the great struggles and labor of John (Vatatzes)
> Ducas who, after him took up the reins of government—God (then)
> looked with favor so that the church's affairs, with respect to its revenues
> and expenses, could again have a beginning.[13]

There follows a bit later a passage vivid in its reflection of the
Greek feeling toward their reconquest:

---

[11] Text, p. 28, col. 1.

[12] See below next page, text of document: "Then by the will of Almighty
God our Majesty entered Constantinople from which the Romans were
expelled because of their sins." Evidently only Gregory of Cyprus, among the
Byzantines, attributed the Byzantine loss of their capital rather to fate.

[13] Text, p. 28 and p. 29, col. 1.

Then by the will of the Almighty Our Majesty entered Constantinople
from which the Romans had been expelled because of their sins, and to
which the mercy of God brought them back. And Our Majesty took care,
first and above all else, to render to God on this occasion of the restoration (ἀποκατάστασις) of the Romans, the first fruits (ἀπαρχάς) of the
return of the Romans to their ancestral lands, which happened during
our reign.[14] Our Majesty had the aim of restoring to the sons and
grandsons of the Romans who had been expelled from Constantinople,
those things the loss of which their fathers and grandfathers had suffered two generations before at the hands of the barbarian dynasty
(βαρβαρικὴ δυναστεία). And I sought to renew our rightful patrimony
which was cut off by the sword of the unlawful hand. Because if, according to Solomon, it is wise to know who partakes of God's grace,
how otherwise could Our Majesty, after our restoration, begin the ap-
portionment of property? For Our Majesty received the grace of God
and so Our Majesty bestows land first on the church of God which was
left neglected during the long period of exile. This is the area of Hagio-
sophitika (literally, "the Hagia Sophian property") which until now
has preserved its name as a clear sign of its previous owner with all its
rights on land and sea.[15]

It is here at this point that the chrysobull begins its detailed, precise
delineation of the various properties being awarded to Hagia Sophia—
material which F. Dölger has cogently summarized in his *Regesten*
and which H. Ahrweiler has carefully studied. I note in passing the
importance of this enumeration of properties for the study of the
development in Byzantium of such protofeudal institutions as the
πρόνοια and χαριστίκιον. It would be useful if other technical terms
employed in this section such as πάροικοι, κομμέρκιον, ἐννόμιον,
τοπιατικόν, etc. could be analyzed for possible importance for Byzantine social and institutional history.[16]

To continue quoting from our document, Michael mentions as now
awarded (or rewarded to Hagia Sophia):

also the buildings located (in Constantinople) around the district of the
famous church of the Wisdom of God (Hagia Sophia) and those which
are within and outside the courtyard of the Augusteion and the area of
the Milion,[17] just as, concerning these, is more fully described in the

----

[14] Text, p. 29, col. 1. The Jews gave the first fruits of their crops to the
Temple. Michael and his people were imbued with the fixed idea that good
acts would bring back God's favor and avert punishment, a view consistent
with the Orthodox faith.

[15] Ahrweiler, *ibid.*, 57f., has dealt in great detail with the *Hagiosophitica*
(the property, as noted, belonging traditionally to Hagia Sophia around
Smyrna).

[16] Text, p. 29, col. 2.

[17] See R. Janin, *La géographie ecclésiastique de l'empire byzantin* 3 (Paris,
1953). In front of the open area of the Augusteon (named for the Augusta
Helen, Constantine's mother), was the Milion, from which all distances were

promulgated ὁρισμὸς (edict) of Our Majesty, along with the area adjoining the old patriarchate of (Hagia) Irene, the Word of God.[18]

These two churches referred to, Hagia Sophia and Hagia Irene, did
in fact constitute the two poles of the district of the patriarchate. [19]
In this same section Michael informs us how the revenues from the
areas mentioned should be allotted—one third to the patriarch's household (πατριαρχικὸν κελλίον), one-third (τὸ δὲ δίμοιρον) to his "offi-
cialion" (his staff of presbyters, deacons, and cantors); we may
recall that in Justinian's time the clerical staff of Hagia Sophia consisted of over four hundred persons and, finally, among other things,
a small part to be set aside for lighting, that is candles to be used in
Hagia Sophia (λυχοκαία). [20]

After more material on Hagia Sophia's properties in Constantinople
being awarded (or rewarded) to the church, comes a passage men-
tioning in strikingly laudatory terms the incumbent patriarch Joseph,
who is referred to as:

> conducting himself during these years . . . honorably, freely offering aid
> to those who needed it, pouring out his mercy like a river to the poor,
> offering in abundance whatever the prelates, clerics, and monks need,
> providing sustenance to those who in everything took care of the
> patriarch (and) showing the same care as before for those who abandoned
> the clerical state, fostering abundant support to the monks who could
> not be nourished from the monasteries (κοινόβια), offering assistance to
> poor girls so that they could marry legally and be spared a life of sin,
> looking out for the lives of widows, and in all he did evoking gratitude.[21]

Several of these references may be to those Greek clerics and monks
who, displaced by the Latin clergy, suffered from want or who, from
religious conviction, refused to continue in their functions while subject
to Latin ecclesiastical authorities.

---

measured. It was originally a column, later a square building on pillars with
a platform on top: D. Rice, *Constantinople. From Byzantium to Istanbul*
(New York, 1965), 18.

[18] Text, p. 29, col. 2 and p. 30, col. 1. Evidently Michael had previously
issued another edict relating to properties granted to Hagia Sophia soon
after entering the capital, in 1261 or 1262. Note text: "as are more fully
described in the (already) promulgated ὁρισμός." St. Irene was the cathedral
church before St. Sophia's erection (hence called here "the old patriarchate").
Both churches together were referred to as "the Great Church": see A. Van
Millingen, *Byzantine Churches in Constantinople* (London, 1912), 84-85.

[19] See Janin, *ibid.*, I pt. I.

[20] Text, p. 30, cols. 1-2. See G. Downey, *Constantinople in the Age of
Justinian* (Norman, Oklahoma, 1960), 113 on Justinian's time.

[21] Text, p. 30, col. 2.

The real reasons for the rich gifts and emoluments, so ostentatiously presented to Patriarch Joseph by Michael in this document, are not mentioned here. But in my view significant is the timing of the issuance of this chrysobull. For Patriarch Joseph's attitude to Michael had recently begun to change. Joseph had earlier in Nicaea earned Michael's thanks for removing the ecclesiastical excommunication levied against Michael by his predecessor Patriarch Arsenios, after Michael's usurpation of the throne at Nicaea and his callous blinding of the legitimate boy-emperor, John Lascaris. But Joseph now had turned openly against Michael's policy of religious union with Rome, a course of action necessitated, Michael believed, by the pressing need to avert the threat of a second Latin occupation of Constantinople by Charles of Anjou, King of Sicily. [22] Sakkelion, who first printed this document in 1864, and Zepos, who reprinted, it, date this chrysobull to 1272. I would agree, though Dölger more cautiously placed it in the period from 1261 to 1271. [23] In the latter year there broke out into the open clerical and monastic opposition to Michael's growing attempts to coerce the Greek clergy and people into acceptance of the *filioque* and other Latin doctrinal and liturgical concessions for religious union demanded by the papacy. In this bitter struggle, the support of Patriarch Joseph and the higher clergy of Hagia Sophia obviously could be of great value to Michael. Thus, through the more than generous grants made by this chrysobull, Michael may well have been seeking to placate Joseph and his prelates, a group already commonly referred to as the faction of "Josephites."

---

[22] On Patriarch Joseph I, who was in office from 1268 to 1274 (and later again from 1282 to 1283) see G. Ostrogorsky, *History of the Byzantine State* (New Brunswick, 1969), 462, 486. Also Geanakoplos, *Emperor Michael*, 262; V. Laurent, "Le serment anti-Latin du Patriarche Joseph Iᵉ, *Echos d'Orient* 27 (1927), 396ff.; a letter of the Emperor to Patriarch Joseph in F. Mikosich and J. Müller, *Acta et diplomata res graecas italasque illustrantia* 5 (Vienna, 1860f.), 247 (where the term ἐπιστημονάρχης is used to refer to the emperor's authority over the church; and, finally, documents from Joseph's patriarchate in V. Laurent, *Les Regestes des Actes du Patriarchat de Constantinople, 1208-1309* (Paris, 1971), 180-210.

[23] On date, 1272, see Sakellion, 32, note a; Zepos, *op. cit.*, 659; and Dölger, *Regesten*, no. 1956, pp. 52-53. It is possible that this document of 1272 may have been a formalization or extension of privileges granted earlier (perhaps in 1261 or 1262) by Michael to the church. See above, text for n. 18, where the document reads: "as are fully described in the (already) promulgated ὁρισμὸς of Our Majesty." Cf. also Pachymeres, 172, 173, stating that Michael presented lavish treasures to Hagia Sophia soon after entering the city. On Charles of Anjou see Geanakoplos, *Emperor Michael*, 189-371.

The next passage is very similar to parts of Michael's two typica (monastic charters) he issued in favor of the monasteries of Sts. Demetrius and Michael, in which, as a kind of apologia, he enumerated the principal steps of his career, presumably thus demonstrating or seeking to justify God's election of him as his chosen instrument. [24] As our chrysobull continues:

> Our Majesty has been crowned by God with the imperial rank, a gift not only extraordinary but superior to anything on earth and more exalted and renowned than any worldly office. We were created ... were nourished by Him who controls life, who provides sustenance. We grew up ... became a man, and were trained in military exercises. We achieved glory through our military virtue; we were honored with senatorial rank; we have with God's help carried out our duties well (καλῶς διεθήκαμεν τὸ ἡμετέραν) and, militarily, we have punished our enemies. We became emperor, something shared by no other of our people (ὁμοφύλων), a rank in which God in his grace has placed us.[25]

Of course Michael does not here mention, nor does he anywhere in his two typika, his usupation of the throne or his earlier excommunication by Patriarch Arsenios (from which Patriarch Joseph had finally absolved him). But he knew only too well the stigma with which these two acts had branded him and the necessity of attempting to erase their memory from Greek minds.

Then, after noting "the shortcomings of my own eagerness," Michael inserts a curious statement about his successors, that is members of his own house:

> And you descendants who will follow—you should not in any way be jealous of my reward from the community (οὐδὲ ὑμεῖς ... μισθοῦ μοι φθονήσετε) for which you may also prepare yourselves if God shall look with favor in your time on your increase of holy votive offerings. ... For, if the favor (ἔλαιος) of God returned us to Constantinople, we did not spare any human effort and treasure in taking care of everything that was necessary and in disposing of affairs, as it seemed to us, in the best military manner. All that we did after our return here could uphold us since acts are more persuasive as evidence than easy words.[26]

In a subsequent passage Michael enumerates one by one his acts after his entering the City. (By the way, before 1261 Michael had evidently never set foot in Constantinople, though Pachymeres relates

---

[24] See *Imperatoris Michaelis Palaeologi de vita sua opusculum necnon regulae quam ipse monasterio S. Demetrii praescripsit fragmentum* (St. Petersburg, 1884); and A. Dmitrievskii, *Opisanie liturgiceskih rukopisej*, vol. 1, pt. 1, *Typica* (Kiev, 1895), 769-94. Both are also cited in Geanakoplos, *Emperor Michael*, 16, n. 1.

[25] Text, p. 31, col. 1.

[26] Text, p. 31, cols. 1 and 2.

that from childhood onward he had fantasies about himself retaking the glorious city. [27] Michael affirms here that, "[First] we repaired the walls all around the city, most of which we found completely ruined and which we re-erected from their very foundations (κρηπίδων), in some other places extending the restored parts for a considerable stretch." This attention to the walls was an act of critical importance if the Venetian fleet, the Latin Empire's chief defense, were (as did in fact happen) to return from Daphnusia, the isle in the Black Sea to which it had been lured, possibly by Michael himself. [28] "In addition," the chrysobull continues, "we restored parts of other sections of the walls, so that no part of the wall of the city remained bereft of care (ἄμοιρον), left, that is, either partly or completely un-rebuilt." Michael stresses, secondly, that "at my orders there was begun the restoration of the holy churches everywhere in the city, the beauty and buildings of which had suffered from the work of destruction by the Latin plot (λατινικῆς ἐπιβουλῆς)." Then, Michael refers, thirdly, to his "reestablishment and rebuilding of the monasteries." And, finally, to "the new luster (αἱ ... νέαι φαιδρότητες) of the palace, which we found a remnant of its former glory and which we took care to renew and make more splendid than before." [29]

All these works of restoration on the part of Michael are corroborated in detail by contemporary Greek sources, by the histories of Pachymeres, Acropolites, and the later Gregoras, and by the official encomia of Holobolos, and that of the later patriarch Gregory of Cyprus. [30] Regarding the monasteries, one of Michael's own two typica relates in particular how he rebuilt the monastery of St. Demetrius, founded earlier by his ancestor George Palaeologus. [31] As for churches, we know from Janin's studies that twenty Greek churches and monasteries, the latter including the Pantokrator and Studius, had been taken over by the Latin clergy during the occupation and that under

---

[27] Pachymeres, *Historia*, 1:128 (cf. Geanakoplos, *Emperor Michael*, 19).

[28] See Geanakoplos, *ibid.*, 99-102.

[29] For this entire paragraph see text, p. 31, col. 2. This agrees with Pachymeres, 161, and Gregoras, 87, who affirm that he moved into the Great Palace, since the Latins had made the Blachernae unfit for habitation. See n. 33 below.

[30] For all these sources and exact citations see Geanakoplos, *Emperor Michael*, 122-37 and cf. also works cited above in n. 4.

[31] Geanakoplos, *ibid.*, 16, n. 1, and cf. above n. 4.

the tutelage of the Cistercian order gold decoration had been placed in Hagia Sophia. [32]

In connection with Michael's repair of the imperial palace, Pachymeres recounts that Michael chose to restore the Great Palace overlooking the Golden Horn rather than the more recently built Blachernae palace, which was deemed uninhabitable because of the smoke and debris of the Latins. As Pachymeres scornfully puts it, "it was filled with thick smoke and Italian fire, which the servants of the uncouth Baldwin had allowed to permeate the palace." [33] Holobolos, Michael's officially appointed panegyrist, refers to this Latin Emperor even more derisively as a "manling" (ἀνδράριον).[34]

In the light of these various examples of repair and reconstruction one can well imagine haw vast must have been the task facing Michael to restore Constantinople to even a semblance of its former condition. Gregoras, perhaps only somewhat exaggeratedly, wrote: "After 1204 Constantinople was then an enormous, desolate city, full of ruins and stones, of houses razed to the ground, and of the few remains of the great fire. Enslaved, it had received no care from the Latins except destruction of every kind day and night." [35]

Our document continues with Michael's lavish praise for the Great Church of Hagia Sophia, termed here the "common metropolitan church of the faithful, the holy sanctuary, the holy abode, the truly divine palace, and Your abode, though we have not learned to make God dwell in houses built of human hands." [36]

At this point there follows a passage of some theological subtlety:

> ... the enhypostatic Wisdom of God (ἐνυπόστατον Σοφίαν Θεοῦ), the self-existent (αὐθύπαρκτον) power of Him who emptied Himself for us and so humbled Himself as to take on the form of a slave and received the whole man so that we could share in the first glory [referring to Adam's life before the fall] and in the more divine life and participate in the divinity (καὶ θεοὶ τῇ μετουσίᾳ γενοίμεθα) ... For what can one add about the essence (οὐσία) which created everything through the λόγος which controls and rules over all ... so that the Roman possessions (σχοινίσματα) would continue to increase forever (εἰς ἄπειρον) and the boundaries (of the Empire) would be immeasurably extended.

---

[32] Janin, "Les sanctuaires de byzance sous la domination byzantine," 134, 172. On the Cistercians in general cf. E. Brown, "The Cistercians in the Latin Empire of Constantinople and Greece, 1204-76," *Traditio* 14 (1958), 63-120.

[33] Pachymeres, 161 (cf. Geanakoplos, *Emperor Michael*, 122).

[34] Holobolos, *Orationes*, ed. Treu, p. 68 (ἀνδράριόν τι βραχύτατον).

[35] Gregoras, *Historia*, 1:87-88.

[36] Text, p. 31, end of page.

This last phrase is consonant with the idea expressed by Michael immediately after his entrance into the capital when he called an assembly together and announced it would be his primary aim to recover the lost territory of his Empire. [37] The document concludes with the following fervent prayer, a desire shared by the entire Greek populace: "May the affairs of the Very Great Church return to their previous prosperity and may (the Empire) with your (God's) consent recover its previous possessions and its former good order (εὐκοσμία) and splendor." [38]

In the concluding sentence, a kind of signature to the chrysobull, the dates of the month and indiction are obliterated. Literally the text reads: "This (document) has been drawn up in the month of ——— in the ——— indiction of the year 1272 (6700), in which year our pious and 'God-impelled' (θεοπρόβλητος) power has signed it." Note the use here of θεοπρόβλητος,[39] a term which then was and today still is applied to a bishop, and which probably was used here by Michael purposely in order to point up once again his selection as the chosen instrument of God's will.

To conclude our remarks—this chrysobull, then, from which we have quoted the more important passages, besides enumerating the specific properties and privileges accorded to the Great Church after the Greek return and expressing Greek emotion over restoration of Constantinople to Byzantine hands, constitutes, from Michael's, that is the author's, point of view—and herein lies its real importance for us—a subtle piece of political-ecclesiastical propaganda. For through issuance of this document Michael hoped, as we can clearly see from other of his public pronouncements, to make Constantinople's recovery redound in Greek minds to his own benefit.

By repeatedly referring to himself as the instrument employed by God to restore Constantinople and its greatest treasure, Hagia Sophia, to the Greeks, and in addition, by according or re-according properties to Patriarch Joseph and his church, Michael sought to make his people, on the one hand, forget his criminal usurpation of the throne and, on the other, to win over Joseph and the Josephite party to his unionist policy. This interpretation of Michael's aim in issuing the

---

[37] Text, p. 32, col. 1. On Michael's oration to the people in 1261 see Pachymeres, 153, line 9 up to 155, line 12 (cf. Geanakoplos, *Emperor Michael*, 120).

[38] Text, p. 32, cols. 1-2.

[39] For θεοπρόβλητος see Lampe, *Patristic Greek Lexicon*, 632.

document—in effect to legitimize his reign through emphasis on God's selection of him as the instrument of God's will, seems pointed up even further in the use made by Michael's chancery (as by other contemporary official Greek sources inspired by Michael) of various titles that were applied to Michael. Thus the use of such Old Testament titles as the "New David," the "New Moses," even the "New Zerubbabel" (who restored the Jewish Temple as Michael did Hagia Sophia) [40]— all express a sense of revivification or renewal as in the work of the Jewish prophets and rulers of old. Even more meaningful, however, is the Christian title, the "New Constantine," [41] which Michael naturally preferred above all. For like Constantine the Great of the fourth century Michael did not see himself as the founder of a new Empire, but, as he repeatedly puts it in this document, as a "restorer" and "reestablisher" of the Roman Empire. In Michael's case, however, the Empire was restored and revived not because of a pagan barbarian threat as in Constantine's time, but, ironically, it was freed from the pollution of other Christians, the Latins and their "heresy," and the purity of the Orthodox faith thereby restored.

---

[40] On these titles see esp. text in Previale, "Un panegyrico inedito per Michele VIII Paleologo," 20; also Geanakoplos, *Emperor Michael*, 121, n. 8.

[41] Pachymeres, 1:300, attributes to Germanos, the future patriarch, the invention of the title the "New Constantine." Cf. Acropolites, *Historia*, 183-84; and Gregoras, *Historia*, 1:86.

THE CHRISTIAN GOSPEL AND SOCIAL RESPONSIBILITY

The Eastern Orthodox Tradition in History

JOHN MEYENDORFF

St. Vladimir's Orthodox Theological Seminary

If the Christian East has any established reputation, it consists in its purported detachment from historical realities, its concern with "mysticism," its one-sided dedication to liturgical contemplation of eternal truths, and its forgetfulness of the concrete needs of human society, as such. The issue is of some importance, because Western Christians, in the midst of their own activistic and society-oriented concerns, often have their own minds so well set on this reputation of Eastern Christianity, that meaningful cross-fertilization becomes impossible. If the study of history can help destroy prejudice, it can certainly be of use in this instance, not only for theologians engaged in ecumenism, but also for all those interested in religious experience. Indeed, the very notions of "Christian East" and "Christian West" have now a merely historical significance: the ideas which for centuries have distinguished East and West, as they were geographically, culturally and politically separated, could now become (and indeed have become already) a common inheritance. There are today many Westerners who are "Eastern" Orthodox Christians, and modern Western culture itself is unthinkable without the impact of a Dostoyevsky. On the other hand, indelibly Western religious phenomena, like the million-strong Baptist movement in Russia, are prominent in the "East," not to speak of Marxism itself, which was conceived in industrial England, but found its radical application in Eastern Europe and, more recently, in the Far East.

Our time, therefore, is a time of confrontations and options. Ideas and values, detached from their historical background, are to be accepted or rejected on the basis of their intrinsic worth. But then the study and understanding of their historical background becomes an even more responsible task. Distinguishing between the permanent and the occasional is particularly indispensable to Orthodox theologians involved in the necessary task of clarifying what is Tradition—the inner consistency of ideas and actions expressed in history with the one apostolic faith—and what are the human "traditions," which reflect the legitimate variety of historical process and, at times, conflict with the unchanging and unchangeable content of the Gospel itself.

The value of the various human "traditions" can be established only on the basis of a faith which gives meaning to history and provides it with a goal, an *eschaton*. Christian initiatives in the life of society are not blind initiatives: they are based on knowledge of what can ultimately be *expected* as the end of human history, and what cannot. Similarly, it is the same *expectation* which provides them with a basis for selection among the initiatives taken by others.

Our discussion of historical developments in the past of Eastern Christianity must therefore start with a definition of eschatological categories.

Three eschatologies

Christianity always rejected the ontological dualism of the Manicheans, and also the idea—common in the Gnosticism of the second century—that visible creation is the work of an inferior Demiurge, distinct from the Transcendent God; instead it affirms the basic goodness of creation, "both visible and invisible." With equal consistency, however, the New Testament maintains an existential dualism between "this world," which is in a state of rebellion against God, and "the world to come," when God will be "all in all." Christians expect "the city to come" and consider themselves only "sojourners" rather than full-fledged citizens in the present world. However, this New Testament eschatology and its practical implications have been lived and understood differently by Christians at different times in history.

(1) The idea that the "Kingdom" will come suddenly, through a single-handed divine *fiat,* in a not-so-distant future was wide-spread in the early Christian communities. This eschatological conception in effect implied that Christians would constantly pray that "the figure of this world may pass away." They would not be concerned at all with the betterment of society, simply because earthly society was destined to an early and catastrophic disappearance. They would consider as unavoidable the ultimate condemnation of the vast majority of mankind and the salvation of only a few. In this perspective even the smallest cell of earthly society, the family, would become a burden; and marriage, though permitted, would not be recommended. The eschatological prayer, "Come, Lord Jesus!" would be understood primarily

as the cry of the "remnant," totally helpless in a hostile world and seeking salvation *from* it, not a responsibility *towards* it.

Such an eschatology provides no basis for any Christian mission to society or to culture. It attributes to God alone, acting without any human cooperation, the task of bringing about a New Jerusalem, which would come down ready-made from heaven. It also forgets those New Testament images of the Kingdom which precisely imply co-operation or "synergy": the mustard seed, which grows into a big tree, the yeast which leavens the whole dough, the fields ready for the harvest. An eschatology of withdrawal is, of course, psychologically understandable and even spiritually justified in times when the Christian community is forced to return to itself through external pressure and persecution, as in the first centuries and in more recent times as well; but if transformed into a system, it clearly betrays the biblical message taken as a whole. The "New Jerusalem" is not only a free gift of God coming from heaven, but also the seal and the fulfillment of all the legitimate efforts and aspirations of mankind, transfigured and transformed into a new creation.

(2) The emphasis on human achievement leads to another and opposite extreme: a pelagianizing and optimistic eschatology based on a belief in the never-ending progress of human society. In strongly maintaining that history has a meaning and goal, this belief in progress—in its capitalistic or marxist forms—is a post-Christian phenomenon. It is still technically an "eschatology" and has inspired much of modern European and American culture during the past three centuries. In the past decade many Christians have also more or less adopted this eschatology. They identify social progress with "new creation," accepting "history" as a guide towards the "New Jerusalem," and defining the primary Christian task in "secular" categories.

This second eschatology, whether or not it calls itself Christian, takes no account of sin and death, from which mankind cannot be redeemed through its own efforts; and thus it ignores the most real and the most tragic aspect of human existence. It seems to aspire after an unending civilization, ever imprisoned by death, which in fact would be "as horrible as immortality for a man who is prisoner of sickness and old age." [1] By accepting historical determinism, it renounces the very center of the Christian message: *liberation* from "the powers and principalities" of history through Christ's resurrection and through

---

[1] G. P. Fedotov, *Novy Grad* (New York, 1952), 323.

the prophetic promise of a cosmic transfiguration, brought by God, not by man.

(3) The biblical concept of "prophecy" leads us to a third form of eschatology which does justice both to God's power and to man's freedom and responsibility. Prophecy, both in the Old Testament and the New, is neither a simple foretelling of the future nor a declaration of inevitability. It is "either a promise or a menace." [2] In other words, as the Russian religious philosopher Fedotov rightly points out, it is always *conditional*. The "good things" of the future are a promise to the *faithful*, while cataclysms are a menace to the *sinners*. Both, however, are ultimately conditioned by man's freedom. God would refrain from destroying Sodom for the sake of ten faithful, and when the Ninevites repented, he pardoned Nineveh, sparing it from the doom promised by Jonah.

For God is not bound by any natural or historical necessity. Man himself, in his freedom, is to decide whether the coming of Jesus will be a frightful judgment or a joyous marriage feast. No eschatology will be faithful to the Christian message unless it maintains both the power of God over history and the task of man, which resides in the very real freedom which was restored to him in Jesus Christ for the building of the Kingdom of God.

These are the initial considerations which will provide us with a point of reference in viewing and evaluating facts of the past.

The legacy of Byzantium

Rome and its imperial tradition exercised an indelible influence, both in the West and in the East, on the way Christians approached all issues involving society and culture. The Christian Church condemned apocalyptic Montanism, with its preaching of withdrawal from history and its negation of culture; but it welcomed the opportunity offered to it by the conversion of Constantine, and in the East even counted him among the saints, "equal to the apostles." This was a clear option taken in favor of assuming responsibility for the whole of the "inhabited earth" (οἰκουμένη). This world was to be influenced not only directly through word and sacrament, but also indirectly though the means which were at the disposal of the State: legislation, administration, and even (more questionably) military force, since now all wars waged against the infidels were seen as holy wars.

---

[2] *Ibid.*, 327.

There are innumerable legislative texts which illustrate the fact that the Christian empire, without any formal objection on the part of the Church, considered the emperor as a direct appointee of God to rule and protect society. "It is in the name of the Lord Jesus Christ," writes emperor Justinian (527-565), "that we always start every undertaking and action. For from Him we received full charge of the empire; by Him, we concluded a permanent peace with the Persians; through Him we have dethroned the fiercest and strongest tyrants; through Him, we have overcome numberless difficulties; by Him it has been given to us to defend Africa and reduce it under our power; by Him, to govern (the state) wisely and keep it strongly under our sway... Hence we place our life under His Providence and prepare to organize our armed troops and our officers..." [3]

As is well known, the tradition of christianized autocracy produced different historical forms in the West and in the East. The West experienced the fall of Rome in the fifth century and after the ephemeral attempts of Carolingians and Ottonians to assume the old Roman imperial power, and after the epic struggles by popes to ensure the Church's independence, the *Roman pontiff* was finally recognized as a legitimate successor of the Caesars, acknowledged both as the religious and the political leader of Christendom. By contrast, in the East the original empire lasted until 1453. But if this is so are historians right in assuming that the system of government accepted by the Byzantine State and Church was a form of "caesaropapism?" This is a serious contention. If it were true, it would imply that in the Medieval period the Orthodox Church did in fact capitulate to the "secular," i.e. did accept the second type of eschatology which sees the Kingdom of God as fully "continuous" with secular history. In that case Orthodox theology today would be inconsistent with its own past in criticizing "secularism."

It would certainly be impossible to present here a full historical discussion of the problem of Church and society in Byzantium, and I will limit myself to a few brief statements, which could easily be backed with texts and facts:

(1) *Byzantine Christianity never accepted the belief that the emperor had absolute authority in matters of faith or ethics.* [4] It could not accept such a belief for the simple and general reason that it never

---

[3] *Codex Just.* I, 27, 2.
[4] I discuss this point at length in my study of "Justinian, the Empire and the Church," *Dumbarton Oaks Papers* 22 (1968), 45-60.

was a religion of authority. The ever-recurring theological controversies continued before and frequently after the meeting of councils
called by the emperors to settle them (cf. the triadological controversies after Nicea; the christological controversies after Ephesus and
Chalcedon, etc.) Imperial edicts did not stop them. At the time of the
Paleologan dynasty (1261-1453), each successive emperor was actively
pushing the Church towards union with Rome. The union, however,
failed to take place.

(2) *It is not by opposing to the emperors another competing
authority* (i.e. *that of the priesthood) that Byzantine society avoided
caesaropapism, but by referring all authority directly to God.* This
theocentric view of the universe and of the Church is well expressed in
the classic text on the subject, the Sixth Novella of Justinian: "The
greatest blessings of mankind are the gifts of God which have been
granted us by the mercy on high—the priesthood and the imperial
authority. The priesthood ministers to things divine: the imperial
authority is set over, and shows diligence in things human; but both
proceed from one and the same source, and both adorn the life of
man." [5]

In the West this famous text provoked an *institutional* struggle
between two legally defined powers, the *sacerdotium* and the *imperium*;
but in Byzantium it was understood in a *christological* context. In Christ,
the two natures are united, without separation or confusion, into one
single *hypostasis*, or person, who is the unique source of their united
(though distinct) existence. The adoption of this christological model
as a pattern for the organization of society illustrates quite well the
contrast between the legally-minded West and the eschatologically
oriented East. [6] Indeed, according to Justinian, the common aim of
the empire and the priesthood is "a happy concord (άρμονία) which
will bring forth all good things for mankind," clearly an eschatological
goal actually undefinable in legal, political, or social terms.

Of course, Byzantine Christians were aware of the fact that all
humans—emperors, patriarchs, priests—would inevitably be in some

---

[5] English tr. in E. Barker, *Social and Political Thought in Byzantium* (Oxford,
1957), 75-76. In spite of the obvious meaning of this solemn text, the idea that
Byzantine emperors attributed to themselves the priestly dignity appears in
authoritative publications today. Cf. Walter Ullmann, *Medieval Political Thought*
(London, 1975), 33-34.
[6] On the consequences, see F. Dvornik, *Early Christian and Byzantine Political
Philosophy: Origins and Background* II. Dumbarton Oaks Studies 9 (Washington, D.C., 1966).

way unfaithful to the Christian ideal set before them, and thus they never
ascribed infallibility to any individual nor even to any legally defined
institution. This is precisely why the history of the Byzantine Church
offers innumerable examples of highly authoritative voices challenging
the arbitrary actions either of emperors or of ecclesiastical authorities.
The examples of St. John Chrysostom, St. Maximus the Confessor,
St. John of Damascus, and St. Theodore of Studios are well-known.
They cannot be considered as exceptions to the rule, because their
writings have been widely read by generations of Byzantine Christians
and were always among the most authoritative patterns of social
behavior in the Christian East. None of them, however, challenged
either the political system or the eschatological ideal defined by Justinian. None of them denied the principle that "divine" and "human"
things are inseparable since the Incarnation, and must become "christ-
like," i.e. the "human" must live in "harmony" with the divine. None
of them preached either an apocalyptic withdrawal from culture or a
separation between the spiritual and the secular which would give
"autonomy" to the latter.

How did this ideal manifest itself in practice? There is no doubt
that Byzantine society, like medieval Western society, made continuous
efforts to integrate Christian principles into its legislative texts and
its daily practice. This applies to both the State and the Church.
"We believe that there is nothing higher and greater that we can do,"
wrote the emperor Leo III in his *Ecloga*, "than to govern in judgment
and justice those who are committed (by God) to our care, to the end
that the bonds of all manner of injustice may be loosened, the oppression imposed by force may be set at naught, and the assaults of
wrongdoers may be repelled." [7] Similarly, the Church was required,
by its canon law, to use its wealth in building and administrating institutions of social welfare. [8] The extent to which both the State and
the Church practiced social welfare is wider than one usually imagines, [9]
even if the negative institutions inherited from pagan antiquity, such
as slavery, were only humanized without being fully suppressed.

The overall concern for the *humanum* implied no clear distinction of
jurisdiction between the State and the Church; unity of purpose was
the very content of the ideal of "harmony" defined by Justinian. This

---

[7] Barker, *op. cit.*, 84-85.

[8] See for example, canons 8 and 10 of the Council of Chalcedon.

[9] See D. J. Constantelos, *Byzantine Philanthropy and Social Welfare* (New
Brunswick, N.J., 1968).

unity of purpose justified the concern and the power of the emperor
to administer practical Church affairs (choice of patriarchs, convocation
of councils, definition of limits of ecclesiastical jurisdiction, etc.) as
well as the participation of Church officials in political responsibility.
Certainly the canon law of the Church forbade both the appointment of
clerics by civil authority (II Nicea, canon 3) and the assumption of any
secular dignity by clerics (Chalcedon, canon 7). But these canons never
served as a guarantee against abuses. On the other hand, the Church
never considered it an abuse to ensure continuity of the Justinianic
"harmony" by buttressing the State in times of need. Thus the "ecumenical patriarch" of Constantinople was, in fact, a political official of
the Empire, the guarantor of imperial legitimacy; and he would automatically assume the regency of the State when the need for this arose.
The roles played either as regents or political leaders by patriarchs
Sergius I (610-638), Nicholas Mysticus (901-907, 912-925), Arsenius
Autoreianus (1255-1259, 1261-1265), and John Calecas (1334-1347)
are examples of this. The typically Byzantine notion of the inseparable
union between a universal Church and an ideally universal Empire
was also expressed in the very last days of Byzantium. Patriarch
Anthony (1389-1390, 1391-1397) was asked by the Great Prince of
Moscow, Basil I, whether the commemoration of the Byzantine emperor's name could be dropped at liturgical services in Russia. "My
son, the patriarch answered, you are wrong in saying: We have a
church but no emperor. It is not possible for Christians to have a
church and not to have an empire. Church and empire have a great unity
and community; nor is it possible for them to be separated from one
another." [10]

The Slavs, spiritual children of Byzantium, certainly learned the
lesson. The Byzantine pattern of relations between Church and society
was faithfully adopted by them with the same ideal of a "harmonious"
union in a common allegiance to Christ. Creating their little "Byzan-
tiums" in Preslav, in Ohrid, in Trnovo, in Kiev and in Moscow, Slavic
tsars and princes recognized the Church as their cultural inspiration
and guide; and the Church assumed this role willingly, translating
Byzantine texts into the venacular, and assuming social and political
responsibility whenever the need arose. Thus St. Alexis of Moscow
became for a time regent of Muscovite Russia (1353-1378), and his
example was later followed by Patriarch Filaret (1619-1634). Even

---

[10] Barker, op. cit., 195.

the great St. Sergius of Radonezh used his spiritual prestige against the factional feuds of Russian princes.

What then is the legacy of Byzantium to the contemporary Orthodox Church? Theologically, it is primarily in the affirmation that just as man, individually, is destined to "deification" and is fully himself when he is in communion with God, a communion which was realized by Jesus Christ, and in Him made accessible to all in the faith, so human society is called to conform itself to God's presence and become the Kingdom of God. The ambiguity of the Byzantine experiment resided, however, on the level of eschatology. Could the Justinianic "harmony," an eschatological ideal, be realized concretely in history? Was Byzantium so fully transformed and transfigured as a society that it found itself in full conformity with God's plan, or was it still a "fallen" society, under the power of evil, sin, and death?

The Byzantine Empire, as a political and cultural entity, never resolved this ambiguity of its claims. The Church, however, always maintained the *distinction* between the priesthood and the empire, between the liturgical, sacramental, and eucharistic anticipation of the Kingdom on the one hand and the empirical life of still-fallen humanity on the other. This polarity between the "already now" and the "not yet" was also constantly proclaimed in the large and prosperous Byzantine monastic movement, whose withdrawal from society and non-conformity to the standards imposed by the empire served constantly as a prophetic reminder that there *cannot* be total "harmony" before the *parousia,* that the Roman Empire is not yet the Kingdom of God, that in order to share in Christ's victory over the world Christians must themselves challenge the laws and the logics of fallen mankind.

Modern times

The survival of Eastern Orthodox Christianity after the fall of Byzantium and of the other Christian empires effectively proves that Orthodox Christians did not believe in the empire as a fully "realized eschatology," but rather—as the monks have always maintained—they discovered the Kingdom in the Eucharist and the personal experience of God, accessible to the members of Christ's body.

History itself forced them into recognizing the "other-worldliness" of Christianity, since the "world" had suddenly become hostile again.

The Ottoman Empire, which during four centuries held under its sway the Balkans, Asia Minor, and the Middle East (much of the former Byzantine territories) was a Moslem state, which tolerated the existence of a large Christian population but forbade all Christian mission and made any cultural or intellectual development practically impossible. During all these centuries the Byzantine liturgy, with its rich hymnography, its explicit eschatological character, and its ability to unite the congregation into a real experience of the body of Christ, became the principle and largely self-sufficient expression of Christianity. Also, following the Byzantine tradition mentioned above, which implied that the patriarch of Constantinople would assume responsibility for society as a whole in the absence of the emperor, the ecumenical patriarch became the *ethnarch*, or civil and religious head of the entire Orthodox Christian population of the Turkish realm by investiture of the Sultan. Thus, while the Church did not actually renounce its mission to society, this mission in practice became limited by the boundaries of a ghetto. This situation, enforced by the tragedy of history, was unfortunately to remain as a habit even when times again became more favorable to mission.

Meanwhile, in Russia a new and powerful Orthodox empire had taken shape and seemed originally destined to assume the role of a second Byzantium or, if one wishes, a "third Rome." However, the political and social ideas which eventually prevailed in Russia were those of a Western secular state, with Byzantine formulae used mainly to justify autocratic power as such. The ecclesial and canonical corrective which had been acknowledged in Byzantium was lacking. It is in Russia, however, at a time when the empire had not yet taken its final turn towards secular ideals, that a significant theological controversy took place precisely on the social role of the Church. The controversy opposed "Possessors" and "Non-Possessors," two monastic and ecclesiastical groups, equally devoted to the idea of a relevant Christian mission to society but standing for different forms of action and witness. [12] The "Possessors," led by St. Joseph of Volotsk (1440-1515) found themselves in the tradition of Byzantine theocratic society. They defended the right of the Church, and particularly of the monasteries, to possess great wealth, which was destined to be used for social action: hospitals, schools, and various forms of welfare. This social witness was seen by them as essential to the very nature of

---

[11] On the Turkish period, see S. Runciman, *The Great Church in Captivity: A Study of the Patriarchate of Constantinople from the Eve of the Turkish Conquest to the Greek War of Independence* (Cambridge, 1968).

[12] For a brilliant analysis of the controversy see G. P. Fedotov, *The Russian Religious Mind* II (Cambridge, Mass., 1962).

Christianity. They were not afraid of the spiritual vulnerability of a rich Church, whose wealth could be used by an inimical State to blackmail it. They believed in the future of a "holy Russia," whose benevolent tsars would support the Church's prosperity and whose ecclesiastical leadership would be forever immune to the temptations of bourgeois comfort, using its wealth only for good works.

The "Non-Possessors," meanwhile, considered that wealth inevitably corrupts, especially that form of wealth which was enjoyed by medieval monastaries: serfs working on immense domains. They saw the mission of the Church primarily as a prophetic witness, pointing to the Kingdom to come. St. Nilus Sorsky (1433-1508) the leader of the "Non-Possessors," inherited the ideals of hesychasm, the mystical and contemplative monasticism of the early Church. He did not trust, as his opponents did, the future of a "holy Russia." He foresaw its secularization and defended the full independence of the Church from the State.

The controversy ended with the victory of the "Possessors." But the "Non-Possessors" were to be largely vindicated by later historical developments. At the time of the secular Enlightenment the Russian Church was deprived of its lands by Peter the Great and Catharine II. It had no means left for a meaningful social witness. Meanwhile, the spiritual heirs of St. Nilus Sorsky—St. Tikhon of Zadonsk (1724-1783), St. Seraphim of Sarov (1759-1833), the *startsy* of Optino— became the most authentic witnesses to Christian experience in the midst of secular society and succeeded in building bridges between traditional Orthodoxy and the religious revival of the *intelligentsia* in the late nineteenth and the early twentieth centuries.

The past two centuries have witnessed tremendous historical changes in the life of the Orthodox Church. The Ottoman Empire disintegrated; and out of this disintegration new nations, whose religious past is rooted in Orthodoxy, were born. Orthodox Russia, after some very hopeful signs of spiritual revival, became the Soviet Union. Millions of Orthodox Christians were dispersed throughout the Western world, where the general frame of reference used in solving "social issues" is determined by Western religious history.

In the midst of this confusion, it was inevitable that the traditional Orthodox values would be severely tested. The new nations in the Balkans, whose cultural identity the Orthodox Church had maintained for centuries of Turkish yoke, had gained their political independence in an atmosphere of secularized Romanticism, which was itself a fruit of the French Revolution. The *nation* itself, not the Christian eschatological and christological ideas, came to be seen as the supreme goal of social action. The Church was frequently unable either to cope with the situation or to discern the spiritual issues at stake. The hierarchs, whose traditional role as "ethnarchs" placed them originally at the forefront of the liberation struggle, soon accepted the comfortable position of obedient civil servants in states led by secularized politicians. Mistaking the new situation for a return to Byzantine theocracy, they identified the interests of the Church with that of secular nationalism. The Church condemned this identification in an official conciliar statement (1872), labeling it as the heresy of "phyletism." But the temptation of religious nationalism remains one of the most basic weaknesses of contemporary Orthodoxy. In fact, it represents a capitulation before a subtle form of secularism, which Byzantium with its universal idea of the empire always avoided.

In Orthodox circles today concern for a social witness of Orthodoxy is frequently voiced. Between the two World Wars, and also after World War II, a remarkable revival of Christian social activism took place in Greece. It achieved significant results in the field of evangelism but was later criticized—with some justification—for its pietistic and protestant-inspired orientation. Meanwhile, on the intellectual level, the Orthodox Church attracted to its fold prominent Russian political economists who had previously been Marxists. This pleiad of "religious philosophers," including S. N. Bulgakov, N. S. Berdyaev, S. L. Frank, P. B. Struve and others, began to exercise its influence in the Church itself; and some of them played an important role in Church affairs just prior to the Revolution. Even if some of them, under the influence of an optimistic Hegelianism, adopted a monistic and static philosophy of the universe, usually know as "sophiology" and not unlike the systems of Tillich or Teilhard, their move "from Marxism to Idealism" is a significant event in the history of Orthodox thought. It still fascinates those involved in the renascent religious thought among Soviet intellectual dissidents today.

What attracted these people back to Orthodoxy? Primarily, its eschatological expectation of a transfigured universe; its belief in "deification" as the ultimate destiny of man; its ability, in its liturgical life and in the spiritual experience of its saints, to anticipate the vision of the second coming. They were drawn to Orthodoxy's ability to maintain a "realized" and not only a futuristic eschatology; to speak of the Kingdom of God not only in terms of concepts, or practical achievements, but also as a real vision of the divine presence.

These are the aspects of the Orthodox Tradition which make it a living hope not only to intellectuals disappointed in Marxist totalitarian socialism but also to those of us whose destiny is to witness to Orthodoxy in the West.

Conclusion

Christian tradition cannot be evaluated only in terms of its "successes" and its "failures." As we all know, the New Testament itself does not offer promises of earthly success to the followers of Jesus. Indeed, this must be so, because the true power of Christ will be manifested to the world only on the *last day*, while the *present* power of the Kingdom is fully revealed only to the eyes of faith. Our brief review of the Orthodox Tradition is certainly not a success story; we have only attempted to suggest the main orientations of Orthodox thought and action *historically*. How these historical facts can find their place in a contemporary doctrinal statement must be left to another occasion.

However, a preliminary conclusion can already be drawn: that a Christian solution of social issues is never either absolute or perfect as long as the *parousia* has not taken place, and that a Christian can live with that imperfection because he knows that the *parousia* will eventually come; but he cannot be reconciled with imperfections as such. The Orthodox Church has condemned the eschatology of "withdrawal," which would justify indifference and inaction. But—and this is particularly important for present dialogues—it will certainly never agree that the Kingdom of God present in the Church as Mystery and as an anticipated eschatological reality, is dependent upon the influence which its members may or may not exercise in secular society. Orthodoxy will always maintain that the starting point, the source, and the criterion for solving social issues are found in the uninterrupted, mysterious, and in a sense transcendent communion of the Eucharistic gathering.

Historically Orthodox Christians frequently looked for substitutes for this initial and basic criterion. The Byzantine Empire provided one; nationalism later presented another. But these historical and spiritual mistakes were ultimately recognized as such. They should not, in any case, justify similar substitutions today.

THE RADICAL REFORMATION

*Essays in Radical, Magisterial, and Catholic
Reformation Church History*

HUMANISM, SCHOLASTICISM, AND THE INTELLECTUAL ORIGINS OF THE REFORMATION

STEVEN OZMENT

Yale University

Biblical Humanists or New Scholastics?

After Luther posted his ninety-five theses in 1517 German humanists became his first identifiable group of supporters. German humanists had long cultivated the liberal arts, opposed religious superstition, and championed a German national culture. The important names here are those of Conrad Celtis (1459-1508), Johannes Trithemius (1462-1516), Willibald Pirckheimer (1470-1528), Conrad Peutinger (1465-1547), Johannes Reuchlin (1455-1522), and Conrad Mutianus Rufus (1471-1526). Those humanists who sided with Luther saw his religious reform as a continuation of their own criticism of scholasticism and efforts to return to the original text of Scripture. While this perception proved in the end to be a misunderstanding of the reformer's full intent, it was initially productive for both sides. [1]

German humanists came to Luther fresh from their own very personal battle with the scholastic theologians of Cologne in the so-called "Reuchlin affair." This was a conflict initiated by a converted Jew named Pfefferkorn, who in 1506 launched an almost successful campaign to suppress Jewish writings. In the course of the campaign Pfefferkorn viciously attacked Johannes Reuchlin, Europe's foremost Christian authority on Hebrew and Jewish learning. Reuchlin had earned Pfefferkorn's wrath by opposing the destruction of Jewish books after the Emperor Maximilian I, under pressure from Pfefferkorn's supporters, ordered Jews in 1509 to surrender their books. Although anti-Semitism rather than hostility to humanist studies was the primary motivation of the Cologne scholastics who backed Pfefferkorn, German humanists interpreted Pfefferkorn's pamphlet attack on Reuchlin as an assault on academic freedom and joined Reuchlin in hot reply. Ulrich von Hutten and the Erfurt humanist Crotus Rubeanus published the most memorable piece in the affair, a gross satire on

---

[1] See the seminal essay by Bernd Moeller, "Die deutschen Humanisten und die Anfänge der Reformation," *ZKG* 70 (1959), 46-61.

scholastics entitled *Letters of Obscure Men*. When Luther was attacked by the church's theologians after 1517 Reuchlin himself drew
a parallel between his own difficulties and those the young reformer
was experiencing. [2]

The breach that later opened between Luther and Erasmus in 1525
did not end collaboration between humanists and Protestant reformers
and this famous confrontation should not be taken as symptomatic of a
larger incompatibility, much less divorce, between humanism and Protestantism. Protestant religious reforms continued to go hand in hand
with humanist educational reforms in Protestant cities and towns
throughout much of the sixteenth century. Protestant reformers did
not abandon humanist belief in the unity of wisdom, eloquence, and
action, even though their views on church doctrine and human nature
gave their educational programs a different content from those of the
humanists. For Protestants everywhere the *studia humanitatis* remained
a more appropriate tool for reform than scholastic dialectic; humanist
studies taught Protestant preachers the languages needed to deal authoritatively with the original text of Scripture and helped them acquire the
rhetorical skills necessary to communicate Protestant doctrine effectively.

There was a fundamental and lasting kinship between humanism
and Protestantism. Neither had been able to find in the dominant late
medieval scholastic traditions either attractive personal models or an
educational program appropriate to the changed society of the sixteenth century. Finding the chivalric and clerical traditions of the
Middle Ages inadequate to both their literary interests and political
aspirations Italian and northern humanists had turned instead to either
classical or Christian antiquity. Protestants, finding medieval religion
incapable of resolving their religious problems, turned back to the
Bible and the Church Fathers. Ignatius of Loyola called attention to

this close connection between humanism and Protestantism and their
common undercutting of church tradition. He warned in his *Spiritual*

---

2 "God be praised that now the monks have found someone else who will give
them more to do than I." Cited by Lewis W. Spitz, "The Course of German
Humanism" in *Itinerarium Italicum: The Profile of the Italian Renaissance in
the Mirror of its European Transformations: Dedicated to Paul Oskar Kristeller
on the Occasion of His 70th Birthday*, eds. H. A. Oberman and T. A. Brady
(Leiden, 1975), 409. A recent study has found humanist association with Reuchlin exaggerated. See James Overfield, "A New Look at the Reuchlin Affair," in
Studies in Medieval and Renaissance Thought, 8, ed. H. L. Adelson (Lincoln,
Neb.; 1971), 167-207.

Exercises against reading the Bible and the Church Fathers directly and apart from the guidance of "scholastic doctors such as Thomas Aquinas, Bonaventure, and the Master of the Sentences (Peter Lombard)"; the latter, Ignatius argued, possess a "clearer understanding" of both Scripture and the Church Fathers inasmuch as they are "of more recent date." [3]

The positive association of humanism and Protestantism, especially in the early years of the Reformation, is only one side of the story, however, as contemporary humanists and kindred critics of mature Protestantism were quick to point out. Erasmus came to view the Lutheran Reformation as a threat to the liberal arts and good learning. [4] Sebastian Franck compared the debate between Luther and Zwingli in 1529 over Christ's presence in the Eucharist with earlier scholastic quarrels between Franciscans and Dominicans over the Immaculate Conception of the Virgin; Franck was personally convinced that the "new scholastics," as he described the Lutherans, would outstrip the papacy in the production of great theological summaries and commentaries on Scripture. [5] Sebastian Castellio accused the Calvinists of reviving the "sophistries of the Sorbonne," while the Lutheran spiritualist Valentin Weigel turned against Philipp Melanchthon, the mind behind the authoritative Lutheran creeds, as a mediocre "Greek grammarian and Aristotelian philosopher." [6]

Biblical humanists or new scholastics—which were the Protestant reformers? Did they begin as humanists only to end up as a new type of scholastic? I would like to argue that in terms of its intellectual history Protestantism can be identified exclusively with neither humanism nor

---

[3] "The scholastic doctors, being of more recent date, not only have a clearer understanding of Holy Scripture and of the teachings of the positive and holy doctors, but also, being enlightened and inspired by the Divine Power, they are helped by the Councils, Canons, and Constitutions of our Holy Mother Church." *The Spiritual Exercises,* trans. by A. Mottola (Garden City, 1964), 140. For an earlier version of this argument cf. Paul L. Nyhus, "Caspar Schatzgeyer and Conrad Pellican: The Triumph of Dissension in the Early Sixteenth Century," *ARG* 61 (1970), 194.

[4] Letter to Martin Bucer (March 2, 1532) in *Erasmus and His Age Selected Letters of Desiderius Erasmus,* eds. H. J. Hillerbrand and M. A. Haworth (New York, 1970), 259-60.

[5] Horst Weigelt, *Sebastian Franck und die lutherische Reformation* (Gütersloh, 1972), 48.

[6] Castellio, *Contra libellum Calvini in quo ostendere conatur Haereticos jure gladij coercendos esse* (1612), L 1 a; Weigel, *Dialogus de Christianismo,* ed. A. Ehrentreich in *Valentin Weigel: Sämtliche Schriften* 4 (Stuttgart-Bad Cannstatt, 1967), 47.

scholasticism, but was rather, from the start, a peculiar blending of both these medieval traditions.

Although the Protestant reformers replaced scholastic dialectic with the rhetorical ideals of humanism when they reformed university curricula (see below), they continued to share the preoccupation of medieval theologians with the definition and defense of church doctrine, albeit on a more homiletical than theoretical level, that is, they were more interested in preaching doctrine than in contemplating it. Protestants made the liberal arts a handmaiden to a continuing medieval theological ideal. The reformers did not take up the educational program of the humanists for its own sake, nor for any latent moral or social possibilities in it, but because they believed it to be the most effective way of achieving the higher end of transmitting Christian doctrine and righteousness to the masses in the vernacular. [7]

The intellectual origins of Protestantism could more easily be outlined if there existed simple, solitary definitions of humanism and scholasticism. This, unfortunately, is not the case. There are today at least four distinct schools of thought on the nature of Renaissance humanism. [8] One builds on the work of Jacob Burckhardt and sees the Renaissance as the birth of modern consciousness and praises humanists as advocates of individualism, secularism, and moral autonomy against medieval Christian culture. A second school follows the reverse thesis of Giuseppe Tofannin and views Italian humanism as an epitome of medieval Christian culture and humanists as true champions of Christian Neoplatonism and Augustinianism against the heterodox and pagan strains in Averroism and Aristotelianism. Still another school of thought, certainly the dominant point of view in the United States, follows Paul Oskar Kristeller in more modestly restricting the definition of humanism to the scholarly pursuit of eloquence, viewing it as strictly an educational and cultural program dedicated to rhetoric, scholarship, good language and literature, with only a secondary interest in metaphysics and moral philosophy, whether Christian or pagan. A final school is that connected with the contro-

---

[7] Cf. Alain Dufour, "Humanisme et Reformation: Etat de la question," *XIIe Congres Internationale des Sciences Historiques Vienne, 29 Aout-5 Septembre 1965: Rapports* III (Horn/Wien, 1965), 57-74.

[8] I have extrapolated this summary from Donald Weinstein, "In Whose Image and Likeness? Interpretations of Renaissance Humanism," *JHI* 33 (1972), 165-76, and Helmar Junghans, "Der Einfluss des Humanismus auf Luthers Entwicklung bis 1518," *Luther-Jahrbuch 1970*, ed. Franz Lau (Hamburg, 1970), 45-51.

versial work of Hans Baron, which portrays Florentine humanists as proponents of republican liberty and civic responsibility, who urged urban elites to study ancient history and literature primarily for its political and moral wisdom. [9] Scholasticism is at least as complex a phenomenon. The article on scholasticism in the *Encyclopedia of Philosophy*, for example, foregoes a definition altogether and directs the reader to "see Augustinianism; Averroism; Medieval Philosophy; Ockhamism; *scientia media* and Molinism; Scotism; and Thomism." [10]

Humanism and scholasticism not only defy simple, solitary definitions, but also resist a prevalent scholarly tendency to depict them as mortal enemies. The two movements actually originated together in Italy in the thirteenth century and developed side by side throughout and beyond the Renaissance; attacks on Aristotelianism by humanists like Petrarch and Leonardo Bruni were, in Kristeller's phrase, only "interludes within a long period of peaceful coexistence." [11] An authority on German humanism has also found the relationship between humanist poets and scholastic theologians at the University of Erfurt, the first north German University to introduce humanist studies in the fifteenth century, to be one of "peaceful coexistence." [12] At the University of Heidelberg humanists and scholastics not only coexisted peacefully, but were also very close to each other in their reform proposals. There scholastics like Johannes Wenck urged biblical studies and stressed the importance of applied knowledge ("nützlich erkenntnis") in an effort to broaden the narrow traditional scholastic curriculum. [13] It has been suggested that in terms of their intellectual

---

[9] Baron's thesis was set forth in *The Crisis of the Early Italian Renaissance*: *Civic Humanism and Republican Liberty in an Age of Classicism and Tyranny* I-II (Princeton, 1955), and has received sharp criticism from Jerrold E. Siegel, "'Civic Humanism' or Ciceronian Rhetoric?," *Past and Present* 34 (1966), 3-48, who found more rhetoric than active defense of republican ideals among Italian humanists. Baron's reply: "Leonardo Bruni: 'Professional Rhetorician' or 'Civic Humanist?'," *Past and Present* 36 (1967), 21-37. A more recent criticism of Baron's work is David Robey, "P. P. Vergerio the Elder: Republicanism and Civic Values in the Work of an Early Humanist," *Past and Present* 58 (1973), 3-37.

[10] Vol. 7 (New York, 1967), 324.

[11] "Humanism and Scholasticism in the Italian Renaissance" in *Studies in Renaissance Thought and Letters* (Rome, 1956), 576-77; "Florentine Platonism and Its Relations with Humanism and Scholasticism," *Church History* 8 (1939), 211. Cf. also R. W. Southern, *Medieval Humanism* (New York, 1970), 49.

[12] Junghans, *Luther Jahrbuch* (1970), 65.

[13] Gerhard Ritter, *Die Heidelberger Universität* I: *Das Mittelaltar (1386-1508)* (Heidelberg, 1936), 421-31, 450.

origins and approach to university studies many fifteenth century thinkers were actually hybrids of scholasticism and humanism— " 'half humanist' and 'half scholastic' in outlook." [14] What Charles Trinkaus has described as "theologia rhetorica," the union of theological theory with practical preaching, was actually as much an ideal of reform-minded scholastics as of the humanist critics of scholasticism. [15]

Not only were humanist attacks on subtlety, ineloquence, and impracticality not without precedent among scholastic theologians (think of Jean Gerson and Nicholas of Clémanges), but humanists also seldom let their criticism of scholasticism lead them to question the basic Christian content of scholastic learning. Critical of scholastic form and method, they became quite docile before the capital points of scholastic doctrine. Lorenzo Valla, for example, one of the most critical humanists, censured Thomas Aquinas's preoccupation with logic and metaphysics and his barbarous Latin style and even described his theology as inferior to that of the Latin and Greek fathers, yet he accepted Aquinas as a saint whose doctrine was sound. [16] Erasmus's answer to those who accused him of undermining scholastic theology expresses much late medieval humanist sentiment on this issue: "As for scholastic theology," Erasmus writes, "it has not been my wish to abolish it, but that it may be more authentic and more serious; in this, unless I am mistaken, I am promoting and not hurting it." [17] Those who chose to abolish scholastic doctrine as well as to criticize scholastic method became Protestants.

Despite the complexity of the concepts and the historical movements, humanism and scholasticism do have definable distinguishing characteristics. The most basic is their different views on the proper method

---

[14] Spitz, "The Course of German Humanism," 375-76.

[15] Charles Trinkaus, *In Our Image and Likeness: Humanity and Divinity in Italian Humanist Thought* II (London, 1970), 770.

[16] Hanna H. Gray, "Valla's *Encomium of St. Thomas Aquinas* and the Humanist Conception of Christian Antiquity," *Essays in History and Literature Presented by the Fellows of the Newberry Library to Stanley Pargellis,* ed. by H. Bluhm (Chicago, 1965), 37-51. Cf. also Lewis W. Spitz, *The Religious Renaissance of the German Humanists* (Cambridge, Mass., 1963), 8, 38, 206, 275; Trinkaus, *In Our Image and Likeness* II, 766.

[17] Letter to Louis Ber (March 30, 1529) in *Erasmus and His Age,* 224. See also Christian Dolfen, *Die Stellung des Erasmus von Rotterdam zur scholastischen Methode* (Osnabrück, 1936), 51, 82. On the threat of humanist method to the scholastic tradition in all fields of learning see Charles G. Nauert, Jr., "The Clash of Humanists and Scholastics: An Approach to Pre-Reformation Controversies," *Sixteenth Century Journal* 4 (1973), 12-13.

and goal of education. Humanists read classical authors (orators, poets, historians, and moral philosophers) directly in their original tongue and urged that such study of primary sources be made the core of the Arts curriculum. This approach to education tended to make the individual scholar rather than an established tradition of interpretation the authority on a subject. Scholastics, on the other hand, approached their subjects, whether biblical, theological, or philosophical, indirectly, by juxtaposing the views of recognized past authorities. For scholastics the scholar's basic task was not to judge tradition from the allegedly superior vantage point of the original source—this was seen to be the constant threat of purely humanist studies—but rather to strive to harmonize divergent opinions on a subject, reconciling authorities rather than exposing and rejecting them. Where humanists engaged in the edition of original sources on the basis of the best manuscripts at hand, scholastics wrote summaries of traditional teaching and concordances of discordant opinions. Even when scholastic theologians edited texts, as the Augustinians did the works of their founder, they continued to be consumed by questions of its doctrinal unity and the continuity of historical interpretation.

A second distinction between humanism and scholasticism is the order or priorities to which their different vocations and educational philosophies led. Humanists, as orators and rhetoricians, gave right living and good deeds—the active civic life—priority over right thinking and correct confession. Scholastics, as defenders of church doctrine and tradition, observed a reverse order of priorities. Humanists were of course not indifferent to either the quality of their thought, the truthfulness of their assertions, or the importance of tradition. [18] But unlike the scholastic theologians, they judged such things by their larger moral ends. Although many later Renaissance thinkers (post 1527) seem to have become jaded intellectuals, at home with abstraction and hierarchical thinking and viewing man as basically a creature of intellect rather than of will, this was a far cry from the early humanist movement and the essence of humanism. Early Renaissance thinkers rejected the abstract man of classical and theological anthropology, with his tiered faculties of reason, will, and sensual appetite.

---

[18] As Sem Dresden summarizes: "One (humanist) writer might lay emphasis on the *vita contemplativa*, another on 'civic humanism,' but all acknowledged the need for and value of both and endeavored to do justice to both at the same time." "The Profile of the Reception of the Italian Renaissance in France" in *Itinerarium Italicum*, 184.

To them man was a complex unity, driven mainly by passion and will, who found self-fulfillment not in withdrawn contemplation of eternal verities, but in active engagement in society. [19] It was not a question of simply making will supreme over intellect within the traditional hierarchical view of man, as Scotists and Ockhamists had earlier done, but of breaking altogether with this traditional conceptual scheme. German humanism in the late fifteenth century has been described as practical, didactic, and moralistic; "action-oriented and people-directed," German humanists rejected abstract and merely antiquarian pursuits. [20] It was characteristic of the early humanist movement generally to scorn scholastics above all for "abstracting from life." Against such abstraction Petrarch made his famous declaration: "It is better to will the good than to know the truth." [21] There is an abiding disinclination among humanists to pursue doctrinal questions beyond a certain point, to make inquiries for what seemed to be the sake of inquiries. This trait stands out especially in Erasmus, who saw the very fall of the church from her true mission in the evolution of church doctrine during the disputatious councils of the Patristic era. [22] When Erasmus challenged Luther on the issue of free will, it was because he considered Luther's doctrine of the will's bondage to sin to be detrimental to morality *even if the doctrine were true.* [23] This reflects the humanist's order of priorities. The consequences of ideas are seen to be more important than the ideas themselves; the effects of a religious doctrine must also be considered when one assesses its truthfulness.

As the church's theologians scholastics had a peculiar stake in tradition and church dogma. They were vocationally inclined to make the abstract pursuit of truth, or correct confession, the overriding preoccupation. In the late Middle Ages scholastic theology became the most disciplined, and unrelenting form of the medieval *fides quaerens*

---

[19] William Bouwsma, "Changing Assumptions in Later Renaissance Culture," *Viator* 7 (1976), 421-40.

[20] Spitz, "The Course of German Humanism," 390-97.

[21] Cited by Hanna H. Gray, "Renaissance Humanism: The Pursuit of Eloquence" in *Renaissance Essays,* eds. P. O. Kristeller and P. Wiener (New York, 1968), 203.

[22] Letter to John Carondelet (Jan. 5, 1522/23), in *Erasmus and His Age,* 168-69.

[23] "Fingamus igitur in aliquo sensu verum esse, quod docuit Vuyclevus, Lutherus asseruit, quicquid fit a nobis, non libero arbitrio, sed mera necessitate fieri, quid inutilius, quam hoc paradoxon evulgari mundo?" *De libero arbitrio* I a 10 in *Erasmus von Rotterdam. Ausgewählte Schriften* 4 (Darmstadt, 1969), 18.

intellectum. Whereas humanists, alert to the ethical consequences of theological doctrines, insisted that good deeds should be a test of creedal truth, scholastics, sensitive to the necessity of an abiding body of truth, insisted that true creeds must be the fount of good deeds. Luther, who received the most intensive scholastic training, considered his doctorate in theology grounds to contest even the pope on matters of doctrine, whereas Erasmus could poke fun at his degree in theology, calling it a "foolish project," no more than an adjustment to the custom of the day. [24] For Luther, if doctrine was true, life had to adjust to it, regardless of the difficulty or the cost. The eternal truth of an idea was more important than its short term temporal consequences.

Protestantism and Humanist Educational Reforms

Protestants came to embrace the humanist program of studies and set it in place of the scholastic. Luther himself had come under humanist influence in the early 1500's during his training in the Arts at the University of Erfurt, the most humanistically progressive German university at the time. He witnessed an open rift between Erfurt's humanists and scholastics after Nikolaus Marschalk had transported the linguistic tools (classical Latin, Greek, and Hebrew) and the rhetorical skills of Italian humanism to the University. Erfurt humanists were also prominent in the Reuchlin affair after 1512. Although they were trained scholastics, Luther's philosophy teachers at Erfurt, Jodocus Trutfetter and Bartholomaüs Arnoldi von Usingen, were also sympathetic to humanism, and one of Luther's closest friends, fellow monk Johannes Lang, an expert Hebraist and Graecist, became prior of the Augustinian order in Erfurt in 1516. Before he went to Wittenberg Luther's own Augustinian order and the Erfurt faculty of Arts had exposed him to a humanism which encouraged the study of ancient languages, especially Greek, and critically juxtaposed the Bible and the writings of the Church Fathers with scholastic theology. [25]

The University of Wittenberg, located according to a contemporary description "in termino civilitatis," was founded in 1502, the second youngest German university of the Age of Reformation (after the

---

[24] Wilhelm Borth, *Die Luthersache (Causa Lutheri) 1517-24: Die Anfänge der Reformation als Frage von Politik und Recht* (Lübeck/Hamburg, 1970), 23; Johan Huizinga, *Erasmus and the Age of Reformation* (New York, 1957), 62.
[25] Junghans, *Luther Jahrbuch (1970)*, 64-76.

University of Frankfurt an der Oder, founded in 1506).[26] Since its
founding the University had favored the *via antiqua* and listed its
courses according to the teaching of Duns Scotus (*via Scoti*) and
Thomas Aquinas (*via Thomae*). The *via moderna* was represented
by Luther's Ockhamist philosophy teacher in Erfurt, Trutfetter, who
taught in Wittenberg between 1507 and 1510. Although the University
had a contingent of academic humanists since its inception, the dominance of the scholastics within the Arts faculty had caused the *studia
humaniora* to be deemphasized. Still, between 1502 and 1514 a number
of humanist reforms were begun. A modern Latin grammar replaced
that of Alexander of Villa Dei; better Latin translations of Aristotle's
works were introduced; Greek was intermittently taught and Greek
texts published; geography and ethnology became part of the curriculum; and mathematics was given a special emphasis. These were
all measures congenial to the reforms later introduced by Luther and
Philip Melanchthon in 1518.[27]

Already before the fateful assault on scholastic theology in September, 1517 in the *Disputation Against Scholastic Theology,* Luther
had described Aristotle, Porphyry, and the scholastic commentaries on
Peter Lombard's *Sentences* as "hopeless studies" (*perdita studia*) and
"tyrants" within the schools. A few months thereafter he boasted to his
friend Lang that a new theology and St. Augustine were ascendant in
Wittenberg and Aristotle's "final doom" only a matter of time.[28] By
May 9, 1518 Luther could pen a famous letter to Trutfetter in which
he not only defended the new direction of the Wittenberg theologians,
but also declared his conviction that the church would never be reformed until canons, decretals, and scholastic theology, philosophy,

[26] G. A. Benrath, "Die deutsche evangelische Universität der Reformations-
zeit," in H. Rössler and G. Franz, *Universität und Gelehrtenstand 1400-1800*
(Limburg/Lahn, 1970), 63-83.

[27] Max Steinmetz, "Die Universität Wittenberg und der Humanismus (1502-
1521)" in *450 Jahre Martin Luther Universität Halle-Wittenberg* (Halle, 1952),
108-10, 112-16; E. G. Schwiebert, "New Groups and Ideas at the University
of Wittenberg," *ARG* 49 (1958), 65, 67; Maria Grossmann, "Wittenberg Printing,
Early Sixteenth Century" in *Sixteenth Century Essays and Studies,* ed. Carl S.
Meyer (St. Louis, 1970), 53-74. The conservative bent of Wittenberg humanism
prior to Melanchthon's arrival is illustrated by Otto Beckmann, a leading humanist,
who, despite his dislike of scholasticism, refused to make sweeping changes in
the curriculum. He decided against the Reformation in 1519. Nikolaus Müller,
Die Wittenberger Bewegung (Leipzig, 1911), 236.

[28] To John Lang (Feb. 8, 1517), *WABr* I, p. 88 = *LW* 48, p. 37; (May 18,
1517), *WABr* I, p. 99 = *LW* 48, p. 41.

and logic were eradicted and new studies put in their place. [29] Between 1518 and 1519 direct efforts were made to eliminate Aristotelian studies from the University curriculum. Luther requested that the course on Aristotle's *Ethics* be made elective "so that students could spend more time with Scripture and true theology." [30] Thrice within as many months he begged permission to drop the traditional scholastic lectures on Aristotle. Writing directly to Elector Frederick the Wise, founder of the University, he asked that the Thomist lecture on Aristotle's *Physics* be removed and a simple historical study of Aristotle (*lectio textualis*) put in its place. He wanted the Thomist lecture on Aristotle's logical writings replaced by a lecture on Ovid's *Metamorphoses* and expressed his hope for a speedy demise of the Scotist lectures on the same body of Aristotle's works. [31] In March, 1519 Luther declared to Georg Spalatin, chaplain and private secretary to Frederick the Wise, that lectures on Aristotle's *Physics, Metaphysics,* and *De Anima* were unworthy of Wittenberg students. [32]

The new curriculum in the University was largely the work of Philip Melanchthon, the great-nephew of Reuchlin, who would earn the title "Teacher of Germany." Melanchthon came to Wittenberg on August 25, 1518 as professor of Greek, and within days of his arrival delivered the traditional inaugural address, choosing the topic, *On Improving the Studies of the Young.* In the name of good letters and classical studies he criticized "those in the schools who... are truly barbarians practicing barbarous arts." He identified them as a terrible progeny—the offspring of Thomas Aquinas, Duns Scotus, Durandus, and Bonaventure (*Thomae, Scoti, Durandi, Seraphici, Cherubici, et reliqui proles*)—who had sprung from the void created by the loss of Greek learning during the long dark night of the Middle Ages. He accused these scholastic theologians of creating contempt for the

---

[29] To Jodocus Trutfetter (May 9, 1518), *WABr* I, p. 170.

[30] To Spalatin (May 18, 1518; Sept. 2, 1518), *WABr* I, pp. 174, 196 = *LW* 48, pp. 63, 82. The criticism of Aristotle's *Ethics* is instructive of the differences the Protestant reformers had with humanists as well as scholastics. Whereas criticism of the *Ethics* was part of the formation of Reformation theology, the embracing of the *Ethics* had been a major feature of civic humanism. See Hans Baron, "Franciscan Poverty and Civic Wealth as Factors in the Rise of Humanistic Thought," *Speculum* 13 (1938), 1-37.

[31] To Spalatin (Dec. 9, 1518; Feb. 7, 1519), *WABr* I, pp. 262, 325. To Frederick the Wise (Feb. 23, 1519), *WABr* I, pp. 349-50. See Karl Bauer, *Die Wittenberger Universitätstheologie und die Anfänge der Deutschen Reformation* (Tübingen, 1928), 109-10.

[32] To Spalatin (Mar. 13, 1519), *WABr* I, p. 359 = *LW* 48, p. 112.

Greek language, causing neglect of mathematics and sacred studies, and corrupting classical rhetoric and dialectic. Melanchthon also traced the fall of piety to the loss of good letters and the broken alliance between the humanities and divinity; curriculum reform would be the key also to a revival of piety. In place of the traditional scholastic curriculum Melanchthon endorsed the study of Greek and Latin philosophers, rhetoricians, and poets, especially Plato, Homer, Virgil, Horace, and "the true historical Aristotle," as distinct from the Aristotle of scholastic commentaries. [33]

By 1520 Luther and Melanchthon had restructured the curriculum. New chairs of Greek and Hebrew were created and the equivalent of a modern language lab was established to assist students with Latin, Greek, and Hebrew. Commentaries on Lombard's *Sentences* were dropped and the old scholastic lectures on Aristotle replaced by straightforward historical study based on the most recent translations. New humanistic lectures on Pliny, Quintilian, and Priscian were introduced. Candidates for theological degrees now defended their views on the basis of their own exegesis of the Bible and studied the ecclesiastical laws of Saxony in place of traditional canon law. [34] Although Wittenberg students continued to be trained in Aristotle's *Logic, Rhetoric,* and *Poetics,* Luther remained hostile to his physical writings (the *Physics, Ethics, Metaphysics,* and *De Anima*), which he believed contained the theoretical foundations of many scholastic theological errors and unchristian teachings. Melanchthon, who would later moderate his views on Aristotle, summarized the fears of Wittenberg theologians by pointing out the danger to theology of such Aristotelian dogmas as the eternality of the world, the immutability of celestial movements, and the mortality of the soul, agreeing with Luther that philosophy and Holy Scripture had opposing views of law, sin, and grace. The greatest fear, however, perhaps prophetic when one looks to the age of Protestant scholasticism in the second half of the sixteenth century, was that theology might once again fall prey to the methods and presuppositions of philosophy, as happened with the Thomists, Scotists, and Ockhamists, and be led back into "irreligious and idolatrous teaching." [35]

---

[33] *Corpus Reformatorum* XI, 15, 17-18.

[34] Steinmetz in *450 Jahre M. Luther Universität,* p. 126; Schwiebert, *ARG* 49 (1958), 71-72; Bauer, *Die Wittenberger Universitätstheologie,* 98-111.

[35] *Corpus Reformatorum* I, 303-05, 307-09. Melanchthon describes Thomas Aquinas as the "leading proponent of impious doctrine." *Ibid.,* 307. Luther spoke

Melanchthon wrote in middle age the most eloquent defense of the Protestant alliance between the humanities and sacred studies. Adopting a device that placed the issue squarely within the framework of the late medieval debates, he replied in 1452 under the name of Hermolao Barbaro to Pico della Mirandola's famous defense of scholasticism. [36] Melanchthon, perhaps unfairly, interpreted Pico's defense of scholastics and criticism of humanist grammarians and rhetoricians as an attack on eloquence and the liberal arts. The ideal of the ancients was not truth awkwardly stated, as he believed Pico had argued, but wisdom eloquently expressed and applied in practice. "I call that man a philosopher," Melanchthon wrote, "who, when he has learned many things that are good and useful to the human race, takes his learning (*doctrinam*) out of the shadow of the school and applies it for the public welfare, teaching people what he knows, whether it be about nature, religion, or civil government." "Of what use to the world," he demanded, "are those monstrous verbal pictures and obscure orations (of the scholastic theologians)? Are they intended to teach men? Do they clarify either civic or religious responsibilities? Are they guides in making decisions? Do they have a role to play in the governance of public and private life?" [37] Those who do not fully understand the words they use and have no practical goal for their craft lose their sense of discrimination and end up creating absurdities, as is attested for Melanchthon by the questions about common natures, quiddities, distinctions, terms of first and second intention, instances, and other "deliramenta," which consume scholastic commentaries. True insight into the nature of things (*iudicium rerum*), that wisdom of the philosophers so highly valued by Pico, is seen by Melanchthon to go hand in hand with eloquent application (*diligentia loquendi*); when one walks in the circles of true philosophers, one does not find wise but ineloquent men, but wise men who converse eloquently about things human and divine (*humanarum et divinarum rerum oratores*). [38]

---

of Aquinas as "autor ... regnantis Aristotelis, vastatoris piae doctrinae." *WA* 8, p. 127.

[36] *Corpus Reformatorum* IX, 689-702. On Pico and Barbaro, see above. On dating Melanchthon's letter see Wilhelm Mauer, *Der junge Melanchthon zwischen Humanismus und Reformation* I (Göttingen, 1967), 224, n. 13. Melanchthon's letter has been translated by Quirinus Breen, "Melanchthon's Reply to Pico," *JHI* 13 (1952), 413-26. For analysis see Breen, "The Subordination of Philosophy to Rhetoric in Melanchthon," *ARG* (1952).

[37] *Corpus Reformatorum* IX, 692.

[38] *Ibid.*, 701.

The other major Protestant educational reformers fully shared Melanchthon's belief in the close connection between the humanities, sacred studies, and true piety, and such is a firm part of the heritage of the Reformation. The Strasbourg educator Jean Sturm portrayed the goal of study as "piety and religion" and praised classical philosophers and rhetoricians as indispensible aids. [39] The French humanist Claude Baduel, who was strongly influenced by the evangelical humanist ideals of Melanchthon and Sturm, said at the founding of the College and University of Nimes in 1540: "Without letters, no good government and no public order; and without them, the churches would neither be able to conserve good doctrine, nor be able to defend themselves against heresies." [40] Theodore Beza embraced this ideal of knowledge leading to righteousness in his address on the occasion of the opening of the Genevan Academy in 1559, exhorting his audience to be "imbued with the knowledge of true religion and of all good arts, to be able to magnify the glory of God, to be an ornament to the fatherland, and also an aid to yourselves." [41]

From such sources one is tempted to agree with William Bouwsma's provocative thesis that "the deepest assumptions of earlier humanist culture found theological expression in the Protestant Reformation," that the Reformation was "the theological fulfillment of the [early] Renaissance." [42] On the other hand, however, the Reformation, as we have seen, was also an important triumph of scholasticism over humanism. The Protestant reformers did adopt the broad educational reforms of humanism and many of them, Melanchthon and Calvin being the most prominent, can, even by the strictest definition, be

---

[39] "Optimum igitur ludi genus est, in quo et doctrinae et morum ratio diligens habetur. Nam tametsi studiorum nostrorum finis sit rerum cognitio, tamen si a doctrina et literis vita dissideat, quid... utilitatis habet elegans ac liberalis institutio? Pietas igitur atque religio in scholis proposita sit, et ad eam iuvenilis animus cultura literarum erudiatur." *De literarum ludis recte aperiendis* (1538) in *Die evangelischen Schulordnungen des 16. Jahrhunderts,* ed. R. Vormbaum (Gütersloh, 1860), 655, 673-74. See also Pierre Mesnard, "La pedagogie de Jean Sturm et son inspiration evangelique (1507-89)," *XIIe Congres Intl. des Sciences Historiques,* 95-100.

[40] In *Transition and Revolution: Problems and Issues of European Renaissance and Reformation History,* ed. R. M. Kingdon (Minneapolis, 1974), p. 179.

[41] *Ibid.,* 181.

[42] *Viator* 7 (1976), 439; "Renaissance and Reformation: An Essay in Their Affinities and Connections" in *Luther and the Dawn of the Modern Era: Papers for the Fourth International Congress for Luther Research,* ed. H. A. Oberman (Leiden, 1974), 129.

described as Christian humanists. [43] But, like the Renaissance, the Reformation also had its cautious, conservative side, one which, on this particular issue, was firmly established from the start.

It is Professor Bouwsma's argument that Renaissance rhetoric, broadly conceived as the union of virtue, wisdom, and the art of persuasion, was the ideal behind Reformation preaching and stress on the Word of God. [44] We can see that ideal applied by Protestants in their educational reforms. But, as with early humanist and Protestant concepts of man, the similarity between humanist and Protestant interest in rhetoric and eloquence is more structural than material. Both saw man as a complex unity, driven by will and passion, but Protestants remained far more skeptical about man's rational, moral, and religious abilities than most humanists ever contemplated. [45] While the reformers set the humanist curriculum in place of the scholastic, the rhetorical arts continued to serve for them the basic scholastic task of defining and defending true doctrine. For Protestants, doctrine was always the rider and the humanities the horse. The humanities became for Protestant theologians what Aristotelian philosophy had been to late medieval Catholic theologians, the favored handmaiden of theology.

There is a further difference between humanists and Protestants

---

[43] According to Kristeller, the term "Christian humanism" is properly applied to "those scholars with a humanist classical and rhetorical training who explicitly discussed religious or theological problems in all or some of their writings"—a definition which excludes Luther, yet embraces, in addition to Melanchthon and Calvin, Erasmus, Vives, Budé, More, Hooker, and many Jesuit fathers. *Renaissance Thought: The Classic, Scholastic, and Humanist Strains* (New York, 1961), 86-87.

[44] "Renaissance and Reformation," 148. Bouwsma even sees the Protestant concept of God as "a transcendent expression of the Renaissance ideal of the orator." *Ibid.* Lewis Spitz has also recently stressed this same point in dealing with the ways the Reformation aided and abetted humanism: "Given Luther's emphasis upon the verbum evangelii vocale and the response of the believer's fides ex auditu, the instrumental importance of rhetoric gained a new dimension of significance during the Reformation era, despite the comeback staged by Aristotelian dialectic." "The Course of German Humanism," 419. Spitz was earlier critical of Bouwsma's thesis: "It would be a fundamental error to equate the fidem facere (verbum facit fidem of Luther) with the humanist persuadere." "Headwaters of the Reformation: Studia Humanitatis, Luther Senior, et Initia Reformationis" in *Luther and the Dawn of the Modern Era,* 115.

[45] Cf. Bengt Hägglund's criticism of Bouwsma by way of a comparison of Renaissance anthropology (*via* Juan Luis Vives and Pico) with that of the Protestant reformers. "Renaissance and Reformation" in *Luther and the Dawn of the Modern Era,* 150-57. There is an important structural similarity here, however, which Hägglund does not acknowledge.

that stems from the persistence of scholasticism within Protestantism. That is the Protestant disinclination to subject their teaching to moral critique. The reformers did not permit ethics to sit in judgment on the truth of their doctrine. It became the hallmark of the Anabaptist, Spiritualist, and rational critics of the Reformation, almost all of whom were deeply influenced by the work of Erasmus, to make good deeds the test of true creeds and to criticize the followers of Luther and Calvin for failing to improve the moral quality of life. [46] The Protestant reformers looked upon sectarian efforts to make ethical considerations the norm of doctrine in the same way that the Council of Constance had looked on the teaching of Wyclif and Hus—as resurgent Donatist heresy. Whereas Erasmus saw in the maturing Reformation a new threat to the humanities, Luther beheld in the Christian philosophy of Erasmus the decline of true doctrine. Luther said of the priority and inviolability of doctrine:

> Doctrine and life are to be distinguished. Life is as bad among us as among the papists. Hence, we do not fight and damn them because of their bad lives. Wyclif and Hus, who fought over the moral quality of life, failed to understand this. I do not consider myself to be pious. But when it comes to whether one teaches correctly about the Word of God, there I take my stand and fight. That is my calling. To contest doctrine has never happened until now. Others have fought over life; but to take on doctrine—that is to grab the goose by the neck! Truly the kingdom and office of the papists is evil. Once we have demonstrated that, it is easy to go on and prove that their lives are also bad. But when the Word of God remains pure, even if the quality of life fails us, life is placed in a position to become what it ought to be. That is why everything hinges on the purity of the Word. I have succeeded only if I have taught correctly. [47]

Life, then, must aspire to true doctrine; the truth of doctrine is not judged by the moral failing of those who profess it—that became the basic Protestant rule. Luther declared that even if Rome had observed the traditional religion with the discipline of the hermits, Jerome, Augustine, Gregory, Bernard, Francis, and Dominic, its false doctrine would still have made the Reformation necessary. [48] Sebastian Castellio complained in a revealing way against the Calvinists in the 1550's: "The Calvinists want men to be judged not on the basis of their morals but according to their beliefs—*non ex moribus sed ex doctrina.*" [49]

---

[46] See my *Mysticism and Dissent: Religious Ideology and Social Protest in the 16th Century* (New Haven, 1973).

[47] *TR* 624 in *Luthers Werke in Auswahl* VIII, ed. O. Clemen (Berlin, 1950), 79.

[48] From the Commentary on Galatians (1545), *WA* 40, p. 687 = *LW* 26, p. 459.

[49] *Contra libellum Calvini*, E 8 b.

As a theological movement Protestantism can be seen as a continuation of the medieval scholastic enterprise of defining true doctrine. This enterprise was streamlined, however, by the *studia humanitatis*. The Protestant reformers were truly *new* scholastics, not only because they approached their task with the tools of humanism, but also because they rejected so many traditional scholastic doctrines as unbiblical. It was a unique blending of movements, as both surviving (and later resurgent) Aristotelianism and the humanities were "confessionalized," that is, taken over and integrated into the larger task of communicating Biblical doctrine to the masses. [50]

It has been argued that without humanism the Reformation could not have succeeded, and it is certainly difficult to imagine the Reformation occurring without the knowledge of languages, the critical handling of sources, the satirical attacks on clerics and scholastics, and the new national feeling which a generation of humanists promoted. [51] On the other hand, the humanist movement also owed something to the Reformation for its long term success. In Protestant schools and universities classical culture found a permanent home, hospitable even in the heyday of Protestant orthodoxy. The humanist curriculum, with its stress on languages and history, became a lasting model for the Arts curriculum in Protestant schools. Classical rhetoric also received a new importance as an aid in the training of Protestant clergy. [52] Although humanist influence attenuated in the later stages of the Reformation and the Protestant confessions became intellectually narrow in the late sixteenth and seventeenth centuries when men with little humanist training assumed positions of leadership, [53] the alliance between sacred and humanistic studies has remained a vital part of the heritage of the Reformation.

---

[50] Cf. H. Liebing, "Die Ausgänge des europäischen Humanismus" in *Geist und Geschichte der Reformation: Festgabe Hanns Rückert* (Berlin, 1966), 370-71.

[51] Moeller, *ZKG* 70 (1959), p. 59; Spitz in *Itinerarium Italicum*, 414.

[52] Spitz, "The Course of German Humanism," 386; Robert D. Linder, "Calvinism and Humanism: The First Generation," *Church History* 44 (1975), 167-81.

[53] Cf. Brian G. Armstrong, *Calvinism and the Amyraut Heresy: Protestant Scholasticism and Humanism in 17th Century France* (Madison, 1969).

LUTHER'S HEXAMERAL ANTHROPOLOGY

CHARLES TRINKAUS

University of Michigan

The following essay examines Luther's views of human nature and the conditions of human existence as he manifested them in his *Lectures on Genesis,* chapters 1-3. [1] Although Luther dealt with man in many writings and contexts, the *Vorlesungen über 1 Mose* is particularly appropriate for study because of the long Christian tradition of treatment of man in the context of both his creation *ad imaginem et similitudinem Dei* of Genesis 1:26 and man's Fall and Curse of chapter 3. Scholarly interest in this work has seemed to focus more on Luther's conceptions and practice of Biblical exegesis and on his theologically crucial conception of the Word than on what it reveals of Luther's views of man. My interest will center on Luther's anthropology and how it compares with the humanistic traditions of the "dignity of man" rather than on his exegetical sources or on the scholastic traditions emphasized by Gerhard Ebeling in his study (now still in progress) of Luther's *Disputatio de homine.* [2]

---

[1] My credentials for this study derive from past efforts to inter-relate Renaissance and Reformation themes and not from the study-in-depth of a life-long Luther scholar. My approach to Luther has been conditioned by study of such works as his *Treatise on Christian Liberty, Secular Government to What Extent Should It Be Obeyed?, The Enslaved Will.* Perhaps more importantly a number of scholars, not necessarily agreeing, have had a syncretistic influence on my understanding of Luther, figures such as: Roland Bainton, F. Edward Cranz, Gerhard Ebeling, B. A. Gerrish, Heiko A. Oberman, Steven E. Ozment, Benjamin N. Nelson, Jaroslav Pelikan, James Samuel Preus, Gordon Rupp, Lewis W. Spitz, Ernst Troeltsch and Max Weber. I have not been able to consult Franz Lau, *"Ausserliche Ordnung" und "Weltlich Ding" in Luthers Theologie,* (Göttingen, 1933). I have used the *Lectures on Genesis* in the following edition and translation: *D. Martin Luthers Werke,* Kritische Gesamtausgabe, 42 Band (Weimar, 1911), hereafter WA 42; and in *Luther's Works,* ed. Jaroslav Pelikan, vol. 1 (St. Louis, 1958), hereafter LW 1. Due to limitations of space Luther's Latin text will not be given, but citations will give page and line numbers of WA 42 and page numbers of LW 1. Translations will be based on those of George V. Schick in LW 1. I have introduced occasional variations where a more literal version seemed stylistically preferable. I have found no places where I would differ with Schick in accuracy of interpretation.

[2] Gerhard Ebeling, *Lutherstudien,* Band II: *Disputatio de Homine,* Erster Teil, *Text und Traditionshintergrund* (Tübingen, 1977). I find Luther's doctrines on man consistent in these two works.

It should be no surprise that on the topic of man, and here in this single work, Luther seems to present more than one point of view, and, as is also usual, it will be our task to compare them and seek to unify them, if that is possible. Although his first significant statement occurs on 1:14, we shall look first at the *locus classicus* for discussions of human dignity: *Faciamus hominem ad imaginem et similitudinem nostram* of Genesis 1:26. [3]

In the exegetical traditions concerning this verse there are three basic questions that are almost always discussed: why the special differentiation in the creation of man of the use of a first person imperative instead of the third person: "Let us"?; why the use of the plural *"Faciamus"*; and the large and extended question of what are the meanings of *imago* and *similitudo* and how they are applied to man. [4] For Luther the use of first person by God indicates a deliberate taking of counsel by God, adding a notable and significant difference between the creation of man and others. The animals have a great similarity to man in that men and animals live together, eat, sleep and rest. "But here the text emphatically separates man since it says God had conceived of making man in a definite deliberation, and not only this but of making man in the image of God." [5]

Luther immediately expands on the meaning of this differentiation in a significant way. He sets forth what would have been the condition of man if his nature had remained unimpaired by the Fall. At a definite time, when the human population had grown to the desired fullness, mankind would have been translated to an eternal and spiritual life. At the same time the physical side of man's life, in which he was similar to the animals (nutrition and reproduction), would have been a pleasing service to God, carried on without lust, sin or fear of death. "This certainly would have been a pleasant and delightful life about which we may indeed think but it may not be realized in this life." [6] Man may still look forward to the spiritual life in paradise through the merit of Christ. This is an important statement of Luther's to which we shall shortly return. Meanwhile, he takes up the second question of the plurality of *Faciamus*, emphasizing against various

---

[3] See below, notes 29, 30, 31.

[4] See my *"In Our Image and Likeness:"* Humanity and Divinity in Italian Humanist Thought* (London and Chicago, 1970), 173-99; and "Renaissance Idea of the Dignity of Man," *Dictionary of the History of Ideas* (New York, 1973), IV, 136-47.

[5] WA 42: 42, 14-16; LW 1: 56.

[6] WA 42: 42, 31-32; LW 1: 57.

Jewish views, the traditional orthodox Christian interpretation that it represented the involvement of the entire Trinity and was an affirmation of the Trinity. [7]

It is in taking up the third traditional question: "What is that image of God according to which Moses said man was made?" that Luther's break with the tradition takes place, and out of this his own position more clearly emerges. The western theological tradition, as Gerhart Ladner has demonstrated, [8] found its classical statement in Saint Augustine's *De Trinitate,* his *De Genesi ad litteram* and other writings. [9] Stressing *imago* rather than '*omoiosis* as the Greek Fathers had tended, Augustine, as is well known, sought a replication of the divine Trinity in an image in the human soul, with a variety of correspondences between Father, Son and Spirit and memory, intellect and will and a number of their equivalences. [10] For Luther, who first spells out the development of this doctrine in some detail (erring only in identifying Augustine's position with Aristotle's), [11] this will not do: "But just as these not unpleasant speculations point to sharp and otiose minds, so they do hardly anything in rightly explaining the image of God." [12] The trouble is that what started out with Augustine as a likely analogy to make the Trinity understandable ended up with other theologians extending this interpretation into a defense of free will which is born from that image: "For they speak as follows: 'God is free, therefore since man is created according to the image of God, he also has a free memory, mind and will.' In this way much comes out which is either spoken improperly or afterwards taken impiously. Thus the dangerous opinion is born in which it is asserted that God governs men in such a way that He allows them to act on their own impulse... From this the conclusion is made that free will concurs as a precedent and efficient cause of salvation. Not unlike these is the more dangerous position of Dionysius when he said, 'Although the demons and man fell, yet the natural powers remained unimpaired, such as mind, memory and will, etc.' But if this is true, it follows that man can so act by the powers of nature that he is saved." [13]

---

[7] WA 42: 43-44; LW 1: 57-59.
[8] Gerhart Ladner, *The Idea of Reform, Its Impact on Christian Thought and Action in the Age of the Fathers* (rev. ed. New York, 1967), Part II, Chap. 5.
[9] *Ibid.*
[10] *De Trinitate,* IX-XII.
[11] WA 42: 45, 3-4; LW 1: 60.
[12] WA 42: 45, 22-23; LW 1: 60.
[13] WA 42: 44, 27-39; LW 1: 61.

It is clear that Luther, although he sees some good in it, cannot accept this traditional conception of the divine image in the creation of man because it opened the doors to the kind of Pelagian soteriology he regarded as most dangerous. It is also clear that on the same grounds he could not accept the Renaissance notions of the dignity of man, which, almost without exception, were either based on, or included as a central ingredient, this conception of the trinitarian powers of the soul. He adds: "I also fear that, after this image has been lost through sin, we are unable properly to understand it. We, indeed, have memory, will and mind, but most corrupted and seriously weakened, indeed, to speak clearly, entirely leperous and unclean. If those powers are the image of God, Satan, it also follows, was created in the image of God, and he has far stronger natural powers than we have." [14]

For Luther, the image of God in man was the general condition of man at his creation before the Fall and Curse, namely: "That Adam had it in his substance, that he not only knew God and believed that He is good but that he also lived a life that was plainly divine, that is that he was without fear of death and of all dangers and was content in the grace of God." It was as though God said: "This is my image by which you will live just as God lives. But if you sin, you will lose this image and you will die." [15] The significance lies in man's faith and trust in God and the psychological security which accompanies it. It followed that when Adam and Eve sinned out of distrust and loss of faith, they instantly lost the image of God. It was only before the Fall that man could have been godlike, not afterwards as Satan falsely told them.

Before the Fall man indeed had the traditional natural powers of memory, intellect and will "in most beautiful security without any fear of death and without any anxiety whatsoever." [16] But this condition, which was lost, did not constitute man's entire possession of the divine image. "To these interior faculties was also added that most beautiful and excellent power of the body and all its members by which man conquered all other animate natures. For plainly I believe that before sin Adam's eyes were so sharp and clear that he excelled the lynx and the eagle. Moreover, he forcefully dealt with lions and bears, whose strength is the greatest, no differently than we deal with

---

[14] WA 42: 46, 4-9; LW 1: 61.
[15] WA 42: 47, 8-17; LW 1: 62-63.
[16] WA 42: 46. 20-21; LW 1: 62.

kittens." [17] Luther never neglects the animal-like capacities and qualities of man, in which he excelled before the Fall as part of the divine
image. But after the Fall "all experience how great is the rage of the
flesh which is not only furious in lusting but also in scorning after
it has had what it wished. Thus in both we see neither reason nor a
will that is whole, but a fury more than beastlike." [18]

After the Fall there is no question of a human dignity resting on
man's creation in the divine image. Within its own premises, however,
the post-lapsarian life was later characterized as not entirely devoid of
advantages. [19] Rather, now, the human condition is described in terms
opposite to what Luther conceived was the pre-lapsarian image of God
in man: "Now therefore we see how many dangers, how many deaths
and occasions of death this wretched nature is driven to experience and
sustain, besides the filthy lust and the other furies of sin and the
excessive emotion which are contained in the souls of all men. Never
are we secure in God; terror and fright also torture us in dreams. These
and similar evils are the image of the Devil who impresses them into
us." [20]

He goes on to argue that the divine image is something "really
unknown, which not only we do not experience but we instead perpe-
tually experience the contrary and hear nothing of it besides the bare
word." [21] Earlier in discussing the beginnings of creation in Genesis
1:2 he argued the incomprehensibility of the divine. "It is madness to
dispute concerning God outside and before time because that would
be to wish to understand bare divinity or the bare divine essence.
Because this is impossible, God involves himself in works and certain
images, just as today he involves himself in Baptism and Forgiveness,
etc." [22] We have to accept God in and through his wrappings and
manifestations, and the Anthropomorphites were not wrong to conceive of God in human terms, but these must clearly be understood as
metaphors. "Therefore such figures of speech are pleasing to the Holy
Spirit and the works of God are put before us which we may apprehend." [23] On the basis of this limited knowledge, he can present the
pre-lapsarian life of Adam, which he will soon argue lasted hardly a

---

[17] WA 42: 46, 21-26; LW 1: 62.
[18] WA 42: 46/31-47/2; LW 1: 62.
[19] E.g. WA 42: 157; LW 1: 210.
[20] WA 42: 47, 18-22; LW 1: 63.
[21] WA 42: 47, 31-33; LW 1: 63.
[22] WA 42: 10, 3-6; LW 1: 11.
[23] WA 42: 37-38; LW 1: 15.

single day, as knowable only in its contrast to the life we now know. An important part of it was its fruitfulness, and Adam's strength to dominate over the beasts and to cause any crop he wished for to grow. But as of the following (seventh) day, after the primal sin, nature itself underwent a change; man was physically weakened in his former natural powers; animals became stronger and more dangerous to man; spines and weeds appeared and increased the difficulty of farming; [24] still later the flood was to make things even worse. [25] Therefore, the dignity of man arising out of his creation in the divine image was something that Luther had to adumbrate from what scriptural hints he had and entertain as an act of faith. It could no longer be fully known.

Similarly, the reformation of the divine image in man through Christ and the Gospel had to be taken on faith. "But now the Gospel has brought about the restoration of that image. Intellect and will indeed have remained, but both very much impaired. And so the Gospel brings it about that we are formed once more according to that indeed better image, because we are borne again into eternal life or rather into the hope of eternal life by faith..." [26] Not only eternal life is restored but also justice.

It should be noted that he states that intellect and will do remain, though much impaired. As he continues this declaration he refers specifically to the trinitarian qualities of memory, intellect and will that he had spurned above as the elements of the divine image of man. Now in the reformed image he admits these qualities: "In this manner that image of the new creature begins to be repaired through the Gospel in this life, but it is not perfected in this life. But when it is perfected in the kingdom of the Father, then the will will be truly free and good, the mind truly illumined and the memory constant; then also it will happen that all the other creatures will be more subject to us than they were in Adam's Paradise." [27]

As he seems frequently to do, he denies a particular interpretation because it seems to have unacceptable theological implications, only to readmit it later in a different context. The restored image centrally includes man's psychic trinity imaging the divine Trinity, along with immortality and renewed domination of the animal kingdom. But man

---

[24] E.g. WA 42: 59; LW 1: 77-78.
[25] *Ibid.*
[26] WA 42: 48, 11-15; LW 1: 64.
[27] WA 42: 48, 27-31; LW 1: 65.

can only dimly know he possesses this restored image before he enters the heavenly life. "Moreover, this which we say, faith and the Word teach, which show, as though from a great distance, that glory of the divine image." [28] Thus Luther manages both to reject and to reaffirm the traditional argument on behalf of human dignity as based on man's possession of the image of the Trinity. But this possession of the image is reserved for man's brief primeval moment of paradisiac life and for his future restoration through Christ in this world, dimly now and only in faith and hope. Yet in the next life, truly and fully realized, and better than in man's beginning.

But he had also extolled the glory of man earlier in his exposition of the creation of the lights and the division of day and night on the fourth day. Taking up the second part of chapter 1, verse 14: "And let them be for signs and for seasons and for days and years," Luther points out that the value of the heavenly lights for mankind indicated in this verse depends on the invention of number and counting, something which children and animals lack and which has to be learned. "Therefore," he says, "counting indicates that man is an extraordinary creature of God." But what man has added through experience and sciences, such as astrology, is more uncertain. Man's interest in the heavenly bodies and their movements and his acquisition of counting and his measuring of time which the scriptures here enjoin upon him are seen as indicators of the immortality of human souls. Such activities reflect glory on man, because the other animals cannot do this. [29]

He develops this thought into a rounded vision of the course of human existence from creation to salvation. "The first human being was made from a clod by God. Thenceforth the human race was propagated from male and female seed from which, little by little, the embryo is formed in the uterus through its single parts and grows until finally through birth it is brought forth into the light of heaven. Afterwards begins the sensitive life and soon that of action and motion. When the body has gained strength, and mind and reason thrive in a healthy body, then that life of the intellect begins to shine, which does not exist in other earthly creatures, so that by the aid of the mathematical disciplines, which no one can deny are divinely revealed, man in his mind soars on high and, leaving behind earthly things, concerns himself with the heavenly and investigates them. Neither cows, nor pigs nor any

---

[28] WA 42: 48, 33-35; LW 1: 65.
[29] WA 42: 33, 15-16—34; LW 1: 44-46.

other animals do this; only man does it. Therefore, man is a creature created to inhabit the celestial regions, leaving the earth behind at some time, and to live an eternal life. For this is why he not only can speak and make judgments (which pertains to Rhetoric and Dialectic) but thoroughly learns all the mathematical disciplines. Now, therefore, from this fourth day our glory begins to be revealed: that God thought of making such a creature who might understand the movements of those bodies which were created on the fourth day and who would delight in such knowledge as though it was proper to his own nature. They should arouse us to give thanks that, as if its citizens, we may belong to that Fatherland which we now see, admire and understand, though as pilgrims and exiles, but which after this life we may examine more closely and understand more perfectly." [30]

Just as he denies that the mental trinity of memory, intellect and will is what Moses meant by the divine image yet reverts to this standard exegesis for the condition of man before the Fall and after his restoration, so also he takes up here the ancient eulogy of man as master of the liberal arts with explicit reference to the trivium and the quadrivium. Moreover, he talks of God making the world in terms analogous to the human arts, asserting that "the Holy Spirit also has His own langauge and way of expression, namely, that God, by speaking, created all things and worked through the Word, and that all His works are some words of God, created by the uncreated Word." I do not intend in this essay to enter into the intricacies of Luther's central theological conception of the Word but wish rather only to point out that he has deliberately constructed it on the analogy of the human languages which, he says, exist within each profession. Each profession has its own vocabulary, and the religious meaning of the scriptural account of the creation parallels but does not either affirm or deny the scientific meaning. "Every science should use its own terminology, ...and they should put their achievements at one another's disposal" just as the various crafts "do to maintain the whole city." [31]

I believe that Luther has revealed here an important echo of the Renaissance (as well as ancient) genre of the dignity of man. In this genre there were two principal arguments supporting man's excellence: first, the magnitude of his mental endowments, reinforced in the Christianizing of the tradition by seeing them (memory, in-

---

[30] WA 42, 33-35, 14; LW 1: 46.
[31] WA 42: 35, 37-38, 36, 12-15; LW 1: 47-48.

tellect and will), as Augustine did, as the image of the divine Trinity; and second, the accomplishments of the human arts, both the mechanical arts of the craftsman and the liberal arts of the intellectual that, as acquired faculties, differentiate man from the animals. Luther does not explicitly or literally follow this tradition but in a round-about way he brings out both of these two major elements of it, though desiring overtly to deny any dignity to man after the Fall for fear of encouraging a false reliance on free will.

On the other hand, man's relationship to animals plays a major role in Luther's thinking. Before the Fall "naked man without arms and fortifications, indeed, also without any clothing, in his naked flesh only, ruled over the birds, the beasts and the fish." He also had a perfect knowledge of all nature over which he was to rule. Moreover, man knew his Creator, his origin and his destination. Whereas "the other animals entirely lacked this knowledge." "Therefore, they entirely lacked that likeness to God." [32] After the Fall there is still a great difference between man and the other animals but it was much greater before. "The things which we accomplish in life are not now done by means of dominion which Adam had but through industry and art." And man because he now has to work for his living becomes more like the animals and overcomes his physical differences by such invention and labor. Also like the animals, man today is prey to the fury of his emotions, whereas before the Fall "there was also a great unity of minds and wills." [33] When Luther comes to the second account of the creation of man in Genesis chapter 2, which he regards as simply an amplification of what is said in chapter 1, [34] he emphasizes the deliberate action of God in shaping man out of earth and breathing into him a living soul. Here again man is seen as like the animals in his physical life but differentiated by the gift of immortality, which today, through Christ, we have in hope. [35]

Lorenzo Valla, the Italian humanist whom Luther so much admired, had also depicted man as in all ways similar to animals except for his gift of immortality. Man and animals both had similar psychic make-ups with the emotions predominating over the intellect, though man's mind was obviously sharper. It was the theological gift that made the

---

[32] WA 42: 49, 27-28, 50, 13-15; LW 1: 66-67.
[33] WA 42: 50, 25-26, 20; LW 1: 67.
[34] See WA 42: 62, 24-25; LW 1: 82; also see WA 42: 91, 8-9; LW 1: 120. "Totum itaque secundum caput consumit in explicatione conditionis hominis."
[35] WA 42: 63-64; LW 1: 83-84.

difference. [36] So also Luther after his text has described man as placed in the Garden of Eden and provided with the tree of life speaks of his pre-lapsarian life as a physical one to which the spiritual is to be added. Also like Valla Luther emphasized man's pleasure and his enjoyment of both eating and procreation, only in Eden, thanks to the tree of life, he would not have aged as the other animals. [37]

Then the tree of knowledge of good and evil is introduced as a form of religious worship. "Adam was created in such a way that if anything troublesome to his nature had happened he would have a protection against it in the tree of life, which preserved his powers and perfect health at all times. And so, completely surrounded as he was by the goodness of the Creator, if he had remained in the state of innocence, he would have acknowledged God as his Creator and would have governed the beasts according to His will without any inconvenience, in fact with extreme joy. For all things were such that they could not harm man but could delight him in the highest degree. And so when Adam had been created in such a way that he was, as it were, intoxicated with rejoicing toward God and was delighted also with all other creatures, there is now created a new tree for the distinguishing of good and evil, so that Adam might have a definite way to express his worship and reverence toward God." [38]

In distinguishing in this way between two aspects of human life, the secular animal side and the religious, Luther sees Moses as in accord with the established intellectual disciplines: "Therefore, what Moses has said up to now has to do with natural philosophy, economic matters, politics, iuridical affairs of medicine. What this statement proposes to Adam about the tree is theological, so that also according to his animality (*animalitatem*) he would have a certain external sign for worshipping God and for yielding obedience in an external work." [39] As he would further develop in great detail in his commentary on chapter 3, Luther regarded the primal sin which ignored the command concerning this tree to be a combination of disobedience to a superior being Who had created man and a reliance by man on his own powers going beyond the bounds of the commanded rule over the animals and guardianship of the garden: "Therefore, let us learn that some external form of worship and a definite work of obedience were necessary for

---

[36] *In Our Image*, 125, 131-32, 155-56.
[37] WA 42: 70; LW 1: 92.
[38] WA 42: 71, 24-34; LW 1: 93-94.
[39] WA 42: 71, 39-41—72, 1-2; LW 1: 94.

man, who was created to have all other living creatures under his control, to know his Creator, and to thank Him. If, therefore, Adam had not fallen this tree would have been like a common temple and basilica to which people would have streamed." And it would also mark man's acceptance of his limitations and subjection to God. [40]

When he comes to verse 15: "Therefore, the Lord God took man and placed him in the garden of Eden that he might work it and guard it," again Luther speaks of the physical life and the spiritual. But now the former was divided into two functions: "Moreover, God assigns to Adam a twofold duty, namely, to work or cultivate the garden and furthermore to watch and guard it." Vestiges of these duties remain today and give us much trouble and inconvenience. "But if you should wish to discuss the matter of food, not only do the animals have [the need for] it in common with us, but men snatch it away from other men and steal it with fraud. Therefore, there is also need for walls, hedges and other defenses, and yet what you have raised with great trouble can be preserved but feebly." [41] Moreover, now, after the Fall, the earth yields its crops only with labor and sweat and is crowded with thorns and weeds when it would have produced easily and with abundance for Adam if he had not sinned. "Work, which in the state of innocence was a game and a pleasure, is a punishment. And now in this wretched state of nature, if anyone has a pleasant garden it is no labor to sow or plant or dig, but it is done with zeal and a certain pleasure!... Moreover, this is a good place to admonish that man was not created for leisure but for labor, even in the state of innocence. Therefore, a life of idleness, such as that of the monks and nuns, is to be condemned." [42]

This is another important statement that aligns Luther with such humanists as Leon Battista Alberti who condemned "ozio" as the greatest of sins and praised a life of activity as the only one fitting for a man of conscience and dignity who wished to fulfill the purpose for which God had created him. [43] It is notable that Luther also made work a duty to be performed in the state of innocence and, though it

---

[40] WA 42: 72, 28-32; LW 1: 95.

[41] WA 42: 77, 29-31, 78, 9-12; LW 1: 102.

[42] WA 42: 78, 21-28; LW 1: 103.

[43] Leon Battista Alberti, *I libri della famiglia, Opere volgari,* ed. Cecil Grayson, I (Bari, 1960), 130: "Chi mai stimasse potere asseguire pregio alcuno o dignitate sanza ardentissimo studio di perfettissime arti, sanza assiduissimo opera, senza molto sudare in cose virilissime e faticossime?... Nulla si truova onde tanto facile surga disonore e infamia quanto dall'ozio."

formally became a punishment after the Fall, it was also a morally desirable and even at times a pleasant state.

Luther's conception of the institutionalizing of human society emerges very specifically in his comments on Genesis 2:16-17: "From every tree of Paradise you shall eat; but from the tree of the knowledge of good and evil you shall not eat." This verse is taken to represent the establishment of the Church, "before there was either an economy or a polity, for Eve was not yet created." [44] The economy is added with the creation of Adam's companion, Eve, and by this he means the household economy, or home, using the term in its old Greek sense. It is the beginning of human society. "Thus the temple is prior to the home just as it is also more important. Moreover, there was no polity before sin, and there was no need for it, for the polity is the necessary remedy against corrupted nature. It is necessary for lust and greed to be constrained by the bonds of law and punishments so that they do not freely wander about. Therefore, you rightly call Polity the kingdom of sin." [45]

Luther's views of the nature of government seem to have changed little here since his treatise on secular government. [46] It is purely protective of the individual home against the rapacious instincts of the others. On the previous verse (2:15) he spoke of government as a vestige of the guard duty commanded by God in Eden. There "it would have been most pleasant." On the other hand: "We have protection today, but it is obviously horrible. It requires swords, spears, cannons, walls, redoubts and trenches; and yet we can hardly be safe with our families." [47] And he adds on the next verse (16): "Therefore, if men had not become evil through sin, there would have been no need for a Polity. ... What need would there have been for laws or a Polity, which is like a cauterizing iron and horrible medicine by which harmful limbs are cut off that the rest might be preserved." [48]

Luther does not seem to have too much confidence in a juridical system where laws are largely self-enforced for mutual benefits, even though he sees that exchange of this sort does take place with the products of craftsmen. He relies far more on the Church and its use of moral exhortation in preaching, which is a remnant of what he

---

[44] WA 42: 79, 2: LW 1: 103.

[45] WA 42: 79, 7-12; LW 1: 103-04.

[46] Cf. my "The Religious Foundations of Luther's Social Views," *Essays in Medieval Life and Thought*, ed. John Mundy et al. (New York, 1955).

[47] WA 42: 78, 30-34; LW 1: 103.

[48] WA 42: 79, 13-19; LW 1: 104.

considers to be God's sermon to Adam at his entrance into Eden. He relies also on the domestic bonds of the family for a softening of the asperities of life after the Fall. [49] Here he makes his usual comparison of what might have happened in Eden and what the relations of the sexes have become. There is a seeming paradox in the contrast between the strict punitiveness of his views of government, and his desire to enhance trust and affection in man's relation to God and in his family. "But who can describe in words the glory of the innocence we have lost? There still remains in nature the longing of the male for the female, likewise the fruit of procreation; but these are combined with the awful hideousness of lust and the frightful pain of birth. Shame, ignominy, and embarrassment arise even among married people when they wish to enjoy their legitimate intercourse. . . . The creation indeed is good and the blessing is good; but through sin they are so corrupted that married people cannot make use of them without shame." [50]

In commenting on the psychological consequences of the original sin in chapter 3, Luther makes some remarkable statements concerning human nudity and the genitalia. He is refuting the claim of the scholastics that man's original justice was not part of his nature and is regained with Christ. Meanwhile, man's natural endowments survive. For Luther it was evidence to the contrary that: "Just as to go nude was of the nature of man, full of trust and security toward God and thus to please God and men, so now after the sin man feels that this nudity of innocent nature displeases God, himself and all creatures. . . . Thus the same members remain in nature, but what were seen to be nude with glory before, now are covered over as though shameful and evil." [51] Adam and Eve "made girdles for covering over that part of the body which by its nature is the most honorable and dignified of all. For what is more noble in nature than the work of generation?" [52] "Should we not therefore feel at last how filthy and horrible sin is, if lust alone can be cured by no remedy, not even marriage which is ordained as a remedy for weak nature?" [53] "Moreover, it is marvellous that no writing by any writer in any language has been found which shows that nudity which was once most virtuous was made shameful through sin. Therefore, we have this one unique master, Moses, who, yet in the

[49] WA 42: 148-149; LW 1: 199.
[50] WA 42: 79, 30-36; LW 1: 104-05.
[51] WA 42: 125, 23-30; LW 1: 167.
[52] WA 42: 125, 35-38; LW 1: 167.
[53] WA 42: 126, 7-9; LW 1: 168.

briefest words, shows that man fallen from faith was confused and that that glory of the genitals was turned into the greatest ignominy, so that man was forced to cover them over with girdles!" [54]

But before we examine Luther's extraordinarily perceptive analysis of the psychology of sinning and of subsequent guilt as paradigmatically illuminated by the story of the Fall and the Expulsion in chapter 3, there are certain relevant passages still in chapter 2, particularly in connection with the creation of Eve. He finds it necessary to argue against the Aristotelian view of the eternity of the world and consequential rejection of any creation *ex nihilo*. Aristotle explains the new creation of reproduction only in terms of its material and formal causes, how one thing reproduces itself. A Christian looks at the efficient and final causes, what brought something into existence and for what purpose or end. From the point of view of reason and philosophy all of this is absurd. "But why does the creation of Adam and Eve seem so unbelievable and miraculous, while man's propagation, which all men know and see, does not seem so miraculous?" [55] Because endlessly repeated, miracles do not seem miraculous, as Augustine more than once pointed out. [56] "Thus it is a great miracle (*magnum miraculum*) that a small seed is planted and that out of it grows a very tall oak." Describing the development of the human fetus, its birth and nourishment by its mother's milk, Luther exclaims: "All these developments afford the fullest occasion for wonderment and are wholly beyond our understanding, but because of their continued recurrence they have come to be regarded as commonplace, and we have verily become deaf to this lovely music of nature. But if we regarded these wonders in true faith and appraised them for what they actually are, they surely would not be inferior to what Moses says here: that a rib was taken from the side of Adam as he slept and that Eve was created from it." It is the greater miracle of man's creation by the Word, a miracle which lifts him above the merely natural such as Aristotle and the other scientists regard him and shows man his divine end: "that man is created according to the likeness of God; in eternity, therefore, he is to live with God, and while he is here on earth, he is to preach God, thank Him, and patiently obey His Word." [57]

---

[54] WA 42: 125, 20-30; 168.

[55] WA 42: 93-94, 94, 29-31; LW 1: 124-26. Cf. *De homine*, theses 12-16, Ebeling, *op. cit.*, 17-18.

[56] E.g. *De civ. Dei*, XXI, capp. 7, 8.

[57] WA 42: 95, 5-6, 12-17; 98, 20-22; LW 1: 126-27, 131.

It would seem not unlikely that in this passage Luther was echoing "Hermes Trismegitus" in the *Asclepius* and Pico della Mirandola [58] in his playing upon the miraculous in man, projecting an ideal of human life transcending nature which had great appeal in the Renaissance. [59] It would also seem, therefore, that Luther, himself, felt some attraction toward the latent theme of man's deification contained in the literature on the dignity of man. But for Luther the aspiration toward deification would have been unnecessary if man had only been able to accept the godlikeness in which he had been created and had followed the commandments of his Maker. It was, ironically, man's striving to emulate the deity (rather than patiently awaiting his elevation to immortality) that led to his downfall. Therefore, we shall appropriately turn now to Luther's comment on chapter 3 of Genesis where he acutely and brilliantly analyzes the motivation and behavior of Adam and Eve in their succumbing to temptation, disobedience, and guilty flight from God.

Luther early on in his discussion of the effect of Adam's and Eve's sin in Genesis 3 attacks the doctrine that man's original justice was extrinsic to his natural endowments (which are referred to above in relation to man's shame about nudity) and that man, therefore, had retained the image of God. This is also why in chapter 1 he had rejected the notion of memory, intellect and will as the trinitarian image of God, as we saw above. He wished to stress that man possessed his dignity in his original creation but lost it with the primal sin and will regain it only through Christ, if he has faith in Christ's work, in the next life. For this reason, man's Fall had best be seen as the loss of faith and trust in God. "Just as reason is overwhelmed by many kinds of ignorance, so the will has not only been confused but has been turned away from God and is an enemy of God. It enjoys rushing to evil, when the opposite should have happened. Therefore, this manifold corruption of our nature should not be weakened but should be amplified. From the image of God, from the knowledge of God, from the knowledge of all the other creatures, and from a very honorable nudity man has fallen into blasphemy, into hatred, into contempt of God, indeed, into what is even more, into enmity against God." [60]

---

[58] *Asclepius* I, 6 in *Hermetica,* ed. W. Scott, I, 294; Giovanni Pico della Mirandola, *Oratio [de dignitate hominis]*, (Indianapolis, 1965), 3.

[59] I refer to Frances Yates' stress on the *"Magus,"* in *Giordano Bruno and the Hermetic Tradition* (Chicago, 1964) and elsewhere.

[60] WA 42: 107, 4-9; LW 1: 142. The actual polemic begins on 123 and 164. The reference to the theological need for rhetoric in the passage cited should be noted.

Correspondingly, as he moves to discuss the serpent's temptation, he argues that: "the serpent directs its attack at God's good will and makes it its business to prove from the prohibition of the tree that God's will toward man is not good. Therefore, it launches its attack against the very image of God and the most excellent powers in the uncorrupted nature." [61] Satan's purpose is to destroy man's trust and faith in God by insinuating that there is deception and inconsistency in His command about the tree. "Therefore, Satan here attacks Adam and Eve in this way to deprive them of the Word and their trust in God. ... Truly, therefore, this temptation is the sum of all temptations; it brings with it the ruin or the destruction of the entire Decalogue. Disbelief is the source of all sins. (*Fons enim omnium peccatorum est incredulitas* .)When Satan aroused this disbelief by driving out or corrupting the Word, there was nothing that would not be easy for him." [62] As he says a little below: "For truly the source of all sin is disbelief and doubt when one departs from the Word. Because the world is full of these [departures], it remains in idolatry, denies the truth of God, and invents a new God." [63]

Luther pursues this theme, describing with great subtlety of psychological insight the steps by which Eve is led to the act of plucking the apple. The sin of disbelief, loss of faith led the way. The act, itself, like a good work, automatically followed. [64] Commenting on Adam's confrontation with God, he continues to project a brilliant literary interpretation of the sparse passage, delineating the psychology of guilt. Parenthetically, it might be said that whatever the merits or shortcomings of Erik Erikson's effort to detect a personal psychological crisis in Luther which was paradigmatic for his vast following, [65] there can be no denial of the deeply psychological quality of his religious thought, and in a certain sense the human condition was typified for Luther by man denying his guilt. I believe a viable interpretation of his entire theology could be constructed around this existential situation. Here he depicts it as follows: "Thus when man has been accused of sin by God, he does not acknowledge his sin but rather accuses God

---

[61] WA 42: 110, 9-12; LW 1: 146.
[62] WA 42: 110-11, 38-41, 1-3; LW 1: 147.
[63] WA 42: 112, 20-22; LW 1: 149.
[64] WA 42: 112-122; LW 1: 149-162.
[65] *Young Man Luther, A Study of Psychoanalysis and History* (New York, 1962). In other words I find Luther's own religious-psychological insights vastly important but wonder whether his personal psychogenesis is very relevant to understanding the historical movement.

and transfers his guilt from himself to the Creator. The outcome is
that in this way sin grows endlessly unless God through His mercy
grants His help. This wickedness and utmost stupidity Adam regards
as supreme wisdom. He has become so confused by his fright that he
does not realize what he is saying or what is doing, and by excusing
himself he accuses himself most seriously and enormously increases
his sin. However, we must not think that this happened to Adam alone.
We, each one of us, do the same thing; our nature does not permit
us to act otherwise after we have become guilty of sin." [66]

Behind his denial of free will lies Luther's vision of guilt-ridden
man. Moreover, Luther sees in his denial of free will no lack of activism on the part of the individual man but rather this pathological
and paralyzed state of unreadiness to accept an accusation of guilt,
this refusal of responsibility for his motives and actions which drives
the individual to all sorts of displacements and covering-over modes
of behavior. The only cure for this panic is a trust which cannot possibly
be self-engendered. Religiously it must come from God. But man's sin
and guilt still remains. Thus Luther's "enslaved will" is so conceived
because it is the common condition of man to be in such a state of
guilty panic as Luther here describes in Adam that he is incapable of
moral choice. Thus also there follows his doctrine of *simul justus et
peccator*. [67] Luther clearly acknowledges the centrality of this conception for his whole religious reform striving: "This is the last step
of sin, to insult God and to charge Him with being the originator of
sin. Unless hearts are given courage through trust in mercy, this nature
cannot be urged on beyond this point if there are successive steps of
sin. That is why the state of the Church was horrible under the Pope.
For then nothing was seen or heard which could encourage a heart in
such distress, except that each year the history of the Passion was
feebly taught, which weakly showed whence forgiveness could be
sought. Everything else led away from the promise of remission of
sins to one's own righteousness. ... Thus these miserable people
wasted away without hope, without counsel, and without any help, in
deepest sorrows of soul. Were these conditions not full of terror?" [68]

---

[66] WA 42: 131, 9-16; LW 1: 175.

[67] Cf. Steven E. Ozment, *Homo Viator, Luther and Late Medieval Theology*,
in *The Reformation in Medieval Perspective*, ed. S. E. Ozment, 142-54, espec.
148-52 and n. 22. My point is that, according to Luther, only in the recognition
of man's sinfulness and loss of godlike qualities which flows from a *fides* conceived
as a total trust in God can human righteousness be restored.

[68] WA 42: 134, 8-21; LW 1: 179-80.

It is, I believe, Luther's sense of the psychological disaster of striving for holiness and self-justification that underlies his denial of the divine image to fallen man, as well as unimpaired natural endowments. It is this psychology which explains his anthropology.

The compensating mercy that was to come with Christ is seen by Luther as already co-present in Adam's confrontation with God in his interpretation of the seed of woman, who will crush the serpent's head, as Christ: "There is not that terrible sight as on Mt. Sinai, where trumpet blasts were mingled with flashes of lightning and peals of thunder. But God comes in a very soft breeze to indicate that the reprimand will be fatherly. ... This shows that even then Christ, our Deliverer, had placed Himself between God and man as a Mediator. It is a very great measure of grace that after Adam's sin God does not remain silent but speaks, and in many words indeed, in order to show signs of His fatherly disposition. ... And so, although the promise concerning Christ is not yet there, it is already noticeable in the thought and counsel of God." [69]

Passing over his remarkable and sympathetic discussion of the fallen state of women, [70] his discussion of chapter 3 fittingly ends with what might be entitled a description of "The Misery of the Human Condition," although he does not deny there are certain compensations such as "the glory of motherhood" and physical pleasures. This, of course, was the medieval and Renaissance counterpart of works on "The Dignity of Man." [71] Luther clearly seems to have the separate stages of his theological vision of the condition of man continuously present in his narration. The time before the Fall, when man was briefly in possession of his dignity (by Luther's calculation hardly a single day) is followed by the Fall and the Expulsion, to be followed in the fullness of time with the coming of Christ and the eventual otherworldly destinies of all men. But in the present, where we and Luther both live, the miserable condition of man in his loss of dignity is brightened both by the retrospective dream of what might have been done through the glorious potential of his one day of innocence and by the hope of future salvation in the time between Adam and

---

[69] WA 42: 135, 8-11, 17-22; LW 1: 180-81.

[70] WA 42: 148-51; LW 1: 198-203.

[71] Adam's curse. WA 42: 152-63; LW 1: 203-19. For discussion and exposition of the inter-relationship of the dignity of man and the misery of human conditions as themes in the Renaissance, see my *In Our Image*, Part II, *passim*. Also see Giovanni di Napoli, " 'Contemptus Mundus' e 'Dignitas Hominis' nel Rinascimento," *Rivista di filosofia neoscolastica*, XLVIII (1956), 9-41.

Christ. Yet the available redemption brought by Christ in these latter days of Christendom is shadowed both by the future conditionality of salvation and the harsh continuation of man's sin-ridden exile. In this simultaneity of the ages, therefore, mankind lives, reminded of the great dignity of the pleasurable and immortal life they might have had, frightened and terrified by the enormity of their ancestral crimes and the burden of guilt that they retain, cheered on, if they have faith, by the promise of salvation and the assurance that their restored dignity will be finer than the original possibility lost. Such are the theological components of Luther's hexameral anthropology.

But encased within this shifting frame were certain elements of historical actuality: the psychology of guilt, self-esteem, dependence and trust; the family and the relationship of husband and wife as the chief scene of our earthly life, inflamed and wounded by pain, anxieties, passion and love, but noble and honorable in Luther's eyes; the state with its harsh punitive function but necessary for the peace of everyman; the learned disciplines and professions by which mankind struggled to make these earthly actions more rational and fulfilling; and finally the Church, with its profession of pastors preaching and guiding the faithful and would-be faithful toward deepened faith and trust in God until they reached their heavenly kingdom. And round about, the idolators, the idlers, the furtive, the larcenous, the murderous who knowingly or unknowingly marched in the hosts of Satan. Here in these lectures on Genesis, chapter 1 to 3, Luther provides this more than usually panoramic view of human destiny. It was a vision which recoiled from the optimism of the Renaissance humanists and Platonists, because, he feared, this very dream of deification (so openly manifested in the writings of Manetti, Ficino and Pico, [72] not likely to have been known to Luther but the substance of similar ideas well known to him) would once again incite men to Adam's sin, namely: "that when he was deprived of his mind by Satan and believed that he would be like God, he became like Satan himself." [73] But Adam, he believed, could have become godlike if he had trusted God in paradise, and now, after Christ, any man could regain the divine image and likeness in his future heavenly home if he believed the divine promises, trusted God's mercy and had faith that Christ had died for him.

---

[72] For analysis see *In Our Image*, chapters VI, IX and X.
[73] See Luther's comments on verse 22 in general: WA 42: 166-68, citation: 166, 29-31; LW 1: 222-25, citation: 223.

THE BAPTISM OF JOHN AND THE BAPTISM OF JESUS IN HULDRYCH ZWINGLI, BALTHASAR HUBMAIER AND LATE MEDIEVAL THEOLOGY

DAVID C. STEINMETZ

Duke University

One of the most curious of all the arguments stimulated by the Protestant Reformation was the paper war between Huldrych Zwingli and Balthasar Hubmaier over the status of the baptism of John the Baptist. The controversy broke out in May, 1525, raged for about six months, and subsided in November, 1525, almost as suddenly as it had erupted. The issue between Zwingli and Hubmaier was whether the baptism of John was equal in power and significance to the baptism of Jesus and, if not, whether a sharp distinction should be drawn between them. Zwingli argued for equality and Hubmaier for distinction.

On the face of it, one would be hard put to find an issue more trivial than the role of John the Baptist in the gospel narratives. In a world in which far weightier issues were at stake, a world divided over the nature of the Church and the possibility of sacraments in anything like the traditional sense, a controversy over the relation of the baptism of John to the baptism of Jesus appears to be a precious dispute over an exegetical issue of doubtful importance.

Yet the debate is far more significant than the limited nature of its subject matter might suggest. John stands between the two testaments and a number of crucial issues intersect in him. It is impossible to discuss the baptism of John in the 1520's without touching on a series of controversial subjects important to the Protestant reformers, such as the nature of the history of salvation, the character of the sacraments or, indeed, the validity of infant baptism. The position one takes on the figure of John colors, if it does not determine, the position one adopts on these other, larger issues.

The problem of the relationship of the baptism of John to the baptism of Jesus was not a new issue sprung on an unsuspecting world by a chorus of enthusiastic Protestant exegetes. The problem was not only traditional, it was the subject of an entire question in the *Sentences* of Peter Lombard (IV *Sent.* d. 2 q. 2). Both Hubmaier and Zwingli are familiar with this distinction, though Hubmaier as a doctor of theology is better trained in scholastic thought than Zwingli, whose formal theological education was painfully brief.

Zwingli is on the warpath against this tradition. In his view the late medieval treatment of John not only distorted the exegetical data but lulled the medieval Catholic Church into embracing wholly erroneous conclusions concerning the nature of baptism. He was floored, then, to discover that Hubmaier, in the name of a radical theology of baptism, had embraced all the old nonsense about John which both of them had learned in the medieval Catholic schools. Zwingli, whose debating manners were no better than they should be, responded to Hubmaier's gentle arguments with a thoroughly uncivil howl of rage.

I. *The Late Medieval Catholic Tradition*

The debate does not make much sense unless one knows what late medieval theologians taught about John. [1] One can find the main lines of this tradition neatly summarized by the fifteenth-century theologian, Gabriel Biel, whose *Collectorium* is a handy compendium of late medieval theological opinions. [2] The position which Biel himself takes on the issues raised in Book IV d. 2 q. 2 is not terribly important for us to note, since it is not likely that Biel as a creative theologian played any role at all in the theological moulding of Zwingli's views. Biel is cited here as an historian who provides the context and background of a sixteenth-century dispute rather than as an original thinker who influenced its outcome.

The question which Lombard raised and which Biel dealt with in three articles is whether people who had been baptized with the baptism of John were required to be baptized with the baptism of Christ. The first article is devoted almost wholly to a clarification of terms. What is meant by the baptism of John? [3] Who were the disciples of John

---

[1] Christof Windhorst, in his admirable study of Hubmaier's theology, makes a brief attempt to place the controversy between Hubmaier and Zwingli in the context of medieval theology, but restricts his discussion to the teaching of Peter Lombard. See Christof Windhorst, *Täuferisches Taufverständnis, Balthasar Hubmaiers Lehre zwischen Traditioneller und Reformatorischer Theologie,* Studies in Medieval and Reformation Thought XVI (Leiden, 1976), 65-68.

[2] References in this essay are to the critical edition prepared by Wilfrid Werbeck and Udo Hoffmann, Gabrielis Biel, *Collectorium circa quattuor libros Sententiarum,* Vol. IV/1 (Tübingen, 1975).

[3] Biel, IV *Sent.* d. 2 q. 2 a. 1 nota. 1, 106-109.

who appear to need rebaptism? [4] Can one draw a distinction between different kinds of rebaptism? [5]

The New Testament is always very careful to label the baptism of John with his own name. That fact is remarkable when one considers that, while Peter and Paul baptized, no one would dream of calling baptism by their names. Their baptism is always called the "baptism of Christ." Only John's baptism is singled out for special treatment. Why is that?

Medieval theologians could think of several reasons, not all equally important. John was the first promulgator and sole minister of his baptism. [6] None of his disciples baptized and the ceremony terminated with his death. Those are the historical reasons why John's baptism carried his name.

More important still are the theological reasons. Nothing finally took place in John's baptism of which John was not the author. [7] In other words, John washed the bodies of his disciples as a sign of penitence for sin, but he was unable to wash their sins away. The weakness of John's baptism is traceable to a defect in its form. [8] John did not baptize in the name of the Trinity, but in the unspecified name of one who was to come. Unless the proper form (the name of the Trinity) is joined to the proper matter (water), no sin is remitted *ex opere operato*.

Biel reports the opinion of Durand of St. Pourçain that John did not use a form at all in the administration of his baptism. [9] While the picture of silent splashings in the Jordan is not a very convincing one historically, Durand believes that since the power of a sacrament depends on its form, the weakness of John's baptism can only be explained by an absence of form.

As far as Biel is concerned either opinion is equally probable. [10] However one explains it, something was amiss with the form of John's baptism. If John had baptized in the proper form, which he could have learned from the disciples of Jesus, then his baptism would have been called the "baptism of Christ" and there would have been no problem of two baptisms to push over.

---

[4] Biel, IV *Sent.* d. 2 q. 2 a. 1 nota. 2, 109-111.
[5] Biel, IV *Sent.* d. 2 q. 2 a. 1 nota. 3, 111.
[6] Biel, IV *Sent.* d. 2 q. 2 a. 1 nota. 1, 106.
[7] Biel, IV *Sent.* d. 2 q. 2 a. 1 nota. 1, 107.
[8] Biel, IV *Sent.* d. 2 q. 2 a. 1 nota. 1, 108.
[9] Biel, IV *Sent.* d. 2 q. 2 a. 1 nota. 1, 108.
[10] Biel, IV *Sent.* d. 2 q. 2 a. 1 nota. 1, 109.

Peter Lombard had tried to draw a distinction between two classes of John's disciples. [11] The first group, described in Acts 19, lacked any knowledge of the Trinity and placed their hope for salvation rather in the baptism administered by John. These people were obviously proper candidates for rebaptism by the apostles. But the second group, mentioned in Acts 8, saw the baptism of John in relation to Christ and shared with the apostles a common faith in the Trinity. There was no need to subject these people to rebaptism and they were given the Holy Spirit by the imposition of hands.

Biel views this distinction with distaste and can hardly wait to announce the result of a quick tabulation of the opinions of the later doctors, who unanimously reject it. [12] The disciples of John are not divisible into two groups. They are not divisible because the baptism of John did not suffice for salvation. Lacking the proper form, it was not a sacrament in the sense of an efficacious sign of grace. The faith of John's disciples was never really at issue. No amount of piety on the part of John's disciples could overcome the unavoidable defect in the essential composition of his baptism. All John's disciples, faith or no faith, were fit candidates for rebaptism by the Church.

Biel does think, however, that one should distinguish between "rebaptize" and "baptize with a repeated baptism." [13] Because the baptism of John was not a true baptism, at least in the sense of its inability to wash away sins, the disciples of John were "rebaptized," but not under any circumstances "with a repeated baptism." Water was applied twice; water joined to the proper form, only once.

If it is true that the baptism of John did not contain grace, was not properly a sacrament, and did not absolve the disciples of John from the obligation to be rebaptized with the baptism of Christ, why on earth was it instituted? [14] What conceivable purpose did it serve?

The question is more than a little embarrassing, especially since the New Testament quite blandly asserts that John was sent by God to preach and baptize, and Biel scurries about to justify the ways of God to man. Biel is even willing to concede that the baptism of John was a sacrament in the loose, though not the strict, sense. It was a sign of a sacred thing; it was a figure of the baptism of Christ. But it would probably be more accurate, and certainly less confusing, to call it a

[11] Biel, IV *Sent.* d. 2 q. 2 a. 1 nota. 2, 109.
[12] Biel, IV *Sent.* d. 2 q. 2 a. 1 nota. 2, 111.
[13] Biel, IV *Sent.* d. 2 q. 2 a. 1 nota. 3, 111.
[14] Biel, IV *Sent.* d. 2 q. 2 a. 3 dub. 1, 116.

sacramental, which prepared people for the grace offered in the baptism of Christ. [15]

The principal role of the baptism of John was to serve as a transitional step between circumcision in the Old Testament and the baptism of Christ in the New. John recalled the Jews from reliance on circumcision and, by doing so, signalled the end of the Old Testament. But he also pointed ahead to the new sacramental dispensation of the Church by offering water as a sign of penitence. The water was not joined to the proper form and so was powerless to absolve the sinner from the guilt and power of its sin. Still it was a step forward to have consecrated and used the matter of the baptism of Christ. [16]

II. *The Controversy*

Zwingli first tackles the subject of John's baptism in 1525 in his *Commentarius de vera et falsa religione*. The treatment is brief, since the *Commentarius* is devoted to an exposition of all the principal topics of Christian doctrine. But even in this brief treatment it is clear that Zwingli is determined to stand the medieval tradition on John on its head and to affirm every proposition which Biel and the brotherhood of medieval university professors took such pains to deny.

There is, Zwingli argues, no significant difference between the baptism of John and the baptism of Jesus. [17] They are the same not merely in matter (no one was prepared to dispute this) but also in form. [18] John, no less than Peter and Paul, taught his disciples to place their hope in Christ and those who put on Christ in John's baptism were dedicated and bound to the Trinity. Not only were the disciples of John not rebaptized but even the disciples of Jesus who were sent out to baptize were first baptized themselves with the baptism of John. [19] Either admit that Peter was baptized with John's baptism

---

[15] Biel, IV *Sent.* d. 2 q. 2 a. 3 dub. 1, 117.

[16] Biel, IV *Sent.* d. 2 q. 2 a. 3 dub. 1, 117.

[17] Citations from the *Commentarius* are taken from the edition by M. Schuler and J. Schulthess, *Huldrici Zuinglii Opera,* III (Zurich, 1832), hereafter abbreviated as *SS* III. Zwingli says exactly, *SS* III, 234: "Quid vero distent Joannis Baptismus et Christi, multa tum olim tum nunc est quaestio; sed inutilis plane, nam discrimen omnino nullum est, quod ad causam ac finem attinet: quamvis quod ad usum sive formam attinent non nihil discriminis sit."

[18] Zwingli, *SS* III, 236: "Quibus adparet, Christum per ministros suos non alia ratione aut forma baptizavisse, quam qua Joannes baptizabat: nam si secus baptizavisset, non potuissent hoc omittere Joannis discipuli." Cf. Zwingli, *SS* III, 239.

[19] Zwingli, *SS* III, 236.

and not rebaptized or admit that the chief of the apostles was un-baptized. *Tertium non datur.*

Acts 19, which is a trump card played by theologians who advocate a sharp distinction between the two baptisms, is challenged by Zwingli, who feels that it is time to call the bluff of medieval exegetes. The New Testament distinguishes between baptism as teaching and baptism as the application of water. The disciples of John at Ephesus had received baptism in the sense of being taught (and badly taught at that!) the rudiments of John's message. But they had not received water. Paul gave them better instruction and sealed it with the external rite of washing. [20]

The theological foundation on which medieval scholasticism distinguished the baptism of Jesus from the baptism of John—namely, that the former conferred grace *ex opere operato* while the latter did not—is airily dismissed by Zwingli. Zwingli did not claim that both baptisms were efficacious signs of grace (which would, of course, be one way to equalize them), but denied that either was. John's baptism did not confer grace *ex opere operato,* but, then, neither does the baptism of Christ. [21]

The principal meaning of baptism for Zwingli in the *Commentarius* seems to be summed up in its role as a sign of a changed life. [22] Baptism signifies that a Christian is bound to a new life and will confess Christ even unto death. In that sense one can accept the medieval definition of a sacrament as a sign of a sacred thing.

Zwingli continues his attack on the medieval consensus in *Von der Taufe, von der Wiedertaufe und von der Kindertaufe,* [23] though he broadens his attack by opening up a second front against the Zurich Anabaptists, who are just as muddled in their treatment of the baptism of John as the scholastics. Zwingli's starting-point is the assertion that baptism is a sign, but only a sign. It is a covenant sign or pledge, like the white cross of the Swiss confederation. [24] But it should never

---

[20] Zwingli, *SS* III, 237-39.

[21] Zwingli, *SS* III, 234: "Nihil efficiebat Joannis tinctio: loquimur autem hic de aquae Baptismo, non de irrigatione interna quae per spiritum sanctum fit. Nihil efficit Christi tinctio: nam Christus Baptismo Joannis contentus fuit, tam in se quam in discipulis."

[22] Zwingli, *SS* III, 239.

[23] The text of this and the remaining Zwingli treatises are found in the edition of Emil Egli et al., *Huldreich Zwinglis Sämtliche Werke,* IV, C.R. XCI (Leipzig, 1927), hereafter abbreviated as *ZW* IV.

[24] *ZW* IV, 218.

be confused with the thing signified, as the scholastics confuse it when
they claim that the waters of baptism contain or convey grace. No
material or external thing can justify. [25] Grace remains in the power
of God, who gives it by an immediate and invisible action. The flesh,
that is, the world of material signs and symbols, profits nothing; it
is the Holy Spirit who makes alive. Anyone who places his confidence
in external rites and ceremonies is an idolator.

Baptism is a word, however, with at least four meanings. Depending
on the context, baptism can be used to signify "water", "Spirit",
"teaching", "faith" or any combination of them. [26] In the ordinary
course of events the Christian will receive baptism in all four senses,
though it is not necessary that these four baptisms coincide and, indeed,
improbable that they will. One can receive water and teaching before
one receives the Spirit and faith and the New Testament does not
seem to require that these four baptisms occur in any particular order. [27]
Baptism in the sense of water can be given to a child before it has
faith as a cowl can be given to a novice in an order before he has
learned the full significance of the discipline which he has embraced. [28]
The New Testament does not require faith before baptism and neither
should we.

The distinction of four meanings for the word "baptism" is important for Zwingli because of his interpretation of Acts 19. [29] Unless
Zwingli can show that the disciples of John were not subjected to
rebaptism (and he can do that only if there is some ambiguity in the
meaning of the term "baptism"), he will be hard-pressed to defend
his argument that there is no essential difference between the baptism
of John and Jesus. Failure here would result in the collapse of his
whole argument.

But Zwingli appears serenely confident that his exegesis of Acts 19
is sound and that his chain of reasoning stands in no immediate danger
of refutation. Indeed, he attacks the medieval position even more vigo-

---

[25] *ZW* IV, 217.

[26] *ZW* IV, 219-20.

[27] *ZW* IV, 222-25.

[28] *ZW* IV, 231: "Für das erst ist der touff ein pflichtig zeichen, das en,
der inn nimpt, anzeigt, das er sin leben bessren und Christo nachvolgen welle.
Kurtz, es ist ein anhab eines nüwen lebens, und ist also ein anheblich zeichen,
ceremonii oder teleta [τελετά] uff griechisch. Glych als wenn die jungen sind
in die örden gestossen, hat man inen die kutten angeschroten; noch habend sy
die gsatz und statuten nit gewüsset, sunder sy erst erlernet in der kutten."

[29] *ZW* IV, 268-77.

rously and with greater gusto than he exhibited in the *Commentarius*. The entire medieval position on the proper form is theologically unsound and rests on very shaky exegetical underpinnings. Medieval theology treated the formula of baptism in the name of the Trinity as though it were a kind of white magic, a formula of incantation. One would think that scholastic theologians had forgotten that the power of baptism does not reside in the words of a form, however orthodox, but in God. [30]

Waving aside the misguided medieval theology of the proper form, there is still the exegetical question whether the baptism of John involved the whole Trinity. Zwingli believes that it does and cites the account of the baptism of Jesus by John as proof of the Trinitarian character of John's baptism: the Father speaks, the Son is baptized and the Spirit descends like a dove. [31]

Besides, it is not at all clear that the disciples of Jesus always baptized their converts with what medieval theologians regarded as the proper form. There is ample evidence that they frequently baptized in the name of Jesus alone. [32] If that is so, it is very difficult to see how John, who baptized in the name of the Lamb of God who takes away the sin of the world, administered a baptism in any way inferior to the baptism administered by the early Church. It is not enough to say that John's baptism was merely a baptism of repentance, because so, according to the New Testament, was the baptism of Jesus.

Attempts to plead the obsolescence of John's baptism on the basis of a particular understanding of the history of salvation are also doomed to failure. John is not a type of Christ and should not be reckoned with the Old Testament. [33] He offered a baptism, not limited to his own lifetime, but which continues in the Church up to the present day. Whenever the Church points to the Lamb of God and administers the covenant sign of water as the pledge of a new life, there the baptism of John is freshly celebrated. It is not stretching the point to say that to follow Christ at all is to be baptized by John. [34]

Zwingli has by this time managed to thumb his nose at every major point made by late medieval theologians in their discussions of the

---

[30] *ZW* IV, 267.
[31] *ZW* IV, 267.
[32] *ZW* IV, 236.
[33] *ZW* IV, 259-60.
[34] *ZW* IV, 266: "So er [Christus] aber imm touff Johansen getoufft ist, so müssen ouch wir im touff Johansen getoufft werden."

significance of the baptism of John. He has also taken several swipes at Anabaptist theology, insofar as Anabaptists also want to distinguish the two baptisms sharply and argue (as medieval theologians did not) for the fixed sequence of teaching, faith, and baptism by the Spirit prior to baptism by water. Even though Zwingli's major target has been the late medieval theology of baptism, it was Hubmaier, rather than a conservative Catholic, who first felt impelled to respond to him.

Hubmaier's response, *Von der christlichen Taufe der Gläubigen*, was published in the middle of the summer. [35] He strikes hardest at the weakest point in Zwingli's argument, his exegesis of Acts 19. [36] The equation of baptism with teaching is an illusion sprung from Zwingli's overfertile imagination. Baptism by water is a public confession and testimony of an inward faith and commitment. [37] As such, it is always preceded by, but never synonymous with, the teaching of the Word and the response of faith. Zwingli is wrong when he denies such a fixed order in the New Testament. The New Testament moves from teaching and preaching to faith and baptism. [38] Because faith is always prior to baptism, the rite can never be administered to children. [39]

Hubmaier identifies John with the Law and the Old Testament. He is unmoved by Zwingli's arguments that John preached the gospel. His preaching is filled with the curse of the Law, with sin, death, devil and hell. [40] Small wonder that he sent his disciples away to follow Christ. [41] Jesus was the physician, not John. John only prepared his listeners for the consolation of the gospel; he did not himself offer it.

Material symbols are more important for Hubmaier than for Zwingli. Water baptism is necessary to salvation as an expression of obedience to Christ. [42] Christ's baptism rather than John's is connected with the

---

[35] References to Hubmaier's works are to the critical edition by Gunnar Westin and Torsten Bergsten, Balthasar Hubmaier, *Schriften*, IX, Quellen zur Geschichte der Täufer (Gütersloh, 1962), hereafter abbreviated as *HS*.

[36] *HS*, 131-33.

[37] *HS*, 121-22.

[38] *HS*, 134-39.

[39] Hubmaier rejects Zwingli's use of monastic imagery as an analogy for infant baptism, though he later introduces a monastic analogue of his own, *HS*, 138: "Dann wie die angeschroten kutten keyn Münch macht und nicht nütz ist, sonder wider Gott geschicht, also macht der kinder tauff keyn Christen, fahet keyn new leben an, geschicht wider die eynsetzung des tauffs Christi."

[40] *HS*, 124, 127.

[41] *HS*, 126-27.

[42] *HS*, 140-46.

remission of sins, not *ex opere operato* (Hubmaier agrees with Zwingli in regarding that rationale as a theological dead-end) but because of the inward yes of the heart to the proclamation of the gospel (*ex fide recipientis*). [43]

Hubmaier brushes aside Zwingli's claim that the baptism of John and the baptism of Christ are, to all intents and purposes, the same. The New Testament makes it clear, Zwingli's strained exegesis of Acts 19 notwithstanding, that everyone baptized by John must be rebaptized by Christ. John is a preacher who drives men to Christ, not an apostle who administers Christ's baptism.

There is, however, an aspect of John's baptism which Hubmaier finds beguiling and regards rather wistfully as he pushes John's baptism back into the sphere of the Old Testament. John, after all, did not baptize children. [44] His baptism was restricted to adults who felt guilt for their sin and could make an outward public confession. Hubmaier believes that this restriction of baptism to adults, characteristic of the baptism of John, is normative for the baptism of Christ as well. But he has seriously weakened his case by the severe contrast which he has drawn between the two baptisms. If analogies are not permissible elsewhere in considering the two baptisms, why should one suddenly be allowed here?

Zwingli was infuriated by Hubmaier's tract and published his own *Antwort über Balthasar Hubmaiers Taufbüchlein* in November, 1525. All this chatter about two baptisms is irresponsible and flies in the face of the assertion of Paul that there is one Lord, one faith, one baptism (Ephesians 4:5). [45] If Paul is right, then the baptism of Jesus and John are the same. If he is wrong, then Hubmaier must embrace a Hobson's choice of distasteful alternatives. [46] Either John's baptism is worthier than ours, since Christ received it rather than the baptism offered by the apostles, or every Christian must be baptized twice, first with John's baptism for repentance of sins and then with Christ's baptism for the forgiveness of sins. Such absurd theological conclusions unmask the hollowness of Hubmaier's specious exegesis.

There cannot be two baptisms because there is an identity between

---

[43] *HS*, 137.
[44] *HS*, 125: "Da würdt aber gesehen, das Johannes nit junge kinder getäufft hat, sonder die, so sich jrer sünden schuldig gaben und erkanten." Cf. *HS*, 127-34.
[45] *ZW* IV, 598.
[46] *ZW* IV, 598.

John and the Church at the central point, the preaching of the gospel. [47]
John stood beside the Jordan and cried: "Behold the Lamb of God who
takes away the sins of the world!" What apostle ever preached a
purer gospel than that?

Hubmaier replied—rather good-humoredly under the circumstances
—with his own *Gespräch auf Zwinglis Taufbüchlein*. He is unmoved
by Zwingli's arguments and clings to the point he made earlier concerning the distinction of the two baptisms: the baptism of John signified the confession of sins; the baptism of Christ signified the forgiveness of sins. [48] That this is not just a contrast of sufficient and
insufficient baptisms becomes clear when Hubmaier associates the
baptism of John with fear, devil, hell and death and the baptism of
Christ with comfort, Spirit, heaven and life. [49] Hubmaier is not the
least disturbed by Zwingli's angry charge that he has remained bogged
down in traditional views of John. [50] If anything, he takes pleasure in
claiming support for his position in the writings of Origen, Cyril,
Theophylact, Chrysostom and Jerome. [51]

Curiously enough, Hubmaier agrees with Zwingli that the practices
of medieval monasticism provide analogies which illuminate the meaning
of baptism. But whereas Zwingli compares baptism to the assumption
of a cowl by a novice, Hubmaier focuses on the monastic vow. [52] Like
a monk the Christian vows to live according to the rule of Christ,
which is not the same thing as the rule of Benedict or Francis.

In short, Hubmaier wants to stay with the plain, old sound exegesis
of medieval scholasticism which acknowledged the fact of two baptisms
in the New Testament and did not try to gloss it over with fancy explanations about four meanings of the verb "to baptize." [53] John had

---

[47] *ZW* IV, 598-99.

[48] *HS*, 196: "Yetz hörstu, das der Tauff Joannis nichts anders ist, denn ein
offenlich zeügknuss vor den Menschen im Wasser, das sich der Mensch bekennt
ein Sünder vor Gott. Mat. 3. Herwiderumb so ist der Tauff Christi ein offen-
liche unnd eüsserliche bekandtnus oder Ayd des glaubens (das ist, das der Mensch
inwendig glaub verzeyhung seiner Sünden durch Christum), der halb er sich
ein schreyben last und eüsserlich verzaichnen under die Christen, dz er wöll
nach der Regel Christi leben."

[49] *HS*, 197.

[50] *HS*, 196: "Gott sey gelobt das wir nit allain Saturnich lätzköpff seind, wie
du unns nennest, sonder all Theologi met uns, dich aussgenommen."

[51] *HS*, 197.

[52] See, for eamxple, footnote 48 above.

[53] *HS*, 197: "Jch waiss doch nit ainen leerer jung oder alt auf erden, der
dir in disem schweren, mercklichen unnd verfierischen Jrsal bey gsteende, das du
redst, predigest und schreibst, Joannis tauff und der Tauff Christi sey ain tauf."

a role, but it was not the role of an apostle. To linger by the baptism of John is to remain in the obsolete world of the Old Covenant.

III. *Conclusion*

There the debate ground to a halt. Events had overtaken both theologians and they turned their energies and attention to other problems. Yet certain conclusions can be drawn from their brief encounter which are important for us to note.

1. Zwingli is not usually studied against the background of late medieval scholasticism. There are good reasons for this neglect, which we need not go into here. But while Zwingli is not so well trained in scholastic theology as Luther or even Hubmaier, he is not entirely ignorant of it, as his polemic on the baptism of John clearly demonstrates. Zwingli knows the scholastic tradition on John in intimate detail and rejects it point by point. The rejection is radical, far more radical in fact than Hubmaier's, and utterly unnostalgic. Zwingli resists vehemently any attempt to drive a wedge between Jesus and John on the question of baptism, even when the purpose of such an attempt is the thoroughly admirable desire to stress the uniqueness of the saving activity of God in Christ.

Hubmaier, on the other hand, prefers to fish in the familiar coastal waters of late medieval religious thought. Zwingli is exactly right when he points out this conservative streak in Hubmaier's Anabaptist theology. Hubmaier is radical on the question of John's baptism only in the sense that he intensifies tendencies already present in late medieval thought. He sharpens the split between John and Jesus by placing John in the Old Testament as a preacher of the curse of the Law. Medieval theology took the gentler position that John was a transitional or intermediate figure between the two testaments.

In one sense and one sense only is John superior to the prophets of the Old Testament. The Old Testament prophets could only preach Christ as one who was to come, while John could point directly to him with his finger. [54] Still that difference does not make John a preacher of the gospel. John fulfils, if you like, the second or pedagogical function of the Law. He is a stern schoolmaster who drags his reluctant pupils to Christ. However, the fact that the Law drives one to embrace the gospel does not make it any less the law. To use a distinction from Luther which Hubmaier does not employ but which is congenial to the

---

[54] Windhorst, *Täuferisches Taufverständnis,* 55.

point he is trying to make over against Zwingli, God does his strange work through John so that he may do his proper work through Christ.

2. From the standpoint of medieval theology Zwingli places the baptism of Jesus and John on the same level, partly by raising the baptism of John and partly by lowering the baptism of Christ. Zwingli elevates the baptism of John by insisting that John preaches the gospel, administers a baptism with which Father, Son and Holy Spirit are associated, and belongs firmly and unequivocally to the world of the New Testament. He lowers the baptism of Christ, again from a medieval perspective, by arguing that it confers no grace *ex opere operato*. Material signs symbolize but do not convey grace.

3. Zwingli and Hubmaier are forced to deal with John the Baptist because of their redefinition of baptism. Medieval theology with its settled definitions of the sacraments had a carefully allotted place for John; Protestant theology, with its new definitions of everything in sight, did not. The new theological definitions had to do more than satisfy the rational test of internal self consistency; they had to make sense of the exegetical data of Holy Scripture.

It was impossible for Zwingli and Hubmaier to talk about John for very long without making clear their vision of the history of salvation and the relationship between the two testaments. Zwingli's tendency is to lessen the distance between the Old Testament and the New in order to justify analogies between circumcision and infant baptism. It is impossible to do this if there is already a sharp division within the New Testament itself between Jesus and John the Baptist. Hubmaier's tendency is to increase the distance between the testaments in order to stress the uniqueness of the saving activity of God in the New Testament and to stifle the arguments for infant baptism at their source. In pressing his case he gladly makes use of arguments from his own Catholic past.

Zwingli is motivated by a vision of one people of God in history, a history stretching from Abraham to the reformed churches of Switzerland. In order to defend that vision he attacks with radical and not always convincing arguments the medieval scholastic tradition on his right and the Anabaptist reappropriation of it on his left. John is a symbol for Zwingli of the continuity between the two testaments and the unity of the people of God in time. The argument over John is passionate because the issue finally at stake is the validity of that vision.

THE ROLE OF NUREMBERG IN THE SPREAD
OF THE REFORMATION

HAROLD J. GRIMM

Emeritus, Ohio State University

In recent years, historians of the Reformation have given considerable attention to reasons for the rapid spread of the movement, especially to the role played by the imperial cities of Germany. Consequently, a number of stimulating generalizations concerning this phenomenon have been offered and numerous urban histories have been published. [1] To be more certain with respect to our generalizations, however, we must examine the cities more closely with particular attention to such matters as their prior political experience, religious and cultural developments within their walls, social unrest among their inhabitants, and the reception of the message of their evangelical preachers.

Nuremberg provides us with an example of an important imperial city which accepted the Lutheran Reformation at an early date. It was a city with a diversified economy, of a population estimated to consist of between 20,000 and 40,000 souls, of townsmen with a great variety of concerns and interests, and a geographical position that assured its importance as an entrepot for ideas as well as material goods. [2] It was governed by a city council which had been freed from all control of the emperor's burgrave, or castellan, who had had charge of the imperial castle overlooking the city and had been made the first margrave and elector of Brandenburg early in the fifteenth century. The council also had freed itself from the authority of the *Schultheiss,* or royal executive and judge. The emperor's confidence in the city was demonstrated by the fact that he usually held his first imperial diet there and entrusted it with the care of the imperial regalia. Furthermore, the city

---

[1] See especially Bernd Moeller, *Reichsstadt und Reformation,* Schriften des Vereins für Reformationsgeschichte, no. 180, vol. 69 (Gütersloh, 1962), tr. from a French edition into English under the title *Imperial Cities and the Reformation*: *Three Essays* (Philadelphia, 1972) ; and Steven E. Ozment, *The Reformation in the Cities*: *The Appeal of Protestantism to Sixteenth-Century Germany and Switzerland* (New Haven, 1975).

[2] Rudolf Endres, "Sozialstruktur Nürnbergs," in *Nürnberg—Geschichte einer Europäischer Stadt,* ed. Gerhard Pfeiffer (Munich, 1971), 194-99 (hereafter cited as Pfeiffer, *Nürnberg*).

had begun to emerge as an important territorial state with the acquisition of the imperial forest, originally under the jurisdiction of the burgrave, and of castles, lands, and towns by purchase or conquest. By exercising extensive administrative and judicial powers and creating a centralized bureaucratic system, the city council maintained a strict control over its territory.

Unlike the situation prevailing in most other imperial cities, the aristocratic patricians retained complete control of the city council. They conscientiously served the general welfare of the community, including the economic interests of the crafts, whose first-rate industry enabled the merchants to exchange goods with people throughout the commercial world. In return, the citizens, bound together by an annual oath, supported the rule of the patricians. Sovereign authority resided in the small council of forty-two members, thirty-four of whom were patricians and eight were representatives of the eight major crafts. A large council of approximately two hundred patricians and other distinguished citizens met occasionally to act on certain major matters such as war or taxation for which the small council desired broad popular support. [3] The concern of this government to provide for the general welfare of its people, both temporal and spiritual, and to maintain peace and order, helps explain its role in the introduction of the Reformation.

The city council's sense of duty with respect to the spiritual well-being of its people was evinced in the late medieval period by its demand for the improvement of morals, support of monastic and parish reforms, participation in the election of its clergy, and administration of ecclesiastical properties, religious endowments, poor relief, and education. These were concerns that grew out of the medieval corporate consciousness and conception of the city as a small *corpus christianum* in which the city corporation and church organization were one. But the development of the city council's authority, the emergence of well educated city clerks and jurisconsults, and the growth of bureaucratic institutions led to the gradual decline of corporate feeling and the increased emphasis on ethics that favored the growth of Protestantism. Luther's doctrine of justification by faith alone, for example, stressed the individual's direct, personal relation to God, while his doctrine of the two kingdoms drew a distinction between the spiritual and temporal

---

[3] For a detailed description of Nuremberg's government, see that of Christoph Scheurl in *Die Chroniken der fränkische Städte*, vol. 5: *Nürnberg* (Leipzig, 1874), 785-804, and parts of it in English translation in Gerald Strauss, *Nuremberg in the Sixteenth Century* (New York, 1966), 58-67.

authorities. Likewise, his emphasis upon the freedom of the individual called attention to man's obligation to serve his neighbor in love because of the love of God, whereas his ennobling of every calling of man tended to break down the medieval sharp distinction between the clergy and the laity.

In many ways, the city council's assumption during the Reformation of the duties of its bishop, who resided at Bamberg, was adumbrated by its activities in behalf of the spiritual welfare of its people during the latter part of the Middle Ages. In the fifteenth century, for example, it assumed the right of protection of its monasteries. It placed them under administrators who had charge of all secular matters, prescribed the number of religious for each of them, established definite rules and regulations for them, and made them render a strict account of all their property and endowments. It went so far as to play an active role in carrying out monastic reforms with the consequence that a number of its monasteries were exemplary institutions at the beginning of the Reformation. By 1500, it also had obtained from the papacy the right of presentation of the provosts of the two parish churches, St. Sebald and St. Lorenz. It selected men trained in law as well as theology whose chief duty was the selection and supervision of the parish clergy. [4] Likewise, the council assumed greater responsibility for its poor and sick by providing proper administration for the city's eleemosynary institutions and the endowments provided for them, so that the reorganization of Nuremberg's poor relief in the spirit of the Reformation was a natural consequence.

The patricians of the small council, the patricians and distinguished members of the large council, and other wealthy and influential citizens of Nuremberg comprised about six to eight percent of the city's population. [5] By background, education, political experience, and commercial

---

[4] See esp. Friedrich Roth, *Die Einführung der Reformation in Nürnberg* (Würzburg, 1885), 35-40. Other excellent sources for the Reformation in Nuremberg are Adolf Engelhardt, *Die Reformation in Nürnberg*, in *Mitteilungen des Vereins für Geschichte der Stadt Nürnberg*, 33 (1936) and 34 (1937) (hereafter cited as Engelhardt, *Reformation*, 1 and 2; Gerhard Pfeiffer, "Die Einführung der Reformation in Nürnberg als kirchenrechtliches und bekenntniskundliches Problem," *Blätter für deutsche Landesgeschichte* 89 (1952), 112-133; and Gottfried Seebass, "The Reformation in Nürnberg," in *The Social History of the Reformation*, eds. Lawrence P. Buck and Jonathan W. Zophy (Columbus, Ohio, 1972), 17-40. For sources, see *Quellen zur Nürnberger Reformationsgeschichte*, ed. Gerhard Pfeiffer, Einzelarbeiten aus der Kirchengeschichte Bayerns, vol. 45 (Nuremberg, 1968) (hereafter cited as Pfeiffer, *Quellen*).

[5] Endres, "Sozialstruktur," in Pfeiffer, *Nürnberg*, 194-99.

contacts men of broad vision, this class was receptive to the religious and cultural currents of their day. Some of them became active members of intellectual circles, or sodalities, that fostered religion and culture. Because the patricians as a whole were conscious of the importance of the crafts for the economic well-being of the city, they encouraged them in every possible way, thereby retaining the good will of the artisans.

The broad middle class, comprising artisans, lesser merchants, and shopkeepers, constituting about sixty percent of the population, was relatively stable at the beginning of the sixteenth century, largely because of the city's prosperity. The boys of this class usually attended school long enough to learn to read and absorb the growing amount of printed material available to them and to participate in the cultural activities of their day. The influence of the cobbler poet Hans Sachs on the development of the Reformation among the members of this middle class is well known.

Approximately a third of Nuremberg's population belonged to the poor, propertyless class of people who were not attached to guilds or lands but were day laborers, unemployed apprentices, and pieceworkers without steady or adequate incomes and thus frequently objects of charity. At the bottom were the professional beggars, outcasts, and members of the proscribed professions such as grave diggers and prostitutes. Although this class was restless and readily listened to left-wing leaders of the Reformation and fomenters of revolt, it was less apt to engage in violence than the poor of most other cities. The city council kept discontent to a minimum by providing the poor with efficiently administered relief, especially after the creation of the Common Chest and Great Almonry of 1522.

Whereas many factors were instrumental in preparing the way for the Reformation in Nuremberg, most important was the message itself, brought to all classes of people by pamphlets of the reformers and sermons of the preachers. It is this that helps explain the important role that Nuremberg played in the movement as a whole, for these materials were published by the city's printers for wide circulation. Furthermore, the advice provided the council by the clergy and legal consultants was passed on to cities and towns in various parts of Germany that were considering adopting the Reformation.

Among the first citizens to be influenced by the Reformation and instrumental in making its doctrines known among their townsmen were the members of the intellectual circle, first named after Conrad

Celtes (1459-1508), a German humanist who had been crowned poet laureate by Emperor Frederick III in Nuremberg. Known as the *Sodalitas celtica,* it soon included Willibald Pirckheimer, one of Germany's outstanding humanists, at whose home the men met; the two influential city treasurers Hieronymus Ebner, to whom Luther later dedicated his *Commentary on Psalm 110,* and Anton Tucher; Kaspar Nützel, who translated Luther's *Ninety-five Theses* into German for use by the common people; Christoph Scheurl, formerly professor of law at the University of Wittenberg and now legal consultant of the city council; Lazarus Spengler, *Ratsschreiber,* or council clerk, who became one of the city's leading lay reformers; and Albrecht Dürer, the illustrious artist.

Influenced to a considerable extent by the piety of late medieval mysticism and the ethical emphasis of Christian humanism, the members of the sodality maintained contacts with intelligentsia throughout Europe, including Erasmus, and sought to improve the moral life of Nuremberg. [6] They also were greatly influenced by the Christian mysticism of Johann Staupitz (ca. 1470-1524), general vicar of the Augustinian Eremites, and his successor Wenceslas Linck (1483-1547). On his visits to Nuremberg, especially in 1516 and 1517, Staupitz, after whom they now named the circle *Sodalitas staupitziana,* preached sermons of simple, practical piety to large audiences, excerpts of which some members of the group copied for subsequent use. They also appreciated having the opportunity of visiting with him in the Augustinian Monastry and jotting down some of the "table talks" on cultural as well as religious subjects. Linck, a life-long friend of Martin Luther and a reforming preacher at the Hospital of the Holy Spirit in Nuremberg from 1524 to his death, was to a large degree responsible for converting the popular name of the circle to "Martinians," or followers and admirers of Martin Luther.

The Martinians became well acquainted with Luther on his stops in Nuremberg on his way to and from his hearings before Cardinal Cajetan in Augsburg in October, 1518. Linck helped give him courage for continuing his dangerous mission, made travel arrangements for the journey, presented him with a new cowl, accompanied him to Augs-

---

[6] An excellent example of such a concern is Lazarus Spengler's *Ermanung und Undterwaysung zu einem tugenthaften Wandel* (Nuremberg, 1520) written for, and dedicated to, Albrecht Dürer. See Harold J. Grimm, "Lazarus Spengler, the Nürnberg City Council, and the Reformation," in *Luther for an Ecumenical Age,* ed. Carl Meyer (St. Louis, 1967), 108-19.

burg, and stayed with him at the Carmelite Monastery there. On his return trip, Luther gained more adherents by preaching in the church of the St. Egidien Monastery. So impressed was Lazarus Spengler by his contacts with Luther that he provided historians with the only contemporary account of the visits and wrote the first pamphlet published in defense of the Reformer, his widely read *Defense and Christian Reply Against Several Opponents with Reasons Why Doctor Martin Luther's Teaching Should not be Rejected But on the Contrary Considered Christian.* [7]

The *Defense* was first published in Augsburg in 1520, about the same time as a brilliant satire against the Ingolstadt Professor Johann Eck, Luther's most formidable enemy, called *The Corner Planed Smooth* (*Eccius dedolatus*). Eck accused Pirckheimer of having written the satire with the assistance of Spengler and included both of them among those threatened with excommunication in the papal bull against Luther, the *Exsurge domine,* and excommunicated in the bull *Decet pontificem romanum.* Although both eventually were granted absolution, they and their city had become deeply involved in Luther's cause.

Nuremberg was officially represented at the Diet of Worms in 1521 by three councilmen, its council secretary, and an experienced jurisconsult. These men were greatly impressed by Luther's stand, as can be seen in their reports to the city council. The city's jurisconsults explained that the Edict of Worms against Luther need not be obeyed because it was unjust and had not been issued with the unanimous approval of the electors, princes, and estates of the Empire, as was required. They added that it would not be wise to publish it before learning the response of other estates. [8] The council took their advice, although it later, in October 1521, posted it at the city hall and forbade the publication of Luther's books, but as a mere formality.

It was in this spirit that the city council permitted the Reformation to take hold in Nuremberg, despite the presence of the *Reichsregiment* (Imperial Council of Regency) and three imperial diets there during the critical years 1522-24. Already in the summer of 1520, it had appointed as provost of the parish church of St. Lorenz Hektor Pömer

---

[7] *Schutzred vnnd christenliche antwurt ains erbern liebhabers gotlicher warheyt der heyligen schrifft auff etlicher vermaint widersprechen mit an zaygung warumb Doctor Martini Luthers leer nit als unchristenlich verworffen sonder mer fur christenlich gehalten werden soll* (Nuremberg: Jobst Gutknecht, ca. 1520).

[8] Staatsarchiv Nürnberg, Repertorium 60b, Ratsbücher 3, p. 80. Although the argument against the legality of the edict was not correct, it proved very effective.

(1495-1541), a young patrician student at the University of Wittenberg who assumed his duties in 1521. It appointed as provost of
St. Sebald Georg Pester (ca. 1470-1536), also a Nuremberg citizen
who had studied law and theology at Wittenberg. Since both were
supporters of Luther, they appointed Lutheran clergy for service in
their respective parishes.

Most influential among the newly appointed clergy was Andreas
Osiander (1496-1552), an able scholar in languages and science as well
as in theology and an effective preacher. He provided the city council
with important memoranda concerning religious matters, played a major
role in developing the Brandenburg-Nuremberg Church Order of 1533,
and won over many people to the Reformation, including persons at-
tending the diets at Nuremberg. In 1524, the council appointed as
preacher of St. Sebald Dominicus Schleupner (d. 1547) upon Luther's
advice. It was under the two provosts that these two reformers gradually
introduced changes in the parish churches that conformed with the basic
Reformation doctrines of Luther. The Augustinian prior Wolfgang
Volprecht (d. 1528) probably was the first to administer the Lord's
Supper in both kinds to the laity, but to a small circle of intimate
friends, in Holy Week, 1523. In May of the next year, he read the
Mass in German to a large congregation. Upon leaving the monastery,
he became a preacher at the Hospital of the Holy Spirit under
Wenceslas Linck. The prior of St. Egidien, Friedrich Pistorius (1486-
1553), also became a vigorous supporter of the Reformation.

The preaching of the Lutheran clergy was accompanied by a number
of changes in customs and ceremonies. During Lent and Easter, 1524,
the city council forbade the setting up of indulgence flags as sinful,
cancelled the passion play at the New Hospital on Good Friday as
harmful to the Christian spirit, and declared the consecration of wine
and water as contrary to the Gospel. It insisted that the continuation of
such ceremonies would lead to turmoil and rebellion among the towns-
people and that the preachers were not followers of Luther or any other
man but of the Gospel and the Word of God. Osiander administered
communion in both kinds to Isabella, sister of Charles V and Ferdinand
and wife of the deposed King Christian II of Denmark. On Pentecost,
the pastors of the two parish churches administered communion in both
kinds to their parishioners and began to baptize and read the Gospels
and Epistles in German. The provosts themselves abolished requiems,
birthdays of the saints, Masses for the dead, singing of the *Salve
regina,* and consecration of water and salt.

The city council, wishing not to proceed too fast in making changes and hoping to avoid difficulties with both the empire and the papacy, requested that the provosts desist from further changes, restore those ceremonies that did not endanger man's salvation, and submit a written statement explaining the changes made. It assured them, however, that it did not object to the reading of the Gospels and Epistles in the vernacular or to celebrating the Lord's Supper in both kinds. [9] It sent a delegation to Archduke Ferdinand in June 1524 that explained that the provosts had acted without its prior knowledge and had not carried out all the emperor's demands because they feared that any action contrary to the Gospel would lead to disunity and revolt.

The city council sent the same delegation to the bishop of Bamberg. It repeated the explanation given Ferdinand, adding that the council had requested the restoration of the old ceremonies but that the citizens had continued to demand the changes. [10] The bishop then summoned the provosts and Prior Volprecht of the Augustinian Monastery to appear before him in September 1524 to be tried in his episcopal court. When they refused to appear, claiming that the matter concerned the city of Nuremberg as a whole and that the bishop was acting as both plaintiff and judge, the episcopal court excommunicated them and deprived them of their offices on the charge of heresy. When the council learned of this action, it ignored it and openly defended the three men. Having defied the bishop by accepting the preaching and changes in worship of the reformers, the council assumed a position of leadership that greatly influenced the spread of the Reformation to other cities and territories.

Meeting of the Council of Regency and of the imperial estates in three diets in Nuremberg from 1521 to 1524 not only brought its leading citizens into touch with influential persons from throughout the Empire, but it gave the latter an opportunity to see how the Reformation took hold in a populous and dynamic urban community. Many members carried an enthusiasm for the movement back to their own cities and territories. Albert of Brandenburg, grand master of the Teutonic Knights, for example, developed a long-lasting friendship with a number of Nuremberg patricians and Andreas Osiander and became Lutheran in 1525.

Although the first Diet of Nuremberg was too poorly attended to

---

[9] Pfeiffer, *Quellen,* 5-7.

[10] The instructions for the delegates to the bishop and his answer are in *ibid.,* 271-76.

accomplish much, the second, which was presided over by Ferdinand and convened in November 1522, came to grips with the Lutheran problem. At a combined session of the diet and the Council of Regency, the papal nuncio, Francesco Chieregati, presented the papal admission, however, that there were serious abuses in the Papal Curia that had permeated the entire church hierarchy and that Luther's demand for reforms was a divine punishment of the church for this state of affairs. This startling statement was used by Luther's defenders to justify their reforms and helped them gain support for the calling of a free church council of secular and ecclesiastical delegates to solve the problem of Lutheranism. Furthermore, the nuncio's demand that the city's clergy be arrested as heretics was met by a popular clamor in support of them and by the council's determination to protect them by force if necessary. His demand that only anti-Lutheran religious books be published was followed by the council's acquiescence but with its choice of Spengler as the chief censor. The recess of the second Diet of Nuremberg contained the important provision that nothing should be preached or published "except the true, clear, and pure Gospel according to the doctrine and interpretation of Scripture as approved and accepted by the Christian Church." [11] The Lutherans interpreted this as the abrogation of the Edict of Worms and as a permission to preach the Gospel.

Nuremberg, Strassburg, Augsburg, and other cities defended this interpretation of the recess of 1523 during the meeting of the third diet in 1524 and agreed to accept the decision of a free church council with respect to the religious differences. [12] The diet in its recess demanded enforcement of the Edict of Worms "as far as possible," a modifying clause that permitted the Evangelicals to claim that enforcement of the edict would be impossible. In July 1524, Charles V issued the Edict of Burgos, forbidding the meeting of a German council to solve the religious question and demanding that the public refrain from discussing religious matters until the meeting of a general church council convened by the pope.

When the diet moved the Council of Regency to Esslingen and disbanded Nuremberg's city council could meet its local problems with little outside interference. Sustained by actions of the diet, it and other evangelical governments interpreted the recess in their favor. The

---

[11] G. A. von Planitz, *Berichte des kurfürstlichen Rates G. A. von Planitz aus dem Reichsregiment in Nürnberg, 1521-1523* (Leipzig, 1899), 357.

[12] *Deutsche Reichstagsakten*, Jüngere Reihe, 4 (Göttingen, 1963), 489-95.

council thereby moved in the direction of the Reformation but within the legal restrictions set by the diet and the emperor. It consistently maintained its loyalty to the emperor to the end of its existence as an imperial city in 1806.

Encouraged by the failure of three diets to find a definite program of action for the enforcement of the Edict of Worms, the city council continued its support of its preachers. At the same time, it became aware of the fact that the persistence of preaching against the evangelical movement by clergy in some of its monasteries was creating disunity and unrest in the city at a time when the storm clouds of the Peasants' Revolt were gathering in Germany. An example of the council's difficulties was provided by the Carthusian Monastery whose prior, Blasius Stöckl, was removed from office for having taught evangelical doctrines. When the council refused as guardian of the monastery to have him replaced by another, Stöckl suggested that charges against him be discussed by a number of theologians.

The city council, realizing that it could not appeal to a German national council, and eager to establish unity of preaching in Nuremberg, asked its preachers to prepare lists of articles of faith that they deemed necessary for salvation. It even had Osiander prepare a list of the most important of those submitted. [13] It asked for a discussion of these articles, twelve in number, "in a friendly colloquy" by the city's clergy witnessed by the members of the small and large councils. The discussion took place in the city hall from 3 to 14 March 1525. When, finally, Osiander presented the Lutheran interpretation and Lienhard Ebner the Catholic, the latter's presentation was so badly received that the final Catholic summary was presented in writing. Osiander followed this with a two-hour address, attacking the views of the Catholic preachers, accusing them of causing disunity and asking the council to settle the religious disputes immediately without waiting for the meeting of a general church council. [14] The council assumed this responsibility immediately, following the wishes of the citizens as interpreted and presented to it by the theologians.

Soon after the colloquy, the council, having assumed complete ecclesiastical authority, demanded that the preachers of the monasteries

---

[13] Gottfried Seebass in *Andreas Osiander d. Ä. Gesamtausgabe,* vol. 1 : *Schriften und Briefe 1522 bis März 1525,* eds. Gerhard Müller and Gottfried Seebass (Gütersloh, 1975), no. 39, 454-63.

[14] The council's explanation of its action to Michel von Kaden for possible use in the Council of Regency is in Pfeiffer, *Quellen,* 360-63.

and convents conform to the Gospel in their sermons or cease preaching and leave the city. It ordered the cessation of the Catholic Mass and the adoption of the liturgy and the Lord's Supper of the parish churches. These actions were followed by the gradual dissolution of monasteries and convents. The council also compelled the clergy to become citizens with public obligations as well as privileges. On the other hand, it assumed complete responsibility for their well-being. It called them, paid their salaries, and regulated their conduct. It also exercised a stricter control than previously over its citizens as a whole by limiting the number of holy days, introducing severe laws against adultery and bigamy, forbidding the playing of cards and dice, and punishing blasphemy.

The city council was particularly successful in developing its care of the poor, thereby playing a significant role in influencing poor relief elsewhere. It placed church property and endowments under the efficiently organized Common Chest and Great Almonry, administered by the Alms Office. This office was divided into two parts, one for the city and one for its territory. Each one administered its respective church and school buildings, endowments, poor relief, pensions of monks and nuns, and salaries of clergy, sextons, and teachers.

Like the reformers of Wittenberg, members of the city council were desirous of maintaining excellent schools for the purpose of improving Christian education and morals, and for training young people for responsible citizenship. To this end, the council not only improved the three Latin schools of the city but established a new, higher school, or Gymnasium to lay the bases for secular as well as religious careers and prepare young men for entrance into universities. Although Philip Melanchthon declined the offer to head this new school, he came in Nuremberg to help organize its curriculum and obtain outstanding teachers for it. He also delivered the address at its dedication on 2 May 1526.

Having achieved relative peace and unity among its people by adopting the Reformation at an early date, the city council sought to avoid future unrest by steering a cautious, conservative course. It sought to avoid disturbances not only by alleviating some of the worst conditions of its peasants and townsmen but also by refusing to condone theological disputes and religious splinter groups. It thereby succeeded in minimizing the effects of the Peasants' Revolt, the Sacramentarian Controversy, and the spread of Anabaptism. [15]

---

[15] See esp. George H. Williams, *The Radical Reformation* (Philadelphia, 1962).

Nuremberg's lower classes became restless during the beginnings of the Peasants' Revolt, but in general they responded favorably to the palliative measures of the city council. This was true even of many of those who had been influenced by their revolutionary leaders but who were assuaged by the council's reduction or elimination of some of the most oppressive tithes and services. Although Nuremberg was a member of the Swabian League that suppressed the movement with a vengeance, it did not resort to brutality. Yet it was firm in its punishment of those responsible for the insurrection.

The council likewise pursued a moderate though firm policy with respect to the radical reformers. When the spiritualist reformer Thomas Müntzer appeared in Nuremberg in 1524 to publish a violent pamphlet against Luther, it confiscated the copies but not without reimbursing the printer. It likewise confiscated a pamphlet written by Andreas Bodenstein von Carlstadt defending the symbolical interpretation of the Lord's Supper and also published in Nuremberg. This initiated the Sacramentarian Controversy in the city. Students of Albrecht Dürer, Georg Pentz and the brothers Sebald and Barthel Behaim, confessed after two weeks in prison and under torture that they adhered to the symbolical interpretation of Baptism and the Lord's Supper. They even admitted that they leaned toward atheism and had denied the council's political authority. Although the council expelled them, it later permitted them to return. It exiled permanently their mentor Hans Denck, the school teacher of Nuremberg who entertained unorthodox views, especially because these included encouragement of social discontent.

Anabaptist views became threatening in the eyes of the council in 1527, especially after it had begun to associate them with the Peasants' Revolt. Among the early leaders in Nuremberg and its territory was Wolfgang Vogel, a person who was especially influential among social revolutionary groups. Convinced that he preached the abolition of secular authority as well as Anabaptist doctrines, it had him decapitated. He was the only Anabaptist who suffered this fate in Nuremberg, for the council consistently opposed the harsh persecution of the Anabaptists meted out by the Swabian League. It decreed the death penalty, supported by an imperial mandate issued at the Diet of Speyer of 1529, only for those who threatened to overthrow the government by violent action. [16]

---

[16] Hans-Dieter Schmid, *Täufertum und Obrigkeit in Nürnberg* (Nuremberg, 1972), 196-97.

Nuremberg's role in the spread of the Reformation is apparent in its correspondence with other cities and territories, the activities of its representatives at the diets of the Empire and the Swabian League, and the influence of its church order. As early as 26 July 1524, the city council of Magdeburg wrote the city council of Nuremberg, asking for information concerning its changes in church services and ceremonies. In its reply, the council enclosed a list of articles concerning these changes, including an explanation of some of them. [17] In March of the following year, Strassburg also asked it for such information. In reply, it sent the city the account of the religious colloquy of that month originally prepared for use in defending its action before the Imperial Council of Regency. [18] In March 1528, Goslar, in a dilemma because of the demands of its citizens for evangelical preachers on the one hand and the determination of the Catholic duke of Brunswick to make the city a part of his territory on the other, sought advice from Nuremberg with respect to Reformation changes. The city council responded by sending Goslar Lazarus Spengler's statement, "Order of and Changes in the Ceremonies in Nuremberg, Prepared in 1528," [19] in which he maintained that it was Christianity's chief responsibility to preach the Gospel and the government's to provide uniformity of preaching and peace. This statement influenced the development of the Reformation not only in Goslar but also in Strassburg and Ulm. A copy also was sent to Transylvania where it had considerable influence. [20]

Although German cities were not represented on a par with the other estates in the imperial diets, their wishes could not be ignored. Accordingly, Nuremberg played an active role in their deliberations through its representatives. This was true of the Diets of Nuremberg, 1522-24, during those critical years of the city's acceptance of evangelical changes. At the Diet of Speyer in 1526, it cooperated with other imperial cities, especially Strassburg and Ulm, for the purpose of obtaining from the emperor clear statement in defense of their right to have the Gospel preached and changes made to conform with it.

---

[17] Pfeiffer, *Quellen,* 277-78, 280-83.

[18] *Ibid.,* 440-47; Gottfried Seebass, "Apologia Reformationis," *Zeitschrift für bayerische Kirchengeschichte* 39 (1970), 25, n. 21.

[19] "Verzeichnus der geenderten misspreuch und ceremonien, so in kraft des wort Gottes zu Nurmberg abgestellt und gepessert seyen," in Pfeiffer, *Quellen,* 440-47. See Seebass, "Apologia," 27-28.

[20] Printed in Erich Roth, *Die Reformation in Siebenbürgen,* 2 vols. (Cologne and Graz, 1962), 1:197-207.

But it would not join the Lutheran princes in the League of Torgau-Gotha, formed to prevent the enforcement of the Edict of Worms. The diet's postponement of the solution of the religious issue until the meeting of a general church council and its provision that every government should meanwhile conduct its religious affairs in accordance with its obligations to God and the emperor gave the Evangelicals respite from strong Catholic pressure. At the Diet of Speyer of 1529, Ferdinand demanded in the name of his brother aid for war against the Turks, suppression of heresy, and nullification of the recess of 1526 that had virtually given each government the right to determine its own course in religious affairs. As a consequence, Nuremberg instructed its representatives at the diet to remain firm in their support of the evangelical cause and to urge the representatives of the other cities to do likewise. [21] Despite the firm position of the cities, Ferdinand and the diet rescinded the concessions of the previous diet. Fourteen cities, like the evangelical rulers, protested against this, thereby earning the name "Protestant." Although the Protestants were unanimous in this and tentatively agreed to cooperate in the event that they were attacked for religious reasons by other estates, the city council of Nuremberg elected not to join an alliance directed against the emperor. It and the margrave of Brandenburg-Ansbach consistently maintained that no estate had the right to resist the emperor with force. In religious matters, it could oppose him only by passive resistance.

When Charles V rejected the Protestation and it looked as though he might enforce the Edict of Worms, the City Council of Nuremberg had to decide whether or not to join the Lutheran electors and princes who were planning an alliance for the purpose of resisting any attempt on the part of the emperor to force them to return to the religious status quo. Meetings of the Protestant rulers and cities at Rodach, Schwabach, Schmalkalden, and Nuremberg 1529-30 strengthened its determination not to join any alliance for the purpose of resisting the emperor by force. [22]

---

[21] See the letter of Spengler to Peter Butz of Strassburg, *Politische Correspondenz der Stadt Strassburg im Zeitalter der Reformation,* eds. Hans Virck and Otto Winkelmann, 2 vols. (Strassburg, 1882-98), 1 : no. 451, pp. 256-57.

[22] Wolfgang Steglich, "Die Stellung der evangelischen Reichsstände und Reichsstädte zu Karl V. zwischen Protestation und Konfession 1529/30," *Archiv für Reformationsgeschichte* 62 (1971), 161-92, based on his edition of the *Deutsche Reichstagsakten,* Jüngere Reihe, 7 ,part 1 (Göttingen, 1970), 76-118; and Ekkehart Fabian, ed., *Die Abschiede der Bündnis- und Bekenntnistage protestierender Fürsten und Städte, zwischen den Reichstagen zu Speyer und zu Augsburg, 1529-1530* (Tübingen, 1960).

Despite Nuremberg's differences with most of the other Protestant rulers and cities with respect to the right of resistance to the emperor, it played a significant role in maintaining Protestant unity at the Diet of Augsburg of 1530. [23] It supported the Augsburg Confession from the outset and refused to accept the Catholic Confutation. During discussions between a committee of Catholics and one of Protestants, designed to work out religious differences, Melanchthon showed a willingness to make concessions with respect to the restoration of episcopal authority and the Mass. To this the City Council of Nuremberg reacted strongly, urging the Protestant princes and cities to make no concessions. The emperor's determination to end the diet terminated attempts at conciliation. He gave the Protestants who had signed the Augsburg Confession until 15 April 1531 to decide whether they would renounce the errors of their confession and reunite with the church, pope, and emperor while awaiting the decisions of a general church council to be convoked in six months.

The provisions of the recess obviously implied that the emperor would use force against those who disobeyed it. Accordingly, the Protestant princes and cities who had signed the Augsburg Confession met in Schmalkalden on 22 December 1530 where they agreed to form the Schmalkaldic League for the purpose of resisting the emperor by force if necessary. Because Nuremberg refused to join, it sacrificed its political leadership to a considerable degree. But for the time being, at least, it could consider its policy of political loyalty to the emperor while adhering to Lutheranism justified, for Charles did not attack the Protestants after April 15, 1531, as he had threatened to do. Beset by problems of such magnitude as the renewed invasion of Hungary by the Turks and the pope's refusal to call a church council, he even concluded with them the Religious Peace of Nuremberg of 23 July 1532. This peace postponed armed conflict until the outbreak of the Schmalkaldic War in 1546.

Although Nuremberg gave up its leadership in political affairs, it continued to play a significant role in religious matters, especially with respect to the organization of Lutheranism. Greatly concerned with problems involved in maintaining unity in preaching, the retention of ceremonies, and ecclesiastical administration, it cooperated with Mar-

---

[23] Adolf Engelhardt, *Der Reichstag zu Augsburg 1530 und die Reichstadt Nürnberg* (Nuremberg, 1929); Hans von Schubert, *Der Reichstag von Augsburg im Zusammenhang der Reformationsgeschichte,* Schriften des Vereins für Reformationsgeschichte, no. 150, vol. 48 (Leipzig, 1930).

grave George of Brandenburg-Ansbach in conducting a thorough visitation in 1528 which gave them considerable material with which to create a common church order. [24] On the basis of these findings, the City Council of Nuremberg appointed a commission which, together with a similar group of clergymen of Brandenburg-Ansbach, produced the Brandenburg-Nuremberg Church Order. Osiander, with the assistance of Johannes Brenz, drafted the final copy, which was printed in Nuremberg and put into effect there and in Brandenburg-Ansbach in 1533. Although it excluded such matters as the right of excommunication and public confession before communion, over which there were sharp differences of opinion, it provided sufficiently clear statements with respect to doctrine, order of services, administration of sacraments, and discipline to play an important part in establishing religious uniformity in Nuremberg and Brandenburg-Ansbach. It was so well organized that it served as a model for church orders elsewhere in Germany. [25]

At the height of its power and influence during the first decade and a half of the Reformation, Nuremberg played a dominant role, not only in the economic and political life of Germany, but also in the spread of the evangelical movement. In this role, it had few equals among the imperial cities of the Holy Roman Empire.

---

[24] Engelhardt, *Reformation*, 2: 69-107.

[25] "Die Kirchen Ordnung, In meiner gnedigen herrn der Marggrauen zu Brandenburg Und eins Erbern Rats der Stat Nürnberg Oberkeyt und gepieten, wie man sich byde mit der Lerr und Ceremonien halten solle. 1533," *Die evangelischen Kirchenordnungen des XVI. Jahrhunderts,* ed. Emil Sehling, vol. 11 : *Bayern,* part 1 : *Franken* (Tübingen, 1961), 140-305.

PETER MARTYR VERMIGLI AND THE MARKS OF THE TRUE CHURCH

ROBERT M. KINGDON

University of Wisconsin, Madison

One of George Huntston Williams' most important contributions to scholarship has surely been in the history of ecclesiology. The distinction, which he first drew more than twenty years ago in his monumental studies of the Radical Reformation, between a "Magisterial Reformation" of Lutherans, Zwinglians, Calvinists, and Anglicans on one hand, and a "Radical Reformation" of Anabaptists, Spiritualists, and Evangelical Rationalists on the other, has influenced an entire generation of specialists on the period. [1] It has made us all more aware of the importance of doctrines of church government in distinguishing among various groups of Christians. In Williams' own work, of course, ecclesiology has been used primarily to distinguish from each other the "Magisterials" with their attempts to co-operate closely with secular governments in the reform of the Church and the "Radicals" with their attempts to purify the Church by avoiding all collaboration with secular institutions. It has also been used, secondarily, to assist in the delicate job of distinguishing from each other the many often ephemeral and protean groups of "Radicals." Ecclesiology can also be used, however, to distinguish with greater precision among various groups of "Magisterials." That is the enterprise to which this article hopes to contribute. It will focus on one ecclesiological doctrine, that of the marks of the true Church of Christ.

When the Reformation of the sixteenth century began, Luther and his associates hoped to reform the entire Church, beginning with those parts of it in western Europe controlled by the Roman Catholic hierarchy. They obviously failed in that objective. Rome did not wish to be reformed along the lines suggested by Luther and resisted both

---

[1] George Huntston Williams, Introduction to Part I of *Spiritual and Anabaptist Writers: Documents Illustrative of the Radical Reformation...*, vol. XXV in *The Library of Christian Classics* (Philadelphia, 1957), 19-38; "Studies in the Radical Reformation: a bibliographical survey," *Church History* 27 (1958), 46 ff.; Introduction to *The Radical Reformation* (Philadelphia, 1962), xxiii-xxxi.

strenuously and successfully all attempts to make it do so. What the early Reformers did do in the end was to stimulate the creation of a number of separate alternative churches in parts of western and northern Europe, each claiming to be the true Church of Christ. These, of course, were the ancestors of many of our modern Protestant denominations. The creation of these new churches led to vigorous competition between them and the Roman Catholic Church and sometimes among themselves as well. On the intellectual level the competition took the form of rival theologies, one important ingredient of which was generally an ecclesiology. And within these ecclesiologies one component was often a doctrine of the notes, or signs, or marks by which the true Church could be distinguished from its false competitors. Polemical exchanges on the marks of the true Church became particularly common and heated late in the sixteenth century and they continued well into the early seventeenth century. They remain useful in helping us understand how ecclesiastical spokesmen of the period wished to distinguish themselves from each other.

Roman Catholic apologists could assemble a considerable variety of marks of the true Church to justify their position. They could point to the numerical superiority of their constituency and the material wealth of their corporations as signs that God in His Providence had selected their institution as His own. More often they pointed to the unbroken history of their Church, stretching back to the time of Christ and His Apostles, sealed by the apostolic succession of its leaders and elaborated by the canonical ordination of its clergy.

"Magisterial" Protestants retorted by insisting that there were two and only two marks of the true Church: (1) the teaching of pure doctrine; (2) the correct administration of the sacraments. This was the general position of most Lutherans. It found particularly authoritative expression in article seven of the Augsburg Confession of 1530, which defines the Church as the congregation of the faithful in which the Gospel is purely preached and the sacraments rightly administered. [2] This position, furthermore, was endorsed by John Calvin. In every edition of his monumental *Institutes of the Christian Religion* from 1541 on, he defined the visible Church as a body in which the Word of God is purely preached and heard and in which the sacraments are

---

[2] For a fine critical edition of both German and Latin texts, which differ somewhat, see *Die Bekenntnisschriften der evangelisch-lutherischen Kirche,* 5th ed. (Göttingen, 1963), 61.

administered according to Christ's instructions. [3] This doctrine of the
marks of the true Church is of obvious utility in developing a reply
to the Roman Catholic position. It denies the importance of numbers,
wealth, and tradition and substitutes the claims of ideology and its
symbols. Since the doctrine is supported by such influential authorities
within both the Evangelical Lutheran and Reformed Calvinist camps,
one might suppose that it was one on which all Protestants could agree.

In fact, however, this two-mark doctrine did not fully satisfy many
Protestants, including not only a good many Radicals, but also an
increasing number of spokesmen for the Reformed Churches, which
are commonly believed to have been founded by Zwingli and Calvin.
These Protestants may have been disturbed by an antinomian tendency
in much of the early theology of their movement, an emphasis on the
doctrine of justification by faith alone so extreme that it left little
room for the encouragement of ethical behavior which is commonly
another important part of Christian teaching. Or they may have been
disturbed by a lack of practicality associated with this doctrine, by its
failure to provide any guidance for the institutional shape the true
Church should take. The task of building new ecclesiastical institutions
became increasingly important to later Reformers, as it became more
and more obvious that nothing would come of early hopes for reform of
the entire Church and that their movement would either have to create
durable institutions to preserve itself or face the likelihood of collapse.

For whatever reason, a number of early "Magisterial" theologians
developed an alternative doctrine of the marks of the true Church.
They argued that there were in fact three fundamental marks. To the
two classical marks suggested by the Lutheran confessions and Calvin
they added the third mark of discipline. One of the earliest statements
of this three-mark doctrine can be found in the writings of Martin
Bucer, that seminal thinker who had such a pervasive influence on
every branch of the Reformation. In his *Scripta duo adversaria D.
Bartholomaei Latomi* . . ., a polemic directed against a Catholic theologian of Cologne and published in 1544, Bucer lists the Word, sacraments, and discipline of Christ as marks of the true Church. [4] The

---

[3] IV:1:9. See particularly in the critical variorum edition of Jean-Daniel
Benoît (Paris, 1957-1963), IV, 20.

[4] Quoted in Tadataka Maruyama, "The Reform of the True Church: the
Ecclesiology of Theodore Beza," Unpublished Th.D. dissertation, Princeton
Theological Seminary, 1973, p. 38, n. 15. This splendid contribution to our
knowledge of Reformed ecclesiology is to be published in 1978 by the Librairie
Droz of Geneva. Hereafter cited as Maruyama.

same triad recurs in other works of his. This three-mark doctrine was later endorsed by such other Reformed theologians as John Knox, Pierre Viret, and Theodore Beza, although not always with consistency. It was also given more formal suport by inclusion in several Reformed confessions of faith, including the Scots Confession, and Belgic Confession, and the Hungarian Confession. [5] One expression of this point of view which was particularly sharp, clear, and influential was that of Peter Martyr Vermigli. It is upon his version of this doctrine that this paper concentrates.

There is a growing recognition among scholars of the value of the writings of Vermigli for a full understanding of early Reformed theology. These writings are comprehensive, covering almost all the topics at issue during the period. They are organized and expressed with admirable clarity, avoiding much of the tendency to rhetorical flourish and tangential argument which characterizes the writing of other Reformers. And they are documented with impressive erudition. These qualities can be explained in part by the unusual strength of Vermigli's training and the unusual variety of positions he filled as a teacher and consultant. A quick sketch of his career should thus help us to understand his thought.

As a boy, Vermigli had entered the Lateran congregation of the Canons Regular of St. Augustine in his native Italy and had been sent to the order's study house at the University of Padua for training in theology and philosophy. He had become particularly interested in the neo-Aristotelian thought for which Padua was then distinguished and had mastered it to a degree rare among early Protestants. Unlike other Reformers, he saw this body of thought as of continuing value after his conversion to Protestantism and used it frequently, explicitly, and expertly in the elaboration of his own theological position. Unlike some Aristotelians of the period, moreover, Vermigli also shared the humanists' interest in the languages of antiquity. He learned Greek while in Padua and Hebrew while in Bologna where he was sent after completion of his formal education. Vermigli first became acquainted with Protestant thought in Naples where he settled next. There he became involved in a group of local Evangelicals and read certain of the books of Bucer and Zwingli. His final assignment from the order took him to Lucca, where through public teaching he stimu-

---

[5] *Ibid.*, 369. Beza's own shifting view is, of course, discussed at some length and summarized on pp. 365-70.

lated a serious attempt at reformation of the city. When this came to the attention of authorities in Rome, it helped provoke the repressive measures which signaled the beginning of the Counter Reformation in Italy. Vermigli fled to the Protestant north in 1542 and spent the rest of his life in exile. Bucer helped him obtain his first position in the north, as a teacher in the Strasbourg Academy. He stayed there until 1547. Thomas Cranmer then persuaded both Bucer and Vermigli to come to England, where Vermigli was assigned to teach at Oxford until 1553, when the accession of Mary forced him to resign and leave the country. He returned to Strasbourg, where he taught until 1556. The growth of orthodox Lutheranism in that city made him increasingly uncomfortable, however, so he moved to Zurich where he again served as a teacher until his death in 1562. [6]

Vermigli's early reading in Protestant theology and the acquaintances he made during his career as a Protestant teacher inclined him to align himself primarily with the theological positions of Bucer and Zwingli. After he settled in the north, he became increasingly interested in the theology of Calvin, entered into a cordial correspondence with him, and found himself in substantial agreement with the Reformer of Geneva on many doctrines in controversy. He also became well acquainted personally with the younger generation of leading theologians in this camp, notably Beza and Henry Bullinger.

Vermigli's teaching at Protestant schools consisted of lectures on books of the Bible. At Strasbourg and Zurich he lectured on books of the Old Testament, at Oxford he lectured on the New Testament.

---

[6] The primary source for biographical information on Vermigli is a funeral oration by Josiah Simler, prepared in consultation with Vermigli's student and secretary, Giulio Santerenziano, and published in a number of editions of Vermigli's Genesis commentary and his *Common Places*. See Philip McNair, *Peter Martyr in Italy: an anatomy of apostasy* (Oxford, 1967), xiv-xv. I have used the version in the 1583 English translation of the *Common Places*. For further and more recent accounts of Vermigli's career, see McNair, which is particularly reliable and detailed but covers only the period to 1452; Joseph C. McLelland, *The Visible Words of God: an exposition of the sacramental theology of Peter Martyr Vermigli, A.D. 1500-1562* (Grand Rapids, 1957), 1-68; Marvin Walter Anderson, *Peter Martyr, a Reformer in Exile (1542-1562): a chronology of biblical writings in England & Europe* (Nieuwkoop, 1975), I, 35-266. See also three expert recent studies of aspects of Vermigli's thought: Klaus Sturm, *Die Theologie Peter Martyr Vermiglis während seines ersten Aufenthalts in Strassburg, 1542-1547* (Neukirchen-Vluyn, 1971); John Patrick Donnelly, *Calvinism and Scholasticism in Vermigli's Doctrine of Man and Grace* (Leiden, 1976); Salvatore Corda, *Veritas Sacramenti: a study in Vermigli's doctrine of the Lord's Supper* (Zurich, 1975). Hereafter cited by author's last name.

He would pick one book for a term, and lecture on it in the usual Protestant way, going from verse to verse in *lectio continuo*. Over the years these lectures were published as Biblical commentaries. In their published form they include many set treatises of a rather formal sort on various topics not always closely related to the Biblical verses they are supposed to explain. These short treatises scattered throughout the commentaries are known as the *loci* or *common places* of Vermigli. Each *locus* can be identified by the Biblical verse or pericope to which it is attached.

During his own lifetime, Vermigli arranged for the publication of several of these Biblical commentaries and some polemical works. Many of his writings remained in manuscript at the time of his death, however, and it was left to his friends and students to arrange for their publication. Many of the printed works of Vermigli, as a consequence, are as much a product of the general Reformed community of scholars as of Vermigli himself. This is particularly true of the most influential of them, the *Loci Communes* or *Common Places*. Shortly after Vermigli's death, Beza asked Bullinger's opinion of a project to abstract the *loci* from Vermigli's Biblical commentaries, arrange them in a systematic form, and publish the collection. [7] It took some time for this project to materialize, but the collected *Loci Communes* of Peter Martyr were finally printed in 1576, in London. In the next eighty years this collection went through some thirteen further editions, some of them considerably expanded with the addition of polemical treatises, correspondence, and biographical material. They appeared in such important Reformed publishing centers as Basel, Zurich, Geneva, and Heidelberg, in addition to London. [8] These *Common Places* were arranged in the same general order as the topics in Calvin's *Institutes of the Christian Religion*. They were consciously designed to complement, expand, and document that theological classic. This collection became a standard textbook for the education of Reformed clergy-

---

[7] Beza to Bullinger, 1 July [1563], in Henri Meylan, Alain Dufour, and Arnaud Tripet, eds., *Correspondance de Théodore de Bèze*, IV (Geneva, 1965), 161-65.

[8] Professor Donnelly and I are gathering material for a full descriptive bibliography of Vermigli's writings. One or the other of us has examined copies of the following editions of his *Loci Communes*. All but one are in Latin. (1) London, 1576; (2) Zurich, 1580; (3) Basel, 1580-1582; (4) London, 1583; (5) London, 1583—in English; (6) Zurich, 1587; (7) Heidelberg, 1603; (8) Heidelberg, 1613; (9) Heidelberg, 1622; (10) Geneva, 1623; (11) Geneva, 1624; (12) Geneva, 1626; (13) Geneva, 1627; (14) Amsterdam and Frankfurt, 1656.

men in the late sixteenth and early seventeenth centuries. It had a pervaise influence on several generations of the leaders of the Reformed movement.

Both the *Common Places* and the *Institutes* devote a fourth and last book to the two human institutions through which God leads men to Christ and His service—the Church and the state. The proportions of the books are somewhat different. Only one chapter in twenty of the fourth book in the *Institutes* is devoted to analysis of the state while nearly half of the fourth book in the *Common Places* deals with politics. Both books begin with discussions of ecclesiology, however, and develop them in significantly parallel ways. Vermigli's *loci* on ecclesiology fill the first twelve chapters of the *Common Places*. The most important of them are drawn from his commentary on First Corinthians, based on a series of lectures at Oxford, 1548-1549. The text of this epistle lends itself to reflection on ecclesiology, dealing as it does with the organizational problems of one of the earliest Christian churches. Vermigli's position in England also encouraged him to reflect on problems of church organization. Archbishop Cranmer frequently consulted his two distinguished guests from the continent, Bucer and Vermigli, for advice on how to go about the extensive reforms in the Church of England to which he was committed after the accession of Edward VI. Cranmer seems to have turned to Vermigli particularly for advice on institutional reform. Vermigli became a member of a committee charged with drafting an entire Reformed code of ecclesiastical laws for England. A surviving manuscript copy of this code contains corrections and annotations in the hands of both Cranmer and Vermigli, suggesting their contributions to the final draft were considerable. The code was never promulgated, to be sure. It was a victim of the abrupt end of the Edwardian reform program caused by the untimely death of the king. Attempts to revive it during the Elizabethan period failed. Even though it never became law, however, it provides striking proof of Vermigli's interest in institutional reform. [9]

Loci drawn from other commentaries are used to fill in the presentation of Vermigli's doctrine of ecclesiology in the *Common Places*. Most of them come from lectures he delivered later in life. They tend, however, simply to confirm and refine the views expressed in the commentary on First Corinthians. The most interesting of them is the

---

[9] James C. Spalding, "The *Reformatio Legum Ecclesiasticarum* of 1552 and the Furthering of Discipline in England," *Church History* 39 (1970), 162-71, especially p. 167 on the surviving manuscript. Hereafter cited as Spalding.

locus De Schismate on I Kings 12, from a lecture delivered in Zurich. His teaching there was interrupted during 1561 for an extended trip to France, where Vermigli joined Beza in the delegation of Protestants summoned by the royal court to a debate with Catholic bishops and theologians at the colloquy of Poissy. Vermigli was used in this debate primarily to argue the Protestant eucharistic position, a doctrine upon which he had become a respected authority as a result of debates in England. But ecclesiology was another important issue at Poissy and led to sharp exchanges between Beza and the moderate Catholic spokesman Claude d'Espence. [10] Perhaps the Poissy debate can be linked to Vermigli's commentaries on I Kings.

Vermigli's doctrine of the marks of the true Church is expressed most concisely in two of these *loci*. One is the *locus De Ecclesia* on I Corinthians 1, with which chapter 1 of book four of the *Common Places* begins. The other is the *locus De Schismate* on I Kings 12, which occupies all of chapter 6 of this book. In the first of these *loci*, Vermigli begins with a definition of the Church which contains the marks: "it [the Church] is a company of believers, and regenerate persons, whom God gathereth together in Christ, by the word and the holy Ghost, and by his Ministers governeth the same with pureness of doctrine, with lawful use of the sacraments, and with discipline." He then goes on to explain with more precision the value and nature of these marks: "But and if thou wilt conclude hereby that the Church shall be unknown, we will deny it to be a firm conclusion; because there be proper marks assigned, by which the same may be very well known, and be discerned from profane conventicles. For wheresoever the pureness of doctrine flourisheth, the sacraments are purely ministered, and discipline exercised, thou hast a congregation whereunto thou mayest safely join thyself." [11] At the end of this *locus* in the English translation, there is a cross-reference to other passages dealing with the marks of the true Church. The most developed of them is in *De Schismate* and reads: "the three marks of the Church which are wont to be shewed by men of our side: namely doctrine, the right administration of the sacraments, and the care of discipline (which these men

---

[10] Maruyama, chapter 3, pp. 63-97.

[11] My quotations are taken out of the 1583 English translation of the *Common Places,* hereafter cited as *C.P.,* compared with the 1583 Latin edition of the *Loci Communes,* hereafter cited as *L.C.,* both published in London, STC nos. 24669 and 24668. I have modernized spelling, capitalization, and punctuation, but have made no other changes. For these particular quotations, see *C.P.,* IV:1:1.

[Catholic opponents] cry out to be feigned by us and cannot be confirmed by the word of God) are very manifestly found in the Epistle to the Ephesians [5:25—which he then glosses]." He continues, in explicit retort to Cardinal Hosius who rejected Protestant arguments on the marks of the true Church, "he seeth that among us the pure word of God is exercised, the sacraments according to the institution of Christ administered, and discipline not altogether neglected," and for that reason Hosius must develop a more complex doctrine of marks to defend the Catholic position. [12]

The entire section on ecclesiology in Vermigli's *Common Places* can be analyzed as being built around the three marks he specifies at the beginning. This principle of organization is not explicit, and the obvious model remains Calvin's *Institutes*. But the three marks provide a useful pattern for analysis of the way in which this block of twelve chapters is assembled. The remainder of chapter 1 consists of a variety of *loci* on the preaching ministry and may be regarded as elaborating on the first mark. So may the next three chapters which are also on the ministry and are rather short, including *loci* on the use of property for the support of ministers, on the authority of ministers in relation to the spiritual leadership of the Church, and on the laws governing ministers. Chapter 5 includes a consideration of discipline and church polity and chapter 6 discusses schism. They may be regarded as elaborating on the third mark. Chapter 7 begins a consideration of the sacraments with discussion of Old Testament circumcision which Vermigli, in company with most "Magisterial" Protestants, sees as a forerunner of baptism, followed by chapters on baptism and communion, the two rites he accepts as sacraments. These chapters may be regarded as elaborating on the second mark.

Of these three subjects, Vermigli's doctrine of the sacraments has attracted the most attention from scholars. His eucharistic theology, in particular, has been subjected to considerable scrutiny and is the subject of two important recent books. [13] This is certainly understandable. Vermigli's treatises on the eucharist are particularly subtle and lengthy, lending themselves to careful analysis. And they were also of considerable influence, for Vermigli was regarded by contemporaries among the Reformed as a leading authority on the subject. He upheld the Reformed position on the eucharist in spirited formal debates with

---

[12] *C.P.*, IV:6:16, 17.
[13] McLelland; Corda.

Catholic theologians at both Oxford and Poissy. And he elaborated and defended this position against certain Lutherans in polemics published after he settled in Zurich. In this study, however, I would rather concentrate on Vermigli's *loci* on discipline. This is the part of his argument which is most novel, it seems to me, flowing as it does from his emphasis on discipline as a third mark of the true Church. It sets him apart in a significant way from Luther and Calvin and makes of him a considerable influence in his own right, given the wide acceptance of this position among the Reformed by the seventeenth century.

The most important statement of Vermigli's position on discipline is to be found in his *loci* on I Corinthians 10:9 and on I Corinthians 5, published as the first eighteen sections of chapter 5 in book four of the *Common Places*. The title of this chapter, *De disciplina & politia Ecclesiae*, is in itself significant, since it makes clear the fact that for Vermigli discipline requires a consideration of church polity. The link is made explicit in his text. The chapter begins with a general discussion of ecclesiastical discipline, moves on to an extended consideration of excommunication as a particularly valuable tool of discipline, then turns to church polity, since "that we may rightly understand who ought to be excommunicate, it is needful to discuss in what sort the society of the Church is." [14] This linkage is important. In much of the Reformed writing on the subject during this period the terms "discipline" and "polity" are used almost interchangeably. This can be confusing to readers accustomed to modern usage. It is important to emphasize the fact that for most of the Reformed the attempt to establish standards of appropriate ethical behavior within the Christian community required the creation of a structure including institutions charged with enforcing those standards.

This chapter begins, as do most of Vermigli's really important *loci*, with a general definition: "Ecclesiastical discipline is nothing else but a power granted to the Church by God, by which the wills and actions of the faithful, are made conformable to the law of God: which is done by doctrine, admonitions, correction, and finally by punishments, and also by excommunication if need require." It then employs, and this again is characteristic, Aristotle's four-fold schema of causes as a method for elaborating the definition. It seeks to discern, in other words, the material, efficient, formal, and final causes of ecclesiastical

---

14 *C.P.*, IV:5:9.

discipline. In Vermigli's own words: "the efficient cause is charity, for that it is no just correction, if it proceed of hatred, wrath, or injury. But the matter wherein it is occupied, be sins, and those grievous sins, seeing lighter faults pertain not to this kind of correction. The form is the manner prescribed by God. The end is, that evil may be taken away from among the faithful." [15]

Of the possible methods of discipline, excommunication clearly concerned Vermigli most. More than half of the chapter on discipline, sections 2-18, is devoted to his *locus De Excommunicatione* on I Corinthians 5. This *locus* begins again with a definition, this time starting with etymologies of the term excommunication, weighing the meaning of both Greek and Hebrew equivalents. It then announces an outline for the rest of the *locus,* promising to consider in turn how necessary excommunication is, what lesser steps should be taken before proceeding to this extreme measure, who should be excommunicated, and how this disciplinary tool should be used. [16] Vermigli sees excommunication primarily as a tool for enforcing standards of behavior and urges that it be used to punish not only "great crimes" like adultery or drunkenness which are matters of public notoriety, but also lesser sins which come to public knowledge. He would not limit its use solely to preventing misbehavior, however, but would also apply it to misbelief, against "they that be infected with ill doctrine." [17] The actual excommunication itself he sees as technically the work of the sinner, a deliberate alienation on his part from God. But this inner and private excommunication should be brought to the attention of the entire community in a public ecclesiastical rite "which is a token of this inward apostasy (indeed not a certain and necessary token, yet a great one and greatly to be feared)," a rite which should be "inflicted by the Church of Christ." [18]

When Vermigli turns to an explanation of how the Church should administer excommunication, he faces the problem of analyzing the polity of the Church, in order to locate within it appropriate responsibility for this type of discipline. Here he again uses Aristotle to structure his analysis, turning this time to the *Politics*. That Vermigli knew the *Politics* well is made abundantly clear in his political *loci,* most of which come from his commentaries on Judges, and many of which

---

[15] *C.P.,* IV :5 :1.
[16] *C.P.,* IV :5 :2.
[17] *C.P.,* IV :5 :5.
[18] *C.P.,* IV :5 :8.

are assembled in the second half of book four in the *Common Places*. He found particularly useful Aristotle's analysis of the types of government into six categories, according to the *locus* of sovereignty in each: three good types—monarchy, aristocracy, and polity—matched by three bad types into which they tend to degenerate—tyranny, oligarchy, and democracy. Near the beginning of his most comprehensive *locus* on politics, *De Magistratu,* which constitutes chapter 13 of the *Common Places,* he makes a statement which is close to a quotation from Aristotle: "the form of magistrates is not of one sort but manifold: as monarchy (the government of one), aristocracy (the rule of many good men), and polity (politic government). Or else tyranny (where one rules for his own commodity), oligarchy (where a few be in authority), and democracy (when the people bear the sway)." While he does not refer specifically to the passage in Aristotle's *Politics* (III.v.i-iv) which contains this analysis, he does give an explicit credit to ancient thinkers by following his own analysis with this comment: "the descriptions and natures of which forms Plato, Aristotle, and other philosophers have elegantly described." 19 This six-part analysis of the forms of government recurs again and again in Vermigli's political *loci.* He did not insist that any single form was the ideal type of secular government. Any one of the three good forms would do. There was sound precedent in the Old Testament for each. He did insist that any one of these good forms was preferable to any of the three bad forms. And this moral distinction is connected later to his interesting and influential arguments for political resistance to established governments.

In analyzing the polity of the Church, Vermigli uses these same Aristotelian political categories. He does not find in Aristotle a model for an appropriate form of church government, however, but rather finds that in another ancient source, the Roman Republic. He argues that the Church, like the Roman Republic, should be a mixed government, adopting the best features of each of the three good forms described by the ancient Greeks, in a careful balance. He may have been following a commentator like Polybius in developing this theory of mixed government but there are a number of other possible sources. Whatever his source, he finds in the Roman Republic a monarchic principle in the institution of the dictator, an aristocratic principle

---

19 *C.P.,* IV :13 :2. I am currently preparing an edition of this and certain other political *loci* of Vermigli.

in the institution of the Senate, and a democratic principle in the practice of referral of laws and decrees to the people for confirmation. [20] His use in this passage of the term "democratic," incidentally, is unusual and interesting. Normally he follows Aristotelian Greek practice in reserving the term "democratic" for the bad form of popular government, rule by the mob, and uses the term "politic" for the good form of popular government. In this *locus* he changes his usage and employs the word "democratic" in a more modern approving sense.

This Roman mixed government, Vermigli feels, is a better model for the government of the Church than any of the simpler forms described by the ancient Greeks. Here is his own full analysis of church polity: "It is not simple, but it is compounded of monarchy, aristocracy, and democracy. From it must be removed pernicious types of government, I mean tyranny, oligarchy, and corrupt domination of the people. If you respect Christ, it is called a monarchy, for He is our king who acquired the Church for himself with his own blood. He is now in heaven, yet rules this kingdom of his, not with a visible presence, but by the spirit and word of holy scriptures. And there are in the Church to execute this office for Him, Bishops, Presbyters, Doctors, and others who rule, in respect of whom it may justly be called an aristocracy. For they who are preferred to the government of churches, because of excellent gifts of God in doctrine and purity of life, must be promoted to these positions . . . . But because in the Church there are matters of very great weight and importance referred to the people (as appears in the Acts of the Apostles), it has an element of polity [here substituted for 'democracy']. But of the most weight are accounted excommunication, absolution, choice of ministers and the like, so it must be concluded that no man can be excommunicated without the consent of the Church." [21]

Observe that Vermigli reserves the right of excommunication to the people as a whole, rather than to more select institutions which represent them. He does not seem to be advocating either excommuni-

---

[20] *L.C.*, IV :5 :9. *C.P.* here supplies explanations of the Latin terms for "aristocratic" and "democratic," rather than using the terms themselves.

[21] *L.C.*, IV :5 :9. I have prepared a fresh translation, because in this instance *C.P.* does not use the significant political terms of *L.C.* For a recent edition of texts of both versions, see Robert M. Kingdon, *Geneva and the Consolidation of the French Protestant Movement, 1564-1572* (Geneva and Madison, 1967), in appendix III, pp. 217-218, hereafter cited as Kingdon.

cation of the Erastian type, limited to secular courts, or of the Calvinist type, limited to ecclesiastical courts on the model of the Genevan Consistory. He rather seems to be advocating congregational excommunication of the sort supported by Jean Morély and other dissidents within the French Reformed Church to the considerable distress of Calvin, Beza, and the other clerical leaders of that Church. [22] There is even some resonance of the Anabaptist approach to excommunication here. And there is more in a later passage in which he discusses appropriate treatment of the excommunicate, urging they be completely shunned, with all good Christians avoiding salutations, conversation, and even eating with them. Unlike the Anabaptists, however, he would make an exception to this general rule of shunning for the children, wives, and legal subjects of an excommunicate, since duty requires them to deal with such a sinner. [23] And elsewhere, to be sure, Vermigli explicitly repudiates many Anabaptist teachings.

This leads us to consideration of the influence of Vermigli's doctrine of the marks of the true Church. That it was considerable is suggested by the publication history of his works. Not only did his *Common Places* go through fourteen editions. Many of the commentaries upon which it is based went through a number of editions. The Commentary on First Corinthians, for example, went through four editions, and the Commentary on Kings through five. Most of these publications were in Latin, the only language that Vermigli normally used himself. They were clearly intended for the educated, not for the general public. A number of his works, however, including the *Common Places,* were translated into English and published in London. English is the only vernacular into which much of his work was translated. This suggests a particularly strong influence in Britain. Most of the Latin editions of his works were printed in such important Reformed publishing centers on the continent as Zurich, Geneva, and Heidelberg. Some of them also appeared in Basel, that great center for all kinds of printings, including a good many works produced by religious refugees from Italy, above all Pietro Perna. It was Perna, in fact, who produced the most complete single edition of Vermigli's *Loci Communes,* 1580-1582. [24]

---

[22] Kingdon, pp. 43-137, deals with the Morély affair. For a summary of Morély's argument on congregational discipline, see pp. 50 ff., specifically p. 52 on limitation of excommunication to the entire congregation.

[23] *C.P.,* IV :5 :18.

Clearly Vermigli had a considerable influence within the Reformed community. It will take a good deal of further work, however, to delineate the precise nature of that influence. In particular it is by no means clear which of the competing factions which developed within that movement were most faithful to the ecclesiological teachings of Peter Martyr. Indeed some influence can be traced in several directions. Several of Vermigli's most devoted students became leading Anglicans. Pre-eminent among them was John Jewel, bishop of Salisbury under Elizabeth I and a leading early apologist for the Church of England as established by Elizabeth. Jewel had become acquainted with Vermigli at Oxford, followed him into exile on the continent, joining him first in Strasbourg and then in Zurich, and maintained a warm correspondence with him after returning to England. [25] Edmund Grindal, Elizabeth I's first bishop of London and her second primate, probably also came to know Vermigli as one of the group of religious refugees in Strasbourg. In fact it seems probable that practically all of the important Elizabethan church leaders who had been members of the colonies of Marian exiles in Strasbourg and Zurich knew Vermigli personally. So did some of those leaders who remained in England during the Marian persecution. This network of personal contacts with the English elite helps to explain the high regard in which Vermigli was held by Elizabethans generally and the number of editions and translations of his work published in London. Since most of these men supported the episcopalian establishment of Elizabeth I, they obviously did not find a great incompatibility between the teachings of Vermigli and the practices of the Church of England.

Others among Vermigli's students and some of his best friends, on the other hand, became leading Presbyterians. Pre-eminent among them was Theodore Beza, Calvin's successor as Moderator of the Company of Pastors in Geneva. Beza was in frequent correspondence with Vermigli during his life and worked with him particularly closely in the

---

[24] See above, n. 8, on editions of the *Loci Communes*. Professor Donnelly or I have also examined copies of the following editions, all in Latin—of the Commentary on First Corinthians: (1) Zurich, 1551; (2) Zurich, 1567; (3) Zurich, 1572; (4) Zurich, 1579, and of the Commentary on Kings: (1) Zurich, 1566; (2) Zurich, 1571; (3) Zurich, 1581; (4) Zurich, again 1581; (5) Heidelberg, 1599.

[25] W. M. Southgate, *John Jewel and the Problem of Doctrinal Authority* (Cambridge, MA, 1962), especially the first two chapters, pp. 3-48. See also John E. Booty, *John Jewel as Apologist of the Church of England* (London, 1963), *passim*.

Protestant delegation at the Colloquy of Poissy. After Vermigli's death, it was Beza who first suggested the compilation of the *Loci Communes*. Beza also obtained possession of most of Vermigli's private library, making it the nucleus of the library of the comparatively new Geneva Academy. [26] Yet Beza became an ardent Presbyterian. On Calvin's death in 1564, he refused to accept the position of Moderator in Geneva on terms that would make it resemble the office of a bishop, insisting on annual election of the Moderator by the entire Company of Pastors. And after he had been routinely elected to the office for a number of years, he finally flatly refused to continue serving in 1580. Beza also worked hard to encourage Presbyterians in Scotland like Andrew Melville and Thomas Cartwright in their strenuous opposition to the rule of bishops in a Reformed Church. [27]

I have not as yet uncovered any direct personal connections between Vermigli and early Congregationalists. Most of them in his own lifetime were tainted with Anabaptism and that would have caused him to spurn their friendship on other theological grounds. But there is a good chance of influence in that direction, too, judging from the content of some of his writing. His opinion that the power to excommunicate should be reserved to the entire congregation, for example, must surely have appealed to later Congregationalists. It comes as no surprise, therefore, that we find copies of Vermigli's works in a place of honor within the libraries constructed in colonial New England to assist in the creation of a Congregational commonwealth. [28]

It might even be argued that, if the specific form of discipline suggested in the legal code Vermigli helped draft for England back in 1552 had prevailed, the later division among the English Reformed into Episcopalians, Presbyterians, and Congregationalists could have been avoided. This code ingeniously combines the guiding principles of these three factions, for example, in the procedure for excommuni-

---

[26] Alexandre Ganoczy, *La Bibliothèque de l'Académie de Calvin* (Geneva, 1969), supplies an inventory of the entire library. Donnelly, appendix, pp. 208-17, abstracts from it all of those items known to have belonged to Vermigli.

[27] On Beza's attitude toward the position of Moderator, see Olivier Labarthe, "Le changement du mode de présidence de la Compagnie des Pasteurs de Genève, 1578-1580," *Zeitschrift für Schweizerische Kirchengeschichte* 67 (1972), 160-86. On Beza's assistance to Presbyterianism in Scotland and England, see Maruyama, chapter 9, pp. 303-41.

[28] Giorgio Spini, "Riforma Italiana e Mediazioni Ginevrine nella Nuova Inghilterra Puritana," in Delio Cantimori, et al., *Ginevra e l'Italia* (Florence, 1959), 451-89, especially pp. 458 ff.

cation, suggesting that it be vested in the local congregation, on re-commendation of a group of elders, with the permission of a bishop. [29]

Even though Vermigli cannot be identified securely with any single one of these three factions seeking different types of church polity, however, he can be connected to the general concern they all shared for Christian discipline and polity. And this brings us back to the marks of the true Church. For it became characteristic of the entire Reformed movement that it was more concerned with questions of order than its main rival within the "Magisterial" camp, the Evangelical Lutheran movement. Vermigli's insistence that discipline must be the third mark of the true Church was surely both a symptom of this Reformed emphasis and a contribution to its growth and persistence.

---

[29] Spalding, p. 170. While Vermigli's ideas on excommunication may lend themselves to compromise of this sort, there are other strands in his thought which would create problems for such a compromise. In particular there is an Erastian strand, pointed out by Erastus himself. See Donnelly, pp. 188-189. I am indebted to Professor Donnelly and Thomas M. Safley for close readings of earlier drafts of this essay.

THE BISHOP CONFRONTS THE QUEEN

John Jewel and the Failure of the English Reformation

JOHN E. BOOTY

Episcopal Divinity School

John Jewel, apologist of the Church of England during the first years of the reign of Queen Elizabeth I, was fearful that the Reformation in England might fail. In his sermons, much neglected by scholars, we find him confronting his Queen and her nobility and gentry, accusing them of endangering true religion by plundering the church, rather than caring for it and raising up a learned and devout ministry. The danger he considered to be very great, for he believed that as true religion is necessary to the building up of the commonwealth, so the lack of it portended national doom. [1]

In a sermon given at Paul's Cross on Haggai 1:2-4, Jewel expressed his concern for the condition of the Church of England: "There lacke already Ministres throughout the Realme, to teach the people, and to build up the walls of Gods Church. One poore hireling is driven to serve two or three Parishes. The sick hath no man to comfort or counsell them: the dead have no man to burie them." [2] He went on to lament the decay of universities and schools "which ever have been nourceries" to raise up a learned and conscientious ministry, and to comment that "Actes of Parliament, and Proclamations, are not enough to content the conscience of the people, and to builde the Temple." What was needed was the active, personal intervention of the supreme governor of the Church of England, the Queen.

At Paul's Cross, the preaching station outside St. Paul's Cathedral, London, Jewel was addressing members of the Queen's Court, Mayor and Aldermen of the city, and the great throng that assembled there each Sunday morning. Before them all, Jewel exclaimed:

> Oh, that the Queenes Maiestie knewe the great scarcitie, and miserable neede of Ministers that is abroade. And I beseech you good my Lordes, and

---

[1] The case was put well by Richard Hooker, who early enjoyed Jewel's patronage. See *Of the Laws of Ecclesiastical Polity*, 5.1.1.

[2] *Certaine Sermons preached before the Queenes Maiestie, and at Paules crosse* (London, 1583), Sig. Gij.ᵛ. Subsequent references are given in the text following each quotation.

other Honourable and worshipfull that are here, that have or may have
accesse to her, to put her in remembrance that her grace will be mindefull
of the house of God, and redresse the greedinesse both of corrupt patrones,
and of such who engrosse and gather into their hands many livings, being
them selves the remnant of the ignorant and persecuting *Babylon*: and
leave to take charge over the people, blinde Syr Johns, not onely lacke-
Latin, but lacke-honestie, and lacke-conscience, and lacke-religion. It would
be a great furtherance to the Church of God, a wonderfull way to encrease
Schooles, and the Universities (Giij.r).

He then turned to the next division of his sermon, leaving a matter
that he considered to be of the utmost gravity.

Jewel was seemingly heard and taken seriously by someone of
importance at Paul's Cross, for he subsequently preached at Court,
in the presence of the Queen, on the plight of the church and in
particular on the desperate need for learned and devout ministers.
We do not know when the sermon was given, although the references to
"your graces late visitation" (Jvj.v) suggests some time after the
Royal Visitation of 1559, while the statement, "Your grace hath alreadie
redressed the doctrine" (Kiij.r) may refer to an early date, for on
November 16, 1559, Jewel informed Peter Martyr Vermigli: "The
doctrine is everywhere most pure". [3] And yet it would seem that he
was speaking out of his experience as Bishop of Salisbury, who, having
struggled largely in vain to improve the clergy of his diocese, came
to London intent upon exposing what he perceived to be the failure of
the English Reformation. He went to his diocese as bishop for the first
time on or about May 24, 1560. On April 13, 1561, he was back in
London, preaching at Paul's Cross. [4] By then Jewel had firsthand
knowledge of his clergy and diocese. In the same year, he reported to
Archbishop Parker that of the two hundred twenty clergymen beneficed
there, only twenty (exclusive of Cathedral clergy) were preachers and
several of these were not licensed to preach. Furthermore, there seemed
to exist a causal connection between those who were well educated
(classified as *doctus*) and those known to be preachers. [5] The overwhelming truth was that the clergy were ill prepared and much blame
for the situation was due to those responsible for their preparation.

---

[3] John Jewel, *Works,* ed. John Ayre, Parker Society (Cambridge, 1845-50),
4:1225.
[4] See Millar McLure, *The Paul's Cross Sermons* (Toronto, 1958), 203, 225;
and *The Diary of Henry Machyn,* ed. John Gough Nichols (London, 1848), 255.
[5] Corpus Christi College, Cambridge, MS 97, ff. 185b-193a; see Anne Whitman,
"The Church of England, 1542-1837," in *A History of Wiltshire,* Victoria County
Histories (London, 1956), 1:33.

It is possible, then, that Jewel preached the sermon on Haggai on April 13, 1561, was heard by someone present with access to the Queen, and that as a result arrangements were made for him to preach at Court, there to convince her majesty of the need for corrective action on her part. There is no way of ascertaining exactly when Jewel made his appearance at Court. He may have had to wait until the next March when it was noted that he preached there. [6]

Nor can we know where Jewel preached this Court sermon. In the vicinity of London it might have been at some palace such as Whitehall, St. James, Windsor, Hampton Court, or Greenwich. At whatever place he preached, if on a Sunday there would have been a procession from the presence chamber, led by the nobility, followed by the Lord Keeper of the Great Seal, the Sword of State, the Sceptre, and finally the Queen and her ladies-in-waiting and maids-of-honor. In the chapel the Queen would have occupied a separate gallery, the music would have been sung by the choristers of the Chapel Royal, a cross and candle-sticks would have been on the altar to the consternation of some, and the service would have been from the Elizabethan *Book of Common Prayer.* The Queen would have listened carefully; she had been known to censure preachers who strayed from their texts, wandering into matters which she considered none of their business. [7] It was in such a setting that Jewel confronted the Queen, sounding an alarm.

Jewel was known to the Queen. He had preached in her presence before and was appreciated as a learned and persuasive preacher. In exile during Queen Mary's reign, greatly influenced by Peter Martyr Vermigli in Zurich, Jewel had returned to England in 1559 full of enthusiasm for the Queen and the revival of the Reformation there. He had been at the center of affairs during the parliament which proclaimed the Queen's supremacy and re-introduced the *Book of Common Prayer,* somewhat amended. He had become impatient with the Queen and her Council for their slowness in moving to extirpate papal influence, but he was loyal and when the parliament ended participated in the Royal Visitation as a member of the commission visiting the Western Counties and was made Bishop of Salisbury. But most importantly he had emerged during the first year of the Queen's reign as the most eloquent and forceful defender of the Queen's settlement of religion. His reputation as an apologist began with the Chal-

---

[6] John Strype, *Annals of the Reformation* (Oxford, 1820-1840), I, i:407.

[7] See Rachel and Allen Percival, *The Court of Elizabeth I* (London, 1976), 43-44.

lenge Sermon at Paul's Cross in November 1559, repeated at Court
in the Spring of 1560, and again, in an expanded form, at Paul's Cross
in March. He had thus gone from Paul's Cross to the Court with a
vital message before. William Cecil, the Queen's principal secretary,
was much impressed by Jewel and set him to work writing the *Apologia
Ecclesiæ Anglicanæ*. The Challenge Sermon and the *Apology* were to
be important instruments of church and state, setting off a literary
controversy between Jewel and English recusants at Louvain.

Jewel did not begin his sermon at Court with an exegesis of his
text, Psalm 69:9 ("The zeale of thine house hath eaten me"), nor
with any reference to the practical purpose of the sermon. He chose,
rather, to establish a convincing foundation, beginning with consideration of the question: "to what ende and purpose mankinde was
create and set in this world" (Hij.^{r}). The generality of mankind has
had its notions from the light of nature, but the Christian, enlightened
by God's Word, possesses the truth: "the very true ende why man
was made was to knowe and to honour God". Or, to put it another
way, the end for which we are made is to serve God, to look beyond
nature, and to "become the Temples of the holy Ghost: that the holy
Spirite of God may dwell in us, and make us fitte instruments of the
glorie of God" (Hij.^{v}). To accomplish this, God provided "his holy
word," and we have "Temples and Churches, places to resort unto
altogether, to honour, to worship, and to acknowledge him to be our
God, to ioyne our hearts and voyces together, and to call upon his holy
name" (Hiij.^{r}). Such places are called "the dwelling place of God"
because it is there that we pray and our prayer is heard; there God's
Word is proclaimed and the sacraments and ceremonies used in the
right way.

The godly, thus, rejoice in the beauty of the church, God's house,
and are full of zeal to protect and preserve it. When they see it
disordered, "the Sacraments of God abused, the trueth troden under
foote," they lament and mourn (Hiiij.^{r}). Zeal, as Jewel explained, "is
an affection and vehement love," a kind of caring or sensitivity such
as God has shown to his people and such as those who truly love God
demonstrate towards God and all that he has created (Hiiij.^{v}). The
preacher then began to press in more closely on those before him. He
pointed out that there are those who claim to have such zeal toward
God who in actuality, while seeming to care for the church, plunder
and destroy it. Their case is clear. Such feelings toward God and
care for the church as they express come not from any understanding

of God's will for them or for the church. Indeed, it must be presumed that their behavior proceeds "not of malice or wilfulnesse, but only of the lacke of teaching and understanding" (Hv.^{v}-vj.^{r}). Zeal alone is not sufficient. Such vehement feeling may lead to superstition, idolatry, and other such enormities; "true and godly zeale proceedeth not from hypocrisie or intention, but is led and trained by understanding, and is molten into the heart, and the vehemencie and heate of it, no man knoweth, but he that feeleth it" (Hvij.^{v}). In such a way Jewel established the right order: knowledge and understanding first and then such zeal as proceeds therefrom, zeal which then consumes both reason and heart. With this Jewel came very near to the center of his concern, but then he backed away to discuss the difference between those with false and destructive zeal and those whose zeal was formed and molded by God's Word, ending this sub-section with a reference to the martyrs of his own day: those consumed by zeal for God's house.

The age of the martyrs was now past. True religion had been restored. The challenge now was to preserve it. The papacy had not been lax in doing that which would preserve the Church of Rome; so much the more should the English be zealous to maintain and build up the church restored to that which it was meant to be when it first began. There are many ways in which this might be done: "I will leave to speake of the rest, and only stay upon learning, which may truly be called the life and soul of the Church, and of the Christian religion" (Jiiij.^{r}). This second approach by Jewel to the subject of his concern (here summarized much more briefly) was more historical than theological, as he reminded those listening of the recent history of England and of the continuing menace of Rome, the epitome of that hypocrisy and ignorance formerly discussed in abstract terms. The inference here is that those who applied his description of false zeal to themselves in the first part of the sermon, now recognize that instead of serving the true church as established in England they serve England's enemy, the Church of Rome. By preventing learning they harm both church and nation.

History testifies to the importance of learning in the promotion of true religion. Charlemagne, the cathedral schools, and the schools and colleges established by the German Lutheran princes and the free cities, were all cited as examples. In every place where the Gospel has reached and been received, learning has prospered. England is the exception, where, "since the Gospel hath bene received, the maintenance for learning hath been decaied. And, the lacke of learning wilbe the

14

decay of the Gospel" (Jv.ʳ). How is this so? Because a learned ministry depends upon the cultivation and maintenance of learning. Furthermore, the well-being of the nation depends upon the maintenance of true religion. The right order of things is clear: learning is needed to produce a ministry capable of nourishing the people of God with understanding, that they may in turn have godly zeal to protect true religion and thus promote the common weal.

Jewel knew that he was treading on dangerous ground and asked the Queen and the others present to have patience, allowing him to speak the truth freely. With this he proceeded to the first accusation: The clergy resident in their parsonages do not receive the income attached to those livings. Such income is claimed by patrons who treat the parish churches as investments for the increase of their personal wealth. Such patrons are more like merchants than patrons, serving their own bellies and not God. The patron should be zealous to provide "a learned Master, who might be able to preach the word," but this is not the case (Jvj.ʳ). The young, who might study and in time enter the ministry, observe how the patrons behave and turn away: "some become prentises, some turne to phisick, some to law" (ibid.). Furthermore, by reason of impropriations some benefices are so poor that none could live on them and thus none wants them. The very large number of vacancies testifies to this fact.

Jewel then directly confronted the Queen:

> Your graces subiectes had hope of amendement, in your graces laste visitation. But yet it standeth stil in case as miserable as it did before. I know, your grace heareth not of these matters. And I hope God wil worke in your gracious heart, to provide some remedy against them. For otherwise, the scholes wilbe forsaken, the Church desolate, the people wilde and dismayed, the Gospel discredited ... (Jvj.ᵛ)

Jewel acknowledged that there were bishops who appointed ignorant clergy with no knowledge of Latin, but he defended them as having to fill vacancies with the best candidates available, no matter how ignorant. He anticipated the argument that ministers should teach without concern for payment, and contended that no one should wish poverty on those who spend years preparing for the ministry. He might have added that the argument is usually made by those laity most at fault, persons who should take seriously the consequences awaiting those who despoil God's house for the sake of their bellies. Foreign powers, now happily excluded from the land shall, as a result of greed and the lack of godly zeal, invade the realm, and "the truth of God shall be taken away, the holy scriptures burnt and consumed in the fire. A marveilous darkenes and calamitie must needes ensue" (Jvij.ᵛ). His warning was unmistakable. For lack of a learned ministry, true religion shall perish from the land, antichrist shall triumph, and God shall be angered, leaving England desolate.

Thus far Jewel had concentrated on the powerful and wealthy who prevented the Church of England from having a learned ministry. Now, in the context of his warning, he pointed out that in places where learned ministers were found, parishioners did not listen to them: "nothing will move them... because the ministerie of God, and thereby God him selfe, is despised" (Kj.ʳ). If this is true, the provision of more university educated clergy cannot be expected to solve England's problem. Hearts must be changed in the village churches as well as in the royal chapel.

Jewel pled for repentance before it was too late. He acknowledged that he could have preached concerning something else, but nothing else so much deserved the attention of his auditory. Once more he directed his words to the Queen: "You are our Governour, you are the Nource of Gods Church. We must open this griefe before you. God knoweth if it may be redressed, it hath growen so long, and is runne so farre. But, if it may be redressed, there is no other besides your Highnesse, that can redresse it" (Kij.ᵛ). As was required, Jewel mixed flattery into his demand. The Queen herself was learned above the learning of any other prince. She had found the church disordered on her accession. "Your grace hath alreadie redressed the doctrine: now cast your eyes towardes the Ministrie, give courage and countenance unto learning, that Gods house may be served: so shall you leave a Church of God, and a testimonie that the zeale of the Lords house hath eaten you up" (Kiij.ʳ). Having addressed the Queen, Jewel turned to the other chief persons of the realm present in the chapel, exhorting them to further the Word and the ministry in deeds and not with words alone. Finally, he spoke to all who despoiled the church: "Let not the Ministerie by your means be despised. You enriched them, which mocked, and blinded, and devoured you: Spoyle not them nowe that feede, and instructe, and comfort you. Let us seeke the glorie of God. Let us at length serve the Lorde and not our bellie, and greedie wantonnesse" (Kiij.ᵛ-iiij.ʳ).

We do not have any record of the discussion which then took place concerning Jewel's words. We can imagine that the bishop's reputation for audacity was enhanced, for only a dullard would have been unaware of the fact that Jewel was attacking the Queen and was impelled to do so out of fear that the Reformation in England was in grave danger. So long as the Queen not only acquiesced in the plunder of the church but actively led in it, an educated ministry could not be had, for there were no adequate funds with which to finance their education or to maintain them in benefices when ordained. Without a learned ministry all would be lost. Jewel's ideal, the Reformation ideal, of an educated ministry capable of edifying the people, was doomed given the circumstances.

How valid was Jewel's concern? Given the Reformation ideal of a learned ministry, it would seem that he had just cause for concern. The church had been plundered. According to the *Valor Ecclesiasticus* of 1535 the total net income of the English Church was £ 320,180. Taking into account underestimates and omissions, it is possible that the total should be closer to £ 400,000 per annum, or one fifth of the yearly national income. [8] For various reasons, including human greed, anticlericalism, a depleted national treasury, and the sincere conviction that the church should not be encumbered with riches, the church's wealth was brought under attack. Reminiscent of Wyclif, schemes were devised for the nationalization of the church, whereby all of the ecclesiastical properties would be in the hands of the Crown. [9] Such schemes were not feasible, if only because Henry VIII did not wish to have his bishops abused and their loyalties alienated. But the attack on the church's wealth commenced, nevertheless. By 1540 the monasteries were dissolved and the various properties of some 650 religious houses (accounting for about 50% of the church's wealth) were seized and redirected through the Court of Augmentations to the benefit of privileged laity. [10] By 1547 colleges and chantries suffered the same fate, although some attempts were made to direct some

---

[8] W. G. Hoskins, *The Age of Plunder: The England of Henry VIII, 1500-1547*, Social and Economic History of England (London, 1976), 124-25.

[9] Public Record Office, SP 1/152, f. 11-13; precis printed in Phyllis M. Hembry, *The Bishops of Bath and Wells, 1540-1640: Social and Economic Problems* (London, 1967), 260. See also pp. 59-61 and L. Stone, "The Political Programme of Thomas Cromwell," *Bulletin of the Institute of Historical Research*, 24:1-18. Cf. G. R. Elton, "Parliamentary Drafts, 1529-1540," *ibid.*, 25: 117-132, esp. p. 129.

[10] See Christopher Kitching, "The Disposal of Monastic and Chantry Lands," *Church and Society in England, Henry VIII to James I*, eds. Felicity Heal and Rosemary O'Day (London, 1977), 119-36.

of the proceeds toward the benefit of those seeking education. [11]

The wealth of the bishops was not seized in the same manner, but it was eroded by the exchange of properties, by forced leases, in some instances by outright seizure, and by various practices of Tudor prelates in providing for children and relatives. [12] It was customary by law (26 Henry VIII, c. 3) for the Crown to collect first fruits on the appointment of a bishop, and for the Crown, should it wish to do so, to exchange properties with the newly consecrated bishops. The Crown would trade so-called spiritual properties, such as parsonages and tenths and the like, usually former monastic properties, for other properties of equivalent book value but actually much more desirable, such as manors and manor lands. [13] Such practice grew during Henry's reign and peaked during the reign of Edward VI. Queen Mary sought to restore what the church had lost, but Elizabeth formalized the process of exchange in a statute (1 Eliz. I, c. 19). At the beginning of her reign many sees were kept vacant for what seemed to be an excessively long time while exchanges were arranged, always to the benefit of the Queen. Matthew Parker, Archbishop of Canterbury-elect, along with other bishops, protested and sought to buy the Queen off with an annual pension of £ 1,000. If she refused, as she did, they hoped that she would be mindful of their needs. [14] The result was that many bishoprics were ransomed and impoverished. [15] The extent of this impoverishment is not fully realized until the high rate of inflation during the sixteenth century is taken into account. Between 1535 and 1595 there was a three-fold increase in costs, a factor which inflicted severe hardship, especially on those with fixed incomes: the church was to an increasing extent dependent upon such income. Giving up long leases on properties at sums fixed at the beginning of the leases, and commuting tithes for fixed sums, benefited the church initially, but in the long run were extremely detrimental, in large part because of the relentless tides of inflation.

The impoverishment of the church on the diocesan level was reflected by the poverty of the clergy. It has been estimated that on

---

[11] In particular see the statutes: 37 Hen. VIII, c. 4, which vested all chantries in the king's hands, and 1 Edw. VI, c. 14, the act dissolving the chantries.

[12] The facts are detailed by Hembry, *Bishops of Bath and Wells,* esp. chapters 3 and 5.

[13] Hoskins, *Age of Plunder,* 138-39.

[14] Hembry, *Bishops of Bath and Wells,* 130; see also pp. 129-32.

[15] See Christopher Hill, *Economic Problems of the Church: From Archbishop Whitgift to the Long Parliament* (Oxford, 1956), 26.

the eve of the Reformation the incumbent of a benefice, with an assistant, would require a minimum of £15 per annum. The *Valor Ecclesiasticus* suggests that "three-quarters of all parochial livings in England were worth less than £15, and that a half of all livings were not worth £10, and many less than £7."[16] During the reign of Elizabeth £30 was considered the minimum necessary annual income for the maintenance of a qualified incumbent and Archbishop Whitgift informed "the queen that not one in twenty of the benefices in the country was worth £30 clear."[17] It is not surprising, then, that competent scholars were not attracted to the ordained ministry, and that so many benefices were cared for, if they received any care at all, by unlearned, incompetent curates. In addition, the psychological damage was very real. The lack of financial support bred a crippling sense of insecurity among the clergy.[18]

How ill-prepared were the clergy? Any consideration of this question must take into account the expectations of those concerned.[19] In fact, expectations had been changing. The ideal priest as depicted by John Myrc before the Reformation was a man of prayer and sanctity whose *regula* was the Scriptures and whose life was the cross. His duties involved saying the canonical hours, celebrating the Mass daily, and educating the people in the rudiments of the faith. The emphasis fell on the Mass, however, the validity of which was not dependent on the erudition or moral excellence of the priest.[20] Well before the Reformation in England began, the actual performance of priests engaged in such ministry was being criticized. Christian humanists complained of priests "that ... can no thyng dow but pattyr up theyr matyns and mas, mumbling up a certayn number of wordys no thynge understoode."[21] Under such pressures as were exerted by learned humanists, concern shifted from the performance of a few basic duties

---

[16] Peter Heath, *English Parish Clergy on the Eve of the Reformation* (London, 1969), 172-73.

[17] Hill, *Economic Problems of the Church*, 202ff., esp. p. 205. See Christopher Haigh, *Reformation and Resistance in Tudor Lancashire* (London, 1975), 237-39.

[18] See Felicity Heal, "Economic Problems of the Clergy," *Church and Society in England*, 113.

[19] See Hugh F. Kearney, *Scholars and Gentlemen: Universities and Society in Pre-Industrial Britain, 1500-1700* (London, 1970), 28-29. Kearney believes that the clergy "could not have been in so depressed a condition as its many critics made out," and that such criticism was "derived from a higher expectation of what the parson had a right to."

[20] See Heath, *English Parish Clergy*, 3-7.

[21] Thomas Starkey, *A Dialogue between Cardinal Pole and Thomas Lupset,* ed. J. M. Cowper (E.E.T.S., extra ser., xii, 1878), 132.

to an understanding of those duties, and more. For the best understanding and performance an university education seemed not only beneficial but essential. To raise the standards of the ordained ministry, colleges were founded at Oxford and Cambridge, criticism of ignorant clergy increased, and pressures were brought to bear on Crown, bishops, and lay patrons to reform the clergy according to the new standards.

The Reformation further emphasized the humanist ideal. Toward the end of the century, John Reynolds, Master of Corpus Christi College, Oxford, friend of Richard Hooker, and leader of the Puritan group at the Hampton Court Conference, wrote a letter to a young man who was seeking advice on how to study divinity. In the letter Reynolds emphasized godliness and learning. Learning was to be concentrated on the study of Scripture and the sound exposition of Scriptural truth, such as that contained in Calvin's *Institutes*. Furthermore, the student should seek an adequate knowledge of Hebrew and Greek; Latin was simply taken for granted.[22] The aim of such education was to produce an able preacher, one capable of teaching the faith and administering the godly discipline. The *Book of Common Prayer* seemingly required such learned ministers. The Ordinal of 1550 associated Word with Sacrament, the new priest being given a Bible as an instrument of office, along with the bread and chalice, the instruments prescribed in medieval ordinals.[23]

As a result of such changing standards, evidence of clerical ignorance increased. About 1530, Stokesley, Bishop of London, examined the curates of his diocese. Fifty-six were brought before him; twenty-two were prohibited from functioning because of ignorance; six were allowed to continue if they submitted themselves to a course of study; six others were barred as unsuitable; and nine were inhibited for various reasons. Thus, out of fifty-six only eleven were approved.[24] Other examples come to mind, including John Hooper's visitation of his diocese in 1551.[25] John Parkhurst, Bishop of Norwich, examined one Thomas Atkinson in 1572, and upon discovering that the priest was

---

[22] Corpus Christi College, Oxford, MS 316, f. 46-48.

[23] Cf. the medieval ordinal, William Maskell, ed., *Monumenta Ritualia Ecclesiæ Anglicanæ*, 2nd ed. (Oxford, 1882), 2:226, and the ordinal of 1550, Joseph Ketley, ed., *The Two Liturgies ... set forth ... in the Reign of King Edward VI*, Parker Society (Cambridge, 1844), 179.

[24] Summarized by Heath, *English Parish Clergy*, 73-74.

[25] Ibid., 74, and see J. Gairdner, "Bishop Hooper's Visitation of Gloucester in 1551," *English Historical Review*, 19:98-124.

ignorant of Latin, could not identify the contents of the third chapter of Matthew, could not answer the question "What is the faith?", and was altogether ignorant of Paul's Epistle to the Romans, finally concluded: "I perceived he was soch an ignorant asse I was wery to talk with him any more." [26] Such incidents were evidently not uncommon.

There was general agreement among reform-minded ecclesiastics in England that incumbents ideally should be graduates of Oxford or Cambridge. Obtainable statistics indicate that while there were increasing numbers of graduates in the ministry, progress was very slow and in some places imperceptible. Margaret Bowker reports that in the diocese of Lincoln the percentage of graduates presented by laymen to livings between 1421 and 1520 rose from $3\frac{1}{2}\%$ to $11\frac{1}{2}\%$. [27] But in Gloucester in 1570 "none of the 36 ordinands had degrees." [28] Later, at the beginning of the seventeenth century, the situation changed dramatically, and even earlier the percentage of graduates on ordination lists in dioceses such as Oxford and Peterborough was impressive. It must be noted here that university graduates were not the only educated men ordained. There were many who studied at the universities, stopping short of the M.A., the degree which identified a person as a graduate. Some proceeded only so far as the B.A., studying the old and new logic, together with grammar and rhetoric, if such had not been acquired at an earlier stage. To obtain the M.A., three further years were required in order to study arithmetic, geometry, music, and metaphysical and natural philosophy. In the course of time this regimen would change, especially in colleges which were under humanist and Protestant influences. In addition, one should note the growth of grammar schools during the sixteenth century. Educational standards and facilities were rapidly improving. [29] Ordinands might very well have gained a solid if rudimentary education in town or village schools. All so educated would learn at least some Latin. Furthermore, as increasing numbers of English men and women were educated, they expected better educated ministers. Finally, printing should be men-

---

[26] *The Letter Book of John Parkhurst*, R. A. Houlbrooke, ed., Norfolk Record Society 43 (1974-1975), 98-99.

[27] *The Secular Clergy in the Diocese of Lincoln, 1495-1520* (Cambridge, 1968), 42.

[28] Rosemary O'Day, "The reformation of the ministry, 1558-1642," *Continuity and Change: Personnel and Administration of the Church of England, 1500-1642* (Leicester, 1976), 67.

[29] *Ibid.*, 70.

tioned. Books were more readily available and certain books were prescribed for reading by clergy, commencing with the Bible. [30]

Various efforts were made to improve the educational and moral standards of the clergy. [31] Mention has been made of the founding of new colleges at the universities. During Elizabeth's reign more colleges were established, such as Emmanuel and Sidney Sussex at Cambridge. Less well known is the Queen's provision in 1560 of income from Crown prebends assessed at less than £20 per annum to provide for theological scholarships. [32] In addition, there were attempts made to educate those who had already been ordained. Especially important were the exercises or diocesan meetings for examination of unlearned clergy and prophesyings or discussions (including preaching and prayers) of doctrine by learned ministers for the benefit of themselves and others not as well educated. These devices, adopted from the practice of the reformed church of Zurich, were regarded as dangerous by Elizabeth when they came to her attention in the 1570s, for she believed they could be used by those of the Puritan faction to advance their cause against the religious settlement. She ordered that they be discontinued, but they were viewed as vitally important by many bishops and there is evidence that they continued beyond the crisis of 1576-7. [33]

Much depended on the bishops and archdeacons and their regular functions, including ordinations, institutions, and visitations. The law demanded that they labor for the reform of the clergy. The Royal Injunctions of 1559 ordered

> that every parson, vicar, curate, and stipendiary priest, being under the degree of master of art, shall provide and have of his own, within three months after this visitation, the New Testament both in Latin and English, with Paraphrases upon the same, conferring the one with the other. And the bishops and other Ordinaries by themselves or their officers, in their

---

[30] See Bowker, *The Secular Clergy,* 48; Heath, *English Parish Clergy,* 193-94; and Lucien Febvre and Henri-Jean Martin, *The Coming of the Book: The Impact of Printing, 1450-1800,* (London, 1976), esp. ch. 8.

[31] See Mark H. Curtis, *Oxford and Cambridge in Transition, 1558-1642* (Oxford, 1959), 167ff.

[32] O'Day, "The reformation of the ministry," 62.

[33] See Stanford E. Lehmberg, "Archbishop Grindal and the Prophesyings," *Historical Magazine of the Episcopal Church,* 34 (1965): 97-128; Ralph Houlbrooke, "The Protestant Episcopate, 1547-1603: The Pastoral Contribution," *Church and Society in England,* eds. Heal and O'Day, 90; Patrick Collinson, *The English Puritan Movement* (Berkeley, 1967), 170-71; and Edward Cardwell, *Documentary Annals* (Oxford, 1844), 1:389-91.

synods and visitations, shall examine the said ecclesiastical persons, how they have profited in the study of Holy Scripture. [34]

The Interpretations of the Bishops 1560/1 further instructed the archdeacons to examine the clergy on prescribed texts of the New Testament and Archbishop Parker in the Advertisements of 1566 confirmed this procedure. [35] The canons of 1571 gave additional support to examinations of the unlearned clergy by archdeacons. [36] The parliamentary statute of 1571 enforcing subscription to the Thirty-Nine Articles of Religion (13 Eliz. I, c. 12), required that clergy subscribe, lead honest lives, and "be able to answer and render to the ordinary an account of his faith, in Latin according to the said Articles, or have special gift and ability to be a preacher..." [37] The canons of 1575 ordered that previously ordained unlearned clergy be prevented from functioning and that bishops diligently examine curates seeking admission to any cure. Again it was insisted that clergy "be able to render to the... bishop and account of his faith in Latin" in accordance with the Articles of Religion. [38]

There is some evidence that all of this was taken seriously. [39] But in spite of the law and the efforts of bishops such as Parker, Parkhurst, Jewel, and others, the Church of England was vulnerable to the criticism that ill-prepared men were being ordained and instituted to benefices. The Puritans, having emerged as a kind of party both within and outside of Parliament, leapt at the evidence of weakness as proof that a further reform of the church was necessary. The petition which they presented to Parliament in December 1584 reminded the Commons that, in spite of legal requirements, the bishops were taking ignorant men into the ministry and were maintaining them in their livings. [40] Whitgift protested that he "had omitted nothing that might perteyne to the reforming of that abuse." He admitted that some were provided with benefices who could not preach but "thought it muche better to have some to reade the service

---

[34] W. H. Frere, *Visitation Articles and Injunctions,* Alcuin Club 16 (London, 1910), 2:13-14.

[35] *Ibid.,* 60, 178.

[36] Edward Cardwell, *Synodalia* (Oxford, 1842), 1:112.

[37] *Ibid.,* 132-34.

[38] Henry Gee and W. J. Hardy, *Documents Illustrative of English Church History* (London, 1914), 479-80.

[39] Haigh, *Reformation and Resistance,* 240.

[40] British Library, Addit. MS 38,492, f. 73-74.

etc., without a sermon, then that the people like unto Brute beastes should bee left without Prayers, Sacraments, reading the Scriptures and Homilies and without Sermons also." He went on to say that it was "against Charitie" to oust unlearnde ministers from their livings when they had no other "trade whereby to lyve." Given the existence of unlearned ministers and the need to provide a more learned ministry, exercises were proposed, "not those unto that which they called Prophecies (which had bene the cause of some troubles in the Churche) but some other more private, such as shall seem best to ourselves, both for the peace of the Churche, and their better instruction." [41]

Such reasoning may seem inadequate, but the evidence suggests that Whitgift was earnestly striving, against great odds, to secure a more learned ministry. One of his greatest challenges involved persuading learned men to enter the ministry, with the possibility that they might spend their lives in poverty. It was in relation to such a predicament that the bishops fought against a bill which would have prohibited pluralism. They were committed to working against the injustices involved in non-residence and pluralism, but they argued that pluralism should not be altogether outlawed since it served to compensate "men of speciall note, and degree in Schoole." [42] It was particularly painful for the bishops to be summoned by the Queen, as they were in 1584/5, to be chastised "in that you have not a greater care in making Ministers." [43] The fault lay as much with the Queen, the nobility, and the gentry, who plundered the church, refusing to make adequate provision for the support of a learned ministry.

As Jewel confronted the Queen, exhorting her to reform the church's ministry, giving "courage and countenance unto learning, that God's house may be served" (Kiij.^{r}), he was not, therefore, expressing some private, peculiar concern. The Reformation in England depended upon the quality of the ministry, its learning and its zeal, and thus, seeing who those were who could effect such reform, it depended upon its powerful laity, the Queen, her nobility and gentry. All must be concerned and all must give that which is necessary to provide an adequate ministry. Failure to do so could only be considered evidence of selfishness and of a lack of godly zeal.

Jewel sounded the clear note of warning which Richard Hooker

---

[41] Inner Temple, Petyt MS 538(38), f. 79-82.
[42] Lambeth Palace Library, MS 2007, f. 123.
[43] Public Record Office, SP 12/176 (68,69), f. 191-93; and see J. E. Neale, *Elizabeth I and Her Parliaments, 1584-1601* (New York, 1958), 69-71.

was to elaborate upon and resound. Hooker, who by his own admission owed much to the older man, agreed with the Puritan opposition that in general, according to natural law, Scripture, canon, decrees, and the wisdom of the ancients, ignorance, non-residence, and pluralism should be condemned. Learning and faithfulness were urgently required. And yet, given the hard realities of Elizabethan England, exceptions must be allowed. It was clear to him that there were not enough learned men to fill all of the livings in the English church; the universities could not provide such numbers; and the finances of the church were such that the required number of learned ministers could not adequately be supported. Such realities required that learning be defined in relation to that degree of learning needed to provide for the basic necessities of ministry. It was far better to have ministers of mean learning than to have God's people untended. He defined the basic needs in terms of the minister able "to perform the service of public prayer, to minister the sacraments unto the people, to solemnize marriage, to visit the sick and bury the dead, [and] to instruct by reading although by preaching" he is not able to serve his people. [44] Likewise, although non-residence and pluralism are not desired in the best reformed church, yet given the circumstances in England they may be allowed. Hooker was clearly irritated by the perfectionism of the Puritans, their lack of realism, and their rigidity, but beneath the irritation there was sympathy, for although Hooker allowed that circumstances might necessitate compromise with principle, yet he feared the danger involved in allowing those who sought exceptions to have their ways. His fear and his aspiration were both revealed as he prescribed means by which to improve the sorry state of the English church. Bishops must "take heed lest unnecessarily and through their default the Church be found worse or less furnished than it might be." Patrons must not destroy the souls for which they are responsible in pursuit of selfish gain. Those with power to dispense from that which is right according to law should do so according to merit alone. The chief personages of the realm who dispense favors must not suffer "their names to be abused contrary to the true intent and meaning of wholesome laws by men in whom there is nothing notable besides covetousness and ambition." Those who enjoy pluralities should "as well remember what in duty towards the Church and in conscience towards God they ought to do, as what

---

44 *Of the Laws of Ecclesiastical Polity*, 5.81..5.

they may do by using to their own advantage whatsoever all see tolerated." [45] While Hooker did not believe that all was lost if a learned ministry could not be obtained, he nevertheless agreed with Jewel that the mark which should be aimed at was a learned and faithful ministry and that all that stood in its way lacked godly zeal and would suffer the consequences.

Finally, what went on in the mind of Queen Elizabeth as she listened to Bishop Jewel? In the end, in the midst of the "Golden Speech" which she made before her last Parliament, she protested: "I have ever used to set the Last-Judgment Day before mine eyes, and so to rule as I shall be judged to answer before a higher Judge, to whose judgment seat I do appeal, that never thought was cherished in my heart that tended not unto my people's good." [46]

---

[45] *Ibid.*, 5.81.16.
[46] Neale, *Elizabeth I and Her Parliaments, 1584-1601,* 390.

PRELIMINARY OBSERVATIONS ON WRITING A HISTORY OF THE ROMAN INQUISITION

JOHN TEDESCHI

The Newberry Library, Chicago

I would have greatly preferred to present George Williams with a completed "History of the Roman Inquisition," [1] than merely the notes which follow. But since that project is still in a rudimentary state, I shall try to do the next best thing and set down the reasons that led me to undertake it and anticipate where it will lead me.

The idea of the "History" probably dates to my first serious encounter with great quantities of Inquisitorial documents at Trinity College, Dublin in the summer of 1967. [2] My original intention, as I began to forage through this important manuscript collection, was to calendar the sixteenth- and early seventeenth-century materials, consisting of sentences pronounced by the Roman and provincial Italian tribunals of the Holy Office. At this time I was interested in the suspects: who they were, the types of heresy they had espoused, and the titles of the books they had possessed. I was pursuing a scholarly interest in the Italian Protestant Reformers first kindled by George Williams during my years in graduate school.

My attention began to wander to other things: monastic or house arrest as the prevailing forms of imprisonment, the weight given to extenuating circumstances and the opinions of learned legal advisers, the relative mildness of witchcraft proceedings, the large number of cases that terminated with abjurations on Cathedral steps, and the infrequency of capital punishment. I became sidetracked. A picture

---

[1] By Roman Inquisition I mean the judicial system which was established on ancient foundations by Paul III with the Bull *Licet ab Initio* (1542) as a response to the Protestant challenge in Italy, "Sacra Congregatio Romanae et Universalis Inquisitionum, seu Sancti Officii." In 1908 it became known as "Congregatio Sancti Officii" and after 1965 as "Congregatio pro Doctrina Fidei" or "S. Congregazione per la Dottrina della Fede." It is a pleasure to express my appreciation to the Institute for Research in the Humanities, The University of Wisconsin, Madison, for a fellowship during the academic year 1976-77 that permitted several months of uninterrupted research and writing on the topic.

[2] The Dublin documents (henceforth abbreviated TCD) are part of the valuable materials removed by order of Napoleon from Roman archives and which were not returned after his fall. For a fuller account of their provenance and contents, see J. Tedeschi, "La dispersione degli archivi della Inquisizione romana," *Rivista di storia e letteratura religiosa* 9 (1973), 298-312.

of Inquisitorial justice began to form in my mind which differed from the traditional view I had always naturally accepted and which is commonly associated with Henry Charles Lea's *A History of the Inquisition of the Middle Ages*. Although Lea's monumental study is addressed to the workings of the institution in a period earlier than my own, it enters a sweeping indictment which was intended to apply also to the sixteenth century: "A few words will suffice to summarize the career of the medieval Inquisition. It introduced a system of jurisprudence which infected the criminal law of lands subjected to its influence, and rendered the administration of penal justice a cruel mockery for centuries." [3]

A change in my thinking occurred very gradually. I can still remember my reaction towards the beginning of my work on the Dublin documents upon encountering this sentence pronounced at the conclusion of a trial: ". . . and because you have conducted yourself more openly and sincerely than the others in confessing your errors, it seems proper for us to proceed against you with greater mercy . . ." [4] The offender was condemned to a *carcere perpetuo*. I was appalled. If this was mild treatment what did Inquisitors do when they were severe? Later, I discovered why the judges in this case thought they were dealing mercifully by sentencing this individual to what seemed to be life imprisonment. Inquisitorial manuals are unanimous in their opinion that this sentence should be commuted, when the convicted heretic had shown signs of real contrition, after a lapse of three years. [5] The failure to understand Inquisitorial terminology has misled more than one well-intentioned scholar and has contributed to the ill-fame of the institution. [6]

---

[3] *A History of the Inquisition of the Middle Ages*, 3 vols., (New York, 1888), III, 650.

[4] TCD, vol. 1224, f. 201: "Et perchè tu sei proceduto più liberamente et sinceramente de gli altri nel confessare gli errori tuoi, ci pare ancora conveniente usarti magiore misericordia . . ." The sentence is against the Bolognese Antonio de' Ludovisi and is dated Rome, 21 September 1567.

[5] See, among many others, Iacobi Simancas, *De Catholicis Institutionibus* (Rome, 1575), 113: "Solet poena perpetui carceris post lapsum triennii plerumque remitti, si eo tempore vincti humiles et veri poenitentes fuerint." I was fortunate to find Ludovisi mentioned in letters addressed by the Roman tribunal to the Bolognese Inquisitor inquiring about his behavior and ordering his release from monastic confinement. In Ludovisi's case the "life sentence" lasted six years. Bologna, Biblioteca dell' Archiginnasio (henceforth abbreviated BA), MS. 1860, ff. clxlv, clxxxxviiii.

[6] See, for example, Franco Gaeta, "Documenti da codici vaticani per la storia della Riforma in Venezia," *Annuario dell' istituto storico italiano per l'età moderna e contemporanea* 7 (1955), 5-53, at p. 7, discussing a carpenter arrested in

If a tentative new perspective was one factor that helped to persuade me of the importance of studying the Inquisition, the second was the fact that, despite the current active interest in the Catholic Reformation and Counter-Reformation, the Roman Inquisition has been generally ignored by modern scholarship. No one, to the best of my knowledge, has approached the organization and procedures of this institution as subjects worthy of critical study on their own account. Of the fifty-four articles which comprise the first *Festschrift* for Hubert Jedin, not one deals with the Inquisition. [7] The two volumes which cover the Counter-Reformation in the authoritative Fliche & Martin *Histoire de l'Église* devote a grand total of six and one half lines to it, [8] and there are only a few words on the subject in the apposite volume of Jedin's otherwise comprehensive manual of church history. [9] The Inquisition fares no better in the distinguished histories of this period by Dickens and O'Connell. [10] The ample historiographical survey by Eric Cochrane fails to turn up a single work on this subject or a single reference to research in progress. [11] The Inquisition apparently was not deemed sufficiently controversial to warrant discussion in a recent symposium volume devoted to religious "problems" in sixteenth-century Italy. [12] Not one recent title is listed in Van der Vekené's admittedly lacunous bibliography [13] or in Bell's survey of

Venice in 1533: "... il 9 e il 10 maggio egli è arrestato e le porte della prigione non gli si apriranno mai più, perchè il 6 giugno dell'anno seguente verrà condannato *ad perpetuos carceres.*"

[7] Erwin Iserloh & Konrad Repgen, eds., *Reformata Reformanda. Festgabe für Hubert Jedin zum 17. Juni 1965*, (Münster, 1965).

[8] Léon Cristiani, *L'Église à l'époque du Concile de Trente* (Paris, 1948); Leopold Willaert, *Après le Concile de Trente. La Restauration Catholique, 1563-1648* (Paris, 1960).

[9] *Handbuch der Kirchengeschichte. IV. Reformation, Katholische Reform und Gegenreformation* (Freiburg, Basel, Vienna, 1967).

[10] A. G. Dickens, *The Counter Reformation* (London, 1968), 106 contains only a few sentences based on the account in B. J. Kidd, *The Counter-Reformation, 1550-1600* (London: 1933), 42 ff; Marvin R. O'Connell, *The Counter Reformation, 1559-1610* (New York, 1974) where the Inquisition is mentioned in passing but nothing is said about its activity. Other agencies of the Roman Church (Jesuits, Council of Trent, Nunciatures) are discussed in the bibliographical essay, but not the Holy Office.

[11] "New Light on Post-Tridentine Italy: A Note on Recent Counter-Reformation Scholarship," *Catholic Historical Review* 56 (1970), 291-319, who laments "the Italian phase of the Counter-Reformation is barely mentioned in most of the recent literature in English" (p. 292).

[12] *Problemi di vita religiosa in Italia nel Cinquecento* (Padua, 1960) where the Inquisition does not even appear in the index.

[13] Emil Van der Vekené, *Bibliographie der Inquisition. Ein Versuch* (Hildesheim, 1963).

current research in legal history. [14] One can also search in vain the published proceedings of recent congresses devoted to the history of law [15] or in such publications on ecclesiastical law in particular as *Studia Gratiana* and the *Bulletin of Canon Law*. Enormous erudition is brought to bear in the pages of these scholarly journals to explicate minute points of legal doctrine, and yet the Inquisition, which immediately comes to mind when one thinks of the administration of justice by the Catholic Church in the medieval and early modern periods, is studiously ignored. One would also never guess leafing through such volumes interested in Dominican and Franciscan history as the *Archivum Fratrum Praedicatorum* and the *Archivum Franciscanum Historicum* that staffing the tribunals of the Holy Office had been the exclusive responsibility of these two mendicant orders. When a recent study mentions "a field of scholarship as well-tilled as the Inquisition under the pontificate of Paul IV" [16] it is not able to support this statement by referring to a single work published since 1959; and in all the writings cited the diffusion of Protestantism in Italy, and not the Inquisition, is the real subject of investigation.

For the moment our knowledge of the organization and procedures of the Roman Holy Office is still largely based on the general chapters devoted to it in Pastor's *History of the Popes*; [17] on the old and diffuse studies of provincial tribunals by Battistella, [18] Fumi [19] and

---

[14] Hugh F. Bell, "Research in Progress in Legal History," *American Journal of Legal History* 17 (1973), 66-84.

[15] For example, the massive *La formazione storica nel diritto moderno in Europa*, (Florence, 1977) (*Atti del Terzo Congresso Internazionale della Società Italiana di Storia del Diritto*).

[16] Christopher Cairns, *Domenico Bollani, Bishop of Brescia. Devotion to Church and State in the Republic of Venice in the Sixteenth Century* (Nieuwkoop, 1976), 121.

[17] Ludwig von Pastor, *The History of the Popes from the Close of the Middle Ages*, 40 vols., (St. Louis, 1898-1953), XII, 503-13; XIII, 210-24; XIV, 259-318; XVI, 305-52, 478-82; XVII, 288-343, 400-04; XIX, 296-322; XXI, 192-97; XXIV, 198-219. Pastor deals with the external history of the institution, not its judicial procedures. More useful, perhaps, is his edition of *Decreta*, decrees issued by the Supreme Inquisition in Rome during its weekly meetings, where the pope himself generally presided: "Allgemeine Dekrete der Römischen Inquisition aus den Jahren 1555-1597. Nach dem Notariatsprotokoll des S. Offizio zum erstenmale veröffentlicht," *Historisches Jahrbuch der Görres-Gesellschaft* 33(1912), 479-549.

[18] Antonio Battistella, "Alcuni documenti sul S. Officio in Lombardia nei secoli XVI e XVII," *Archivo storico lombardo*, ser. 3, vol. 3, a. 22 (1895), 116-32; *Il S. Officio e la Riforma religiosa in Friuli* (Udine, 1895); *Processi d'eresia nel Collegio di Spagna (1553-1554). Episodio della storia della Riforma in Bologna* (Bologna, 1901); "Notizie sparse sul Sant'Officio in Lombardia durante i secoli

Amabile; [20] on the brief sketch in Niccolò del Re's survey of the Roman
Congregations; [21] on the somewhat apologetic observations in Angelo
Mercati's editions of the trials of Giordano Bruno and Niccolò
Franco; [22] and, above all, on the precious information that can be
gleaned from almost every page in several writings by Luigi Firpo,
especially in his important reconstruction of the trial of Giordano
Bruno. [23] Inquisitorial sources have been relied upon heavily by
students of Italian heresy, witchcraft, popular religion, and censorship
of the press. Extremely useful insights into the administration of
Inquisitorial courts are furnished *indirectly* by the exemplary studies
and documents published recently by such scholars as Aldo Stella, [24]

XVI e XVII," *Archivio storico lombardo,* ser. 3, vol. 17, a. 29 (1902), 121-38;
Il S. Officio e la Riforma religiosa in Bologna (Bologna, 1905).

[19] Luigi Fumi, "L'Inquisizione romana e lo stato di Milano. Saggio di ricerche
nell' Archivio di Stato," *Archivio storico lombardo,* ser. 4, vol. 13, a. 37 (1910), 5-
124, 285-414; vol. 14 (1910), 145-220.

[20] Luigi Amabile, *Il Santo Officio della Inquisizione in Napoli. Narrazione con
molti documenti inediti,* (Città di Castello, 1892).

[21] *La Curia romana. Lineamenti storico-giuridici,* 3rd. ed., (Rome, 1970), 89-100
(the account is taken from the beginnings to the reign of Paul VI).

[22] Angelo Mercati, *Il Sommario del processo di Giordano Bruno, con appen-
dice di documenti sull'eresia e l'Inquisizione a Modena nel secolo XVI* (Vatican
City, 1942); *I Costituti di Niccolò Franco (1568-1570) dinanzi l'Inquisizione di
Roma esistenti nell'Archivio Segreto Vaticano* (Vatican City, 1955).

[23] "Il processo di Giordano Bruno," *Rivista storica italiana* 60 (1948), 542-97;
61 (1949), 5-59; reprinted separately with an index of names (Naples, 1949).
In "Una relazione inedita su l'Inquisizione romana," *Rinascimento* 9 (1958), 97-
102, Firpo publishes an account from an early seventeenth-century manuscript
describing the composition and routines of the Supreme Congregation in Rome.
A recent unpublished paper by him ("Due esecuzioni capitali di eretici a Roma
nel 1595") presented at a historical meeting in Torre Pellice is described as
"uno studio dei metodi inquisitoriali e delle procedure del Sant'Uffizio alla fine
del Cinquecento": Achille Olivieri, "Permanenze nella storiografia religiosa italiana: il XV Convegno di studi sulla Riforma e i movimenti religiosi in Italia
(Torre Pellice, 1-3 settembre 1975)," *Bollettino della Società di Studi Valdesi,*
a. XCVI, no. 138 (1975), 131-48, at p. 144.

[24] Aldo Stella's two monographs *Dall' Anabattismo al Socinianesimo nel Cinquecento Veneto* (Padua, 1967) and *Anabattismo e Antitrinitarismo in Italia nel
XVI secolo* (Padua, 1969) are based on Venetian Inquisitorial documents as are
his "Ricerche sul Socinianesimo: Il processo di Cornelio Sozzini e Claudio Textor
(Banière)," *Bollettino dell'Istituto di Storia della Società e dello Stato Veneziano*
3 (1961), 77-120; "Il Processo veneziano di Guglielmo Postel," *Rivista di storia
della chiesa in Italia* 22 (1968), 425-66. Disappointingly general is Stella's "L'Inquisizione romana e i movimenti ereticali al tempo di San Pio V," *San Pio V e
la problematica del suo tempo* (Alessandria, 1972), 65-82.

Antonio Rotondò, [25] Carlo Ginzburg, [26] Valerio Marchetti, [27] Paul Grendler, [28] and Pasquale Lopez, [29] among others.

In the light of the many modern works devoted to the Jesuits and other religious orders, to the Council of Trent, to the reforming measures of the episcopacy, and to the nunciatures, [30] the neglect which surrounds the Roman Inquisition is indeed curious. It can not be explained in terms of its relative unimportance. On the contrary, in the sixteenth century it held a place of honor among the various bodies and programs which were called into being or revitalized by the Catholic Church as bulwarks against the spread of heresy and as agents of reform. Cardinals vied with one another to secure appointments as members of the Holy Office, [31] quite understandably when one

---

[25] Antonio Rotondò, "Per la storia dell'eresia a Bologna nel secolo XVI," *Rinascimento*, ser. 2, 2 (1962), 107-54; "Nuovi documenti per la storia dell' 'Indice dei Libri Proibiti' (1572-1638)," *Rinascimento*, ser. 2, 3 (1963), 145-211; *Camillo Renato, Opere, documenti e testimonianze* (Florence & Chicago, 1968), are based primarily on documents preserved in the Archivio di Stato, Modena and the Biblioteca dell'Archiginnasio, Bologna.

[26] Carlo Ginzburg has made effective use of Inquisitorial sources preserved in the Archivio di Stato, Venice and in the Archivio della Curia Arcivescovile, Udine in his studies of sixteenth-century heresy and in his more recent pioneering work on Italian popular culture. About him see Anne J. Schutte, "Carlo Ginzburg," *Journal of Modern History* 48 (1976), 296-315.

[27] A part of Valerio Marchetti's important research on early Socinianism is now conveniently gathered in his *Gruppi ereticali senesi del Cinquecento* (Florence, 1975), based heavily on Sienese Inquisitorial documents, a longlost *fondo* which he personally rediscovered. See his "L'Archivio dell'Inquisizione senese," *Bollettino della Società di Studi Valdesi*, a. 93, no. 132 (1972), 77-83.

[28] Paul Grendler, *The Roman Inquisition and the Venetian Press, 1540-1605* (Princeton, 1977), based on Inquisitorial materials in Venice, the Vatican and other Italian and foreign archives. Regrettably, the judicial procedures of the Holy Office are not a central concern of the book and occupy only a few pages (42-62).

[29] Ample use of Inquisitorial documents, preserved primarily in the Archivio Storico Diocesano of Naples, *Sant'Ufficio*, is made by Pasquale Lopez, *Inquisizione, stampa e censura nel Regno di Napoli tra '500 e '600* (Naples, 1974), a book which it would be interesting to compare with Grendler's, cited in the note above, as to sources, methods and conclusions.

[30] See Cochrane "New Light on Post-Tridentine Italy," *passim*.

[31] See the autobiography of Giulio Antonio Santorio, Cardinal of S. Severina, a senior member of the Holy Office: "Gli diedi (to Pope Urban VII) una nota dei Signori Cardinali e Consultori del Sant'Ufficio acciò non aggiungesse, ne mutasse senza saputa della Congregazione le persone, poichè molti pretendevano quel loco, si de' cardinali, come de' prelati..." Newberry Library, MS. Case 6A 35, f. 862. Santorio's *Life* has been published by G. Cugnoni in the *Archivio della società romana di storia patria* 12 (1889), 329-72; 13 (1890), 151-205, and studied by Hubert Jedin, "Die Autobiographie des Kardinals Giulio Antonio Santorio," *Akademie der Geistes- und Sozialwissenschaftlichen Klasse*, (1969), no. 2, pp. 15-47.

thinks of the succession of sixteenth- and early seventeenth-century
popes who served apprenticeships as Inquisitors.[32] The construction
of St. Peter's was brought to a standstill and its workforce diverted
to speed the completion of the new palace of the Holy Office begun
by Pius V in 1566.[33] This position of preeminence received formal
recognition in 1588 when Sixtus V elevated the Inquisition to the
first position among the fifteen departments or Congregations into
which papal government was divided.[34]

Nor can this neglect by current scholarship be explained in terms of
the relative inactivity of the institution. On the contrary, the full involvement of the Roman tribunal and its provincial chapters in the
conflicts and controversies of the age are attested by the voluminous
nature of the surviving records. Despite the fact that the archives
contained in the Palace of the Holy Office remain barred to scholars,
we possess, in abundance, the sources necessary to undertake the study
of the Roman Inquisition. A full discussion of the many different types
of primary materials which may be considered pertinent occupies a
central place in my ongoing investigation. For the moment I should
like only to call attention to the obvious sources of direct Inquisitorial
provenance: the thousands of trials surviving in the libraries and
archives of Bologna, Modena, Naples, Udine, Venice and elsewhere;
the hundreds of sixteenth- and seventeenth-century sentences in Trinity College, Dublin; the correspondence between the Roman Congregation and several provincial Inquisitors preserved in a number
of depositories (virtually intact from the year 1571 onward in the
case of Bologna); the many memoranda, *pratiche*, summaries of proceedings and decrees copied for the personal use of high officials of
the Holy Office which, with the rest of their papers, found their way
into various public libraries and archives in Italy and abroad; newly
discovered Inquisitorial archives, such as in Siena and Pisa; or those

---

[32] Pastor, *Popes, passim*: Marcello Cervini, Marcellus II (1555); Gianpietro
Carafa, Paul IV (1555-59); Michele Ghislieri, Pius V (1566-72); Felice Peretti,
Sixtus V (1585-90); Giovanni Battista Castagna, Urban VI (1590); Giovanni
Antonio Facchinetti, Innocent IX (1591); Camillo Borghese, Paul V (1605-21).
Adrian VI (1522-23) had served as Grand Inquisitor of Spain in 1516.

[33] Pastor, *Popes*, XVII, 289, quoting from an "Avviso di Roma" dated 5
October 1566: "La fabrica della Inquisizione tuttavia si sollicita, et per formarla
presto, hanno levato li muratori et scarpellini di S. Pietro, nel qual hora si fa
niente."

[34] By virtue of the Bull "Immensa Aeterna Dei," dated 22 January 1588. It is
published in many collections. See Carolus Cocquelines, *Bullarum, Privilegiorum
ac Diplomatum Pontificum Amplissima Collectio* (Rome, 1747), IV⁴, 393.

finally rendered accessible thanks to cataloguing, such as the *fondo Inquisizione* in the Curia Arcivescovile, Naples. [35]

Studies on the medieval phase of the Inquisition seem to have been more plentiful; [36] but this does not justify and can not be used to explain the absence of attention to the restructuring of that body which Paul III set in motion in 1542. The Inquisition, far from being a monolithic structure, was an institution which experienced development and change, in terms of organization, procedures, and definitions of the law throughout its long history. The two stages, medieval and modern, must not be understood as a single phenomenon. [37]

Though the Roman Inquisition has never been studied for its own sake, numerous writers have discussed "the Inquisition" and have used sources connected with its activity in their research. Although several were dealing with the medieval Inquisition, they made sweeping generalizations, as did Lea, intended to encompass also the later history

---

[35] For a preliminary brief description, see J. Tedeschi, "La dispersione degli archivi." On the Neapolitan documents, see the articles by Luciano Osbat, "Sulle fonti per la storia del Sant' Ufficio a Napoli alla fine del Seicento," *Ricerche di storia sociale e religiosa* 1 (1972), 419-27; "I Processi del Sant'Ufficio a Napoli. Alcuni problemi di metodo," *La società religiosa nell-età moderna* (Naples, 1973), 941-61; "Un importante centro di documentazione per la storia del Mezzogiorno d'Italia nell'età moderna: l'archivio storico diocesano di Napoli," *Melanges de l'École française de Rome* 85 (1973), 311-59.

[36] See, for example, the useful anthology of documents by Kurt-Victor Selge, *Texte zur Inquisition* (Gütersloh, 1967) and the excellent editions of legal handbooks by Alexander Patschovsky, *Die Anfänge einer Ständigen Inquisition in Böhmen. Ein Prager Inquisitoren-Handbuch aus der ersten Hälfte des 14. Jahrhunderts* (Berlin, 1975); and by Lorenzo Paolini, *Il "De Officio Inquisitionis." La procedura inquisitoriale a Bologna e a Ferrara nel Trecento* (Bologna, 1976).

[37] One of the best ways I know to get at the differences between medieval and modern Inquisitorial practices and teachings is to study closely the commentary by the noted Curial jurist, Francesco Pegna (d. 1612), to his editions of the authoritative manual, the *Directorium Inquisitorum* composed by the fourteenth-century Inquisitor of Aragon, Nicolas Eymerich. Pegna never missed an opportunity to indicate the development and change from Eymerich's day to his own. For the various editions of this famous work, see Emil Van der Vekené, *Zur Bibliographie des Directorium Inquisitorum des Nicolaus Eymerich* (Luxemburg, 1961); Idem, "Die Gedruckten Ausgaben des *Directorium Inquisitorum* des Nicolaus Eymerich," *Gutenberg Jahrbuch* (1973), 286-97. The recent French abridgment by Louis Sala-Molins, *Le Manuel des Inquisiteurs* (Paris, 1973) should be used with caution. On Pegna, see Edward M. Peters, "Editing Inquisitors' Manuals in the Sixteenth Century: Francisco Peña and the *Directorium Inquisitorum* of Nicholas Eymeric," *The Library Chronicle* 40 (1974), 95-107 (*Bibliographical Studies in Honor of Rudolf Hirsch*).

of the institution. [38] The results are confusing. Serious scholars—I am excluding from consideration sensationalist writers and apologists—[39] can be found taking diametrically opposed positions on almost every imaginable issue. Their disagreement ranges from such specific and readily verifiable questions as whether defense counsel was permitted in trial proceedings, [40] to broader ones such as whether the Spanish and Italian Inquisitors of the sixteenth and seventeenth centuries were agents fueling the witch persecutions or among the few not sharing in the excesses; [41] whether, in fact, the administration of law by the Inquisition was a mockery and perversion of justice or, by contemporary standards at least, a painstaking and honest effort to reach a correct verdict. [42] The confusion is compounded when we

---

[38] Jeffrey B. Russell, *Witchcraft in the Middle Ages* (Ithaca, 1972), 158: "The principles by which the Inquisition would operate for centuries were established in the thirteenth"; Edward M. Peters, Introduction to H. C. Lea, *Torture* (Philadelphia, 1973), xvii.

[39] They are frequently unwittingly one and the same. See, most recently, John A. O'Brien, *The Inquisition* (New York, 1973), a work which accepts uncritically the tales of horror associated with the Inquisition but tries to explain them in "the special context of medieval society, culture and tradition" (p. 3).

[40] The denial of counsel to the defendant in Inquisitorial proceedings is asserted by Russell, *Witchcraft,* 158; Peters, Introduction to Lea, *Torture,* xii, and many others. Cf. Walter Ullmann, "The Defense of the Accused in the Medieval Inquisition," *The Irish Ecclesiastical Record,* ser. 5, 73, (1950), 481-89, at p. 481: "Canonistic scholarship was unanimous in its demand that the accused must not be deprived of legal aid... the inquisitor was bound to grant him legal aid in the person of a qualified advocate." See also below at notes 49 and 68.

[41] Rossell Hope Robbins, Introduction to *Catalogue of the Witchcraft Collection in Cornell University Library* (Millwood, N.Y., 1977), xxvii: "The Inquisition continued to provide the intellectual and religious sanction for judicial murder, and issued many manuals on witch hunting throughout the seventeenth century." Cf. H. C. Lea, *Minor Historical Writings, Edited by Arthur C. Howland* (Philadelphia, 1942), p. 3 (a letter from Lea to George Lincoln Burr): "It is a very curious fact which I have nowhere seen recognized, that in both Spain and Italy the Holy Office took a decidedly sceptical attitude with regard to the Sabbat and the *Cap. Episcopi.,* that preserved those lands from the madness prevailing elsewhere."

[42] As spokesmen for the negative view, considered applicable also to the later Inquisition, see Peters, Introduction to Lea, *Torture,* xvii; Russell, *Witchcraft,* 158; Leonard W. Levy, "Accusatorial and Inquisitorial Systems of Criminal Procedure: The Beginnings," *Freedom and Reform: Essays in Honor of Henry Steele Commager,* eds., H. M. Hyman & L. W. Levy (New York, 1967), 16-54. On the painstaking efforts made by sixteenth-century Spanish and Italian Inquisitors to separate the innocent from the guilty, on their methods which were "honest, simple, and straightforward," see Henry Kamen, *The Spanish Inquisition* (London, 1965), 173. In basic agreement are Cecil Roth, "The Inquisitional Archives as a Source of English History," *Transactions of the Royal Historical Society,* ser. 4, 18 (1935), 107-22, at p. 107; Richard E. Greenleaf, *The Mexican Inquisition of the Sixteenth Century* (Albuquerque, 1969), 4; Paul Grendler, *The Roman Inquisition,* 56.

encounter contradictory points of view in the works of single individuals. [43] The issue is complicated further because some of these
writings do not always meet the critical standards one expects in
serious works of history. They misuse sources, [44] fail to substantiate
claims, [45] and, on rare occasions, even seem to be perpetrating willful
distortions. [46] It is difficult to imagine a situation in modern scholarship where greater uncertainty prevails, where the sure and fixed
guidelines are so few. The unresolved disputes which continue over
these questions also must be counted among the reasons which led me to
undertake the specific study of the phenomenon known to history as
the Roman Inquisition, in its sixteenth- and seventeenth-century form.

One of the principal assignments of my research, then, has been to
analyze the surviving evidence, as it exemplifies both theory and
practice, at first hand, and to examine step by step, from the initial

[43] See Walter Ullmann, "The Defence," 486: "For the innocence of the accused
was always taken for granted, so long as the prosecutor did not bring forth
convincing proof of the defendant's guilt"; and see the contrary view by the
same author in his Introduction to H. C. Lea, *The Inquisition of the Middle
Ages, its Organization and Operation* (London, 1963), 29: "There is hardly one
item in the whole inquisitorial procedure that could be squared with the demands
of justice; on the contrary, every one of its items was a denial of justice or a
hideous caricature of it."

[44] There is a tendency on the part of several writers to see the aberration as
the rule. They hold up abuses on the part of provincial officials, against which
Rome was reacting, as the normal and accepted *modus operandi*. For example, an
investigatory commission sent out by Clement V in 1306 had discovered inhuman
conditions in the prison of Carcassonne. Lea generalized from this: "Starvation, in fact, was reckoned as one of the regular and most efficient methods to
subdue unwilling witnesses or defendants." (*History of the Inquisition of the
Middle Ages,* I, 142).

[45] See, for example, H. C. Erik Midelfort, *Witchhunting in Southwestern
Germany, 1562-1684. The Social and Intellectual Foundations* (Stanford, 1972),
19: "In fact, the Inquisition conducted trials in secret, used torture frequently,
denied counsel or defense to the accused and demanded the names of accomplices." When one turns to the accompanying note (p. 234, n. 50) for the supporting
documentation one finds only: "Actually, the sixteenth-century Italian and Spanish Inquisitions did conduct moderate witchcraft trials, since they forbade the
use of torture to discover accomplices."

[46] A recent glaring example of this occurs in R. H. Robbins, *Encyclopedia of
Witchcraft and Demonology* (New York, 1974) which at pp. 267, 268, 270 reproduces a series of torture scenes labeled "Horrors of the Inquisition," "Tortures
of the Inquisition," and "More tortures of the Inquisition," all "according to
Samuel Clarke, *Martyrology* 1651)." The reader who troubles himself to actually
consult Clarke's *Martyrology* will be surprised to find that there the illustrations are intended to depict something quite different. The subjects are, in turn,
"The Tenth Primitive Persecution which began anno Christi 308"; "The Persecution of the Albigenses" (i.e. of the seventeenth-century Waldensians by the
Dukes of Savoy); "The Persecution of the Church in France."

summons to its final disposition, the unfolding of a trial before an Inquisitorial court. I have come to the conclusion that, while *moral* justice was impossible in a context where the Catholic Church felt, together with virtually all other secular and religious authorities on both sides of the Alps, that it had the right, even the duty to persecute those who differed in their religious beliefs, *legal* justice in sixteenth-century terms was dispensed by the Roman Inquisition. It was not a drumhead court, a chamber of horrors, or a judicial labyrinth from which escape was impossible. Capricious and arbitrary decisions, misuse of authority, and wanton abuse of human rights were not tolerated. [47] Rome watched over the provincial tribunals, enforced the observance of what was for the times an essentially moderate code of law, [48] and maintained, to the extent that a consensus existed, uniformity of practice.

It may not be an exaggeration to claim, in fact, that in several respects the Holy Office was a pioneer in judicial reform. The defense attorney was an integral part of Roman trial procedure [49] at

---

[47] When abuses or inconsistencies in trial procedures were discovered the supreme Congregation rarely failed to take corrective action. I can cite, among many other cases, a letter from Cardinal Pompeo Arrigoni, a member of the Roman tribunal, to the Inquisitor of Bologna (29 July 1606; BA MS. 1863, f. 34) which discusses the case of a certain Bartolomeo Betti. Betti had been tried in Ferrara but this case was ordered reopened and transferred to Bologna because the Roman officials, after a careful study of the proceedings "are not satisfied with the confession made by Betti before the Inquisitor of Ferrara and fear that it has been extorted from him *con mali modi*."

[48] To cite one example, in the procedure of the Holy Office witchcraft was treated as a category of heresy. This meant that the penitent first offender (one who had not formally abjured on a previous occasion) was permitted to be reconciled with the Church and generally punished with a prison sentence of short duration. And it was not until the decree *Omnipotentis Dei* issued by Gregory XV on 20 March 1623 that consignment to the secular arm (*debitis poenis puniendus*) was prescribed for witches who had apostatized to the devil and had caused injury or death through their *maleficii*. See *S.mi D.N.D. Gregorii Papae XV. Constitutio adversus Maleficia, seu Sortilegia Committentes* (Rome, 1623).

[49] See, for example, Eymerich's *Directorium Inquisitorum*, p. 446: "Et sic concedentur sibi (to the suspect) advocatus, probus tamen, et de legalitate non suspectus, vir utriusque iuris peritus, et fidei zelator..." And in the case of an indigent defendant, counsel had to be provided by the court. See the letter from a Cardinal of the Roman Congregation to the Inquisitor of Florence (16 August 1603; Brussels, Archives of State, MS. II 290, vol. I, f. 118): "Se per la povertà loro non haveranno il modo di fare la spesa dell' avvocato et pro-curatore, V.R. gliene proveda ex officio acciochè non restino indifesi." The Inquisitor's obligation to the indigent extended to providing travel expenses for defense witnesses who might have to be summoned from distant parts. See Eliseo Masini, *Sacro Arsenale, overo prattica dell' officio della Santa Inquisitione* (Genova, 1621), 268.

a time when he played only a ceremonial role in the great Imperial legal code, the *Constitutio Criminalis Carolina* (1532), [50] and was being deliberately excluded by the French Ordinance of Villers-Cotterets (1539). [51] In England felons were denied the right to counsel until 1836. [52] Whereas in Inquisitorial courts the defendant received a notarized copy of the entire trial (with the names of the prosecution witnesses deleted) and was given a reasonable period of time to prepare his reply to the charges, [53] in secular courts the evidence against him was read and he had to make his defense on the spot. [54] Skepticism in regard to witchcraft invaded Roman legal circles at a time when other parts of Europe remained in the grip of a witchhunting mania. Not least among the reasons which spared Italy the epidemics of bloody persecutions which ravaged northern Europe from the late sixteenth through much of the seventeenth century, was the insistence by the Inquisition that the testimony of a suspected witch was of extremely limited validity as a basis for prosecution against others. Judges were instructed, for example, to discount testimony of a witch against persons whom she named as participants at Sabbats since frequently they were transported to these nocturnal reunions not physically but in illusions inspired by the devil. [55] And, if

---

[50] See John H. Langbein, *Prosecuting Crime in the Renaissance*: *England, Germany, France* (Cambridge, Mass., 1974), 189. An "orator" for the accused did not appear on the scene until the judgment day, "Rechttag," after the offender had been convicted.

[51] *Ibid.* 313, Article 163 of the Ordinance: "In criminal matters the parties shall in no wise be heard through counsel or the agency of any one else, but they shall answer the charges of which they are accused through their own mouths..."

[52] David Melinkoff, "Right to Counsel: the Message from America," in Fredi Chiappelli, ed., *First Images of America,* (Berkeley, 1976), I, 405-13, at p. 406, by provision of the "Prisoners' Counsel Bill." Until 1695 the same rule had applied to indictments for high treason.

[53] On the defense phase of the trial (known as the *processo repetitivo*) as opposed to the prosecution phase (the *processo informativo*), see, among others, Masini, *Sacro Arsenale,* 85ff, who emphasized the care with which the judge should govern the proceedings: "E perchè tal repetitione è molto difficile, dee con somma isquisitezza e diligenza maneggiare; percioché da essa pende l'honore, la vita & i beni de' rei."

[54] Langbein, *Prosecuting Crime,* 247. See also Gaetano Cozzi, "Note su tribunali e procedure penali a Venezia nel '700," *Rivista storica italiana* 77 (1965), 931-52, at p. 945.

[55] See, for example, the chapter "De Sortileghi" in the widely diffused (but still unpublished) Inquisitorial manual, "Prattica per le cause del Sant'Officio," usually attributed to Cardinal Desiderio Scaglia (d. 1639), for many years one of the most influential members of the Roman Congregation: "Si procede contro li complici, eccetto contro quelli che esse dicono haver veduto nel giuoco ò tripudio. Sopra di che vi è decreto speciale del Supremo Tribunale che non si proceda contro

it is true, as John Langbein asserts in his book, *Prosecuting Crime in the Renaissance,* that the beginning of imprisonment for punishment, rather than for the purpose of custody during the trial, can only be traced back on the continent to the closing decades of the sixteenth century, then the Inquisition, through its centuries-long practice of incarcerating *ad poenam,* must be regarded also as a pioneer in the field of penology, at a time when secular judges, in pronouncing sentence, only had as alternatives the stake, mutilation, the galleys and banishment. [56]

The Roman Inquisition needs to be studied as a legal system, in its organizational and judicio-procedural aspects. The composition of the central tribunal in Rome, of its provincial chapters and the qualifications and backgrounds of the officials who staffed them should be examined, together with the establishments which housed them and how they were supported. Attention should be given to the crucial jurisdictional issues and resulting tensions, as they manifested themselves in several different ways: in the relationship of the Inquisition to the episcopal courts, with whom the former enjoyed an ancient but uneasy association; [57] to the secular tribunals who were, at least in theory, relegated to a position of inferiority but who disputed the competence of the Holy Office in such cases as witchcraft, sorcery, blasphemy and bigamy where the heretical implications of the crime frequently were difficult to establish; [58] to secular rulers at whose

---

essi potendo le deponenti ingannarsi circa le persone nominate per illusione del Demonio." Biblioteca Apostolica Vaticana (henceforth abbreviated BAV), *Borg. Lat.* MS. 660, pp. 29-42, at p. 39.

[56] *Prosecuting Crime in the Renaissance,* 195. In a later work (*Torture and the Law of Proof. Europe and England in the Ancien Regime* [Chicago, 1976], 29), the earlier use of incarceration by the Church to punish crime is recognized.

[57] Despite centuries of collaboration in the pursuit of heresy between Bishop and Inquisitor and thousands of pages written attempting to work out the rights and spheres of jurisdiction of each, doubts and confusion on the subject persisted to the end. See, for example, the interesting letter from the Cardinal Inquisitor d'Ascoli to the Inquisitor of Bologna reprimanding him for an excessive cooperation with the officials of the episcopal court: "... essendo senza essempio che gl'Inquisitori dipendono da gl'ordinarii, o, faccin con essi un sol tribunale nelle cose della fede..." (4 June 1588; BA, MS. 1861, f. 64).

[58] See, for example, the compendium of Inquisitorial procedure, BAV *Barb. Lat.* MS. 1370, f. 24: "Carcerati in S.to Officio non sunt interim pro aliis causis molestandi... Causa S.ti Officii prius terminanda quam aliae." Individuals in a secular prison denounced to the Inquisition as suspected heretics had to be consigned to the latter immediately "aliorum criminum cognitione suspensa." (Bull of Pius V, undated but 1566, in Cocquelines, *Bullarum* IV², 276). Secular judges were obliged to carry out sentences pronounced by the Holy Office without access to the trial records. See Pegna's commentary in Eymerich, *Directorium Inquisitorum,* 563.

pleasure the Inquisition functioned, if it was permitted to function at all, outside the papal states; [59] to the Franciscans and Dominicans who controlled the monasteries where the local Inquisitions had their quarters and to whose officials Inquisitors remained bound by the rules of their Order; [60] and, finally, in the relationship between Rome and the local Inquisitorial courts. The extent of the authority possessed by the latter to act independently of the supreme tribunal, at least in so-called routine matters, was the subject of recurring discussion and recrimination. [61]

---

[59] For instance, the Holy Office was never admitted into the Republic of Lucca and in Naples had to operate under the cloak of the episcopal courts. In Genoa, Savoy, Venice and later in Tuscany lay officials were either members of the court, contrary to customary procedure, or interfered freely in given cases. In these states any serious action contemplated by any ecclesiastical judge, such as arrest, extradition of a suspect to Rome, and confiscation of property depended on the assent of the secular authorities. There is no comprehensive modern study dealing specifically with these questions. For individual states, see G. Bertora, "Il tribunale inquisitorio di Genova e l'Inquisizione romana nel '500 (alla luce di documenti inediti)," *La Civiltà Cattolica*, a. 104, vol. 2 (1953), 173-87; Marino Berengo, *Nobili e mercanti nella Lucca del Cinquecento* (Turin, 1965), Ch. VI "La Vita religiosa." For Tuscany, see Marchetti's *Gruppi ereticali, passim.,* and Niccolò Rodolico, *Stato e chiesa in Toscana durante la reggenza lorenese (1737-1765)* (Florence, 1910), 182-266. For the vicissitudes of the Holy Office in Naples, Savoy, and Venice, see the apposite volumes of the *Nunziature d'Italia* in the course of being published by the Istituto di Storia Moderna e Contemporanea, Rome.

[60] Inquisitors frequently complained that the heads of monasteries interfered with their duties. Priors accused Inquisitors of needlessly taking advantage of their special positions to escape from the common discipline. Some of the problems and abuses existing in their relationship are discussed in an interesting letter from the Roman Congregation to the General of the Dominicans (4 September 1580; Pastor, "Allgemeine Dekrete," p. 546). From a letter written to the Inquisitor of Bologna by the *Commissario Generale* of the Roman Holy Office (28 July 1623; BA MS. 1866, f. 119) one gains the impression that disaffection between his provincial officials and the rulers of monasteries was a general problem: "Sono molto pregiuditiali le liti e dissentioni non convenevoli che vertono fra gli Inquisitori e Priori alla riputatione della Religione, al buon governo de' conventi, et agli interessi proprii di essi." In the present case he ordered "che si dovesse correggere il P. Inquisitore di Modena, e cassare il Priore..."

[61] Much ink was spilled by Rome trying to help its lower officials to distinguish what was ordinary from critical business. But the issue was never resolved satisfactorily. See the patient letter from Antonio Balduzzi, Commissioner of the Roman Congregation, to the Inquisitor of Bologna (11 March 1573; BA, MS. 1860, f. cxx) who had written asking to be instructed on the question. Balduzzi replied that it was impossible to make general rules and that the Inquisitor's own judgment should be able to tell him how to regulate himself, adding: "Certo è che non ogni minutia, ne ogni depositione s'ha da scrivere. Ma quando le cause sono fondate o volete venire a qualche atto importante come di sentenza, o simile, è bene d'avisarne..." Later in the century the Cardinal of S.ta Severina

Examination of the judicial side of the Inquisitorial system needs to focus especially on those issues, connected with the definition of heresy as a public, capital, or "excepted" crime, which introduced important procedural disabilities (of which one of the most famous perhaps was the concealment of the names of prosecution witnesses), intended to favor the prosecution in support of the interests of the faith. [62] Whether these exceptions had this effect in reality, when offset by compensating safeguards, [63] whether they were consistently employed in the Roman courts, is not so certain. Even Lea spoke of "theoretical severity and practical moderation." [64] Moreover, jurists were unanimous that in view of the seriousness of the crime of heresy, the gravity of the consequences, and the exceptions in the legal procedure, proof of guilt had to be without question, clearer than the light of mid-day. [65] There were some who did not hesitate to assert that it was preferable to allow the guilty to go unpunished than to see an innocent person condemned. [66] In no case should the disabilities be permitted to impair the conduct of proper and legitimate proceedings. [67]

---

was still repeating for the benefit of another provincial official, the Inquisitor of Florence, that the latter possessed the authority to pronounce judgments "nelle cause ordinarie, et che non sono gravi per la qualità delle persone et delli delitti." (21 May 1594; Brussels, State Archives, MS. II 290, vol. II f. 170).

[62] Onofrio Ruffino ("Ricerche sulla condizione giuridica degli eretici nel pensiero dei Glossatori," *Rivista di storia del diritto italiano* 46 [1973], 30-190) describes the appropriation by canon law, beginning with the decretal *Vergentis in senium* (1199), of the Roman concept of *crimen maiestatis*.

[63] See, for example, Masini, *Sacro Arsenale*, 283: "Essendo la facoltà che si da al reo di difendersi in causa d'heresia in un certo modo manchevole, posciache non se gli fanno sapere i nomi de' testimoni, è necessario, che le prove per convincerlo siano chiarissime e certissime."

[64] *Materials Toward A History of Witchcraft*, ed., Arthur C. Howland, (Philadelphia, 1939), II, 952.

[65] See, among many other authorities, Cesare Carena, *Tractatus de Officio Sanctissimae Inquisitionis et Modo Procedendi in Causis Fidei* (Cremona, 1642), 338: "Criminalistae omnes clamant in criminalibus iuditiis probationes debere esse luce meridiana clariores ... [when] de vita hominis agatur probationes clarissimae esse debent ..."; *Repertorium Inquisitorum Pravitatis Haereticae* (Venice, 1575), 635: "Quanto magis crimen est grave, maiores praesumptiones & evidentiora indicia requiruntur."

[66] "... ad nullius vero condempnationem sine lucidis et apertis probationibus, vel confessione propria procedatis. Sanctius enim est facinus impunitum relinquere, quam innocentem condempnare." (From the fourteenth-century manual *De Officio Inquisitionis* cited above at n. 36).

[67] Pegna, in his commentary to Eymerich's *Directorium*, 583: "Ordinem et solemnitates à iure alias requisitas non esse necessario observandas (in heresy trials): ille tamen omittendae non sunt, quae ad substantiam causae spectant,

The attempts of succeeding generations of lawyers to accommodate theories, hammered into being under the stress and violent conditions of the thirteenth century, to a more rational and equitable system of law, [68] as well as their attempts to reconcile contradictory opinions are, in my opinion, among the more interesting findings emerging from this research. Inquisitorial law was not always uniform and its manuals not necessarily unswerving procedural guides. I have encountered many issues where a precise definition was not attained, over which jurists of equally great reputation disagreed, [69] where the practice of Rome differed in some instances, but not in others, from the opinions of such revered authorities as Iacobo Simancas (d. 1583), resulting in predictable uncertainty and confusion for the practicing judge. [70]

Above all, it must be recognized that there was development and change in the interpretation of legal procedure. Those modern scholars are in error, for example, who assume that the notorious *Malleus Maleficarum*, the work of two German Dominicans first published in 1486, remained "the standard manual for the persecutors of the

hoc est illae, sine quibus nec iuste, nec recte aut commode negotium tractari posset." Among the essentials which could not be eliminated were those "sine quibus aut vere delictum probari non posset, aut reus non posset se iure defendere."

[68] Jurists, for example, had to contend with the pronouncement of successive medieval popes: "Concedimus, quod in Inquisitionis haereticae pravitatis negotio, procedi possit simpliciter et de plano, et absque advocatorum ac iudiciorum strepitu et figura (in Eymerich, *Directorium*, p. 111). Inquisitors circumvented the apparent prohibition of the defense attorney by distinguishing between the pertinacious "hacreticus" who wanted to defend the validity of his heresy and the "causa haeresis." See, for example, the *Repertorium Inquisitorum*, 35: "Advocatus dandus est imputato de haeresi, nisi constet illum esse haereticum & in haeresi persistere..."

[69] Symptomatic of this uncertainty are the several briefing books, *pratiche*, listing precedents on questions of Inquisitorial procedure, compiled from various sources, but usually from Rome's correspondence with provincial Inquisitors. One such is contained in BAV, *Barb. Lat.* 1370 where the law has been searched to resolve such questions as "Sponte comparente, an possint expediri a solo Inquisitore sine Ordinario?" (p. 72); "Disputationes inter Catholicos et Haereticos an admittendae?" (p. 101), etc.

[70] For example, the teaching of the great Spanish jurist denying to the defense in trial proceedings the possibility of cross-examining prosecution witnesses was in direct conflict with the practice of the Holy Office where "sine dubio totum contrarium observetur" (Carena, *De Officio Sanctissimae Inquisitionis*, 372). And yet, in a letter from the supreme tribunal in Rome to the Inquisitor of Bologna (7 November 1573; BA MS. 1860 f. 160) the latter is reminded not to let himself be persuaded by anyone to "fare cose nuove," that he should be cautious about proceeding to arrest a suspect "come ben insegna il Simanca."

next two centuries, not only in Catholic but in Protestant countries as well." [71] On the contrary, a philosophy entirely opposed to that of the *Malleus* was gaining ascendancy in the tribunals of the Holy Office throughout the second half of the sixteenth century and was made normative thanks to the *Instructio pro formandis processibus in causis strigum, sortilegiorum & maleficiorum* which began to circulate in manuscript at least as early as 1624 and was incorporated into the *Sacro Arsenale* (beginning with the edition of 1625), the most widely followed Italian Inquisitorial handbook of the age. [72] At the end of the sixteenth century, even Martinus Del Rio, an unquestioning enemy of witchcraft, had separated himself from many of the teachings pronounced by the *Malleus Maleficarum* a hundred years before. [73]

A reappraisal of the Inquisition should not gloss over its many weaknesses and deficiencies, the chief of which, perhaps, was the fact that the entire legal fabric patiently constructed over several centuries, in practice, if not in theory, was at the mercy of one man, the pope. During the pontificate of that zealous persecutor, Paul IV (1555-59), due process was placed under an almost unbearable strain, and the Church during his reign did fall into the grip of a witchhunting mentality. Paul gladly would have departed from strict judicial procedure and would have exchanged the seemingly endless deliberations for more summary forms of justice. [74] Although many of his excesses disappeared with him there is no doubt that they must be counted among the factors contributing to the unfavorable reputation which the Holy Office has endured for centuries.

---

[71] Gustav Henningsen, "The European Witch-Persecution," *DFS Translations* I (1973), 12; also Russell, *Witchcraft*, 231.

[72] The earliest evidence for its diffusion is a letter from Cardinal Millino of the Roman Congregation to the Bishop and Inquisitor of Lodi (9 May 1624; BAV, *Borg. Lat.* 660, no. 130, modern numbering) accompanying a copy of the Instructions. The letter, itself a remarkable document, begins "La materia de' maleficii è qui sempre stata stimata fallace, et incerta assai, come è in effetto..."

[73] Del Rio, *Disquisitionum Magicarum Libri Sex* (Lyons, 1612), 323: "Praxis vero illa, quam Sprengerus ponit [p. 3 *Mallei* q. 14] ut damnetur non ad torturam iterandam, sed ad eandem alio die continuandam, & hoc posse fieri non ortis novis indiciis; mihi callidior, quam verior; & crudelior, quam aequior videtur."

[74] Pastor, *Popes*, XIV, 306 n., quoting from Bernardino Pia's report on Paul's attitude toward the trial of Cardinal Giovanni Morone: "Dice (it is not clear to whom this refers) che el papa quattro dì sono bravò gagliardamente saper i casi suoi, che non occorrevano tanti processi, scritture ne giustificationi, ne servar termini, che saveva benissimo come si stesse il fatto, che esso era il giudice vero che senza altro poteva et doveva dar la sentenza et altri simili et terribili parole..."

The results of a careful examination of Inquisitorial procedure and law should be useful not only to legal historians, but also to those seeking to bridge the gap between seemingly irreconcilable views of the Roman Church in the sixteenth century. [75] Our understanding of the Counter-Reformation necessarily must be affected by any new light cast on one of its most controversial institutions.

---

[75] The leading Catholic scholarly spokesman for a negative assessment of Counter-Reformation religion is Romeo de Maio, for example in his *Riforme e miti nella Chiesa del Cinquecento* (Naples, 1973), whose views John W. O'Malley justly observed (*Catholic Historical Review* 62 [1976], 113-15), appear irreconcilable with the much more benign interpretation by another distinguished Catholic authority, H. O. Evennett (*The Spirit of the Counter-Reformation . . . Edited with a Postscript by John Bossy* [Cambridge, 1968]).

FAUSTO SOZZINI AND JUSTIFICATION

JOHN C. GODBEY

Meadville/Lombard Theological School

One of the problems in understanding Fausto Sozzini's relationship to the Reformation centers on the doctrine of justification, which is in certain formulations the doctrine of justification by faith through grace. [1] Although this doctrine is one of the cornerstones of the Reformation in its varied forms, it transcends that complex movement. As Lowell C. Green has noted, Erasmus provided a part of the impetus for the formulation of the doctrine. [2] Sozzini vigorously opposed interpretations of the doctrine formulated as "faith imputed as righteousness for the sake of Christ," [3] but he insisted that a doctrine of justification by faith was a central part of his theology. The polemically-charged context in which he wrote and the influence of confessional perspectives in subsequent centuries have presented difficulties in understanding his views. Despite these difficulties, his doctrine of justification deserves to be acknowledged as a legitimate variant within the Reformation.

A continuing tendency found in studies by earlier and more recent scholars has been to interpret his theology as centered on a doctrine of human obedience to divine commands in such a form that faith is identified with obedience. Otto Fock regarded the Socinian view as "in essential points the catholic *fides formata.*" [4] Ludwik Chmaj por-

---

[1] "... justified by faith is he who, excluded from the righteousness of works, grasps the righteousness of Christ through faith, and clothed in it, appears in God's sight not as a sinner but as a righteous man." John Calvin, *Institutes of the Christian Religion,* ed. John T. McNeill, LCC 20-21, (London, 1960), I :726-27. Cf. "Solafideism" in George Huntston Williams, *The Radical Reformation* (Philadelphia, 1962).

[2] Lowell C. Green, "The Influence of Erasmus upon Melanchthon, Luther and the Formula of Concord in the Doctrine of Justification," *Church History* 43 (1974), 185.

[3] Sozzini's extensive attacks upon the doctrine of the imputation of the righteousness of Christ can be found in *De Jesu Christo Servatore* (which will be discussed below), 4.8. Cf. John Charles Godbey, "A Study of Faustus Socinus' *De Jesu Christo Servatore*" (Ph.D. diss., University of Chicago, 1968), 229.

[4] "Wie haben hier im Wesentlichen die katholische fides formata..." Otto Fock, *Der Socinianismus nach seiner Stellung in der Gesammtentwicklung des christlichen Geistes, nach seinem historischen Verlauf und nach seinem Lehrbegriff dargestellt* (Kiel, 1847), 682.

trayed the young Sozzini as being influenced by Castellio's "thesis that the religion of Christ is the teaching of obedience to his commands for the purpose of attaining salvation" [5] and the mature Sozzini as emphasizing "the efficacy of man's moral efforts"; [6] yet Chmaj acknowledged that both Sozzini and John Niemojewski, "the two most important religious thinkers of that time [1587] in Poland," [7] agreed on the centrality of faith as confidence and trust in Christ and conceived of obedience as dependent upon and derivative from such faith. [8] Zbigniew Ogonowski portrayed the Socinians' view as "that trusting in God we fulfill his commands and we trust that we shall receive immortality as a reward for our obedience." [9] According to him, their conception of faith was one that embraced both trust and obedience. [10] Such an interpretation virtually identifies Sozzini's view with that of Samuel Przypkowski, according to whom works were the soul of faith. [11] When one compares this view with a view that emphasizes trust and confidence as the nature of justifying faith, with works dependent upon and flowing from that faith, a lively tension emerges between the two positions. Was Sozzini's doctrine of justification in essence "only a modification of justification by works"? [12]

---

[5] Ludwik Chmaj, *Faust Socyn (1539-1604)* (Warsaw, 1963), 22.

[6] *Ibid.*, 396.

[7] *Ibid.*, 262.

[8] "Both professed in agreement that... [the believers'] obedience to Christ's commands and their attitude toward religion were going to depend on that confidence." *Ibid.* 263. (Chmaj's summary of the argument in the exchange of letters is on pp. 262-73. Cf. Ludwik Chmaj, ed., *Faust Socyn. Listy* [Letters] 2 vols., Biblioteka Pisarzy Reformacyjnych, no. 2 [Warsaw, 1959] 2:7-81 and 2:86-87 for a succeeding letter of 1588, with the relevant footnotes on pp. 2:313-18.)

[9] Zbigniew Ogonowski, *Socynianizm polski* (Warsaw, 1960), 80.

[10] Zbigniew Ogonowski, *Z Zagadnień Tolerancji w Polsce XVII wieku* [On the Problem of Tolerance in Poland in the Seventeenth Century] (Warsaw, 1958), 242-43.

[11] "Nor verily shall you finde in the whole compass of our Faith, that more duties are required of believers, then [sic] Assent to the promises of Jesus Christ, and Obedience to his Precepts. The first of which the Apostle *James,* ch. 2 very aptly intimateth to be the Body of Faith; and the second, the Soul thereof." [Samuel Przipcovius], *Dissertatio de Pace, & c. or, A Discourse Touching the Peace & Concord of the Church* (London, 1653), 8. Cf. Ogonowski, *Z Zagadnień Tolerancji,* 246.

[12] "Faith is [for Socinus] obedience to the commands of Christ in the hope of the reward of life eternal. It justifies, because God naturally approves such an attitude, and 'if a man does what in him lies' does not exact more. Justification by faith thus becomes only a modification of justification by works." Robert S. Franks, *A History of the Doctrine of the Work of Christ,* (New York, 1918), 2:30.

De Jesu Christo Servatore

De Jesu Christo Servatore was written in 1577 and 1578 while
Sozzini was in Switzerland. It was published in Poland in 1594. Circulating in Poland in manuscript form, it strongly influenced the younger
generation of ministers and markedly increased Sozzini's influence. In
this work Sozzini submitted the satisfaction theory of the atonement to
a devastating criticism. This critical attack was preparatory to his basic
concern, which was to present his own view of justifying faith. [13] He
opposed the view of Jacques Couvet, his opponent in this exchange,
and of other Reformed churchmen, that justifying faith is a belief
that our sins have been taken away by Christ's sufferings. The main
line of Sozzini's argument was that faith is *fiducia* or *confidentia,* trust
and confidence, not *assensus,* assent to a proposition. Both in *De Jesu
Christo Servatore* and years later, in *Tractatus de Justificatione,* he
distinguished between assent ("to believe God") and trust ("to believe in God"). He held that both assent and trust can be rendered to
God and to Christ. Justifying faith is by its very nature such confidence and trust. [14]

Sozzini noted that both he and his opponents agreed that faith
cannot exist without good works. [15] He pointed out that his opponents
sometimes presented faith as if it had nothing to do with good works.
Those who thought they were justified by a belief that Christ's death
took away their sins often manifested little or no good works in their
own lives. Neither scripture nor reason will support the view that,
by the action of the Holy Spirit, God reforms a justified man's will
so the man thereafter abstains from sin and devotes himself to good
works. Hence the opponents' view is contradicted by their own words,
by scripture, by reason, and by their own lives.

Sozzini presented his own view of the nature of justifying faith.

---

13 Godbey, "A Study," 32-35, 273, 358, 434-50.

14 "...aperte à me exposita fuit, in disputatione illa mea de Jesu Christo
Servatore, in ipso ferme initio ejus partis, ubi explicatur, quidnam sit ea fides
in Christum, qua justificamur." Faustus Socinus, "De Fide & Operibus," *Tractatus
de Justificatione* in *Bibliotheca Fratrum Polonorum qui Unitarii Appellantur...
Socini Opera,* (Irenopoli [Amsterdam] : Post annum Domini, 1656), 1:624. (Cf.
Jeroom Vercruysse, " «Bibliotheca fratrum polonorum» Histoire et bibliographie,"
Odrodzenie i Reformacja w Polsce [Renaissance & Reformation in Poland] 21
[1976], 197-212.)

15 "...as you yourselves do not deny, this faith in Christ by which we are
justified cannot exist without good works." Faustus Socinus, *De Jesu Christo
Servatore,* in *Socini Opera,* 2:232.

> Therefore the faith in Christ that makes us righteous in the sight of God is, as the words themselves clearly indicate and reason absolutely requires, nothing else than that we trust in Christ, as we have said long before; that is, not only that we, meditating on those things which Christ said to us, believe them to be true, but also that we regard those things as so great that if he should command us to do something, we would do it, if he commanded us to hope for something, we will hope for it, or, so that I might speak more specifically and clearly, if he affirmed that we are going to attain to a certain good if we do something we would not only be persuaded that this is true, but we would not hesitate to do it in order that we might attain to that good. [16]

Taken out of context in this way, such a passage is subject to serious misunderstanding. It requires to be considered within the context of his previous statements and subsequent statements on the nature of justifying faith. He used many examples to rule out assent as the meaning of justifying faith, for the latter is confidence and trust in God (and in Christ). "Now to have confidence in God always renders man righteous in God's sight, by the benevolence of God himself . . ." [17]

Sozzini also sought to rule out obedience as the meaning of, or as a part of, justifying faith. This point must be noted with care, for other scholars have concluded that, in fact, he does end by identifying faith with obedience. Serious misunderstandings result if one quotes out of their full context his statements that Abraham's faith was perfected by his works and that someone "is said to have confidence because he obeys." [18] He agreed with the Reformed churchmen that works must be present, for justifying faith cannot exist without them. He conceived of their relationship as such that good works depend on confidence and trust for both their existence and their value. The words "perfected by obedience" and "is said to have confidence" are said from the human point of view because the behavior known as obedience makes faith visible to other men.

But Sozzini does not believe this is precisely the way to describe how God regards a man, for God is capable of seeing into the heart of a man. As we shall see later in our discussion of the *Tractatus de Justificatione,* Sozzini noted that God can and will justify a man who has confidence in him even prior to an occasion that calls forth from that man the resulting, corresponding obedience. (Although it is not there explicit, this point is implicit in the portion of *De Jesu Christo Servatore* that refers to Abraham's faith.)

---

[16] *Ibid.,* 2:234.
[17] *Ibid.*
[18] *Ibid.,* 2:235.

Sozzini distinguished *fiducia* from *assensus,* for the former is justifying faith. Obedience flows from and is dependent upon such justifying faith. This understanding emerges from the text of his major work, *De Jesu Christo Servatore,* if one does not focus only on isolated sentences, read apart from their proper context, which is the structure of the argument as it is presented in Parts One, Two, Three, and Four of the book.

Tractatus de Justificatione

The *Tractatus de Justificatione* was written nearly a decade and a half after *De Jesu Christo Servatore.* The origin of the book is to be dated between 1587, when Sozzini wrote to John Niemojewski that the synod of Chmielnic was scheduled to discuss his treatise on the redemptive sacrifice of Christ, [19] and 1591, when *Iustificationis nostrae per Christum . . .* was published. [20] The *Tractatus de Justificatione,* as such, was published in 1611 and in 1616.

Within this collection of essays there are several definitions of justification, but the one that best embraces the different aspects that he considered essential to this concept is to be found in his "Dialogue on Justification." [21] Sozzini acknowledged that in scripture, *justitia* sometimes means holiness, but it also means justification. Justification is "the condition of human actions and divine will from which it comes about that someone is pronounced righteous by God himself, or is regarded as righteous." [22] He believed all the relevant Pauline passages had this meaning. Distinguishing between the righteousness of man (or of the Law) [23] and "a certain righteousness of

---

[19] Chmaj, ed., *Faust Socyn. Listy* 2:19. (Cf. n. 11: "Wdaje się, że Socyn ma tu na myśli swój niewielki traktat, który pt. *Justificationis nostrae per Christum syn opsis* [*sic*] *prima,* wyszedł w r. 1591 pod pseudonimem Gratiana Turpio, a który wraz z innymi drobnymi pismami Socyna wydali Bracia Polscy w Rakowie w r. 1616. *Bibl. Fr. Pol.* I, s. 601-603." *Listy* 2:314.)

[20] *Listy* 2:157. This is a letter to Christopher Morsztyn, dated Febr. 3, 1595. The footnote indicates that the text, *Iustificationis nostrae,* was published in 1591. *Ibid.,* 2:327, n. 9.

[21] Chmaj believed Sozzini wrote the "Dialogue" at about the same time as the two synopses, for the "Altera Synopsis" states: "His quae hactenus exposuimus, per convenientes aptasque interrogationes & responsiones explicatis, . . ." Socinus, "Altera Synopsis," *Socini Opera* 1:603.

[22] ". . . id est, eam conditionem, ut sic dixerim, humanarum actionum, eamque divinam voluntatem, ex qua fiat, ut quis justus coram Deo ipso pronuncietur, seu pro justo habeatur: . . ." Socinus, "De Justificationis Dialogus," *Socini Opera* 1:615, n. 55.

[23] Cf. Lowell C. Green, "Influence of Erasmus," 188.

God," [24] Sozzini emphasized the latter, whereby in the relationship between human actions and the divine will, justification is God's action of pronouncing a man as righteous or regarding him as righteous. In the "Altera synopsis" he stated "our justification before God is that we are regarded by God as just, or righteous." [25] Shortly thereafter he emphasized that it is faith in Christ which "renders us righteous in God's sight." He explicitly rejected the view that justification involves making a man righteous, that is, virtuous and holy. [26] Justification means to pronounce a man righteous, that is, to judge that he is as if he ought not to be condemned, or to pronounce that he is as if he had never sinned. Sozzini gave examples to show that both scripture and ordinary language used *facere* to mean "to declare to be." [27]

Thus Sozzini agreed entirely with the Pauline view that we are justified by faith alone without our righteousness or good works, but he was concerned that the serious ambiguities that had arisen over the word *works* be clarified. These ambiguities have been so interpreted as to place Paul and James in opposition, for at the end of chapter two of his epistle James wrote that we are justified not only by faith but also by works. By *works* Paul meant such actions as are meritorious and justifying by their own power, constituting a perfect fulfillment of the Law. This form of justification is impossible. By *works* James meant "that obedience without which God does not wish to regard a man as dear to him." Such works need not be perfect. [28] Justifying faith, for Paul, contains obedience in the sense that we trust in God, or in God through Christ, to such an extent that the trust leads to, or results in, obedience. [29] Sozzini's repeated emphases show that he does not regard obedience as a part of faith; rather, obedience naturally

---

[24] "...hanc justitiam eam esse, quae per fidem Christi est: quae quidem qualitate quadam, nova Dei justitia erat... & [in contrast to the righteousness of man] divina illa demum hac ratione inspecta, dicenda, quae à Dei misericordia, praeter id, quod sensus humanus omnino dictat, proficiscitur, qualis est justitia per Christi fidem..." Socinus, "De Justificatione Dialogus," 1:615-16.

[25] Socinus, "Altera synopsis," 1:602.

[26] Socinus, "Fragmenta de Justificatione: De significationibus vocabuli Justificationis," 1:619.

[27] *Ibid.* He stressed the juridical meaning of *facere*.

[28] Socinus, "Fragmenta de Justificatione: Quid sit, sub Euangelio non ex operibus, sed ex fide justificari?" 1:621.

[29] "...& propterea cum Paulus affirmat, nos per ipsam fidem justificari, fidem intelligere, qua obedientia ista contineatur, & vicissim apparet, satis esse, si obedientia nostra mandatorum Dei, ejusmodi fuerit, ut merito affirmari possit, nos fide, nempe in Christum, sive in Deum per Christum, esse praeditos; hoc est, nos Christo, sive Deo per Christum, confidere." *Ibid.*

flows from complete trust and is dependent on it. When misunderstandings of Paul's view were clarified, Sozzini completely agreed with Paul that our justification is by God's pure grace without any works, including the works of the Law. [30] (When addressing an epistle to the Jews, Paul had to add "of the Law" in Romans 4 when he referred to Abraham and David, for the Jews wanted to be justified by a fulfillment of the Mosaic Law.) Paul excluded both the ceremonial works and the moral works of the Mosaic Law. [31] But Paul's highly compressed language did not mean that he excluded all works whatsoever and however considered. His meaning was as follows.

> There are no works which are so great that we can be justified because of their merits. Since it is certain that there is no one who performs those works which were commanded under the Old Testament or the New Testament most perfectly and entirely throughout his whole life, which was, however, without doubt, required or would be required in order that, on this ground, in some meritorious way, justification could occur through these works. [32]

Sozzini explained that he wrote "aliquo modo meritoria" (in some meritorious way) in order to exclude both an absolute merit based on the excellence of the works per se and even a relative degree of merit that would derive from God's promise. One should never say that justification is granted to us for the merit of our works, for our obedience is always imperfect. What one can say, in relation to works, is that God wished to pronounce us as justified if we have good works, but not for the sake of the works themselves. [33]

"De Fide et Operibus"

One of the documents in *Tractatus de Justificatione* is a portion of a letter [34] which responded to several questions. First, the questioner assumed that without faith no one can attain to eternal life. Works have no such efficacy. What efficacy did Sozzini attribute to works

---

[30] Socinus, "De Justificatione Dialogus," 1:607.

[31] Socinus, "Fragmenta de Justificatione," 1:620.

[32] *Ibid.*

[33] *Ibid.*, 1:620-21.

[34] Socinus, "De Fide et Operibus, quod attinet ad Justificationem nostram...," 1:622-26. Chmaj suggested that the inquirer was Andreas Dudith. ("...którym był prawdopodobnie Dudycz." *Listy* 2:327, n. 10.) Later he thought it was Francesco Betti. ("Adresatem owego listu był prawdopodobnie Betti, któremy Socyn posłał później rękopis swej rozprawy o powadze Pisma św." Chmaj, *Faust Socyn*, 305.)

before faith? Sozzini responded that works that occur before faith have no efficacy for attaining to eternal life. Only complete trust in Christ (*fiducia*) justifies man. Works are visible; faith is not visible. Faith can be distinguished from works only by an intellectual analysis, but the distinction is real. Behavioral expression of faith gives it perfection of form and, so to speak, life. This behavior (works) is *always* imperfect. God forgives and justifies on the basis of what He can see (and we cannot see), complete trust in Christ. [35] (God notes the presence of justifying faith in a man and will regard him as righteous even before he expresses his trust by his obedience to God. [36])

In his second question the inquirer assumed that all works derive their value from faith, so he concluded that one should preach "that Jesus is the Messiah, the Son of God, etc." before one preached the necessity of penitence and a holy life. Did Sozzini think "to believe in Christ" meant the same as "to believe his doctrine with regard to works"? In his reply Sozzini noted that scripture describes three successive modes of faith: belief in a proposition asserted about Christ, belief in a proposition asserted by Christ, and trust in Christ. Neither of the first two modes justifies one; only *fiducia* does so.

Third, the inquirer asked whether Sozzini considered works equal to faith, or whether they were the effects of faith. Could a man be justified by God in that God gave him the living spirit of faith before the man performed any works? Sozzini acknowledged that most good works are in fact only the effects of justification (sequels or appendices to justification). Our justification (the forgiving of our sins) can be preceded by penitence and conversion, which also conserve justification. Sometimes scripture uses *bona opera* to refer to penitence and conversion, and in this sense *bona opera* are interchange-

---

[35] Socinus, "De Fide et Operibus," 1:623-24. Sozzini's answer to this question gives Fock and others a basis for claiming that Sozzini defines works as a part of faith, but the answer needs to be read in the light of the long preface, which shows that the distinction between *fiducia* and behavior is real. The justifying element is *fiducia*. In his answer to the second question, Sozzini wrote: "Ex fide quidem praestantia & dignitas operum pendet, si fidei nomine fiduciam intelligamus quae in Christo collocetur, & in Deo per ipsum, *& ratione intellectus hanc fiduciam ab ipsis operibus distinguamus*, quemadmodum in responsione ad primam quaestionem dictum est." (Italics supplied.) *Ibid.*, 1:624-25.

[36] "JOH[ANNES]. Ille autem reipsa nondum est justus, quoniam adhuc nihil fecit? 31. CHR[ISTOPHOR]. Imo reipsa justus est. Non enim Deus tam opus ipsum quam animum ascipit hominis, qui jam jam vellet omnia facere, si in sua essent facultate, quae Deo placent: idcirco ad omnes probationes fidei sustinendas paratus est, nullique se subducit occasioni, in qua fidem suam Deo, ejusque fide duci probare possit. 32." Socinus, "Dialogus de Justificatione," 1:606.

able with faith. [37] Now Sozzini explicitly held that penitence [38] and
conversion [39] are not in the powers of the natural man. They require
divine action as a part of the event, [40] in which we participate. In
this sense *bona opera* (penitence and conversion) are equal to faith.

In his fourth question the writer assumed "that nothing can be
found in us except material of condemnation" and that "the whole
cause of our salvation is outside of us." What did Sozzini mean
when he wrote "that it is more necessary to inquire what things
ought to be in us than to inquire what things are outside of us"?
Did Sozzini believe "that there is some free will or faculty of
attaining to heaven by our works"? In his reply Sozzini emphasized
that God's goodness and his gracious will expressed in Christ are
the more important side of our justification; yet our concern should
be that whatever God requires in us will, in fact, be found in us. A
true and living faith must be "in us." This expression does not
mean in our sovereign power; it means "within us, and that not
without our will and action." [41] The difficulty with the teim *free
will* is that any use of this term immediately leads others to think
one is asserting a Pelagian view, and this results in great misunderstanding. Sozzini here acknowledged, but sharply restricted, a certain
scope for human will and action. He knew he would have to write
another treatise to clarify this matter. [42]

---

[37] Socinus, "De Fide et Operibus," 1:625.

[38] "This penitence does not come [to anyone] except through faith in Christ."
Socinus, *De Jesu Christo Servatore,* 2:192. Those who fall back into sin require
grace: "Verum iterata poenitentia ista, non in nostra potestate est; sed Deus,
ut eam habere possint, illis concedit, quibus vult, ipsique videtur." Socinus,
"Theses de Justificatione," 1:604.

[39] "For you had done nothing before on account of which you would have
merited to have so great a salvation decreed for you or that it should be made
known to you rather than to others.:... Inasmuch as *it is God who,* by his own
benevolence, being moved to this by no work of ours, *created us in a spiritual
manner through Christ Jesus* and the preaching of his Gospel, and who similarly
brought it about that we should walk in that holiness and newness of life which
he commanded..." (Italics supplied.) Socinus, *De Jesu Christo Servatore,* 2:242.
This same point can be found in Part Two, chap. seventeen, where the divine
action necessary for conversion is described as the inscription of the divine Law
in our hearts by God and by God through Christ.

[40] This is a central point.

[41] "Sic enim, ut supra attigi, accipienda sunt verba illa mea *In nobis,* non
autem ut significent idem, quod, *In potestas nostra,* quemadmodum fortasse tu
acceperas, cum ego tamen semper hoc sensu ea extulerim, ut videlicet idem
significent, quod *Intra nos,* idque non sine voluntate atque actione nostra:
...Verum ego penitus mihi persuadeo, voluntatem istam atque actionem nostram,
aliqua saltem ratione in nostra esse potestate..." (Sozzini's italics.) Socinus,
"De Fide et Operibus," 1:626.

[42] Cf. the "Raków Lectures" discussed below.

The "Theses"

The last part of the *Tractatus de Justificatione* is a document entitled "Theses on the Cause and Basis [43] in Man Himself of that faith in God, by which Holy Scripture testifies man is justified." [44] Sozzini argued that man may be depraved by education or custom, but if he has some distinction of right and wrong, of what should or should not be done, he can be guided by reason and do those things that are right even if he thinks that to do so will be less than beneficial for him. By nature man desires what he thinks is good for him and does not desire what he thinks is harmful to him. If man's natural instincts were infallible, desire and reason would be in harmony, so neither virtue nor vice could really exist. Man's natural instincts are not infallible, so desire and reason are in conflict. If he adheres to reason he can easily come to a belief that a God exists who rewards those who do good and punishes evildoers; yet he who obeys desire will scarcely, or never, be persuaded of this. Adherence to a persuasion that God exists, and that he rewards those who do good, is not enough. In addition there must be a strong will to follow the commands of reason, to do the right. Hence God gave mankind his commands and reason, which discerns that one should obey God's commands.

> But since the faith in God by which scripture testifies that man is justified before God contains this persuasion and obedience, it can now be sufficiently established from the things that have been said what is the cause and ground in man himself of that faith: namely, love and zeal of doing right and avoiding wrong.
>
> Now this love and zeal are able to be present already either before man heard anything of the commands given to him by God or before he was awakened through this hearing. But if neither occurs this faith of which we speak will never be able to exist in man. [45]

This argument moves from an assumption that man has some distinction of right and wrong to the conclusion that the cause and

---

[43] Or: "Ground."

[44] "Theses de Causa et fundamento in ipso homine, ejus fidei in Deum, qua hominem justificari, Sacrae Literae testantur," *Socini Opera* 1:626-27. Delio Cantimori transcribed this work from manuscript 3421 of the Krasiński Library of the University of Warsaw, which bore the date 1604. He published it in Delio Cantimori & E. Feist, *Per la storia degli eretici Italiani del secolo XVI in Europa* (Rome, 1937), 236-38. The manuscript perished in World War II; Chmaj dates this "w czasie powstania warszawskiego..." (at the time of the Warsaw Uprising). Ludwik Chmaj, "Wykłady Rakowskie Fausta Socyna," *Studia Nad Arianizmem* (Warsaw, 1959), 173, n. 18.

[45] Socinus, "Theses," 1:627.

ground of justifying faith is love and zeal of doing right and avoiding wrong (obedience). [46] The passage appears to mean that justifying faith is *assensus* and *obedientia*. Has Sozzini adopted a view of rationalism and moralism?

Ludwik Chmaj stressed "the efficacy of man's moral efforts" and regarded Sozzini as seeking "to exonerate God of all responsibility for man's life" by placing that responsibility on man himself. [47] Zbigniew Ogonowski emphasized *amor ac studium* by putting the words in italics and connecting them with the initial assumption of some distinction between right and wrong. Ogonowski interprets this as the beginnings of a naturalistic ethic. [48]

But Sozzini does not say that the love and zeal of doing right and avoiding wrong are, per se, in man by nature; only the potentiality (*potest . . adesse*) for them is in man by nature. [49] Such love and zeal can be present, but they are not inevitable. They can even be present before man hears and is awakened by God's commands. But such love and zeal of doing right and avoiding wrong are *not* identical with justifying faith. As Sozzini has reiterated in his many documents, justifying faith is *fiducia*, complete trust and confidence in God or in God through Christ. Such love and zeal will be moved to *confidentia* only after man has heard God's word and has been awakened through hearing it.

Sozzini was concerned that we inquire "what things ought to be in us," as he wrote in his letter "On Faith and Works." He has previously emphasized that "those things which are outside of us," God's goodness and his gracious will expressed in Christ, are "more important in our justification than those things which are in us." Hence the "Theses" should not be read from a view that biases the theses toward an excessive emphasis on man's will and action. A distinction of right and wrong, a decision to adhere to reason, the ability to be persuaded that God exists and that he rewards those who do good, love and zeal of doing good and avoiding wrong—all

---

[46] ". . . recta faciendi & prava vitandi amor ac studium." *Ibid.*

[47] Chmaj, *Faust Socyn*, 22, 396.

[48] ". . . *pragnienie i gorliwość czynienia tego, co prawe, a unikanie tego, co niegodziwe* . . ." (Ogonowski's italics.) Ogonowski, *Z Zagadnień*, 250. ". . . już u Socyna znajdują się zaczątki poglądu o powszechności zbawienia w oparciu o etykę naturalną." *Ibid.*, 260.

[49] "*Potest* autem amor iste atque studium, vel jam adesse, antequam homo de Deo ejusque sibi datis praeceptis quidquam audiat, vel per ipsam auditionem excitari." (Italics supplied.) *Socini Opera* I :627. (Cantimori, *Per la storia degli eretici Italiani*, 238.)

these things must be in us; yet they are not enough. They do not constitute justifying faith, for, as we shall see, such faith depends on the grace of divine revelation.

The "Raków Lectures" of 1601 and 1602

In his "Raków Lectures" of 1601, Sozzini rejected the Pelagians who maintained that man can obey the Law by his natural powers. Appealing to Romans 7, he stressed the divine aid that is necessary to enable one to obey God. This aid consists in the promise of eternal life through the gospel. Under the Gospel, men can seek God and anticipate his grace. He even says men have whatever is necessary to will the good and to will to do that which is good. But these resources are not enough. If men were left to themselves, these human resources would be useless. God's revelation through Christ awakens in men the will to do the good, which He perfects. [50] (He concluded this section by noting that many learned men have acknowledged that the passages in scripture that seem to destroy all human free will are are very few and are obscure.) [51]

In his "Raków Lectures" of 1602, [52] Sozzini maintained that under

---

[50] "Notandum est hominem perfecte quidem posse velle recte facere, *ut vero ad actum deducat, auxilio Dei indiget.* Quod verum esse et ratio et experientia et scriptura sacra demonstrant... *Errant pelagiani, qui putant hominem naturalibus viribus solis posse servare legem*... Quam autem nobis necessarium sit ad Deo oboediendum eius auxilium, documento est 7 cap. ad Rom. Non est autem auxilium Dei tale, ut nos necessitet et cogat ad Deo oboediendum. *Auxilium enim illius est nihil aliud quam promissa vitae aeternae,* quo auxilio carebant ii, qui sub lege, quae tota minas detonat... Et sic sub novo testamenta nulla opus est gratia, quae sit extra evangelium, quia et vires naturales habemus et praeterea non deest Deus iis, qui ipsum quaerunt... Gratiam suam exsequitur Deus in iis, qui id faciunt, quod possunt. *Est enim in nobis bene velle et recte velle facere.* Sed nisi Deus spem nobis fecisset et alicuius insignis boni, istud velle in nobis latuisset et otiosum fuisset, quia nulla occasio illud exercendi se obtulisset. *Spe autem facta Deus excitavit in nobis illud bene velle.* Prorsum autem Deus non tantum incipit in nobis operari, *verum etiam perficit* et nunquam deserit nos. Unde fit, ut homo, qui naturaliter potest bene velle, Deo spem alicuius insignis boni faciente etiam velit recte facere et re ipsa faciat." (Italics supplied.) Lech Szczucki and Janusz Tazbir, eds., *Epitome Colloquii Racoviae Habiti Anno 1601,* Biblioteka Pisarzy Reformacyjnych, no. 5 (Warsaw, 1966), 53-54.

[51] *Ibid.,* 54.

[52] These lectures, "Acta Synodi Racoviensis. Anno domini 1602..." began on October 7, continuing for (at least) eighteen sessions. The manuscript from which Delio Cantimori transcribed them bore notations which indicated it was prepared at Altdorf from February 13, 1608 to "Ultima Febr. 1608." Cantimori transcribed only parts of the (now lost) text. Cantimori, *Per la storia degli eretici Italiani,* 258-75.

the Law men were able at least to will the good. But under the Gospel, according to Romans 7 and 8, men are able to will and to do the good without any prevenient grace (i.e., "absque illa speciali gratia sub lege existente"); the grace of the Gospel, a message giving the hope of eternal life, frees men's powers in a way the Law could never do. Under the Gospel grace is necessary if men are to resist temptations and to persevere.[53] As the 1601 Lectures included Sozzini's awareness that God's action in the human situation is necessary for men to make any effective use of their human powers to will and to do the good, so the 1602 Lectures include his recognition of the importance of the revelation in Christ and of men's need of grace that they may use those human powers (or resources).

In the "Theses" and in the "Raków Lectures," Sozzini analyzed in some detail the manward side of justification; yet he maintained distinctions that stress man's need of grace, i.e., God's goodness and his gracious will expressed in Christ, which constitute the more important side of our justification. In the "Theses," he described "the things which ought to be in us"; love and zeal, in us, must be awakened in man by divine revelation. The "Raków Lectures" show that, shortly before his death, Sozzini held that God's revelation awakens and frees in man, and his grace perfects in man, the will to do the good.

Conclusion

Sozzini's thought contains neither the language of *meritum de congruo, meritum de condigno,* and *fides formata* nor real analogues to those concepts. He rejects the idea of merit by obedience. He does not consider obedience the soul of faith. Obedience flows from and depends upon *fiducia,* which is justifying faith. *Fiducia* is only intellectually distinguishable by men from the behavior which flows

---

[53] "De virious autem agendi est alia quaestio. De quo Rom. 7. Ubi quidem non de singulis omnibus hominibus loquitur; sed in genere de humano genere. Nam non est impossibile ut possit inveniri qui non tantum velit sed et obediat (non quidem plenissime; nam nemo talis) absque illa speciali gratia sub lege existente, non sub Evangelio. Nam sub illo possunt non tantum velle, sed et facere, sine ulla gratia praeveniente, quod docetur ad Romanos 7 et 8 cap. *Nam sub lege est sub hac captivitate, ut velit sed facere non possit. At sub Evangelio spes vitae aeternae mille modis confirmatas dat vires exequendi quod Deus vult,* quam tamen postea Deus confirmat in rebus arduis ... *ita ut sub ipsa lege, posset saltem velle, sed sub Novo testamento, non tantum velle, sed et ipsa re agere ... Opus autem habemus gratia Dei, ad persistendum in omnibus tentationibus,* ad perseverandum, etc., et certi esse debemus quod nobis Deus succurret." (Italics supplied.) *Ibid.,* 269-70.

from it; yet God makes the distinction and justifies a man who places full trust in Him even prior to the man's encounter with occasions that elicit from him obedience. Penitence and conversion, which are essential for a living, justifying faith, must be awakened in man by Christ. This faith is "within us, not without our will and action." Man's natural potentiality for love and zeal to do the right must be awakened by revelation, and grace is necessary if man is to attain to the full trust that is justifying faith.

Sozzini also rejected ideas of natural religion and a natural, saving knowledge of God. All saving knowledge of God comes from divine revelation. [54] Thus he excluded any form of incipient religious humanism; all human good actions require divine grace. Justifying faith is "under the Gospel," not the life of the natural man.

One is reminded of Heiko Oberman's words concerning Robert Holcot: "Without this gift of grace man is *helpless*; but it is just as true that without the full use of man's own natural powers, the offer of grace is *useless*." [55] Yet there is a difference. Holcot wrote: "...qua si homo vellet facere quod in se est ad penitentiam, deus facit quod in se est ad misericordiam." [56] Sozzini denied that man could be penitent of his own natural power; yet he believed that God would awaken man to penitence and to full trust in Christ, and that from such trust would flow obedience, which God would work to perfect.

Sozzini believed that sixteenth-century oppositions of Paul to James worked misunderstanding. As a disciple of Paul, he sought to correct this misunderstanding of the nature of justifying faith. As Moffatt wrote in his commentary on James, "the notion that religious belief justified by itself arose out of a misapprehension of Paul's antithesis between faith and works." [57] Robert Grant made

---

[54] "Tak więc negacja religii naturalnej, i to w każdej formie, jest konsekwentna i zupełna. Cała wiedza o Bogu, jaką ludzie posiadali lub posiadają, pochodzi wyłącznie z bożego objawienia." Zbigniew Ogonowski, *Socynianizm a Oświecenie* [Socinianism and the Enlightenment] (Warsaw, 1966), 88.

[55] Heiko A. Oberman, "Facientibus quod in se est Deus non denegat gratiam. Robert Holcot, O. P. and the Beginnings of Luther's Theology," *Harvard Theological Review* 54 (1961), 328 (Oberman's italics).

[56] "'...talis [malus senex] penitens in articulo mortis habet propositum satisfaciendi sub conditione "si posset" et hoc sufficit divine misericordie; quia si homo vellet facere quod in se est ad penitentiam, deus facit quod in se est ad misericordiam.' Sap. Lect. [Super Libros Sapientie] 48 C." *Ibid.*, n. 50.

[57] James Moffatt, *The General Epistles. James, Peter, and Judas,* The Moffatt New Testament Commentary (Garden City, New York, 1928), 43.

a similar judgment: " 'Faith apart from works is dead.' Paul would have expressed this point differently, but he would not have disagreed." [58]

---

[58] Robert M. Grant, *A Historical Introduction to the New Testament* (New York, 1963), 223.

WILDERNESS AND PARADISE

Essays in Modern Church History

RELIGION AND BACON'S NEW LEARNING

From Legitimation to Object

J. SAMUEL PREUS

Indiana University

The "Great Instauration" that Francis Bacon proposed to the world in such works as his *Novum Organum* (1620) [1] prophesied a brilliant new age of learning, secular and scientific. Yet this modernist vision was laced with traditional religious and even eschatological symbols of legitimation. Hence Bacon's work constitutes an interesting moment in the complex story of changing relationships between religion and learning in the west. Professor Williams has traced the roots of Harvard University through explicitly theological traditions of New England, Geneva, medieval Paris and beyond, showing how richly laden with religious intent and eschatological pretension the enterprise of university education, and the calling of the professor, have been in some contexts.

Bacon's vision of learning was couched in similar wilderness/paradise metaphors, but his *New Atlantis* may be studied as an ideological alternative to New England, and symptomatic of an important break in western intellectual history. Although charged with hopes for restoration of dominion lost in the fall, and fraught with expectation of a new age of human possibilities, [2] Bacon's schema was theologically shaped by a fundamental division between creation and redemption, which in turn underwrote a basic division in the labor of learning. His new learning had as its goal nothing less than gradual restoration of man's broken dominion over nature—but nothing more than that either, for the knowledge of the restoration of fellowship with God through the redemptive work of Christ was separate and already complete, and left to the essentially custodial care of theologians. [3]

---

[1] The organization of the work is laid out by Fulton H. Anderson, *The Philosophy of Francis Bacon* (Chicago, 1948), 145.

[2] Paolo Rossi, "Baconianism," *Dictionary of the History of Ideas* (New York, 1973), I, 173. Loren Eiseley, "Francis Bacon," *Horizon* 6 (1964), 43. Benjamin Farrington, *Francis Bacon, Philosopher of Industrial Science* (New York, 1949), 146.

[3] Theodore K. Rabb, "Bacon," *International Encyclopedia of the Social Sciences* (n. p., 1968), I, 494-98. Bacon emphasizes that the fall was not the

Thus theology, although still looked to for the legitimating *framework* of learning, had no integral role in its actual *advancement*. Meanwhile, in opening up the vista of a total reconstruction of knowledge, Bacon was outlining a plan that would create new theoretical space for— among other things—a study of religion itself quite distinct from theology.

To elaborate this general picture, I shall examine religious dimensions of Bacon's thought from three perspectives: first, the theological framework that he explicitly provided for the scientific enterprise in his paradigmatic *New Atlantis*; second, his strict distinction (in the tradition of the "counter-Renaissance" [4]) between theology and his own "instauration," wherein theology, although proper in its own realm, was separated utterly from the actual content and dynamics of that new learning; [5] and finally, the extent to which Bacon created space on his intellectual map, and laid important groundwork, for scientific study of religion itself as a new field of inquiry. [6]

*

Bacon's *New Atlantis* (c. 1618) remained—perhaps appropriately— unfinished, yet emphatically displays the author's sense of religion as underwriter of a society dedicated to the advancement of learning. His fable begins somewhere in the vast wilderness of the north Pacific. A lost ship espies land, and at length discovers an island paradise. Less abstract in conception than More's *Utopia*, Bacon's Bensalem constituted an actual social paradigm of what he believed could happen:

> a model or description [as Bacon's contemporary, W. Rawley observed] of a college instituted for the interpreting of nature and the production of great and marvelous works for the benefit of man, under the name of Salomon's House, or the College of the Six Days' Works. [7]

---

result of man's knowledge and mastery of nature: *Advancement of Learning* (hereafter *AL*) I; *The Works of Francis Bacon*, (hereafter *Works*) ed. J. Spedding *et al.* (Boston, 1860-64), repr. St. Clair Shores, Michigan, n.d.), VI, 92. Cf. Moody E. Prior, "Bacon's Man of Science," *Journal of the History of Ideas* 15 (1954), 359, on the importance of this point.

[4] Hiram Haydn, *The Counter-Renaissance* (New York, 1950), 251-76.

[5] Anderson, *op. cit.*, 298.

[6] See the discussion below at n. 20. Cf. my articles, "Zwingli, Calvin and the Origin of Religion," *Church History* 46 (1977), 186-202, and "Machiavelli's Functional Analysis of Religion: Context and Object," *Journal of the History of Ideas* (scheduled for Spring, 1979).

[7] *New Atlantis* (hereafter *NA*); *Works* V, 357.

This paradisic island, "beyond both the old world and the new," [8] was the sort of place where Bacon's program of cooperative, organized research could proceed with careful division of labor and without the constraints of traditional authorities or civil disruptions. Yet in Bacon's portrayal it was fully supported by religious beliefs and symbols which had been generated by a straightforward and unmistakable divine revelation. As the names already indicate, Bacon took his Bible straight, and even drew clues from it regarding proper procedure. Yet, as we shall see, biblical data in no way affected the method, the content or the actual findings drawn from the systematic study of nature by the citizens of this society. God the Creator of nature was in no sense part of its content. [9]

In the story, Bacon's travelers are told that Salomon's House was founded some three-hundred years before the Christian era for the purpose of studying "the works and creatures of God." [10] Its founder, King Solamona, had somehow been informed of the Hebrew creation story "that God had created the world and all that therein is within six days."

> Therefore he instituting that House for the finding out of the true nature of all things (whereby God might have the more glory in the workmanship of them, and men the more fruit in the use of them) did give it also that second name [, College of the Six Days' Works]. [11]

Thus, the glory of the Creator and the use of man provide the axiological and teleological framework of the whole enterprise. But the knowledge of Christian redemption comes to the people only much later, saving them from "infidelity" but in no way altering their original intent (only one of many indications of Bacon's strict distinction of the spheres of creation and redemption). The purpose of the House of Salomon is described by one of its Fathers (interviewed by the reporter) as "the knowledge of Causes, and secret motions of things; and the enlargement of the bounds of Human Empire, to the effecting of all things possible." [12]

The Bensalemites collect information from every corner of the globe, remaining undetected by others, but far ahead of them all. De-

---

[8] *Ibid.*, 367, 369.

[9] *De Augmentis Scientiarum* (hereafter *DAS*) III.4; *Works* VIII, 509f. Cf. *Great Instauration* (hereafter *GI*), Pref.; *Works* VIII, 31.

[10] *NA*; *Works* V, 382.

[11] *Ibid.*, 383.

[12] *Ibid.*, 398. Prior offers a detailed portrait of Bacon's almost priestly man of science (*op. cit.*).

tached from the turmoil of Europe, they have surpassed it in useful knowledge. Bensalem does not itself require any great "instauration" (restoration) such as is required for Europe; rather, it is intended as a model for what might be done, and among founders of Britain's Royal Society and other learned societies it did in fact provide such a model. [13]

Bacon wanted to make clear that his project could be carried on within bounds of strictest (Protestant) orthodoxy; yet he managed to suggest at the same time that the scientific, experimental mind was best suited to make intelligent theological (as well as scientific) judgments. Our travelers are told how the people of Bensalem became Christian: shortly after the Ascension of Christ, they were vouchsafed a special (special delivery!) revelation. [14] Their Christian conviction was arrived at quite "scientifically," i.e., by careful observation and intelligent interpretation of some rather compelling evidence that God was trying to tell them something. This conclusion was inferred by one of the wise men of Salomon's House from a divinely-produced visible spectacle. This wise man was trained to recognize divine causality when he saw it, and thus to "discern . . . between miracles, works of nature, works of art, and impostures and illusions of all sorts." [15] What Bensalemites got, delivered by sea in a small ark, was the Bible and a personal letter from St. Bartholomew. These unimpeachable credentials settled all religious questions once for all, freeing the citizens to continue uninterrupted in their investigations, but now "saved from infidelity (as the remains of the old world was from water) by an ark, through the apostolical and miraculous evangelism of St. Bartholomew." [16]

This knowledge of redemption neither adds new dimension to, nor places restraints on, the study of the created order; the people continue in their recovery of "that right over nature which belongs to it by divine bequest." [17]

---

[13] Thomas Sprat, History of the Royal Society, eds. J. I. Cope & H. W. Jones (St. Louis, 1958), xii: "Joseph Glanvill commented that Lord Bacon's 'Salomon's House in the NEW ATLANTIS was a Prophetick Scheam of the ROYAL SOCIETY.' Our age has amply documented the assertion." Bacon appears on the Frontispiece of Sprat's work as the society's patron saint. Cf. T. K. Rabb, op. cit., 497.

[14] NA; Works V, 370ff. The Jews of Bensalem had also received a special revelation of their own, and remained loyal to it; ibid., 390f.

[15] Ibid., 371.

[16] Ibid., 373. The multi-lingual populace enjoyed their own pentecost experience as well.

[17] Novum Organum (hereafter NO) I. 129; Works VIII, 163.

For man by the fall fell at the same time from his state of innocency *and* from his dominion over creation. Both of these losses, however, can even in this life be in some part repaired; *the former by religion and faith, the latter by arts and sciences.* 18

Thus, Bacon reinterprets the divine response to the fall as a dual one, and the arts and sciences become a significant part of the "sweat of Adam's brow" through which the "curse" is gradually overcome, and the paradisic, harmonious relationship between man and nature is progressively restored as learning steadily advances through time. 19

*

Bacon used religion to underwrite a program of learning that was entirely secular, in the sense that all of creation—both as nature, and as the creative productions of humanity—was to be opened to scrutiny as a realm distinct from, even though parallel to, theological learning. 20 Each realm, separated by an "absolute chasm," 21 would have its place, but there would be no mixing. Like his theological counterpart Martin Luther, 22 Bacon was a believer in two separate spheres, two "kingdoms," and the scholar must render to each its due: to faith what belongs to faith, and to reason what belongs to reason. 23 Unlike Luther, however, Bacon's commitment to "liberty" bore on experimental philosophy, while Luther's concern was theology. In common, they maintained that a "mixing" of the two spheres inevitably resulted in the corruption of both. 24

For Bacon, Scripture and nature constituted a sort of dual "revelation" from God to man. 25 Two consequences immediately followed

---

18 *Ibid.* II. 52; *Works* VIII, 350 (italics mine).

19 *Ibid.* The Enlightenment idea of progress depended on the belief that man could change his environment for the better—only one implication of the pregnant axiom that "truth is the daughter of time."

20 *DAS* II. 1; *Works* VIII, 407.

21 Anderson, *op. cit.,* p. 148.

22 Cf. Haydn, *op. cit.,* on Luther.

23 *NO* I. 65; *Works* VIII, 93f. For example of Bacon's strict revelationism, see *DAS* IX. 1; *Works* IX, 347ff

24 *NO* I. 62; *Works* VIII, 91; cf. *Ibid.,* 65; 93f. See Prior's careful summary, *op. cit.,* 363.

25 *AL* I; *Works* VI, 144: "For our Saviour saith, 'You err, not knowing the Sriptures, nor the power of God;' laying before us two books or volumes to study, if we will be secured from error; first the Scriptures, revealing the will of God, and then the creatures expressing his power..." Cf. *Natural and Experimental History* (hereafter *NEH*), Introduction; *Works* IX, 371.

from this—consequences that functioned as presuppositions for like-minded *virtuosi* of Bacon's time: the two revelations could not contradict each other, and the study of nature could be pursued as a genuinely "religious" calling. [26] This doctrine also implied a single methodology for all inquiry: whether in theology or in the study of nature, one came to the truth through inductive means. [27] Bacon insisted that the mind, by itself, was virtually powerless. He wanted to deflate the claims of the mind's innate powers made by rationalistic philosophers and scholastic theologians of the past, radically limiting valid and certain knowledge (*including* knowledge of God) to that which arose from direct observation:

> Man... can do and understand so much and so much only as he has observed in fact or in thought of the course of nature; beyond this he neither knows anything nor can do anything. [28]

It is as little children that we must come into the kingdom, whether natural or supernatural. [29] Thus, for him, the difference between theological and scientific inquiry was not based on the notion that there was some qualitative difference in the way it was conducted but rather in the sort of questions that were asked, and the objects of each. Theology was rooted in the unimpeachable evidence of a word from God, and had as its object the nature and will of God; science would draw from ongoing, cumulative experience of the world, and was not to be interfered with or imposed upon by theological claims. [30] In a sense, *all* truth, even that of Christian theology, was the "daughter of time," but it would remain static, once delivered, while knowledge and mastery of creation would progress without regard for a definitive antiquity. [31]

---

[26] *Parasceve* IX; *Works* VIII, 369: "For I want this primary history to be compiled with a most religious care, as if every particular were stated upon oath; seeing that it is the book of God's works..." Basil Willey, *Seventeenth Century Background* (Garden City, 1955), 42: "To study nature... cannot be contrary to religion; indeed, it is part of the duty we owe to the great artificer of the world."

[27] Rabb, *op. cit.*, 497.

[28] *NO* I. 1; *Works* VIII, 67. Cf. *Ibid.* 36; 75, and *DAS* II. 13; *Works* VIII, 456.

[29] *NO* I. 68; *Works* VIII, 99. Cf. *DAS* V. 2; *Works* IX, 69.

[30] *NO* I. 84; *Works* VIII, 117: "And with regard to authority, it shows a feeble mind to grant so much to authors and yet deny time his rights, who is the author of authors, nay rather of all authority. For rightly is truth called the daughter of time, not of authority."

[31] Theological truth is the dauther of time in the sense that revelation happens in time, but not in the progressive, open-ended sense with which Bacon thinks of other knowledge.

So emphatic was Bacon in his insistence on observation that he criticized Galileo and his like, who saw mathematics as the key to the universe, for wishing to impose on nature more order than was actually there. Given the opportunity, Bacon says, these theorists would arrange the stars into a system more orderly than actually exists, creating a cosmos such "as we see in the vaulted roofs of palaces... so great a difference is there betwixt the spirit of man and the spirit of the universe." [32] Bacon was off base here, [33] and his contribution to the actual progress of learning was intellectually limited by his underestimation of the importance of hypotheses as well as of mathematics; [34] yet he was not unaware of the inadequacy of pure induction, and in fact aspired to get beyond it, as his famous metaphor of the ant, spider and bee shows:

> Those who have handled sciences have been either men of experiment or men of dogmas. The men of experiment are like the ant; they only collect and use: the reasoners resemble spiders who make cobwebs out of their own substance. But the bee takes the middle course; it gathers its material from the flowers of the garden and the field, but transforms and digests it by a power of its own... Therefore from a closer and purer league between these two faculties, the experimental and the rational (such as has never yet been made) much may be hoped. [35]

Moreover, he could cite Plato with approval on the necessity of general notions by which we recognize things and organize our world. [36] Still, Bacon did not provide a complete theory of knowledge. His commitment to a description of the real world, and accumulation of hard and useful knowledge in contrast to the scholastic "spiders" [37] and

[32] *DAS* V. 4; *Works* IX, 99f. Cf. *NO* I. 45; *Works* VIII, 79.

[33] E.g., Thomas S. Kuhn, *The Structure of Scientific Revolutions* (2d ed., Chicago, 1970), 16.

[34] Mary Hesse provides a balance-sheet of Bacon's achievements and errors from a scientific point of view in Brian Vickers, ed., *Essential Articles for the Study of Francis Bacon* (Hamden, Conn., 1968). On his neglect of hypotheses and mathematics, see among others G. V. Benson, "Francis Bacon," *Dictionary of National Biography* (London, 1917 ff.), I, 828; J. H. Randall, *The Career of Philosophy from the Middle Ages to the Enlightenment* (New York, 1962), 254.

[35] *NO* I. 95; *Works* VIII, 131f.

[36] *DAS* V. 3; *Works* IX, 86. This only seems to be contradicted by *DAS* II. 13; *Works* VIII, 456: "...that is the true philosophy which echoes most faithfully the voices of the world itself, and is written as it were at the world's own dictation; being nothing else than the image and reflexion thereof, to which it adds *nothing of its own,* but only iterates and gives it back" (italics mine). Here, Bacon is warning against distortion by addition of traditional preconceptions, and therefore not quite contradicting the idea that the mind's own inherent "power" may "transform and digest" what is observed.

[37] *AL* I; *Works* VI, 122, 132.

the "confident and dogmatical" Aristotelians [38] led him to eschew

> the serene tranquility of abstract wisdom.... For I am building in the
> human understanding a true model of the world, such as it is in fact, not
> such as a man's own reason would have it to be...[39]

In this connection, he admired Machiavelli "and other writers of that
class, who openly and unfeignedly declare or describe what men do,
and not what they ought to do." [40] Bacon's extreme sensitivity to the
errors of preconception, of tradition, of abstract speculation, etc., led
him to much closer scrutiny of the *distortions* of knowledge (gathered up in the notorious "idols") than to its legitimate foundations.
As he himself stated, "interpretation is the true and natural work of the
mind when freed of impediments." [41] His conviction that all knowledge
was derived from experience led him to see those impediments in a
new way, and thus to attempt a social explanation of philosophical
errors, together with the first "typology of the sources of distortion
in human understanding." Along these lines he is credited with laying
groundwork for the sociology of knowledge, [42] a critical component
of sociology of religion.

*

On the basis of the above, I wish now to describe what a study of
religion itself might look like, within the boundaries of a Baconian
perspective, and also to see the extent to which he actually entertained such a study, with religion itself as its object. We have already
seen, given his normative considerations regarding the scope of in-

---

[38] *De sapientia veterum* (hereafter *DSV*) 26; *Works* XIII, 150.

[39] *NO* 124; *Works* VIII, 156.

[40] *DAS* VII. 2; *Works* IX, 211. George H. Nadel, "History as Psychology in
Francis Bacon's Theory of History," in Vickers, *op. cit.*, 243, writes: "Bacon
and Machiavelli have long been recognized as the principal exponents of the
proposal to reorient the study of moral philosophy towards an empirical or
historical study of behavior...."

[41] *NO* I. 130; *Works* VIII, 164. Cf. *GI*, Proemium; *Works* VIII, 17f. Bacon's
lack of anxiety about *how* we know exactly reflects (as elsewhere) William
of Ockham: see Gordon Leff, *William of Ockham: The Metamorphosis of Scholastic Discourse* (Manchester, 1975), 123.

[42] Irving L. Horowitz, *Philosophy, Science and the Sociology of Knowledge*
(Springfield, Ill., 1961), 18. Cf. James E. Curtis & John W. Petras, eds.,
The Sociology of Knowledge: A Reader (London, 1970), 7. I am indebted to
Prof. James T. Richardson for suggesting this connection upon hearing an
earlier version of this paper at a meeting of the Society for the Scientific Study
of Religion, October, 1977.

quiry, that any study of religion would have to be strictly separate from theology. That contention is reinforced when we look at those areas of Bacon's thought most pertinent to this issue: first, his ideas about natural theology, and then, two areas that would shape the content of a scientific study of religion, viz., his idea of "natural histories" as the building blocks for the advancement of knowledge, and his discussion of the imagination (rather than reason) as the psychological locus of religiousness.

Bacon's tendency is to discount those innate resources on which natural theology depends. Just as he rejected the rationalism represented by Galileo (and as he would be the bedrock of English resistance to Cartesian philosophy) so also, consistently, Bacon did not see religiousness as a natural quality rooted in human reason. His outlook thus anticipates not the rationalistic Deism that would soon be articulated by Herbert of Cherbury, whose *De Veritate* appeared two years before Bacon's death, but rather the critique of natural theology, and the psychological theory of religion itself, that would be offered later by David Hume. [43]

Bacon would not have shared Herbert's confidence in the constructive theological potential of so-called "common notions" of religion. [44] As Anderson observes,

> Bacon is unable to see in the human creature any natural faculty or faculties capable of discerning either the inner thoughts or the nature of God.... He maintains that wisdom respecting the Supreme Being cannot be attained by reason and sense but only through the revelation contained within his inspired Word. [45]

Thus, *reason's* only access to the divine dimension of reality (existence of which Bacon did not doubt) is through straightforward, empirical appropriation of divine revelation—described with ideal clarity in the *New Atlantis* (discussed above). Apart from such revelation reason has no specific knowledge of the divine at all. Such a relic as remains, after the Fall, of the divine "spark," is too feeble to provide knowledge of divine things; hence, "religion, whether considered with regard to morals or mysteries, depends on revelation from God." [46]

Despite this apparent denial of a rational natural theology, Bacon

---

[43] The former in his *Dialogues Concerning Natural Religion* (1777), the latter in his *Natural History of Religion* (1757).

[44] Bacon describes their extremely attenuated role in *NO* 64, 66 and 97; *Works* VIII, 92f., 94, 132.

[45] Anderson, *op. cit.*, 53.

[46] *DAS* IX. 1; *Works* IX, 348.

acknowledged that human beings possess an appetite or desire for self-transcendence, and he affirmed that "the assumption or approach of man to the Divine or Angelical nature is the perfection of his form." [47] But how could this be, given Bacon's denials of reason? Bacon's answer, such as it is, lies in his discussion of imagination, to which we shall come shortly.

Bacon's Great Instauration included two essential elements: the making of natural histories, and the method of induction, as presented in the *Novum Organum*. The natural histories would gather up the essential data, while the method of induction would pyramid these materials into eventual mastery of nature for man's benefit. The fundamental importance of the natural history in Bacon's scheme is established by the mythic status it receives in the *New Atlantis*; King Solamona himself, the founder, had launched their enterprise by writing a natural history of "all plants . . . and of all things that have life and motion." [48] "History and experience," Bacon believed, form the base of the "pyramid" of knowledge, and "natural history" was the basis of natural philosophy. [49] Natural history, he declared, would be "the nursing mother of philosophy, to furnish the stuff and matter of true lawful induction, and thus become a solid and eternal basis of true and active philosophy." [50]

As to specific topics that Bacon prescribes for these "histories," more of them are natural than cultural, historical or psychological, since mastery of the natural environment (rather than the psychological or social one) dominated Bacon's vision. Nevertheless, Bacon regarded his program as universal in scope, and mapped the terrain of knowledge to include full treatment of the "History of the intellectual faculties; reflexion, imagination, discourse, memory, etc." [51] Bacon's contribution in this area would prove fruitful for later authors more specifically interested in religion—most obviously David Hume, whose *Natural History of Religion* (1757) is a classic in the study of religion.

Bacon's anticipation of that line of inquiry will be more fully evident

---

[47] *DAS* VII. 2; *Works* IX, 204.
[48] *NA*; *Works* V, 383.
[49] *DAS* III. 4; *Works* VIII, 507.
[50] Paraphrased by Richard F. Jones, *Ancients and Moderns: A Study of the Rise of the Scientific Movement in Seventeenth-Century England* (St. Louis, 1961), 53ff., in the context of discussion of the important place of natural histories in Bacon's program.
[51] *Parasceve*, Catalog; *Works* VIII, 378.

when we turn to his discussion of imagination, but it should be noted
first that Bacon's *Essays* are an integral contribution to the natural
histories, [52] and among these essays are discussions of religion as a
social problem treating religious conflict, sects, atheism and superstition. By treating such subjects, Bacon showed how his empirical
approach would operate in areas other than natural science. He
tried always to isolate historical causes, and took social, psychological
and political factors into account. [53] Also, he tried to derive laws or
axioms from the study of many specific examples—induction at
work. [54]

Like all thoughtful men of his time, Bacon was disturbed by the
extent to which religious conflict seemed to be a peculiar affliction of
Christianity. He seems close to the insight of Herbert of Cherbury
in his analysis of this situation: conflict arises from rival and mutually
exclusive claims to divine revelation. In the pithy formulation of the
early (1612) *Essays,* Bacon noted that

> the quarrels and divisions for religion were evils unknown to the heathen;
> and no marvel, for it is the true God that is the jealous God; and the gods
> of the heathen were good fellows. [55]

Bacon also pinpointed the savagery of Christian religious conflict as a
major cause of atheism in his own time. Ideas such as these would
of course get full airing in Hume's work, but Hume would put his
material in a fuller theoretical, psychological framework than Bacon
did. Still, Hume may have learned from Bacon's notions of the imagination, and from his attempts to penetrate the hidden meaning of
ancient myths. This brings us to Bacon's treatment of the imagination.

*

Imagination is one of the three human faculties from which all
cultural endeavor springs. The other two sources are memory, which

---

[52] Ronald S. Crane, "The Relation of Bacon's *Essays* to his Program for the
Advancement of Learning," in Vickers, *op. cit.,* 272-92.

[53] E.g., the analysis of the causes of atheism (*Essays* XVI; *Works* XII, 133f.),
listing the many divisions of religion, the scandal of priests, lack of reverence,
learning, peace and prosperity ("for troubles and adversities do more to bow
men's minds to religion"). Cf. discussion of the causes of superstition (*Ibid.*
XVII, 136) or the rise of sects (*Ibid.* LVIII, 276).

[54] E.g., "If a new sect have not two properties, fear it not; for it will not
spread. The one is, the supplanting or the opposing of authority established;
for nothing is more popular than that. The other is, the giving license to
pleasures and voluptuous life" (*Ibid.,* 276ff.).

[55] *Works* XII, 315.

gives rise to history, and reason, the source of philosophy. [56] Thus, imagination is a major category in Bacon's organization of the resources for the advancement of learning. We saw above that Bacon denied an innate rational-religious faculty. Here we find his alternative: in his description of the poetic imagination he located the most basic religious faculty of human beings, and attempted to penetrate the meaning of its productions. Put another way, Bacon seems to have suggested that the psychological mechanism of self-transcendence is the imagination, rather than reason. [57] Constructively, reason is feeble and without immediate contact with the divine; yet it comes into its own in its ability to organize and analyze empirically the products of the imagination—images, poems, stories. This critical and interpretive use of reason complements that of Bacon's "wise man" of Bensalem, as he sorts out an authentic "miracle" of divine revelation: in both cases, reason operates on data provided through the senses directly, or upon literary material characterized by its use of sensual language to offer and at the same time conceal some deeper truth.

Bacon proposed that the data of imagination were the avenues for understanding religion, because in matters "of faith and religion, our imagination raises itself above our reason." [58] This would seem to be what Bacon meant when he said elsewhere that "the assumption or approach of man to the Divine or Angelical nature is the perfection of his form." [59] Bacon did not spell that out. But he did assert that imagination, one major area of scientific inquiry, was also the sphere in which to locate religion. He seems to have been trying to develop a general theory of religion without denying the accepted *theological* doctrine of his time: thus, he was careful to assert on the one hand (protecting his flank from orthodox critics) that specific divine revelation comes from God to the "very citadel of the mind," but, in a more general way, he allowed that "divine grace uses the motions of the imagination as an instrument of illumination, just as it uses the motions of the will as an instrument of virtue." [60]

Imagination's peculiar form of discourse is poetry, which is in turn

---

[56] *DAS* II. 1; *Works* VIII, 407. Anderson, *op. cit.,* 148ff., gives a full description.
[57] We must leave aside the question of how, or whether, these "faculties" can be separated in a real person.
[58] *DAS* V. 1; *Works* IX, 61f.
[59] *DAS* VII. 2; *Works* IX, 204.
[60] *DAS* V. 1; *Works* IX, 62.

subdivided by Bacon into three areas: parables, and narrative and dramatic poetry. [61] Parable is the typical vehicle and proper language of religious expressions: "religion," Bacon writes, "ever sought access to the mind by similitudes, types, parables, visions, dreams." [62] The peculiar use of the word "religion" (instead of "God") here suggests that Bacon was looking for an appropriate non-theological term—i.e., a term that need not presuppose the specific action of God (a matter of faith) but that would account for the undeniable fact that such occurrences are habitually and rightly identified as religious. At any rate, Bacon has begun to talk about a realm of human consciousness distinct from reason that manifests to us what Bacon calls "religion." This imaginative faculty is worthy of attention even though it does not, according to Bacon, produce real knowledge in the scientific sense. [63] Through it, we may come to some wisdom of consequence. Here Bacon is vague, and perhaps confused. On the one hand, he seems close to a clear conception of non-theological religion study—close, in fact, to an outright reductionist thesis that religion is a product of the imagination, or fantasy. [64] But that is not the direction in which he carries his discussion of ancient myths. Wedded still to a Renaissance reverence for antiquity, he claims that the ancient parables conceal insights or echoes of a pristine ancient natural philosophy; [65] but at the same time, as a "modern," he is convinced that through his superior new methods, the long-hidden truth of these fables can be deciphered and recovered. [66]

Man's religious imagination raises consciousness to a higher than ordinary level, in Bacon's view, for

---

[61] *DAS* II. 13; *Works* VIII, 440.

[62] *DAS* V. 1; *Works* IX, 62.

[63] *Ibid.,* cf. *Essays* XLII; *Works* XII, 223; *DSV,* Preface; *Works* XIII, 76: "*religion* delights in" the "veils and shadows" of parable.

[64] Paolo Rossi, *Francis Bacon, from Magic to Science,* tr. Sacha Rabinovitch (London, 1968), 87, says that Bacon's treatment of fables foreshadows "a notion that was to become a turning point in the development of European thought: the notion that religion stems from fantasy."

[65] Charles W. Lemmi, *The Classic Deities in Bacon: a Study in Mythological Symbolism* (Baltimore, 1933), 41.

[66] *NO* I. 84; *Works* VIII, 116f. This is Bacon's famous argument setting the reverence for antiquity on its head by pointing out that the moderns are really the ancients—since "the old age of the [present] world is to be accounted the true antiquity," and much more might be expected from it than from the ancient times, "inasmuch as it is a more advanced age of the world, and stored and stocked with infinite experiments and observations."

there is agreeable to the spirit of man a more ample greatness, a more
perfect order, and a more beautiful variety than it can anywhere (since
the Fall) find in nature.... Whence it [poetry] may be fairly thought
to partake somewhat of a divine nature; because it raises the mind and
carries it aloft, accommodating the show of things to the desires of the
mind, not (like reason and history) buckling and bowing down the mind
to the nature of things. [67]

Bacon's reference to the fall reminds his readers of the religious-
eschatological justification for his Instauration; deciphering the ancient myths (to which he devoted a special treatise, the *De sapientia
veterum*), will aid in fulfillment of the divine promise that man may
eventually overcome the consequences of the Fall and reclaim his
intended dominion over Nature. The ancient myths seem to him to be
the "veils" between our fallen state and that primitive purity of knowledge that, if recovered, would contribute to the promised "kingdom of man." [68]

Exactly what Bacon hoped to learn from the ancient stories is not
entirely clear, categorically: he found in them wisdom about all sorts
of things, including religion. But he regarded them with a respect
approaching his reverence for revelation (which means, of course,
"unveiling"), as can be seen in his peculiar (and I think deliberate)
use of the ark-metaphor. In two separate contexts Bacon uses the
image of the ark as the bearer of revelation. One we have already
seen, in the "special delivery" of the Christian message to the people
of Atlantis. In a second context, in praise of ancient parables, Bacon
says that "parable has ever been a kind of ark, in which the most
precious portion of the sciences were deposited . . ." [69] We are reminded
of Bacon's notion that Scripture and nature parallel "revelations";
here, (ancient) culture may also be revelatory in its own way. For
these poems, parables, or stories were a medium of "communion
between divinity and humanity." [70] Vaguely, he felt that in some
extraordinary way "the [ancient] world had brought forth greater
things than it remembered"! [71] The ancient myth was thus an "ark"

---

[67] *DAS* II. 13; *Works* VIII, 440f.

[68] Rossi, *Francis Bacon*, 127-30, relates the interpretation of fables to the
recovery of ancient wisdom, but perhaps does not emphasize enough its link with
the advancement of learning. The two are tied together by Bacon's traditional
theological framework, whereby recovery of the lost Golden Age has, at the
same time, eschatological significance.

[69] *DSV*, Dedication; *Works* XIII, 69.

[70] *DSV*, Preface; *Works* XIII, 76. *DAS* II. 13; *Works* VIII, 442.

[71] So James Spedding, in his introduction to *NA*; *Works* V, 352.

launched on the flood of history, and its message could be deciphered now, thanks to the new Baconian method available to the "moderns." [72]

After all that, Bacon's attempts to reinterpret specific ancient stories seem far-fetched. Yet his conviction that they bore meanings beyond their surface, and that these meanings reflected some profound experience of reality, would take later scholars beyond his allegorizations in the direction of more modern psychological and social interpretations (e.g. Bernard Fontenelle and Giambattista Vico). [73] David Hume's psychological account of the origin of religion, although transposed into a different conceptual framework, may have been specifically informed by Bacon's interpretation of the myth of Pan. Bacon described the capacity of nature, as man's environment, beyond his control, to excite terror. Such fear and dread was a useful survival instinct when it promoted man's self-preservation:

> But the same nature knows not how to keep just measure—but together with salutary fears ever mingles vain and empty ones; insomuch that all things (if one could see into the heart of them) are quite full of Panic terrors; human things most of all; so infinitely tossed and troubled as they are with superstition ... especially in seasons of hardship, anxiety and adversity. [74]

Hume, appreciative of the degree of religious toleration among the polytheistic heathen, may also have drawn on Bacon's observations regarding the social consequences of Christianity. Quarreling over religion was unknown to the heathen, Bacon observes,

> because the religion of the heathen consisted rather of rites and ceremonies, than in any constant belief. For you may imagine what kind of faith theirs was, where the chief doctors and fathers of their church *were the poets*. [75]

But religious conflict appears with the revelation of the true God, because "the true God hath this attribute, that he is a jealous God; and

---

[72] See the text quoted above, n. 66.

[73] On Vico, see Enrico de Mas, "Vico's Four Authors," in Giorgio Tagliacozzo ed., *Giambattista Vico: an International Symposium* (Baltimore, 1969), discussing how he adapted Bacon's method to the study of society. On Fontenelle, see L. M. Marsak, *The Achievement of Bernard le Bovier de Fontenelle* (New York, 1970).

[74] *DSV* VI; *Works* XIII, 99. Fear and anxiety in face of a life-situation that he cannot control, and under threat of an uncertain future, constitute the psychological roots not only of "superstition," but of religion itself, according to Hume (in the *Natural History of Religion*). Anderson recognizes dependence on Bacon in Hume's interpretation of the "structure of all experience in terms of psychological history" (Anderson, *op. cit.*, 303).

[75] *Essays* III; *Works* XII, 86; my italics.

therefore his worship and religion will endure no mixture nor partner." [76] This observation comes from his essay "Of Unity in Religion" (1625), but Bacon also claimed to find it hidden in the ancient
myth of Diomedes, or Zeal—something unknown to the ancients, yet
foreseen in their imagination, so that they seem to have prophesied the
mixed blessings of knowing the "true" God. [77]

*

There is an unbridged gap between the contemporary study of
religion (as distinct from theology) and its peculiar roots in intellectual history. Such a gap does not exist for theologians, who from
the time of Eusebius have been able to trace their pedigrees back to
the creation of the world. To fill that gap (albeit in more modest
degree)—to understand the emergence of a scientific inquiry into religion out of its historical context—is the broad aim that motivates
and shapes the present study.

Bacon excluded nothing in the natural and human realms from his
program, although he gave only fragmentary attention to study of
religion in his reconstruction of knowledge. Lacking sustained interest in systematic study of society, Bacon's mind was attuned mainly
to understanding and mastery of nature. Yet his very preoccupation
with a method of inquiry that would be totally free from traditional
philosophical and theological preconceptions, yet legitimate for believers, heralded a thoroughly modern era of learning. His presuppositions and method were available to anyone who wished to develop
them and apply them to religion, and thinkers such as Vico, Fontenelle
and Hume would do so.

His most pertinent suggestions, it seems to me, would be first,
his clear sense of the difference between theology and other areas of
inquiry, which invites careful consideration of exactly what sort of
problems one wishes to solve, and what sort of questions one hopes
to answer, before research actually begins. Bacon had a clearer sense
than some modern students of religion who keep the lines fuzzy
between theology (especially "natural theology") and the study of
religion, working both sides of the street at once, mingling justification with explanation, prescription with description, indoctrination
with information. Bacon's approach would support clear distinctions
here. He would also not try to identify a common essence of all

---

[76] *Ibid.*, 86ff.
[77] *DSV* XVIII; *Works* XIII, 127.

religion by *a priori* invocation of an innate religious sense or idea, out of which one might propose normative definitions of religion. These are never spacious enough to account for all the evidence, and therefore must undergo endless revision. [78] Rather, Bacon would try to observe religious phenomena as they actually appear, confident (naively, perhaps) that not only could he identify "religious phenomena" when he saw them, but that his eye for them would improve the more he observed.

In addition to these normative considerations, Bacon's two substantive pointers (his proposal for natural histories, and his identification of pertinent data of religion study with works of the imagination) would both yield interesting fruit in the work of subsequent students of religion.

In a way, Bacon lacks awareness of the possibilities of a study of religion, indeed, lacks interest in such a study. I think the reason for this is related to the note on which we began: his fervent religious legitimation of the scientific enterprise. Bacon was still uncritically committed to divine revelation as a satisfactory *explanation* for the existence and phenomena of religion. For him, the origin of religion lay in the initiative of the God of the Christians; hence, despite his restless curiosity about practically everything, Bacon was rather complacently satisfied with the traditional (protestant) explanation of religion. He thus stands as negative evidence for my broad hypothesis about the rise of the study of religion, viz., that the study of religion arose from the criticism of religion (more exactly, from criticism of specific religious traditions, or aspects thereof); that such criticism resulted, in turn, from the perception of the failure of religion; that this critical impulse, already surfacing in the Renaissance and Reformation period, became increasingly generalized so as finally to embrace religiousness *per se* in its critical and analytical purview. [79] Lacking such sense of failure of religion, or of conflict between it and the values he envisioned, Bacon felt little need for sustained critical analysis of it.

An observation by Richard S. Westfall seems to support this line of interpretation. He notes that Thomas Hobbes fit the general outlook of the Royal Society *virtuosi* (all of whom acknowledged Bacon

---

[78] Melford E. Spiro, "Religion: Problems of Definition and Explanation," in Michael Banton, ed., *Anthropological Approaches to the Study of Religion* (London, 1966), 86ff.

[79] This interpretation is expanded in my articles cited above, n. 6.

as their patron saint), except that he alone *rejected* their view (and Bacon's) that "science did not challenge Christianity." [80] Hobbes, then, was unique among that group in seeing essential conflict between the new outlook and the theological tradition, *and* it is Hobbes alone that offered a critical socio-political analysis of religion as such, in his *Leviathan*. Hobbes made a contribution to a functional analysis of religion integral to his thought (as Machiavelli had before him) whereas, by contrast, Bacon's contributions to a scientific approach to religion were fragmentary and peripheral to his interest. For Bacon, religion remained the legitimating *context* of thought; he had not yet brought it into focus as an *object*: as the given providential framework of his entire program, it could not be, at the same time, the object of critical analysis in any comprehensive sense. His inclination, rather than reducing religion study to a science, was to elevate study of nature to a religion.

Yet, those who came later and shared his scientific outlook, but who were dissatisfied with or sceptical of traditional accounts of the origin and roles of religion could walk through the door he opened by his proposal of natural histories, and his insights about imagination, and proceed toward new ways of studying and attempting to explain religion.

---

[80] Richard Samuel Westfall, *Science and Religion in Seventeenth-Century England* (New Haven, 1958), 20ff.

SOCINIAN HISTORIOGRAPHY
IN THE LATE 17TH CENTURY

Benedykt Wiszowaty and his "Medulla historiae ecclesiasticae"

LECH SZCZUCKI

University of Warsaw

I

Although the history of the Polish Brethren, or Socinians, has been the subject of a number of studies—from the now classic work by Earl Morse Wilbur [1] to a whole string of authoritative and comprehensive publications by Janusz Tazbir [2]—we still know relatively little about the intellectual legacy of this emigration and the direct impact it made on philosophical and theological debates of the late 17th century.

It should at once be emphasized that the Sejm edict of 1658 which required the Socinians to leave Poland within three years (this time limit was moved back the following year and the date of banishment was ultimately set for 10 July 1660) proved disastrous for the Socinian church which soon disintegrated into a number of groups and factions dispersed over almost the whole of Europe. The two largest centers of the Socinian emigration—Transylvania and East Prussia—never played an intellectual role of any consequence in its history (the last great thinker among the Polish Brethren, Samuel Pryzpkowski, died in Prussia in 1670), while the attempt made by Stanisław Lubieniecki, Jr. (1625-75) to plant a Socinian colony in Northern Germany was firmly resisted by Protestant orthodoxy.

In these circumstances it was Holland which became the intellectual

---

[1] E. M. Wilbur, *A History of Unitarianism: Socinianism and its Antecedents* (Cambridge, Mass., 1945).

[2] Of which I shall list only the most important: *Stanisław Lubieniecki, przywódca ariańskiej emigracji* [*Stanisław Lubieniecki, Leader of the Socinian Emigration*] (Warszawa, 1961); but see K. E. Jordt-Jørgensen, *Stanisław Lubieniecki. Zum Weg des Unitarismus von Ost nach West im 17. Jahrhundert* (Göttingen, 1968); *Bracia Polscy w Siedmiogrodzie 1660-1784* [*The Polish Brethren in Transylvania 1660-1784*] (Warszawa, 1964); *Bracia Polscy na wygnaniu. Studia z dziejów emigracji ariańskiej* [*The Polish Brethren in Exile. Studies in the History of the Socinian Emigration*] (Warszawa, 1977).

hub of the Socinian diaspora, its moving spirit being the outstanding leader and thinker, Andrzej Wiszowaty (1608-78), who arrived in Amsterdam in 1666, although here, too, the difficulties with which the exiles had to contend were acute. 3 Quite apart from their in many cases severely straitened circumstances, they found themselves up against the utterly basic problem of lacking formal legalization of their denomination. As a result they had to fall back on the support of sympathetic Remonstrant, Collegiant and Mennonite circles. Although there can be no doubt of the help and consideration which they received from the Remonstrants in particular, the fact remains that, for want of an independent church organization of their own, the exiles were also hard put to maintain a separate identity. The example of various "near-Socinian" thinkers like Jeremiah Felbinger or Daniel Zwicker, who, after leaving Poland, plunged vigorously into the swirl of religious life in the United Provinces, is highly typical in this respect. Last but not least, it must be added that at the time that Wiszowaty appeared in Amsterdam, Socinianism as a doctrinally and organizationally formalized religious movement was in the throes of a profound crisis, the cause of which did not stem solely from its dissolution in Poland. I am thinking of the discussions within the Socinian church itself, which revealed serious dissensions over fundamental questions of dogma (Christology) and over socio-political issues (attitudes to the state and temporal institutions). But I am thinking above all of the new philosophical currents of Cartesianism and Spinozism, since they posed questions and problems basically beyond the intellectual horizons of Polish Socinianism which owed its avantgarde character largely to sixteenth-century inspirations. By the mid-seventeenth century these had become, at any rate in part, anachronistic. However, this crisis has not yet been sufficiently investigated 4 and until the work of the last Polish Socinians, including the Amsterdam edition

3 Cf. L. Szczucki, "Z dziejów emigracji socyniańskiej w Holandii" [From the History of the Socinian Emigration in Holland], *Odrodzenie i Reformacja w Polsce*, 20 (1975), 202-09 (where I published three hitherto unknown letters of Andrzej Wiszowaty).

4 But cf. K. Pomian, "Piotr Bayle wobec socynianizmu" Pierre Bayle and Socinianism, Archiwum Historii Filozofii i Myśli Społecznej, 6 (1961), 101-82; Z. Ogonowski, *Socynianizm i Oświecenie. Studia nad myśla filozoficzno-religijna arian w Polsce XVII wieku* [*Socinianism and Enlightenment. Studies in the Philosophical and Religious Thought of the Unitadians in Seventeenth-century Poland*] (Warszawa, 1966); M. Firpo, "Pierre Bayle, gli eretici italiani del Conquento e la tradizione sociniana," *Rivista storica italiana*, 65 (1973), 612-66.

of the Racovian Catechism, [5] has been analyzed there is little that can be said on the subject.

Nevertheless, it is quite apparent that Andrzej Wiszowaty was thoroughly aware of all these problems and that he endeavored with great single-mindedness to face them squarely. In the field of dogma he took an extremely moderate line, opposing all attempts at doctrinal revision. Moreover, and significantly enough, these were controversies of a strictly internal nature known only to a trusted few. Wiszowaty's principal concern (he was, after all, bound by ties of warm friendship with Remonstrant quarters and regarded Holland as his second homeland) seems to have been to preserve the Polish complexion of the diaspora and to codify on a grand scale the ideological and historical patrimony of the Polish Brethren. As it happens, the publishing ventures directed after his death by his son, Benedykt, which comprised the monumental *Bibliotheca Fratrum Polonorum*, [6] numerous editions of the writings of individual Socinians, landmarks of history like the second edition of *Slavonia reformata* by the Polish Calvinist, Andrzej Węgierski (1679), the *Bibliotheca antitrinitariorum* by Christopher Sandius (1684) and the *Historia reformationis Polonicae* by Stanisław Lubieniecki (1685), fanned a singular revival of interest in Socinianism, though this interest by then was to a large extent academic in flavour.

The phototype editions of the last three works, each furnished with lengthy introductions, [7] as well as the other studies that have appeared of late on the subject of Socinian historical scholarship [8] make it

---

[5] Cf. E. M. Wilbur, *op. cit.*, p. 583, n. 43. Needless to say, the painstaking study by W. Burger Van Wyk, *Die Versoeningsleer in die Rakouer Kategismus* (Ampen, 1958), does not tackle this question.

[6] Cf. J. Vercruysse, "Bibliotheca Fratrum Polonorum. Histoire et bibliographie," *Odrodzenie i Reformacja w Polsce*, 21 (1975).

[7] Christophori Sandii, *Bibliotheca antitrinitariorum*, praefatione et indice nominum instruxit L. Szczucki (Varsoviae, 1967); Stanislai Lubieniecii, *Historia reformationis Polonicae*, praefatione instruxit H. Barycz (Varsoviae, 1971); A. Wengerscii, *Libri quattuor Slavoniae reformatae*, praefatione instruxit J. Tazbir (Varsoviae, 1973).

[8] I am thinking primarily of Janusz Tazbir's monograph on Lubieniecki (see n. 2 above); H. Barycz, "Stanisław Lubieniecki jako historyk reformacji" [Stanisław Lubieniecki as Reformation Historian], in L. Szczucki, ed., *Wokół dziejów i tradycji arianizmu* [*Of the History and Traditions of Socinianism*] (Warszawa, 1971), 77-94; and, last but not least, G. H. Williams, "The Sarmatian Myth Sublimated in the *Historia Reformationis Polonicae* (1664/85) of Stanislas Lubieniecki and related documents," in V. Erlich, ed., *For Wiktor Weintraub. Essays in Polish Literature, Language and History offered to Wiktor Weintraub on his Sixty-fifth Birthday* (The Hague, 1974), 567-79.

unnecessary to describe it in greater detail. Only a few observations
are in order. Polish Socinianism's actual historical achievements were
never on a par with what it could claim in the realm of theology and
philosophy. The Sandius-Benedykt Wiszowaty work is, after all, virtually no more than a bibliography, athough it is an extremely valuable
one not only for its abundance of source data, but also for its historical excursuses. The uncompleted history by Stanisław Lubienicki, Jr.,
which is as important as the *Bibliotheca* (if not more so) because of its
wealth of source material, represents nevertheless, especially when set
against the great erudite historiography of the seventeenth century, a
middling opus, part apologetic, part hagiographical, part sectarian. This
last quality, which derives from the Anabaptist heritage of the sixteenth century (the social doctrines of Anabaptism, be it remembered,
exerted a strong influence on Polish Antitrinitarianism), was to be
echoed in the Amsterdam edition of the Racovian Catechism (1680)
prepared by Benedikt Wiszowaty. Plagued by debacles and setbacks,
Polish Socinianism went back to its roots which had been heavily fertili-
zed by Anabaptism and which, to be sure, had never been entirely
forgotten, when it renounced the "world" and pursued an austere, egalitarian program of moral reconstruction.

These brief and perforce stereotyped remarks seem necessary in order
to put into better perspective Benedykt Wiszowaty's hitherto unknown
Medulla historiae ecclesiasticae. This is probably the last serious work
to come from the Polish Socinians, one which winds up their contribution for good and is in a sense their parting shot. It seems worth
studying therefore, at greater length, though I am well aware that my
own study of it can be neither exhaustive nor fully qualified, since I
am a historian of ideas and not a theologian and since my command
of history of dogma is extremely scant.

II

What we know of the life of Benedykt Wiszowaty (who died some
time after 1704) is very meagre. It amounts, in effect, to only the
sketchiest information. There is no record of his birth, nor of the
academic centers which, to judge by his remarkable historical and
theological learning, he presumably attended. What can, however, be
said for certain is that the basic influence in the moulding of his
personality was his father, Andrzej Wiszowaty. It was under the
guidance of Andrzej, that Benedykt embarked on and then carried out
the publishing ventures referred to earlier. He remained in touch with

Remonstrant circles with which he had been connected since his earliest days, after he left Holland and settled in East Prussia where in 1684 he became minister of the Socinian exiles' community in Kosinowo. [9]

Wiszowaty's correspondence during the years 1682-1704 with the Remonstrant theologian Philip van Limborch is really the sole source from which we can learn a little more about this unassuming, even deliberately self-effacing Polish Socinian who, despite his remoteness from Dutch intellectual centers, made a point of keeping in contact with them. [10] He read the works of Remonstrant theologians, requested news of the latest publications, discussed various exegetical problems and, last but not least, took a lively interest in the progress of the publishing projects undertaken by the Remonstrants in conjunction with the edition of the works of the distinguished Socinian thinker, Samuel Przypkowski. Nevertheless it cannot help striking the eye that, despite the efforts of Benedykt himself and the good will of his Dutch friend, this correspondence was subject to continual interruptions. Obviously Wiszowaty, who was wholly immersed in the arduous life of his small community, had little time for independent studies of his own and for establishing a genuine dialogue with the Dutch world.

But in the early years of his sojourn in Prussia, Wiszowaty did not confine himself solely to the role of reader or commentator of the writings of his Dutch friends. He was busy also with an extensive work of history, which is extant in two manuscripts. The first, now located at the University Library in Hamburg (ms. Theol. 1879/4⁰/) [11]

---

[9] Cf. J. Tazbir, *The Polish Brethren in Exile,* 132-3. It is possible, however, that Wiszowaty left for Prussia earlier, since in a letter to Philip van Limborch of 11 March 1682 he wrote: "Et quoniam propositum meum in Prussiam brevi proficisci, operam dabo, ut si illic quaedam lucubrationes eius [scil. S. Prypcovii-L.S.] adhuc haerent, itidem ad clarissimum virum transmittantur" (The University Library in Amsterdam, ms. III e. 3, f. 88 a).

[10] B. Wiszowaty to P. van Limborch, Amsterdam, 11 March 1682; Kosinowo, 25 July 1691; Kosinowo, 1 February 1697; Kosinowo, 27 June 1704. The University Library in Amsterdam, ms. III E. 3, f. 88 a-d. I am grateful to Prof. Janusz Tazbir for microfilms of these letters.

[11] Cf. F. S. Bock, Historia antitrinitariorum, t. I, pars 2, Regiomenti et Lipsiae 1776, p. 1028. My attention was drawn to the Hamburg MS in 1956 by the distinguished historian of Polish culture, S. Kot, who died in 1976. It is worth giving the chapter headings of *Medulla*: 1. De Nazaraeis et Ebionitis; 2. De patribus saeculi 1 et ultra; 3. De haereticis saeculi 1 et ultra; 4. De Artemonitis et Alogis; 5. De patribus a medio ad finem saec. 2; 6. De haereticis a medio ad finem saec. 2; 7. De beryllo et Paulo Samosateno saec. 3; 8. De patribus saec. 3; 9. De haereticis saec. 3; 10. De homousianorum et Arianorum dissidiis saec. 4; 11. De Photino, Priscilliano et eorum homodoxis saec. 4; 12. De patribus a Concilio Nicaeno usque ad initia saec. 5; 13. Controversiae circa

and dating to the late seventeenth or early eighteenth century, bears
the following title: *C.D.O.M. Medulla historiae ecclesiasticae s.
Problema s. Tractatus de origine et progressu verae et falsae de Deo
Patre et Filio eius Iesu Christo Domino nostro nec non Spiritu Sancto
doctrinae auctore Andrea Wissowatio Sociniano.* It runs to 347 pages.
The other is in the library of the Romanian Academy of Sciences in
Cluj (ms. Kéz 130). It is an eighteenth century copy, as it contains
the postscript: "Finis. Anno Christi crucifixi 1734 20 Martii." [12] The
text displays minor variations compared with the Hamburg manuscript,
chiefly of a stylistic nature, although, as in the latter, there are also
errors. Moreover, the chapters are additionally sub-divided into sections
and the pages are not numbered. Another interesting point is that
the transcriber was ignorant of the author's name, for the words here
underlined were added later in a different hand: *Benedicti Wissowatii
Medulla Historiae Ecclesiasticae, seu De origine et processu verae et
falsae de Deo Patre et Filio eius Iesu Christo Domino nostro nec non
Spiritu Sancto doctrinae.*

Thus the first problem posed in confronting these two manuscripts
is that of authorship. It does not, however, seem a particularly complicated problem since the following arguments add up, I think, to a
conclusive case for the author having been *Benedykt Wiszowaty.*

First, in the *Bibliotheca antitrinitariorum* (1684), which, as we know,
was edited by Benedykt Wiszowaty, there is no reference in the article
(very meticulously compiled) [13] "Andreas Wissowatius" to a *Medulla
historiae ecclesiasticae.* Further, it would be stretching credulity to
suppose that Benedykt, who cherished the memory of his father so
devotedly, would have unabashedly purloined his work. Second, it is
made absolutely clear by the text of *Medulla* itself that it was written

---

doctrinam de Spiritu Sancto; 14. De Nestorii doctrina eiusque sectatoribus; 16.
Continens saeculum 6; 17. Continens saeculum 7; 18. Continens saeculum 8;
19. Continens saeculum 9; 20. De ecclesiis in Aegypto saec. 10; 21. Continens
saeculum 11; 22. Continens saeculum 12; 23. De Albigensibus et Valdensibus
et aliis purioris doctrinae propugnatoribus saec. 12 et 13; 24. Continens saeculum
14 et 15; 25. Continens saeculum 16 et 17.

[12] The existence of this manuscript was intimated by J. Tazbir, *The Polish
Brethren in Transylvania,* 130. It also contains the *Religionis Christianae brevis institutio secundum Unitarios* (with the following legend above the title: "Anno
1731 16 Cal. 9 bris"), incomplete, for that matter, and *Prolegomena ad historiam
ecclesiasticam Novi Testamenti.* It has proved impossible to establish the authorship of these two treatises, though there is evidence suggesting that they were
written in the Hungarian rather than Polish Unitarian world.

[13] Cf. C. Sandius, *Bibliotheca antitrintariorum,* 145-49.

after the appearance of *Bibliotheca,* which, as is noted at the end, "nuper in lucem prodiit."

What clinches the argument, however, is this passage from a letter written by Benedykt himself to Philip van Limborch on 25 July 1691:

> Eadem occasione vellem etiam rescire ex te, vir clarissime, an visus sit a te tractatus quidam m.s. sub titulo *Medulla historiae ecclesiasticae,* quem frater noster Christophorus Zagorski ante aliquot annos huc per vestras oras ex Gallia redux penes se habuit; et, nisi mea memoria fallit, retulit mihi tibi etiam ab ipso fuisse communicatum et tuae, vir reverende, subiectum censurae. Quod si ita sit, rogo, ut et de hoc scripto, si vel ad manus est, vel contenta eius in memoria haerent, velis, vir doctissime, tuum promere iudicium. [14]

This passage leaves no doubt as to the intentions of the writer, and it is highly typical of his character: though on terms of friendship with Limborch, Benedykt was loth to inhibit his judgment and he skirted around the question of authorship. Unfortunately, Limborch's answer is not known to us, although it is legitimate to surmise that it was none too complimentary. The author, therefore, left his work in manuscript form, although that did not prevent it from circulating among Polish and Hungarian Unitarians. It will not be beside the point to note that the Krzysztof Zagórski referred to in the letter was in the years c. 1702-06 minister of the Polish and subsequently Hungarian Unitarian community in Kolozsvár before eventually moving to Prussia. [15] In view of the close ties between the communities in Prussia and Transylvania, it can safely be assumed that the Transylvanian Unitarians were properly informed as to the authorship of the *Medulla.* But ascribing it to Benedykt Wiszowaty does not by any means rule out a certain, as it were, "ideal," contribution from his father, a matter that will be gone into later.

This still leaves the dating of the work to be established, if only approximately. Unfortunately, we do not know when it was that Krzysztof Zagórski paid his visit to Limborch, but the phrase "a few years ago" ("ante aliquot annos") in Benedykt Wiszowaty's letter of 1691 indicates that it must have been towards the end of the 1680's at the latest. Since, as we have seen, the *Medulla* was completed "shortly" after the appearance of Sandius' *Bibliotheca* (1684), all the odds are that it was in the second half of the 1680's.

---

[14] The University Library in Amsterdam, ms. III E. 3, f. 88 b (25 July 1691).
[15] Cf. J. Tazbir, *The Polish Brethren in Exile,* 125-27 and *passim.*

III

The very title, *Medulla historiae ecclesiasticae*, seems an allusion to a celebrated work of the second half of the seventeenth century, the *Nucleus historiae ecclesiasticae* by Christopher Sandius, Jr., (1644-80). This fascinating figure was a "proof-reader" in Dutch printing shops, a student of Christian antiquity and a thinker in his own right. Towards the end of his life he tried to wed his decidedly Platonist-inspired philosophical outlook with the ideas of Spinoza, whom, for that matter, he knew personally. He has already been the subject of a study of mine and I intend to return to him given that interesting new evidence about him has now come to light. [16] Here it is enough to say that his *Nucleus historiae ecclesiasticae* (first ed., 1668, second ed. enlarged and revised, 1676; *Appendix addendorum, confirmandorum et emendandorum ad Nucleum historiae ecclesiasticae*, 1678), which claimed the attention of the likes of Spinoza and Newton, represented an attempt to reinstate the "Arian" and "Arianizing" currents in the history of Christianity, the basic accent being placed on Christological rather than Trinitological issues. Despite the warm feelings he entertained for the Socinians (he himself never belonged to any church) and despite his intimate friendship with many of them and with Andrzej and Benedykt Wiszowaty in particular, Sandius repeatedly emphasized the point where he and the Polish Brethren parted company. A firm believer in the pre-existence of Christ (it is worth stressing in passing that the description of Sandius as an "Arian" is none too accurate), he also insisted that Faustus Socinus' doctrine *de Verbo* was an utterly new and completely unprecedented development in the history of Christianity. Andrzej Wiszowaty took issue with Sandius' Christological views in a separate treatise, now lost, and he answered his *Nucleus* in a dissertation, also lost, entitled *In Christophori Sandii Nucleum historiae ecclesiasticae animadversiones.* [17] It seems likely, therefore, that Benedykt Wiszowaty, having inherited his father's papers, could have found in them the inspiration to write his treatise.

It was this that I had in mind in speaking of Andrzej Wiszowaty's probable contribution to *Medulla historiae ecclesiasticae.*

From the point of view of the "historical genealogy" of Socinianism, the problem raised by Sandius was of undoubtedly basic significance.

---

[16] L. Szczucki, "W kręgu spinozjańskim (Krzysztof Sandius, Junior)" ("In Spinozan Circles—Krzysztof Sandius, Junior"), *Studia i materiały z dziejów nauki polskiej,* seria A, zesz. 12 (1968), 157-73.

[17] C. Sandius, *Bibliotheca antitrinitariorum,* 147-48.

Attribution of the "kernel" (nucleus!) of the history of Christianity to its various "Arian" or "Arianizing" manifestations, together with the categorical exclusion of Socinian Christology from this patrimony, was bound to provoke a rejoinder from the Socinians themselves, an additional reason being that this was propounded by a writer known and highly esteemed in all sorts of circles, Catholic, Protestant, and heterodox.

This is in no way to imply that Benedykt Wiszowaty's chief object was a refutation of Sandius. Nevertheless, the parallelism of the titles (*Nucleus* and *Medulla* are, after all, synonyms for "kernel", "core", "marrow") seems revealing.

Let it be said at once that Benedykt Wiszowaty's work cannot possibly bear comparison with Sandius' magnum opus, which represents the best traditions of seventeenth-century ecclesiastical history. It was for good reason that the author of the *Nucleus* enjoyed a high standing among scholars of various denominations who by no means shared his doctrinal views. Yet it must be added in fairness that Wiszowaty does not seem to have nursed any such high-flying ambitions. After all, the *Medulla*'s philological-historical documentation is relatively modest compared to that of *Nucleus*. Although thoroughly conversant with the Fathers of the church and with ancient ecclesiastical writers, and although well versed in historical and theological literature of the fifteenth-seventeenth centuries, Wiszowaty was primarily a historian (and at times simply a chronicler) and he was less of a theologian and philosopher of history than was Sandius. If he nevertheless merits some attention, it is chiefly as a conscientious compiler of critical motifs long present in the sixteenth- and seventeenth-century Antitrinitarian tradition, motifs which, and this is a point which deserves emphasis, he tried to enrich with his own reflections. [18]

In twenty-five chapters Wiszowaty traced the rise of the dogma of the Trinity and orthodox Christology (i.e., belief in the eternal preexistence of Christ). At the same time he sought to prove that both these dogmas were completely unknown in the first centuries of Christianity and that for a long time after they were finally accepted they were understood in a manner basically different from that of contemporary theologians. The second theme of the *Medulla historiae ecclesiasticae*—and it is of an apologetic nature—consists of an analysis of the various Antitrinitarian currents in the history of Christianity

---

[18] Cf. L. Szczucki, "Aspetti della critica antitrinitaria sociniana," Archiwum Filozofii i Myśli Społecznej, 12 (1966), 141-59.

which, according to Wiszowaty, demonstrate that the true doctrine had
never been forgotten and that its adherents had continually served re-
minders of its existence. This of course is an application of a by then
classic proposition of Protestant historiography (with its antecedents
in Matthias Flacius Illyricus' *Catalogus testium veritatis*), tailored in
this instance to Wiszowaty's own Unitarian outlook.

The author's general intentions are, therefore, perfectly clear. He
was bent on demolishing the historical pedigree of Trinitarian orthodoxy
and showing that its current doctrine, established as a result of abuses
of various kinds, was a mass of errors or, at best, of confusions that
bore no relationship to the Apostles' Creed (which Wiszowaty regarded
as containing the essence of Christian doctrine) or to the teachings of
the ancient Church.

As Wiszowaty saw it, the adulteration of the simple, original precepts began even during the lifetime of the apostles, though it was
only after the death of these implacable keepers of the divine truth
that the process began to assume alarming proportions. For it was
then that the stage was seized by the alumni of a completely different
school, Greek philosophy, who were determined to interpret the revealed
truth according to their own lights. Loyal to the traditions of sixteenth-
and seventeenth-century Polish (and Italian) Antitrinitarianism, Wiszowaty was a resolute opponent of Neoplatonism, to which he attached
the chief blame for introducing the presumptuous and impious speculations underlying the dogma of the Trinity and the pre-existence of
Christ. This meditation on the history of a church gradually losing its
doctrinal unity and becoming an arena of fierce and unedifying strife
reveals also the sectarian nature of Wiszowaty's views. Only a select
few, says Wiszowaty, can in effect discover the supreme good, which is
divine truth; the masses, on the other hand, especially when false beliefs
closely match previously shaped views, as was the case with pagans
converted to Christianity, will never choose "the best things." [19] For

---

[19] "Postquam autem sacer apostolorum chorus differentem sortitus est finem
et generatio illa praeteriit quae divinam sapientiam ipsis auribus audire meruerat,
tunc impii erroris conspiratio per seductionem eorum qui alienam doctrinam trade-
bant initium cepit. [...] Nemo igitur miretur, sequentibus temporibus tam paucos
veritatis fuisse confessores. Numquam enim, ut praeclare ethnicus dixit sapiens,
cum rebus humanis tam bene agitur ut optima pluribus placeant. Praesertim cum
multo plausibiliora fuerint falsa quam vera dogmata, his maxime qui e gentilismi
tenebris Christi doctrinam amplectabantur. Qui variis et miris philosophorum,
imprimis Platonicorum, imbuti erant opinionibus ad quas poetarum fabulae ac-
cesserunt, apud quos omnes Iesus Christus crucifixus, verus ille Deus et filius

Wiszowaty, therefore, the history of the Church is the history of a minority, one defeated, persecuted and suffering, but one which nevertheless, dauntlessly convinced of the justice of its cause, passes on to succeeding generations the torch of divine truth.

However, it must also be emphasized that this pessimism, easy to understand given the situation of Polish Socinianism in the seventeenth century, is articulated in a flexible manner with varying degrees of intensity. By and large, the period running up to the Council of Nicaea and even, in a certain sense, to the sixth century (and this is the subject of almost three-quarters of the work) is treated by Wiszowaty as a time of, as it were, relative doctrinal equilibrium. The real decline of the Church began with the adoption of Christianity by Constantine the Great. For it was then that a religious community still, despite all its blunders, autonomous vis-a-vis the "world" was stricken by an acute blight, and brute force and violence replaced the "spiritual" weapons employed previously. The institutionalization of the Church, which as Wiszowaty repeatedly and deploringly notes, opened the way for the pagan temporal power to intcrefere unwarrantably in matters of faith, had a number of baleful consequences in the purely doctrinal sphere. Wiszowaty the historian has no doubt that the terms "orthodoxy" and "heresy" were frequently exploited in the Church by wielders of authority capable of imposing their will. Orthodox was simply the side that won and that reserved the appellation "orthodox" for itself, branding the losers as heretics and then, on the strength of purely arbitrary decisions, introducing new doctrinal dispensations which might be totally at variance with hitherto universally accepted beliefs. [20]

It is now time to examine in very general outline the principal substantive themes of the *Medulla historiae ecclesiasticae*. But before doing so, it is perhaps worth drawing attention to the reasonable, even dispassionate tone of the work. Wiszowaty keeps a tight rein on contentiousness and never indulges in vituperation. He contents himself with terse observations without the slightest streak of the *rabies theologica*,

---

hominis, stultitia erat, secundum id quod legimus 1 Cor. 1, 22, remanserant tamen et posterioribus saeculis antiqua vestigia et primaevae veritatis testes." (*Medulla*, cap. 1).

[20] "Hodie etiam apud nos qui catholici et orthodoxi appellari amant vix aliquod punctum vel punctillum esse quod non aliquando male, immo haeresos nomine audierit. Verum ii qui praevalebant rerumque potiebantur ceteros cum dogmatibus eorum tanquam haereticos pro lubito traducebant. Saepenumero iam quod antea plurimis placuerat postea vix aliquos diffusores inveniebat. Et vice versa ea dogmata quae prius vel ignota vel ab eventis fere improbata fuere, postea apud plerosque summam invenerunt venerationem." (*Medulla*, Prologus).

then so widespread. Evidently, he is confident that the evidence he has assembled will be more persuasive than vehement assertion.

The first theme of the *Medulla historiae ecclesiasticae* consists, as has been mentioned, of arguments demonstrating the groundlesness of the tenets of the orthodox Trinitology and Christology of Wiszowaty's day. These he continually confronts with the views of ancient ecclesiastical writers, who are usually quoted at length, and he shows that even those of them acknowledged by Trinitarian orthodoxy in actual fact expressed wholly discordant beliefs. Needless to say, his chief emphasis is put on the testimony of Ante-Nicene writers with chapter and verse cited from Hermas, Justin, Irenaeus, Clement, Tertullian and Lactantius, among others. [21] They, Wiszowaty maintains, always flatly underlined the pre-eminence of God the Father and the inequality of Christ in relation to Him. Indeed he goes even further. Without in the least concealing his disapproval of the Council of Nicaea and the confession it decreed, he nevertheless stresses that the theologians of that time continued to believe in the pre-eminence of the Father and did not refer to the Holy Ghost as God (such was the opinion of Hilary of Poitiers, for instance), a view "unknown to the Scriptures and antiquity" and one which was only established by the Council of Constantinople in 381. Generally speaking, however, the Post-Nicene Fathers (Wiszowaty here quotes the authority of Hilary of Poitiers, Basil the Great, Victorinus Afer, Gregory of Nazianzus, Augustine, Cyril of Alexandria, etc.) "nequaquam eandem, quae nunc viget, fovisse sententiam de Trinitate et Filii cum Deo Patre consubstantialitate, quem non eiusdem numeri (prout hodie creditur), sed tantum eiusdem speciei clare professi sunt." [22] Although he frequently draws attention to the gradual accretion of errors in the doctrine concerning God and Christ

---

[21] Which is not to say, of course, that Wiszowaty's attitude to these writers was uncritical. Take St. Justin, for instance, who, knowing no Hebrew, read the Gospels through the glasses of Neo-Platonism, although "de tali quae hodie colitur Trinitate ne somniasse quidem luce meridiana clarius est" (*Medulla,* cap. 2); Irenaeus "Filium Dei et Spiritum Sanctum nequaquam Deo Patri coequales statuisse, prout hodierni faciunt theologi" (*ibid.,* cap. 5); "Clementis libri [...] demonstrant eum nequaquam Filium Dei ipsum Deum Patrique aequalem esse credidisse" (*ibid.*). Cf. the following assessment of the doctrine of Lactantius: "Ex his et quae superius allegavimus patet manifeste Lactantium non unum numero Deum Patrem et Filium esse credidisse, sed tantum concordiae et voluntatis unitatem inter eos statuisse. Ex cunctis vero, quae protulerimus, clare liquet Lactantium qui antenicaenorum Patrum agmen claudit una cum aliis quos memoravimus docuisse Filium Dei minorem esse Patre secundum divinitate" (*Medulla,* cap. 8).
[22] *Medulla,* cap. 12.

proposed by these writers, it is quite clear from what he says that the period up to roughly the fifth century was, *summa summarum,* a time when the spark of divine truth still glittered even in the pronouncements of the theologians who sided with the doctrine of the ever more powerful Roman Church. As for subsequent centuries, he discusses them very perfunctorily, concentrating chiefly on the witness they give to the "primeval truth," a matter to which we will return.

It is, however, the second, though parallel, theme of the *Medulla historiae ecclesiasticae* which seems much more pertinent and original. This is an account of the history of various "heretical" doctrines, treated of course in their relation to Trinitological and Christological problems. There can be no doubt that Wiszowaty wished in this way to indicate the ideological sources of Socinianism and at the same time its deep roots in the history of the Church, as is clearly evidenced, for that matter, by a certain thrust at Sandius. [23] But it is probable that he also had other aims in mind than those dictated by the interests of the denomination which he represented. In the process of systematically demolishing the historical foundations of Trinitarian orthodoxy, he sought to reinstate a certain ideological patrimony, one which was not only close to Socinianism, but which also then engaged liberal religious groups and intellectual quarters associated with the "republic of learning." Wiszowaty does not by any means treat Socinianism as the sole depository of divine truth. He simply sketches in its historical credentials which, to his mind, entitled it to an important and significant part in this discussion.

Wiszowaty's choice of "historical genealogy" was carefully considered. There was no question whatsoever of uncritical acceptance of all instances of Antitrinitarianism in the history of the Church. "Primeval truth" or "healthy teachings" were to be found, as he saw it, only in those doctrinal pronouncements which underlined the absolute pre-eminence of God the Father and roundly denied the pre-existence of Christ. This criterion, applied fairly rigorously where the first five centuries of Christianity are concerned, is thereupon more or less abandoned; nor, for that matter, could the historical material have sustained it. This accounts for the distinct aloofness (once again it

---

[23] "Pro conclusione hoc tantum dicimus Sandium ex his omnibus quae conservavit, ut probaret Socinum novam atque inauditam sententiam de persona Christi protulisse, nihil aliud exculpare atque concludere posse quam aliter Samosatenianos initium Evangelii S. Ioannis explicasse ac nunc hi qui vulgo Sociniani vocantur facere solent." (*Medulla,* cap. 7).

will not be amiss to recall his anti-Platonist cast of mind) with which he treats the views, for example, of various Gnostics, the reason being that they denied the humanity of Christ and maintained that he had a "corpus phantasticum et impatibile." [24] Hence also his mixed feelings about Arians who, though vastly preferable to the Nicene parties, had no scruples (and this seems to have been Wiszowaty's chief objection) about resorting to violence against adherents of "primeval truth." [25]

Let us, therefore, now take a somewhat closer look at these exponents of "primaeva veritas," since they play a very important role in the *Medulla historiae ecclesiasticae*. In the period of primitive Christianity Wiszowaty singles out the Nazarenes and Ebionites. He considered that both these ancient Judeo-Christian sects (remember how much store he set by "ex antiquitate" argumentation) were of basic importance in the history of Christianity, since they had preserved intact the legacy of the pure faith on two fundamental matters: the monotheism of God the Father and the elevation of Christ, born a man, to the status of Son of God in reward for his merits. It is worth noting in passing that Wiszowaty makes much of the topographical location, as it were, of both these groups, obviously assuming that propinquity to the cradle of the Christian religion had enabled them to safeguard the patrimony of the true faith. Here he seems to share the view, fairly frequently encountered during the Renaissance, that as Christianity spread farther afield, the divine light, hitherto focussed on strictly specified lands (Palestine, Syria), underwent increasing etiolation and dissipation. [26]

The historical merits of all these observations seem less to the point than are the conclusions that Wiszowaty draws from them. He not only emphasizes the influence of the Nazarenes and Ebionites on ancient ecclesiastical writers (like St. Ignatius or pseudo-Barnabas), but he also derives in direct line from them the whole great tradition of the Eastern heresies which so heavily stressed the question of the humanity

---

[24] Porro ex hoc Cerinthii errore manasse videntur opiniones eorum, qui duas personas vel naturas seu substantias completas intelligentes in Christo esse docuerunt ac proinde filium Dei antesaecularem non vere natum sed tantum incarnatum nec vere mortuum esse statuere necesse habuerunt." (*Medulla,* cap. 3).

[25] "Dum sic de memoratis opinionibus ac controversiis Homousiani et Ariani, non tantum spirituali sed et carnali modo, strenue digladiantur, interim propugnatores veritatis ac simplicitatis primaevae plectuntur et utrisque invisi pro lubitu vexantur." (*Medulla,* cap. 10). Here Wiszowaty was thinking mainly of the Arians' dislike of Photinus.

[26] Regarding echoes of these ideas in sixteenth-century Transylvania Antitrinitarianism, see L. Szczucki, *W kręgu myślicieli heretyckich* [*Among Heretic Thinkers*] (Wrocław, 1972), 88-89.

of Christ—the tradition of Artemon, Paul of Samosata, Photinus, Nestorius, and their followers. These were the very men, falsely accused of heresy and persecuted, who, according to Wiszowaty, expressed "healthy and rightful views" on the subject of God and Christ, and their adherents' churches preserved these teachings. Hence his huge interest in various Eastern churches and sects—Samosatenians, Photinians, Nestorians, Monophysites—and also his frequent, and occasionally none too judicious [27] attempts to draw a parallel between this "Ebionite-Nazarene" tradition and later Antitrinitarian manifestations.

The impression is hard to resist that, having established the historical pedigree of "primeval truth" interpreted, as we have seen, in a Unitarian spirit, Wiszowaty ran out of steam and proceeded, sometimes superficially, sometimes diffusely, and with an excess of superfluous detail, to record the various attacks on the Trinity or Nicene-Chalcedonian Christology. As far as the Middle Ages are concerned, he discusses at some length—in keeping, for that matter, with the sixteenth-century Antitrinitarian tradition [28]—the refutations of the nominalists (Roscellinus, Abelard, Gilbertus Porretanus), and also devotes much attention to the Antitrinitarian strands in the history of various sects, such as the Bogomiles (noting their affinities with the doctrine of Photinus), Albigenses, Waldenses or Hussites. As for the sixteenth and seventeenth centuries, which are scrutinized in only one brief chapter, one is struck by the complete omission—no doubt on ecumenical grounds—of the names of the great reformers and by the exceedingly curt, not to say baldly factual, account of the origins of Antitrinitarianism in Italy, Transylvania, Germany and Poland, which does not in effect go beyond the sixteenth century but repeats the information to be found both in Sandius' *Bibliotheca antitrinitariorum* and in the dissertations appended to it. Moreover, Wiszowaty deliberately leaves out the names of all the Polish Antitrinitarians and deals with Faustus Socinus himself in just one short sentence. One cannot help feeling that in the course of writing this chapter (which gainsays its title by comprising only the sixteenth century) Wiszowaty

---

[27] I am thinking in particular of *Epistola Ioannis Smerae ad Regem Russorum Vlodimirium*, an apocryphal work originating in Polish-Lithuanian sixteenth-century Antitrinitarian circles (cf. I. Malyshevskiy, "Podlozhnoye pismo polovca Ivana Smery k vyelikomu knazyu Wladimiru svyatomu," *Trudy Kievskoy Dukhovnoy Akademii* 17 [1876]) and purporting to describe the doctrine of the Christians of Alexandria in the tenth century. Wiszowaty gives it a separate, enthusiastic chapter, surmising that they were an offshoot of the Nazarenes.

[28] Cf. L. Szczucki, "Aspetti della critica antitrinitaria sociniana," 149ff.

realized that the topic he had embarked upon transcended both his principal purpose and his powers. This seems to be evident in the closing passages of the work, where he explains to the reader the reasons for his brevity, and in short but pointed phrases, steeped with melancholy, though not without a tinge of unveiled pride, where he recounts the fortunes of sixteenth- and seventeenth-century Unitarianism. They are, I think, worth quoting in full: [29]

Silentio hic veneror omnes quorum in Hungariae et Transylvaniae regnis a praeterito saeculo ad haec usque tempora permultae florent ecclesiae ob unius Dei Patris unicique Filii eius professionem Unitariorum titulo gaudentes.

Missos etiam facio eos, qui hodiernis temporibus in diversis locis eandem fidei confessionem amplectuntur, ut et hos, qui titulos tantum hominibus invisos, non dogmata ipsa repugnant. Praetereo insuper florentes illas ecclesias quae in Polonia eique adnexis provinciis praeterito et praesenti saeculo ad invidiam usque per totum Christianum orbem illustres fuerunt, praeditae in paucitate sua non paucis sapientibus, potentibus et nobilibus viris. Quos vel ipsa generosa Sarmatarum gens protulit, vel aliunde ortos ad se seu ad asylum confugientes tamquam suos, ambabus excepit ulnis. Ex his eorum qui verbi divini gladio primaevam tutati sunt veritatem, catalogum exhibet *Bibliotheca antitrinitariorum,* quae nuper in lucem prodiit. Horum vero, qui huius veritatis professoribus patrocinium praebuere, series recensetur in *Vindiciis pro Unitariorum* libertate eidem *Bibliothecae* adiunctis.

Praetereo denique, veterem novumque non renovando dolorem, atroces illas oppressiones ac persecutiones, quas superiori et hoc saeculo in iisdem potissimum oris eiusdem veritatis passi sunt propugnatores.

Si enim haec cuncta, prout par est, enarranda essent, hic emergeret labor, qui novas etiam posceret vires. Quibus cum impares nos esse sentiamus, in praesentia, proposito nostro functi, tanta testium nube producta, quam ex ipsorum adversariorum (quod iterum notandum) monumentis collegimus, hic pedem figimus atque lampada hanc aliis iam tradimus.

---

[29] *Medulla,* cap. 25.

WILDERNESS EXPERIENCES OF RELIGION IN AMERICA

ROBERT T. HANDY

Union Theological Seminary

American religious life through much of colonial and national history has been numerically dominated by Christianity originating in Europe. The European Christian invaders of North America were so sure of the superiority of their religion and civilization that they pushed aside the religions and civilizations of the native "Indian" populations and planted their own institutions. Soon persons from other continents, Africa and later Asia, were brought into the mix, and their influence on religion in America must not be overlooked. Yet in full awareness of Charles H. Long's warning that "a great deal of the writings and discussions on the topic of American religion has been consciously or unconsciously ideological, serving to advance, justify and render sacred the history of European immigrants in this land," [1] I think we are in accord with the facts in simply noting at the outset the predominant influence for three centuries of Western European Christianity in shaping the patterns of religion in the New World.

The ships that brought Christianity to this continent came from Spain and the Netherlands, from Sweden and France, from Germany and Switzerland as well as from the British Isles; they brought Catholics as well as Anglicans, Puritan Congregationalists, Presbyterians, Dutch Reformed, Lutherans, Baptists, Quakers and many others. They also brought Jews—not in great numbers until the nineteenth century. And they brought those who belonged to no religious movement, and who seemed to be quite indifferent to religious claims.

Though they came from many places, those early settlers were well aware that they were on the edge of a great wilderness—uncharted, mysterious, dangerous. Those Christians who located in Jamestown and Williamsburg, in St. Augustine and New Amsterdam, in Plymouth and Boston believed that they had been sent by divine providence to carry out certain tasks of civilizing and Christianizing this wilderness. In the very first history of Massachusetts, Edward Johnson has his "typical Puritan" declaring as he leaves England, "I am now prest for the service

---

[1] "Civil Rights—Civil Religion: Visible People and Invisible Religion," in Russell E. Richey and Donald G. Jones (eds.), *American Civil Religion* (New York, 1974), 212.

of our Lord Christ, to re-build the most glorious Ediface of Mount
Sion in a Wildernesse." [2] The idea was spelled out many times, as in
an election sermon preached by Samuel Danforth in 1670, "A Brief
Recognition of New England's Errand into the Wilderness," from which
Perry Miller drew the title of one of his best-known writings. [3] So
strong were the first impressions, and so long were the vast spaces
of the new land resistant, that the feeling of being peoples in a wilderness has long persisted in the life of American religionists. In one
of his most imaginative essays, Sidney E. Mead observed that

> Americans during their formative years were a people in movement through
> space—a people exploring the obvious highways and the many unexplored and
> devious byways of practically unlimited geographical and social space. The
> quality of their minds and hearts was formed in that great crucible—and
> in a very short time. [4]

Not only has the feeling of living in a wilderness persisted; it has been
transferred from the geographic to quite other experiences which people
of faith had in America. Those experiences in various wildernesses
had their great moments as deeds were done and faith was clarified;
they had their moments of failure when higher principles were compromised in the face of cultural pressures. Some of the wounds received in wildnerness encounters by churches and synagogues have not
yet healed.

Five wilderness experiences stand out, beginning with that initial
encounter with sheer geographical space.

The Western Wilderness

At the outset and for three centuries, wilderness meant first and
foremost the North American continent with its forests and wastes, its
mountains and deserts, its rivers and swamps, its plains and prairies.
The early settlers and their descendants for many generations were
determined to conquer that wilderness, to plant churches there and to
transform it into a garden. Though we are now sensitive to some of
the mistakes of these pioneers, let us not minimize the magnitude of
their achievement. They planted religious institutions in every village,

---

[2] *Johnson's Wonder-Working Providence, 1628-1651* ("Original Narratives of
Early American History," ed. J. Franklin Jameson [New York, 1910]), 25.
For a rich analysis of the wilderness imagery, see George H. Williams, *Wilderness
and Paradise in Christian Thought* (New York, 1962).

[3] *Errand into the Wilderness* (New York, 1964), see esp. p. 2.

[4] *The Lively Experiment: The Shaping of Christianity in America* (New York,
1963), 7.

town and city across this vast continent; they erected a chain of local, regional and national units which we inherit and can use or neglect. They endeavored to communicate the faith they knew to all types of persons, carried Bibles and books into areas before they were explored, founded educational institutions from humble Sabbath schools to vast universities, erected a network of missions and then used the institutional framework they had shaped into a base for overseas mission. In any history of the expansion of western religion, their deeds are notable. Done largely on a voluntary basis, theirs was an impressive accomplishment of faith.

What they did has set a strong activistic stamp on most forms of religion in America. Lefferts A. Loetscher has declared that "amazing activity in Christian service at home and abroad has been the chief glory of American Christianity." [5] And Willard L. Sperry once remarked that "of the Roman Catholic orders, those concerned with propaganda and good works are in the great majority." [6] The activism of the American Jewish community is well known; Will Herberg once remarked that it "has no over-all organization, and every attempt to give it one so as to eliminate 'overlapping' has failed .... And yet this community without central control is capable of great communal efforts." [7] In emphasizing this important aspect of religion, however, others were neglected. For activism has often been stressed at the expense of the contemplative, mystical, and intellectual aspects of religion; it has given a one-sidedness to many religious styles in America.

There was another and more serious limitation in the drive of the European Christian invaders to conquer this wilderness. They virtually identified Christianity and western civilization, a civilization which they believed was far superior to any other and which did not hestate to call itself Christian. Most of them also believed in the superiority of European peoples, and felt that other civilizations and peoples should be grateful for their leadership. Hence, with a few happy exceptions, they had great difficulty in relating in any positive way to native Indian populations and cultures, and contributed to the tragic and dishonorable history of that encounter. They also dealt very unjustly with the Black people whom they pressed into service as slaves,

---

[5] *The Broadening Church: A Study of Theological Issues in the Presbyterian Church since 1869* (Philadelphia, 1954), 92.

[6] *Religion in America* (New York, 1946), 135.

[7] *Protestant—Catholic—Jew: An Essay in American Religious Sociology* (Garden City, N.Y., 1955), 212.

and co-authored the most painful and inexcusable chapters of American history. And when their descendants have interpreted their conquest of the wilderness, too often have they passed over the difficult places lightly, and neglected to tell the story of the contributions of others to the winning of the west.

We must record one more problem. While many persons of zeal who battled the physical wilderness decade after decade were sincerely trying to advance religious faith, others got that mixed up with conquering the land for profit. Some of the hard chapters in the sobering tale of how religious faith gets involved in and is sometimes displaced by hunger for land and wealth were written in this country. [8]

The story of the march of religious faith and institutions across the continent is one of impressive achievement—but it is also one accompanied by compromises and capitulations, some tragic. That today there are so many congregations across this land is evidence of remarkable accomplishments; unfortunately some of those accomplishments were stained by diseases of giantism, hyper-activism, and racism.

A Wilderness of Sects

These early settlers who thrust their way onto this continent and their descendants ever since have had to face quite another kind of wilderness, that of a broad and ever-widening spectrum of churches, sects, cults, groups, communities, fellowships, societies and organizations. That diversity was initially a very serious problem for those who were trying to build Christian states in the American wilderness, for almost everyone at the beginning assumed that churches should be established by law in the European state-church tradition. As Perry Miller once summarized the seventeenth-century situation, "No nation of Europe had yet divided the state from the church; no government had yet imagined that religion could be left to the individual conscience. Society, economics, and the will of God were one and the same, and the ultimate authority in human relations was the ethic of Christendom." [9] But immigrants were arriving from various national churches into the same colonies, and clashes were not long in developing. Also among the settlers were a few persons who were suggesting some radical

---

[8] E.g., see Bernard Bailyn, *The New England Merchants in the Seventeenth Century* (Cambridge, 1955); Frederick B. Tolles, *Meeting House and Counting House: The Quaker Merchants of Colonial Philadelphia, 1682-1763* (Chapel Hill, 1948).

[9] *Errand into the Wilderness*, 105.

departures from customary church-state systems, persons who were children of the left wing of the Reformation—chiefly Mennonites—and of the left wing of Puritanism—Baptists and Quakers. The architects of the Puritan Bible commonwealths of New England soon had to face the demands of the latter groups for religious freedom, while the leaders of southern Anglican church establishments had to deal with Puritans in their midst who might still have gone along with an establishment if it could have been their own.

A bewildering religious wilderness of competing groups was soon in the making. When Governor Dongan reported on religious conditions in the City of New York nearly three hundred years ago, in 1687, he said:

> New York has, first, a Chaplain belonging to the Fort, of the Church of England; secondly, a Dutch Calvinist; thirdly, a French Calvinist; fourthly, a Dutch Lutheran. Here bee not many of the Church of England, few Roman Catholicks; abundance of Quaker preachers, men and Women especially; Singing Quakers; Ranting Quakers; Sabbatarians; Anti-Sabbatarians; some Anabaptists; some Jews: in short, of all sorts of opinions there are some, and the most part of none at all. [10]

A half-century later when the Moravian leader Count Nicholas Von Zinzendorf arrived in Philadelphia he was amazed at the religious diversity he found there. He noted that "All shades of sectarians exist here down to open infidelity," for, as Julius Sachse observed,

> Besides the English, Swedish, and German Lutherans, and the Scotch, Dutch and German Reformed, there were Arminians, Baptists, *Vereinigte Vlaaminger en Waterlander*, Mennonites from Danzig, Arians, Socinians, Schwenkfelders, German Old Tunkers, New Tunkers, New Lights, Inspired, Sabbatarians or Seventh-Day Baptists, Hermits, Independents, and Free Thinkers. [11]

Certainly that great diversity was unusual for the time, and probably could have happened only in freedom-loving Pennsylvania, but with the passing decades other groups arrived up and down the colonies.

There were many reasons why the new nation as it broke its ties with the mother country and made good its claims to independence decided to adopt what had once been the heresy of the Christian left and moved toward religious freedom and the separation of Church and state. Economic interests, the influence of Enlightenment philosophy, the contributions of those who offered biblical and theological argu-

---

[10] As quoted by Edward T. Corwin, *A History of the Reformed Church, Dutch* (New York, 1895), 87-88.

[11] *The German Sectarians of Pennsylvania* (2 vols., Philadelphia, 1899), I, 442.

ments for freedom, the example of the four colonies which had no established churches and showed it could be done, and the sheer number of competing groups are all part of that story. With varying degrees of enthusiasm most religious bodies not only went along with but began positively to affirm the values of religious liberty. Many saw some dangers: that without the influence of the coercive power of the state vast numbers would fall away from religion entirely. As Dongan sarcastically put it, "of all sorts of opinions there are some, and the most part of none at all." But on the whole believers were willing to run the risks, trusting that by persuasion they could do better what coercion had so often failed to do. Just as the American churches in general supported the struggle for independence, although all of them were troubled by some inner divisions on the issue, so also did most of them come around to accepting belief in and practice of religious freedom. Leaders of churches which retained established status in other countries sometimes grew enthusiastic about the American experiment. John Carroll, the first American Roman Catholic bishop, spoke many times of his "earnest regard to preserve inviolate forever in our new empire the great principle of religious freedom." [12] And John Henry Hobart, an ardent High Church Episcopal bishop in the early years of the nineteenth century, is remembered among other things for his sharp criticism of most other Christian groups in this pluralistic wilderness. But when he was abroad he sang the praises of the new way of liberty, saying "It is the *religious freedom* of my country that constitutes, in my view, one of her proudest boasts." [13] This new experiment, at the time a novel departure in western civilization, was soon to exert its influence widely across the globe, and to help others to work toward a similar solution. By taking the route of freedom, it was hoped that the wilderness of sects would become a garden and not a jungle.

The American history of religious freedom has been marred by some serious lapses. Some of those who loudly praised it in the early nineteenth century were afraid things would not turn out their way. They wanted freedom for themselves, of course, but were so sure that

---

[12] Letter from Pacificus to Mr. Fenno (Publisher), 10 June, 1789, in *Gazette of the United States,* 10 June 1789, p. 65, col. 3; cited in Peter Guilday, *The Life and Times of John Carroll* (2 vols., New York, 1922), I, 368.

[13] Quoted in "Bishop Hobart's Estimate of the Church of England: A Review of *The United States of America Compared with Some European Countries, Particularly England* (New York, 1825), pages torn from a book and bound as a pamphlet in the Union Theological Seminary Library, New York, 120-21.

they were following the way of truth and goodness that when they found themselves unable to win others to their views they too easily became convinced that those who opposed them were somehow purveyors of error and evil and could be brought into line by the pressure of public opinion and the law. [14] So many of the Roman Catholic and Jewish immigrants who swarmed into the new land of liberty soon found that there were some damaging holes in the protective shield of religious freedom; only slowly did some Protestants learn that you can't have the cake of freedom if you consume it whenever you run into opposition. They found that true freedom for oneself means freedom for all, and that persuasion must remain that and not slide over into covert coercion. The lessons came hard, for it meant that persons of all national, racial, and religious backgrounds, even those for which one had antipathy, must be given full freedom. But David S. Schaff spoke for the great majority of the church people of this land when in 1912 he declared that the first mission of American Christianity "seems plainly to be to demonstrate that the complete separation of church and state, as we have practiced it, is the principle most favorable for the development of the Christian religion. The self-government of the American church stands for a voluntary return to the condition in which the church found herself placed prior to the conversion of Constantine." [15]

A number of groups seized on the opportunities provided by religious freedom to press for liberation in other areas. So after the Civil War freed Black persons poured into their own churches, the first and for long decades the only major community institutions they could call completely their own. These citadels of freedom have served as a source of strength and encouragement in a land that has so long deprived Black people of other freedoms; their churches have often served as bases for the advancement of other rights.

Another consequence of the experiment in religious freedom in this land had been its influence in other parts of the world; it was no accident that one of the principal thinkers and authors behind the historic Declaration of Religious Freedom passed by the Second Vatican Council in 1965 was an American, Fr. John Courtney Murray. Something of the American experience is blended with others in that great milestone of church history which declares "that the human person has

---

[14] I have tried to summarize this story in *A Christian America: Protestant Hopes and Historical Realities* (New York, 1971), esp. chap. ii.

[15] "The Movement and Mission of American Christianity," *The American Journal of Theology*, XVI (Jan., 1912), 63.

a right to religious freedom. This freedom means that all men are to be immune from coercion on the part of individuals or of social groups and of any human power, in such wise that in matters religious no one is to be forced to act in a manner contrary to his own beliefs." [16]

So Americans have accepted the principle of religious freedom as a proper way of dealing with the wilderness of churches and religious institutions of all kinds. This course has had some important consequences. The corollary of religious freedom, as Mead has so clearly explained in his seminal book, *The Lively Experiment,* is voluntaryism in religion. [17] With the coming of freedom and the separation of church and state, each religious group has been on its own, dependent on its own inner resources for survival and growth. One result of this has been to intensify that activism of religion in America to which attention has already been called. But it has also served to bring out some other qualities, mentioned by David Schaff in his discussion of the churches as "sincerity in Christian profession, the wide participation of the laity in Christian activities, and a ministry choosing its vocation from spiritual motives." [18]

The wilderness of sects has also been faced by various movements which have sought to bring about cooperation and a deeper understanding among the variety of religious groups. To cite just a few examples: the Plan of Union of 1801, the Evangelical Alliance, the healing of divisions within denominational families, the Federal and National Councils of Churches, one major merger across denominational lines, the increasing of Eastern Orthodox and Roman Catholics in ecumenical life, and the broadening of interfaith dialogue to include groups of many backgrounds. The great diversity of American religious life continues, but much of the bitterness and isolation of past periods has been significantly qualified.

The Wilderness of War

Periodically, American religious institutions have been plunged into the wilderness of war. Especially in the times of the Revolutionary, the Civil, and the Vietnam wars, churches and synagogues have had to face agonizing decisions in a crisis. In all wars, the problems of how to deal with pacifist minorities have arisen. [19] But the most

---

[16] Walter M. Abbott, S.J. (ed.), *The Documents of Vatican II* (N.Y., 1966), 678-79.

[17] See esp. p. 113.

[18] *Loc. cit.,* 65.

[19] See, e.g., Peter Brock, *Pacifism in the United States from the Colonial Era to the First World War* (Princeton, 1968).

terrible of all the wildernesses of war was that of the strife between sections over slavery that led to the bitterness of civil war.

Today it seems so unthinkable that a country which thought of itself in religious terms had to undergo a frightful war before its slaves might be emancipated, that we have to go over again and again the story of how strong those sectional and economic interests were which held most religious institutions within the dominant sentiments of their localities. Happily there are those records of valor, all too rare, when persons went against prevailing interests to oppose slavery, often at the cost of mob action and banishment. Years ago Clement Eaton wrote that "from the Southern ministry came a larger portion of outspoken critics of slavery than from any other professional group. Such a group of insurgents, isolated though they were, indicates that perhaps the strongest force in producing free lances was moral conviction." [20] Many Black Christians played important roles in abolitionism and in the famous underground railroad to freedom, drawing on resources of faith in their courageous actions. Some outstanding advocates of the women's rights movement of that period identified themselves with abolitionism.

Though there were those persons who drew on their religious principles to oppose the evil of their time, on the whole the behavior of many religious institutions during the ordeal of sectional strife and division adds up to an unpleasant tale. It is one that must not be forgotten, for it describes in stark terms the temptations into which churches and synagogues can fall when they depend too much on public opinion and not enough on their own deeper commitments to faith and righteousness. The active pro-slavery stance of many southern churches, the long compromising and temporizing of many northern churches before they finally swung late to accepting emancipation, the continuing stain of racial prejudice even in antislavery circles—these we must remember, not so much to condemn those who were actors in that bitter contest but to have a mirror to hold up to the religious institutions of our time.

How do these bodies see themselves in today's struggles for freedom, as moral leaders or followers? In facing the moral crises of our own time do they think first of the principles they profess or of the expectations an environing culture places upon them? When the war spirit sweeps across the land, can they deal creatively with the minorities

---

[20] *Freedom of Thought in the Old South* (Durham, 1940), 271.

who may refuse to fight for conscience's sake? What resources can
they bring to try to avoid that "next" war which could turn the land
into wilderness again—a terrible burned-out wilderness.

An Urban Wilderness

Americans tamed the physical wilderness they found when they
arrived as immigrants, but by the late nineteenth century they found
themselves faced with a sprawling and burgeoning wilderness which
remains untamed, the modern metropolis. As Sam Bass Warner puts it
in a book he boldly entitles *The Urban Wilderness,* Americans "live
in one of the world's most urbanized countries as if it were a wilderness
in both time and space." His book describes our collective inability to
resolve the tension between the goals of open competition, community,
and innovation, and explains how our "unwillingness to move beyond
the confines of private land ownership, have produced today's disordered, inhumane, and restricted city." [21] American religionists generally have had a hard time coming to terms with the urban setting that
has come to dominate the nation. In the late nineteenth and early twentieth centuries a romanticized rural nostalgia long persisted in religious life; conventional wisdom of the time often said "God made the
country, man made the city." In his famous book of ninety years ago,
Our Country, Josiah Strong described the seven perils facing America,
picturing the city as the seventh peril and the epitome of all the others. [22]
At about the same time John Lancaster Spalding, Catholic Bishop of
Peoria, contrasted the country and the city, showing how vastly better
it was to live in the rural rather than the urban scene. He concluded
by saying, "If those I love were rich I should not wish them to live
in the city; and if they were poor, and made it their dwelling-place,
I should despair of them." [23] The bishops of the Methodist Episcopal
Church at the dawn of the present century recognized the American
city as "a conglomerate of all races, nations, tongues, faiths, customs
and political ideas," and labelled it "the menace of the American State
and Church." [24]

---

[21] *The Urban Wilderness: A History of the American City* (New York,
1972), 4, 15.
[22] *Our Country: Its Possible Future and Its Present Crisis* (New York,
1885), esp. chap. x.
[23] As quoted in Robert D. Cross (ed.), *The Church and the City, 1865-1910*
(Indianapolis, 1967), 28.
[24] David S. Monroe, (ed.), *Journal of the General Conference of the Methodist
Episcopal Church held in Chicago 1900,* 63-64.

Though attitudes have changed but slowly, the religious forces of America in the twentieth century generally came to see the urban scene with all its complexities, mysteries and dangers as the new frontier for faith, for it is there that people are concentrated. The immigrants of the colonial period often regarded the physical frontiers they faced as places of mystery, complexity, and danger. Though in their haste and determination they made mistakes, some costly, yet they did face courageously the reality before them. Many of the twentieth century Christian and Jewish pioneers in the urban wilderness have struggled with their new tasks of making faith vital in seemingly impossible settings; the other side of the coin has been the flight of so many congregations to more viable settings. Leaders of local and national missions in both denominational and ecumenical contexts have learned a lot about faith and the city in recent decades; there is a wealth of information and insight available. What is needed now is the imagination to see that the present wilderness situation is far greater in magnitude than those faced by any previous generation. To deal with it, the religious forces will need both courage and a willingness to cooperate with many others.

A Wilderness of Conflicting Ideas

The churches and synagogues have passed through another wilderness in their journey across American history. The whole series of intellectual revolutions that have swept over the modern world have created a tangled wilderness of conflicting ideas and perspectives about the nature of the universe in which we live, and about the nature of those of us who live in it. These developments, many of them spectacular, could not help but impinge on the thought of religious persons and institutions, with their historic concerns for trying to understand ultimate realities and for seeking to probe the mysteries of human nature and destiny. In most forms of religion in America there is a broad spectrum covering those who have accepted many of the insights into reality suggested by modern science and philosophy, those who tend to reject many of them, and those representing very broad ranges of opinion strung out in between. One could point to Reform, Orthodox, and Conservative Judaism for example, but here I want to focus on the way this wilderness of conflicting ideas has affected Christian thought.

Through the centuries leaders of Christian thought have struggled with the necessities of attempting to express the faith in the terms of dominant intellectual frames of reference in order that it could be communicated to the mind of particular periods. So Christian faith has been stated in terms of (for example) Platonism, Aristotelianism, the Enlightenment, Romanticism, Idealism, Pragmatism, Naturalism, Realism, Existentialism, and Processism. Most of those who have labored at these theological tasks have realized that Christian faith can never be fully expressed in such intellectual syntheses. They have found, however, that without the continual effort to understand and interpret the faith by using available patterns of thought and methods of analysis, Christian insights will not be relevantly illumined for those whose minds are informed to greater or less degree by the dominant intellectual scientific and philosophical patterns of their time. The various efforts to explain faith from the perspective of differing intellectual traditions has also often illumined in fresh ways facets of the gospel itself in ways that had not previously been so clearly seen. Part of the role of the churches is to engage in these continuing theological tasks. But they become very difficult and controversial in a time of intellectual revolutions, and the image of a wilderness becomes very appropriate.

The record of the adventures of the churches in this wilderness of ideas is a quite mixed one. The churches were originally immigrant churches and the dominant thought patterns of European theology long persisted through much of their history and into the present, so much so that it is sometimes hard for people schooled in that tradition to see other theological patterns, such as those from Asia, Africa, or the Americas, as requiring equally serious attention. Then, the facing of the physical and urban wildernesses has absorbed much of the attention and energy of the churches; the tasks set before them were so formidable and insistent that they seemed to demand priority and evoked the characteristic activistic style of so much of American Christianity. America has not produced many great theologians; the lists of the native giants are short: the names of Jonathan Edwards, Horace Bushnell, Walter Rauschenbusch, the Niebuhrs and Martin Luther King would appear on many of them. Of the first of these, Jonathan Edwards, eighteenth-century Congregational pastor, missionary to the Indians and briefly college president, Perry Miller once wrote,

> He is the last great American, perhaps the last European, for whom there could be no warfare between religion and science, or between ethics and nature. He was incapable of accepting Christianity and physics on separate premises. His mind was so constituted—call it courage or call it naiveté—that he went directly to the issues of his age, defined them, and asserted the historical Protestant doctrine in full cognizance of the latest disclosures in both psychology and natural science. [25]

[25] *Jonathan Edwards* (Cleveland, 1959), 72.

It may be coincidence, but I suspect it is more symbolic of a deeper problem of American Christian life that this scholarly pastor was dismissed from his Northampton church after more than two decades of service.

It *has* been hard for American churches fully to understand and accept the importance of the ongoing intellectual and theological tasks. Mead has forcefully called attention to the way Protestant thought failed to deal creatively enough with the tension between Pietistic and Enlightenment ways of interpreting faith in the eighteenth and early nineteenth centuries. While calling religious freedom American religions' outstanding accomplishment, he finds theological structure to be its outstanding failure, and has deplored the "prevalence of a fuzzy and amorphous intellectual structure in the religious groups." [26] Hence the churches were ill-prepared to deal with the onslaught of the intellectual revolutions that so influenced American thought in the period following the Civil War. The general impact of scientific and evolutionary thought and the particular pressures of critical and historical analyses of the Bible and tradition brought about serious tensions in the world of religion. So opened the complex rift in many congregations and denominations between liberal and conservative perspectives. It is easy to draw an oversimplified picture here; on each side of the rift were various strands of thought, and there have been various moderating forces throughout the past stormy one hundred years of theological history. Yet the differences have been real and persistent. Henry Ward Beecher, eloquent and controversial pastor of Brooklyn's Plymouth Church in the later nineteenth century, could welcome the theory of evolution as a great truth which was bringing to "religious truth as set forth in the life and teachings of Jesus a new and powerful aid, fully in line with other marked developments of God's providence"; more than thirty years later William Jennings Bryan, lay statesman, could exclaim that "The evolutionary hypothesis is the only thing that has seriously menaced religion since the birth of Christ; and it menaces all other religions as well..." [27] Periodically the deeper tension has exploded in some dramatic polarizations, as in the Briggs case of the 1890's, in the suppression of Catholic modernism a decade later, and especially in the bitter Fundamentalist/Modernist controversies within Protestantism in the 1920's. That these polariza-

---

[26] *The Lively Experiment*, 141, cf. p. 15.
[27] Beecher, *Evolution and Religion* (Boston, [1886]), preface; Bryan as cited in Willard B. Gatewood, Jr. (ed.), *Controversy in the Twenties: Fundamentalism, Modernism, and Evolution* (Nashville, 1969), 137.

tions could become so sharp and produce such intense bitterness within
denominational families suggests some serious limitations in the churches' way of dealing with intellectual issues.

The theological record shows significant strengths as well as limitations, however. There have been American theologians of world
renown, and there have been creative theological movements which have
continuing influence. Sydney E. Ahlstrom has called attention to and
provided impressive documentation for what he has called "a sustained
theological achievement—an achievement that is, in fact, made all
the more remarkable by the immense obstacles that were raised up for
a new nation of immigrants and their descendants who migrated westward to tame and people a continent." [28]

Today we live in a time when the intellectual revolutions in almost
every field of thought continue to challenge, to inform, to stimulate
and to disrupt. Familiar opinions about the universe and its complexities are under almost constant revision; conventional wisdom
about human life and morals is almost daily challenged. To be sure,
humans do not live by intellect alone, and faith is fed by the many
springs of emotion and intuition as well as by the mind. But there
is much unfinished business here for people of faith; there are both
impressive resources and pressing questions to be faced if religious
institutions are to deal with the wilderness of conflicting ideas in
any way comparable to the achievement of forebears in facing the
physical wilderness.

*

It has been a difficult journey through various wildernesses that
religious peoples and their institutions have taken across nearly four
centuries of history in this land. Mistakes have been made and wrong
turns taken. Some of the achievements that looked good at the time
have later shown serious limitations. Yet churches, synagogues, and
religious associations of many kinds have faithfully tried to communicate their religious visions and resources even as they themselves failed to follow their own insights fully. They brought inspiration, direction, guidance, and comfort to millions, have entrusted
to this generation a network of congregations, communions, and organizations rich in potential. What this generation does or fails to do
with its rich and varied religious inheritance may have a lot to do
with the direction of our journey into the wilderness experiences the
future may have in store for us.

---

[28] (Ed.), *Theology in America: The Major Protestant Voices from Puritanism
to Neo-Orthodoxy* (Indianapolis, 1967), 12.

ANNUIT COEPTIS: AMERICA AS THE ELECT NATION

The Rise and Decline of a Patriotic Tradition

SYDNEY E. AHLSTROM
Yale University

Historical events, upon close analysis, almost always lose their simplicity and explode into multiplicity. A street murder in the headlines becomes a macabre conspiracy. A third-rate burglary exposes a complex network of political malfeasance that brings a national administration to its fall. But the inverse is also true. The slow transformation of a civilization, viewed from a great distance, becomes a single event. Classical civilization "declines" for a millennium and a half— from Caesar's coup d'état to the Ottoman conquest of Constantinople— but historians yet speak of the Fall of Rome. In the same manner the four-hundred-year story of an ideological tradition can be apprehended as a unitary event. It is not only from a divine perspective that a thousand years are as the twinkling of an eye. In any event it is in this spirit that a quadricentennial view of this nation's present crisis is here being undertaken. The scope may seem vast; yet we benefit from the telling of the whole story. Even though the denouement lies beyond us, historical reflection may lead us to valuable resources within the tradition itself. [1]

Among the leading thinkers of the revolutionary generation it was probably John Adams who took the most seriously historical stance. In 1818, long after his retirement from political life, he asked himself in a thoughtful letter to Hezikiah Niles, "What do we mean by the American Revolution?" He then quickly dismissed the notion that it was the War and went on almost in the manner of modern phenomenologists: "The Revolution [he said] was in the minds and hearts of the people. It was a change in their religious sentiments, of their duties and

---

[1] On my title see note 26. National ideologies and the structures that support them are a fundamental concern of the historian of religion; and for the historian of the American nation the ideological tradition is of especially explicit and acute importance. My own long-term interest in these matters was made more specific by many lectures delivered on diverse aspects of American history in connection with observances of the American Bicentenary. I hope in the near future to enlarge upon and more fully document the many broad generalizations on the American experience which I have made in these pages.

obligations. This radical change in the principles, opinions, sentiments, and affections of the people was the real Revolution." Nor was this the first time that Adams had pondered the meaning of America's spiritual transformation. In his most extended published exposition of the fundamental issues he condemned the anti-democratic implications of the canon and the feudal law, which to his mind still held English society in relative bondage. He spoke of the "execrable race of the Stuarts" [King James I and King Charles I] and pointed to the Puritan Revolution as the time when "the struggle between the people and the confederacy of temporal and spiritual tyranny became formidable, violent, and bloody." It was this great struggle, he said, that peopled America. And "after their arrival here they began their settlement and formed their plan, both of ecclesiastical and civil government, in direct opposition to the canon and the feudal systems." [2]

And, of course, Adams was right in his assertion that this "land of the pilgrims' pride" was grounded on Puritan conviction. It might be said, moreover, that one of the great historiographic revisions of the last decade or two has tended to confirm John Adams' judgment and render obsolescent Herbert Butterfield's animadversions on the so-called "Whig Interpretation" of history. [3]

Four hundred years ago, to be sure, the vast land that is now the United States—from Cape Cod Bay to Drake's Bay—was, from the perspective of Western Europe, no more than a vision—or a fantasy. But in Elizabethan times it began to became the object of concrete intentions which grew strong and definite as Spain's gains in the south and her neglect of the north came to be recognized. Then in 1607 the first enduring colony was planted by the Virginia Company. This and other momentous Anglo-American events of the seventeenth century will remain incomprehensible, however, if we do not consider a revolution in the Christian Church which had begun to be realized under Elizabeth's relatively lenient rule. The revolution referred to was at the outset chiefly a matter of theology and piety, and the term Puritanism

---

[2] Adrienne Koch and William Peden, eds., *The Selected Writings of John and Quincy Adams* (New York, 1946), 203-05; 11-15.

[3] I refer to that view of post-reformation history which viewed the rise of Protestantism, democracy, and capitalism in the English-speaking world as a succession of Good Things. It was best delineated by Herbert Butterfield in *The Whig Interpretation of History* (London, 1931). One may agree with his criticism of over-confident value judgments but yet support the general line of historical interpretation which explains the rise of modern bourgeois civilization.

is usually applied to it. 4 But because this radical movement was in fact an extension or extrapolation of that Reformed tradition so often linked with John Calvin's name, we have no recourse but to confront the social implications of that biblical revival which occupied so central a place in the Reformation as a whole. Indeed we must see the truth of Jacob J. Finkelstein's assertion that the Word of God which Moses transmitted at Sinai contains the "most revolutionary sentence in the Bible: 'You are a kingdom of priests, and a holy nation.' " (Exodus 19:6). 5 It is Israel's radical sense of peoplehood, its stern monotheism, and its conviction that earthly reality is an inexorable linear movement from Creation to the messianic kingdom, that gives Christianity its fundamental structure and which conveys what is most distinctly "western" to Western civilization. 6 What made this Judaic impulse especially powerful was the explicit claim of the Christian Church to *be* the New Israel: "Ye also as lively stones are built up a spiritual house, an holy priesthood . . . ye are a chosen generation, a royal priesthood, a holy nation." (I Peter 2:1-10).

At the time of this writing Christians were, of course, a "pilgrim people," harrassed and persecuted. Even among educated Romans they were not quite clearly distinguished from observant Jews. But with a rapidity that was often considered a special sign of God's favor, the church converted the empire. In the early fourth century the Emperor Constantine himself had to capitulate if he wished to rule. In another century, under Theodosius, the old Roman temples would be forcibly closed and Christianity made the empire's official religion.

One great entailment of the Church's evangelistic triumph was its assimilation or appropriation of many fundamental motifs of Classical philosophy (notably the Platonic and Stoic) and various forms of pagan religion (notably mytic and gnostic forms of otherworldliness). These

---

4 Over against the views of Charles and Katherine George in *The Protestant Mind of the English Reformation, 1570-1640* (Princeton, 1961) and many others, one must eschew the notion that Puritanism was a mere X in the algebra of abuse. It was a discrete and revolutionary religious movement whose appearance and growth had large, long-term effects on the subjective and social life of Western civilization.

5 See Jacob J. Finkelstein, "The Goring Ox: Some Historical Perspectives," *Temple Law Quarterly* 46 (1973), 253. Quoted further in my "Religion, Revolution and the Rise of Modern Nationalism: Reflections on the American Experience," *Church History* 44 (1975), 497. The influence on western thought of Israel's linkage of faith, religious cult, and national covenant is incalculable.

6 The vast continuing impact of the Hebrew Scriptures derives especially from the way many fundamental biblical motifs remain essential to Christianity, Islam, and the Marxist impulse.

otherworldly attitudes, in turn, were carried over into the great medieval millennium which followed. Accompanying them was a strong syncretistic tendency which facilitated the conversion of new peoples to the faith, but which also conduced to a loss of the characteristically Hebraic aspects of the Christian message. Roman law meanwhile put its mark on ecclesiastical polity. Perhaps most sharply differentiating the medieval Church from the church of the martyrs was its tendency to make the Christian Church co-terminus with the civilized world and to insist that everyone be an orthodox church member—even on pain of death. [7]

Then in the sixteenth century came those cataclysmic events that shattered the idea of Catholic universalism. In the name of a return to the Bible the Reformers repudiated many major elements of medieval religious practice. Christians now had to face many stark religious alternatives. Complicating this process, moreover, was an awakening of national feeling which in many quarters led various political entities to be imbued with a sense of holy peoplehood, especially among those who committed themselves to the Reformed tradition. This, in turn, was due to the extraordinary thoroughness with which Zwingli, Calvin, and others repudiated the institutional structures of Catholicism as well as the worship-forms, religious attitudes and life styles that had animated the medieval world. Despite Calvin's assurances to Francis I in his preface to his *Institutes of the Christian Religion* (1536), even the idea of sacral kingship was profoundly threatened by a movement which in its conviction of God's absolute sovereignty sought to banish magic and superstition from religion. [8]

Yet all that was torn down had to be replaced according to God's specific provision as set forth in Holy Scripture. And on the Continent this Reformed program of theological and ecclesiastical reconstruction

---

[7] The extirpation of the Albigensian Cathari is one signal example among many. This passion for orthodoxy, of course, continued in the Protestant churches, as, indeed, also in the communist movement.

[8] Max Weber spoke long ago of "that great historic process in the development of religion, the elimination of magic from the world." He saw the Reformation as vital to this process, the Reformed more so than the Lutheran, and the Puritans most of all. "The genuine Puritan even rejected all signs of religious ceremony at the grave...in order that no superstition, no trust in the effects of magical and sacramental forces should creep in." *The Protestant Ethic and the Spirit of Capitalism* (London, 1930), 105. The first German edition appeared in 1905. When this inner revolution is coupled with the vast institutional, religious, and behavioral transformations required by Reformed theology, the modern imagination is challenged to conceive an equivalent in contemporary terms that would be equally revolutionary.

was accomplished with a considerable degree of consensus in those lands where "Calvinistic" doctrines were accepted. It is of vast significance for the future of America, however, that in England this grand enterprise went awry—for a variety of important reasons. The primary fact may be that King Henry VIII severed his highly unified kingdom from Rome, despoiled the monasteries, and made himself supreme head of the national church while yet still maintaining that England was an essentially Catholic land. By the time of his death in 1547, however, the Protestant movement had become so strong that under Edward VI both the Book of Common Prayer and the Forty-Two Articles of Religion had explicitly aligned England with the Reformed cause. The chief leaders of this Edwardian reformation were burned or forced into exile during Queen Mary's brief and bloody reign (1553-58); but with the accession of Elizabeth in 1558 the tide turned again—and this time with decisive effect.

Now with hostility to Rome at a new peak of intensity the exiles returned, while John Foxe's *Book of Martyrs* fired the zeal of Protestants with vivid pictures of the Marian horrors and assigned to England the responsibilities of an Elect Nation. [9] Puritanism then took shape as an answer to that great summons, with the Bible as never before shaping both piety and polity. Attacks on popish vestments and ceremonies came first; followed soon after by radical "presbyterian" demands for thorough restructuring of the church, including the abandonment of episcopacy itself. Then emerging more gradually and effectively was a far more profound and outwardly more benign and gradualist impulse which made matters of faith and morals the prime consideration, and it was this more distinctly spiritual form of the Puritan movement that proved ultimately to be most subversive.

Its unmistakable leader was the Cambridge theologian William Perkins, whose thoughts on the inner implications of Reformed theology gradually produced a revolution in Christendom, and a tradition which finally would become a counter-cultural movement of immense force. [10]

---

[9] Foxe's book was first published in 1559 at Basle in Latin; but in that same year he returned to England where an English edition was published in 1563, after which a succession of revised editions appeared, and continued so to do long after his death, as Dissenters and Methodists turned it to their purposes. See William Haller, *The Elect Nation: The Meaning and Relevance of Foxe's Book of Martyrs* (New York, 1963).

[10] Perkins (1558-1602) was by no means alone in shaping this new tradition; William Ames (1576-1633) with his *Marrow of Sacred Divinity* (Latin, 1623; English, 1638) provided a systematic account, and a long line of distinguished pastor-theologians deepened and extended the movement: Laurence Chaderton,

Central to this new piety was the problem of assurance: If God's sovereign will determines all that happens in this world and the next, and if salvation itself is according to God's will, how do Christians know if they have received God's effectual call? The answer to this question, which arose over and over again in a minister's pastoral care, was that the perception of faith came through an inward experience of God's redeeming grace—and not a mere profession of faith or a godly walk, or regular attendance on the ordinances of the church. In and around this soul-searching a whole new form of Christian piety arose, and with it, by an inexorable logic, there emerged also a new mark of the saint—and a new and revolutionary way of purifying the church. A subjective warrant—a conversion experience—entered into Christian history as a decisive and normative aspect of personal and ecclesiastical affairs.

In the great debates at Cambridge during the 1590's the historian may now discern what the controversialists of that day could not: namely, that the Episcopal and Puritan parties were taking positions which were irreconcilable. From the Puritan point of view the old medieval notion of baptizing everyone into the church and inviting all to the Lord's Supper became increasingly unacceptable. There then followed a great winnowing of the spirits that rapidly added numbers to the Puritan party. The result of this process during the turbulent reigns of James I and Charles I was a gradual separation of constituencies and the emergence of a broad and powerful Puritan movement, marked by a stern but this-worldly asceticism. Intrinsic to this process, moreover, was the way in which its individualistic emphases in matters of religion gradually permeated the social, economic and political realms as well. The conversion experience, in other words, brought about a reordering of values and hence of personal comportment. [11]

Richard Sibbes, John Cotton, William Preston and many others. See David D. Hall, *The Faithful Shepherd :A History of the New England Ministry in the Seventeenth Century* (Chapel Hill, N.C., 1972).

[11] Max Weber's many works stimulated much of the succeeding scholarship on this process. More recently Christopher Hill has done likewise. Especially valuable in itself and for its bibliographical commentary is David Little, *Religion, Order and Law* (New York, 1969). My own emphasis is placed on the conversion experience and on the way in which attitudes, values, and behavior are reoriented—with renewed determination. In this regard three great commonwealth founders are especially interesting: John Winthrop, William Penn, and above all Oliver Cromwell. Kenneth Shipps in a recent article delineates three types of Puritans according to their dominant interests: political, ecclesiastical, and ethical. He sheds valuable light on the first but does not sufficiently stress how the other two groups generate social and political concerns. *Church History* 45 (1976), 196-205.

When James I became king in 1603 he recognized the danger to his throne and warned active dissidents that they would be harried out of the land: no bishop, no king. During his reign, a policy of compromise, corruption and connivance staved off the almost inevitable confrontation and allowed Puritanism to grow in numbers and militancy. It was James' inadroit son, Charles I (1625-1649) who had to face a Parliament that would no longer tolerate arbitrary rule and popish policies. Then with the summoning of the "long" Parliament in 1640, events that expose the meaning and implications of Puritanism began to unfold with the inexorability of a Greek tragedy.

Oliver Cromwell, who more than any other would lead this revolution, had become sure of God's effectual call only two years before. And probably no conversion portended more for England's and America's future. He wrote of this great turning point in his life to his cousin in 1638, when he was 28 years old and the father of five children:

> Blessed be [God's] name for shining on so dark a heart as mine. You know what my manner of life has been. Oh, I lived in and loved darkness and hated the light.... Yet God had mercy on me. Oh, the riches of his mercy. Praise Him for me, pray for me, that He who hath begun a good work would perfect it to the day of Christ. [12]

With Parliment assuming control, the Earl of Strafford was executed in 1641. In 1642 at Nottingham, King Charles raised his standards. In 1643 the Westminster Assembly was convened with instructions to prepare a confession of faith, catechisms, and a directory of worship for the realm. In 1644 and 1645 came those two decisive victories of Cromwell's New Model Army, at Marston Moor and at Naseby. In 1645 Archbishop Laud was executed. In the following year episcopacy was abolished. Finally in December 1648 came Colonel Pride's purge of Parliament's remaining moderates—and then by a direct sequence of events, the ultimate act, the execution of King Charles in January, followed by the abolition of the House of Lords and the abrogation of monarchy. Religious freedom was declared amid many claims for further political and social reforms. All told, it was an awesome course of events. And in reviewing the Puritan Revolution as a whole we must concur with Antonia Fraser's judgment that "It is at least possible to claim Cromwell as the greatest Englishman." [13]

The revolution, of course, did not in the immediate sense issue in permanent reform. In 1658 Cromwell died, and within two years

---

[12] See Maurice P. Ashley, *Oliver Cromwell and His World* (New York, 1972), 13.
[13] Antonia Fraser, *Oliver Cromwell the Lord Protector* (New York, 1974), xiii.

Charles II was crowned. A period of retributive oppression followed, most notably on St. Bartholomew's day in 1662 when over 2,000 of England's beneficed clergy were ejected from the Church for their Puritanism. Yet after the Restoration of 1660 neither Charles II nor his brother James II could rule effectively, even with large subsidies from France; and in 1688-89, with the Catholic issue again a provocation, came the Glorious Revolution. James fled to France and now Parliament asserted *its* authority by making William of Orange King and his Stuart wife Queen. The word "Glorious" as a description of this event has been criticized—possibly because there was so little bloodshed—but it is surely one of the most decisive events in British constitutional history, even though it left England's social structure intact and kept dissenters from the established religion in demeaning circumstances. Since American colonials had likewise felt the force of James II's arbitrary rule, the Glorious Revolution also erupted there. And this fact provides an occasion for turning our attention to the American phase of the Puritan Revolution.

*

One of the cliches of history has it that the "free aire" of America made democrats out of all who came. But it is false. Columbus, Cortez, and Pizzaro did not bring freedom to New Spain, nor did Champlain and Count Frontenac to New France. There is considerable truth, on the other hand, in the contention that the "American Revolution" (as distinguished from the War for Independence) began with the earliest English settlements in America. And the basic reason is that most of these early settlers and nearly all of their leaders were part of that great English constituency which had tended toward the Puritan's cause during the great winnowing provoked by the Stuart kings. Now in America the various religious, social, economic, and political implications of their piety and their anti-popery were being worked out in mind and in deed.

Virginia, to be sure, is a considerable exception in that the settlers recruited by the Company in London sought easy wealth, not work. Slavery and the plantation system soon led, in the tidewater region at least, to a social order of a more paternalistic caste than was to obtain in the middle and northern colonies. [14] There is thus a certain justice

---

14 It is hard to comprehend how European Christendom, having ended Roman slavery, could renew the practice of capturing and buying Black Africans and then sell them into slavery, but they did—in the Spanish and Portuguese em-

in the way that Americans in their search for national origins have shown a sentimental preference for the "Pilgrims" who signed the Mayflower Compact in 1620. The classic statement of the form of intentionality which underlay the great swarming of the Puritans, however, is the "Model of Christian Charity" which Governor John Winthrop delivered in 1630 while yet aboard the *Arbella*. In it we see not only the coordination of civil and religious concern that has conditioned all later phases of American history but also his deep conviction that the Model being projected had a distinct place in God's plan for the redemption of the world.

> We shall find that the God of Israel is among us, when ten of us shall be able to resist a thousand of our enemies, when He shall make us a praise and glory that men shall say of succeeding generations: "The Lord make it like that of New England." For we must consider that we shall be as a city upon a hill, the eyes of all people are upon us. So that if we shall deal falsely with our God in this work we have undertaken, and so cause Him to withdraw his present help from us, we shall be made a story and a byword through[out] the world. [15]

The piety of those who landed in New England was a mature development of that which Perkins and, somewhat later, William Ames had expounded in pulpit and treatise; and among the emigre pastors in their midst were at least a dozen major Puritan spokesmen of this tradition. In their churches the ideal of congregations of "visible saints" was sought and in the Cambridge Platform of 1648 was made official. In all of this great fervor prevailed, and many were convinced that they were in fact living out a final chapter of *Heilsgeschichte*, fulfilling God's plan for the later days.

As the years and decades went by, the great migration to America continued. New colonies were founded, from Maine to South Carolina, with the last great venture in Puritan statecraft being William Penn's "Holy Experiment" in Pennsylvania—a vast and benignly governed asylum which rapidly became a populous paradigm of future forms of

---

pires first, and then in the English. Ancient assumptions on social hierarchicalism prevailed. The origins of American slavery are best described by Edmund S. Morgan, *American Slavery, American Freedom: The Ordeal of Colonial Virginia* (New York, 1975). See also, Lester B. Scherer, *Slavery and the Churches in Early America* (Grand Rapids, 1975). The basically Puritan caste of the Virginia Company leadership was manifest in many of their acts, including the ordering of a legislative assembly in 1619. But in 1623 the charter was vacated and Virginia became a royal colony and increasingly paternalistic.

[15] "Christian Charity, A Model Hereof," quoted from the final portion. Alden T. Vaughan, ed., *The Puritan Tradition in America* (New York, 1972), 139-46. The conditional nature of the covenant should be noted.

American pluralism. [16] Even the most daring hopes of these early
founders were surpassed. Within this vast diaspora, moreover, one
could find almost the full spectrum of European belief, even in the
Bay Colony itself and in supposedly Anglican Virginia. Baptists and
Quakers and Presbyterians were almost everywhere, though perhaps
especially in Pennsylvania and the Jerseys. Various radical groups
persisted in Rhode Island and Pennsylvania, but there were also rigid
Puritans in East Jersey, Dutch Reformed in New York, and Catholics
in Maryland—though after 1649, more Puritans than Catholics. By the
century's end religious freedom had become a practical reality in most
areas. Yet the overwhelming religious disposition of these diverse
peoples was fiercely anti-Catholic, Reformed and broadly Puritan;
memories of coercion and oppression were vivid; antipathy for arbitrary powers in state and church were correspondingly strong. Individualism as a general point of view prevailed.

What was in fact coming into existence in these many straggling
settlements was a form of social existence such as the world had never
seen. People were buying farms, setting up in trade, founding churches
and defining their life styles more or less as they pleased. Nearly
everywhere, moreover, they were becoming involved in politics both at
the local and commonwealth levels. Perhaps most important of all they
were acquiring property! Indeed a new kind of social and economic
order was gradually emerging. Though the hideous anomaly of chattel
slavery was firmly established in its midst, a basically capitalist civilization was taking shape within a British imperial context that almost
guaranteed the emergence of political conflict and a renewal of Crom-
wellianism.

The Glorious Revolution in America was the first major manifestation. While the arbitrary rule of James II was being overthrown in
England there were disturbances in every American colony—most
seriously in New England and Maryland—and when it was all over
Americans (they can be called that by then) were intensely aware
of the need for better guarantees of their cherished liberties than they
then possessed.

This quest was interrupted, however, by the great "French and
Indian" Wars that King William to a considerable degree provoked.
Yet even this "Seventy Years War" in many ways conduced to inter-
colonial solidarity against a common Catholic threat. France, Spain,

---

[16] Pennsylvania's rapid expansion also illustrated how immigration policy
(first English, later American) conditioned the course of American Indian policy.

and more remotely Austria were beheld as minions of the anti-Christ. Even more momentous was the emergence during these years of what Nathan Orr Hatch has called "civil millennialism," which is to say the transformation of traditional views of the coming Kingdom of God from the purely religious realm to the political realm. [17] Very interesting, moreover, is the way in which the rhetoric of execration heaped upon Catholic rulers and their oppressive institutions was creating a point of view that after 1765 would be turned against King George III and England's oppressive colonial rule. On these more secular premises Protestants of all sorts could agree. The rationalistic Unitarian Jonathan Mayhew could gain widespread approbation when he celebrated the centennial of the execution of Charles I.

Giving much additional potency to the notion of America's providential destiny was that "Great and General Revival" which swept through the colonies from Georgia to New Hampshire between 1734 and 1745. Amidst the tumults of this vast rejuvenation of colonial piety a fervent form of millennial expectation arose. Jonathan Edwards himself proclaimed most clearly of all that there was both scriptural and rational warrant for believing that the Great Awakening was itself a sign that the Kingdom of God was beginning in the very events then being experienced—not only the spiritual upheaval, but even the military events. If Jonathan Edwards had lived one more year and beheld General Wolfe's great victory at Quebec in 1759 or had seen New France *and* the Floridas as well as India transferred to Protestant hands in 1763, he would have interpreted it as the greatest blow to the Anti-Christ since the Reformation itself! [18]

Richard Bushman is not exaggerating when he describes the Great Awakening as a huge earthquake which changed the entire colonial landscape. And he rightly warns us not to compare that revival with one of Billy Graham's genteel affairs—but rather with urban riots, the student movement of the 60's and the great anti-War demonstrations rolled into one. [19] "The New Lights," declared Ezra Stiles, "are

---

[17] "The Origins of Civil Millennialism in America: New England Clergymen, War with France, and the Revolution," *William & Mary Quarterly* 31 (1974), 407-30. See also his book, *The Sacred Cause of Liberty* (New Haven, 1977); and also, James Davidson, *The Logic of Millennial Thought* (New Haven, 1977).

[18] On Edwards' millennial expectations see Clarence C. Goen, ed., *The Works of Jonathan Edwards: The Great Awakening* (New Haven, 1973), 353-58. Edwards frequently discerned "signs of the times" in political and military events, even very minor ones. See Stephen Stein, ed., *The Apocalyptic Writings,* same edition, vol. 5 (1977).

[19] Richard L. Bushman, *From Puritan to Yankee: Character and the Social*

subversive of peace, discipline, and government." After 1745 the standing order in New England had in effect been overturned. Baptists and Separatists were forming new churches regardless of the laws of New England and Virginia. American evangelicals had discovered their *national* solidarity and power. New attitudes toward the conversion of slaves had even brought the anti-slavery movement into the distant view; and a new destiny for America was being proclaimed.

Given all of these American developments historians are seeing more clearly than ever before that by the 1730's or even more surely by the 1740's nearly every major claim to be made by the Founding Fathers of 1776 had already become a matter of practical principle in the various colonies. So strong were these convictions, moreover, that even before the great Treaty of Paris of 1763 had been signed, the Revolutionary epoch had begun. James Otis was already taking his radical libertarian stand. [20]

There is no need to rehearse the familiar course of events that unfolded between the Stamp Act riots and the battles at Concord Bridge and Bunker Hill. Like the Puritan Revolution of the 1640's it moved inexorably toward its now over-familiar denouement and was everywhere apprehended, by deists and Puritans alike, as a providential work of God.

We must recognize, however, that the "American Revolution" was not in the strict sense a revolution in America. By and large the persons, families, and classes who were in power remained in power. There was no great social overturning—except for the loyalist who fled the country. (As for those who stayed or returned, nearly all were able to rehabilitate their reputations and resume their place in the social order.) Before the war members of the social elite provoked, led, or applauded the rioting throngs. During and after the war they went on to frame constitutions for the several states and then for the federal government. Throughout the revolutionary era they were being elected as governors and representatives of the people.

In the light of these circumstances we are enabled to see more clearly the very great importance of more than a century's social and political experience. Informing this growing libertarian tradition,

---

Order in Connecticut, 1690-1765 (Cambridge, MA, 1967), 187 and chapters following. See also his *The Great Awakening: Documents on the Revival of Religion, 1740-1745* (New York, 1970), xi.

[20] Writs of Assistance (general search warrants) were the immediate objects of Otis's attack, but he soon turned to the larger issues of oligarchic rule and illicit taxation.

moreover, were the old claims of the Puritan Revolution in England, and in a more moderate way, the theory and practice that issued from the Glorious Revolution. England's liberal policies on immigration to the colonies had done the rest. Suspicious of encroachments on the liberties already enjoyed, Americans separated themselves from British rule in a manner and spirit which Bernard Bailyn has succinctly described in his impressive study of *The Ideological Origins of The American Revolution*:

> The primary goal of the American Revolution, which transformed American life and introduced a new era in human history was not the overthrow or even the alteration of the existing social order but the preservation of political liberty threatened by the apparent corruption of the [English] constitution, and the establishment in principle of the existing conditions of liberty.... What was essentially involved in the American Revolution was not the disruption of American society, with all the fear, despair, and hatred that entails, but the realization, comprehension and fulfillment of the inheritance of liberty and of what was taken to be America's destiny in the context of world history. [21]

After the Battle of Yorktown had been won on both land and sea, Lord North's government wisely concluded that with 20 percent interest being charged on a rapidly growing national debt, further fighting was pointless. In 1783 at Paris the American confederacy gained international recognition of its independence. With national sovereignty established the next item on the revolutionary agenda was the preparation and ratification of a national constitution so that the increasingly manifest shortcomings of the Articles of Confederation could be corrected and a stable form of government established. And on March 4, 1789 this process was solemnly documented by the inauguration of George Washington as President of the United States of America.

Thirty five years had elapsed since the First Continental Congress had published its Declaration and Resolves, and during that time one of the world's great debates on political theory had ensued, with countless disagreements being registered on innumerable issues, great and small. Yet the most outstanding feature of that great American debate, when reviewed from a two century's perspective, is the degree to which it was conducted within the context of a libertarian individualism in which property rights were an unquestioned good. By the same token one must insist on the essential consonance between the Declaration

---

[21] Bernard Bailyn, *The Ideological Origins of the American Revolution* (Cambridge, MA, 1967), 19-21.

and Resolves, the Declaration of Independence, and the Constitution with its Bill of Rights. For the first time in history a democratic people had constitutionalized its culture and its ideals. [22] So satisfied were Americans with the effectiveness of this momentous deed that within another fifteen years their patriotism had elevated the Constitution virtually to the transcendent level of Holy Writ.

Nothing in the foregoing account of the Revolution is meant to denigrate the thoughtful men who guided the country through trying times or the ideas which informed their work. At the same time, however, it is important that we fully recognize their immense indebtedness to the actual practice of previous generations in America and to the dissenting tradition in English political thought. Certainly one of the chief characteristics of the revolutionary generation as a whole was its wholehearted acceptance of the laissez-faire principles which were given classic expression by Adam Smith in the very year 1776. In his first inaugural address George Washington had insisted that "no people can be bound to acknowledge and adore the Invisible Hand which conducts the affairs of men more than those of the United States." He then went on to say that "the propitious smiles of Heaven can never be expected on a nation that disregards the eternal rules of order and right which Heaven itself has ordained." In his Farewell Address he also reverted to these notions. saying that "with slight shades of difference you [the American people] have the same religion, manners, habits, and political principles," whereupon he enlarged on the blessings that would accrue if commercial freedom between the various regions of the country were maintained. On all of these matters Washington was voicing the conventional wisdom of the new republic. [23]

In this context a realistic estimate of the Enlightenment's revolutionary significance is also in order, if only because it is so often

[22] A declaration of independence and a federal constitution serve very different functions; but the whole process of creating a new democratic republic can and should be viewed as a relatively unitary accomplishment. Stanley Elkins and Eric McKitrick provide a valuable historical account of changing views on this matter in "The Founding Fathers: Young Men of the Revolution," *Political Science Quarterly* 76 (1961), 181-216.

[23] The economic principles which Smith expounded with such astonishing clarity had long since been widely practiced in America, yet the appearance of the book in the year of Independence is an illuminating coincidence. The moral, political, and economic theories leading to Smith's great synthesis lead back to the early seventeenth century; and they were constantly reinforced by Puritan views of vocation, work, and self-denial, as well as their disaprobation of indolence, vain display, and useless recreation.

exaggerated. The fact is that many of Europe's most despotic rulers were proud sponsors of the Enlightenment. Similarly many of the philosophes were often very comfortable in autocratic company, politically conservative and intellectually condescending. Indeed, many of the more prominent Tories were as rationalistic as Jefferson or Franklin, while some of the most radical revolutionaries, on the other hand, were conservative in theology. A profound awareness of human depravity may in fact be a major legacy of Reformed and Puritan thinking to the distinctive work of America's founding fathers.

What the Enlightened tradition of thought achieved in a positive sense was a new mode of political discourse, inspired by the age's scientific achievements and hence more universal in its appeal. It thus proposed a "scientific" basis for dealing with the problems of human government. In framing constitutions for the several states and the federal union the Founding Fathers undoubtedly profited from a vast body of Enlightened theory and then passed it on to later reformers in Europe and elsewhere. [24] Yet the Enlightened outlook itself—like the firm faith in written constitutions which it engendered—soon yielded on one level to the great evangelical revivals that began during Jefferson's administration, and at another level to the romantic movement which burgeoned during the 1830's. [25] Despite this great shift in American attitudes, however, the revolutionary leaders were revered without restraint by later generations. They were seen as having been divinely led. Even more remarkable is the degree to which they themselves, over and over again, ascribed their success to the providence of Almighty God. Of the three deistic rationalists who were on the committee to draft the Great Seal (Jefferson, Franklin, and John Adams) at least two proposed scenes from Israel's flight from

---

[24] Clinton Rossiter, Caroline Robbins, and Bernard Bailyn have rightly stressed the importance for American political thought and practice of the older dissenting tradition to which Algernon Sidney made so large a contribution and which John Trenchard and Thomas Gordon did so much to propagate after 1719. See especially Bernard Bailyn, "Political Experience and Enlightenment Ideas in Eighteenth-Century America," *American Historical Review* 67 (1962), 339-51.

[25] The early eclipse of the Enlightenment in America is not sufficiently stressed. The great resurgence of evangelicalism which began with the Second Great Awakening tended to exclude rationalists, infidels and masons from the Protestant establishment during the ante-bellum period. Daniel Boorstin, quite appropriately, entitles his study of the Revolutionary Generation *The Lost World of Thomas Jefferson* (New York, 1948). In non-evangelical circles the romanticism of Emerson, the Transcendentalists, and popular romantics such as Henry Wadsworth Longfellow performed a similar function.

Egyptian bondage for depiction on the seal's reverse side. And in
the device finally adopted the same ideas are expressed, though not in
biblical language. Beneath a depiction of God's all-seeing eye are two
phrases:

ANNUIT COEPTIS
[*Heaven smiles on our undertaking*]
NOVUS ORDO SECLORUM
[*A new order of the ages*] [26]

Where the Founding Fathers showed a measure of restraint, however, the leading evangelical interpreters of the nation's destiny shared
the unmeasured extravagance of a patriotic citizenry. Timothy Dwight
while a chaplain in the revolutionary army had tried to provide an
anthem for the new nation in 1777, before the continental army had
won a single significant battle. Yet his claims were literally boundless:

> Columbia, Columbia, to glory rise,
> The queen of the world, and child of the skies:
> Thy reign is the last, and the noblest of time...

Ezra Stiles of Yale had somewhat better grounds for enthusiasm in
1783 when he delivered his famous sermon, "The United States Elevated
to Glory." After Washington's death the tradition gathered strength,
building on the millennial visions of the colonial era and stimulated by
the Second Great Awakening. After Andrew Jackson had become the
hero of New Orleans in 1815 even more extravagant language became
common as Protestants came to regard America's millennial destiny as a
certainty; it was God's New Israel. By the time of Lafayette's trium-
phant tour in 1824-1825 patriotism and Christian eschatology were being
fused; the nation's destiny was manifest. [27]

---

[26] The eye in the pyramid symbolizes God or Heaven. George Washington used
the words "heaven smiles" in his First Inaugural. When these phrases are linked
with E PLURIBUS UNUM [From many, one] on the other side of the seal,
the United States is clearly being proclaimed to be a providentially favored nation
and to inaugurate a new age in human history. See a One Dollar bill.

[27] See Fred Somkin's fine account of the Lafayette celebrations, *The Unquiet
Eagle: Memory and Desire in the Idea of American Freedom* (Ithaca, N.Y.,
1967). The idea of *Manifest Destiny* has deep colonial roots. After Independence
it became an article of patriotic faith. Andrew Jackson gave it new force in his
farewell message of 1838. John L. O'Sullivan popularized the idea and coined
the slogan between 1838 and 1845. See Albert K. Weinberg, *Manifest Destiny*
(Baltimore, 1953), 107-11. After 1830 the South developed its own paternalistic
view of the millennium, while black slaves in their spirituals nurtured still
another hope "over Jordan."

As a result of this process the Union itself came to occupy an extraordinarily exalted status in American hearts and minds. It became an object of genuine reverence and veneration, a source of moral norms, and in some sense a transcendent entity. Probably nobody evpressed these convictions in a more popular way than Samuel Francis Smith, the Andover seminarian who in a single moment of inspiration wrote "My country 'tis of thee" in 1832. George Washington was the first saint of America's civil religion even before his death in 1799, but the others were soon similarly recognized—notably Adams and Jefferson—after their almost simultaneous deaths in 1826, on the 50th anniversary of the Declaration. By this time the evangelical resurgence together with the steady westward flow of native Americans and immigrants was inspiring even grander visions of America as a beacon to the world. Governor Winthrop's image of America as a "city on a hill" was fused with Edwards' prophecy of the coming Kingdom. Lyman Beecher, the leading spokesman for this "Benevolent Empire," had no doubts but that "our own republic, in its constitution and laws is of heavenly origin." [28]

The glorious visions, on the other hand, had the effect of raising up the spectre of subversion. As a result the great campaigns of the "evangelical united front," whether missionary or reformist in their intent, were accompanied by a great outpouring of anti-Catholic slander and organized opposition to other non-evangelical religious movements. [29] In the vast literature of nativism, however, few, if any, stated the case for bigotry more eloquently than did the Reverend Samuel M. Campbell of Rochester, New York, who also reveals the intimate connection of millennialism and counter-subversionary thinking.

> [It is] the good common sense of the American people that it is perfectly fair to keep up certain things that mark us as a Protestant Christian people. And this decision is undoubtedly right, for the freedom there is among us is so entirely the fruit of our Christianity that we can not let our religion go without losing our liberty with it. This is a Christian Republic, our religion being of the Protestant type. People who are not Protestants dwell among us, and people who are called Christians but who are not Protestants. We have never shut our doors against them but if they come they must take up with such accommodations as we have.... If this disturbs anyone's mind we are sorry for this disturbance, but we can not change our plan. If anyone coming among us finds that this arrangement is uncomfortable, perhaps

---

[28] *Lyman Beecher's Works* (Boston, 1852), 1.189.

[29] See especially David B. Davis, ed., *The Fear of Conspiracy: Images of UnAmerican Subversion from the Revolution to the Present* (Ithaca, N.Y., 1971). Crèvecoeur's fateful metaphor of the United States as a great "melting pot" of the world's races undoubtedly encouraged this trend.

he will do well to try some other country. The world is wide and there is more land to be possessed; let him go and make a beginning for himself as our fathers did for us; for as for this land we have taken possession of it in the name of the Lord Jesus Christ and if he will give us grace to do it, we mean to hold it for him, till he come. [30]

By far the most serious threat to both the nation's expansionist vision and its moral integrity was the concomitant growth of the slavocracy. This fact had begun to alienate Southerners from the northern understanding of the Coming Kingdom at least since 1776. Conversely, the antislavery crusade and the ensuing war brought Northern fervor to its highest pitch—captured by nobody with such obvious genius as in Julia Ward Howe's "Battle Hymn of the Republic." Then as at no other time the Federal Union came to be understood as God's instrument of retributive justice. And in Abraham Lincoln the times found a person who could expose the expiatory meaning of a terrible war and direct the national conscience toward a "new birth of freedom." [31]

Yet Lincoln's summons went unheeded, with the result that the nation's centennial was celebrated in 1876 amid the corruptions of the Grant administration and, worse still, the abandonment of southern Reconstruction in 1877. Thereafter Americans moved into the multiple crises of the Gilded Age: massive immigration, urban dislocation, industrial strife, and the machinations of the robber barons. In a rapidly changing urban ethos church life and traditional moral attitudes were put under stress, to the great discomfiture of many. Perhaps most upsetting of all was the simultaneous impact of science, evolutionary theory, biblical criticism, historical theology and the modern religious ideas that grew out of these developments. [32]

In this troubled atmosphere American evangelicalism for the first time became seriously divided on theological grounds. In the new

[30] Samuel M. Campbell, "Christianity and Civil Liberty," *American Presbyterian and Theological Review* 5 (1867), 390-91.

[31] The crusade against slavery was the one great reform movement to which the libertarion tradition was explicitly and inescapably committed. No contradiction of freedom and equality could be greater than a vast system of chattel slavery. In Abraham Lincoln the nation gained a leader of prophetic insight who even in the midst of tragedy could declare that "the purposes of the Almighty are perfect, and must prevail," Letter to Eliza Gurney, in William J. Wolf, *The Almost Chosen People: A Study of the Religion of Abraham Lincoln* (New York, 1959), 155. On northern Protestants and the War see James H. Moorhead, *American Apocalypse* (New Haven, 1978).

[32] Paul A. Carter illuminates many of these stresses in *The Spiritual Crisis of the Gilded Age* (DeKalb, Ill., 1971).

fundamentalist outlook that began to emerge social reform and millennial optimism faded away. Dwight L. Moody in his great revival campaigns categorically inverted the accepted vision of American destiny. He depicted this world as a wrecked vessel and pointed to a safe pre-millennial lifeboat. [33]

Among those who revelled in the new liberal theology and marvelled at the new technology, on the other hand, an aggressively optimistic notion of the coming kingdom arose, more secular and more political than ever. As the head of the Evangelical Alliance and a major promoter of the Social Gospel, Josiah Strong gained an especially wide hearing. Seeing America as the successor to Greece, Rome, and Great Britain he envisioned nothing less than a Christian Anglo-Saxonization of the world. [34] America, moreover, proved to be very ready for this imperialistic message; and Presidents McKinley, Theodore Roosevelt and Wilson, each in his way, proceeded to make the United States a decisive military and economic force in world affairs. In fact it was during the surge of patriotism that followed upon the country's entering World War I that the identification of the United States as the world's Redeemer Nation reached its extreme expression.

Only with the crash of 1929, the Great Depression, the Dust Bowl, and the New Deal did a more realistic estimate of America's national purpose begin to emerge. By this time, however, the rifts in American Protestantism that had appeared in the Gilded Age began to take the form of an enduring schism with very considerable political implications. [35] The traditional patriotic claims for America began to lose their hold on the hearts, minds, and social imagination of the people as a whole.

The years of the Great Depression and the "Third American Revolution" [36] over which FDR presided did in fact experience a major transformation of outlook. New urban values came to predominate in the nation's counsels; the welfare state became an accepted reality, and

---

[33] "The Return of Our Lord" (1877), in William G. McLoughlin, ed., *The American Evangelicals, 1800-1900* (New York, 1968), 180-85.

[34] See Strong's *The New Era, or, The Coming Kingdom* (New York, 1893), 79-80.

[35] Out of the controversies and litigation over evolution in the schools, and in the virulent opposition to the New Deal during the 1930's there emerged a form of religio-political conservatism which is still recognizable in the 1970's.

[36] In retrospect Franklin Roosevelt does not appear as a radical, yet Heinz Eulau's perception of a "Third Revolution" is justified. See his essay on the New Deal in Bernard Sternsher, ed., *The New Deal: Doctrines and Democracy* (Boston, 1966), 197-211.

hitherto ignored ethnic minorities gained a degree of recognition that
began to mitigate the power of the Protestant establishment. Within
Protestantism, moreover, a "Neo-Orthodox" movement in theology
brought serious criticism to bear on traditional theology and ethics.
World War II, of course, did provide an all-encompassing sense of
national purpose. Despite the provocations of Hitler and Pearl Harbor,
however, the excesses of the First war were avoided.

Under the Truman and Eisenhower administrations, on the other
hand, the intensifying Cold War created an atmosphere which nourished
the rise of many counter-subversionary activities, among which the
depredations of Senator Joseph McCarthy were the most sensationally
irresponsible. During the decade 1956-1966 it was probably the civil
rights movement and the leadership of Martin Luther King that provided most of what moral dignity the post-war period experienced. The
election of a Roman Catholic President in 1960 also had the effect
of reducing prejudice and making the national faith a more inclusive
one.

The promising aspect of these developments, however, was radically
undone in 1965 when President Johnson initiated a drastic escalation
of the war in Vietnam which gradually led in turn to a concomitant
escalation of racial protest and anti-war agitation that was duly carried
into the Nixon Administration in 1968. Then during the election campaign of 1972 came the culminating event of the post-war era. The
White House itself was implicated first in a political burglary, and then,
many frantic months later, in a vast skein of governmental malfeasance.
On Thursday August 8, 1974, Richard M. Nixon, after a vote of im-
peachment, became the first American president to resign from office.
Then in April 1975 almost simultaneously with President Ford's official
inauguration of the Bicentennial Era at Lexington and Concord, came
the tumultuous collapse of the American regime in South-East Asia.
Amidst energy problems, unemployment, inflation, corruption and a
grievous lack of political leadership the American people were experiencing a greater degree of ideological confusion than at any time
since the Republic's centennial year.

Even dramatic events of this magnitude, however, are not a sufficient explanation of the protracted decay of a national ideological tradition. In its ante-bellum heyday this tradition was regarded by such
acute observers as Alexis de Tocqueville and Wilhelm von Humbolt
to be one of the wonders of the modern world. But in the 1970s this
condition no longer obtained. It would appear, therefore, that ideological

reconstruction was one of the nation's most urgent needs. The country as a whole was experiencing the predicament of a garden club that has lost its interest in flowers. Desperately needed therefore is an examination of both the sources of the republic's earlier vitality and the reasons for its latter-day uncertainty. In either case we are driven back to a reconsideration of the American Revolution itself, for that event not only created the political nation but in many crucial ways defined the central and enduring characteristics of the social order which developed.

What came to pass can be simply stated. A migrant dissatisfied people imbued with the principles of England's Puritan revolution planted a civilization on the thinly populated American shore, where they were soon joined by a host of others who also sought an asylum from oppression and an unpromising future in Europe. After becoming alienated from a British government that would or could not share their aspirations, the American people won their independence and founded the world's first democratic republic. In framing their government they secured what they wanted most, equality before the law, untrammeled civil rights, religious freedom, and, above all, the protection of property. They wanted to do what they pleased; in this broad land they exercised that right with abandon, as did a steady flow of immigrants.

This is not to say that the American Revolution was an insignificant event. The bourgeois revolution which it constitutionalized was the most momentous thing that had happened in Western history; and the United States was the place where it was most fully accomplished. Arbitrary rule, sacral kingship, authoritarian religious establishments, feudal class structures, and the institutionalized denial of intellectual liberty—all of this was put on borrowed time in 1776. In the moral ethos which this *laissez-faire* mentality nourished the institution of slavery, and the southern paternalism which sustained it, was a standing affront which was swept away by force of arms and three constitutional amendments.

Undergirding and legitimating this great libertarian enterprise was a conviction, rooted in Puritan theology, that this country was uniquely chosen and favored by God. And it was during the civil war this special form of patriotism reached its ultimate expression. At just this juncture, however, serious difficulties begin to darken the picture. The prevailing economic anarchy was not bringing freedom and justice to all. Blacks, Catholics and Jews felt the brunt of discrimination. Farmers, labor, slum-dwellers, and many of the later immigrants faced misery and neglect, while the great "captains of industry" gained the solitude of

government. Entrepreneurial liberty was creating disparities of wealth
and opportunity that were making the ideal of equality a legal fiction.
When such conditions were aggravated by rapidly changing mores and
radical changes in religion and ethics, America's covenantal relationship
with God appeared to be breaking down, or so it increasingly seemed
to those generations who bridged the decades between the Civil War and
the Great Depression. And these disturbing signs became even more
apparent during the national tribulations of the Sixties and Seventies.
By this time the chief underlying cause of uneasiness was the massive
fact of poverty and the destruction of "domestic tranquility" which it
produced. Millions of Americans were not only persistently out of
work but were in effect living outside the social covenant. To them, in
fact, the social order had become an enemy with whom the bonds of
loyalty and obligation were severed. They had become simply the
detritis of an "efficient" industrial system, a waste product being
stacked in slums and inhumane housing projects. As a consequence a
kind of unorganized guerilla warfare was rendering the cities unsafe
and spreading to suburban and rural areas.

In an increasingly secularized culture, moreover, the patriotic theology of nationalized redeemerism was losing its hold. To many non-
Protestants and non-Christians, indeed, this ideology was apprehended
as an exclusionistic threat. [37] Extreme cognitive dissonance meanwhile
was producing frenetic and irrational behavior. Perhaps most serious
of all manifestations was the pervasive weakening of those inner
restraints on self-indulgence and the pursuit of wealth which Puritan
ethics had always emphasized and which even Adam Smith in 1776
was taking for granted. Even according to a modest estimate made in
1976 the annual public cost of the white collar rip-off going on within
corporate structures was $ 21 billion, with tax evasion not included.
Another major sign of unrestraint was the tendency of business and
political leaders to regard natural resources as inexhaustible and the
environment as indestructible. Posterity was being left to fend for
itself.

*

---

[37] As America began to observe its Bicentennial Era, its most urgent ideological need was a credible conception of nationhood which is universal in its
scope and which is free of those attitudes, claims, and doctrines that exclude
or antagonize many Americans. Ideologies, however, are not simply summoned
into existence, or minted like coins. They arise from the depths of corporate
experience and are upheld or sustained by the beliefs, and acceptances, and
behavior of the people.

In 1787 Benjamin Rush had confidently predicted that the War was only the first act in the ongoing American Revolution. He predicted that many more acts would follow. Had he been correct, the nation's ideological canopy would still be holding out the rain. But Rush was wrong. Only two acts have been played. The first was the belated Emancipation which was from the start drastically compromised by racism. The social legislation of the 1930's has fared better and in many cases (as with social security) has become an accepted aspect of American life. On the other hand the New Deal's control of corporate power and its egalitarian use of the tax power have been all but undone by the rise of huge conglomerates and world-ranging multinational corporations. Commercial banks now control urban redevelopment and dictate the fiscal policies of cities. Genuine tax reform is not legislated.

In other words, while the fundamental structures of American life changed drastically, the assumptions of the eighteenth century were being left largely uncriticized.

Hence the national ideology collapses under the weight of anomalies: massive poverty, insolvent cities, and bankrupt hospitals in the world's most affluent nation; inequality in the land of the free. The country, alas, has answered the worst fears of Mercy Otis Warren, a remarkable member of the generation of 1776 who also wrote an important history of the revolution:

> A regard to private interest has ever operated more forcibly on the bulk of mankind than the ties of honor or the principles of patriotism; and when the latter are incompatible with the former, the balance seldom hangs in equilibrio. Thus it is not uncommon to see virtue, liberty, love of country, and regard to character, sacrificed at the shrine of wealth.

All of which leads us to a self-evident truth for the republic's third century: justice is the first virtue of any government and any state. If it happens that this country awakens to that truth, then its ideological health will also be restored, but not otherwise. As we look back on the episode of God's New Israel in America and put it in a world-historical perspective we may hope, therefore, that a new dialectic of liberty and equality will come to life and that substantial content will in due time be given to the country's historic commitment to the "general welfare."

JOHN COTTON WASHED AND MADE WHITE

CONRAD WRIGHT

Harvard Divinity School

A half-century ago, the conventional judgment on the controversy between Roger Williams and John Cotton was unambiguous. Williams was an apostle of religious freedom, an early advocate of the separation of church and state, and hence an "irrepressible democrat." Cotton, by way of contrast, was a "steward of theocracy," himself perhaps possessing "sweetness of temper," yet one who "allowed himself to be coerced by narrower-minded men." [1]

One half of this contrast—the picture of Roger Williams as a liberal born before his time—was sharply challenged in the 1950s by Mauro Calamandrei, Perry Miller, and others. [2] Edmund S. Morgan's *Roger Williams: The Church and the State* (1967) advanced the process of reassessment; so that now Williams is understoond more clearly than before, not as a misplaced democrat, but as "a man of his time and very much a part of it." [3] But the other half of the contrast has not been similarly restructured. While there has been recent scholarly attention directed toward Cotton, it has been concerned mainly with his views of the doctrines of grace and the question of preparation for salvation, and with his writings on congregational polity. [4] His controversy with Williams has been discussed in terms of the theological concepts and literary conventions that shaped the presentation of the arguments, and so divergent views of typology have been explicated in detail; [5] but there has not been a re-examination of the structure of

---

[1] Samuel H. Brockunier, *The Irrepressible Democrat* (New York, 1940); Vernon L. Parrington, *The Colonial Mind* (New York, 1927), 28, 29.

[2] Mauro Calamandrei, "Neglected Aspects of Roger Williams' Thought," *Church History* 21 (1952), 239-258; Perry Miller, *Roger Williams: His Contribution to the American Tradition* (New York and Indianapolis, 1953).

[3] Edmund S. Morgan, *Roger Williams: The Church and the State* (New York, 1967), 5.

[4] Larzer Ziff, *The Career of John Cotton* (Princeton, 1962); Norman Pettit, *The Heart Prepared* (New Haven, 1966); Larzer Ziff, ed., *John Cotton on the Churches of New England* (Cambridge, 1968).

[5] Sacvan Bercovitch, "Typology in Puritan New England: The Williams-Cotton Controversy Reassessed," *American Quarterly* 19 (1967): 166-191; Jesper Rosenmeier, "The Teacher and the Witness: John Cotton and Roger Williams," *William and Mary Quarterly* 25 (1968), 408-431; Richard Reinitz, "The Separatist

the arguments themselves. Hence even a partisan of Cotton can declare with respect to the dispute over liberty of conscience that "John Cotton's reputation has suffered badly because of the brilliant response he drew from Roger Williams." [6] That leaves the conventional judgment little modified: even if Williams cannot be claimed as a twentieth-century liberal, it will still be taken for granted that he got the better of the argument.

It is time for a fresh look at the exchange between Cotton and Williams, and especially for consideration of Cotton's side of the argument, which has been the more neglected. The burden of the present essay is that, while Cotton reaches some practical conclusions that we reject, his basic assumptions would be widely acceptable even today. Once allowance is made for the fact that he was addressing a social situation very different from our own, his position emerges as a rather admirable and humane one. In any case, the opportunity to see how his assumptions work in different times and under different circumstances may be illuminating.

I

If Cotton has been misunderstood, why is this so? Two reasons are apparent: a) while Williams's writings have long been available in full, as a practical matter Cotton's position has been known only through Williams's quotation of him for purposes of refutation; and b) certain of the words crucial to the discussion have changed their meanings, although the ordinary reader has not been sensitive to this fact. "Conscience" is one of them; "persecution" may be another. If Roger Williams tells us that Cotton believes in persecution for cause of conscience, he immediately conjures up for us the image of a bigoted theocrat, and some equivalent of the martyrdom of Servetus seems close at hand. But before we accept that conclusion, we need to take account of Cotton's denials, and especially to watch how the words "conscience" and "persecution" are being used.

Included in Williams's *Bloody Tenent of Persecution* is the text of Cotton's answer to an inquiry as to his views on liberty of conscience. This document has generally been taken to be a fair statement of Cotton's position. It was, however, an immediate and compact res-

---

Background of Roger Williams' Argument for Religious Toleration," in Sacvan Bercovitch, ed., *Typology and Early American Literature* (Amherst, MA, 1972), 107-137.

[6] Ziff, *Cotton on the Churches*, 35n.

ponse to inquiry, rather than a carefully worked out exposition of his views. Hence it was less clearly phrased than it might otherwise have been, and was liable to misconstruction. It has to be read in the light of his *Bloudy Tenent Washed,* which is a full-scale reply to Williams. But the *Bloudy Tenent Washed* was never reprinted until the facsimile edition of 1972, and was long available only in rare book collections in research libraries. For every scholar who might read Cotton, there were doubtless a dozen who had William's full text available to them, and scores who were familiar with anthologized passages from it. [7]

Cotton himself complained that Williams's publication of the early document containing his views was unauthorized, and that his position was thereby misrepresented. [8] Williams at times follows a pattern of argument such as this: Cotton says thus and so; the obvious inference from such a position is this conclusion; therefore Cotton is to be condemned for holding such a conclusion. To which Cotton may be found replying, in effect: the inference you think is obvious from my statemetns is not obvious at all; it is a faulty inference, which leads to a conclusion I do not hold.

Thus at the beginning of the *Bloudy Tenent Washed,* Cotton says of Williams:

> ...he taketh Liberty to his Conscience openly to publish, That I do professedly maintaine Persecution for cause of Conscience, When I doe in expresse tearmes professedly Renounce it....
> *Object.* But it may be, by consequence, I doe maintaine Persecution for cause of Conscience, though in expresse tearmes I professedly Renounce it.
> Ans. 1. What if such a thing might be inferr'd by consequence? mens judgements and professions are not so be taken up from every unwary consequence, against their owne positive and expresse Declarations, and Professions. [9]

What Cotton is protesting is exemplified in Chapter Twelve, where the question arises of the punishment of a person who holds wrong views on a fundamental point of doctrine. Cotton originally said: "for

---

[7] Williams's *Bloudy Tenent* was reprinted by the Hanserd Knollys Society (London) in 1848, and again in 1867 as volume three of the six-volume collection of his writings published by the Narragansett Club (Providence, R.I.). This latter edition was the basis for the 1963 edition (New York). Citations from the *Bloody Tenent* in this essay may be found in either the 1867 or the 1963 edition. The selected passages with which most readers are familiar may be found in several anthologies, as, for example, in Perry Miller and Thomas H. Johnson, eds., *The Puritans* (New York, 1938), or Alpheus Thomas Mason, ed., *Free Government in the Making* (New York, 1949).

[8] John Cotton, *The Bloudy Tenent, Washed* (London, 1647), 2.

[9] *Ibid.,* 3.

an *Erronious* and *blind Conscience,* (even in fundamentall and weighty Points) It is not lawfull to persecute any, till after *Admonition* once or twice: and so the Apostle directeth, *Tit.* 3.10 . . . ." [10] When Williams quotes Cotton, he adds the following phrase, as though it were Cotton's: "and then such consciences may be persecuted . . . ." [11] But these are Williams's words, not Cotton's; they represent his inference from what Cotton said, and they subtly transform the thrust of the argument. Cotton was not arguing at that point for punishment; he was asserting that *if* punishment were meted out under the stated circumstances, whether by church discipline or by the civil authorities, it would not properly be defined as persecution for cause of conscience. This does assume that punishment *may* be meted out under certain circumstances—that such a course is one possible option. But in the phrase Williams adds, "may" suggests permission at last to do what one has all along eagerly sought to do; and furthermore, action by civil authority is taken for granted. "But it was no part of my words or meaning," Cotton protests, "to say, that every Heretick, though erring in some Fundamentall and weighty Points; and for the same excommunicated, shall forth with be punished by the Civill Magistrate . . ." [12]

II

If so simple a word as "may" can be misunderstood, what of a more difficult one, like "conscience"?

What does the word mean to us today? Conscience is an inner guide to right and wrong action. We have an inward sense of peace with ourselves when we do what we know in our hearts is the right thing to do; we have a sense of guilt when we violate our consciences.

The eighteenth and nineteenth centuries taught us to believe that the monitions of conscience are, in a special way, of divine authority. Conscience is the voice of God speaking inwardly, telling us what we must do, regardless of public opinion or social pressure. George Washington wrote in his copybook: "Labour to keep alive in your breast that little spark of celestial fire,—conscience." [13] Even when there is reluctance to speak of God, conscience is thought of as the individual soul expressing itself with the deepest integrity. There is a sacredness ascribed to it, as there is to the soul itself, so that compulsion

---

[10] Williams, *Bloody Tenent,* 42.

[11] *Ibid.,* 84.

[12] Cotton, *Bloudy Tenent Washed,* 27.

[13] John Bartlett, *Familiar Quotations,* 13th ed. (Boston, 1955), 366b.

of the individual conscience is seen as a violation of the deepest sanctities.

This is not what the word has always meant, however. The term comes from the Latin *conscientia*, meaning knowledge shared with others. Often the proper translation is simply "consciousness." As applied to moral concerns, it has to do with standards of right and wrong shared within a group: an individual's conscience is his or her capacity to apprehend a shared consciousness of what constitutes right and wrong behavior, in accordance with natural law or the revelation of Scripture. This understanding of the word stresses the intellectual side of achieving correct moral judgments, rather than individual feelings or intuitions of what is right or wrong.

Authorities seem to be uncertain as to the dating of the shift in conscience from an awareness of an external shared rule of law to an inner tribunal; but they agree that it was well under way in the early eighteenth century. Perhaps the rise of Pietism and related forms of evangelical religion is a parallel tendency, which gives a clue to the timing of the shift. But that a shift has occurred is obvious when we go back to the seventeenth century, and look at a book like William Ames's *De Conscientia* (1622). The book deals with issues involving moral judgment, subjected to rational analysis and determination. So Ames defines "conscience" as "a mans judgement of himselfe, according to the judgement of God of him," and goes on to say, "I call Conscience *Iudgement,* First, to shew that it belongs to the Vnderstanding, not to the Will." Later he adds: "By *Judgement* therefore, in the definition of Conscience, (I understand most properly with the best Schoolemen) an act of practicall judgement, proceeding from the Vnderstanding by the power or meanes of a habit." [14]

Ames has much more to say, and many distinctions to make; but the important thing here is the definition of conscience as falling in the sphere of intellectual or rational discourse common to all, rather than as some sort of individual intuition. The judgments of the individual conscience are as much subject to argument and correction as any other intellectual proposition; they are not immune to criticism as if based on an inward and private apprehension of God's will. All of which means that our feelings of dismay when we hear of someone compelled against his or her conscience are anachronistic if projected into the Williams-Cotton debate.

---

[14] William Ames, *Conscience, with the Power and Cases Thereof* (London, 1643), 1, 3.

If the word "conscience" needs clarification, so too does the word "persecution."

Cotton himself points out that the word is being used in two ways in the discussion, and that the two have not been properly discriminated. Rightly used, "persecution" means the punishment of an innocent person. That is always wrong, and Cotton invariably rejects it. "I expressly professe," he declares at the outset. "1. *That no man is to be persecuted at all (much lesse for Conscience sake:) because all persecution is oppression for Righteousnesse sake.*" [15]

The punishment of a guilty person, of course, is legitimate; and when an offender is punished who is in the wrong, and knows perfectly well that he has been caught doing something he ought not to do, no question of persecution arises.

But, says Cotton, Williams uses the term "persecution" in another, looser way, to apply to all cases where a person pursues an immoral or unrighteous course of action, but through blindness or stubbornness or misplaced sincerity is unwilling to acknowledge his fault. And he complains that Williams does not discriminate as to the various ramifications of such situations:

> ...if persecution be taken properly for affliction or oppression for righteousnesse sake I knew it was out of Question, all persecution was unlawfull, whether by the Church, or the Magistrate: an unjust excommunication is as true persecution, as an unjust Banishment. But if persecution be taken more largely, and loosely, (as it is by the Author of the Letter, and by the *Discusser,* for any affliction, or persecution for cause of Conscience (whether good Conscience, or evill, whether rightly informed, or erroneous) If that be the intent of the Letter (as it seemed to me) to beare witnesse against that, then any testimony of Scripture, that justifieth a lawfull censure of false and erroneous Teachers, doth evince the scope of the Letter to be erroneous, which is against all persecution for cause of Conscience. [16]

This involved passage may be simply summarized. Cotton is saying that if the word "persecution" is used in its narrow and proper sense, all persecution is wrong. But if Williams wishes to use the term loosely to apply to the punishment of all sorts of wrongdoers who insist that what they have done is perfectly all right, then such "persecution" may be necessary.

Since Cotton was constantly responding to Williams, chapter by chapter and paragraph by paragraph, he himself often uses the word

---

[15] Cotton, *Bloudy Tenent Washed,* 3.

[16] *Ibid.,* 117. In this passage, the "Author of the Letter" refers to the prisoner in Newgate whose remarks were sent to Cotton for comment, thereby occasioning his first compact statement of his views; the "Discusser" is Roger Williams.

"persecution" in this larger and looser sense. We think of the term as applying to a deliberate policy of harrassment of harmless individuals or groups, and so the term connotes bigotry or malevolence. So it does also in Cotton's first example, the punishment of an innocent person. But in the larger and looser use that Cotton has pointed to in Williams, and which he himself cannot avoid at times, it means no more than punishment or restraint for erroneous behavior, with none of the overtones of animus that we automatically associate with the word.

III

These considerations as to how the words "conscience" and "persecution" are to be understood bring us to the crux of the debate. The central issue may be stated thus: how should the civil magistrate act towards an individual who sincerely, or conscientiously, adheres to religious beliefs or follows religious practices that are generally held by society at large to be wrong? Cotton's answer is that there are times and circumstances when it is absolutely necessary to curb religiously-motivated behavior; but when the magistrate does so, he should be under the check of certain specific restraints.

Cotton gives two examples of the kind of religiously-motivated behavior he has in mind. The first of these is given by way of illustration of a man with a "seared conscience," who persists in his view despite all attempts at persuasion. If he is punished, it is not properly persecution for conscience' sake, since persecution is punishment of the innocent, while conscience refers to the common rationally-grounded moral judgment of society as to what the law of God requires.

> And though it be true, there is a seared conscience in some, to which God hath in his judgement, given them up, that they may never see light, how cleare soever, both in Scripture and nature: and though this seared conscience doe not extenuate, but aggravate sinne; and though a man by this seared conscience may commit some notorious capitall crime (as he that in *Ireland* burnt his owne sonne in the fire, in the imitation of *Abraham,* and called in his Neighbours to rejoyce in beholding the power of his faith:) and though such a man was justly put to death: yet it may not be said, he was punished for his conscience, but for that unnaturally barbarous cruelty and murther, which he committed, and which his conscience could never have blinded him to commit, out of any naturall humane ignorance, or infirmity, but out of poenall and judiciall blindness, which God never leaveth men unto, but upon habituall and customary sinning against light of conscience. [17]

What Cotton is grappling with here, in the example of the man in Ireland who burned his own son, is the kind of problem that arises when

---

[17] *Ibid.,* 22.

a Jehovah's Witness refuses to permit a blood transfusion for a minor child; or a Charles Manson family engages in ritual murder; or a Mormon in the mid-nineteenth century outrages the moral standards of most Americans by practising polygamy; or an Amana colony refuses to conform to public school requirements; or an opponent of the Vietnam war breaks into the office of a draft board and spills blood on the records. Some of these examples may win our sympathy for the conscientiously-motivated behavior; others will not. Yet the problem is the same in every case.

It is a very difficult thing at times to do justice both to the conscientious scruples of the person involved, and to the protection of the body politic. Yet not all religiously-motivated behavior can automatically be accepted as right. There are times when all of us will acknowledge that the conscientiously-informed behavior of persons must be restrained. It is not obvious, therefore, that Roger Williams was always right in his plea for soul liberty, while Cotton was wrong in arguing that social control is sometimes necessary. When we get to the basic structure of the problem, apart from the particular circumstances, we find the issues to be far from clean-cut.

Cotton had another kind of issue in mind besides the one illustrated by the father in Ireland who burned his son. It was the political threat to the realm of England from Catholic power. Most of us do not respond sympathetically to this concern, and may wish to deplore the anti-popery of those times; but the problem was not peculiar to Cotton's day. The problem stated in general terms is this: under what circumstances and in what way is it legitimate for the civil magistrate to restrain persons whose sincerely-held beliefs undermine the accepted value system that makes the society a going concern, and whose conscientiously-motivated behavior may destroy that society?

For example: was it legitimate for white citizens' councils, the members of which sincerely believed in racial superiority, to prevent blacks from getting equal educational opportunities? Was it proper for the civil magistrates in Washington, D.C. to intervene? Was that persecution for cause of conscience? Or again, was it legitimate for people, who sincerely believed that the re-election of Richard Nixon in 1972 took priority over all else, to engage in criminal activity? If the consciences of such men approved their actions, did that make them right? Or did they have what Cotton termed a "blind conscience?"

What lies behind Cotton's position is the conviction that civil society is possible only when there is a prevalent standard of civil behavior among people in their dealings with one another. Society at large cannot but be concerned with the attitudes and values people hold, to the extent that they affect behavior. And moral behavior can hardly be separated from religious values.

Where we differ from Cotton is not so much with respect to the basic argument, as with respect to the range of values insisted on and the violations of accepted behavior that seem important enough to correct. We may no longer worry about blasphemy; but how about racism? We may not be concerned with infidelity; but what of male chauvinism? We may have stopped talking about religious heresy; but what about political heresies—Communism (if one is a John Bircher) or neo-Nazism (if one is a Jew in Skokie, Illinois)?

IV

What, then, should the magistrate do? Cotton's answer is: Nothing—unless three conditions are satisfied.

The first of these conditions is that fundamental issues must be at stake. Civil magistrates should not promote a common set of attitudes or restrain deviant behavior on trivial matters. Interference can be justified only when the civil peace is basically jeopardized, and when the danger is clear and obvious. *"I Professe further,"* Cotton writes, *"That none is to be punish'd for his Conscience sake, though Erroneous, unlesse his Errors be fundamentall..."* [18]

One may respond that one man's fundamentals are another man's trivia, and this is why Roger Williams was banished: the magistrates of Massachusetts Bay were making an issue of trivial matters, such as Williams's refusal to hold communion with churches that had not separated completely from the Church of England. Trivial this may seem to us; but not so either to the Massachusetts Bay Puritans or to Williams. Indeed, by modern standards it is Williams rather than Cotton who has the greater capacity for turning small matters into issues of no compromise. It is clear that Cotton would not define as fundamental any doctrines of religion that were obscure, or in debate among theologians. He did not even consider the matter of congregational polity, which concerned him greatly, so fundamental as to call for punishment of dissent. He almost comes to the point of asserting that if there is an issue on which there is any real debate among the theologians, it cannot be fundamental:

---

[18] *Ibid.*, 3.

... the cases of Religion, wherein we allow Civill Magistrates to be Judges, are so fundamentall, and palpable, that no Magistrate studious of Religion in the feare of God, but, if he have any spirituall discerning (as all truly Christian Magistrates have, and even Pagans have discerned between innocent Christians, and turbulent Seducers) he cannot but judge of such grosse corruptions as are unsufferable in Religion.... [19]

It may be argued that Williams readily assumes that Cotton is of a persecuting spirit because he himself has so much more rigorous a notion of what is not to be compromised. If punishment were meted out to maintain Williams's standards of correctness in religious matters, almost no one would escape. It is because his standard of right behavior is rigorous, and the level of jeopardy correspondingly high, that the legitimacy of punishment is brought into question. If every small difference between adversaries has to be a life and death affair, then either they should be kept far apart, or they should be denied recourse to sanctions. Hence separation of church and state as Williams defined it, denying to the magistrate the power to punish infractions of the first Table of the Laws, is the necessary result, not of Williams's tolerance, but of his intolerance. Cotton's more relaxed levels of expectation mean a lower level of jeopardy, so punishment becomes not an immediate recourse but a last resort.

Cotton's second condition is that punishment for conscientious error is appropriate only when the error produces turbulent and disruptive behavior. Even here, his argument is qualified and restricted.

I would not say, That every man that holdeth forth Error in a boisterous and arrogant spirit to the disturbance of Civill Peace, ought to be punished with death. This is too Bloody a Tenet, unlesse the boisterous Arrogancy were such as did disturbe the Civill Peace to the destruction of the lives and soules of men. [20]

Here we may be reminded that the Puritans never authorized magistrates to ferret out and punish doctrinal error privately held. The Cambridge Platform states: "The object of the powr of the Magistrate, are not things meerly inward, & so not subject to his cognisance & view, as unbeliefe hardness of heart, erronious opinions not vented; but only such things as are acted by the outward man ..." [21] Cotton even goes beyond that restriction to say that the magistrate may not restrain the public utterance of heresy or blasphemy except under cer-

---

[19] *Ibid.,* 101-102.

[20] *Ibid.,* 35.

[21] Williston Walker, *The Creeds and Platforms of Congregationalism* (New York, 1893), 236.

tain circumstances: "not simply because it is evill, unless it be also
notorious, and evident, and convicted by sufficient witnesses, and held
forth with publick offense, and disturbance." [22]

Thirdly, Cotton declares that there should be no punishment for
erroneous conscientious behavior unless persuasion does not succeed.
Titus 3:10 states: "A man that is an heretick after the first and
second admonition reject." Cotton actually turns around the exclu-
sionary thrust of this verse, and makes it permissive rather than man-
datory.

> Where though I say, That it is not lawfull to persecute any, though erring
> in Fundamental and weighty Points, till after once or twice admonition: I doe
> not therefore say, (as the *Discusser* reporteth me) that after once or twice
> admonition, then such Consciences may be persecuted: *But if such a man after*
> *such Admonition shall still persist in the Error of his way, and be therefore*
> *punished, He is not persecuted for cause of Conscience, but for sinning against*
> *his own Conscience.* [23]

One further qualification was placed by Cotton on the use of force
by the magistrate to restrain the turbulent or boisterous expression of
error. Punishment of the offender must be "according to the quality
of the disturbance raised by him." [24] The evil nature of the crime of
heresy or of blasphemy does not provide the measure of the punishment,
but rather the degree of threat to the civil peace, arising from the
manner in which the error is spread abroad. Cotton is even ready to
tolerate Jews, Indians, and Roman Catholics, so long as they keep their
errors to themselves.

> And for the Civill State, we know no ground they have to persecute *Jewes,*
> or *Turkes,* or other *Pagans* for cause of Religion, though they all erre in
> Fundamentalls. No nor would I exempt Anti-Christians [*i.e.*, Roman Catholics]
> neither, from Toleration, notwithstanding their Fundamentall Errors, unlesse
> after conviction they still continue to seduce simple soules into their damnable,
> and pernicious Heresies: as into the Worship of false Gods, into confidence
> of their owne merits for Justification, into seditious conspiracyes against the
> lives and States of such Princes, as will not submit their Consciences to
> the Bishop of *Rome.* [25]

IV

When all these qualifications are made, it becomes clear what Cotton
means when he says that a person who is punished for holding erro-

---

[22] Cotton, *Bloudy Tenent Washed,* 110.
[23] *Ibid.,* 27.
[24] *Ibid.,* 36.
[25] *Ibid.,* 33.

neous views in a violent way, as a threat to civil order, despite attempts at persuasion, is not punished for cause of conscience but for sinning against conscience. He is not punished because of the views he may conscientiously hold, but because his behavior violates the common conscience of society, which his warped and twisted or "seared" conscience rejects. Nor does Cotton say that such a person should be punished inexorably, without exception, and forced to pay the uttermost farthing. Rather, he says that if it becomes necessary to restrain or punish such a person, that is not properly to be regarded as persecution for cause of conscience.

The *Bloudy Tenent Washed* is not a license to magistrates to pursue and root out heresy wherever it may be found. It is not advocating a crackdown on offenders; it is concerned rather with establishing restraints on the authority of the magistrates. As a political theorist, Cotton may be seen on other occasions as well opposing the unlimited authority of magistrates as leading to arbitrary government. "Let all the world learn to give mortall men no greater power then they are content they shall use," he wrote, "for use it they will: and unlesse they be better taught of God, they will use it ever and anon . . ." Or again:

> It is therefore most wholsome for Magistrates and Officers in Church and Common-wealth, never to affect more liberty and authority then will do them good, and the People good; for what ever transcendant power is given, will certainly over-run those that give it, and those that receive it: There is a straine in a mans heart that will sometime or other runne out to excesse, unlesse the Lord restraine it, but it is not good to venture it: It is necessary therefore, that all power that is on earth be limited, Church-power or other: If there be power given to speak great things, then look for great blasphemies, look for a licentious abuse of it. It is counted a matter of danger to the State to limit Prerogatives; but it is a further danger, not to have them limited: They will be like a Tempest, if they be not limited . . . [26]

We noted at the outset the difficulty the modern reader has in grasping Cotton's argument because of the changes in the use of terms like "conscience" and "persecution." We must remind ourselves in conclusion that there are broader difficulties, related to our changed perceptions of what may threaten the social order and the value system that holds it together. There is no fear now that Roman Catholicism will subvert American democracy, and it takes an act of the imagination

[26] Edmund S. Morgan, ed., *Puritan Political Ideas* (Indianapolis, 1965), 174-75. The quotation is from Cotton's *Exposition Upon the Thirteenth Chapter of the Revelation* (London, 1655).

for us to appreciate why Englishment in 1640 viewed Popery as a threat
to social order. There is no fear now that violations of the First Table
of the Law will result in the collapse of civilized society; but in the
small, relatively homogenous society in which Cotton lived, based as
it was on a broad assent to religiously phrased common values, this
was a part of the central value system.

   The situation has changed; the threats to social order are different
now. But when one penetrates through the historical particularities of
the 1640s, to concentrate on the structure of Cotton's argument, he
seems to be giving some very sensible and humane advice on how to control the exercise of civil authority with respect to some rather difficult issues that confront human societies in one form or other in
every time and place.

AMERICAN MISSIONARY IDEOLOGIES

"Activism" as Theory, Practice, and Stereotype

WILLIAM R. HUTCHISON
Harvard University

The 1925 Stockholm Conference on "Life and Work" set itself almost naively to an impossible task: that of discussing Christian social action without raising theological issues. Organizers had failed to realize that merely to call such a conference raised theological issues which if not vented in the official papers and proceedings would be argued in the halls and the public press. In the event, the presentation of social issues at Stockholm aroused vigorous debate in all those arenas. The main point in contention was whether what was called "activism" should be considered a healthy emphasis in religion, or must be seen as a distortion of the Gospel and a dangerously disproportioned understanding of the relations between Divine and human initiatives.

German and other European detractors of Christian activism (also called simply "Americanism") had in mind a fairly definite set of characteristics. The term referred fundamentally to a certain busy-bodied optimism about bringing in the Kingdom—largely through human effort, allegedly, and with little more than consultative assistance from the Deity. Beyond that, activism connoted practically, a quantitative habit of mind, excessive individualism, and some form of imperialism. In negative terms, the activist was defined as someone who knows little of the contemplative, the theological, the churchly. With all his heedless involvement in the world, he occupied an opposite pole from the "quietist" who supposedly withdraws from all involvement. By the same token, the activist stood as the religious representative of what the American culture as a whole was commonly perceived to be. He represented the American at prayer; or, better, the American on his way to church—running.

After the Stockholm Conference—and partly because of it—controversy in these matters became focused on the Social Gospel. But even then the issues reached beyond the social question; and certainly they had done so during the quarter-century before Stockholm. Critics earlier in the twentieth century had detected the alleged "Americanist" traits in revivalism fully as much as in the Social Gospel. Dwight

Moody had been thought to embody them even more, perhaps, than Washington Gladden or Walter Rauschenbusch. The supreme exemplars, in fact (or perhaps just the most visible and therefore troublesome ones), had been neither revivalists nor social gospellers, but rather a whole generation of American leaders who seemed to combine important features of each. The real thoroughbreds of the species were John R. Mott, Robert E. Speer, and a score of other Americans prominent in international missionary and student organizations. To a critic of "American activism" and its supposed influence, nothing was quite so frightening as the Student Volunteer Movement.

Once one realizes that religious social reform—despite the tenor and preoccupations of the Stockholm controversies—was not the phenomenon most deeply in question, it becomes possible to understand the position of some disputants whose stance might otherwise be inexplicable. The most impassioned attack on *Amerikanismus* in the early 1920s, for example, came not from a theological conservative or an opponent of social action, but from Dr. Heinrich Frick, a champion of ecumenism and the history-of-religions movement who would shortly, without any fundamental reversal, become a fan of Archbishop Söderblom—the great Swedish champion of the Life and Work Movement—and even of the dreaded Americans. Frick's *Die Evangelische Mission* (1922) took a stance athwart the usual dichotomies of liberal vs. conservative, or social vs. evangelical. It spoke, instead, to a more fundamental tension in Christianity and its missionary enterprise: the tension between what the Pope (in his own brief against "Americanism" in 1899) had called the active and the passive virtues. [1]

Frick, later a Professor at Marburg but at this time *Privatdozent* at Giessen, opened his book with the observation that "es gibt Mission, und es gibt Propaganda"; and he spent nearly one hundred pages deploring the shift from "mission" to "propaganda" that he thought the Anglo-Americans had instigated within the world missionary movement. [2] Frick took as frighteningly symbolic the title and illustrations that he had found on the cover of a book celebrating the hundredth anni-

---

[1] *Testem benevolentiae*, January 22, 1899, John T. Ellis, ed., *Documents of American Catholic History* Volume II (New York, 1967), 544-45.

[2] Heinrich Frick, *Die Evangelische Mission: Ursprung, Geschichte, Ziel* (Bonn, 1922), 5, 352-429. I have been told by Frick's students and friends from his later years in Marburg (Prof. and Mrs. Helmut Koester of Harvard, Prof. Hans-Werner Gensichen of Heidelberg), not only that Frick later became pro-American, but that he wished everyone would forget his early diatribes against *Amerikanismus*. He nonetheless did write them; and the views, however extreme or recanted, were far from singular.

versary of a London missionary society. The Union Jack, the Star-spangled Banner and the Cross were pictured together on this book cover. Above them one read the words: "The Spiritual Expansion of the Empire." That had been in 1901; the book had provided a fitting culmination, he asserted, not for the "Missionsjahrhundert" it was supposed to celebrate, but rather for a "Jahrhundert der Weltpropaganda." [3]

Since that time, according to Frick, conditions had become steadily worse. The Americans, nurtured in the hopelessly individualistic revivalism and sectarianism of their crude frontiers, had aggravated the worst British influences. With their naive Bible societies, their rough itinerating methods, their superficial approaches to unity and cooperation, their failure to distinguish between unchurched heathen and Christians who simply belonged to the wrong church, the Americans had confirmed that their aims were fundamentally not religious at all. What they really wanted to do was to convert everyone, Hottentots and Germans alike, to an American style of religion and civilization. If the British had produced the rather dangerous Hudson Taylor, with his itinerating, unstable China Inland Missionaries, the Americans had produced a more frightening example in Taylor's namesake, the rough-hewn Bishop William Taylor of the Methodists. [4]

Frick's criticism of Americanism, like that voiced by Leo XIII two decades earlier, sought to avoid injustice by emphasizing that insofar as Americanism was making progress on the Continent, European churches must share the blame. Their weakness and vulnerability had prepared the ground for this evil infestation. The Scandinavian contribution to the notorious "free missionary" movement—to give an extreme example—could scarcely be blamed on the Americans at all. Frick thought that the fishermen of the northern coasts—kin, perhaps, of the American frontiersmen—were "at the same time superstitious and given to clairvoyance." They "submerge themselves fervently in the Bible and champion political radicalism." In such an atmosphere the crudities of Anglo-American individualism could thrive especially well. Unsound missionary practices like those of the Liebenzellers in Germany, while owing much to the activist example from abroad, were responding to this example because their own principles of action had been shaky to begin with. [5]

---

[3] *Ibid.*, 352-53.
[4] *Ibid.*, 369-76.
[5] *Ibid.*, 384-85.

The World Missionary Conference at Edinburgh in 1910 had, according to Frick, signalled Anglo-American dominance and demonstrated the spread of activism into European missions. The missionary clauses in the Versailles Treaty had then confirmed, much more overtly, the newly imperialistic character of the missionary movement. Article 438, which placed the property and operations of German missionary establishments effectively under the control of the Allied governments, superficially had seemed at odds with the spirit of pacific internationalism surrounding the Edinburgh Conference; but in a deeper sense Versailles had revealed what *really* had been happening at that earlier conference, whose sessions and "continuation committees" had been so heavily dominated by English-speaking delegates. [6]

Frick's ultimate objection—despite this pointed attack, and despite his bitter feelings in the backlash of war and defeat—was an objection not to the personal dominance of English-speaking people or governments, but rather to the identification of missions with national-cultural objectives of whatever sort. He was deploring a shrill, super-organized, quantity-minded evangelical Protestantism of which, according to his information and understanding, the Americans were the leading representatives.

Other German and Swiss commentators such as Rene Heinrich Wallau, Erich Stange, and Adolf Keller found Frick unduly negative about the Americans, yet concurred in depicting them as this-worldly, practical and, for the time at least, domineering. [7] Johannes Weise, typically for these more moderate observers, mixed admonition and gentle reproof with appreciation as he assessed John R. Mott's enthusiasm for world evangelization. Weise noted with some relief that Mott, at the end of a book on the world student movement, had acknowledged the necessity of divine aid in the fulfillment of these great projects. Weise thought that German readers, perhaps because they were simply accustomed to a different rhetorical style, would miss this sort of acknowledgment in the earlier portions of Mott's book. [8]

European discussion of American activism—whether as a mere fact of international life or as a dreaded evil, whether as a needed comple-

---

[6] *Ibid.*, 390-92.

[7] Wallau, *Die Einigung der Kirche* (Berlin, 1925), 246-52; Stange, *Vom Weltprotestantismus der Gegenwart* (Hamburg, 1925), 20-55; Keller, *Dynamis* (Tübingen, 1922).

[8] Weise, "Ein Buch von Dr. Mott," *Mitteilungen zur Förderung einer deutschen christlichen Studentenbewegung*, Nr. 262-63 (1921), 138-43.

ment to European modes or as a quality that hampered collaboration—was thus a prominent feature in international conversation in the earlier 1920s; and it became much more so in the years immediately following the Stockholm Conference. [9] So far as the slogans and allegations relating to Americanism reflected any sort of reality—so far, even, as they affected real relationships in the international Christian community—questions about their accuracy and effect must be pursued seriously. One must ask to what extent activism had a real existence as theory, as practice, and as a possibly influential stereotype. In asking such questions about the activist image, one is also inquiring into the accuracy of larger generalizations held and utilized, by Americans as well as by Europeans, about the nature of religion and culture in the United States.

First, then: activism in theory or theology. My impression, based upon preliminary forays into the writings of the most articulate spokesmen for "mainline" American Protestant missions, is that such spokesmen, rather than being oblivious to the dangers in what Europeans called activism, were aware of at least some of those dangers, and were troubled by them. I also find, however, that an overwhelming sense of the rightness, glory and Providentiality of their own Christian civilization made it nearly impossible for these American theorists to stifle the cultural and national elements in their message. As theory, and even as a kind of "proclamation," American activism was surely a reality.

The terms in which such emphases were expressed could of course vary. Professor Robert Handy identifies an argument over "civilization" as the key to many nineteenth-century efforts to Christianize America. [10] As Handy indicates, it was also a prominent element in discussions about the rationale and the appropriate instrumentalities for foreign missions. The theorists of missions did not usually discuss activism as such. They scarcely made use of that term, nor did they worry about all the tendencies to which it refers: the religious individualism that troubled Frick, for example, seems seldom to have been a matter of debate at home. What American theorists argued about was the extent to which—if at all—"civilizing" must precede or accompany evangelization. Participants in this debate displayed considerable awareness of the implications—both theological and tactical—of what nowadays would be called cultural imperialism.

---

[9] See W. A. Visser 't Hooft, *Background of the Social Gospel in America* (Haarlem, 1928), 2-10.

[10] *A Christian America* (New York, 1971).

During the middle years of the nineteenth century, the most prominent American spokesman for missions, Rufus Anderson, was a
person adamantly opposed to "civilization" as the goal or method of
the enterprise. As one who had been Secretary (from 1832 to 1866)
of the American Board of Commissioners for Foreign Missions,
Anderson in 1869 noted with dismay that the Board's earliest statements of purpose had reflected an improper sense of priorities. Home
missions, which the ABCFM originally had included in their operations, had aspired in 1816 to make the American Indians "English in
their language, civilized in their habits," and only thirdly "Christian
in their religion." [11] He allowed that the mistake had perhaps been a
natural one for modern missionaries who, unlike those of apostolic
times, faced civilizations less developed than their own. Whatever the
excuses, however, Anderson believed the modern attempts to place
language, education, and civilization ahead of Christianization were
clearly failing. He therefore had made himself the prime American
spokesman for a policy that would eliminate or subordinate all lay
activities in relation to those of the evangelist, and that would also
place native churches as rapidly as possible on their own. While the
reasoning behind such emphases was partly pragmatic—alternative
schemes had brought meager results—Anderson operated from a strong
conviction that the Christian message is confused and sullied by its
involvement with civilizing objectives, from whose bondage it must
be separated if it is to be preached in its full purity and power. [12]

The reader, knowing these views and taking for granted their
sincerity, is likely to be astounded when the same author repeatedly
pays homage to the wonders of American and Western civilization, or
when he stresses the reliance of the entire missionary effort upon
advantages conferred by modern learning, arts and technology. Anderson was highly impressed, as were missionary spokesmen throughout
the century, with the apparently Providential developments in technology, commerce and military conquest that had, one way and another,
opened doors and broken down walls throughout the world for the
introduction of Christianity. He fell easily into phraseology about "the
blessedness of a Christian civilization," and he gave credit for reducing
the cost of missionary conquests "to the human enterprise of men of
the world, as seen in steamships, railways, and other signs of progress

---

[11] Rufus Anderson, *Foreign Missions: Their Relations and Claims* (New
York, 1869), 97.
[12] *Ibid.*, 94-95.

in civilization too numerous to specify." All of these amenities had been, he said, "doubtless providentially intended to facilitate the Church in its great work of evangelizing the world of mankind." [13]

It may seem that no one holding such views of the preparatory function of civilization ought to have chided others for placing civilizing efforts among the obligations of missions. Anderson would have replied, of course, that civilizing should be—and was being—taken care of by someone else, not by the missionary. But I think we must also grasp the considerable extent to which the missionary spokesmen took the values of their own culture for granted; and then the extent to which that presumption enabled them to hope for the exportation of a "pure Gospel." They thought that it had required the force of Western culture to break down the walls surrounding heathendom, but that once this had been accomplished, the superiority and Providential triumph of Western culture were so plain, to the heathen as to everyone else, that no special advocacy was needed. One was free, in other words, to preach an allegedly pure Gospel in relation to which the Western culture was at most a silent partner.

In spite of such deep-rooted assumptions and perhaps delusions, it is still fair to say that Anderson's theory of missions was antiactivist. He campaigned so vigorously against the teaching of English in missionary schools, and against the commissioning of lay persons as missionaries, that he literally split the great organization he headed. [14] A half-century later, however, at a time much nearer to Frick's assault and the acute European criticism of American missions, the mainline theory (so far as it had been represented by Anderson) had altered. In the generation of John Mott, Robert Wilder, James Dennis, Robert E. Speer and the Student Volunteer Movement—the generation leading to Edinburgh and Stockholm—the missionary ideology of the most vocal and most publicized American leaders clearly had become more explicitly activist.

This did not mean, as many critics insisted, that missionary theory now ignored the work of conversion in favor of schools or journalism, or even in favor of soup kitchens. Evangelization was still the aim, just as Mott's famous watchword ("The Evangelization of the World in This Generation") said it was. But the civilizing activities of missions had acquired new prestige and, often, primacy: Anderson had begun with an assumption that doctors and teachers are *not* to be sent,

[13] *Ibid.*, 1-19, 124, 208-9.
[14] Cyrus Hamlin, *Among the Turks* (New York, 1878), 274-86.

and then had allowed some exceptions. The men of Speer's generation, by contrast, were themselves in many cases laymen who presupposed a full acceptance of ancillary forms of missionary activity, but who then qualified their activism with stern warnings against cultural hubris, against superficial social amelioration, and against any ignoring of evangelism or the Church.

The Presbyterian and ecumenical leader Robert E. Speer, probably the most broadly representative and most sensitive of the prominent missionary theorists in the early twentieth century, reflected this full, unapologetic incorporation of civilizing motives and methods in the theory of missions. In his *Christianity and the Nations,* he rested much of the defense of the enterprise on evidence that missionized peoples were advancing in the arts and morality of civilization as understood in the West. This was a contention that had been extensively documented, a few years before, in James Dennis's *Christian Missions and Social Progress,* and in the almost yearly surveys, atlases, and gazeteers of missions appearing around the turn of the century. Speer himself, though he insisted that the supreme aim of missions is "the proclamation of Christ" and that missionary objectives "must include . . . as little beside that as is possible," plainly had given up any serious attempt to divorce conversionist and civilizing aims. [15]

American missionary theory, in other words, as one observes it in prime spokesmen of the mainline churches and boards, had become more explicitly, if still cautiously, activist in the time between the leadership of Rufus Anderson and that of Mott, Speer, and Dennis. Whether one glorified in the leadership of these men or regretted and deplored it, their stated principles were not grossly divergent from the Americanist ideology Europeans were discussing.

It would seem, perhaps, that enough has now been conceded to make the case clear: that Frick and the others were right; that the American missionary movement and American Protestantism were indeed, for good or ill, singularly activistic.

That may well be the conclusion when further investigation has been completed. But I suggest, despite the obvious importance of Protestant leaders like Speer and the unequivocal nature of their message, that the matter cannot be left there. I think we must take the trouble to look into sources that in some instances are far more recondite and scattered. The first question to be asked is whether activism as theory

---

[15] Robert E. Speer, *Christianity and the Nations* (New York, 1910), 60, 17-85.

was so clearly "American" as was commonly supposed. We must try, secondly, to determine how much difference the so-called Americanist principles made in practice—for example, to what extent the assumptions and methods of American missionaries in the field (a) corresponded with the theories of American spokesmen, and (b) varied from the practices of European colleagues. We must, finally, ask about the capacity of the American mainline churches and boards to speak authoritatively for the entire American missionary movement (to say nothing of their ability to represent "American religion" itself).

It is because of such questions that the title of this article refers to mission "ideologies" in the plural; and why the subtitle suggests that historians eventually must examine practice and stereotype as well as theoretical expression.

How singular, really—either in theory or in practice—was this American activism whose existence and occasional stridency I have conceded? One warning was voiced by Professor Adolph Deissmann of Berlin when the dispute over this matter reached its height in 1927. These hopeful theologies of the Kingdom, Deissmann pointed out, had scarcely originated with the Americans. He suggested sardonically that if Wichern, the mid-nineteenth-century German champion of social Christianity, had appeared anonymously at Stockholm and expressed his theology of the Kingdom, many at that conference would immediately have denounced his opinions as examples of the new and dangerous Americanist influence. [16] On such grounds the singularity of Americanism as theory must at least be questioned.

To answer queries about activism in actual practice, one might begin by examining comparatively the relative weight given to evangelistic and other operations in the American, British, and Continental missions at the time when these questions were raised. Judging from statistics gathered by the Student Volunteer Movement about the time of the Edinburgh Conference, there is a *prima* facie case for doubting whether American and British missions were very different from Continental ones in their intermixing of evangelistic and civilizing operations. In India, to be sure, Continental mission societies showed a higher proportion of ordained missionaries to the total missionary force than did the Anglo-American societies—41% as against 28% for the British and 32% for the Americans and Canadians. But for China the percentages were comparable: in Continental societies, 33%

---

[16] Deissmann, *Die Stockholmer Bewegung* (Berlin, 1927), 94.

were ordained; among the British the figure was 25%; among North Americans, 29%. In West Africa, the Continental societies and the North American ones showed precisely the same percentage of ordained workers: 40%. (Here the British reported 35%). [17]

Finally—to come to the matter of stereotyping—one must investigate, within the pattern of American missionary groups, the possible differences between the mainline ideologies voiced by Speer, Mott, or comparable international celebrities, and those of the spokesmen for other mission societies. A number of churches and missionary organizations, with numerous representatives in the field, sent few delegates or none to international meetings. Their theories of missions, when expounded at all, reached relatively narrow constituencies.

Even casual attention to the lists of Stockholm delegates reveals that the Americans at that meeting represented a minority—however significant—of Protestants in the United States. [18] The same is true for the Edinburgh meeting of 1910. Of the approximately 90 American societies that might have been represented at Edinburgh, only 35 actually were. Among these 35, most of the delegates (345 out of 412) came from the nine mainline mission boards; and these nine boards provided virtually all of the numerous American speakers at Edinburgh. [19]

One might surmise, in answer, that this over-representation of the American white Protestant establishment reflected the actual numerical situation at the mission stations. The field statistics suggest otherwise. In some mission areas such as Korea and Brazil, the dominance of the mainline societies was indeed almost complete (in Korea 232 missionaries out of 240; in Brazil 190 out of 204). But in most others the "sects" were quite heavily represented. They provided 30% of the total American personnel in Japan, 26% in China, 30% in

---

[17] James S. Dennis, et al., *World Atlas of Christian Missions* (New York, 1911), 88-94. Such figures of course do not tell a definitive story. One would need to discover how many ordained persons may have been engaged in non-evangelistic work; inquire how many lay persons were devoting themselves to some form of evangelism; and consider a number of other variables.

[18] William R. Hutchison, "The Americanness of the Social Gospel: An Inquiry in Comparative History," *Church History*, 44 (1975), 380.

[19] World Missionary Conference, *History and Records of the Conference* (Edinburgh, 1910), 35-107. James A. Scherer's assertion that "the participation of virtually every non-Roman missionary agency in Christendom had been secured" would seem to be wildly wrong, at least with respect to the United States. Sherer, "Ecumenical Mandates for Mission," in Norman A. Horner, ed., *Protestant Crosscurrents in Mission: The Ecumenical-Conservative Encounter* (Nashville, 1968), 21.

India, 70% in West Africa, 20% in Southwest Africa, 55% in South Africa, and so on. [20]

In some cases, we know almost before we begin serious investigation that the non-mainstream groups in question conformed to the patterns visible in the dominant organizations. Alexander Crummell and certain other leaders of the American Black churches, for example, far outdid most White advocates in their enthusiasm for carrying Anglo-American language, technology, and culture to the heathen. [21] And many other sectarian groups will be found, in their dissent from the American mainstream, to exemplify that very individualism that formed such an important part of the activist stereotype.

But beyond those instances there are literally dozens of others—some of them, like the Adventists, responsible for very large contingents in the mission areas—which may or may not support the stereotypes in question. We should find out.

Meanwhile, we must recognize that those voluble, terribly earnest American speakers at Edinburgh and Stockholm—whether or not they really represented "American religion"—did convey an American self-image that was seen and taken seriously throughout the world, and that is not to be under-rated. Their sense of themselves and their role constituted a further twist or transmutation in the American self-image that Professor Perry Miller found developing and changing in the seventeenth century.

The Puritans, Miller wrote, having seen their experiment ignored by the rest of the world, drew back from their original errand—which had been both exemplary and tutelary—and resolved to come to terms with the American wilderness. [22] Their nineteenth-century missionary successors, at least from the generation of Anderson to that of Speer, managed to rationalize a return to something like the early intent. They shaped a new "errand" into the howling wilderness of the world. While painfully aware that America had still not fully come to terms with itself and its Judeo-Christian heritage, they considered that process sufficiently advanced that the word of its impending success could be transmitted to those still sitting in utter or relative darkness.

Once again, as in the very earliest years of the Puritan experiment, there was reluctance simply to let the "city on a hill," the aspiring Christian Commonwealth, stand and shine as a light to the

---

[20] Dennis et al., *World Atlas*, 86-102.
[21] See, for example, Crummell's *The Future of Africa* (New York, 1862).
[22] Perry Miller, *Errand Into the Wilderness* (Cambridge, Mass., 1956).

nations. The managers of the experiment, or their agents, would go out
to persuade others to follow the light. They might even influence the
political process, as American Puritan leaders had hoped to do in
Cromwellian England. Whether John Mott—refusing the political leve-
rage even of an ambassadorship—or any other American religious
leaders yearned for much political influence remains doubtful. But their
exuberant sense that they were reaffirming and extending the original
errand must, I think, be appreciated if we are to begin to understand
this tumultuous phase of the history that has shaped the modern international order and modern consciousness.

THE ECUMENICAL COMMITMENT TO A TRANSFORMING SOCIAL JUSTICE

JOHN C. BENNETT

Emeritus, Union Theological Seminary

In recent decades there has been a remarkable converging of the ecumenical movement with its structure in the World Council of Churches and the leadership of the Roman Catholic Church in their commitment to a transforming social justice. I contrast transforming justice with justice that is no more than fair application of existing rules. This common commitment is in radical contrast to the dominant tendencies in both world-wide Protestantism and Roman Catholicism in the nineteenth century. Commitment to a transforming social justice is not new and it has many precedents in Christian history including particular movements such as the anti-slavery movement in the nineteenth century. What is new is the extent to which there is this convergence in the teaching of most churches.

First, I shall give some evidence for what I have said about the previous neglect of social justice in the churches. In the United States there was a very strong tendency before the rise of the Social Gospel in the last decades of the nineteenth century for theologians and leaders in the Protestant churches to identify Christian faith with capitalistic individualism and to discourage interference with the law of supply and demand by legislation or by labor unions. The laws of *laissez faire* economics were believed to be the laws of divine providence. There was a strong tendency to assume that the poor were so generally responsible for their poverty that poverty was said to be a sin by such a popular preacher as Henry Ward Beecher [1] and wealth was seen to be

---

[1] Quoted in Sidney Ahlstrom, *A Religious History of the American People* (New Haven, 1972), 789. I recommend the following three volumes for a more extended coverage of the material in this chapter and for bibliography: Edward Duff, S. J., *The Social Thought of the World Council of Churches* (New York, 1956); Paul Bock, *In Search of a Responsible World Society* (Philadelphia, 1974); and Joseph Gremillion, *The Gospel of Peace and Justice* (Maryknoll, N.Y., 1976). The last mentioned volume includes major documents that cover the Roman Catholic developments from Pope John until 1975. The reader may be interested to know that I was a participant in all of the conferences and assemblies on the Protestant-Orthodox side mentioned in the text except Stockholm and Nairobi.

a sign of virtue. [2] Henry F. May in his *Protestant Churches and In-dustrial America* makes the following generalization: "In 1876 Protestantism presented a massive, almost unbroken front in its defense of the social *status quo*." [3] 1876 is not only the end of our nation's first century; it also is a good date for the beginning of the influence on American Protestantism of the Social Gospel which, whatever its defects as seen from our vantage point, did undermine the complacent economic individualism which dominated American Protestantism for so long. It also was an important factor in preparing the way for the later ecumenical commitment which I am emphasizing.

In 1948 a section of the Lambeth Conference which brings together all the bishops of the Anglican communion made a very frank statement about the contrast between their views and the dominant tendencies in the Church of England and in many other European churches in earlier periods:

> We have to admit that the Christian Church through the formative decades of the industrial era showed little insight into what was befalling human society. It was still thinking in terms of feudalism. The Church of England was identified almost completely with the ruling classes, as were the churches of central and eastern Europe. Its own economy had the marks of a dying feudalism or latterly of bourgeois society. [4]

Archbishop William Temple confirms this judgment. In a chapter in which he shows that there have been important social teachings in Christian history involving what I call a commitment to transforming social justice, he is driven to say: "There was nearly a century during which the social witness of the Church was almost unheard." [5] That century came to an end in his judgment with the revival of Christian social doctrine by Frederick Denison Maurice and his Christian Socialist colleagues.

It is however important to avoid the tendency of many enthusiasts for social forms of Christianity to assume that Christian history has

---

[2] See as a startling account of the complacency about wealth the chapter entitled "The Gospel of Wealth of the Gilded Age" in Ralph Henry Gabriel, *The Course of American Democratic Thought* (New York, 1940).

[3] Henry F. May, *Protestant Churches in Industrial America* (New York, 1949), 91. Martin Marty (*Righteous Empire* [New York, 1970], 145) says of this quotation that "it is difficult to find documentation that would lead one to alter May's judgment."

[4] *The Lambeth Conferences - 1867-1948* (London, 1948). Section on the Lambeth Conference of 1948, Report on the Church and the Modern World, Part 2, p. 21.

[5] William Temple, *Christianity and Social Order* (New York, 1942), 35.

been almost entirely a history of social apostasy. There have been those in many periods who have witnessed to God's identification with the poor and oppressed and who have clearly taught that human need has the right of way over the rights of property. It is interesting to see how one expression of this witness has reappeared among Christian teachers. I refer to the well known statement of St. Ambrose: "You are not making a gift of possessions to the poor person. You are handing over to him what is his. For what has been given in common for the use of all you have arrogated to yourself. The world is given to all, and not only to the rich." St. Thomas quotes a very similar passage from St. Ambrose. [6] Pope Paul VI in his encyclical, *Populorum Progressio* (Par. 23) lifts up that passage again for emphasis in his strong plea for justice for the poor in the third world. Many sectarian or minority movements in Christian history have witnessed to the Biblical teaching about justice and have embodied this same commitment. George Williams in his *The Radical Reformation*, which has done so much to give us a broader and richer view of the Reformation, has brought to the fore this radical ferment in Christian history. In a later period the left-wing Calvinists of the English revolution spoke to our concern for a transforming social justice.

I am in this chapter emphasizing the convergence of both Protestants and Catholics. In spite of much emphasis on social justice in Catholic teaching, the dominant tendency in the nineteenth century seems to have been a fear of social change. Catholic authorities seemed to have been traumatized by the French Revolution and for some decades greatly inhibited by the fear of all forms of Marxism. Pope Leo XIII marks the beginning of a new period in which the plight of the victims of the industrial revolution came to haunt the Church and the rights of the organizations of industrial workers came to be much emphasized. Leo shared the fear of Marxism and he seemed preoccupied to a great extent with defense of the Church against rising forces of social change but he did begin a new period. The Catholic support for the rights of the industrial workers (now in this country of the farm-workers) which has had a great effect on our history goes back to the inspiration of Leo's social encyclicals. John XXIII and Paul VI speak without the old fears and inhibitions to the problems of social justice in our time.

I shall begin this study with ecumenical developments outside the

---

[6] *Summa Theologiae* 2a2ae, Q 66, Art. 7.

Roman Catholic Church after the first world war. What happened then was made possible by the momentum of Christian social teaching associated with the Social Gospel in this country and parallel movements in Europe, especially in Britain. The international ecumenical movement that dealt with the problems of "Life and Work" became significant as a result of the Stockholm Conference in 1925. There has been a tendency to discount that conference because it represented to a great extent the outlook of the liberal Social Gospel and Anglo-Saxon activism. It took place at the beginning of the revival of Reformation theology for which Karl Barth was the great stimulus and quite soon it was regarded as theologically superficial, though the major theological conflict over the tendency to identify the Kingdom of God with achievements in history did come to the surface at Stockholm. The criticisms of Stockholm should not obscure its importance as the beginning of an ecumenical process. The idea of Christian unity based upon cooperation in areas of agreement without raising the ultimate theological issues proved to be a mistake only in part. It has remained true to this day that Christian unity both in common social commitments and in areas of common Christian faith can be achieved without waiting for unity on the particular theological issues which stand in the way of full organic union of the churches. The mistake at Stockholm was that it did not take seriously enough other theological issues which impede cooperation on social issues. Some of them were raised at Stockholm and in the next period the ecumenical movement began to put these theological issues on its agenda while it continued to seek bases for cooperation on issues of social justice and peace. The Faith and Order Movement continued to study the theological differences that were directly relevant to the quest for full organic union.

Growing out of the Stockholm Conference and the work of its "Continuation Committee" the Universal Christian Council of Life and Work was formed in 1930. This provided the institutional framework for future ecumenical cooperation on social issues and in 1938 it joined with the Faith and Order Movement in forming the World Council of Churches. [7] The major event before the formation of the World Council of Churches was the Oxford Conference on Church, Community and State in 1937.

---

[7] In 1938 the World Council began its existence under the title "The World Council of Churches in process of formation." World War II interrupted the process and the World Council came fully and formally into existence at Amsterdam in 1948.

In the preparations for the Oxford Conference it was determined that Oxford would be different from Stockholm in giving major attention to the theological differences most closely related to Christian social ethics and social policy. Volumes were written in preparation for the conference on the Christian understanding of man, the Kingdom of God and history, the theology of the state, and the function of the Church in society.

The report of the Oxford Conference on the economic order laid the foundation for most subsequent ecumenical thinking about social justice. [8] New emphases did come later as the struggles of the third world for social justice came to the fore in ecumenical thinking for the Oxford Conference was almost entirely western in its make-up. Now that the World Council has become a sounding board for the third world this is seen as Oxford's serious limitation but I doubt if its most fundamental teaching has been superceded. The following is my summary of its statement of the dialectical relationship between justice and love: Love transcends justice but love must seek justice in the social sphere. Justice is necessary in the restraint of evil but it is also a guide toward the transformation of society under the judgment of love and in the direction of greater harmony and brotherhood. Social systems are never to be identified with the Kingdom of God but the opposite error must also be avoided that assumes that the ideals of the Kingdom provide no guidance for social decisions and structures. The section of the Conference that made this report included both believers in a reformed capitalism and advocates of various forms of socialism and the section refused to identify Christian faith or the church with either.

Yet the report emphasized four points at which the Christian understanding of man was "affronted by the assumptions and operations of the economic order of the industrialized world." They were as follows: "The enhancement of acquisitiveness," "inequalities," "irresponsible possession of economic power" and "the frustration of the sense of Christian vocation." In each case the criticism of capitalism was drastic though that label was not used. Most important for our purpose was the discussion of inequalities. It is clear that Oxford taught

---

[8] My references are to the report of Section Three on "The Church, Community and State in Relation to the Economic Order" of which I was the secretary. This section of the report shows the influence of Reinhold Neibuhr and the paragraphs dealing with inequalities show the influence of R. H. Tawney. Both were on the drafting committee.

that justice should be under the pressure of equality, equality of opportunity and equality of condition, without advocating a system that seeks to guarantee complete equality. It saw clearly that inequalities of condition are often so serious that they undermine equality of opportunity. Emphasis was put on "the primary duty of insuring that the conditions required for full personal development are enjoyed by the whole of the rising generation." As an anticipation of so much later teaching it was noted that disadvantages are often the result of race. What was said about irresponsible possession of economic power was also important for the achievement of justice. Such power "often makes them (those over whom it is exercised) servile; fear of losing their jobs and a vague belief that the richer members of society always hold the whip hand, tends to destroy their spiritual vitality." Under "the frustration of Christian vocation" one major concern mentioned is the effect of unemployment on people.

The report also includes teaching about property which involve far-reaching criticisms of the institutions based upon economic individualism. The relativity and contingency of all human property rights are emphasized. Much is made of the distinction between property for personal use and property that gives the owners power over other persons with the latter seen as the more problematic. The point is made that "every argument in defense of property rights which is valid for Christian thinking is also an argument for the widest distribution of these rights." [9]

Taken together all that was said by this conference supported a view of justice as a source of radical criticism of existing capitalistic institutions and as a guide for the transformation of society in the interests of the victims of present structures and policies. There was no ideological commitment to any total system. Communism was criticized for its utopianism, its one-sided materialism, and its "disregard for the dignity of the individual," and was seen as a warning against the substitution of irresponsible political power for irresponsible economic power. There are very slight indications of a concern that later came to dominate ecumenical thinking: the contrast between rich and poor nations.

The Amsterdam Assembly did not retreat from what was said at Oxford but sharpened the criticism of Churches for the neglect of the

[9] I remember showing this section on property to William Temple (then Archbishop of York) who was in another section, and he suggested this very important sentence.

struggles of the victims of injustice. It dealt with the conflict between capitalism and communism with more precision than Oxford. The experience of Christians from the third world was beginning to be felt. Also, at Amsterdam there was more said about racism than at Oxford though it was not until the Evanston Assembly in 1954 that racism became a major subject of Assembly discussion, and after that time it has been one of the two or three chief concerns of the World Council both in its teaching and in its policies.

The Amsterdam report stressed the failures of the Churches in the past: "our churches have often given religious sanction to the special privileges of dominant classes, races and political groups, and so they have been obstacles to changes necessary in the interests of social justice and political freedom." One result of the failure of the churches has been the development of "communism in its modern totalitarian form" and its atheism. It was significant that as early as 1948 the delegates at Amsterdam repudiated the idea of a holy cold war against communism. They saw communism as a judgment on the churches and they called the churches to "recognize the hand of God in the revolt of multitudes against injustice that gives communism much of its strength" and to recognize that "the atheism and anti-religious teaching of communism are in part a reaction to the chequered career of a professedly Christian society."

The Amsterdam report received most publicity in this country because of the way in which it dealt with both communism and what it called *"laissez faire* capitalism." Its criticism of "the atheistic Marxian communism of our day" was entirely negative both theologically and ethically. For example, it referred to "the belief that a particular class by virtue of its role as the bearer of a new order is free from the sins and ambiguities that Christians believe to be characteristic of all human existence" and to "the ruthless methods of communists in dealing with their opponents," to the demand of the party on its members for an exclusive and unqualified loyalty which belongs only to God, and "to the coercive policies of communist dictatorship in controlling every aspect of life." The only communism known at the time was Stalinism and it could be said at a later time that these criticisms did not apply to the same extent to all forms of communism.

The criticisms of capitalism with the use of that label were similar to those made at Oxford with the addition of the criticism that "it has kept the people of capitalist countries subject to a kind of

fate which has taken the form of such social catastrophes as mass
unemployment." Its criticisms of capitalism were not theological: they
were criticisms of its effects and especially of its tendency to "subordinate what should be the primary task of any economy—the
meeting of human needs—to the economic advantages of those who
have most power over its institutions." The delegates at Amsterdam
agreed with the judgment made at Oxford that Christianity should not
be identified with either capitalism or socialism as ways of organizing
society. However the specific criticisms of capitalism were stronger
than anything said about socialism as distinguished from "communism
in its modern totalitarian form." It did speak of those who fear that
the socializing of the means of production will "lead to new and in-
ordinate combinations of political and economic power, culminating
finally in an omnicompetent state." In one sentence it offered a
criticism of the ideologiec of both *"laissez faire"* capitalism and communism. This sentence caused some consternation in the United States.
The following was said about these ideologies: "Communist ideology
puts the emphasis upon economic justice, and promises that freedom
will come automatically after the completion of the revolution. Capitalism
puts the emphasis upon freedom, and promises that justice will follow
as a by-product of free enterprise." The statement about capitalism is
true of its ideology as this was very generally taught before the development of welfare capitalism. Perhaps most of all in the United States a
continuing belief in this ideology creates an inhibition against direct
efforts of the community to act for the sake of justice. Even here
what can be called *"laissez faire* capitalism" no longer exists but the use
of that qualification of the meaning of capitalism did not seem to
reduce the resentment in many American circles against Amsterdam and
the World Council. 10

The idea of "the responsible society" which was given currency
at Amsterdam dealt chiefly with political structures but it had strong
implications for social justice as well as political freedom. It includes
the idea that those who hold either political or economic power "should
be responsible to God and to the people who were affected by it." It
was said that power should be distributed as widely as possible through

---

10 Section three of Amsterdam of which I was also secretary chose to speak
of capitalism without the limiting words, *laissez faire,* in relation to four criticisms which indicate tendencies in capitalism. The limiting words were added at
another point to the original draft after considerable debate. At Evanston the
word "capitalism" was widely dropped because of its ambiguity.

the whole community. And this was linked with economic justice and equal opportunity.

It is not necessary to write as fully about the subsequent Assemblies because there was no retreat from the affirmations concerning a transforming justice made at Amsterdam. At Evanston (1954) there was a broadening of the range of this commitment. This was most pronounced in regard to race. A whole section of the Assembly was devoted to racial and ethnic tensions. Racial discrimination and segregation in both South Africa and the United States were in the minds of everyone. The extent to which the churches mirrored in their life the racial pattern of society was much emphasized. The report of the section said: "When we are given Christian insight the whole pattern of racial discrimination is seen as an unutterable offense against God, to be endured no longer so that the very stones cry out." The Assembly passed the following resolution: "The Second Assembly of the World Council of Churches declares its conviction that any form of segregation based on race, color or ethnic origin is contrary to the Gospel, and is incompatible with the Christian doctrine of man and with the nature of the Church of Christ." [11]

A study conference had been held in Lucknow, India, prior to the Evanston Assembly and one of the sections of Evanston appropriated some of its statements about the need for change in the so-called "under-developed regions." [12] Immediately after the assembly the World Council initiated a study of what were called areas of "rapid social change." Rapid social change is present in western industrialized countries as well as in Asia and Africa and Latin America but this phrase was in practice a euphemism to refer to areas of economic and related forms of underdevelopment. Often the word, "developing," has been used as being less invidious. This study with the help of a foundation grant continued for six years and it became the means by which the World Council prepared itself intensively to deal with the contrast between rich and poor nations and with the problems of development and liberation at later Assemblies. [13] Since the next

---

[11] The first draft of the report on race was in large part of the work of Alan Paton.

[12] The East Asia Christian Conference came to be an important agency under the umbrella of the World Council of Churches, and it often pioneered on questions of justice.

[13] The results of this study are summarized and interpreted by Paul Abrecht in *The Churches and Rapid Social Change* (London, 1961). He has been the prime mover in most of the activities of the World Council related to social justice from 1954 to the present.

Assembly met in New Delhi this concern came to the center of its
attention. Also, during those years the World Council's membership
increased steadily and more and more the churches from Asia, Africa
and Latin America made themselves felt.

This new trend was supported by the fact that the International
Missionary Conference at the New Delhi Assembly was integrated with
the World Council of Churches. This meant a unification of the
ecumenical activities that were related to those continents.

In 1966 a conference that was in the succession of the conferences
that had met in Stockholm and Oxford and which had dealt with
problems of life and work met in Geneva. Its special subject was defined
as "Christians in the technical and social revolutions of our time." It
was deliberately set up to give the churches from Asia, Africa and
Latin America a number of delegates (47%) that were out of proportion to the size of the churches on those continents so that the human
interests of those vast areas would be fully represented. This conference
caused the World Council to move more intensively than ever before into
the technical problems of economic development and into the political
problems of revolutionary change. The majority of the delegates were
lay men and women and of these a great many were economic or social
experts and politicians. At this conference there were no more articulate
representatives than those from Latin America. The actual reports of
the conference are moderate documents but in the plenary sessions and
on many other occasions the issues raised by revolutionary struggles
were greatly emphasized. From this time on the World Council in both
its teaching and its policies moved away from preoccupation with the
issues raised by Europeans and North Americans and from major
attention to east-west problems and came to give special attention to the
global problems of poverty, hunger and racial discrimination.

The Geneva Conference though officially called did not represent
the churches officially as do the Assemblies. It was called to speak
for itself to the World Council of Churches. It had great influence
upon the subsequent official life of the Council. The Uppsala Assembly
(1968) which met two years later reflected the spirit of Geneva to a
remarkable extent.

All that has followed Uppsala in the history of the World Council
gives additional support to my contention concerning the commitment of
the ecumenical community to a transforming justice. There is no space
for an account of the explosion of meetings, specialized and regional,
of actions both symbolic and substantial which illustrate the depth of

this commitment. [14] Between Uppsala and Nairobi (1975) these meetings and activities gave special emphasis to racial justice especially in the context of Africa. They also extended the range of interests related to this commitment involving the quite recently recognized limits of resources, the peaceful uses of nuclear power, the kinds of technology best suited to the development of nations with large populations, the reality of hunger and the threat of its catastrophic increase. Problems of economic justice are no longer as simple as they were at Oxford or Amsterdam when it seemed that the chief issue was to find the best place on the spectrum between capitalistic individualism and socialism. A whole range of technical problems created by limited resources and inflation complicate all efforts to find systemic solutions.

Priorities differ from region to region and it is still the case that many Christians live in situations where the overwhelming problem is to find ways to overcome political and economic institutions of oppression and the emphasis is on the necessity of revolution. The more technical issues for them can wait until they have displaced the political and economic powers of which the vast majority of their populations are at present victims. Here the issue of revolutionary violence is central and perplexing. [15] Churches and their ecumenical institutions are deeply divided on this issue and the divisions are between people who are equally committed to transforming justice. Debates on this level only underline the basic commitment.

---

[14] One of these many conferences in which I was a participant was on theology and social ethics and was held in 1968 in the Theological Seminary in Zagorst near Moscow under the auspices of both the Church and Society unit and the Faith and Order unit of the World Council of Churches. It included Russian Orthodox and several Roman Catholics and produced one of the best statements of which I know about the ethics of revolution. One of the most publicized actions of the World Council was its program to combat Racism which made grants to liberation movements in many parts of the world though the early emphasis was on Africa. This was one of the most controversial of any of the actions of the World Council, but its leaders believed that more than by words this act identified the World Council with those struggling for justice against great odds.

[15] Because of the relation of some of the activities of the World Council and of many Christians to liberation movements that are involved in revolutionary violence a commission appointed by the Council worked for several years on the subject of violence. Its report which canvasses the issues and shows that some disagreements cannot be overcome was published in *The Ecumenical Review* (October, 1973).

II

The new relationship between Roman Catholics and Protestants is the most momentous change that has come in the life of organized Christianity in my lifetime. I shall emphasize the converging of the ecumenical movement that has its structure in the World Council of Churches and the Roman Catholic leadership on this commitment to transforming justice. The encyclicals of the Popes from Leo XIII to the present day have on this commitment moved ever more decisively in one direction. Since the Second Vatican Council there has been a truly amazing removal of obstacles to social justice which had been present in the political teaching of the Church, especially teaching about religious freedom. The declaration of the Vatican Council on religious freedom came when the Church was clearly ripe for it and it speedily changed teaching, policies and climate in the Church everywhere. In Latin America where the Catholic Church had been a persecuting Church not many years ago it has become the courageous and effective defender of the rights, not only of Christians or Catholics, but of all persons. Until this change came the Church could not be a reliable defender of economic justice for all people. So long as it was engaged in defending itself against non-Catholics it tended to ally itself with the conservative political and economic powers. This new openness of the Church and its readiness to support political democracy and freedom for all represent an extraordinary change. The Church is no longer defending itself anxiously against socialism as was the case with the social stance of previous popes. Since John XXIII the Church has moved away from its rigid hostility toward Marxism in all forms. Dialogue with Marxists and negotiations with Communist regimes and even greater tolerance of Italian Communism have removed the temptation always to support the *status quo* as a way of defending the Church against communism. As I write there is a struggle within the Church concerning the way the highest authorities should respond to the Liberation Theologians in Latin America who make considerable use of Marxism in their diagnosis of their situation and who favor alliances between Christians and Marxists in their countries. [16] Yet,

---

[16] The conference of Latin American bishops in 1968 in Medillin gave considerable encouragement to the liberation theologians. There is a strong effort on the part of some Latin American bishops in cooperation with a faction in the Curia to blunt the radicalism of Medillin at the next conference of the bishops in 1978. This struggle is described in articles by Gary MacEoin in *Latin America Press*, January 5, 1978 and by Peter Hebblethudite in *The National Catholic Reporter*, March 24, 1978. This suggests that the Pope meets obstacles in his own commitment to radical changes in Latin America.

the larger picture does enable me to write confidently about the present convergence between Catholic thinking on problems of social justice and the teaching of the World Council. Pope John's encyclicals, *Mater et Magistra* and *Pacem in Terris* and Pope Paul's encyclical, *Populorum Progressio* and his Apostolic Letter entitled *Octogesima Adveniens* and the statement by the Synod of Bishops that met in Rome in 1971 on "Justice in the World" taken together provide a consistent and far-reaching commitment of the Church.

The openness of the Church toward what we might call in general the "left" in contrast to its defensiveness against all movements and institutions influenced by Marxism or even by democratic forms of Socialism was very important in freeing the Church for a reliable commitment to justice. Pope John in a famous passage in *Pacem in Terris* provided the basis for this openness. He wrote as follows:

> It must be borne in mind, futhermore, that neither can false philosophical teachings regarding the nature, origin and destiny of the universe and of man be identified with historical movements that have economic, social, cultural or political ends, not even when these movements have originated from those teachings and have drawn and still draw inspiration therefrom.... This is so because the teachings, once they are drawn up and defined, remain always the same, while the movements, working in constantly evolving historical situations, cannot but be influenced by these latter and cannot avoid, therefore, being subject to changes, even of a profound nature. (159)

Pope Paul quotes this passage with approval in *Octogesima Adveniens* but he gives a mild warning against being led by the desirable aspects of movements influenced by Marxism to an acceptance of the Marxist ideology. As in many papal documents what is said is almost on a knife edge in the warning given against moving too far in a direction which has a rather tentative approval. [17] The pope couples a warning against Marxist ideology with a warning against "liberal ideology," a position similar to the common American trust in the self-sufficiency of free-enterprise.

The sense of global responsibility and especially concern for the poor in the third world are very pronounced in the utterances of Paul VI. His rigidity about birth control, which is not unrelated to the problems which cause poverty, and about women and about sex are disappointing but this Pope remains very progressive on matters of social justice. His encyclical, *Populorum Progressio,* shows more passion than most encyclicals. While on the issue of revolutionary violence it takes a negative position, except for one paragraph which seems to

---

[17] *Octogesima Adveniens,* 30-34.

provide permission for it under extreme conditions (par. 31), the Pope
in this encyclical provides a launching pad for the liberation theologians and others who go farther in their radicalism than the encyclical. [18]

I have referred to Pope Paul's quotation from St. Ambrose which
ends with the words "the world is given to all and not only to the rich."
The encyclical adds the following comment:

> That is, private property does not constitute for anyone an absolute and un-
> conditioned right. No one is justified in keeping for his exclusive use what
> he does not need when others lack necessities. In a word, according to the
> traditional doctrine as found in the Fathers of the Church and the great
> theologians, the right to property must never be exercised to the detriment
> of the common good.

And then he says that when there is a conflict between property rights
and the common good it is the responsibility of "public authorities to
look for a solution, with the active participation of individuals and
social groups."

Populorum Progressio is the strongest trumpet-call for truly radical
change in third world countries in any of the encyclicals. It still uses
the word, development, which is widely rejected in Latin America
because it is regarded as involving imitation of the so-called "developed
countries" and because it is seen to be on the agenda of those countries
serving their interests. The Pope, however, makes clear that "to speak
of development, is in effect to show as much concern for social progress
as for economic growth. It is not sufficient to increase overall wealth
for it to be distributed equitably." This is in sharp contrast to the
kind of development taking place with what is regarded as success in a
country like Brazil.

The responsibility of the richer nations is greatly emphasized: "We
repeat once more that the superfluous wealth of rich countries should
be placed at the service of poor nations." Then there follows a principle
that has the most far-reaching implications: "the rule which up to now
held good for the benefit of those nearest to us, must today be applied
to all the needy of this world." This can be bracketed with the following
statement from the Uppsala Assembly that was quite representative of
the spirit and teaching of that body: "It is one world and the gross
inequalities between the people of different nations and different
continents are as inexcusable as the gross inequalities within nations."

---

[18] Gustavo Gutierrez in his most influential *A Theology of Libertation* makes
use both of this encyclical and of the reports of the Medillin conference in this way.

(Section III) In one sentence which could have been written by the liberation theologians the Pope says of churches and nations that if they do not live according to this principle "their continued greed will certainly call down upon them the judgment of God and the wrath of the poor, with consequences no one can foretell."

All the teachings from the World Council and from Popes which I have cited would be of little importance if they represented an occasional statement arrived at hurriedly under the emotional pressure that often takes place in religious meetings. Their significance comes from the fact that they represent a cumulative development over several decades. This general direction is reflected in the work of So-De-Pax (Society, Development and Peace), the only agency which actually unites the World Council and the Vatican. It is interesting that this one agency relating the World Council and the Vatican is in the area of the common concern for justice and peace. [19]

This trend at the highest level of ecumenical life receives strong support from national and regional councils of churches and from the teaching of many denominations. It seems of particular significance that Lutherans who were so critical of the Social Gospel for its optimism concerning the embodiment of the Kingdom of God in institutions of this world and for confusing Law and Gospel have done much to support the positions taken by the World Council of Churches. This is especially true of the work of the Lutheran World Federation. [20]

Any churchman in any country and in any denomination knows that there is a great contrast between the trend about which I have written and the attitudes that are present in many, probably most, congregations. This is true of both Roman Catholics and Protestant congregations. There is a tendency for local churches to reflect the dominant attitudes in the national or even local culture. Yet, there is continuous interaction between the teaching at the ecumenical level and many groups, agencies, journals, Schools of Theology which influence Christians in the various countries. There is a steady process of education that goes on as more and more churchmen participate in the many processes of corporate thinking and policy-making beyond the local church. One must not claim

[19] The Vatican has a Pontifical Commission on Peace and Justice and there is in many countries a national commission of the Church with the same name. So-De-Pax links this commission with the World Council of Churches.

[20] The movement within Lutheranism away from the inhibitions in regard to social and political action resulting from the Two-Realms doctrine can be seen in many selections in a volume edited by Karl H. Hertz, *Two Kingdoms and One World* (Augsburg, 1976).

too much for this in terms of changes in public opinion throughout the churches but it is a reality that should be affirmed and its effect depends a good deal on how particular issues of justice come into focus as a result of events. An illustration of the effectiveness of this inter-action is the very great change within churches on issues of racial justice.

As one who is not an historian I am diffident about making genera-lizations which involve most of Christian history, especially in a book that is in honor of a great historian, but I want to conclude this chapter with a suggestion concerning what seems to be the meaning of what I have written. If one regards as significant, regardless of the extent to which it needs qualification, the basic contrast that Ernst Troeltsch drew between church and sect, [21] can we not say that some tendencies which were chiefly characteristic of sects with roots among the dispossessed are now present in the life and teaching of the great churches? When has their leadership, both theological and ecclesiasti-cal, responded so sensitively to the poor and oppressed of the world and to their struggles for more just structures? No longer is there a viable response in terms of philanthropy alone. Pressure on the churches by people in many countries who have been oppressed or neglected has been a major factor in this change. They have become articulate and have often gained the power to push if not to overthrow the powers that have kept them dependent and in poverty. Within the churches this pushing has changed attitudes and commitments especially when the consciences have been prepared to accept change. Who can estimate the relative importance of this pushing and of the Christian resources which have prepared consciences? There are and there will continue to be widespread conflicts within the Christian community over these issues of transforming justice but they will not be chiefly conflicts between sects and churches; rather they are and will continue to be conflicts within the churches.

---

[21] See especially Ernst Troeltsch, *The Social Teaching of the Christian Churches* (New York, 1931), I:328-43.

MODEL MAN, MODERN MAN, REFORMATION MAN

LEWIS W. SPITZ

Stanford University

The church historian in a modern university lives and works in an overwhelmingly humanistic and scientific environment. He might well ask whether he is an anachronism in such a context. He must take stock on occasion of whom it is that he is being historical about. He must probe his own self-conscious depths as well as listen to the views of his colleagues as to what man, the major subject and object of history, really is. He can contribute to the conversation the dimension of historical perspective, which here can best be done by presenting the most popular current models of man, the western conception of modern man, and Reformation man as the refurbished image of Christian man, the ideal church man.

A great company of earnest men share this concern, few so learned in theology and the social and natural sciences as Wolfhart Pannenberg, who formulates the problem in this way:

> We live in an age of anthropology. One of the principal goals of contemporary thought is a comprehensive science of man. Many different scholarly disciplines are united in this goal. In connection with the question about man, the particular investigations within different disciplines have frequently brought these disciplines into unexpected contact with one another. Biologists and philosophers, jurists and sociologists, psychologists, physicians, and theologians have found related insights and to some extent even a common language in the question about man. The specialized methods appear, before our eyes, to contribute to overcoming their own fragmentation by constructing a new comprehensive understanding of man. Today the sciences concerned with man are following the best route toward taking the place in the general consciousness held in earlier centuries by metaphysics. The fundamental change that man's consciousness has experienced in recent times is expressed in this: man is no longer willing to fit into an order of the world or of nature, but wants to rule over the world. [1]

---

[1] Wolfhart Pannenberg, *What Is Man? Contemporary Anthropology in Theological Perspective* (Philadelphia, 1970), 1. (The literature is enormous, but two statements deserving special notice are Jürgen Moltmann, *Man: Christian Anthropology in the Conflicts of the Present* (Philadelphia, 1974), and Abraham Joshua Heschel, *Who Is Man?* (Stanford, 1965). Heschel observes (p. 19) that "psychology, biology, sociology have sought to explore the nature of man. And yet man remains an enigma." Two valuable collections of sources and essays on the problem of man are Crane Brinton, ed., *The Fate of Man* (New York, 1961) and Joseph K. Davis, ed., *Man in Crisis: Perspectives on the Individual and His World* (Glenview, IL., 1970).

Anthropology has served as a focal point for interdisciplinary discussions for well over a century. In his famous lectures entitled *Weltgeschichtliche Betrachtungen* Jacob Burckhardt announced: "We, however, shall start out from the one point accessible to us, the one eternal center of all things—man suffering, striving, doing, as he is and was, and ever shall be. Hence our study will, in a certain sense, be pathological in kind." Friedrich Nietzsche confided after hearing one of Burckhardt's addresses that for the first time in his life he had enjoyed listening to a lecture. What is different about the present discussion is the extent to which the natural sciences have joined in the conversation.

Many of the emerging post-modern models of man have ancient historical embryonic antecedents. The zoomorphic view of man which sees people as mere animals has a root in western culture as far back as ancient Greece. One need merely recall the famous instance recorded by Plato. In response to the definition of man as a two-legged animal lacking feathers, Diogenes the next day brought to the encounter group a plucked cock. The sophists defined man as a living being (ZOON) having the power of speech. To Aristotle man was variously a rational or a political animal. Popular books today describe man as a naked ape or "an ingenious assemblage of portable plumbing." One elemental cynical analysis of man reads like this: "The human body contains a sufficient amount of fat to make seven cakes of soup, enough iron to make a medium-sized nail, a sufficient amount of phosphorous to equip two thousand match-heads, enough sulphur to rid one's self of one's fleas." Human beings can truthfully be described as living organisms which are highly complex chemical machines consisting chiefly of colloidal material and possessing the peculiarity of preserving and reproducing themselves.

Thomas Hanna created quite a stir with his assertion that neglect of the somatic side of man, inflicted by the Platonic and idealist tradition, was the cause of man's basic ills. Morality or immorality is most evidently an expressive somatic response to something within the individual's environment. To say that another man's behavior is "immoral," he argued, is to say rather that you experience a particular complex of neuromuscular events in response to his behavior. *What,* then, and *where* is the "immorality" itself? Without question, the *where* is the body and the *what* is an automatic neuromuscular activity of the body. [2] Hanna is able to cite University of Chicago psychologists

---

[2] Thomas Hanna, *Bodies in Revolt: A Primer in Somatic Thinking* (New York, 1970), 23.

and others who showed by experiments that subjects experienced an automatic adaptational reflex to sensuous stimulation that was quite uncontrollable by act of will. [3] One thrust of behavioral science research has indeed been to minimize the extent of rational control in man's decisions and responses. Fascinating work is being done with electro-encephalographs and the research on biofeedbacks, the alpha wave (relaxed alertness), and other physiological phenomena. Since Pareto's recognition in *Mind and Society* of the extent to which behavior is determined by inherited or conditioned patterns and allowed by man's near infinite capacity for rationalizations, derivations and residues, a major emphasis in the behavioral sciences has been toward a zoomorphic view of man.

Reflecting the imagery of an industrial society as well as the engineering and technological segments of the university, a second popular view of man is that of the machine model. Benjamin Franklin coined the term *homo faber*, one of his great verbal inventions. Possibly in the Hellenistic period of science and ingenious devices some thinker unknown to us drew analogies between man and the machine. Seneca in 61 A.D. spoke of the air pollution in Rome, caused by smoke and refuse as well as by horses drawing carts and chariots, but the machine model is essentially a modern artifice. In opposition to Descartes' argument in the *Discourse on Method*, V, that man cannot be conceived of as a machine, La Mettrie (1709-1751) in *L'Homme Machine* described human psychical activities as mechanical functions of the brain. Industrialization added to the force of the analogy. Adam Smith and Karl Marx were in agreement that the simple repetitive functions of production, even before the assembly line, primitivized and alienated man. Carl Sandburg's poem *The Hammer* (1910) pointed to a dismal future for a mechanized society.

In the present early stages of the second industrial revolution, futurologists point to an intimate symbiosis between man and the machine accelerated by the rapid development of computer science and cybernetics. Robert Heinlein, science fiction writer, described man's first lunar landing, made possible by computer science, as the "beginning of the adulthood of the human race," which will lead to the subjugation of man's extraterritorial environment and the creation of an electronic global village. The society of the future will not be the grey megalith of totally industrialized people, envisioned and feared in

---

[3] *Ibid.*, 279.

the nineteenth century, but a highly fluid, rapidly changing society which has already shown the bewildering and disorienting effects of the new electronic industrial surge. [4]

The historian is pleased to note the antiquity of the operative word cybernetics. Homer used it in the *Odyssey* for the helmsman. It can be found in Pindar and Aeschylus and Plato used it in the *Republic* for the prudential aspects of government. In his *Essay on the Philosophy of Science,* 1843, the French physicist Ampère used the term cybernétique for the science of civil government. It appears with supreme dignity in the motto of Phi Beta Kappa, Philosophy the Guide of Life. Already whole production processes are controlled by the artificial intelligence of electronic machines. Recent experiments at the Stanford medical school have so delicately connected human brains to computers that they are able by thought to give positive or negative commands to the machine with a high positive correlation between mental command and computer reaction. It is a very real question as to whether the brain's superiority, which rests upon the greater complexity of its neural system and the greater sensitivity and efficiency of human memory, is an essential difference or one which can be overcome with the progress of technology. One scientist. John von Neumann, has asserted that "there is no essential gap between man and machine. For every human activity we can conceive a mechanical counterpart." [5] There are machines already which can reproduce themselves. The implications are crucial and far-reaching for anthropology.

The biophysicists have introduced yet a third model, that of the fabricated man. The assumption is that modern living leads to biological entropy and that molecular biology or controlled heredity by clonal reproduction is necessary to improve the genetic pool. It is a thought worthy of Nietzsche's moving beyond man. Donald Fleming, historian of science, has used the phrase "messianic positivism" to describe the mind-set of certain molecular biologists. Joshua Lederberg has raised the question of clonal reproduction as a diversion to be introduced

---

[4] Alvin Toffler, *Future Shock* (New York, 1970), is the best known of the recent books projecting such a development.

[5] John Von Neumann, *Machines and Man,* quoted by the editor, *Scientific American* (New York, 1955), cited in Kenneth Vaux, *Subduing the Cosmos. Cybernetics and Man's Future* (Richmond, VA, 1970) 19. Marshall McLuhan in *Understanding Media: The Extensions of Man* (New York, 1964), 21, argues that each new medium that influences us permanently alters our psychic environment, "imposing on us a particular pattern of perceiving and thinking that controls us to an extent we scarcely suspect." See Vaux, p. 20.

into human evolution in an effort to control the future of the species. He combines somatic, psycho-sociological and genetic criteria for the selection of the phenotypes to be perpetuated in reproduction with a great variety of techniques. Cloning has been done on lesser forms of life, such as frogs, and although the obstacles for human cloning are formidable and a recent book claiming it had been done is fraudulent, eventual success is very possible and even probable. Cloning aside, well over a million babies have been given life by artificial insemination, which involves some conception of genetic improvement in some cases. [6]

Perhaps the most daring call for mankind to set long term goals for its own development has come from Gerald Feinberg, a Columbia professor of physics, in his book *The Prometheus Project*. [7] An existential humanist, he urges mankind to set goals to be realized over several generations in an effort to organize its own Providence and escape from its own history. He points to three such targets, the creation of super-intelligent machines and their association with organic systems, the conquest of aging, and the increase of intelligence by biological engineering and controlled environmental changes. The ultimate goal should be the expansion of human consciousness until it becomes coterminous with the universe. He is ready for species suicide in favor of creatures beyond present human parameters. We may ask whether or not the desire to attain a human consciousness or transhuman consciousness coterminous with the universe is not the same as the primordial desire to eat of the fruit of the tree of the knowledge of good and evil and to be like God. But as the rehabilitated heretical

---

[6] Paul Ramsey, *Fabricated Man: The Ethics of Genetic Control* (New Haven, 1970), 62. C. Judson Herrick, *The Evolution of Human Nature* (New York, 1961), 461-66, discusses the cleavage in our culture between the spiritual and natural, declaring that we live by faith in the order of nature, in ourselves, and in our fellow men.

[7] Gerald Feinberg, *The Prometheus Project* (New York, 1968), 15-19, on long range goals. He (p. 146) holds that the roots of man's discontent lie in his sense of his own finitude, his inability to accomplish all that he wills, and his feelings about the meaninglessness of life: "In order to overcome its limitations, consciousness would have to transform itself into a single, universal entity.... The ultimate range of consciousness would be, essentially, a conscious universe, each part of which plays a role in the overall consciousness and no part of which is regarded as the external world by that consciousness. A poet might say that consciousness must become coextensive with creation. Such a universal consciousness would be no more finite than the universe itself.... There would be nothing outside the universal consciousness, and so this source of unhappiness would be eliminated."

church father Origen believed, there may be an infinity of universes, so that even with a full knowledge of one universe man still will not have become God.

The many drives operative in the scientific pursuit remind the historian of the utopians with their varying visions of the future. To have as a colleague a physicist such as Burton Richter, who two years ago won the Nobel Prize for the discovery with the Stanford Linear Accelerator of the Psi particle, a new class of matter which acts independently of and, indeed, contrary to basic Newtonian laws, is to gain a special insight into the scientific mentality. It includes whimsy, for he named the new substance Charm Quark, the German word for cottage cheese. There is a sense of wonder in him, though he is a cold scientist, and a sense of the poetry of physics.

The futurism of science is in some scientists regularly combined with a utopian mentality, not meliorism but optimism. It is interesting to note the differences between the utopias of Russian and of American science fiction writers, the former with orderly, square or rectangular cities, the latter disorderly, weird and imaginative. In *The Radical Papers* Lewis Coser and Irving Howe say of the utopianists that these dreams and system makers have one thing in common, their desire to storm history. [8] In discussing the spiritual problem of modern man, C. G. Jung observed that to be "unhistorical" is the Promethean sin and in this sense modern man lives in sin. A higher level of consciousness is like living with a heavy burden of guilt. [9]

It is not difficult to see that the tendencies which Alfred North Whitehead perceived to be at the root of much that is half-hearted and wavering in our civilization are operative today in an extreme form. Scientific realism, based on mechanism, is conjoined with an unwavering belief in the world of men and of the high animals as being composed of self-determining organisms, which has introduced a radical

---

[8] Irving Howe, ed., *The Radical Papers* (Garden City, N.Y., 1966), 14. The great popularity of William Irwin Thompson's weird book *At the Edge of History: Speculations on the Transformation of Culture* (New York, 1971), with its slashing at liberal humanists, "ordinary" scientists, speculations on outer space invasions, the theory of the Olmecs in Yucatan, suggests that the temper of the reading public requires books that are not only beyond history and the present, but beyond science and beyond all belief.

[9] Ernst Cassirer, *An Essay on Man: An Introduction to a Philosophy of Human Culture* (New Haven, 1944), 61, argued that utopian thinking has been important for the development of the modern world and relates such thought to the ethical world which is never given, but forever in the making. He cites Goethe's sentence: "To live in the ideal world is to treat the impossible as it if were possible."

inconsistency at the basis of modern thought. [10] The developments of recent years have, in fact, exaggerated the dichotomy. In response to the crisis, humanists argue that man should not feel belittled by the vastness of the universe or the interminable corridors of time, since it is only through the light of consciousness that the universe becomes visible, and should that light disappear, only nothingness would remain. Without man's cumulative capacity to give symbolic form to experience, to reflect upon it, refashion and project it, the physical universe would be as empty of meaning as a handless clock: its ticking would tell nothing, for the mindfulness of man makes the differences. [11] Many scientists are acutely aware of the great but still limited role to be played by science. For a man of the stature of Max Planck science is a way of measuring knowledge, not a means of discovering truth itself in the sense of that which always is. [12] Mathematicians now assert that formulas prove the impossibility of solving all mathematical problems. On a positive note, Norbert Wiener, the father of cybernetics, near the end of his life began a rather elementary dialogue between the science of cybernetics and theology by discussing three points in cybernetics relevant to religion: machines which learn, machines which reproduce themselves, and the coordination of machine and man. [13] If religion is the special subject matter of the church historian, his task may not be over yet. As a matter of fact, the historian and specifically the church historian are needed for balance and perspective in the present intellectual milieu more urgently than ever before. They should conceive of history, however, not only as the dialogue of the past and the present, but of the past and the future.

The church historian has a unique advantage in analyzing the predicament of modern man, for not only is he aware of the present difficulties emerging as the modern moves into the post-modern period,

---

[10] Alfred North Whitehead, *Science and the Modern World* (New York, 1925), 106.

[11] Lewis Mumford, *The Myth of the Machine,* I (New York, 1967), 29-35: The Light of Consciousness.

[12] Max Planck, *The Meaning and Limits of Exact Science.* 1941.

[13] Norbert Wiener, *God and Golem, Inc: A Comment on Certain Points Where Cybernetics Impinges on Religion* (Cambridge, MA, 1964), 11. His pioneering book is also germane to the historian concerned with problems of social control, *Cybernetics or Control and Communication in the Animal and the Machine* (Cambridge, MA, 1948; 2nd ed., 1961). Wiener warned of the social dangers of automata in a small popular book, *The Human Use of Human Beings* (Boston, 1950). The social concern aroused by cybernetics is reflected in such books as V. H. Brix, *Cybernetics and Everyday Affairs* (London, 1967).

but he understands many of the processes at work in history which made modern man what he has become. The heart of the matter is man's image of himself. The French socio-anthropologist Lévi-Strauss speaks of the neolithic paradox, the phenomenon that man's self-image, as he first realized that he was the kind of creature who could make fire, was of greater civilizing force than the discovery itself. Given the Biblical Archimedian point and the three great ages of church history as a base, the church historian can offer a perspective on man that the university and the intellectual world sorely need. He must not, then, conceive of his task as narrowly institutional, but as consequentially anthropological as well as theological.

The modern view of man has lost its wholeness and has been bifurcated by a tendency on the one hand to stress his rationality, individuality, moral nature, responsibility, and essential goodness, and on the other hand to emphasize his irrational nature, emotional side, conformism, and amoral, immoral and selfish propensities. The one tendency is represented by the tradition in modern times of idealism and liberalism, the other by that of anthropological realism. The church historian has a unique contribution to make by way of restoring soundness to modern man's concept of man and stability to post-modern man's experimentation with and projection of the future of man. Not only is his enterprise justifiable to the presentist insofar as the church remains a significant component of contemporary society, but it is authenticated by the fact that the Christian understanding of man has been a major contributor to that past from which the present has emerged and into which the future is rapidly tumbling. The church historian can bring to bear upon contemporary human problems the vast resources of the church's spiritual reservoir and of all of Christendom's millennia of human experience, good and bad.

By reconstructing an authentic picture of the Reformation view of man, which was only an intensified and refurbished Christian view of man, the church historian can instruct contemporary man without a special program or design. The reformers were, as Aldous Huxley observed, sweaty realists about sinful man. Yet, by intensifying the Christian message they underlined the basic worth and dignity of man on the Christian grounds of creation, incarnation, and regeneration. What an impact that idea of man's worth in God's eyes has had upon man's self-image! That is true not only of the encomia on man by a Nemesius of Emessa, Lactantius, Pico della Mirandola and other fathers and intellectuals later in the tradition, but it is true of the message brought home to every peasant in the village churches for centuries when they heard and had explained to them the words of the priest in the mass: *Deus qui humanae substantiae dignitatem mirabiliter condidisti et mirabilius reformasti.* The Reformation view emphasized man's special place in the great scheme of things by linking man and God, on God's terms.

As the modern western picture of man fades away it is reason that needs all the defenders it can get. Reinhold Niebuhr observed that men no longer put faith in reason but faith in history. Luther, who at Worms appealed to *ratio evidens,* regenerate reason, declared reason to be God's greatest creation and the judge of all things. Along with his emphasis upon faith as trust, not credulity as a short circuit around reason, he remained in the main stream of western Christian rationalism from St. Augustine on down. Moreover, while Luther retained the tripartite division of man into body, soul and spirit, the force of his theology was to see man whole, the *totus homo* under the law or under grace. "In my temerity," he said, "I do not distinguish body, soul and spirit, but present the whole man unto God." *Caro* or flesh meant theologically man under the law and *anima* or spirit meant reborn man rightly trusting in God. The major source of that soul-body dualism which has aroused such ire of late is to be found in Platonism and, as Luther observed in the *Operationes in Psalmos,* the philosophers have given the terms their own meanings. [14]

Victor Hugo commented that science has long sought the secret of perpetual motion and it has found it—it is science itself. The church historian can add a blessing to the cultivation of science and secular culture by the positive reinforcement of ancient precedent. A reading of book XXII of St. Augustine's *City of God* might for some scientists place their enterprise within a meaningful spiritual context. Augustine sees creation as a continuing action which will go on into the future. God's presence gives coherence and direction to all reality, this first church father to discuss technology explained. Divine power energizes human cultural creativity. Man becomes a coworker with God, sharing in his nature and power. There is even an eschatological note which

---

[14] *Martin Luthers Werke,* Weimar Ausgabe 5, 207, 34-36. A compact overview of the problem from antiquity to contemporary philosophy to be commended for its precision and clarity in brief scope is C. A. Peursen, *Body, Soul, Spirit: A Survey of the Body-Mind Problem* (London, 1966). The contemporary pressure against rationalism is summarized in the discussion of integral versus rational man in William Barrett, *Irrational Man: A Study in Existential Philosophy* (Garden City, N.Y., 1958), 265-80.

388 LEWIS W. SPITZ

suits the temper of modern science, or at least of many modern scientists. As a later Augustinian, Luther, put it, the world is the sphere of faith's works. All cultural activity like life itself is a *negotium cum deo,* a business to be carried on together with God. For the believer there is nothing profane, for, Luther declared, *in Christo omnia sunt spiritualia.*

As for science fiction utopias, there is a long tradition of utopian thinking and dreams beginning with the Hebrew prophets. In addition to formal utopias such as Johann Valentin Andreae's *Reipublicae christianopolitanae descriptio* or Thomas Neogeorgus's *Pammachius,* the whole long wilderness motif proves that the impulse to imagine and seek the "good society" and "perfect world" and to cultivate a garden in the desert virtually coincides with human history. [15]

What of the future? The church historian who has seen the limited progress and stunted achievements of men, even of those gifted with the very best of spiritual endowments through the long centuries past will be realistic in his expectations for the future. He is apt to agree with the prediction of that exquisite humanist, Thomas Mann, an emigré and a refugee from his native land, a country notable for its scientific achievements and the homeland of the Reformation. In a letter addressed to the men of a far distant future which was buried in a time capsule at the 1939 New York World's Fair, Mann wrote of man:

> We know that the idea of the future as a "better world" was a fallacy of the doctrine of progress. The hopes we center on you, citizens of the future, are in no way exaggerated. In broad outline you will actually resemble those who lived a thousand or five thousand years ago. Among you, too, the spirit will fare badly—it would never fare too well on this earth, otherwise men would need it no longer. That optimistic conception of the future is a projection into time of an endeavor to approximate to his idea of himself, the humanization of man.

In pointing to these reassuring precedents, genial parallels, and sanctions in the tradition for post-modern developments, the church historian must make one fact quite clear, that there is an essential Christian understanding of man that is unique and generically related to the essential Christian message. Every philosophical view of man's whole being, every sociological system, many branches of natural

---

15 George H. Williams, *Wilderness and Paradise in Christian Thought: The Biblical Experience of the Desert in the History of Christianity* (New York, 1962), suggests that creating a garden in the wilderness has a kind of utopian aspect to it.

science, every mechanistic theory of life in the final analysis seeks to place man within its vision of the world. This effort becomes religion only when it combines with its view of life a perception of God. The religious view of life is more than a *Weltanschauung,* it is also a *Gottanschauung.* A sense of the transience of life, so dreaded by modern man, is given major attention in all the higher religions. But God-consciousness is still not in itself essentially Christian. The uniquely Christian view of man first emerges from the general religious view when man is seen as sinful under the law of God and redeemed by Christ the Savior. Whether the words are those of the prophet, "Woe is me! for I am undone; because I am a man of unclean lips!" (Isaiah 6:5), the *Kyrie eleison* of Greek Orthodoxy, the *mea maxima culpa* of the Latin church, or Luther's cry of despair, "out of the depths have I cried unto Thee," the recognition of responsibility and failing *coram deo,* the need for redemption, belong to the essence of the Christian view of man. The concept of regenerate man, the theology of joy and hope, belong quite as much to that distinctively Christian view of man. [16] There is, then, a very real difference between church history and secular history and between church history in a properly defined context and the history of religions in general. It is a difference in spiritual anthropology.

We have surveyed some ultra-modern or post-modern models of man. We have referred briefly to the bifurcation in the western intellectuals' understanding of man: idealistic and anthropological realistic. And we have presented Reformation man as an archetype of the Christian understanding of man. The church historian does indeed deserve a secure and well rewarded place in the modern university. He, like his secular historian colleague, is very much needed for his contribution to anthropology, for man is the measurer, if not the best measure, of all things. The church historian whose views of man are firmly grounded in Biblical realism and whose ideal of man is the One who was also true man can teach and write the kind of history needed by the church, the university, and the world today. That is what our celebrant has done for many long years, an inspiration to all of us.

---

[16] Heinrich Bornkamm, "Der protestantische Mensch nach dem Augsburgischen Bekenntnis (1530)," *Das Jahrhundert der Reformation: Gestalten und Kräfte,* 2nd ed. (Göttingen, 1966), 125-26. To conclude with and on an ecumenical note, a book to be highly recommended for essays which touch here and there on the themes of this paper, see Walter J. Ong, S.J., ed., *Knowledge and the Future of Man* (New York, 1968), especially the brilliant pages by Father Ong himself, "Knowledge in Time," 3-38.

A LETTER FROM ROLAND BAINTON
ON IMMORTALITY

Dear George:

The possibility of life after death has been for us both a matter of poignant concern. Therefore, I thought it might be well to review the Ingersol lectures on this theme from 1896 through 1947. Later numbers are not in the Yale library and the main issues have certainly been canvassed in the earlier.

Every discussion must inevitably confront the mind-body problem. If a moderate blow on the head will make a man an idiot will a heavier blow make him an angel? Using other terminology, Plato asserted that the soul can survive without the body and this Aristotle denied. The Apostle Paul devised a compromise by distinguishing two varieties of body, terrestrial and celestial. With this in mind Tillich was able to subscribe to the resurrection of the body, though not of the flesh. Throughout the Middle Ages the resurrection of the flesh was current and animals which had eaten men were portrayed disgorging the necessary parts for the reconstruction. The Platonic-Aristotelian divergence reappeared in the Renaissance with Ficino and Pico on the Platonic side and Pomponazzi on the Aristotelian, though he would submit to the pronouncement of the Church.

Modern behaviorism, untramelled by ecclesiastical authority, asserted that the brain causes emotions and ideas. Obviously, then, if there were no brain there could be no emotions and ideas. This view was countered by William James in his Ingersol lecture ("Human Immortality," 1897), who as a psychiatrist regarded the brain not as the creator but as the transmitter of nonphysical impacts from without, as in the case of telepathy. The brain simply passes on what it has received to the nervous system. This view may be psychologically correct, but beside the point as to immortality, because the brain, though only the transmitter, is still needful for sentient life. The same objection can be brought against the suggestion of William Pepperell Montague ("The Chances of Surviving Death," 1934) that the mind is like the harper who plays upon the harp. The brain is only the harp. Yes, but what can the harper do without the harp?

Pre-existence as a warrant for believing in post-existence is not taken seriously in these essays. There is no reference to Wordsworth's *Intimations of Immortality* where the boy comes "trailing clouds of glory from heaven which is his home." The poem most quoted is Tennyson's wistful *In Memoriam*. Metempsychosis is treated as a historical curiosity.

Attention is given to the claims of Sir Oliver Lodge and F. B. Meyer that actual communications have been received from the dead through a medium. The claim in these essays is dismissed on the ground that the banal communications, if valid, would prove only that the dead have experienced no intellectual improvement. Another reason for rejecting the reports is that throughout the period of recorded history they have been so rare. If it were as easy for the billions of the dead to reach us as it is from Cambridge, Massachusetts to ring up Texas, Alaska or London would they have so little availed themselves of the possibility? Charles R. Brown ("Living Again," 1920) testified that for fifty years he had been in the most intimate touch with his mother. During the two years since her death she had not once, so to speak, rung him up.

A medical argument has been advanced too recently to have been considered in the above essays, namely that during the interval between medical death and resuscitation patients have testified to pleasant sensations. The question here to be asked is how dead is medically dead? Certain parts of the bodily organism can function after others have ceased. A chicken with its head cut off can run once around the barnyard. Medical death is not *rigor mortis*. If it were there would be no resuscitation.

The authors of these essays rejected table rappings and I am confident would have been no less disinclined to accept the testimony of the "medically dead." But they did not on that account reject belief in immortality. Their line of approach was religious in the broad sense. William Wallace Fenn ("Immortality and Theism," 1921) pointed out that if one believes in God as intelligence, will, justice, love and compassion, and not housed in a body with a brain and nervous system like ours, then we are back with Plato, concluding that an incorporeal mind can exist and operate. The inference is not invalidated if for God one should substitute a cosmic intelligence, which no one can deny. The regularity of the heavenly bodies, which makes possible the prediction of an eclipse to a second, bespeaks a cosmic mind of high intelligence, not to mention the complex adjustments of molecules, atoms and cells in the inorganic and organic areas. The very mind of

man, able "to think God's thoughts after him," points to an endow-
ment by some generative force. The cosmic intelligence is not altogether disembodied. There is the physical universe which may be
termed the body of God, but it is certainly not constructed on the
model of human anatomy. The possibility, then, of the existence of a
soul without the body is not excluded, though the actuality cannot
be demonstrated.

Another line of argument proceeds not from the possibility of a soul
without a body but from the evidence of the beneficent purpose of
God, or if you will, the cosmos, to develop ever more advanced and
superior forms of life. There is an upward thrust, an *élan vital* from the
inorganic to the organic, from the plant to the animal, from the animal
to man. This is a process in which man is not caught in an ineluctable
chain but in which he can participate. By reason of memory and
foresight man can make decisions and influence the future. Possibly
in the laboratory he can even manipulate genetics (a very dangerous
procedure). The general feeling is, however, that man has reached a
plateau of physical advance so that the body cannot be further improved. The process will then have to be on the level of the soul,
intellectually and morally. This can never be fully achieved in the
present life. Man is endowed with potentialities which in a single span
of years can never be realized. Death leaves us always incomplete.
Bartok succeeded in composing the third concerto for piano and
orchestra prior to death save for the last seventeen bars. John Haynes
Holmes ("The Affirmation of Immortality," 1947) wonders whether
God will leave us all with unfinished concertos. May we not rather
assume that the process will continue after death? Is not this the point
of Teilhard de Chardin's omega point?

One observes that in the above discussion the consummation appears
to be conceived in individual terms. Each person is to realize the total
potential. The quest is self-centered. Others, such as Wilhelm Ostwald
("Individuality and Immortality," 1906), have suggested that the
genuine realization of the potential lies in the forgetfulness of the
self: "The happiest moments in life are associated with a certain loss
of personality . . . . When I am sketching, sitting quietly in the open,
there comes to me in a happy moment complete forgetfulness of my
poor self." The extreme forms of mysticism see the ideal in the
submerging of the self in the great abyss of being. The philosophical
idealist finds the realization of individuality through the loss of individuality. However, Josiah Royce ("Conception of Immortality," 1899)

finds a way to combine the singularity of the person and the subordination of the person to the whole. It is by union with God that we attain
our full individuality. The point is illustrated in the case of a stone
in a cathedral. It is an individual stone. There is no other stone just
like it. It first precisely into the position in which it is set. But there
would be no such position if there were no cathedral. Others ask just
what is this cathedral in the case of the individual person? The answer
is the Christian community. C. H. Dodd ("The Communion of the
Saints," 1936) phrases it as the "communion of the saints."

Some argue that immortality is necessary not only for the realization
of our potential but also for that of God. Life is so full of inequities
that God is not good unless in the life to come he will make some
rectification. The argument is not convincing because the plain fact is
that there can be no rectification. Was there any rectification for Job
when to replace his children destroyed by the tornado he was given
twice as many? Would he not always grieve for those taken? The
inequities of life remain a profound mystery. God cannot compensate.

The acceptance of organic evolution had helped theology by opening
up the possibility of extending the process beyond death but had created
a difficulty at the beginning. The usual assumption has been that animals are mortal, men immortal. At what point then in the evolutionary
process did immortality enter? Shall we wipe out the line by saying
that all animals are immortal or that all men are mortal? Or shall we
say that some animals are immortal and some men mortal? Montague
observed that "The love of a dog for its master has in it an absolute
poignant beauty . . . and there would be more point in the continuance
through eternity of the poor brute . . . than of the cleverest human
rogue who ever lived." J. Fiske ("Life Everlasting," 1900) relates
from Walter Scott the story of a dog that died of starvation while
watching over the body of its master, dead on a Highland moor.

We are confronted thus with the problem of conditional immortality.
Henry Drummond said that life depends on correspondence with the
environment. The human body needs food, drink and oxygen to
breathe. But if the body is gone and the environment is spiritual what
correspondence can there be on the part of one who has lived only for the
needs and the lusts of the body? Conditional immortality is implied in
the liturgy of the Eucharist. "Take, Eat." These elements are to "preserve thy body and soul unto *everlasting life*."

The resurrection of Jesus is often cited as proof for the resurrection
of all men. But if immortality is conditional it would prove only that one

man rose again. In any case the resurrection is first of all an alleged fact of history and as such is subject to all of the tests of rigorous historical evidence. The presence of Christ in the hearts of believers is abundantly testified through the ages but the problem then comes to be as to the truth value of interior experiences.

Another question is the desirability of immortality. Luther raised the question with Melanchthon of what there would be to do up there. Melanchthon told him enjoyment of the vision of God. "Oh yes," he agreed, but one wonders whether he would not soon have wearied of just looking. Lowes Dickinson ("Is Immortality Desirable?," 1909) desired immortality for the attainment of moral perfection. But if one made it then the excitement of the effort would disappear.

Curiously in these lectures by intellectuals I have found little concern for an enlargement of knowledge in the life to come. Moses Stuart, who was not one of them, said he hoped to live long enough to be able to read, when it came out, the next volume of Dorner's work on the person of Christ, but added that he would soon be where he would know more about it than Dorner. How fascinating it would be, unencumbered by gravity and immune to temperatures, to soar to the sun and explore its interior, to be able in the flick of an eye to traverse light years and converse with the nebulae! The epistle of John says that when we see him we shall be like him. Would we not have to be like him to make immortality endurable?

Some adduce the desire for permanence as the stimulus for creative endeavor. Would Raphael, we are asked, have painted the Sistine Madonna had he thought that it would be shredded by a vandal? Probably not if he thought it likely soon to happen, but if he thought it would never happen he was naive. The men of antiquity built for eternity and in what state now are their monuments? Where is the Colossus of Rhodes? Where are the arms of the Niké of Samothrace? Nothing earthly is permanent. But that may be the point of the argument. We desire permanence. It is not attainable here. Will it not be granted then in the hereafter? How can we tell?

Another question is as to which stage in our life we should wish to be restored. "To infancy?" Certainly not. "To senescence?" Certainly not. Presumably we desire to drink of the elixir of eternal youth. But what will happen to the stages after death? My sister Gladys died before I was born. I think of her as in the photo of the babe in mother's arms. But if we meet within the heavenly places she will be older than I. Will she have learned English? Will she have learned so much that

I'll not know enough to converse? May we not do better to cease prying into the inscrutable?

To what degree has belief in immortality profited mankind? It has been an enormous comfort to the bereaved and a great support to heroic endeavor. In Holland of the sixteenth century a husband and wife were in prison awaiting execution for adherence to Anabaptism. They were in the same building, not allowed to visit, but permitted to exchange letters. The husband wrote, "My darling lamb, fear not the torments. Not a hair of your head shall perish without the Father's will. My dear wife, I take leave of you, for I do not expect to see you again. But after many days we shall be united before the altar of Christ." I have the feeling that Sir William Osler's ("Science and Immortality," 1904) belief in immortality was prompted by his clinical experience of comfort to the dying and, for the bereaved, the consolation that through faith some day they would gather at the river that flows by the throne of God.

On the other hand the belief has done great harm, not so much the belief itself as the kind of immortality expected. Those who deviated from the creed of the Church were thought to be destined to everlasting torment from which they might be saved if the prospect of burning at the stake did not wean them of their obstinate error. And if they were allowed to live, God would visit his wrath upon the community which suffered them.

Again I have known belief in immortality used to justify killing in war on the ground that it did not destroy the individual but merely changed his setting to another sphere where God would take him in hand.

Where then are we? We cannot know the distant scene. One step is enough. Julius Bixler ("Immortality and the Present Mood," 1931) rightly observes that the significance of life is not determined by a future state, but by our capacity for loyalty now. If life is a tragedy let it be heroic. Time is not to be measured by length of days. Methusaleh is recorded to have lived 969 years and he died. That's all. Charles R. Brown gave a sermon on this text with the title "A life of one dimension: length." Bixler summarized: "Life counts for more than death, spirit for more than matter, loyalty more than cowardice or sloth."

Can it be that God has left us in such ignorance that we should serve him only for himself in the spirit of the lines attributed to Saint Teresa of Avila?

I love thee not, my God, for heaven's reward.
I fear thee not for hell's eternal flame.
Were there no hell still would I fear thee, Lord.
I'm moved to see thy lacerated side.
I'm moved to look when hands and feet are nailed.
I'm moved to see thy body so impaled.
To look upon thee mocked and crucified.

Ours so to live that we can join in the old gospel hymn, "Are you ready?" "Oh yes, I'm ready. I'll be ready when the great day comes."

Roland Bainton
Emeritus, Yale University

BIBLIOGRAPHY * OF THE WRITINGS OF GEORGE HUNTSTON WILLIAMS

1940

"Priest, Prophet, and Proletariat: a study of the theology of [sin in] Paul Tillich," *Journal of Liberal Religion* 1 (1940), 25-37; cf. *Protestant Digest* 3, 6 (1940), 67-78.

1945

"Current Trends in Unitarian Theology," *Christian Register* 124 (1945), 41-44; cf. "Contemporary Trends in Unitarian Thinking," with Horace Westwood, *ibid.* 127 (1948), 17-20, 23.

1949

"The Church, the Democratic State, and the Crisis in Religious Education," *Harvard Divinity School Bulletin* 14 (1949), 35-61.

Rethinking the Unitarian Relationship with Protestantism: An Examination of the Thought of Frederic Henry Hodge (1805-1890) (Boston: Beacon, 1949).

1951

Public Aid to Parochial Education: Presented by the Harvard Law School Forum, Addresses by George H. Williams, et al. (Cambridge: Harvard Law School, 1951).

"Christology and Church-State Relations in the Fourth Century," *Church History* 20 (Sept. and Dec., 1951), 3-33, 3-26.

The Norman Anonymous of 1100 A.D.: Toward the Identification and Evaluation of the So-Called Anonymous of York, Harvard Theological Studies 18 (Cambridge: Harvard University, 1951).

"Church History: From Historical Theology to the Theology of History," *Protestant Thought in the Twentieth Century,* ed. Arnold Nash (New York: Macmillan, 1951), 147-78.

---

* Revision by James D. Smith, III of a bibliography by Dr. Maria Grossmann, *Harvard Theological Review* 67 (1974), 139-53. The bibliography does not contain book reviews, except in a few cases where they take on the character of a review article. Reprints or revised versions of articles appear under the entry of the original article. Within each year, writings are grouped topically.

1952

"Katholieken en Protestanten in de Verenigde Staten van Amerika,"
Wending: Maandblad voor Evangelie en Cultuur 7 (1952), 65-75.

1953

"What Has Jerusalem to do with Athens?," *Universalist Leader* 135
(1953), 195-97.
"Decanal Report, 1952-53," *Report of the President of Harvard College and Reports of Departments* (1952-53), 468-71.

1954

Ed., *The Harvard Divinity School: Its Place in Harvard University and
in American Culture* (Boston: Beacon, 1954).
"The Three Recurrent Conflicts," *ibid.*, 3-18.
"Theology and Integrity of the University," *ibid.*, 230-48.
"Church, Commonwealth, and College: The Religious Sources of the
Idea of a University," *ibid.*, 295-351.
"Issues Between Catholics and Protestants at Mid-Century," *Religion
in Life* 23 (1954), 163-205.
*American Critical Pluralism as the Emerging Middle Ground in Inter-
faith Relations* (Boston: Division of Publications, American Uni-
tarian Association, 1954).
"Comment on the Religious Education Association Meetings," *Religious
Education* 49 (1954), 11-12.
"Willard Learoyd Sperry," Faculty Minute with Henry J. Cadbury
and Arthur D. Nock, *Harvard Gazette* (Oct. 30, 1954), 38-39.
"Decanal Letter, 1954," *Harvard Divinity School Bulletin* 19 (1953-
54), 75-81.
"Decanal Report, 1953-54," *Report of the President of Harvard College and Reports of Departments* (1953-54), 99-116.

1955

"The Elect of All Mankind," *Christian Register* 134 (1955), 23, 26.
"Religious Education in a Pluralistic Democracy," *Religious Education*
50 (1955), 38-44.
"Decanal Letter, 1955," *Harvard Divinity School Bulletin* 20 (1954-
55), 99-116.

1956

"The Ministry in the Ante-Nicene Church," *The Ministry in Historical*

Perspective, eds. H. Richard Niebuhr and Daniel D. Williams (New York: Harper's, 1956), 27-59, 290-97.

"The Ministry in the Later Patristic Period," *ibid.,* 60-81, 297-301.

"Harvard and Hinduism," *Prabuddha Bharata or Awakened India* 61 (1956), 55-59.

"The Place of Professor Wolfson's Philosophy of the Church Fathers," *Harvard Divinity School Bulletin* 21 (1955-56), 81-91.

"Church-State Separation and Religion in the Schools of our Democracy," *Religious Education* 51 (1956), 369-77; abridged in *Selected Readings in the Philosophy of Education,* ed. Joe Park (New York: Macmillan, 1958), 413-429; second ed. (1963), 503-25; cf. *Crucial Issues in Education,* eds. Henry Ehlers and Gordon Lee (New York: Henry Holt, 1959), 108-17; and, *Federal Aid to Education,* ed. Ronald Steel (New York: Wilson, 1961).

1957

"The Spontaneous Missionary Church: A Lesson from Ancient Church History," *Laity* 4 (Nov., 1957), 3-14.

"The Philosophy of the Church Fathers by Harry Austryn Wolfson: A Review Article," *Church History* 26 (1957), 156-68.

"The Sacramental Presuppositions of Anselm's *Cur Deus Homo,*" *Church History* 26 (1957), 245-74.

Spiritual and Anabaptist Writers, ed. with Angel M. Mergal, Library of Christian Classics XXV (Philadelphia: Westminster, 1957); pb. reprint, *idem.,* 1977.

"Michael Servetus and Sebastian Castellio: A Review of a Multilingual Tribute to Pioneers of Tolerance," *Proceedings of the Unitarian Historical Society,* 11, 2 (1957), 29-35; also *Erasmus* 10 (1957), 278-81.

"The Reluctance to Inform," *Theology Today* 14 (1957), 229-55.

"Unitarian Christianity and a Christian Unitarianism," *Unitarian Christian* 13, 1 (1957), 3-7; cf. *Faith and Freedom* 11 (1958), 119-27.

"Harvard and Hellas," *Greek Orthodox Theological Review* 3 (1957), 23-25.

"The Golden Priesthood and the Leaden State," *Ricerche di Storia Religiosa: Studi in onore di Giorgio La Piana* 1 (1957), 291-310; cf. *Harvard Theological Review* 50 (1957), 37-64.

1958

"The Role of the Layman in the Ancient Church," *Ecumenical Review*

10 (1958), 225-48; also with notes in *Greek and Byzantine Studies* 1 (1958), 9-42; cf. Spanish trans. "El Papel de los Laicos en la Iglesia Antigua," *Cuadernos Teologicos* 27-28 (1958), 45-66.

"Studies in the Radical Reformation (1517-1618): A Bibliographical Survey of Research Since 1939," *Church History* 27 (1958), 46-69, 124-60.

"A Century of Church History at Harvard, 1857-1957," *Harvard Divinity School Bulletin* 23 (1957-58), 85-102.

The Theological Idea of the University (New York: National Council of Churches, 1958).

"The Christian College Today: Situation, Dilemma, and Call," *Christian Scholar* 41 (1958), 193-209.

"Interreligious Relationships: Conflict, Competition, and Cooperation, with special reference to public education," *Religious Education* 53 (1958), 381-86.

"To the Junior Class of 1958: A Glance Backward Before You Press Ahead," *Unauthorized Version*, Harvard Divinity School (Sept, 1958), 3-4; cf. "Entering HDS 16-17-18-1958," *Harvard Divinity School Bulletin* 24 (1958), 2, 6-7.

"Letter to President Pusey," *Harvard Crimson* (Apr. 18, 1958), 3, 5.

1959

"Anabaptism and Spiritualism in the Kingdom of Poland and the Grand Duchy of Lithuania: An Obscure Phase of the Pre-History of Socinianism," *Studia nad Arianizmen*, ed. Ludwik Chmaj (Warszawa: Pánstwowe Wydawnictwo Naukowe, 1959), 215-62.

"The Wilderness and Paradise in the History of the Church," *Church History* 28 (1959), 3-24.

"The Seminary in the Wilderness: A Representative Episode in the Cultural History of Northern New England," *Harvard Library Bulletin* 13 (1959), 369-400; 14 (1960), 27-58.

"Prayer on the Occasion of His Father's Farewell Sermon," *Unitarian Register* 138 (1959), 6.

"Robert H. Pfeiffer," Faculty Minute with Harry Wolfson, et al., *Harvard Gazette* (Jan. 31, 1959), 92-93.

1960

Anselm: Communion and Atonement (St. Louis: Concordia, 1960).

"Georg Florowski," *Weltkirchen-lexikon*, eds. Franklin Littell and Hans Hermann Walz (Stuttgart: Kreuz, 1960), col. 414.

"Sebastian Franck," *ibid.*, cols. 416-17.
"Unitarier," *ibid.*, cols. 1514-15.
"Universität," *ibid.*, cols. 1516-19.

1962

"Camillo Renato (c. 1500-c. 1575)," *Proceedings of the Unitarian Historical Society* 14 (1962-63): Italian Reformation Studies in Honor of Laelius Socinus (1562-1962), ed. John A. Tedeschi, 103-95; cf. *Collana dei Studi Pietro Rossi* IV (Florence: Le Monnier, 1965).

The Radical Reformation (Philadelphia: Westminster, 1962). 924 pp.

"Reflections on the Radical Reformation," *Bulletin of the Congregational Library* 14, 1 (1962), 5-10; 14, 2 (1963), 5-10.

"Theologische Ausbildungsstätten," Vereinigte Staaten von Amerika, *Religion in Geschichte und Gegenwart*, 3rd ed., VI (Tübingen: J. C. B. Mohr, 1962), cols. 1309-14.

Wilderness and Paradise in Christian Thought: The Biblical Experience of the Desert in the History of Christianity and the Paradise Theme in the Theological Idea of the University (New York: Harper & Brothers, 1962).

A Time to Rend and a Time to Sew: A Sermon on the Second Vatican Council, Phase I: Oct. 11-Dec. 8, 1962, first preached at the First Church in Cambridge, Dec. 9, 1962; preached in revised version at First Church in Boston, Dec. 16, 1962; cf. *Catholic Messenger*, National Edition (Mar. 7, 1963), 5-6; *Unitarian Christian* 18, 3 (Mar., 1963), 3-7, 15; *North Carolina Catholic* (Mar., 24, 1963), 3A-4A.

1963

"[The Role of the Layman in] the Ancient Church, A.D. 30-313," *The Layman in Christian History*, eds. Stephen Neill and Hans R. Weber (London: SCM, 1963), 28-54.

"Harry Wolfson as Stylist," Tributes to Harry Wolfson on the Occasion of His Seventy-Fifth Birthday, *Mosaic* 4 (Winter, 1963), 36-38.

"Commemorative Sermon on Pope John XXIII," *Unitarian Christian* 18, 4 (1963), 2-6; cf. [Boston] *Pilot* (Aug. 10, 1963), 8; separately printed with order of services at The Cathedral Church of St. Paul, Boston (June 9, 1963), 8-14.

1964

"Michael Servetus and a Theology of Nature," *Journal of the Liberal Ministry* 4 (1964), 121-42.

The Word, the Church, and the University (Cambridge: Student Christian Movement in New England, 1964).

"Introduction [of the Stillman Lectures and the Lecturer, Augustin Cardinal Bea]," *Ecumenical Dialogue at Harvard: The Roman Catholic-Protestant Colloquium*, eds. Samuel H. Miller and G. Ernest Wright (Cambridge: Belknap, 1964), 3-24.

Commencement Address, Regis College, Weston, Massachusetts (June 14, 1964).

Review article on *The Catholic Church and Nazi Germany*, by Guenter Lewy, *Harvard Divinity School Bulletin* 28, 4 (1964), 117-18.

1965

"Camillus Renatus Called Also Lysias Philaenus and Paolo Ricci (c. 1550-c. 1575): Forerunner of Socinianism on Individual Immortality," *Harry Austryn Wolfson Jubilee Volume*, ed. Saul Lieberman (Jerusalem: Central, 1965), II, 833-70.

"Unitarian Universalist Association," *Encyclopedia Americana* (New York: Americana Corporation, 1965), XXVII, 431-32.

"Unitarianism," *ibid.*, 432-34.

"Universalism," *ibid.*, 773-75.

Report of the Special Non-Legislative Commission [on Birth Control] (Boston: Legislative Printers, 1965), chairman.

"The Parable of the Elder Brother: Reflections on the Protestant Response to Catholic Ecumenism," *Harvard Divinity School Bulletin*, 29, 3 (1965), 1-11; cf. *9th Naval District Chaplain's Newsletter* (Aug., 1965), 1-9.

"Vatican Council: A Look Ahead," with Richard Cardinal Cushing, Boston *Sunday Herald* (Dec. 12, 1965), IV, 1-4.

"Living Stones," a memorial dedication sermon, *Unitarian Christian* 20, 2 (1965), 3-10.

"Friends of God and Prophets," convocation address of Sept. 29, 1965, *Harvard Divinity School Bulletin* 30, 1 (1965), 1-24.

"Journal of a Soul," review article, Boston *Herald* (June 13, 1965), VI, 8.

Dimensions of Catholic Ecumenism, Occasional Papers, I (The Hague: I.A.R.F., 1965); also mimeographed for Round-Table on Second Vatican Council, New York City (Jan., 1966).

"Georges Vasilievich Florovsky: His American Career (1948-65)," *Greek Orthodox Theological Review* 11 (1965), 7-107.

1966

Chart of Christian History and Culture with accompanying Manual of Church History for the Sunday School Curriculum of the United Church of Christ (Boston-Philadelphia: United Church Press, 1966), consultant.

"Anabaptists," *American People's Encyclopedia* (New York: Grolier, 1966), I, 441-42.

"There Was a Division (Schisma) Among Them," convocation address, *Greek Orthodox Theological Review* 11 (1965-66), 209-16.

"The Religious Background of the Idea of a Loyal Opposition," *Voluntary Associations,* ed. D. B. Robertson (Richmond: John Knox, 1966), 55-89, 402-08.

"*Translatio Studii*: The Puritains' Conception of their First University in New England, 1636," *Festschrift für Heinrich Bornkamm = Archiv für Reformationgeschichte* 57 (1966), 152-81.

1967

"Anabaptists," *Encyclopedia Britannica* (Chicago: William Benton, 1967), I, 838-39.

"Ludwig Haetzer," *ibid.,* XI, 466.

"Melchior Hoffman," *ibid.,* XI, 574.

"Michael Servetus," *ibid.,* XX, 257.

"Sanctification in the Testimony of Several So-Called Schwärmer," *Kirche, Mystik, Heiligung und das Natürliche bei Luther,* Vorträge des Dritten Internationalen Kongresses fur Lutherforschung, ed. Ivar Asheim (Göttingen: Vanderhoeck & Ruprecht, 1967), 194-211; cf. *Mennonite Quarterly Review* 42, 1 (1968), 5-25.

"Popularized German Mysticism as a Factor in the Rise of Anabaptist Communism," *Glaube, Geist, Geschichte: Festschrift für Ernst Benz,* eds. Gerhard Müller and Winfried Zeller (Leiden: Brill, 1967), 290-312.

"Giorgio Blandrata," *New Catholic Encyclopedia* (Washington: Catholic University of America, 1967), II, 604.

"Franz David," *ibid.,* IV, 660.

"Jean LeClerc," *ibid.,* VIII, 598.

"Stanislaw Lubieniecki," *ibid.,* VIII, 1053.

"Bernardino Ochino," *ibid.,* X, 630.

"Socinianism," *ibid.*, XIII, 397-98.

"Sectarian Ecumenicity: Reflections on a Little Noticed Aspect of the Radical Reformation," [Baptist] *Review and Expositor* 64 (1967), 141-60.

"Michael Servetus," *Encyclopedia of Philosophy* (New York: Macmillan and Free Press, 1967), VIII, 419-20.

"Socinianism," *ibid.*, VIII, 474-75.

"Foreword," Ephraim Isaac, *The Ethiopian Church* (Boston: Henry N. Sawyer, 1967), 9-11.

"The 'Congregationalist' Luther and the Free Churches," *Lutheran Quarterly* n.s. 18 (1967), 283-94; cf. "The 'Congregationalist' Luther and Radical Reform," *Harvard Divinity School Bulletin* n.s. 1 (Sept., 1967), 9-12.

"The Attitude of Liberals in New England toward Non-Christian Religions, 1784-1873," *Crane Review* 9, 2 (1967), 59-89.

"Christian Unity: The Road Since 1910," review of *The Ecumenical Revolution: An Interpretation of the Catholic-Protestant Dialogue*, by Robert McAfee Brown, Boston *Sunday Globe* (Aug. 20, 1967), A, 15.

"The Pilgrimage of Thomas Hooker (1586-1647) in England, The Netherlands, and New England," *Bulletin of the Congregational Library* 19, 1 (1967), 5-15; 20, 2 (1968), 9-13.

"The No. 2 Moral Issue of Today [Abortion]," *America* 116 (Mar. 25, 1967), 452-53.

"An Unjust War: Vietnam," *Articles and Issues* 1, 1 (Andover-Newton Theological School) (Oct. 27, 1967), 20-23.

That All the Peoples of the Earth May Know Thy Name, a sermon on Jerusalem, preached at the First Church in Boston (July 23, 1967).

1968

"The Ministry and the Draft in Historical Perspective," *Perspectives* (Students and Faculty of the Harvard Divinity School) (April 1, 1968), 40-76; cf. *Una Sancta* 25, 1 (1968), 3-40; reprinted, in part, *Sanctuary: Special Report* of the Division of Social Responsibility of the Unitarian-Universalist Association (Boston: Beacon, 1968), 33-34; also *The Religious Situation, 1969* ed. Donald R. Cutler (Boston: Beacon, 1969), 464-512.

"Peace in the History of the Church," *Colloquy* 1, 6 (1968), 28-30.

"Joseph Priestley on Luther," *Interpreters of Luther: Festschrift in*

Honor of Wilhelm Pauck, ed. Jaroslav Pelikan (Philadelphia: Fortress, 1968), 121-58.

"Called by Thy Name, Leave Us Not: The Case of Mrs. Joan Drake, A Formative Episode in the Pastoral Career of Thomas Hooker in England," *Harvard Library Bulletin* 16 (1968), 111-28, 278-300.

"A Homily for Communion," *Unitarian Christian* 24, 1 (1968), 14, 16.

Ed., *Church, State, and Education: a new look* (Boston: Beacon, 1968).

"Laurentian in Action . . . Dr. David C. Williams '40: Blind Osteopath Doesn't Dwell on His Limitations," *St. Lawrence Bulletin* 26, 2 (1968), 15.

"Samuel Howard Miller, 1900-1968 in Seven Books: Practical Mystic and Curer of Souls," *Harvard Divinity School Bulletin* n.s. 1, 3 (1968), 2-8.

"Tribute to James Luther Adams," *Godbox* 2, 3, Meadville Student Association (1968), 22-31.

1969

"Erasmus and the Reformers on Non-Christian Religions and Salus Extra Ecclesiam," *Action and Conviction in Early Modern Europe: essays in memory of E. H. Harbison,* eds. Theodore K. Rabb and Jerrold E. Seigel (Princeton: Princeton University, 1969), 319-70.

"For Three Transgressions and for Four (Amos 1 and 2)," Moratorium Day meditation at Harvard Memorial Church, *November Moratorium Addresses, November 13 & 14, 1969*; also *Harvard Crimson* (Jan. 5, 1970), 3-4; this is Prof. Williams' only full length sermon published in the *Crimson.*

"Harvard in Upheaval," *Harvard Divinity School Bulletin* n.s. 3, 1 (1969), 6-14.

"A People in Community: Historical Background," *The Concept of the Believers' Church,* ed. James L. Garrett, Jr. (Scottdale, Pa.: Herald, 1969), 97-142.

1970

"Loyalty and Dissent: Perspectives from History," *America* 122 June 27, 1970), 669-71.

"In Response—The Middle East," *Unitarian-Universalist World* (Nov. 1, 1970), 5.

"Christian Attitudes towards Nature," *Colloquy* 3, 4 (1970), 12-15; cf. "Guilty?," *Alice* 2, 4 (1971), 10-13, 24.

"Nixon Asked to Act on Abortions," [Boston] *Pilot* (Nov. 28, 1970), 1, 3; collaborator.

"Religious Residues and Presuppositions in the American Debate on Abortion," *Theological Studies* 31 (1970), 10-75.

"The Sacred Condominium," *The Morality of Abortion: Legal and Historical Perspectives,* ed. John T. Noonan, Jr. (Cambridge: Harvard University, 1970), 146-71; pb. reprint, 1972.

1971

American Universalism: A Bicentennial Historical Essay = Journal of the Universalist Society 9 (1971), 1-94; reprint as *American Universalism* (Boston: Skinner House, 1976).

"The Chaplaincy in the Armed Forces of the United States of America in Historical and Ecclesiastical Perspective," *Military Chaplains: From a Religious Military to a Military Religion,* ed. Harvey Cox (New York: American Report Press, 1971), 11-57; 149-54; to be revised by Prescott Wintersteen.

"Christian Attitudes Toward Nature," *Christian Scholar's Review* 2 (1971-72), 3-35; 112-26.

"Protecting the Unborn," Boston *Herald-Traveler* (Feb. 26, 1971), 7; cf. "Retain Present Abortion Law," [Boston] *Pilot* (Mar. 6, 1971), 7.

"Testimony Against Abortion," *Metanoia* 3 (1972), 4-7.

"Should We Repeal the Abortion Laws? No!," with Arthur Dyck, Boston *Globe* (Oct. 29, 1971), 17; cf. "[A] Harvard Statement on Abortion," *Catholic Digest* 36, 5 (1972), 29-32.

"Response [to Jean MacRae]," with Marjorie Derr Williams, *Unauthorized Version,* Harvard Divinity School (Nov. 29, 1971), 2, 6, 8.

1972

"The Two Social Strands in Italian Anabaptism, c. 1526-c. 1565," *The Social History of the Reformation,* eds. L. P. Buck and J. W. Zophy (Columbus: Ohio State University, 1972), 156-207.

"The Course of Jewish-Christian Relations," *Unitarian-Universalist Christian* 27, 1 (1972), 5-10.

"Ecology and Abortion," *New England Sierran* 3, 6 (1972), 2, 6.

"Foreword: The Democratization of a Near Constant in History," *Abortion and Social Justice,* eds. Thomas W. Hilgers and Dennis J. Horan (New York: Sheed & Ward, 1972), ix-xix.

1973

"Christopher Dawson, 12 October 1889—25 May 1970: First Incumbent of the Charles Chauncy Stillman Chair at Harvard," with Daniel Callahan, et al., *Harvard Theological Review* 66 (1973), 161-76.

"Creatures of a Creator, Members of a Body, Subjects of a Kingdom," *To God be the Glory: Sermons in Honor of George Arthur Buttrick,* ed. T. Gill (Nashville: Abingdon, 1973), 98-108.

"Professor George LaPiana (1878-1971), Catholic Modernist at Harvard (1915-1947)," *Harvard Library Bulletin* 21 (1973), 117-43.

Wolfson, Harry Austryn. *Studies in the History of Philosophy and Religion,* I, ed. with Isadore Twersky (Cambridge: Harvard University, 1973).

1974

"Baptismal Theology and Practice in Rome as Reflected in Justin Martyr," *The Ecumenical World of Orthodox Civilization: Essays in Honor of Georges Florovsky,* III, eds. Thomas Bird and Andrew Blane (The Hague: Mouton, 1974), 9-34.

"Justin Glimpsed as a Martyr among Roman Contemporaries," *The Context of Contemporary Theology: Essays in Honor of Paul Lehmann,* eds. Alexander McKelway and E. David Willis (Atlanta: John Knox, 1974), 99-126.

"German Mysticism in the Polarization of Ethical Behavior in Luther and the Anabaptists," *Mennonite Quarterly Review* 48 (1974), 275-304.

Documents in Free Church Origins, series ed. with Franklin Littell (Philadelphia: Temple University, 1974-   ); 12 volumes projected.

"The Sarmatian Myth Sublimated in the *Historia Reformationis Polonicae* (1664-85) of Stanislas Lubieniecki and Related Documents," *For Wiktor Weintraub: Essays in Polish Literature, Language, and History offered to Wiktor Weintraub on His 65th Birthday,* ed. Victor Erlich (The Hague: Mouton, 1974), 567-79.

"Sobor Watykanski II, i Sytuacja Ekumeniczna w Polsce w Oczach Obserwatora Protestanckiego," *Katolicki Uniwersytet Lubelski, Zeszyty Naukowe* 17 (1974), 13-21.

"Omnium christianorum pastor et doctor: Vatican I et l'Angleterre victorienne," *Nouvelle Revue Theologique* 96 (1974), 113-46; 337-65.

"Four Modalities of Violence, with Special Reference to the Writings of Georges Sorel," *Journal of Church and State* 16 (1974), 11-30; 237-61.

"G. H. Williams finds stamina, hope in Poland 25 years after World War II," *Harvard Divinity School Bulletin* 4 (1974), 1, 3.

1975

"A Colonial Rector of Harvard University and Stanislas Lubieniecki; a note on one of the first books written by a Pole known to have been read by an American, 1689," *Studia Anglistyczne*, ed. Henryk Zins (Warsaw: Lubelskie Towarzystwo Naukowe, 1975), 41-47.

"Socinianism and Deism: From Eschatological Elitism to Universal Immortality," *Historical Reflections/Reflexions Historiques* 2, 2 (1975), 265-90.

"A History of Speaking in Tongues and Related Gifts," with Edith L. Waldvogel, *The Charismatics: Confusion or Blessing?*, ed. Canon Michael Hamilton (Grand Rapids: Eerdmans, 1975), 61-113.

"Introduction," to James Freeman Clarke, *Ten Great Religions: An Essay in Comparative Theology* (Boston, 1871) in the series: The Rise of Modern Religious Ideas in America, ed. Sidney Ahlstrom (Hicksville, N.Y.: Regina, 1975), 3t-5t.

"Patterns of Thought: Political Perspectives," with Rodney L. Petersen, *The Evangelical Resurgence (1925-1975)*, eds. David Wells and John Woodbridge (New York/Nashville: Abingdon, 1975), ch. 9; rev. pb. edition (Grand Rapids: Baker, 1977).

"New England Puritan Interest in the Christian East," *Andover Newton Quarterly* (special issue in honor of Gerald Cragg) 15, 4 (1975), 267-77.

Thomas Hooker: Writings in England and Holland, 1626-1633, ed. with intro. essays by George H. Williams, et al., Harvard Theological Studies 27 (Cambridge: Harvard University, 1975); distrib. through Scholars' Press, Missoula, Montana.

"Harry Austryn Wolfson," Faculty Minute with Isadore Twersky, et al., *Harvard Gazette* (June 6, 1975), 11.

1976

"The Antitrinitarians in the Polish-Lithuanian Commonwealth of the Sixteenth and Seventeenth Century," *Minutes* of the Seminars in Ukrainian Studies held at Harvard University 6 (1975-76), 87-90.

"Harry Austryn Wolfson (1887-1974)," biographical memoir, American Philosophical Society *1975 Yearbook* XXVIII (Philadelphia: 1976), 178-86; cf. "Harry Austryn Wolfson," *Profiles from the Beloved Community,* ed. Peter Gomes (Cambridge, 1976), 3-12.

"Henry Joel Cadbury: A New Testament Scholar and Nobel Laureate," Faculty Minute by George H. Williams, et al., *Harvard Gazette* (Feb. 6, 1976), 7.

"James Luther Adams," *Andover Newton Quarterly* 16 (1976), 173-85.

"Pope's Proposed Visit Defended," [Boston] *Herald American* (Feb. 28, 1976); cf. [Boston] *Pilot* (Mar. 5, 1976).

"The Revolutionary Plight of Russian Orthodoxy, 1917-1977, in the Soviet Union and in the Diaspora," with Frederick C. Webster, *Unitarian Universalist Christian* 31, 3-4 (1976) 71-109.

"Transition as Part of Religious Change," *Faith and Forum: Journal of the Guild of Religious Architecture* 9 (Fall, 1976), 14-17; 26-28.

1977

"Erasmianism in Poland 1518-1605," *Polish Review* 22 (1977), 3-50; also in *Renaissance East and West,* ed. Cyriac Pullapilly (New Rochelle, N.Y.: Caratzas Brothers, 1978).

"Foreword," Alvin J. Beachy, *The Concept of Grace in the Radical Reformation* (The Hague: Nieuwkoop, 1977), xiii-xiv.

Wolfson, Harry Austryn. *Religious Philosophy,* II, ed. with Isadore Twersky (Cambridge: Harvard University, 1977).

"The Idea of the Wilderness of the New World in Cotton Mather's *Magnalia Christi Americana,*" *Magnalia Christi Americana,* I, eds. K. Murdock and E. Miller (Cambridge: Harvard University, 1977), 49-58.

"Introduction," Prescott B. Wintersteen, *Unitarian Christology in American Unitarianism: An Anthology* (Boston: Unitarian Universalist Christian Fellowship, 1977), ix-xv.

"Anti-abortionist Alive and Well at Harvard University," *National Catholic Register* (Mar. 13, 1977), 1.

1978

"Liberal Christianity: Past and Future," *Unitarian Universalist Christian* 33 (1978), 5-19.

The Polish Brethren: Documentation of the History and Thought of Unitarianism in Poland and the Diaspora, 1601-1685, Harvard Theological Studies 30 (Missoula, Montana: Scholars, 1978). 1200 pp.

"A Priestly Kingdom and a Royal Priesthood: A Sermon in Commemoration of the 150th Anniversary of the Founding of the Church, and of the 125th Anniversary of the Founding of the Edifice of the Prospect Street Congregational Church," *150th Anniversary Booklet,* ed. Frank M. Weiskel (Cambridge, 1978), 21-29.

"Robert Ulich: Poet, Historian, Philosopher, and Educator," Faculty Minute, *Harvard Gazette* (May 19, 1978), 11.

"The Philosophy of Pope John Paul II," [Boston] *Pilot,* CIL (3 November 1978), p. 12, all six cols.

"The Humanitarian Vision of Pope John Paul II," *Polish Review* 24 (1978).

1979

"An Intellectual Portrait of Pope John Paul II," *Worldview* 22: 1 (January, 1979), pp. 1ff.

"From Freedom, Reason, and Tolerance toward a Liberal Christian Conception of Man," *Collegium Conference Proceedings 1978,* ed. Peter Kaufman (Chapel Hill, N.C.), ch. 1.

"Reforming Currents from within and without the Ukrainian Lands in the Sixteenth and Seventeenth Century," *Church and Religion in Early Modern Ukraine,* ed. Zenon Kohut (Cambridge: Harvard University, 1979).

"The Polish-Lithuanian Calvin," *Festschrift for Ford Lewis Battles,* ed. Brian Gerrish (Pittsburgh: Pickwick, 1979), ch. 11.

"The Religious History of the Chaplych Family of Volhynia," *Essays in Honor of Omeljan Pritsak,* ed. Francis Cleaves, Ihor Ševčenko, *et al.* (Cambridge: Harvard University, 1979).

"The Christological Issue between Faustus Socinus and Francis Dávid in 1579," *Antitrinitarianism in the Second Half of the XVI. Century,* Proceedings of the Center of Renaissance Studies, ed. Róbert Dán (Budapest, 1979).

Forthcoming

"The Neo-Patristic Synthesis of Georges Florovsky: Its Present Stage" *The Ecumenical World of Orthodox Civilization: Essays in Honor of Georges Florovsky,* I, eds. Andrew Blane and Masha Vorobiov (The Hague: Mouton).

"Cardinal Stanislas Hosius, 1504-1579," *Shapers of Traditions in Germany, Switzerland, and Poland, 1564-1600,* ed. Jill Raitt (Princeton: Princeton University).

"Father Peter Skarga, S. J., 1536-1618," *ibid.*

"Protestantism in the Ukraine During the Polish-Lithuanian Commonwealth," *Harvard Ukrainian Studies*, II, 1 (March, 1978, pp. 44-72) and 2 (June, 1978, pp. 178ff); in modified form in *Church and Religion in the Seventeenth and Eighteenth Centuries,* Papers of the Ukrainian Research Institute, ed. Zenon E. Kohut.

"Preface," Carl Cohen, *The Impact of the Protestant Reformation on the Jews* (Heidelberg: Lambert-Schneider).

"The Sabbath and the Lord's Day," *Andover Newton Quarterly* 19, 2 (1978).

Reformación Radiál, substantially revised edition in Spanish of *The Radical Reformation* (1962), with the assistance of José Nieto (Mexico City: Fondo de Cultura Economica); Italian revision (1975) in galleys only.

"The Polish-Lithuanian Commonwealth," *The Reformation Experience: The Diversity of Theology and Settlement During the Sixteenth Century,* ed. David. P. Daniel.

Lubieniecki, Stanislas (d. 1675), *The History of the Polish Reformation,* and five related documents, transl. and ed. with Earl Morse Wilbur (d. 1959) and Marek Wajsblum (d. 1962), assisted by Jean Martin; text introduced by a History of All Confessions and Judaism in the Polish-Lithuanian Commonwealth, 1518-1601, Harvard Theological Studies (Missoula, Montana: Scholars).

INDEX OF SUBJECTS

Abolitionism, 307-09, 332
Abortion
G. H. Williams' opposition to, 12-13
Adventists, 361
American Revolution, 322, 326-31
Anabaptism (*See* also Radical Reformation)
conception of history in, 21-27
sacramental practice of, 22
role of church discipline in, 22
influence of Erasmus on, 148
theology of baptism in, 177-81
opposed by Peter Martyr, 211
influence of social doctrines of in Polish Antitrinitarianism, 288
Anthropology
Luther's conception of, 150-68
in Bacon, 275-76
Antitrinitarianism, *See* Unitarianism
Apostles' Creed, 294
Arianism, 292-93, 298
Aristotelianism, 136-37, 149, 201, 274, 312
opposed by Luther, 163
Asceticism, 85
Astrology, 156
Atonement, *See* Christ, work of
Augsburg Confession, 196, 199
Averroism, 136-37

Baptism, 42, 60, 154
replaced by Eucharist as root metaphor for the Atonement, 72-73
priority over the Eucharist in Calvin, 92
of Jesus and John the Baptist in late medieval theology, 169-73
debated by Zwingli and Hubmaier, 173-81
analogous to monastic vow, 179
(infant) compared to circumcision, 181
Baptists, 12, 118, 301, 303
Book of Common Prayer (Elizabethan), 217, 225, 319

Calvinism, 135, 148, 211, 317-20, 365
Cartesian Philosophy, 275, 286

Catholic (Counter) Reformation, 202, 234-35
Chalcedon, Council of, 123, 125
Christmas
not a true sacrament, 102
Christ
Ascension of, 25, 270
Person of
in Clement of Rome, 46-47
in Clement of Alexandria, 52-55
relation of poverty of Christ of, 83-86
relation of Eucharist, 40, 93-94, 99-100
controversies over, 123
relation of church and state, 123-26
hypostastic union, 123
dissensions within Socinianism over, 286
inequality of in relation to the Father, 296
Dorner's work on, 394
pre-existence of, 293
Work of (Atonement), 14
in Guibert of Nogent, 74-76
Sozzini's argument against satisfaction theory of, 252-54
Second Coming of, *See* Eschatology
Church
visible, 92
as Eucharistic fellowship in medieval theology, 92-103
relation of Eucharist to Augustine, 102-03
Peter Martyr on the marks of, 198-214
as the New Israel, 317
as Body of Christ, 10
Church — and State
theory of Kantorowicz on, 4-5, 71-72
in Roman Empire, 64
in Eastern Orthodox tradition, 121-30
"caesaropapism," 122
in Calvin and Peter Martyr, 204-05
separation of in America, 304-08, 338, 347-48
sacral kingship, 318

unity of described as "harmony" by Justinian, 124-25
Luther's views on the relation of, 161-62
Church History, 6
G. H. Williams' conception of, 3-17, 19-20
of Eusebius of Caesarea, 62-67
Socinian perspective of in Benedykt Wiszowaty, 285-300
in a university context, 388-89
Civilization, as preparation for Christianity in Eusebius, 62-70
Cloning, 383
Colloquy of Poissy, 205, 207
Communism, 11, 13, 20-21, 346, 369-70, 374
Congregationalism, 8-9, 15, 213, 301, 312
Conscience
meaning of in John Cotton, 341-44
Constance, Council of, 148
Constantinople
fall of in 1204, 109
recovery of in 1261, 104-17
ecumenical patriarch of, 125
fall of in 1453, 29, 315
Corpus christianum, 20, 183
Covenant
the New, 51
Crusades, 90

Didache, 46-47
Diet of Speyer of 1529, 193, 195
Donatism, 101, 148

Eastern Orthodoxy, 83, 118-30, 389
in modern times, 126-30
Ecumenism, 308
and efforts toward social justice, 263-78
in the thought of F. H. Hedge and Philip Schaff, 13-14, 17
Edict of Worms, 190-91
Election, doctrine of (Free Will, Predestination), 158, 166, 258
Luther and Erasmus on, 140
English Reformation, 319-22
Peter Martyr's influence on, 212
John Jewel's critique of, 215-31
Eschatology, 267
Second Coming of Christ, 25, 28
premillennialism of D. L. Moody, 333
delay of parousia, 28, 39-40, 126, 130

Paul's teaching on in I Thessalonians, 33-44
implications for in the Eucharist, 94
three interpretions of, 119-21
Eucharist (Lord's Supper), 8, 16, 49, 60
identified with priestly sacrifices in Irenaeus, 50-52
theology of in Guibert of Nogent, 71-82
doctrine of real presence, 73, 95-103
manducatio indignorum, 81
three levels of in Thomas Aquinas, 93
Augustine's doctrine of the, 101-103
debate between Luther and Zwingli over, 135
administered in both kinds, 188-89
Carlstadt's symbolical interpretion of, 193
conditional immorality implied in the liturgy of, 393
Excommunication, 187, 208
Ex opere operato, 171, 174, 181

Faith, 155
fides quaeruns intellectum, 140
Socinian's conception of, 251
as fiducia or assensus, 252
Fall, The, 62
Luther's interpretation of, 150-68
effect of upon reason, 275
Filioque, 112
Free Churches, 23
Alexander Campbell's "Restoration Movement," 21
French Revolution, 128
Fundamentalism, 12
controversy with modernism, 313

Gnosticism, 48, 119, 298
Grace, 16, 278
conveyed by baptism, 175
and justification, 261-64

Hesychasm, 128
Holocaust, 20, 29-30
Holy Roman Empire, 24, 29, 133, 194-97
Holy Spirit, 25, 36, 51
relation of to baptism, 175-76
action of in justification, 252
agent in sanctification, 43
Humanism
relationship to Protestantism, 133-49
the nature of Renaissance, 136

relation of to scholastic theology, 137-41

influence upon Luther at Erfurt, 141

Melanchthon's espousal of, 143-46

Beza influenced by, 146

optimism of Renaissance, 168

Imitatio Christi, 84

Immortality

Lorenzo Valla on, 158

as a reward for obedience, 251

the Ingersol lectures on, 390-96

Inquisition (Roman), 232-49

Islam, 16, 23, 25-26

Jehovah's Witnesses, 345

Joachimitism

and radical periodization, 24-27

Judaism, 16, 26, 133, 301-03, 307, 311, 317

Hellenistic, 42

Justification

Luther's doctrine of, 183

Fausto Sozzini on, 250-64

Liberalism, 11-12, 366, 375

Lutheran Reformation

adoption of in Nuremberg, 182-97

Manicheans, 119

Marian exiles, 212, 217

Martyrdom, 47-48, 54, 56-57, 81

Marxism, 129-30, 365, 374-75

Mennonites, 286, 305

Methodists, 308, 353

Monasticism, 84-85, 184

Monophysitism, 299

Monotheism, 298

Montanism, 58-59, 121

Moravians, 305

Mysticism, 392

relation to Eastern Church, 118

in Russian Christianity, 128

Nazism, 1-2, 5, 20-27, 65, 346

Neoplatonism, 136-37, 294

of Ficino and Pico, 390

Nestorianism, 299

Nicea, Council of (I), 22, 123, 295-96

Nicea, Council of (II), 125

Norman Anonymous of 1100 A.D., 6, 71

Ordination, 226

of G. H. Williams, 8

Ottoman Empire, 126, 128

Peasants' Revolt of 1525, 192-93

Pelagianism, 120, 153, 258, 261

Pietism, 21, 26, 313, 342

Polish Brethren, 15, 285f.

Polity

occasioned by the Fall, 161

Peter Martyr Vermigli's conception of, 198-214

"Possessors"

led by St. Joseph of Volotsk, 127-28

Prayer, 49, 51, 54

Preaching, 82, 92, 178, 188

Presbyterians, 212-13, 301, 358

Priesthood of all believers, 317

doctrine in patristic era, 45-61

in Paschasius Radbertus, 99

Protestant Missions

controversy over American "activism," 351-62

Protestant orthodoxy, 144, 149, 270, 285

Providence, 301

Puritanism, 5, 21, 225-27, 230, 301, 305, 316, 319-22, 335

Quakers, 301, 305

Racovian Catechism, 287

Radical Reformation (*See* also Anabaptism), 2, 7, 14-15, 20-23, 365

ecclesiology, 198-200

Recapitulation, doctrine of in Irenaeus, 51

Relics

relation to Eucharist, 79-80

Religious Toleration, 281, 304-08, 321-24

Roger Williams an advocate of, 338-50

Renaissance

Burckhardt's view of, 136

relation to Reformation of, 146-47

reverence for antiquity in, 279

optimistic humanism of, 168

Resurrection, 28

Roman Catholicism, 11, 20-21, 235-39, 306-07, 310, 331, 334, 349, 374, 263-66

Romanticism, 128, 312

Sanctification

Paul's teaching on in I Thessalonians, 42-43

Scholastic Theology and the origins of
the Reformation, 133-49, 272
Erasmus' opposition to, 138
Luther's treatise against, 142
Zwingli's relation to, 180
Scripture, 280
and nature as dual sources of revelation in Bacon, 271-72
pattern for church government in,
209-11
commentaries of Peter Martyr on,
203-04
Second Advent, *See* Eschatology
Sin
Tillich's doctrine of, 2
psychological consequences of, 162-68
release from in the Anselmian view
of redemption, 74-76
Spinozism, 286, 292
Thirty-nine Articles of the Church of
England, 92
Trent, Council of, 21, 237
Trinity, 11
relation to concepts of periodization,
25-27

controversies over, 122
defined as dogma at Nicea I, 22
Augustine's treatise on, 152
imaged in the memory, intellect, and
will, 152-55
baptism in the name of, 171-72
dogma of in Socinian historiography,
292-300

Unification Church, 26
Unitarianism, 4, 10, 13, 15, 299
Hungarian and Transylvanian, 291

Vatican Council II, 307
G. H. Williams observer at, 11
Virgin Mary
as *mediatrix*, 76-77
Immaculate Conception of, 78-79, 135
assumption of, 78, 79

Westminster Assembly, 321
Wilderness (theological sense), 267-68
as metaphor of experiences of religion
in America, 301-14
Witchcraft, 232, 236, 243, 248

INDEX OF SELECTED NAMES

Adams, John, 315f., 329, 331
Ahrweiler, H., 104, 110
Ambrose, Saint, 97, 365, 376
Ames, William, 323, 342
Anderson, Rufus, 356ff.
Anselm of Canterbury, 71ff.
Aquinas, Thomas, 93ff., 103, 135, 138, 142f., 365
Aristotle, 95, 142ff., 152, 163, 207ff., 380, 391
Augustine, Saint, 29, 73, 78, 80, 97, 100ff., 142, 152, 158, 163, 296, 387

Bacon, Francis, 267-284
Bailyn, Bernard, 327
Baldwin of Canterbury, 95ff.
Barth, Karl, 366
Beecher, Henry Ward, 313, 363
Beecher, Lyman, 331
Berengar of Tours, 72ff.
Bernards, Matthäus, 84, 89
Beza, Theodore, 146, 201ff., 205, 211ff.
Biel, Gabriel, 170ff.
Bonaventure, Saint, 82, 135, 143
Bouwsma, William, 146f.
Brown, Charles R., 392, 396
Browne, Sir Thomas, 16
Bruni, Leonardo, 137
Bryan, William Jennings, 313
Bucer, Martin, 200ff.
Bullinger, Henry, 202f.
Bultmann, Rudolf, 28, 52
Burckhardt, Jacob, 136, 380

Calvin, John, 21, 92, 146, 148, 199f., 202, 206f., 211ff., 225, 317f.
Castellio, Sebastian, 135, 148, 251
Catherine the Great, 128
Channing, William Ellery, 11, 14
Charles I, 316, 320f., 325
Charles II, 322
Charles V, 188, 190, 195f.
Chmaj, Ludwik, 250f., 260
Clement of Alexandria, 28, 52ff., 61, 63, 66, 296
Clement of Rome, 46, 47
Constantine the Great, 29, 68, 117, 295, 307, 317

Cotton, John, 338-350
Cranmer, Thomas, 202, 204
Cromwell, Oliver, 321
Cyprian, 46, 61

Dennis, James, 357f.
Descartes, Réné, 381
Dickinson, Lowes, 395
Diogenes, 380
Dodd, C. H., 394
Dürer, Albrecht, 186, 193

Eastwood, Cyril, 51, 54
Eddy, Mary Baker, 26
Edward VI, 204, 223, 319
Edwards, Jonathan, 312, 325, 331
Elizabeth I, 212, 215, 223f., 227, 231, 316, 319
Erasmus of Rotterdam, 134f., 138, 140f., 148, 186, 250
Erikson, Erik, 165
Eusebius of Caesarea, 29, 62-70, 282

Fedorov, G. P., 121
Ferdinand III, 188ff., 195
Florus of Lyon, 94, 98
Fontenelle, Bernard, 281f.
Foxe, John, 319
Francis of Assisi, Saint, 25, 89, 179
Franck, Sebastian, 22, 135
Franklin, Benjamin, 329, 381
Frick, Dr. Heinrich, 352ff., 357f.
Funk, Robert, 34, 37

Galilei, Galileo, 273, 275
Grégoire, Réginald, 72, 84, 89
Guibert of Nogent, 71-82

Hedge, Frederick Henry, 13ff.
Henry VIII, 222f., 319
Herbert of Cherbury, 275, 277
Hippolytus, 61, 64
Hitler, Adolf, 27, 65, 334
Hobbes, Thomas, 283f.
Holmes, John Haynes, 393
Homer, 144, 382
Honorius of Autun, 72, 76, 82
Hooker, Richard, 225, 229ff.

Hubmaier, Balthasar, 169-181
Humbolt, Wilhelm von, 334
Hume, David, 275ff., 281f.
Hus, John, 148

Ignatius of Loyola, Saint, 134, 298
Irenaeus of Lyons, 50ff., 61, 69, 296
Isocrates, 63ff.

James (Apostle), 255, 263
James I, 316, 320f.
James II, 322, 324
James, William, 391
Jefferson, Thomas, 329, 331
Jerome, Saint, 83ff., 179
Jewel, John, 212, 215-231
Joachim of Fiore, 24ff.
John the Baptist, 169ff.
John XXIII, 365, 374f.
Joseph (Patriarch), 112f., 116
Jung, C. G., 384
Justin Martyr, 28, 48ff., 61, 69, 296
Justinian, 122ff.

Kantorowicz, Ernst, 4f., 71f.
King, Martin Luther, 312, 334
Knox, John, 201
Kristeller, Paul Oskar, 136f.

Lactantius, 296, 386
Lea, Henry Charles, 233, 239, 246
Leo XIII, 353, 365, 374
Lévi-Strauss, Claude, 386
Limborch, Philip van, 289, 291
Linck, Wenceslas, 186, 188
Lombard, Peter, 135, 142, 170, 172
Lubieniecki, Stanislaw, Jr., 285, 287f.
Lucretius, 66
Luther, Martin, 21, 29, 133ff., 140ff.,
    148, 150-168, 180, 183, 187ff., 198, 207,
    271, 387f., 395

Machiavelli, Niccolo, 274, 284
Mann, Thomas, 5, 388
Marx, Karl, 381
Mary I, 202, 217, 223, 319
Mather, Cotton, 26
Mead, Sidney E., 302, 308, 313
Melanchthon, Philipp, 135, 142ff., 192,
    196, 395
Melito of Sardis, 50, 61
Michael VIII Paleologus, 104-117
Miller, Perry, 302, 304, 312, 338, 361

Montague, William P., 391, 394
Moody, Dwight L., 333, 352
More, Sir Thomas, 268
Mott, John R., 352, 354, 357f., 360, 362
Müntzer, Thomas, 22, 26, 193
Murray, John Courtney, 75, 307

Newton, Sir Isaac, 292
Niemojewski, John, 251, 254
Nietzsche, Friedrich, 380, 382
Nixon, Richard M., 334, 345

Ogonowski, Zbigniew, 251, 260
Origen, 55ff., 61, 64, 179, 384
Osiander, Andreas, 188f., 191, 197

Papias, 47, 69
Parker (Archbishop), 216, 223, 228
Parkhurst, John, 225, 228
Paschasius Radbertus, 78, 97ff.
Pauck, Wilhelm, 4, 11
Paul (Apostle), 28, 33-44, 97, 171, 173f.,
    255ff., 263f., 391
Paul III, 239
Paul IV, 235, 248
Paul VI, 365, 375f.
Penco, Gregorio, 84, 89
Penn, William, 323
Perkins, William, 319, 323
Peter the Great, 128
Petrarch, Francesco, 137, 140
Pico della Mirandola, Giovanni, 145,
    164, 168, 386, 391
Pirckheimer, Willibald, 133, 187
Pius V, 238
Plato, 144, 209, 273, 380, 382, 391f.
Porphyry, 63, 68, 142
Przypkowski, Samuel, 251, 285, 289

Ratramnus, 98ff.
Rauschenbusch, Walter, 312, 352
Reuchlin, Johannes, 133, 143

Sandius, Christopher, 287, 292f., 297,
    299
Schaff, David S., 307f.
Schaff, Philip, 13, 17
Scotus, Duns, 142f.
Sixtus V, 238
Smith, Adam, 328, 336, 381
Sozzini, Fausto (Socinus, Faustus), 250-
    264, 292, 299
Speer, Robert E., 352, 357f., 360f.

Spengler, Lazarus, 186f., 190, 194
Sperry, Willard L., 4, 303
Spinoza, B., 292
Stiles, Ezra, 325, 330
Strong, Josiah, 310, 333

Teilhard de Chardin, Pierre, 129, 393
Tertullian, 28, 58ff., 296
Tillich, Paul, 2, 129, 391
Tocqueville, Alexis de, 334
Troeltsch, Ernst, 15, 378
Trutfetter, Jodocus, 141f.

Valla, Lorenzo, 138, 158f.
Vermigli, Peter Martyr, 198, 201-214, 216f.
Vico, Giambattista, 281f.
Virgil, 144

Volprecht, Wolfgang, 188f.

Washington, George, 327f., 331, 341
Wentworth, Thomas, Earl of Strafford, 321, 326
Whitehead, Alfred North, 384
Whitgift (Archbishop), 224, 228f.
William of Orange, 322, 324.
Williams, George H., 1-19, 33, 71ff., 81, 198, 232, 267, 365.
Williams, Roger, 338-350
Winthrop, John, 123, 331
Wiszowaty, Andrzej, 286-89, 292
Wiszowaty, Benedykt, 285, 287-299
Wyclif, John, 148, 222

Zwingli, Huldrych, 135, 169-181, 200ff., 318